Life of Beethoven

ALEXANDER THAYER

Life of
Beethoven

Revised by
ELLIOT FORBES
Edited with an Introduction by
IAN CURTEIS

London
THE FOLIO SOCIETY
2001

Alexander Thayer's *Life of Beethoven*, revised by
Elliot Forbes – the text of which forms the basis
for the present edition, edited by Ian Curteis –
was first published by Princeton University
Press in two volumes in 1964.

This edition reproduced by kind permission of
Princeton University Press.

Frontispiece: Beethoven composing his *Missa Solemnis*,
by Joseph Karl Stieler, 1820

Binding illustration: Ludwig van Beethoven.
Engraving by an unidentified artist, 19th
century. (*Royal Academy of Music/Lebrecht
Collection, London*)

Endpaper illustrations: manuscript scores by
Ludwig van Beethoven. Front: Op. 68, Sixth
Symphony. Rear: Op. 90, Pianoforte Sonata in
E minor. (*Beethoven-Haus Bonn*)

Indexes compiled by Frank Pert

Typeset in Granjon at The Folio Society.
Printed at St Edmundsbury Press, Bury
St Edmunds, on St Paul's Wove paper.
Quarter-bound in two shades of Feincanvas
cloth by Cambridge University Press.

Contents

Illustrations

Introduction

An astonishing sight greeted the visitor to Vienna in 1902: a spectacular monument of marble, ivory, precious stones, gold and bronze, crowned by an over-life-sized statue of Beethoven, semi-naked and in classical pose, brow massively furrowed in profound thought, seated on a throne adorned with angels' heads. Gustav Klimt had provided a thirty-four-metre-long frieze, depicting mystical scenes inspired by 'the master'. It was sensational.

The sculpture was the centrepiece of a huge Beethoven celebration and exhibition in a city which had been remarkably indifferent towards him in his lifetime and about which he had frequently been savage. For the opening ceremony, Mahler rearranged and conducted the Ninth Symphony, with gigantic orchestra augmented by extra brass instrumentation and massed chorus. All Vienna attended. The whole occasion marked the height of Beethoven worship, which had been growing apace for some seventy-five years.

The composer had begun to acquire mythological proportions even in his own lifetime. At his dramatic, almost theatrical, funeral in 1827, the actor Heinrich Anschütz had, at the cemetery gates, declaimed a funeral oration written by the poet Franz Grillparzer:

'We who stand here at the grave of the deceased one are in a sense the representatives of a nation, the entire German people, come to mourn the passing of one celebrated part of that which remained to us from the vanished radiance of the art of our homeland, of the spiritual efflorescence of the fatherland.

'The hero of poetry in the German language [Goethe] still lives – and long may he live. But the last master of resounding song, the gracious medium through which music spoke; the man who inherited and magnified the immortal fame of Handel and Bach, of Haydn and Mozart, has ceased to be; and we stand weeping over the broken strings of an instrument now silenced . . .'

In the years that followed, Beethoven was to grow rapidly into a powerful symbolic figure and his simple humanity became increasingly hard to discern. The romantic exaggerations of Bettina Brentano (who, in 1839, published three letters purportedly addressed to her by Beethoven but which are generally held to be, at best, part-forgeries) were followed in 1840 by Schindler's glossy, sentimental soap-opera of a biography wherein the great man could do no wrong. An icon was being created, rather than a uniquely vulnerable human being who could inspire exceptional admiration, loyalty and love on the one hand and on the other could be churlish and foul-tempered, with a positive genius not just for music but also for frenziedly working himself into situations that could only cause acute suffering to all. The picture being presented appeared increasingly false.

It was a sense of this falseness that first engaged Alexander Wheelock Thayer (1817–97) while still an undergraduate at Harvard. He became fascinated by what he had learned of the composer, first, from struggling to read Schindler's *Life* in German – though as he had only a poor grasp of the language what he learned was, to say the least, patchy – and, later, from the Moscheles translation. The book haunted him, and after he had graduated at the age of twenty-six, he conceived the odd idea of learning German simply so that he could make and publish a proper English translation.

In April 1849 he sailed for Europe with precisely this purpose and in Bonn and Berlin soon acquired enough German to read Schindler fully in the original. He then realised that it was a greatly flawed work as a piece of scholarship: it steadfastly suppressed Beethoven's darker and less attractive traits. It dwelt on the noble and sublime in the man and ignored the violence with which, for example, the composer would seize an unsatisfactory dish and hurl it at the waiter, screaming abuse.

Yet there was a great need for an unsentimental biography in English. Clearly, research would have to start from scratch and immediately, while those who knew the great man were still alive. Thayer resolved to write it himself. It became his life's work, begun in his thirties, and with only the third of the eventual five volumes complete when he died aged eighty; and it is a triumph.

Thayer himself recorded how the work progressed in a biographical note written to his German translator, Hermann Deiters, now in the Beethoven-Haus in Bonn:

'. . . In the summer of 1854, I returned to Berlin to work out a plan I had now formed of a pretty exhaustive biography of Beethoven for *American* (not for German) readers, with the hope of supporting myself by writing for the Tribune and one or two other papers. I studied the Beethoven Conversation Books and all the materials then in the Royal Library. But the sickness in my head became very bad again, and after several months of incapacity for labour, I went back to America (Spring of 1856), as my Berlin friends believed – to die!

'In the autumn of 1856 I had a long and severe illness – fever – I was an invalid from August to December. In 1857 I had earned a small sum of money to bring me back to my Beethoven work in Germany. One day in New York I learned that the man who had this money in his hands was bankrupt! I was left with about £2 sterling in my possession.

'By the aid of the gentleman and lady to whom my Beethoven biography is dedicated, I was enabled to return to Europe in August 1858.

'I remained in Berlin the following winter labouring hard; in the summer of 1859 I went to Vienna – Autumn of 1860, Bonn, thence to Paris, thence to London – I returned in August to Vienna, where I was employed in the American Legation. I remained in that position until the end of 1864 when I moved to Trieste and assumed the function of US Consul on 1 January 1865.'

No one in those days thought it strange that a literary man should be appointed a consul. It was the civilised fashion of the times to make such appointments – and there are many examples – as it provided the office-holder with security, light duties and a great deal of free time on his hands to write.

Trieste in those days must have been a quiet spot – Thayer was to live there for thirty-two years until his death. He hired a young man to carry out the office routine while he spent most of his time on the biography. The more deeply Thayer probed into the Beethoven material, the more speedily his feeling of kinship for the German mind and character grew. By this time he spoke German so flawlessly he was often taken for a national.

As Elliot Forbes describes in his Preface to the Princeton edition of Thayer's work: '[His] material came from these different sources: court records . . . contemporary notices and accounts, Beethoven's own documents – letters, sketches, memoranda, and Conversation Books – and reminiscences from anyone he could visit who had been in any way associated with Beethoven or had personal recollection of him.' Prodigious research went into it and its accuracy is incontestable. And it possesses another sovereign virtue: its objectivity is Olympian. In contrast to the conflicting fashions of debunking or over-romanticising, from both of which Beethoven has suffered as much as any subject of biography, Thayer was factual, conscientious and balanced; his own personality and predilections rarely intrude into the narrative. He presented Beethoven as a man of ever-evolving genius and of different moods, many noble but some, to say the least, less so. He was not going to blink away his foibles, his erratic emotions, his relentless capacity for stirring up trouble. He would show him warts and all.

This was in distinct contrast to the biographical fashion of the time, exemplified by his friend Otto Jahn's classic biography of Mozart. Thayer does not offer us interpretative responses to the music; his sole concern is to provide as objective an account of Beethoven the man as possible through the facts available to him. This in no way robs Thayer's work of its extraordinary value but enhances it: for the more one understands the true nature and human complexity of the man, the more one loves, is moved by and understands the music.

And Beethoven, more than any other composer, speaks music constantly from the heart and across a Shakespearean range of emotions. Many described his custom when playing of looking directly at the listeners, as if the music were his method of speaking to them of emotions, experiences, beliefs, deep within his heart. The more haunting movements of the last quartets, which many hold to be the summit of his achievement, come close to the later self-portraits of Rembrandt. The music looks at you, as Rembrandt looks at you from the canvas, with complete revelation. Both seem to say: 'This is me; this is what I believe; this is what I am.'

That the climax of Beethoven's career should coincide with the Congress of Vienna, that great celebration following twenty-five years of war and the overthrowing of the tyrant Bonaparte, once his hero – and that he should be present with kings, princes and statesmen paying respectful court to him – meant little to Beethoven compared to what he saw as his *raison d'être*. He was, at all stages, a believer in freedom and the rights of man. That, to him, is all an artist should care about. Alongside an unconcealed desire for personal glory, which at times resulted in great arrogance, was a genuine hope that his work might in some way lead to a bettering of ordinary human conditions. Thus in 1801 he told his old friend, Franz Wegeler, with obvious feeling: '... When you see me again it will be only as a great man, not only a greater artist but a better and more accomplished man. If conditions are improved in our fatherland, my art will be used only in the service of the poor.'

In his lifetime, many of the immediate driving forces behind the state of mind that produced the music were unknown. Paradoxically, Beethoven who, musically, could wear his heart on his sleeve, was also a private and solitary man with a prodigious internal life. He was, we are told, constantly and deeply in love with a series of women; yet his contemporaries never realised it, let alone who was currently the object of his passions. Sometimes, the objects of those passions were unaware of it themselves. Some commentators have put this down to gallantry, but the reason may be more complex.

Beethoven's biographer, Alexander Wheelock Thayer,
photographed in Bonn, 1890

The so-called 'Immortal Beloved' letter,* those fervent outpourings to a woman yet to be identified with any certainty, was found only after Beethoven's death in a secret drawer *in his house*; so it seems it was never sent. The 'Heiligenstadt Testament',† that equally passionate torrent of grief, despair and contemplation of suicide on the realisation that, at the age of thirty-two, he was irreversibly going deaf – he, of all people! – though addressed to both his brothers, yet only one is named; where the name of the other should be written, he has left blanks. Why? This extraordinary document, with death so close you can smell it on the page, never ceases to remind me of van Gogh's 'Crows over a Cornfield', that dark picture he painted shortly before his own suicide, with black crows wheeling menacingly over a cornfield apparently shaken by storm. The 'Heiligenstadt Testament' was also only discovered after Beethoven's death, also unsent.

That his relentlessly approaching deafness should force Beethoven to abandon his greatly successful career as a performer and concentrate entirely on his lonely future as a composer, dealing with music he would only ever hear inside his head, and thereby make his supreme contribution to the world, was, I believe, the process that restored him to that deep belief in divine purpose and divine love which irradiates passages of religious triumph in his most mature work. He could celebrate Easter – and what a celebration! – only after he had suffered Good Friday.

Although Thayer's notes were all written in English, his great work was first published in German. The reasons for this are that at the time English publishers were not in the practice of bringing out individual volumes of a work over as many years as they were written, and that based in Trieste Thayer was too far removed from the presses to steward an English edition. In Germany, however, neither of these problems presented themselves.

Elliot Forbes gives a precise account of the work's history:

'. . . Although accomplished in German, [Thayer] did not feel confident as to the manner of presentation to a German-reading public. Therefore he chose his friend Hermann Deiters . . . to translate his English text into German and use it as he thought best. The first result of this collaboration was an edition of the work actually completed by Thayer in three volumes [published in Berlin] in 1866, 1872 and 1879 – that is, Beethoven's life through [to the end of] 1816 . . . Increasing ill health which had been bothering Thayer since 1852, was responsible for the fatal delay of the work to follow . . .'

* See pp. 289–91.   † See pp. 144–6.

Thayer died in 1897, leaving a rich collection of source material including transcriptions he had made in Berlin of all the surviving Conversation Books, but no more actually written. Deiters set about completing the work, but in 1907, with the proof sheets of volume IV in his hands, he too died. The publishers then commissioned Hugo Riemann to complete the work and the fifth and final volume appeared in 1908.

Forbes continues:

'... By the time Riemann was at work, a demand for scholarly books on music was growing in America, and Thayer's niece, Mrs Jabez Fox, persuaded Henry Edward Krehbiel to undertake the job [of an English edition]. Krehbiel's aim was to base the English *Life of Beethoven* as much as possible on the original Thayer manuscript from which Deiters had worked. For the last ten years of Beethoven's life he felt as free as his German counterpart to choose his own method of presenting the material. The result was Krehbiel's English version, which was published by the Beethoven Association of New York in 1921.'

But that is far from the end of the story. Such parallel works as Jahn's *Life of Mozart* are very much of their time, in that they combine pure biography with musical analysis according to the musical thinking current and fashionable when they were written. But Thayer's method consisted of the objective presentation of documents and personal testimony of various degrees of reliability, and a good deal less linked musicology; so as new circumstantial evidence came to light – for instance, the discovery in 1949 of the passionate Beethoven–Josephine Deym love letters* – so the need for an updated edition of Thayer's great work grew.

The monumental task of updating within the spirit of the original was undertaken by Elliot Forbes in the 1960s. The extent of the research that went into it is staggering. It was an intricate job to dig back into one edition after another, weighing Thayer's words or the words and judgement of someone using Thayer's material in an attempt to relate it to the underlying original letter, document or recorded anecdote made contemporaneously, a year later or long after. It resembled an archaeological excavation into the many period layers of an ancient city.

Professor Elliot Forbes's splendid two-volume edition was published by Princeton University Press in 1964 and I urge those who find this edited version absorbing to turn to the full text. I have shortened it to a little over half the length, boldly trimming or cutting such sections

* See pp. 190–1 and 224.

as the history of the Beethoven family and that of the Electoral Court at Bonn from 1257; in the same spirit much of the musicology has been cut in order to throw emphasis on Beethoven the man.

It is good to be able to conclude this account with the story of a discovery of another sort.

It was known that Thayer had been buried in Trieste but by 1965 his tomb had long been counted as lost. None the less the US Consulate administrative officer of the day decided that a search ought to be made for it, or the site of where it had once been, recorded.

He combed the Anglican cemetery of that city, which is not large and contained some forty graves scattered over a large area, most with headstones completely overgrown with ivy. He cut away with a penknife and, the following week, a much heavier cutting tool – with many a glance over his shoulder for the police or the custodian.

Drawing a series of blanks, he contacted the administrator of the cemetery, who got the old burial records out of his safe and searched through them. Many fascinating things came to light; but no mention of the name Thayer.

On the point of abandoning the search, as a last throw the administrative officer tracked down a Mr d'Incontrera who had once written a pamphlet which referred to seeing the tomb. That gentleman was persuaded to return to the cemetery after thirty years and, if he could remember, indicate where it was. And this he did. It was built against and into a retaining wall, again completely covered in thick ivy which was stripped so that the inscription could once again be read:

'Alexander Wheelock Thayer
born in Nantick, Mass., USA October 22, 1817
Died in Trieste, Austria July 15, 1897'

The US Consulate took the tomb into its care. Arrangements were made so that it would be kept in good order and clear of ivy in perpetuity. A ceremony was held at the tomb by the current Consulate staff, flowers were laid and two new lines added to the inscription:

'American Consul in Trieste 1865–1882'

and

'BIOGRAPHER OF LUDWIG VAN BEETHOVEN'

IAN CURTEIS

Further Reading

The Beethoven Companion, ed. Barry Cooper (London, 1991).

Breuning, Gerhard von, *Memories of Beethoven*, ed. and trans. Maynard Solomon, and trans. Henry Mins (Cambridge, 1992).

Kinderman, William, *Beethoven* (Oxford, 1995).

The Letters of Beethoven, ed. and trans. Emily Anderson, 3 vols (London, 1961).

Matthews, Denis, *Beethoven* (London, 1985).

Tovey, Donald Francis, *Beethoven* (London, 1944).

Wegeler, Franz, and Ferdinand Ries, *Remembering Beethoven*, trans. Frederick Noonan (London, 1988).

Wyn Jones, David, *The Life of Beethoven* (Cambridge, 1998).

Note on Sources

Sources are often referred to by simple name. The following are among the most frequently mentioned:

Czerny, Carl (1791–1857). Took lessons from Beethoven in the period 1801–3 and by 1820 was considered one of the foremost pianists of his day. He constantly performed Beethoven's work and was a prolific composer himself. He assisted the great man and stayed loyal to him to the end. Many of Beethoven's surviving letters are to him.

Fischer, Gottfried (1780–1864). Childhood friend of Beethoven's, who lodged with his family in the Fischer house in Bonn from the age of ten. In old age, Fischer jotted down his reminiscences of the composer to which he added memories, of varying degrees of accuracy, for a further twenty years until his death. He was uneducated and the manuscript which bears his name is in badly written German, a strange mixture of notes, often repetitious and based on hearsay. It none the less gives a vivid description of three generations of the Beethoven family.

Fischoff, Joseph (d. 1857). Never himself knew Beethoven, but well after the composer's death acquired a copy of some sixty pages of miscellaneous Beethoven notes, letters, journal jottings, recorded remarks and memoranda, the compiler of which has not been identified. The original documents are largely lost, as is also the original copy, but the accuracy of the Fischoff manuscript is considered reliable.

Jahn, Otto (1813–69). Personal friend of Thayer's and author of the monumental biography of Mozart.

Moscheles, Ignaz (1794–1870). Distinguished pianist, conductor and composer. He was Beethoven's friend from 1808 to 1820. In 1841 he published an English translation of Schindler's biography with invaluable new facts and comments of his own.

Ries, Ferdinand (1784–1838). Came to Vienna in 1801 and took lessons from Beethoven. He subsequently played an influential part in the composer's life, particularly in promoting performances of his work in London. Beethoven wrote numerous letters to him. As an old man, Ries collaborated with Wegeler to produce their memoir, *Biographische*

Notizen über Ludwig van Beethoven (recently published in English translation under the title *Remembering Beethoven*), often quoted by Thayer.

Schindler, Anton Felix (1795–1864). Lawyer and violinist, was Beethoven's friend, amanuensis and first biographer. They met in 1814 and by 1819 he had become the composer's unpaid secretary and servant, at one stage sharing the same house. His biography first appeared in 1840. Much in it is inaccurate but he was so close to Beethoven that much is also of absorbing interest.

Seyfried, Ignaz Xavier Ritter von (1776–1841). Very popular Viennese conductor, teacher and composer. He was at all stages a staunch friend and active supporter of Beethoven's, after whose death he published his collection of documents entitled *Ludwig van Beethovens Studien im Generalbasse*.

Wegeler, Franz Gerhard (1765–1848). Great friend of the Breuning family. He had a distinguished medical career and was often in Beethoven's company until 1796. They corresponded frequently towards the end of the composer's life. He collaborated with Ries on the memoir mentioned above.

To
Mrs Mehetabel Adams
(of Cambridge in Massachusetts)
and Lowell Mason, Doctor of Music
(of South Orange in New Jersey)
this work, the researches for which
they so essentially aided,
is inscribed by
Alexander Thayer

Life of Beethoven

CHAPTER 1

The Electoral Court at Bonn

One of the compensations for the horrors of the French Revolution was the sweeping away of many of the petty sovereignties into which Germany was divided, thereby rendering a union of the German People and the rise of a German Nation possible. It was in the court of one of those tiny nations, the Electoral Court of Bonn, that Ludwig van Beethoven was born in 1770 and it is where he spent the first twenty-two years of his life, following in the footsteps of his father and grandfather, both Bonn Court Musicians; and it is in that little city, therefore, that we begin.

The first of the sovereignties to fall were the numerous ecclesiastical-civil members of the old, loose confederation, some of which had played no ignoble nor unimportant part in the advance of civilisation; but their day was past. The people of these states had in divers respects enjoyed a better lot than those who were subjects of hereditary rulers. At the least, they were not sold as mercenary troops; their blood was not shed on foreign fields to support their princes' ostentatious splendour, to enable mistresses and ill-begotten children to live in luxury and riot. But the antiquated ideas to which the ecclesiastical rulers held with bigoted tenacity had become a barrier to progress. These member states of the Holy Roman Empire were ruled with few or no exceptions by men who owed their positions to election by chapters or other church corporations, whose numbers were so limited as to give full play to every sort of intrigue; but they could not assume their functions until their titles were confirmed by the Pope as head of the Church, and by the Emperor as head of the confederation.

Those sees, without exception, were bestowed upon men of noble birth. They were benefices and sinecures for younger sons of princely houses. In general, as men owing their places wholly to political and family influences, so they assumed the vows and garb of churchmen as only necessary steps to the enjoyment of lives of affluence and pleasure.

So late as far into the eighteenth century, travelling was slow, laborious and expensive. Hence journeys, at long intervals, to a council, an imperial coronation or a diet of the empire, were the rare interruptions to the monotony of their daily existence. Not having the power to transmit their sees to their children, these ecclesiastics had the less inducement to rule with an eye to the welfare of their subjects: on the other hand, the temptation was very strong to augment their revenues for the benefit of relatives and dependants, and especially for the gratification of their own tastes and inclinations, among which the love of splendour and ostentatious display was a fruitful source of waste and extravagance.

Confined so largely to their own small capitals, they were far more dependent upon their own resources for amusement than the hereditary princes: and what so obvious, so easily obtained and so satisfactory as music, the theatre and the dance! Thus every little court became a conservatory of these arts. The ecclesiastical prince leaving the civil administration, as a rule, in the hands of ministers, had little to occupy him officially but a tedious routine of religious forms and ceremonies; to him therefore the theatre, and music for the mass, the opera, the ballroom, and the salon, were matters of great moment. They filled a wide void.

The three German ecclesiastical princes who possessed the greatest power and influence were the Archbishops of Mainz, Trèves and Cologne. Peace appears hardly to have been known between the city of Cologne and its earlier archbishops; and, in the thirteenth century, a long-continued and even bloody quarrel resulted in the victory of the city. The archbishops retained no civil or political power within its walls, not even the right to remain there more than three days at any one time. Thus it happened that in the year 1257 Archbishop Engelbert selected Bonn for his residence, and formally made it the capital of the electorate, as it remained until Elector and court were swept away in 1794.

It is fortunate that the electoral archives recently discovered and now preserved at Düsseldorf consist so largely of documents relating to the musical establishment of the court at Bonn during this time. They rarely afford information upon the character of the music performed, but are sufficiently complete to determine with reasonable correctness the number, character, position and condition of its members. The records need not concern us now until we reach the following, which forms part of the history of the grandfather of the subject of this biography:

'March 1733

DECRETUM

For Ludovicum van Beethoven as Electoral Court Musician
'*Cl. A.* Whereas His Serene Highness Elector of Cologne, Duke Clemens August in Upper and Lower Bavaria, etc. Our Gracious Lord having, on the humble petition of Ludovico van Beethoven, graciously declared and received him as Court Musician, and assigned him an annual salary of 400 fl. [florins] Rhenish, the present decree under the

gracious hand of His Serene Electoral Highness and the seal of the Privy Chancellor, is granted to him, and the Electoral Councillor and Paymaster Risack is herewith commanded to pay the said Beethoven the 400 fl. *quartaliter* from the beginning of this year and to make a proper accounting thereof. B——— March 1733.'

Filed under 1756 occur several papers which have a double interest. They relate to the Beethoven family and are so complete as to exhibit the entire process of appointment to membership in the electoral chapel, and they give us the clue to the correct pronunciation of the name Beethoven.

'To His Electoral Serenity of Cologne, etc. My most Gracious Lord
the humble petition and prayer of
Joan [Johann] van Biethoffen
'Most Reverend, most Serene Elector,
Most Gracious Lord, Lord, etc.
'May it please your Electoral Serenity graciously to hear the humble representations how in the absence of voices in Your Highness's Court Chapel my insignificant self took part in the music for at least four years without the good fortune of having allotted by Your Serene Electoral Highness a small *salario*.

'I therefore pray Your Serene Electoral Highness most humbly that it graciously please you (in consideration of my father's faithful service for 23 years) to rejoice me with a decree as Court Musician, which high grace will infuse me with zeal to serve Your Serene Highness with the greatest fidelity and zealousness.
Your
Serene Electoral Highness's
Most humble-obedient-faithful servant,
Joan van Biethoffen'

'To the Music Director Gottwaldt for a report of his humble
judgement. Attestation by the most gracious
sign manual and seal of the Privy Chancellery
Bonn, 19 March 1756
(Signed) Clemens August (LS)'

'Most reverend, most serene Elector,
Most Gracious Lord, Lord, etc.
'Your Serene Electoral Highness has referred to my humble judgement the petition of Joan van Piethoffen, the supplicant prays Your

Electoral Highness for a gracious decree as accessist in the court music, he has indeed served for two years with his voice on the Duc Sall [doxal], hopes in time to deserve the good will of Your Serene Highness by his industry, and his father who enjoys the grace of serving Your Highness as bass singer prays his appointment, I pray most humbly and obediently for instruction concerning Your Highness's good will in the matter, submit myself humbly and obediently to Your Serene Highness's grace and remain in greatest humility.

> Your Serene and Electoral Highness's
> Most humble and obedient servant
> Gottwaldt, Director of the Chamber Music'

Johann van Beethoven, father of our Ludwig, was sixteen years old at this time. Slender success has rewarded the search for means of determining the character and quality of that opera and music, upon which Clemens August lavished such large sums, and in the performance of which father and son – the grandfather and father of our great composer – spent their professional lives.

The period embraced in that Elector's rule (1724–61) was precisely that in which the *old* Italian opera, the oratorio and the sacred cantata reached their extreme limits of development through the genius of Handel and J. S. Bach. It closes at the moment when Gluck, C. P. E. Bach and Joseph Haydn were laying the immovable foundations of a new operatic, orchestral and pianoforte music, and before the perfected sonata-form, that found universal adoption in all non-vocal compositions of the better class.

Composers had to furnish music on demand and as often as was necessary, as the hunter delivered game or the fisherman fish. What a volume of music was produced in this manner can be seen in the case of Joseph Haydn at Esterhaz, whose fruitfulness did not, in all probability, exceed that of many another of his contemporaries. The older Telemann furnished compositions to the courts of Bayreuth and Eisenach as well as the Grey Friars at Frankfurt-am-Main, and also performed his duties as musical director and composer at Hamburg. His easy flow of complex polyphony was greatly admired by Handel.

Following the death of Clemens August in 1761, the Electorship passed to Maximilian Friedrich of the Swabian line Königsegg- (or Königseck-) Rothenfels. For a century or more this house had enjoyed fat livings in the Church at Cologne, in which city the new Elector was born on 13 May 1708. He was by nature an easy, good-tempered, indolent, friendly man, of no great force of character – qualities which, in the incumbent of a rich sinecure just completing his fifty-third year, would be too fully confirmed and developed by habit to change with any change of circumstances; and which made him unusually popular throughout the land.

The condition of the court finances had become such through the extravagant expenditures of Clemens August that very energetic measures were necessary during the first few years of Max Friedrich's rule for its treasury to survive.

It was fortunate for the Elector's subjects that his indolence was made good by the activity and energy of a prime minister who found his beau ideal of a statesman in Frederick II of Prussia. To Kaspar Anton von Belderbusch the new Elector owed his elevation; to his care he entrusted the state; to his skill and strength of character he was indebted for release from the pecuniary difficulties which beset him and for the satisfaction, as the years rolled by, of seeing his states numbered among the most prosperous and flourishing in Germany.

Belderbusch's first care was to reduce the expenditure. He put a stop to building, dismissed a number of the actors, restricted the number of concerts and court balls, dispensed with the costly hunts, reduced the salaries of court officials, officers and domestics, lessened the *état* for the kitchen, cellar and table of the prince, turned the property left by Clemens August into money and comforted the latter's creditors with the hope of better times. But though economy was the rule, still, where the Elector considered it due to his position, he could be lavish.

Henry Swinburne, whose letters to his brother were published long after his death under the title of *The Courts of Europe*, writes under the date of 29 November 1780:

'Bonn is a pretty town, neatly built, and its streets tolerably well paved, all in black lava. It is situated in a flat near the river. The Elector of Cologne's palace faces the South entry. It has no beauty of architecture and is all plain white without any pretensions.

'We went to court and were invited to dine with the Elector (Königsegge). He is 73 years old, a little, hale, black man, very merry and affable. His table is none of the best; no dessert wines handed about, nor any foreign wines at all. He is easy and agreeable, having lived all his life in ladies' company, which he is said to have liked better than his breviary. The captains of his guard and a few other people of the court form the company . . . The palace is of immense size, the ballroom particularly large and low . . . The Elector goes about to all the assemblies and plays at Tric-trac. He asked me to be of his party but I was not acquainted with their way of playing. There is every evening an assembly or play at court.'

A curious proof of the liberality, not to say laxity, of the Elector's sentiments in one direction is the possession of a mistress in common by him
and his minister Belderbusch – the latter fathering the children – and
this mistress was the Countess Caroline von Satzenhofen, Abbess of
Vilich!

The reductions which were made by Belderbusch upon the accession of Max Friedrich in the expenses of the theatre and other amusements do not appear, except in the case of the kapellmeister, to have
extended to the court music proper, nor to have been long continued
in respect to the 'operetta and comedy'. The first in order of the documents and notices discovered relating to the musical establishment of
this Elector are of no common interest, being the petition of our composer's grandfather for the vacant office of kapellmeister and the
decree appointing him to that position. They are as follows:

'Very Reverend Archbishop and Elector
      Most Gracious Lord, Lord!
   'May it please Your Electoral Grace to permit a representation of my
faithfully and dutifully performed services for a considerable space as
vocalist as well as, since the death of the kapellmeister, for more than a
year his duties *in Dupplo*, that is to say by singing and wielding the
baton concerning which my demand still remains *ad referendum*; much
less have I been assured of the position. Inasmuch as because of particular *recommendation* Dousmoulin was preferred over me, and indeed
unjustly, I have been forced hitherto to submit to fate.
   'But now, gracious Elector and Lord, that because of the reduction
in salaries Kapellmeister Dousmoulin has already asked his demission
or will soon do so, and I at the command of Baron Belderbusch am to
begin *de novo* to fill his office, and the same must surely be replaced –
Therefore
   'There reaches Your Electoral Grace my humble petition that you
may graciously be pleased . . . to grant me the justice of which I was
deprived on the death of Your Highness's *antecessori* of blessed memory, and appoint me kapellmeister with some augmentation of my
lessened salary because of my services . . . For which highest grace I
shall pour out my prayers to God for the long continuing health and
government of your Electoral Grace, while in deepest submission I
throw myself at your feet.
                    Your Electoral Grace's most humble servant
                              Ludwig van Beethoven
                                    "Passist" '

'*M.F.* Whereas We, Maximilian Friedrich, Elector of Cologne, on the demission of our former kapellmeister Touche Moulin, and the humble petition of our bass singer Ludwig van Beethoven, have appointed the latter to be kapellmeister with the retention of his position as bass singer and have added 97 rthlr. [reichsthalers] *species 40 alb.* to his former salary of 292 rthlr. *species 40 alb.* per annum divided in *quartalien*, which appointment is hereby made and payment ordered by our grace, our exchequer and all whom it may concern are called on to observe the fact and do what is required under the circumstances.

Attest, etc.   Bonn, 16 July 1761'

Next in order, at an interval of rather more than a year, is the following short paper in reply to a petition, not preserved, of the new kapellmeister's son:

'*Supplicanten* is hereby graciously assured that in the event of a *vacatur* of a court musician's salary he shall have special consideration. Attest our gracious sign manual and the impress of the seal of the Privy Chancellery.

Bonn, 27 November 1762   Max Fried. Elector
                                                                     v. Belderbusch (LS)'

Several papers, dated 26 April 1768, although upon matters of very small importance, have a certain interest as being in part official communications from the pen of Kapellmeister van Beethoven, and illustrating in some measure his position and duties. They show, too, that his path was not always one bordered with roses.

I
'Most Reverend Archbishop and Elector,
Most Gracious Lord, Lord
'Will Your Electoral Grace deign to listen to the complaint that when Court Singer Schwachhofer was commanded in obedience to an order of His Excellency Baron von Belderbusch to alternate with Jacobina Salomon in the singing of the solos in the church music as is the custom, the said Schwachhofer in the presence of the entire chapel impertinently and literally answered me as follows: I will not accept your *ordre* and you have no right to command me.

'Your Electoral Grace will doubtless recall various *disordre* on the part of the court chapel indicating that all respect and *ordonance* is withheld from me, each member behaving as he sees fit, which is very painful to my sensibilities.

'Wherefore my humble prayer reaches Your Electoral Highness that the public affront of Schwachhofer be punished to my deserved *satisfaction* and that a decree issue from Your Highness to the entire chapel that at the cost of Your Gracious displeasure or punishment according to the offence my *ordre* shall not be evaded.

Your Electoral Grace's
Humble and Most Obedient Servant
Ludovicus van Beethoven'

II

'To Kapellmeister van Beethoven
Concerning the Court Musicians
     M. F. E.
  'Receive the accompanying Command to the end that its contents be conveyed to all of our court musicians or be posted on the 'toxal'. We remain, etc.

Bonn, 26 April 1768'

III

'Command respecting the Court Musicians

'Having learned with displeasure that several of our court musicians have tried to evade the *ordre* issued by our kapellmeister or refused to receive them from him, and conduct themselves improperly amongst themselves, all of our court musicians are hereby earnestly commanded without contradiction to obey all the commands given by our kapellmeister in our name, and bear peaceful relations with each other, since we are determined to proceed with rigour against the guilty to the extent of dismissal in certain cases.

Sig. Bonn, 26 April 1768'

On 17 November 1769, Johann van Beethoven submitted a petition in which he exhibited anew his genius for devising methods for varying the spelling of his own name. That he could no longer live on 100 rthlr. salary is evident when it is remembered that he had now been married two years.

'To His Electoral Grace
of Cologne, etc., etc.

The Humble Supplication
     and Prayer   of
        Johann Bethof, Court Musician
   Most Reverend Archbishop and Elector,
    Most Gracious Lord, Lord
'May Your Most Reverend Electoral Grace, graciously permit the pre-

sentation of this humble *supplicando*, how for many years I have served Your Highness faithfully and industriously on the 'Duc saahl' and the theatre, and also have given instruction in various *subjecta* concerning the aforesaid service to the entire satisfaction of Your Electoral Grace, and am engaged now in study to perfect myself to this end ... [As] it is impossible for me to live on the salary of 100 rthlr. graciously allowed me, I pray Your Electoral Grace to bestow upon me the 100 rthlr. left at Your gracious disposal by the death of Your court musician Philip Haveck; to merit this high grace by faithful and diligent service shall be my greatest striving.

Your Electoral Grace's most humble
Joannes Bethof,
Court Musician'

In answer to this there came the following decree:

'Whereas we, Max. Frid. p. on the death of Court Musician Philipp Haveck and the submissive petition of our court musician Philipp Salomon bestowed upon him the grace of adding 50 fl. for his two daughters to the salary which he already enjoys out of the salary of the above mentioned Haveck per year; we confirm the act hereby; wherefore we have graciously issued, this decree, which our Electoral Court Exchequer will humbly observe and make all necessary provisions.

Attest. p. Münster, 17th 9bris 1769'

On the margin was written 'Gracious addition of 50 fl. for the court musician Philipp Salomon' and, besides Brandt and Meuris also, '*in simili* for Court Musician Joann Bethoff 25 fl.'

A note of 23 January 1773, 'the bass singer van Beethoven is incapacitated and can no longer serve as such,' suggests that the old gentleman's appearance as Brunoro in Lucchesi's *L'Inganno scoperto* in May 1773, was a final compliment to his master, the Elector, upon his birthday. He did not live to celebrate another; the death of 'Ludwig van Beethoven, Hofkapellmeister', is recorded at Bonn under the date 24 December 1773. Since the Court Calendar for 1774 had already been printed, his name still stood at the head of the court musicians in this edition.

'Musique du Cabinet, de la Chapelle
et de la cour
Intendat – vacat
Maître de la Chapelle – Mons. Louis* van Beethoven
Musiciens Respectives

Voix	Violons
Mess. Lucas Charles Noisten	Mess. Jean Ries
Jean van Beethoven	Erneste Riedel
Christophe Herm. Jos. Brandt	Erneste Haveck
[Joseph] Daumer, accessist	Ferdinand Trewer
Mad. Anne Marie Ries	Philippe Salomon
Maximil. Valentine Delombre,	Ignace Willmann
née Schwachhofer	Louis Toepser, accessiste
Anne Marie Geyers,	
née Salomon	Basse de Viole
Anne Jacobine Salomon	Jean Joseph Magdefrau
Elisabeth Trewers, accessistin	Francois Tussy

Organiste	Contre Basse
Mess. Gilles van den Eeden	Math. Ant. Marie Poletnich
Joseph Clement Meuris, adj.	

Bassons	Braccistes
Jean [Jos.] Antoine Meuris	Jos. Clem Belserosky
[Theodor] Zillicken	Jean Gottlieb Walter'

It is noteworthy that except for two bassoons there are no wind-instruments. The company of Life Guards had two trumpeters: Diederich Baumgarten and Ludwig Toepser (violinist above); these two, along with Franz Bayer and Wilhelm Stumpff, also court trumpeters, are listed *bei dem Hof-Fuder-Amt*; besides these there is still Joh. Bap. Reynard (or Renard), court kettledrummer.

Let an attempt follow to describe the little city of Bonn as it appeared in 1770 when our composer was there born. The population was 9,560 souls, a number which probably for a long series of years had rarely varied beyond a few score, more or less. For the town had neither manufactures nor commerce beyond what its own wants supported; it was simply the residence of the Elector – the seat of the court, and the people depended more or less directly upon that court

* 'Louis', or 'Luis', was an accepted colloquialism for 'Ludwig': Beethoven was often addressed thus by his friends.

for subsistence – as a wag expressed it, 'all Bonn was fed from the Elector's kitchen'. The old city walls were already partially destroyed. Within them the whole population seems to have lived. Outside the city gates it does not appear that, save by a chapel or two, the eye was impeded in its sweep across gardens and open fields to the surrounding villages which, hidden in clusters of walnut and fruit trees, appeared, when looked upon from the neighbouring hills, like islands rising upon the level surface of the plain. Steam as a locomotive power was unknown, and the commerce of the Rhine floated by the town, gliding down with the current on rafts or in clumsy but rather picturesque boats, or impelled against the stream by the winds, by horses and even by men and women.

To the stranger, coming down from Mainz, with its narrow dark lanes, or up from Cologne, whose confined and pestiferously dirty streets, emitting unnamed stenches, were but typical of the bigotry, superstition and moral filth of the population, little Bonn seemed a very picture of neatness and comfort. Even its ecclesiastical life seemed of another order. The men of high rank in the Church were of high rank also by birth; they were men of the world and gentlemen; their manners were polished and their minds enlarged by intercourse with the world and with gentlemen; they were tolerant in their opinions and liberal in their views.

Let the fancy picture, upon a fine Easter or Pentecost morning in those years, the little city in its holiday attire and bustle. The bells in palace and church tower ringing; the peasants in coarse but picturesque garments, the women abounding in bright colours, come in from the surrounding villages, fill the market-place and crowd the churches at the early masses. The nobles and gentry – in broad-flapped coats, wide waistcoats and knee-breeches, the entire dress often of brilliant coloured silks, satins and velvets, huge, white, flowing neckcloths, ruffles over the hands, buckles of silver or even of gold at the knees and upon the shoes, huge wigs becurled and bepowdered on the heads, and surmounted by the cocked hat, when not held under the arm, a sword at the side, and commonly a gold-headed cane in the hand (and if the morning be cold, a scarlet cloak thrown over the shoulders) – are daintily picking their way to the palace to kiss His Transparency's hand or dashing up to the gates in heavy carriages with white-wigged and cocked-hatted coachmen and footmen. Their ladies wear long and narrow bodices, but their robes flow with a mighty sweep; their apparent stature is increased by very high-heeled shoes and by piling up their hair on lofty cushions; their sleeves are short, but long silk gloves cover the arms. The ecclesiastics, various in name and costume, dress as now, save in the matter of the flowing wig. The Elector's company of guards is out and at intervals the thunder of the artillery on the walls is heard. On all sides, strong and brilliant contrasts of colour meet the eye, velvet and silk, purple and fine linen, gold and silver – such were the fashions of the time – costly, inconvenient in form, but imposing, magnificent and marking the differences of rank and class. Let the imagination picture all this, and it will have a scene familiar to the boy Beethoven, and one in which as he grew up to manhood he had his own small part to play.

CHAPTER 2

Beethoven's Birth and Childhood, 1770–1784

There is no authentic record of Beethoven's birthday. His old Bonn friend Dr Franz Wegeler, on the ground of custom in that city, dates it the day preceding the ceremony of baptism – an opinion which Beethoven himself seems to have entertained. It is the official record of this baptism only that has been preserved. In the registry of the parish of St Remigius the entry appears as follows:

'Parentes:	'Proles:	'Patrini:
D: Joannes van	17ma Xbris.	D: Ludovicus van
Beethoven & Helena	Ludovicus	Beethoven &
Keverichs, conjuges		Gertrudis Müllers
		dicta Baums'

The sponsors, therefore, were Beethoven's grandfather, the kapellmeister, and the wife of the next-door neighbour, Johann Baum, clerk of the electoral cellar. Since it was the custom at the time in the Catholic Rhine country not to postpone the baptism beyond twenty-four hours after the birth of a child, it is in the highest degree probable that Beethoven was born on 16 December 1770.

Of several certificates of baptism the following is copied in full for the sake of a remark written upon it by the master's own hand:

'Department de Rhin et Moselle
Mairie de Bonn
Extrait du Registre de Naissances de la Paroisse
de St Remy à Bonn
'Anno millesimo septingentesimo, de decima septima Decembris baptizatus est Ludovicus, Parentes D: Joannes van Beethoven et Helena Keverichs, conjuges. Patrini, D: Ludovicus van Beethoven et Gertrudis Müllers dicta Baums.

Pour extrait conforme
délivré à la Mairie de Bonn.
Bonn le 2 juin 1810
[Signatures and official seals]'

On the back of this paper Beethoven wrote:

'1772   'The baptismal certificate seems to be incorrect,
                              since there was a Ludwig born before me.*
                              A Baumgarten was my sponsor, I believe.
                                        Ludwig van Beethoven'

The composer, then, even in his fortieth year still believed the correct date of his birth to be 1772, which is the one given in all the old
biographical notices, and which corresponds to the dates affixed to
many of his first works, and indeed to nearly all allusions to his age in
his early years. Only by keeping this fact in mind can the long list of
chronological contradictions, which continually meet the student of
his history during the first half of his life, be explained or comprehended. Whoever examines the original record of baptism in the
registry at Bonn sees instantly that the certificate, in spite of Beethoven, is correct; but all possible doubt is removed by the words of
Wegeler:

'Little Louis clung to this grandfather . . . with the greatest affection,
and young as he was when he lost him, his early impressions always
remained lively. He liked to speak of his grandfather with the friends
of his youth, and his pious and gentle mother, whom he loved much
more than he did his father, who was only severe, was obliged to tell
him much of his grandfather.'

Had 1772 been the correct date the child never could have retained
personal recollections of a man who died on 24 December 1773.
    I conjecture that the boy's age was purposely falsified by Johann,
who may well have had the recent career of the Mozart children in
mind. There exists an official report of 1784 in which the age is given
correctly as an example of where untruth could not be risked. But one
wonders whether the falsification of age could be purposely any the
more risked in a dedication to the Elector; yet the boy composer in dedicating three piano sonatas to Maximilian Friedrich in 1783 wrote 'by
Ludwig van Beethoven, eleven years old'. That family records were
imperfectly kept at that time is amply illustrated by the discrepancies
of birth dates mentioned in contemporary writings.
    Johann van Beethoven thus describes the pecuniary condition in
which he found himself upon the death of his father:

* In 1769. He lived but six days.

'Most Reverend Archbishop,
Most Gracious Elector and Lord, Lord

'Will Your Electoral Grace be pleased to hear that my father has passed away from this world, to whom it was granted to serve His Electoral Grace Clemens August and Your Electoral Grace and gloriously reigning Lord, Lord 42 years, as kapellmeister with great honour, whose position I have been found capable of filling, but nevertheless I would not venture to offer my capacity to Your Electoral Grace, but since the death of my father has left me in needy circumstances my salary not sufficing and I compelled to draw on the savings of my father, my mother still living and in a cloister at a cost of 60 rthlr. for board and lodging each year and it is not advisable for me to take her to my home. Your Electoral Grace is therefore humbly implored to make an allowance from the 400 rthlr. vacated for an increase of my salary so that I may not need to draw upon the little savings and my mother may receive the pension graciously for the few years which she may yet live, to deserve which high grace it shall always be my striving.

Your Electoral Grace's
Most humble and obedient
Servant and musicus Jean van Beethoven'

There is something bordering on the comic in the coolness of the hint here given that the petitioner would not object to an appointment as his father's successor. The hint was not taken; what provision was granted him, however, may be seen from another petition of 8 January 1774, praying for an addition to his salary from that made vacant by the death of his father, and a pension to his mother who is kept at board in a cloister. A memorandum appears on the margin to the effect that the Elector graciously consents that the widow, so long as she remain in the cloister, shall receive 60 rthlr. quarterly. The death of the mother followed and was thus announced in the *Intelligenzblatt* of Bonn on 3 October 1775: 'Died, on September 30, Maria Josepha Pols, widow van Beethoven, aged 61 years.' In a list of salaries for 1776 (among the papers at Düsseldorf) the salary of Johann van Beethoven is given at 36 rthlr. 45 alb. payable quarterly. The fact of the great poverty in which he and his family lived is manifest from the official documents.

On their marriage in 1767, Johann and Maria van Beethoven, then aged twenty-seven and nineteen, took humble lodgings in what was described as 'the rear of the Clasen house in the Bonngasse' (now maintained as a Beethoven museum) and it was there that their great son was born.

From there the Beethovens removed, when is uncertain, to a house

No. 7 or No. 8 on the left as one enters the Dreieckplatz in passing from the Sternstrasse to the Münsterplatz. They were living there in 1774, for the baptism of another son on 8 April of that year is recorded in the register of the parish of St Gangolph, to which those houses belonged. This child's name was Caspar Anton Carl.

Thence the Beethovens migrated to No. 934 in the Rheingasse, so long held to be the composer's birthplace and long thereafter distinguished by a false inscription to that effect. Whether the removal took place in Ludwig's fifth or sixth year is not known; but at all events it was previous to 2 October 1776, for upon that day another son of Johann van Beethoven was baptised in the parish of St Remigius by the name of Nikolaus Johann. Apparently the family removed from this house in 1776 for a short time to one in the Neugasse, but returned again to the house in the Rheingasse in 1777. One thought which suggests itself in relation to these removals of Johann van Beethoven may, perhaps, be that in expectation of advancement in position upon the death of his father he had exchanged the narrow quarters of the lodging in the rear of the Clasen house for the much better dwelling in the Dreieckplatz; but upon the failure of his hopes had been fain to seek a cheaper place again, in the lower part of the town down near the river.

There is nothing decisive as to the time when the musical education of Ludwig van Beethoven began, nor any positive evidence that he, like Handel, Haydn or Mozart, showed remarkable genius for the art at a very early age. But it is clear that Johann van Beethoven gave his son instruction upon the pianoforte and violin in his earliest childhood. In the dedication of the pianoforte sonatas (1783) to the Elector, the boy is made to say: 'Music became my first youthful pursuit in my fourth year', which might be supposed decisive on the point if his age were not falsely given on the title-page. The child had his daily task of musical study and practice given him and in spite of his tears was forced to execute it. 'Cäcilia Fischer', declares a letter in the *Kölnische Zeitung* in 1838, 'still sees him [in her memory] a tiny boy, standing on a little footstool in front of the clavier to which the implacable severity of his father had so early condemned him ... The patriarch of Bonn, Head Burgomaster Windeck ... saw the little Louis van Beethoven in this house standing in front of the clavier and weeping.'

It must be supposed that the father had seen indications of his son's genius, for it is difficult to imagine such a one remaining unperceived; but the necessities of the family with the failure of the petition for a better salary — sent in just at the time when the Elector was so largely increasing his expenditures for music — are sufficient reasons for the inflexible severity with which the boy was kept at his studies. There is but one road to excellence – unremitted application. To this young Ludwig was compelled, sometimes, no doubt, through the fear or the actual infliction of punishment for neglect; sometimes, too, the father, whose habits were such as to favour a bad interpretation of his conduct, was no doubt harsh and unjust. Thus the boy at an early date acquired so considerable a facility upon the clavier that his father could have him play at court and when he was seven years old produce him with one of his pupils at a concert in Cologne.

'AVERTISSEMENT

'Today, 26 March 1778, in the musical concert-room in the Sternengass the Electoral Court Tenorist, BEETHOVEN, will have the honour to produce two of his scholars; namely, Mdlle Averdonc, Court Contraltist, and his little son of six years. The former will have the honour to contribute various beautiful arias, the latter various clavier concertos and trios, in which he flatters himself that he will give complete enjoyment to all ladies and gentlemen, the more since both have had the honour of playing to the greatest delight of the entire Court.
Beginning at five o'clock in the evening.'

Unfortunately we learn nothing concerning the pieces played by the boy nor of the success of his performance.

The father's main object being the earliest and greatest development of his son's musical genius so as to make it a 'marketable commodity', he gave him no other school education than such as was afforded at one of the public schools. Among the lower grade establishments in Bonn was the so-called Tirocinium, a Latin school. To this place young Beethoven was sent; when, is uncertain. His contemporary and schoolfellow Wurzer relates the following in his memoirs: 'One of my schoolmates under Krengel was Luis van Beethoven, whose father held an appointment as court singer under the Elector. He was distinguished by uncleanliness, negligence, etc. Not a sign was to be discovered in him of that spark of genius which glowed so brilliantly in him afterwards.'

Wurzer entered the gymnasium in the autumn of 1781; Beethoven did not. This, therefore, must have been the time at which all other studies were abandoned in favour of music. When Johann stopped the boy's education after the public elementary schools, he was following the pattern set by the majority of parents in Bonn. This had been the pattern of his own life: he started as soon as possible, from the bottom, upon the career of court musician. He was in no position to provide the boy with any other kind of schooling; but since the earliest evidences of his son's talent, it had been clear to him that Ludwig was a born musician.

The lack of proper intellectual discipline is painfully obvious in Beethoven's letters throughout his life. In his early manhood he wrote a fair hand, so very different from the shocking scrawl of his later years as to make one almost doubt the genuineness of autographs of that period; but in orthography, the use of capital letters, punctuation and arithmetic he was sadly deficient all his life long. He was described by Dr Müller as 'a shy and taciturn boy, the necessary consequence of the life apart which he led, observing more and pondering more than he spoke, and disposed to abandon himself entirely to the feelings awakened by music and (later) by poetry and to the pictures created by fancy'. Of those who were his schoolfellows and who in after years recorded their reminiscences of him, not one speaks of him as a playfellow, none has anecdotes to relate of games with him, rambles on the hills or adventures upon the Rhine and its shores in which he bore a part. His friend Gottfried Fischer writes specifically of playful boyish pranks that Ludwig carried out with his brother Carl over which Ludwig could laugh heartily; and he would have us believe that these capers were not always of a harmless character. Further on Fischer states, 'Later one could not say that Ludwig cared much for companions or society. And then, when he had to turn his mind to music or set to work by himself, he assumed quite another demeanour and insisted on due respect. His happiest hours were those when he was free of all company, when his parents were all away and he was left alone by himself.'

Music and ever music; hence the power of clothing his thoughts in words was not developed by early culture, and the occasional bursts of eloquence in his letters and recorded conversations are held not to be genuine, because so seldom found. As if the strong mind, struggling for adequate expression, should not at times break through all barriers and overcome all obstacles! Urged forward thus by the father's severity, by his tender love for his mother and by the awakening of his own tastes, the development of his skill and talents was rapid; so much so that in his ninth year a teacher more competent than his father was needed.

The first to whom his father turned was the old court organist van den Eeden, who had been in the electoral service about fifty years and had come to Bonn before the arrival there of Ludwig van Beethoven, the grandfather. One can easily imagine his willingness to serve an old and deceased friend by fitting his grandson to become his successor; and this might account for the story that at first he taught him gratis, and that he continued his instructions at the command and expense of the Elector.

It is not known whether his instruction was on the organ but it is unlikely that the boy, who was destined for a more systematic instruction in pianoforte playing, was put at the organ at so early an age. Beethoven often spoke of the old organist when discoursing upon the proper position and movement of the body and hands in organ and pianoforte playing, he having been taught to hold both calm and steady, to play in the connected style of Handel and Bach. Van den Eeden when seventy sent the boy Louis, between eleven and twelve years old, to accompany the mass and other church music on the organ. His playing was so astonishing that one was forced to believe he had intentionally concealed his gifts. While preluding for the Credo he took a theme from the movement and developed it to the amazement of the orchestra so that he was permitted to improvise longer than is customary.

It is our conjecture that van den Eeden taught the boy chiefly pianoforte playing, he being a master in that art; but his influence was small. It must be remembered that van den Eeden was a very old man who died in June 1782. Nowhere does he, like the other teachers of Beethoven, disclose individual traits; he is a totally colourless picture in the history of Beethoven's youth.

A fitter master, it was thought, was obtained in Tobias Friedrich Pfeiffer, who came to Bonn in the summer of 1779 as tenor singer in Grossmann and Helmuth's theatrical company. Pfeiffer was a skilful pianist and oboist, and gave the boy lessons, but not at any regular hours. Often when he came with Beethoven, the father, from the wine-house late at night, the boy was roused from sleep and kept at the pianoforte until morning.

About this time the young court musician Franz Georg Rovantini lived in the same house with Beethoven. He was related to the Beethoven family. The young musician was much respected and sought after as a teacher. The boy Beethoven was among his pupils, taking lessons on the violin and viola. But these lessons, too, came to an early end; Rovantini died on 9 September 1781, aged twenty-four.

A strong predilection for the organ was awakened early in the lad and he eagerly sought opportunities to study the instrument. In the cloister of the Franciscan monks at Bonn there lived a friar named Willibald Koch, highly respected for his playing and his expert knowledge of organ construction. We have no reason to doubt that young Ludwig sought him out, received instruction from him and made so much progress that Friar Willibald accepted him as assistant. In the same way he made friends with the organist in the cloister of the Minorites and 'made an agreement' to play the organ there at 6 o'clock morning mass. On the inside of the cover of a memorandum book which he carried to Vienna with him is found the note: 'Measurements (*Fussmass*) of the Minorite pedals in Bonn.' Still another tradition is preserved in a letter to the author from Miss Auguste Grimm. It relates that already at that time Ludwig composed pieces which were too difficult for his little hands. 'Why, you can't play that, Ludwig,' his teacher is said to have remarked, and the boy to have replied: 'I will when I am bigger.'

The feeling for nature which manifests itself later with Beethoven and forms a stimulation for his compositions was already being cultivated at Bonn. Ludwig derived great pleasure, according to Fischer, from the beautiful view of the Rhine and the Siebengebirge* to be seen from the back of his house; 'for Beethoven loved the Rhine.' It can be safely assumed that Beethoven tramped around the lovely outskirts of Bonn at an early age, and there are stories handed down to confirm it. One relates that during the Elector's absences, at which time the musicians were free, father Johann van Beethoven would travel into the country with his son Ludwig and the young Rovantini at the invitation of various music-lovers. In Siegburg, a tradition has been preserved of a later time when the young Beethoven played the organ in the abbey there. In Oberkassel there was the estate of a Herr von Meinertzhagen who is known to have been a patron of the young Beethoven. Since several of the persons invited were noted as friends of music, it is to be supposed that the father visited there with the special purpose of exhibiting his youthful prodigy.

Mother and son undertook a voyage to Holland in the beginning of the winter of 1781. The widow Karth, one of the Hertel family, born in 1780 and still living in Bonn in 1861, distinctly remembered sitting, when a child, upon her own mother's knee, and hearing Madame van Beethoven – 'a quiet, suffering woman' – relate that when she went with her little boy Ludwig to Holland it was so cold on the boat that she had to hold his feet in her lap to prevent them from being frostbitten; and also that, while absent, Ludwig played a great deal in great houses, astonished people by his skill and received valuable presents.

Christian Gottlob Neefe succeeded the persons mentioned earlier as Beethoven's master in music. When this tutorship began and ended, and whether or not it be true that the Elector engaged and paid him for his services in this capacity, as affirmed by divers writers – here again positive evidence is wanting. Neefe came to Bonn in October 1779; received the decree of succession to the position of Court Organist on 15 February 1781, and was thus permanently engaged in the Elector's

* The mountain range with seven peaks on the other side of the Rhine.

service. The unsatisfactory nature of the earlier instruction, as well as the high reputation of Neefe, would render it highly desirable to Johann van Beethoven to transfer his son to the latter's care. It was more than ever necessary that the boy's talents should be put to profitable use, for the father found his family still increasing as he was gradually sinking in social position. The baptism of a daughter named Anna Maria Franziska is recorded in the St Remigius register on 23 February 1779, and her death on the 27th of the same month. The baptism of August Franciscus Georgius van Beethoven follows nearly two years later – 17 January 1781.

The truth seems to be that Johann van Beethoven had now determined to make an organist of his son as the surest method of making his talents productive. The appointment of Neefe necessarily destroyed Ludwig's hope of being van den Eeden's successor; but Neefe's other numerous employments would make an assistant indispensable, and to this place the boy might well aspire. It will be seen in the course of the narrative that Beethoven never had a warmer, kinder and more valuable friend than Neefe proved throughout the remainder of his Bonn life; and that, in fact, his first appointment was obtained for him through Neefe.

Dr Wegeler remarks: 'Neefe had little influence upon the instruction of our Ludwig, who frequently complained of the too severe criticisms made on his first efforts in composition.' The first of these assertions is evidently an utter mistake. In 1793 Beethoven himself, at all events, thought differently: 'I thank you for the counsel which you gave me so often in my progress in my divine art. If I ever become a great man yours shall be a share of the credit. This will give you the greater joy since you may rest assured,' etc. Thus he wrote to his old teacher. As to the complaint of harsh criticism it may be remarked that Neefe, reared in the strict Leipzig school, must have been greatly dissatisfied with the direction which the young genius was taking under the influences which surrounded him, and that he should labour to change its course. He was still a young man, and in his zeal for his pupil's progress may well have criticised his childish compositions with a severity which, though no more than just and reasonable, may have so contrasted with injudicious praise from other quarters as to wound the boy's self-esteem and leave a sting behind; especially if Neefe indulged in a tone at all contemptuous, a common fault of young men in like cases.

But to return from the broad field of hypothesis to the narrow path of facts. 'On this day, 20 June 1782,' Neefe writes of himself and the Grossmann company, 'we entered upon our journey to Münster, whither the Elector also went. The day before my predecessor, Court Organist van den Eeden, was buried; I received permission, however, to leave my duties in the hands of a vicar* and go along to Westphalia and thence to the Michaelmas fair at Frankfurt.' The Düsseldorf documents prove that this vicar was Ludwig van Beethoven, now just eleven and a half years of age.

In the course of the succeeding winter, Neefe prepared that very valuable and interesting communication to Cramer's *Magazin der Musik* in which occurs the first printed notice of Beethoven. He writes, under date of 2 March 1783:

'Louis van Betthoven, son of the tenor singer mentioned, a boy of eleven years and of most promising talent. He plays the clavier very skilfully and with power, reads at sight very well, and – to put it in a nutshell – he plays chiefly *The Well-Tempered Clavichord* of Sebastian Bach, which Herr Neefe put into his hands. Whoever knows this collection of preludes and fugues in all the keys – which might almost be called the *non plus ultra* of our art – will know what this means. So far as his duties permitted, Herr Neefe has also given him instruction in thorough-bass. He is now training him in composition and for his encouragement has had nine variations for the pianoforte, written by him on a march – by Ernst Christoph Dressler – engraved at Mannheim. This youthful genius is deserving of help to enable him to travel. He would surely become a second Wolfgang Amadeus Mozart were he to continue as he has begun.'

This allusion to Mozart, who had not then produced those immortal works upon which his fame now principally rests, speaks well for the insight of Neefe and renders his high appreciation of his pupil's genius the more striking.

It is particularly to Neefe's credit that he brought Sebastian Bach's *Well-Tempered Clavichord* to his pupil's attention, because with it he provided the young genius with material to offset the shallowness of many of the compositions of the day with which Beethoven, because of his professional duties, could not escape contact. From Bach's preludes and fugues, which he was also to play a great deal later in life, he not only derived considerable instruction, but he found, as is evidenced in many of his later works, a pattern for imitation. In general, however, his model was not Bach but Mozart. That Beethoven early became familiar with Mozart's music in his own home may be regarded as certain. From 1784 on, he was in a position to become acquainted almost

* A locum or assistant.

at once with Mozart's latest major works and the latter's influence upon his own music can be traced almost everywhere.

It must be assumed that Neefe, his character being what it was, proceeded conscientiously, carefully, and 'as best he could' methodically with his instruction of the young genius. If nevertheless there were gaps in his instruction it was due to limitations in his own knowledge and ability. He himself, it must be remembered, had by his own admission never had a complete course in composition. Being in the theatre, and having the kind of mind that he did, what he valued most was the achievement of simplicity and intelligibility in music. He was not quite secure in the more difficult polyphonic forms and so could not teach them. For this lack Beethoven had to make up later with Albrechtsberger in Vienna. On the other hand, Neefe brought to the young artist another element which was extremely valuable in the development of his particular talent. Having studied philosophy, he liked to relate musical forms to the spiritual life of man, and in this direction exercised a decisive influence on Beethoven's artistic philosophy. Perhaps also by his suggesting graceful melodic and harmonic touches and by counselling variety in the repetition of an idea, etc., he may have awakened in Beethoven that critical sense which later we find developed to so high a degree. Whether we should go further and assume that he exerted a moral influence upon Beethoven's character is questionable It is not inconceivable that, from the human standpoint, the constant association with an admirable man who was also enthusiastic about his art may have been important to Beethoven, particularly in view of the less pleasant experiences of his home.

A second work belonging to this period was a two-part fugue in D for the organ, which was probably played at his trial for the post of second court organist.

The place of assistant organist to Neefe was no sinecure; although not involving much labour, it brought with it much confinement. The old organ had been destroyed by fire in 1777, and a small chamber instrument still supplied its place. It was the constantly recurring necessity of being present at the religious services which made the position onerous. According to the Court Calendar:

'On all Sundays and regular festivals high mass at 11 a.m. and vespers at 3 (sometimes 4) p.m. The vespers will be sung throughout in *Capellis solemnibus* by the musicians of the electoral court, the middle vespers will be sung by the court clergy and musicians in plain chant with the exception of the *Magnificat*, which will be performed in concerted music. On all Wednesdays in Lent the *Miserere* will be sung by the chapel at 5 p.m. and on all Fridays the *Stabat Mater*. Every Saturday at 3 p.m. the Litanies at the altar of Our Lady of Loretto. Every day throughout the year two masses will be read, the one at 9, the other at 11 – on Sundays the latter at 10.'

Such a programme gave the organist something at least to do, and when Neefe left Bonn for Münster, 20 June 1782, he left his pupil no easy task.

Before the close of the theatrical season of the next winter (1782–3) the master was obliged to call upon the boy for still further assistance. 'In the winter of 1784,' writes the widow Neefe, 'my husband of blessed memory was temporarily entrusted with the direction of the church music as well as all other music at the court while the Electoral Kapellmeister L[ucchesi] was absent on a journey of several months.' Thus overwhelmed with business, Neefe could no longer conduct at the pianoforte the rehearsals for the stage, and Ludwig van Beethoven, now twelve years old, became also 'cembalist in the orchestra'. In those days, every orchestra was provided with a harpsichord or pianoforte, seated at which the director guided the performance, playing from the score. Here, then, was in part the origin of that marvellous power, with which in later years Beethoven astonished his contemporaries, of reading and playing the most difficult and involved scores at first sight. The position of cembalist was one of equal honour and responsibility. Moreover, it was a place in which Ludwig could, even in boyhood, hear to satiety the popular Italian, French and German operas of the day and learn to feel that something higher and nobler was necessary to touch the deeper feelings of the heart; a place which, had the Elector lived ten years longer, might have given the world another not merely great but prolific, nay inexhaustible, operatic composer.

The cembalist's duties doubtless came to an end with the departure of the Elector for Münster in May or June, and he then had time for composition. A song, 'Schilderung eines Mädchens', by him was printed this year, and a Rondo in C for pianoforte, which immediately followed, was also of his composition. A more important work, which on 14 October 1783 was announced as published by Bossler with a magniloquent dedication to Max Friedrich, was the three sonatas for pianoforte, 'composed by Ludwig van Beethoven, aged eleven years'. Beethoven wrote on a copy of the first sonatas: 'These Sonatas and the Variations of Dressler are my first works.' He probably meant his first published works.

The widow Karth perfectly remembered Johann van Beethoven as a tall, handsome man with powdered head. Others described Ludwig to Dr Müller 'as a boy powerfully, almost clumsily built'. In the Fischer manuscript he is described as 'short of stature, broad shoulders, short neck, large head, round nose, dark brown complexion; he always bent forward slightly when he walked. In the house he was called *der Spagnol* (the Spaniard).' How easily fancy pictures them – the tall man walking to chapel or rehearsal with the little boy trotting by his side, through the streets of Bonn, and the gratified expression of the father as the child takes the place and performs the duties of a man!

To turn again to the Beethoven family matters. This summer (1783) had brought them sorrow again. The child Franz George, now just two and a half years old, died on 16 August. This was another stroke of bad fortune which wounded the heart of the father at a time when his pecuniary difficulties were increasing; he was now losing his voice, and his character is described in an official report made the next summer by the words 'of tolerable conduct'.

If the duties of Neefe during the last season had been laborious, in the coming one, 1783–4, they were still more arduous. It was the first under the new contract by which the Elector assumed all the costs of the theatre, and a woman, Mme Grossmann, had the direction. It was all-important to singers, actors and whoever was concerned that the result of the experiment should be satisfactory to their employer; and as the opera was more to his taste than the spoken drama, so much the more difficult was Neefe's task. Besides his acting as kapellmeister in the place of Lucchesi, still absent, there was 'every forenoon rehearsal of opera', as Mme Grossmann wrote to Councillor Tabor, at which, of course, Neefe had to be present. There was ever new music to be examined, arranged, copied, composed – what not? – all which he must attend to; in short, he had everything to do which could be imposed upon a theatrical music director with a salary of 1,000 florins. It therefore became a busy time for his young assistant, who still had no recognition as member of the court chapel and consequently no salary from the court. But he had now more than completed the usual year of probation to which candidates were subjected, and his talents and skill were well enough known to warrant his petition for an appointment. The petition has not been discovered; but the report made upon it to the privy council has been preserved, together with the endorsement.

'Most Reverend Archbishop and Elector,
Most Gracious Lord, Lord
'Your Electoral Grace has graciously been pleased to demand a dutiful report from me on the petition of Ludwig van Beethoven to Your Grace under date the 15th inst.

'Obediently and without delay [I report] that suppliant's father was for 29 years, his grandfather for 46, in the service of Your Most Reverend Electoral Grace and Your Electoral Grace's predecessors; that the suppliant has been amply proved and found capable to play the court organ as he has done in the absence of Organist Neefe, also at rehearsals of the plays and elsewhere and will continue to do so in the future; that Your Grace has graciously provided for his care and subsistence (his father no longer being able to do so). It is therefore my humble judgement that for these reasons the suppliant well deserves to have graciously bestowed upon him the position of assistant at the court organ and an increase of remuneration. Commending myself to the good will of Your Most Reverend Electoral Grace I am Your Most Reverend Grace's

most humble and obedient servant
Bonn, 23 February 1784   Sigismund Altergraff zu
Salm und Reifferscheid'

The action taken is thus indicated:

'High Lord Steward Count v. Salm, referring to the petition of *Ludwig van Betthofen* to become assistant to court organist Neefe, is of the humble opinion that the grace ought to be bestowed upon him, also that a small increase to his present support be granted.

Ad. sup.
Ludwig van Betthoven
'On the obedient report the suppliant's
submissive prayer, rests.'
'Bonn, 29 February 1784'

The appointment was made, but the salary had not been determined upon when an event occurred which wrought an entire change in the position of theatrical affairs at Bonn: the Elector died on 15 April, and the theatrical company was dismissed with four weeks' wages. Lucchesi returned to Bonn; Neefe had nothing to do but play his organ, cultivate his garden outside the town and give music lessons.

CHAPTER 3

First Visit to Vienna – The Years 1784–1792

The youngest son of Maria Theresia, Maximilian, had been elected Coadjutor to the ageing Elector in 1780. In this position he awaited, and was eventually rewarded by, the death of the older man four years later. Thus he succeeded to the Archbishopric and Electorate of Cologne, resident at Bonn, to the court of that city and to the musical establishment thereof – including the family Beethoven.

He was thirty-two, of middle stature, strongly built and already inclining to that corpulence which in his last years made him a prodigy of obesity. If all the absurdities of his eulogists be taken for truth, the last Elector of Cologne – for so it transpired – was endowed with every grace of mind and character that ever adorned human nature. In fact, however, he was a good-looking, kindly, indolent, somewhat choleric man; fond of a joke; affable; a hater of stiff ceremony; easy of access; an honest, amiable, conscientious ruler, who had the wisdom and will to supply his own deficiencies with enlightened and skilful ministers, and the good sense to rule, through their political foresight and sagacity, with an eye as much to the interests of his subjects as his own.

In his boyhood he was rather stupid. The brilliant, witty, shrewdly observant Mozart wrote to his father (17 November 1781):

'To whom God gives an office he also gives an understanding. This is really the case with the Archduke. Before he became a priest he was much wittier and more intellectual and talked less, but more sensibly. You ought to see him now! Stupidity looks out of his eyes; he talks eternally, always in falsetto; he has a swollen neck – in a word, the man is completely transformed.'

His mother had supplied him with the best instructors that Vienna afforded, and had sent him travelling pretty extensively for an archduke in those days. One of his journeys was to visit his sister Marie Antoinette in Paris, where his awkwardness and breaches of etiquette caused as much amusement to the anti-Austrian party as they did annoyance to the Queen.

The rigid economy which he introduced at court immediately after his accession in 1784 gave rise to the impression that he was penurious. It may be said in his defence that the condition of the finances required retrenchment and reform; that he was simple in his tastes and cared nothing for show and magnificence, except upon occasions when, in his opinion, the electoral dignity required them. Then, like his predecessors, he was lavish. His personal expenses were not great, and he waited until his revenues justified it before he indulged to any great extent his passion for the theatre, music and dancing (stout as he was, he was a passionate dancer), and his table. He was, through the nature of his physical constitution, an enormous eater, though his drink was only water.

The influence of a ruler upon the tone and character of society in a small capital is very great. One can well understand how Wegeler in his old age should write: 'In fact, it was a beautiful and in many ways active period in Bonn, so long as the genial Elector, Max Franz, Maria Theresia's youngest son and favourite, reigned there.' How strongly the improved tone of society impressed itself upon the characters of the young is discernible in the many of them who, in after years, were known as men of large and liberal ideas and became distinguished as jurists, theologians and artists, or in science and letters. These were the years of Beethoven's youth and early manhood; and though his great mental powers were in the main exercised upon his art, there is still to be observed through all his life a certain breadth and grandeur in his intellectual character, owing in part, no doubt, to the social influences under which it was developed.

Maximilian had become personally acquainted with Mozart in Salzburg in 1775, where the young composer had set Metastasio's *Il Re pastore* to music to be performed in his honour (23 April); from which time, to his credit be it said, he ever held the composer and his music in kindest remembrance. When in 1781 Mozart determined to leave his brutal Archbishop of Salzburg and remain in Vienna, Maximilian showed at all events a desire to aid him.

On 17 November 1781, the composer writes:

'Yesterday the Archduke Maximilian summoned me to him at 3 o'clock in the afternoon. When I entered he was standing before a stove in the first room awaiting me. He came towards me and asked if I had anything to do today. "Nothing, Your Royal Highness, and if I had it would always be a grace to wait upon Your Royal Highness." "No, I do not wish to constrain anyone." Then he said that he was minded to give a concert in the evening for the Court of Wurtemburg. Would I play something and accompany the aria? I was to come to him again at 6 o'clock. So I played there yesterday.'

Jahn, in his biography of Mozart, continues in the same vein: 'Mozart was everything to him; he signallised him at every opportunity and said, if he were Elector of Cologne, Mozart would surely be his kapellmeister.' Jahn gives no reason why Mozart was not engaged for Bonn at the time of Maximilian's succession. Perhaps he would have been if Lucchesi had resigned in consequence of the reduction of his salary; but he kept his office of kapellmeister and could not very well be dismissed without cause.

Was it the good or ill fortune of the boy Beethoven that Mozart came not to Bonn? His marvellous original talent was thus left to be developed without the fostering care of one of the very greatest of musical geniuses, and one of the profoundest of musical scholars; but on the other hand it was not oppressed, perhaps crushed, by daily inter-course with that genius and scholarship.

Maximilian, immediately upon accession as Elector, ordered full and minute reports to be made out concerning all branches of the administration, of the public and court service and of the cost of their maintenance. Upon these reports were based his arrangements for the future. Those relating to the court music give us details which carry us instantly into the circle which young Beethoven had just entered. They are three in number, the first being a list of all the individuals constituting the court chapel; the second a detailed description of the singers and players, together with an estimate of their capabilities; the third consists of recommendations touching a reduction in salaries.

'J. van Beethoven, age 44, born in Bonn, married; his wife is 32 years old, has three sons living in the electorate, age 13, 10 and 8 years, who are studying music, has served 28 years, salary 315 fl.

'Johann Beethoven has a very stale voice, has been long in the ser-vice, very poor, of fair deportment and married.'

Among the organists:

'Christ. Gottlob Neefe, age 36, born at Chemnitz; married, his wife is 32, born at Gotha, has two daughters in the electorate, aged 5 and 2, has served three years, was formerly kapellmeister with Seiler; salary 400 fl.

'Christian Neffe, the organist, in my humble opinion might well be dismissed, inasmuch as he is not particularly versed on the organ, moreover is a foreigner, having no *Meritten* whatever and of the Calvinist religion.

'Ludwig van Beethoven, age 13, born at Bonn, has served two years, no salary.

'Ludwig Beethoven, a son of the Beethoven sub No. 8, has no salary, but during the absence of the Kapellmeister Luchesy he played the organ, is of good capability, still young, of good and quiet deportment and poor.'

One of the items of the third report, proposing reductions of salaries and removals, has a very special interest as proving that an effort was made to supplant Neefe and give the post of court organist to young Beethoven. It reads:

'*Item*. If Neffe were to be dismissed another organist would have to be appointed, who, if he were to be used only in the chapel could be had for 150 florins, the same is small, young, and a son of one of the court *musici*, and in case of need has filled the place for nearly a year very well.'

This brings to light the ticklish situation Beethoven was in: the student was obviously caught between gratitude for his teacher's help and his own self-interest.

The temporary resolution of this conflict is indicated by the list of 'annual salaries of the Court Chapel and Music', dated 27 June 1784, which includes Neefe, organist, 200 florins in salary, and directly afterwards, Beethoven, organist, 150 florins in salary. This appears to be a compromise decision in which the salary for the boy had clearly been taken out of the salary of his teacher.

Schindler records that he heard Beethoven attribute the marvellous developments of Mozart's genius in great measure to the 'consistent instruction of his father', thus implying his sense of the disadvantages under which he himself laboured from the want of regular and systematic musical training through the period of his childhood and youth. Czerny also related that Beethoven had spoken to him of the harsh treatment and insufficient instruction received from his father. 'But', he added, 'I had talent for music.' It is, however, by no means certain that had Ludwig van Beethoven been the son of Leopold Mozart, he would ever have acquired that facility of expression which enabled Wolfgang Mozart to fill up the richest and most varied scores almost as rapidly as his pen could move, and so as hardly to need correction. Handel said of the elder Telemann that he could compose in eight parts as easily as he (Handel) could write a letter; and Handel's own facility in composition was something astonishing. Beethoven, on the contrary, as his original scores prove, earned his bread by the sweat of his brow. It should be mentioned here that Beethoven now or soon afterwards began to give lessons. That this happened before the death of his mother and that the purpose was to increase the slender family income we learn from Beethoven himself and from Wegeler.

One family event is recorded in the parish of St Remigius – the baptism of Maria Margaretha Josepha, daughter of Johann van Beethoven, on 5 May 1786.

From Dr Wegeler we learn of Beethoven's early friendship with the von Breuning family:

'Ludwig received his first acquaintance with German literature, especially poetry, as well as his first training in social behaviour in the midst of the von Breuning family in Bonn . . . In this house reigned an unconstrained tone of culture in spite of youthful wilfulness. Christoph von Breuning made early essays in poetry, as was the case (and not without success) with [his son] Stephan von Breuning much later. The friends of the family were distinguished by indulgence in social entertainments which combined the useful and the agreeable. When we add that the family possessed considerable wealth, especially before the war, it will be easy to understand that the first joyous emotions of Beethoven found vent here. Soon he was treated as one of the children in the family, spending in the house not only the greater part of his days, but also many nights. Here he felt that he was free, here he moved about without constraint, everything conspired to make him cheerful and develop his mind.'

*

There is a letter from Bonn, written by Neefe, dated 8 April 1787, which contains a passing allusion to Beethoven, and it affords another glimpse of the musical life there.

'Our residence city is becoming more and more attractive for music-lovers through the gracious patronage of our beloved Elector. He has a large collection of the most beautiful music and is expending much every day to augment it. It is to him, too, that we owe the privilege of hearing often good virtuosi on various instruments. Good singers come seldom. The love of music is increasing greatly among the inhabitants . . . The youthful Baron v. Gudenau plays the pianoforte right bravely, and besides young Beethoven, the children of the kapellmeister deserve to be mentioned because of their admirable and precociously developed talent.'

'This young genius deserves support to enable him to travel,' wrote Neefe in 1783. In the springtime of 1787 the young 'genius' was at length enabled to travel. Whence or how he obtained the means to defray the expenses of his journey, whether aided by the Elector or some other Maecenas, or dependent upon the small savings from his salary and – hardly possible – from the savings from his music lessons painfully and carefully hoarded for the purpose, does not appear.

The approximate dates of the journey have been established from the midweek reports of visitors in the *Münchener Zeitung* in the spring of 1787. On 1 April is listed the arrival of 'Herr Peethofen, Musikus von Bonn bei Kölln', again on 25 April staying at the tavern 'zum schwarzen Adler' is 'Herr Peethoven, Kurköllnischer Kammervirtuos von Bonn'. To reach Munich on 1 April, Beethoven must have started his trip about 20 March and reached Vienna on 7 April. But clearly he spent another night in Munich on 25 April, which suggests his having left Vienna to return to Bonn about 20 April. Thus he was in Vienna less than two weeks. On that visit two persons only were deeply impressed upon the lifelong memory of the youth of sixteen years: the Emperor Joseph and Mozart.

Mozart, recently returned from Prague, was already deeply engrossed in the composing of *Don Giovanni*. On 4 April he was writing to his father, having just received news of his poor health. (Leopold Mozart died within two months.) It was not an auspicious time for lessons with the master.

The oft-repeated anecdote recorded by Otto Jahn of Beethoven's introduction to Mozart runs thus: Beethoven, who as a youth of great promise came to Vienna in the spring of 1787, but was obliged to return to Bonn after a brief sojourn, was taken to Mozart and at that musician's request played something for him which he, taking it for granted that it was a show-piece prepared for the occasion, praised in a rather cool manner. Beethoven observing this, begged Mozart to give him a theme for improvisation. He always played admirably when excited and now he was inspired, too, by the presence of the master whom he reverenced greatly; he played in such a style that Mozart, whose attention and interest grew more and more, finally went silently to some friends who were sitting in an adjoining room, and said, vivaciously, 'Keep your eyes on him; some day he will give the world something to talk about.'

The lessons given were few — a fact which accounts for the circumstance that no member of Mozart's family in after years, when Beethoven had become world-renowned, has spoken of them.

According to a communication from Czerny to Otto Jahn, Beethoven had explained to him that he had heard Mozart play: 'he had a fine but choppy [*zerhacktes*] way of playing, no *ligato*.' Czerny adds that Beethoven played this way at first, treating the pianoforte like an organ.

The earliest discovered letter of Beethoven, written to his friend Joseph Wilhelm von Schaden, fully explains the causes of his sudden departure from Vienna and the abrupt termination of his studies with Mozart.

'Well-born, especially worthy friend!

'I can easily imagine what you must think of me, and I cannot deny that you have good grounds for not thinking favourably of me. I shall not, however, attempt to justify myself, until I have explained to you the reasons why I hope my apologies will be accepted. I must tell you that from the time I left Augsburg my cheerfulness as well as my health began to decline. The nearer I came to my native city the more frequent were the letters from my father urging me to travel with all possible speed, as my mother was not in a favourable state of health. I therefore hurried forward as fast as I could, although myself far from well. My longing once more to see my dying mother overcame every obstacle and assisted me in surmounting the greatest difficulties. I found my mother still alive but in the most deplorable state; her disease was consumption, and about seven weeks ago, after much pain and suffering, she died. She was such a kind, loving mother to me, and my best friend. Ah, who was happier than I when I could still utter the sweet name, mother, and it was heard? And to whom can I say it now? Only to the silent images of her evoked by the power of the imagination. I have passed very few pleasant hours since my arrival here, having during the whole time been suffering from asthma, which may, I fear, eventually develop into consumption. To this is added melancholy, almost as great an evil as my malady itself. Imagine yourself in my place, and then I shall hope to receive your forgiveness for my long silence. You showed me extreme kindness and friendship by lending me three carolins in Augsburg, but I must entreat your indulgence for a time. My journey cost me a great deal, and I have not the smallest hopes of earning anything here. Fate is not propitious to me here in Bonn.

'Pardon my detaining you so long with my chatter; it was necessary for my justification.

'I do entreat you not to deprive me of your valuable friendship; nothing do I wish so much as in some degree to become worthy of your regard.

'I am, with the greatest respect
Your most obedient servant and friend,
L. v. Beethoven,
Court Organist to the Elector of Cologne'

A petition of Johann van Beethoven, offered before the death of his wife, describing his pitiable condition and asking aid from the Elector, has not been discovered; but the substance of it is found in a volume of *Geheime Staats-Protocolle* for 1787 in form following:

'24 July 1787

'Your Elec.   'Court Musician makes obedient representation that he has
Highness   got into a very unfortunate state because of the long-
has taken   continued sickness of his wife and has already been com-
possession   pelled to sell a portion of his effects and pawn others and
of this   that he no longer knows what to do for his sick wife and
petition.'   many children. He prays for the benefaction of an advance
of 100 rthlr. on his salary.'

No record is found in the Düsseldorf archives of any grant of aid to the distressed family; hence, so far as now appears, the only successful appeal for assistance was made to Franz Ries, then a young man of thirty-two years, who generously aided in 'every way' his unfortunate colleague.

'My journey cost me a great deal, and I have not the smallest hopes of earning anything here. Fate is not propitious to me here in Bonn.' In poverty, ill, melancholy, despondent, motherless, ashamed of and depressed by his father's ever increasing moral infirmity, the boy, prematurely old from the circumstances in which he had been placed since his eleventh year, had yet to bear another 'sling and arrow of outrageous fortune'. The little sister, now a year and a half old – but here is the notice from the *Intelligenzblatt*: 'Died, 25 November, Margareth, daughter of the Court Musician Johann van Beethoven, aged one year.' And so faded the last hope that the passionate tenderness of Beethoven's nature might find scope in the purest of all relations between the sexes – that of brother and sister.

Thus, in sadness and gloom, Beethoven's seventeenth year ended.

*

Wegeler writes:

'The first, and in every respect the most important, of the Maecenases of Beethoven was Count Waldstein, Knight of the Teutonic Order, and (what is of greater moment here) the favourite and constant companion of the young Elector . . . He was not only a connoisseur but also a practitioner of music. He it was who gave all manner of support to our Beethoven, whose gifts he was the first to recognise worthily. Through him the young genius developed the talent to improvise variations on a given theme. From him he received much pecuniary assistance bestowed in such a way as to spare his sensibilities, it being generally looked upon as a small gratuity from the Elector. Beethoven's appointment as organist, his being sent to Vienna by the Elector, were the doings of the Count. When Beethoven at a later date dedicated the great and important Sonata in C major, Op. 53, to him, it was only a proof of the gratitude which lived on in the mature man. It is to Count Waldstein that Beethoven owed the circumstance that the first sproutings of his genius were not nipped; therefore we owe this Maecenas Beethoven's later fame.'

Wegeler's testimony concerning the warm relationship between the Count and the Elector is borne out by their correspondence. On the other hand, Wegeler is not reliable concerning the extent that the Count helped the young composer. It is likely, however, that if the Count, in the name of the Elector, helped Beethoven to reach Vienna it was for his second trip – and what turned out to be his final move there – in 1792.

It was in the cultivated circle of the von Breuning family that the friendship between Beethoven and the Count was allowed to develop. By this time Ludwig was seventeen, and the role of this family in his life was constantly increasing in value to him both morally and intellectually.

The recent loss of his mother had left a void in his heart which so excellent a woman as Madame von Breuning could alone in some measure fill. He was at an age when the evil example of his father needed a counterbalance; when his mental powers, so strong and healthy, would demand some change, some recreation, from that constant strain in the one direction of music to which almost from infancy they had been subjected; when not only the reaction upon his mind of the fresh and new intellectual life now pervading Bonn society, but his daily contact with so many of his own age, friends and companions now enjoying advantages for improvement denied to him, must have cost him many a pang; when a lofty and noble ambition might be aroused to lead him ever onward; when, the victim of a despondent melancholy, he might sink into the mere routine musician, with no lofty aims, no higher object than to draw from his talents means to supply his necessities and gratify his appetites.

The association between Waldstein and the von Breunings during the spring of 1788 grew rapidly into friendship, as is confirmed by the fact that already in June the Count knew the family well enough to borrow from them a sum of money to help defray the expenses of the ceremony of his induction into the Teutonic Order. Furthermore, the von Breunings for generations had held positions in the order. One can imagine much music-making at that lively house on the city side of the Münsterplatz in which both Beethoven and Count Waldstein could participate, for this nobleman had had the best of musical education in Vienna during his childhood.

We have seen that relations between Waldstein and the Elector became close; both were great admirers of Mozart, and the Elector must have welcomed someone with whom he could talk about the Austrian Court.

After the death of the mother, says Frau Karth, a housekeeper was employed by the family Beethoven, and father and sons remained together in the lodgings in the Wenzelgasse, to which they had moved around 1785. Carl was intended for the musical profession; Johann was put apprentice to the court apothecary, Johann Peter Hittorf. Two years, however, had hardly elapsed when the father's infirmity compelled the eldest son, not yet nineteen years of age, to take the extraordinary step of placing himself at the head of the family. One of Stephan von Breuning's reminiscences shows how low Johann van Beethoven had sunk: viz., that of having seen Ludwig furiously interposing to rescue his intoxicated father from an officer of police.

Here again the petition has disappeared, but its contents are sufficiently made known by the terms of the decree dated 20 November 1789:

'His Electoral Highness having graciously granted the prayer of the petitioner and dispensed henceforth wholly with the services of his father, who is to withdraw to a village in the electorate, it is graciously commanded that he be paid in accordance with his wish only 100 rthlr. of the annual salary which he has had heretofore, beginning with the approaching new year, and that the other 100 rthlr. be paid to the suppliant's son besides the salary which he now draws and the three measures of grain for the support of his brothers.'

It is probable that there was no intention to enforce this decree in respect of the withdrawal of the father from Bonn, and that this clause was inserted *in terrorem* in case he misbehaved himself.

Early in the year 1788, the mind of the Elector, Max Franz, was occupied with the project for the founding of a National Theatre. His finances were now in order, the administration of public affairs in able hands and working smoothly, and there was nothing to hinder him from placing both music and theatre upon a better and permanent footing; which he now proceeded to do. A comparison of the lists of the theatrical establishment with that of the court chapel, as printed in the Court Calendars for 1778 and the following years, shows that some of the singers in the chapel played in the theatrical orchestra, while certain of the players in the chapel sang upon the stage.

As organist the name of Beethoven appears still in the Court Calendar, but as viola player he had a place in both the orchestras. Thus, for a period of full four years, he had the opportunity of studying practically orchestral compositions in the best of all schools – the orchestra itself. This body of thirty-one members, many of them young and ambitious, some already known as virtuosi and still keeping their places in musical history as such, was a school for instrumental music such as Handel, Bach, Mozart and Haydn had not enjoyed in their youth; that its advantages were improved both by Beethoven and others of the younger men, all the world knows.

Beethoven's eighteenth birthday came around during the rehearsals for the first season of this theatre; his twenty-second just after the beginning of the fifth. During four years (1788–92) he was adding to his musical knowledge and experience in a direction wherein he has usually been represented as deficient – as active member of an operatic orchestra; and the catalogue of works performed shows that the best schools of the day, save that of Berlin, must have been thoroughly mastered by him in all their strength and weakness. Beethoven's titanic power and grandeur would have marked his compositions under any circumstances; but it is very doubtful if, without the training of those years as member of the orchestra, his works would have so abounded in melodies of such profound depths of expression, of such heavenly serenity and repose and of such divine beauty as they do, and which give him rank with the two greatest of melodists, Handel and Mozart.

CHAPTER 4

The Move to Vienna

As a pendant to the preceding sketches a variety of notices belonging to the last three years of Beethoven's life in his native place are here brought together in chronological order.

Prof. Dr Wurzer communicated to the *Kölnische Zeitung* of 30 August 1838, the following pleasant anecdote:

'In the summer of the year 1790 or 1791 I was one day on business in Godesberger Brunnen. After dinner Beethoven and another young man came up. I related to him that the church at Marienforst (a cloister in the woods behind Godesberg) had been repaired and renovated, and that this was also true of the organ, which was either wholly new or at least greatly improved. The company begged him to give them the pleasure of letting them hear him play on the instrument. His great good nature led him to grant our wish. The church was locked, but the prior was very obliging and had it unlocked for us. B. now began to play variations on themes given him by the party in a manner that moved us profoundly; but what was much more significant, poor labouring folk who were cleaning out the debris left by the work of repair, were so greatly affected by the music that they put down their implements and listened with amazement and obvious pleasure.'

The greatest musical event of the year (1790) in Bonn occurred just at its close – the visit of Joseph Haydn, on his way to London with the brilliant violinist and conductor, Salomon. Haydn's own account was recorded by his biographer A. C. Dies.

'In the capital, Bonn, he was surprised in more ways than one. He reached the city on Saturday [Christmas, 25 December] and set apart the next day for rest. On Sunday, Salomon accompanied Haydn to the court chapel to listen to mass. Scarcely had the two entered the church and found suitable seats when high mass began. The first chords announced a product of Haydn's muse. Our Haydn looked upon it as an accidental occurrence which had happened only to flatter him; nevertheless it was decidedly agreeable to him to listen to his own composition. Towards the close of the mass a person approached and

Beethoven's grandfather and namesake, the kapellmeister
Ludwig van Beethoven, *c.*1773

Two engravings commonly held to represent Beethoven's parents, Johann and Maria Magdalena, although the authenticity of these is now in some doubt. *Below left*, a drawing made in 1889 of the house in the Bonngasse where Beethoven was born, and, *below right*, a silhouette of the composer in his sixteenth year, then 'a shy and taciturn boy . . . disposed to abandon himself entirely to the feelings awakened by music'

asked him to repair to the oratory, where he was expected. Haydn obeyed and was not a little surprised when he found that the Elector, Maximilian, had had him summoned, took him at once by the hand and presented him to the virtuosi [who had performed the mass] with the words: "Here I make you acquainted with the Haydn whom you all revere so highly." The Elector gave both parties time to become acquainted with each other, and, to give Haydn a convincing proof of his respect, invited him to dinner. This unexpected invitation put Haydn into an embarrassing position, for he and Salomon had ordered a modest little dinner in their lodgings, and it was too late to make a change. Haydn was therefore fain to take refuge in excuses which the Elector accepted as genuine and sufficient. Haydn took his leave and returned to his lodgings, where he was made aware in a special manner of the good will of the Elector, at whose secret command the little dinner had been metamorphosed into a banquet for twelve persons to which the most capable musicians had been invited.

Was our young musician one of these 'most capable musicians'? It seems possible: Beethoven was listed as one of the chapel musicians to the Elector in 1791.

At Aschaffenburg-am-Main was the large summer palace of the Electors of Mainz; and here dwelt Abbé Sterkel, now a man of forty years; a musician from his infancy, one of the first pianists of all Germany and without a rival in this part of it. His style both as composer and pianist had been refined and cultivated to the utmost, both in Germany and Italy, and his playing was in the highest degree light, graceful, pleasing and, as it was described to Wegeler, 'somewhat ladylike'. Beethoven and others were taken to pay their respects to the master, 'who, complying with the general request, sat himself down to play. Beethoven, who up to this time', says Wegeler, 'had not heard a great or celebrated pianoforte player, knew nothing of the finer nuances in the handling of the instrument; his playing was rude and hard. Now he stood with attention all on a strain by the side of Sterkel'; for this grace and delicacy, if not power of execution, which he now heard were a new revelation to him. After Sterkel had finished, the young Bonn concert-player was invited to take his place at the instrument; but he naturally hesitated to exhibit himself after such a display. The shrewd Abbé, however, brought him to it by a pretence of doubting his ability.

A year or two before, Kapellmeister Vincenzo Righini, a colleague of Sterkel in the service of the Elector of Mainz, had published *Dodeci Ariette*, one of which, 'Vieni (Venni) Amore', was a melody with five vocal variations, to the same accompaniment. Beethoven, taking this melody as his theme, had composed, dedicated to the Countess of Hatzfeld and published twenty-four variations for the pianoforte upon it. Some of these were very difficult, and Sterkel now expressed his doubts if their author could himself play them. His honour thus touched, 'Beethoven played not only these variations so far as he could remember them (Sterkel could not find them), but went on with a number of others no less difficult, all to the great surprise of the listeners, perfectly, and in the ingratiating manner that had struck him in Sterkel's playing.'

Carl Ludwig Junker, Chaplain at Kirchberg, the residence of Prince Hohenlohe, wrote thus to Bossler's *Musikalische Correspondenz* in 1791:

'I heard also one of the greatest of pianists – the dear, good Bethofen . . . But, what was infinitely preferable to me, I heard him extemporise in private; yes, I was even invited to propose a theme for him to vary. The greatness of this amiable, light-hearted man, as a virtuoso, may in my opinion be safely estimated from his almost inexhaustible wealth of ideas, the altogether characteristic style of expression in his playing, and the great execution which he displays. I know, therefore, no one thing which he lacks, that conduces to the greatness of an artist. I have heard Vogler upon the pianoforte – of his organ playing I say nothing, not having heard him upon that instrument – have often heard him, heard him by the hour together, and never failed to wonder at his astonishing execution; but Bethofen, in addition to the execution, has greater clearness and weight of idea, and more expression – in short, he is more for the heart – equally great, therefore, as an adagio or allegro player . . . Yet he is exceedingly modest and free from all pretension. He, however, acknowledged to me, that, upon the journeys which the Elector had enabled him to make, he had seldom found in the playing of the most distinguished virtuosi that excellence which he supposed he had a right to expect. His style of treating his instrument is so different from that usually adopted, that it impresses one with the idea, that by a path of his own discovery he has attained that height of excellence whereon he now stands.'

During the last years in Bonn when he could find little joy or satisfaction at home, it became his habit to spend evenings at the tavern. At that time the favourite place of resort for the professors of the new Bonn university and for young men whose education and position at court or in society were such as to make them welcome guests, was the house on the Market-place later known as the Zehrgarten; and there Beethoven was accustomed also to go. Its mistress was the widow Koch who spread also a table for a select company of boarders. Her name, too, often appears in the *Intelligenzblatt* of Bonn in advertisements of books and music. Of her three children, a son and two daughters, the beautiful Barbara – the Babette Koch mentioned in a letter of Beethoven's – was the belle of Bonn. Wegeler's eulogy of her reads thus:

'She was a confidential friend of Eleonore von Breuning, a lady who of all the representatives of the female sex that I met in a rather active and long life came nearest the ideal of a perfect woman – an opinion which is confirmed by all who had the good fortune to know her well. She was surrounded not only by young artists like Beethoven . . . but also by the intellectual men of all classes and ages.'

About the time Beethoven left Bonn for Vienna, the wife of Count Anton von Belderbusch, nephew of the deceased minister of that name, had deserted her husband for the embraces of a certain Baron von Lichtenstein, and Babette Koch was engaged as governess and instructress of the motherless children. In process of time Belderbusch obtained a divorce (under the French law) from his adulterous wife and married the governess on 9 August 1802.

But it was in the Breuning house that Beethoven enjoyed and profited most. The mother's kindness towards him gave her both the right and the power to urge and compel him to the performance of his teaching duties; and this power over him in his obstinate and passionate moods she possessed in a higher degree than any other person. Wegeler gives an anecdote in point: Baron Westphal von Fürstenberg, until now in the service of the Elector, was appointed minister to the Dutch and Westphalian Circuit and to the courts of Cologne and Trèves, his headquarters being at Bonn. He resided in the large house which is now occupied by the post office, directly behind the statue of him who was engaged as music teacher in the Count's family. The Breuning house was but a few steps distant diagonally across a corner of the square. Here Madame von Breuning was sometimes compelled to use her authority and force the young man to go to his lessons. Knowing that she was watching him he would go, but sometimes at the very door would turn back and excuse himself on the plea that today it was impossible to give a lesson – tomorrow he would give two; to which, as upon other occasions when reasoning with him was of no avail, the good lady would shrug her shoulders with the remark: 'He has his *raptus* again,'

an expression which the rapt Beethoven never forgot. Most happy
was it for him that in Madame von Breuning he had a friend who
understood his character thoroughly, who cherished affection for him,
who could and did so effectually act as peacemaker when the harmony
between him and her children was disturbed. Schindler wrote:

'In his later days he still called the members of this family his guardian
angels of that time and remembered with pleasure the many repri-
mands which he had received from the lady of the house. "She understood", said he, "how to keep insects off the flowers." By insects he
meant certain friendships which had already begun to threaten danger
to the natural development of his talent and a proper measure of artistic consciousness by awakening vanity in him by their flatteries. He
was already near to considering himself a famous artist, and therefore
more inclined to give heed to those who encouraged him in his illu-
sions than such as set before him the fact that he had still to learn everything that makes a master out of a disciple.'

Beethoven's remarkable powers of improvising were often exhibited
at the Breuning house. Wegeler has an anecdote: 'Once when Beethoven was improvising at the house of the Breunings (on which
occasions he used frequently to be asked to characterise in the music
some well-known person) Father Ries was urged to accompany him
upon the violin. After some hesitation he consented, and this may have
been the first time that two artists improvised a duo.'

Beethoven had in common with all men of original and creative
genius a strong repugnance to the drudgery of forcing the elements of
his art into dull brains and awkward fingers, namely, the teaching of
pupils of little talent. He was, in 1791–2, just at the age when the
desire for distinction was fresh and strong; he was conscious of powers
still not fully developed; his path was diverse from that of the other
young men with whom he associated and who, from all that can be
gathered now on the subject, had little faith in that which he had
chosen. He must have felt the necessity of other instruction, or, at all
events, of better opportunities to compare his powers with those of
others, to measure himself by a higher standard, to try the effect of his
compositions in another sphere, to satisfy himself that his instincts as a
composer were true and that his deviations from the beaten track were
not wild and capricious. Waldstein, we know from Wegeler, had faith
in him and his works. To this add the restlessness of an ambitious
youth to whom the routine of duties, which must long since in great
measure have lost the charm of novelty, had become tedious, and the

natural longing of young men for the great world, for a wider field of action, had grown almost insupportable.

Or Beethoven's *raptus* may just then have had a very different origin; Jeannette d'Honrath, or Fräulein Westerholt, was perhaps the innocent cause – two young ladies whose names are preserved by Wegeler of the many for whom he says his friend at various times indulged transient, but not the less ardent, passions. The former was from Cologne, whence she occasionally came to Bonn to pass a few weeks with Eleonore von Breuning. Wegeler says of her: 'She was a beautiful, vivacious blonde, of good education, and amiable disposition, who enjoyed music greatly and possessed an agreeable voice; wherefore she several times teased our friend by singing a song, familiar at the time, beginning:

> 'Mich heute noch von dir zu trennen
> Und dieses nicht verhindern können,
>   Ist zu empfindlich für mein Herz!'*

for the favoured rival was the Austrian recruiting officer in Cologne, Carl Greth, who eventually married the young lady.

The passion for Miss d'Honrath was eclipsed by a subsequent fancy for a Fräulein von Westerholt. The Court Calendars of these years name 'Hochfürstlich Münsterischer Obrist-Stallmeister, Sr. Excellenz der Hochwohlgeborene Herr Friedrich Rudolph Anton, Freyherr von Westerholt-Giesenberg, kurkölnischer und Hochstift-Münsterischer Geheimrath'. This much betitled man 'played the bassoon himself and maintained a fair band among his servants, particularly players of wind-instruments'. He had two sons and two daughters. The elder daughter, Maria Anna Wilhelmine, was born on 24 July 1774, married Baron Friedrich Clemens von Elverfeldt, called von Beverföde-Werries, on 24 April 1792, and died on 3 November 1852. She was an excellent pianist. In Münster, Neefe heard 'the fiery Mad. von Elverfeldt' play 'a difficult sonata by Sardi [Giuseppe Sarti] with a rapidity and accuracy that were marvellous'.

It is not surprising that Beethoven's talent should have met with recognition and appreciation in this musical family. He became the young woman's teacher, and as the chief equerry Count Westerholt had to accompany the Elector on his visits to Münster, where, moreover, he owned a house, there is a tradition in the family that young

* 'To part from you again today,
    And to be unable to prevent this
        Is too painful for my heart!'

Beethoven went with them before the young lady's marriage, thus probably around 1790. He had the disease violently, nor did he 'let concealment, like a worm i' the bud', feed upon his cheek.

To the point of Beethoven's susceptibility to the tender passion let Wegeler again be cited:

'The truth as I learned to know it . . . is that there was never a time when Beethoven was not in love, and that in the highest degree. These passions, for the Misses d'Honrath and Westerholt, fell in his transition period from youth to manhood, and left impressions as little deep as were those made upon the beauties who had caused them. In Vienna, at all events so long as I lived there, Beethoven was always in love and occasionally made a conquest which would have been very difficult if not impossible for many an Adonis.'

A relationship that was deeper and more enduring was Beethoven's feeling for Eleonore von Breuning. In December of 1826 Beethoven wrote in a letter to Wegeler: 'I still have the silhouette of your Lorchen, so you see how precious even now are all the dear, good memories of my youth.' Of this Wegeler says: 'In two evenings the silhouettes of all the members of the von Breuning family and more intimate friends of the house were made by the printer Neesen of Bonn. In this way I came into the possession of that of Beethoven [who] was probably in his sixteenth year at the time.'

Two letters from Beethoven to Eleonore – one dated 2 November 1793, the other undated but written in 1794 – show that a quarrel or rift had occurred between them at some time before his departure from Bonn. The cause of it is not known, but these letters, to which we shall return, sought to re-establish and affirm their close friendship.

A review of some of the last pages shows that for the most part after 1789 the life of Beethoven was a busy one, but that the frequent absences of the Elector, as recorded in the newspapers of the day, left many a period of considerable duration during which, except for the meetings of the orchestra for rehearsal and study, he had full command of his time. Thus he had plenty of leisure hours and weeks to devote to composition, to instruction in music, for social intercourse, for visits to neighbouring places, for the indulgence of his strong propensity to ramble in the fields and among the mountains, for the cultivation in that beautiful Rhine region of his warm passion for nature.

The new relations to his father and brothers, as virtual head of the family, were such as to relieve his mind from anxiety on their account.

His position in society, too, had become one of which he might justly be proud, owing, as it was, to no adventitious circumstances, but simply to his genius and high personal character. These were evidently happy years, in spite of certain characteristic and gloomy expressions of Beethoven in letters hereafter to be given, and years of active intellectual, artistic and moral development.

The probability is that in July 1792 it had been proposed to Haydn to take Beethoven as a pupil; and it is pretty certain that the suggestion did not come from the Elector, who, there is little doubt, was in Frankfurt at the coronation of his nephew Emperor Franz (14 July) at the time of Haydn's visit. Whatever arrangements may have been made between the pupil and master, they were subject to the will of the Elector, and here Waldstein may well have exerted himself to his protégé's advantage. At all events, the result was favourable and the journey determined upon.

The Elector, although Archduke of Austria, was also head of a neighbouring state to France. Thus, while criticising France's intentions, he behaved more as a neutral than did Austria or Prussia. But when in October 1792 Mainz fell to the French and the whole left bank of the Rhine appeared to have surrendered defenceless to the enemy, the archives and valuables at Bonn were packed ready if necessary to be removed by ship. The Elector left his residence on 22 October but soon returned since danger for the upper Rhine had disappeared with the timely intervention of the Prussians at Coblenz. But with the French occupation of the Netherlands by the middle of December, combined with the inconvenient behaviour of the Austrians in his own province, the Elector felt compelled to move to Münster on 21 December, where he spent the winter. By March the Netherlands were again in Austrian hands, and the Elector returned to Bonn on 21 April 1793. But the French victories in the summer of 1794 filled Bonn with those in flight, and Maximilian Franz was forced to leave Bonn for the last time on 2 October 1794, from whence he went to Münster, then Frankfurt, and finally Mergentheim by the first half of December.

The fact that by the autumn of 1792 towns were being deserted by the upper classes may explain why Beethoven was able to obtain permission to leave Bonn for Vienna just before the start of the theatrical and musical season. He was given only enough money with which to travel and the promise that more would be forwarded thither.

Beethoven's departure from Bonn called forth lively interest on the part of his friends. The plan did not contemplate a long sojourn in the Austrian capital; it was his purpose, after completing his studies there, to return to Bonn and thence to go forth on artistic tours. This is proved by an autograph album dating from his last days in Bonn, which some of his intimate friends, obviously those with whom he was wont to associate at the Zehrgarten, sent with him on his way. The majority of the names are familiar to us, but many which one might have expected to find, notably those of the musicians of Bonn, are missing. Eleonore von Breuning's contribution was a quotation from Herder:

'Freundschaft, mit dem Guten,
Wächset wie der Abendschatten,
Bis des Lebens Sonne sinkt.'*

Most interesting of all the inscriptions in the album, however, is that of Count Waldstein. It proves how great were the writer's hopes, how strong his faith in Beethoven:

'Dear Beethoven! You are going to Vienna in fulfilment of your long frustrated wishes. The Genius of Mozart is mourning and weeping over the death of her pupil. She found a refuge but no occupation with the inexhaustible Haydn; through him she wishes to form a union with another. With the help of assiduous labour you shall receive *Mozart's spirit from Haydn's hands*.

Your true friend
Bonn, 29 October 1792   Waldstein'

The dates in the album prove that Beethoven was still in Bonn on 1 November 1792, and indicate that it was the last day of his sojourn there. In Duten's *Journal of Travels*, as translated and augmented by John Highmore, Gent. (London, 1782) – a Baedeker's or Murray's handbook of that time – the post-road from Bonn to Frankfurt-am-Main is laid down as passing along the Rhine via Andernach to Coblenz, and thence, crossing the river at Ehrenbreitstein, via Montabaur, Limburg, Würges and Königstein – time twenty-five hours, forty-three minutes.

This was the route taken by Beethoven and some unknown companion. Starting from Bonn at 6 a.m. they would, according to Dutens and Highmore, dine at Coblenz about 3 p.m. and be in Frankfurt about 7 next morning.

The first three pages of a small memorandum book kept by Beethoven during the journey contain a record of the expenses of this journey as far as Würges. One of the items is this: 'Trinkgeld at Coblenz

* 'Friendship, with that which is good,
   Grows like the evening shadow,
   Till the setting sun of life.'

because the fellow drove us at the risk of a cudgelling right through the Hessian army going like the devil, one small thaler.' This army marched from Coblenz on 5 November; but on the same day a French corps, having advanced from Mainz beyond Limburg, took possession of Weilburg. The travellers could not, therefore, have journeyed through Limburg later than the night of the 3rd. We conclude, then, that it was between 1 and 3 November that Beethoven bade farewell to Bonn, and at Ehrenbreitstein saw Father Rhine for the last time.

Ludwig Schiedermair has summed up the state of our knowledge of Beethoven's creative efforts in Bonn in his book *The Young Beethoven*:

'If we reckon along with the compositions that have been preserved and are genuine, that portion, probably not inconsiderable, which today is irreparably lost, although perhaps a piece or two might still come to light amongst the papers in the archives of some European or American library; if we further imagine that many an idea, first conceived in Bonn, is scarcely recognisable for us today as it is reshaped for a later work in Vienna in which it becomes gloriously transformed, then we are faced with the fact that a productivity has started around 1785, bursting forth with ever increasing strength, which must be considered unusually rich despite the fact that the actual number of works that have survived is lower than that found in the similar period of life of other great musicians. It goes without saying that neither the activity within a limited period of a man's life nor the quantity of work constitute the significance of an artist. Besides, as we consider Beethoven's official duties, his family cares, the rewarding intercourse with friends in which his sense of companionship was not always carefree, we are perceiving the life of a youth filled with indefatigable work and constant effort.'

CHAPTER 5

Beethoven's Teachers in Vienna – The Years 1793–1795

It would be pleasant to announce the arrival of Ludwig van Beethoven in Vienna with, so to speak, a grand flourish of trumpets; but, unluckily, there is none of that lack of data which is favourable to that kind of composition; none of that obscurity which exalts one to write history as he would have it and not as it really was. The facts are too patent.

Like the multitude of studious youths and young men who came thither annually to find schools and teachers, this small, thin, dark-complexioned, pockmarked, dark-eyed, bewigged young musician of twenty-two years had quietly journeyed to the capital to pursue the study of his art with a small, thin, dark-complexioned, pockmarked, black-eyed and bewigged veteran composer. In the well-known anecdote of Haydn's introduction to him, Anton Esterhazy, the prince, is made to call the composer 'a Moor'. Beethoven had even more of the Moor in his looks than his master. His front teeth, owing to the singular flatness of the roof of his mouth, protruded, and, of course, thrust out his lips; the nose, too, was rather broad and decidedly flattened, while the forehead was remarkably full and round – in the words of Court Secretary Mähler, who twice painted his portrait, a 'bullet'.

'Beethoven', wrote Junker, 'confessed that in his journeys he had seldom found in the playing of the most distinguished virtuosi that excellence which he supposed he had a right to expect.' He now had an opportunity to make his observations upon the pianists and composers at the very headquarters, then, of German music, to improve himself by study under the best of them and, by and by, to measure his strength with theirs. He found very soon that the words of the poet were here also applicable: ' 'Tis distance lends enchantment to the view,' and did not find – now Mozart was gone – 'that excellence which he supposed he had a right to expect'. For the present, however, we have to do but with the young stranger in a large city, seeking lodgings, and making such arrangements for the future as shall not be out of due proportion to the limited pecuniary means at his command.

Turning again to the small memorandum book, the first entries which follow the notes of the journey from Bonn to Würges are merely of necessities to be supplied – 'wood, wig-maker, coffee, overcoat, boots, shoes, pianoforte-desk, seal, writing-desk, pianoforte-money' and something illegible followed by the remark: 'All beginning with next month.' The next page gives a hint as to the day of his arrival. It contains the substance of two advertisements in the *Wiener Zeitung* of pianofortes for sale, one near the Hohen Markt and two 'im Kramerschen Breihaus No. 257 im Schlossergassel, am Graben'. The latter appears *for the last time* on 10 November; Beethoven was, therefore, then in Vienna.

But he intended to cultivate the Graces as well as the Muses. The next page begins with this: 'Andreas Lindner, dancing-master, lives in the Stoss am Himmel, No. 415', to which succeeds a note, evidently of money received from the Elector, possibly in Bonn but more likely in Vienna: '25 ducats received of which, expended on November (?) half a sovereign for the pianoforte, or 6 florins, 40 kreutzer – 2 florins were of my own money.' The same page also shows him in the matter of his toilet preparing even then for entrance into society: 'Black silk stockings, 1 ducat; 1 pair of winter silk stockings, 1 florin, 40 kreutzers; boots, 6 florins; shoes, 1 florin, 30 kreutzers.' But these expenses in addition to his daily necessities are making a large inroad upon his '25 ducats received'; and on page 7 we read: 'On Wednesday the 12th of December, I had 15 ducats.' Omitting for the present what else stands upon page 7, here are the interesting contents of page 8 – and how suggestive and pregnant they are: 'In Bonn I counted on receiving 100 ducats here; but in vain. I have got to equip myself completely anew.'

Several pages which follow contain what, upon inspection, proves evidently to be his monthly payments from the time when 'all was to begin next month', of which the first may be given as a specimen: 'House-rent, 14 florins; pianoforte, 6 florins, 40 kreutzers; eating, each time 12 kreutzers; meals with wine, 16½ florins; 3 kreutzers for B. and H.; it is not necessary to give the housekeeper more than 7 florins, the rooms are so close to the ground.' Beethoven's first lodgings were in an attic-room which he soon exchanged for a room on the ground floor of a house, No. 45 Alserstrasse, occupied by one Strauss, a printer. Another occupant of the house was Prince Lichnowsky, who soon after took him into his lodgings. He remained in this house until May 1795.

Beethoven was hardly well settled in his lodgings, the novelty of his position had scarcely begun to wear off under the effect of habit, when startling tidings reached him from Bonn of an event to cloud his Christmas holidays, to weaken his ties to his native place, to increase his cares for his brothers and make an important change in his pecuniary condition. His father had suddenly died – '1792, Dec. 18, *obiit* Johannes Beethoff,' says the death-roll of St Remigius parish. The

Elector-Archbishop, still in Münster, heard this news also and conse-crated a joke to the dead man's memory. On 1 January 1793, he wrote a letter to Court Marshal von Schall in which these words occur: 'The revenues from the liquor excise have suffered a loss in the deaths of Beethoven and Eichhoff. For the widow of the latter, provision will be made if circumstances allow in view of his 40 years of service [in the electoral kitchen] . . .'

The consequent lapse of Johann van Beethoven's pension of 200 thalers, was a serious misfortune to his son, particularly since the 100 ducats had not been forthcoming. The correspondence between Beet-hoven and Ries not being preserved it can only be conjectured that the latter took the proper steps to obtain that portion of the pension set apart by the electoral decree for the support of the two younger sons; but in vain, owing to the disappearance of the original document; and that, receiving information of this fact, Beethoven immediately sent from Vienna the petition which follows. While, as is mostly the case with that class of papers in the Bonn archives, it is without date, it was presumably written at the beginning of May 1793:

'Most Worthy and Illustrious Elector!
Most Gracious Lord!
'Several years ago Your Serene Electoral Highness was pleased to retire my father, the tenor singer van Beethoven, from service, and by a most gracious decree to set aside 100 thalers of his salary to me that I might clothe, nourish and educate my two younger brothers and also to discharge our father's debts.

'I was about to present this decree to Your Highness's Revenue Exchequer when my father urgently begged me not to do so inasmuch as it would have the appearance in the eyes of the public that he was incapable of caring for his family, adding that he himself would pay me the 25 thalers quarterly, which he always did promptly.

'However, upon the death of my father in December of last year, when I wished to make use of Your Highness's grace by presenting the above-mentioned gracious decree I learned to my horror that my father had made away with the same.

'With most obedient veneration I therefore pray Your Electoral Highness for the gracious renewal of this decree and that Your High-ness's Revenue Exchequer be directed to pay over to me the sum graciously allowed to me due for the last quarter at the beginning of last February.

Your Electoral and Serene Highness's
       Most obedient and faithful
              Lud. v. Beethowen, Court Organist'

The petition was duly considered by the Privy Council and with the result indicated by the endorsement:

'ad. sup.
of the
Court Organist
L. van Beethoven'

' "The 100 reichsthaler which he is now receiving annually is increased by a further 100 reichsthaler in quarterly payments beginning with 1 January, from the 200 rthlr. salary vacated by the death of his father; he is further to receive the three measures of grain graciously bestowed upon him for the education of his brothers." The Electoral Court Chancellery will make the necessary provisions. Attest p.'

'Bonn, 3 May 1793'

According to the accounts of the office of revenues that still exist at Düsseldorf, Beethoven received the salary of fifty thalers in quarterly payments until March 1794. From this time onward no hint has been discovered that Beethoven ever received anything from the Elector or had any resources but his own earnings and the generosity of newly found friends in Vienna. These resources were soon needed. The remark that two florins of the payment towards the pianoforte were out of his own money proves that he possessed a small sum saved up by degrees from lesson-giving, from presents received and the like; but it could not have been a large amount.

In what manner Beethoven was already in 1794 able to remain 'in Vienna without salary until recalled', to quote the Elector's words, will hereafter appear with some degree of certainty; but just now he claims attention as pupil of Haydn and Albrechtsberger. The letters of Neefe and others prove how strong an impression Beethoven's powers, both as virtuoso and composer, had made upon Joseph Haydn immediately after his reaching Vienna; and no man then living was better able to judge on such points. But whether the famous kapellmeister, just returned from his English triumphs, himself a daring and successful innovator and now very busy with compositions in preparation for his second visit to London, was the man to guide the studies of a headstrong, self-willed and still more daring musical revolutionist was a very doubtful question. The result proved that he was not.

The memorandum book has a few entries which relate to Haydn. On page 7, which contains the entry of fifteen ducats on 12 December 1792, there is a column of numerals (mostly two groschen), the first of which reads, 'Haidn 8 groschen'; and on the two pages which happen to have the dates of 24 and 29 October 1793, are these two entries: '22 kr. [kreuzers] chocolate for Haidn and me'; 'Coffee, 6 kr. for Haidn and me.' These notes simply confirm what was known from other sources, namely, that Beethoven began to study with Haydn very soon after reaching Vienna and continued to be his pupil until the end of the year 1793, or the beginning of 1794, since Haydn left Vienna on 19 January of that year. They indicate, also, that the scholar, whatever feelings he may have indulged towards the master in secret, kept on good terms with him, and that their private intercourse was not confined to the hours devoted to lessons in Haydn's room in the Hamberger house, No. 1275 on the Wasserkunstbastei.

Beethoven's studies with the master were of strict counterpoint. Haydn had made an abstract of Fux's *Gradus ad Parnassum*, a book which he valued highly, and this was used also by Beethoven. The exercises were undertaken in the different species of counterpoint upon six plain chants (from the six old modes). Two hundred and forty-five such exercises are extant, but there can well be more, since the manuscript is not complete. Forty-two of these exercises have changes or indications of mistakes by Haydn. The mistakes indicated refer to parallel fifths and octaves, the handling of parts which accompany a suspension, crossing of voices and treatment of the leading tone, and others which strict counterpoint does not allow. But Haydn has not consistently found all the mistakes in the great majority of the exercises in which corresponding errors are to be found. They lack his corrections. It is apparent that on account of the claims of his own works he was not exacting or systematic as a teacher nor did he devote the necessary time to the continuous training of his student.

Beethoven very soon discovered that also in Haydn, as a teacher, he had not found 'that excellence which he supposed he had a right to expect'. Ries remembered a remark made by him on this point: 'Haydn had wished that Beethoven might put the word, "Pupil of Haydn", on the title of his first works. Beethoven was unwilling to do so because, as he said, though he had had some instruction from Haydn he had never learned anything from him.'

Still more in point is the oft-repeated story of Johann Schenk's kindness to our composer: among Beethoven's earliest acquaintances in Vienna was the Abbé Joseph Gelinek, one of the first virtuosi then in that city and an amazingly fruitful and popular composer of variations. It was upon him that Carl Maria von Weber, some years afterwards, wrote the epigram:

> 'Kein Thema auf der Welt verschonte dein Genie,
> Das simpelste allein – Dich selbst – variirst du nie!'*
>
> * 'No theme on earth escaped your genius airy,
>   The simplest one of all – yourself – you never vary.'

Czerny told Otto Jahn that his father once met Gelinek tricked out
in all his finery. 'Whither?' he enquired. 'I am asked to measure myself
with a young pianist who is just arrived; I'll work him over.' A few
days later he met him again. 'Well, how was it?' 'Ah, he is no man; he's
a devil. He will play me and all of us to death. And how he improvises!'

It was in Gelinek's lodgings that Schenk heard Beethoven improvise
for the first time,

'. . . a treat which recalled lively recollections of Mozart. With many
manifestations of displeasure, Beethoven, always eager to learn, complained to Gelinek that he was never able to make any progress in his
contrapuntal studies under Haydn, since the master, too variously
occupied, was unable to pay the amount of attention which he wanted
to the exercises he had given him to work out. Gelinek spoke on the
subject with Schenk and asked him if he did not feel disposed to give
Beethoven a course in composition. Schenk declared himself willing,
with ready courtesy, but only under two conditions: that it should be
without compensation of any kind and under the strict seal of secrecy.
The mutual agreement was made and kept with conscientious fidelity.'

We shall now permit Schenk to tell his own story:

'In 1792, His Royal Highness Archduke Maximilian, Elector of
Cologne, was pleased to send his charge Louis van Beethoven to Vienna
to study musical composition with Haydn. Towards the end of July,
Abbé Gelinek informed me that he had made the acquaintance of a
young man who displayed extraordinary virtuosity on the pianoforte,
such, indeed, as he had not observed since Mozart. In passing he said
that Beethoven had been studying counterpoint with Haydn for more
than six months and was still at work on the first exercise; also that His
Excellency Baron van Swieten had earnestly recommended the study of
counterpoint and frequently enquired of him how far he had advanced
in his studies. As a result of these frequent incitations and the fact that
he was still in the first stages of his instruction, Beethoven, eager to
learn, became discontented and often gave expression to his dissatisfaction to his friend. Gelinek took the matter much to heart and came to
me with the question whether I felt disposed to assist his friend in the
study of counterpoint. I now desired to become better acquainted with
Beethoven as soon as possible, and a day was fixed for me to meet him in
Gelinek's lodgings and hear him play on the pianoforte.

'Thus I saw the composer, now so famous, for the first time and
heard him play. After the customary courtesies he offered to improvise

on the pianoforte. He asked me to sit beside him. Having struck a few chords and tossed off a few figures as if they were of no significance, the creative genius gradually unveiled his profound psychological pictures. My ear was continually charmed by the beauty of the many and varied motives which he wove with wonderful clarity and loveliness into each other, and I surrendered my heart to the impressions made upon it while he gave himself wholly up to his creative imagination, and anon, leaving the field of mere tonal charm, boldly stormed the most distant keys in order to give expression to violent passions . . .

'The first thing that I did the next day was to visit the still unknown artist who had so brilliantly disclosed his mastership. On his writing desk I found a few passages from his first lesson in counterpoint. A cursory glance disclosed the fact that, brief as it was, there were mistakes in every mode. Gelinek's utterances were thus verified. Feeling sure that my pupil was unfamiliar with the preliminary rules of counterpoint, I gave him the familiar textbook of Joseph Fux, *Gradus ad Parnassum*, and asked him to look at the exercises that followed. Joseph Haydn, who had returned to Vienna towards the end of the preceding year, was intent on utilising his muse in the composition of large masterworks, and thus laudably occupied could not well devote himself to the rules of grammar. I was now eagerly desirous to become the helper of the zealous student. But before beginning the instruction I made him understand that our co-operation would have to be kept secret. In view of this I recommended that he copy every exercise which I corrected in order that Haydn should not recognise the handwriting of a stranger when the exercise was submitted to him. After a year, Beethoven and Gelinek had a falling out for a reason that has escaped me; both, it seemed to me, were at fault. As a result Gelinek got angry and betrayed my secret. Beethoven and his brothers made no secret of it longer.'

The relations between Haydn and his pupil did not long continue truly cordial; yet Beethoven concealed his dissatisfaction and no break occurred. Thoughtless and reckless of consequences, as he often in later years unfortunately exhibited himself when indulging his wilfulness, he was at this time responsible to the Elector for his conduct, and Haydn, moreover, was too valuable and influential a friend to be wantonly alienated. So, whatever feelings he cherished in secret, he kept them to himself, went regularly to his lessons and, as noted above, occasionally treated his master to chocolate or coffee. Neefe tells us that Haydn wished to take him to England on the master's second visit. Why was that plan not carried out? Did Maximilian forbid it? Would

Beethoven's pride not allow him to go thither as Haydn's pupil? Did
zeal for his contrapuntal studies prevent it? Or, finally, was it his ambition rather to make himself known as Beethoven the composer than as
Beethoven the pianoforte virtuoso? At all events, the relationship was
broken off when the master departed for London on 19 January 1794,
and Beethoven's studies were transferred to Albrechtsberger.

These questions may be further considered in connection with three
letters recently discovered which add to our knowledge of the relation
of Haydn's student at this time to his past employer, the Elector at
Bonn. The first letter, from Haydn to the Elector, gives evidence of the
high regard that Haydn had for his pupil and his great desire to help
him.

'Most Reverend Archbishop and Elector,
   'I am taking the liberty of sending to your Reverence in all humility
a few pieces of music . . . composed by my dear pupil Beethoven
who was so graciously entrusted to me. They will, I flatter myself, be
graciously accepted by your Reverence as evidence of his diligence
beyond the scope of his own studies. On the basis of these pieces,
expert and amateur alike cannot but admit that Beethoven will in time
become one of the greatest musical artists in Europe, and I shall be
proud to call myself his teacher. I only wish that he might remain with
me for some time yet.
   'While I am on the subject of Beethoven, may your Reverence permit me to say a few words concerning his financial affairs. For the past
year he was allotted 100 ducats. That this sum was insufficient even for
mere living expenses your Reverence will, I am sure, be well aware.
Your Reverence, however, may have had good reasons for sending him
out into the great world with so small a sum. On this assumption and
in order to prevent him from falling into the hands of usurers, I have
on the one hand vouched for him and on the other advanced him cash,
so that he owes me 500 fl., of which not a kreutzer has been spent
unnecessarily. I now request that this sum be paid him. And since to
work on borrowed money increases the interest, and what is more is
very burdensome for an artist like Beethoven, I thought that if your
Reverence would allot him 1,000 fl. for the coming year, your Reverence would be showing him the highest favour, and at the same time
would free him of all anxiety. For the teachers which are absolutely
indispensable to him and the expenses which are unavoidable if he is to
be admitted to some of the houses here, take so much that the barest
minimum that he needs comes close to 1,000 fl. As to the extravagance
that is to be feared in a young man going out into the great world, I

think I can reassure your Reverence. For in hundreds of situations I have always found that he is prepared, of his own accord, to sacrifice everything for his art. This is particularly admirable in view of the many tempting opportunities and should give your Reverence the assurance that your gracious kindness to Beethoven will not fall into the hands of usurers. In the hopes that your Reverence will graciously accept this request of mine on behalf of my dear pupil, I am, with deepest respect, your Reverence's most humble and obedient servant

Joseph Haydn
Kapellmeister of Prince Nikolaus Esterhazy'
'Vienna, 23 November 1793'

On the same day Beethoven also wrote to the Elector as follows:

'Most Reverend, most high and gracious Elector and Master!

To be worthy of the highest favour of Your Electoral Highness is my single concern. For this I have used all my mental powers in the common purpose of music this year in order to be able to send to Your Electoral Highness in the coming year something which more nearly approaches your kindness to me and your nobility than that which was sent to Your Electoral Highness by Herr Heiden. In the confidence that Your Electoral Highness will not deprive me of the kindness once granted I am in deepest respect Your Electoral Highness's most humble and most obedient

Ludwig van Beethoven'
'Vienna, 23 November 1793'

Only the Elector's reply to Haydn has survived, and the embarrassing position into which it put the composer would indicate a less than complete understanding between Haydn and Beethoven at the time that the compositions were sent.

'The music of young Beethoven which you sent me I received with your letter. Since, however, this music, with the exception of the figure, was composed and performed here in Bonn before he departed on his second journey to Vienna, I cannot regard it as progress made in Vienna.

'As far as the allotment which he has had for his subsistence in Vienna is concerned, it does indeed amount to only 500 fl. But in addition to this 500 fl. his salary here of 400 fl. has been continuously paid to him, he received 900 fl. for the year. I cannot, therefore, very well see why he is as much in arrears in his finances as you say.

'I am wondering therefore whether he had not better come back here in order to resume his work. For I very much doubt that he has made any important progress in composition and in the development of his musical taste during his present stay, and I fear that, as in the case of his first journey to Vienna, he will bring back nothing but debts.'

The fact that of all of the works sent to the Elector only one may have been written in Vienna suggests that in his first year of study in Vienna Beethoven concerned himself almost solely with theory, laying the foundation for his future technique as a composer; and although he was revising works written in Bonn, he probably did not compose any works of importance during this time. Undoubtedly Haydn could not have realised that these were Bonn works, but since Beethoven mentioned in his letter what 'was sent to Your Electoral Highness by Herr Heiden' one wonders whether Beethoven knew which works were sent or not. The stiffness of the Elector's reply could not have pleased Haydn and perhaps the awkwardness of this situation contributed to Haydn's leaving for England without Beethoven.

Johann Georg Albrechtsberger was born in 1736 at Klosterneuburg and died in Vienna in 1809. In 1772 he was appointed Court Organist and in 1792 kapellmeister at St Stephen's in Vienna. He was not only a celebrated teacher of music theory, about which he wrote a number of books and pamphlets, but also a very prolific composer of masses, symphonies, quartets and many other chamber combinations.

The instruction which Beethoven received from him began with simple counterpoint, in which Beethoven now received more detailed directions than had been given him by Haydn. Albrechtsberger wrote down rules for him, Beethoven did the same and worked out a large number of exercises on two *cantus firmi* which Albrechtsberger then corrected according to the rules of strict writing. There followed contrapuntal exercises in free writing, in imitation, in two-, three- and four-part fugue, choral fugue, double counterpoint in the different intervals, double fugue, triple counterpoint and canon. The last was short, as here the instruction ceased. Beethoven worked frequently in the immediate presence and with the direct co-operation of Albrechtsberger. The latter laboured with obvious conscientiousness and care, and was ever ready to aid his pupil. If he appears at times to have been given over to minute detail and conventional method, it must be borne in mind that rigid schooling in fixed rules is essential to the development of an independent artist, even if he makes no use of them, and that it is only in this manner that freedom in workmanship can be achieved. Of this the youthful Beethoven was aware and every line of his exercises bears witness that he entered into his studies with complete interest and zeal.

(Once Beethoven writes an unprepared seventh-chord with a suspension on the margin of an exercise and adds the query: 'Is it allowed?')

The third of Beethoven's teachers in Vienna was the Imperial Kapellmeister Anton Salieri; but this instruction was neither systematic nor confined to regular hours. Beethoven took advantage of Salieri's willingness 'to give gratuitous instruction to musicians of small means'. He wanted advice in vocal composition, and submitted to Salieri some settings of Italian songs which the latter corrected in respect of verbal accent and expression, rhythm, metrical articulation, subdivision of thought, mood, singableness, and the conduct of the melody which comprehended all these things. Having himself taken the initiative in this, Beethoven devoted himself earnestly and industriously to these exercises, and they were notably profitable in his creative work. That Salieri's influence extended beyond the period in which Beethoven's style developed itself independently cannot be asserted, since many other and varied influences made themselves felt later.

This instruction began soon after Beethoven's arrival in Vienna and lasted in an unconstrained manner at least until 1802; at even a later date he asked counsel of Salieri in the composition of songs, particularly Italian songs. According to an anecdote related by Czerny, at one of these meetings for instruction Salieri found fault with a melody as not being appropriate for an air. The next day he said to Beethoven: 'I can't get your melody out of my head.' 'Then, Herr von Salieri,' replied Beethoven, 'it cannot have been so utterly bad.'

Ries, speaking of the relations between Haydn, Albrechtsberger and Salieri as teachers and Beethoven as pupil, says:

'I knew them all well; all three valued Beethoven highly, but were also of one mind touching his habits of study. All of them said Beethoven was so headstrong and self-sufficient that he had to learn much through harsh experience which he had refused to accept when it was presented to him as a subject of study. Particularly Albrechtsberger and Salieri were of this opinion; the dry rules of the former and the comparatively unimportant ones of the latter concerning dramatic composition (according to the Italian school of the period) could not appeal to Beethoven.'

It is now known that the 'dry rules' of Albrechtsberger could make a strong appeal to Beethoven as appertaining to theoretical study, and that the old method of composition to which he remained true all his life always had a singular charm for him as a subject of study and investigation.

Here, as in many other cases, the simple statement of the difficulties suggests their explanation. Beethoven the pupil may have honestly and conscientiously followed the precepts of his instructors in whatever he wrote in that character; but Beethoven the composer stood upon his own territory, followed his own tastes and impulses, wrote and wrought subject to no other control.

He had arrived in a city where the quality of opera was of outstanding excellence. It was exclusively Italian but its execution of the first order. Church music was, perhaps, at a low point. Public subscription concerts were of the highest standards, the stages being filled with some of the best musicians and vocalists in Europe. Instrumental music was of a new, unprecedented excellence, unknown in any other city.

In short, Vienna provided a prolific garden of music, in which our young genius could feed and flourish.

However quiet and 'without observation' Beethoven's advent in Vienna may have been at that time when men's minds were occupied by movements of armies and ideas of revolution, he could hardly have gone thither under better auspices. He was Court Organist and Pianist to the Emperor's uncle; his talents in that field were well known to the many Austrians of rank who had heard him in Bonn when visiting there or when paying their respects to the Elector in passing to and from the Austrian Netherlands; he was a pupil of Joseph Haydn – a circumstance in itself sufficient to secure him a hearing; and he was protected by Count Waldstein, whose family connections were such that he could introduce his favourite into the highest circles, the imperial house only excepted.

Dr Burney, in closing his *Present State of Music in Germany*, notes the distinction in the styles of composition and performance in some of the principal cities of that country, 'Vienna being most remarkable for fire and animation; Mannheim for neat and brilliant execution; Berlin for counterpoint and Brunswick for taste'. Since Burney's tour (1772) Vienna had the highest example of all these qualities united in Mozart. But he had passed away, and no great pianist of the first rank remained; there were extraordinary dilettanti and professional pianists 'of very neat and brilliant execution', but none who possessed great 'fire, animation and invention', qualities still most valued in Vienna and in which the young Beethoven, with all the hardness and heaviness of manipulation caused by his devotion to the organ, was wholly unrivalled. With all the salons in the metropolis open to him, his success as a virtuoso was, therefore, certain. All the contemporary authorities, and all the traditions of those years, agree in the fact of that success, and that his playing of Bach's preludes and fugues especially, his reading of the most difficult scores at sight and his extemporaneous performances excited ever new wonder and delight. Schindler records that van Swieten, after musical performances at his house, 'detained Beethoven and persuaded him to add a few fugues by Sebastian Bach as an evening blessing', and he preserves a note without date, though evidently belonging to Beethoven's first years in Vienna, which proves how high a place the young man had then won in the old gentleman's favour:

'To Hr. Beethoven in Alstergasse, No. 45, with the Prince Lichnowsky: If there is nothing to hinder next Wednesday I should be glad to see you at my home at half-past 8 with your nightcap in your bag. Give me an immediate answer.

Swieten'

It is clear with what industry and energy he engaged in his new career, with what zeal and unfaltering activity he laboured to make the most of his opportunities. In one year after leaving Bonn he felt his success secure, and no longer feared Hamlet's 'slings and arrows of outrageous fortune'.

At this time he wrote to his old friend, Eleonore von Breuning, in Bonn.

'Vienna, 2 November 93

'Most estimable Leonore!
My most precious friend!

'Not until I have lived almost a year in the capital do you receive a letter from me, and yet you were most assuredly perpetually in my liveliest memory. Often in thought I have conversed with you and your dear family, though not with that peace of mind which I could have desired. It was then that the wretched quarrel hovered before me and my conduct presented itself as most despicable, but it was too late; oh what would I not give could I obliterate from my life those actions so degrading to myself and so contrary to my character. True, there were many circumstances which tended to estrange us, and I suspect that tales whispered in our ears of remarks made one about the other were chiefly that which prevented us from coming to an understanding. We both believed that we were speaking from conviction; whereas it was only in anger, and we were both deceived. Your good and noble character my dear friend is sufficient assurance to me that you forgave me long ago, but we are told that the sincerest contrition consists in acknowledgement of our faults; and to do this has been my desire. – And now let us drop a curtain on this whole affair, only drawing from it this lesson, that when friends quarrel it is much better to have it out face to face than to turn to a go-between.

'With this you will receive a dedication from me to you concerning which I only wish that the work were a larger one and more worthy of you. I was plagued here to publish the little work, and I took advantage of the opportunity, my estimable E., to show my respect and friendship for you and my enduring memory of your family. Take this trifle and remember that it comes from a friend who respects you greatly. Oh if it but gives you pleasure, my wishes will be completely fulfilled. Let it be a reminder of the time when I spent so many and such blessed hours at your home. Perhaps it will keep me in your recollection, until I eventually return to you, which, it is true, is not likely to be soon, but oh how we shall rejoice then, my dear friend. You will then find in your friend a happier man, from whose visage time and a kindlier fate shall have smoothed out all the furrows of a hateful past.

'If you should chance to see B. Koch, please say to her that it is not nice of her never once to have written to me. I wrote to her twice and three times . . . In conclusion I venture a request; it is this: I should like once again to own a waistcoat knit of hare's wool by your hands, my dear friend. Pardon the immodest request, my dear friend, but it proceeds from a great predilection for everything that comes from your hands. Privately I may acknowledge that a little vanity is also involved in the request; I want to be able to say that I have something that was given me by the best and most estimable girl in Bonn. I still have the waistcoat that you were good enough to give me in Bonn, but it has grown so out of fashion that I can only treasure it in my wardrobe as something very precious because it came from you. You would give me much pleasure if you were soon to rejoice me with a dear letter from yourself. If my letters should in any way please you I promise in this to be at your command so far as lies in my power, as everything is welcome to me which enables me to show how truly I am

Your admiring true friend
L. v. Beethoven'

Next we come to the fragment of another letter to Eleonore von Breuning. It also shows how bitterly Beethoven's conscience could be troubled by his own impulsiveness or acts of temper, which were always to threaten his relationships with his friends. Particularly interesting because of the postscript, it was probably written in May or June 1794.

'How surprised I was by the beautiful cravat made by your own hand. The thing itself was so pleasant, at the same time it awoke in me a feeling of sadness. Its effect was to bring back the former times of the past, and, moreover, a sense of shame because of your generous behaviour towards me. In truth, I did not think that you still thought me worthy of your remembrance. Oh, if you could have been witness to the way I reacted yesterday to this incident, you would certainly not find that I am exaggerating when I tell you that your remembrance made me weep and feel very sad. – However little I may deserve consideration in your eyes, I beg of you, *my friend* (let me ever call you so), to think of me as one who has suffered very much and continues to suffer through the loss of your friendship. I shall never forget you and your dear mother, you were so good to me that this loss to me cannot and will not easily be restored. I know what I have lost and what you were to me, but I would have to recall scenes, were I to fill in these gaps, which are unpleasant both for you to hear and for me to describe to you.

'As a slight return for your kind remembrance of me I take the liberty of sending these variations and the rondo for violin. I have a great deal to do or I would have transcribed the sonata I promised you long ago, it is a mere sketch in manuscript, and to copy it would be difficult even for one as skilled as Paraquin.* You could have the rondo copied and then send the score back to me. This is all that I can send to you now which would be at all useful to you; since you are now travelling to Kerpen, I thought that these trifles might perhaps give you some pleasure.

'Farewell, my friend, it is impossible for me to call you otherwise. However little you may think of me, please realise that I revere you and your mother just as much as formerly, and if I could contribute in any other way to your pleasure, I beg of you not to forget me. This is still the only means which is left for me to express my gratitude for the friendship which I have received from you. A happy journey, and bring your dear mother back again in sound health. Think occasionally of one who continues to venerate you,

your true friend, Beethoven'

'PS The V. [variations] you will find a little difficult to play, especially the trills in the coda; but don't let this alarm you. It is so contrived that you need play only the trill, leaving out the other notes because they are also in the violin part. I never would have composed it so, had I not often observed that here and there in V. [Vienna] there was somebody who, after I had improvised of an evening, noted down many of the peculiarities, and made parade of them the next day as his own. Foreseeing that some of these things would soon appear in print, I resolved to anticipate them. Another reason that I had was to embarrass the

* A musician in the Electoral Orchestra.

local pianoforte masters. Many of them are my deadly enemies, and I wanted to revenge myself on them, knowing that once in a while somebody would ask them to play the variations and they would make a sorry show of them.'

The instant and striking success of Beethoven as virtuoso by no means filled up the measure of his ambition. He aspired to the higher position of composer, and to obtain this more was needed than the performance of variations, however excellent. To this end he selected the three Trios afterwards published as Opus 1, and brought them to performance at the house of Prince Lichnowsky, to whom they were dedicated. Happily for us, Beethoven related some particulars concerning this first performance of these compositions in Vienna to his pupil Ries, who gives us the substance of the story thus:

'It was planned to introduce the first three Trios of Beethoven, which were about to be published as Op. 1, to the artistic world at a soirée at Prince Lichnowsky's. Most of the artists and music-lovers were invited, especially Haydn, for whose opinion all were eager. The Trios were played and at once commanded extraordinary attention. Haydn also said many pretty things about them, but advised Beethoven not to publish the third, in C minor. This astonished Beethoven, inasmuch as he considered the third the best of the Trios, as it is still the one which gives the greatest pleasure and makes the greatest effect. Consequently, Haydn's remark left a bad impression on Beethoven and led him to think that Haydn was envious, jealous and ill-disposed toward him. I confess that when Beethoven told me of this I gave it little credence. I therefore took occasion to ask Haydn himself about it. His answer, however, confirmed Beethoven's statement; he said he had not believed that this Trio would be so quickly and easily understood and so favourably received by the public.'

More than two years passed by, however, before the composer thought fit to send these Trios to the press; perhaps restrained by a feeling of modesty, since he was still a student, perhaps by a doubt as to the success of compositions so new in style, or by prudence, choosing to delay their publication until they had been so often performed from the manuscript as to secure their comprehension and appreciation, and thus an adequate number of subscribers. In the meantime he prepared the way for them by publishing a few sets of variations. Those on 'Se vuol ballare', revised and improved with a new coda, came out in July 1793, with a dedication to Eleonore von Breuning. Then the thirteen variations upon the theme 'Es war einmal ein alter Mann', from Dittersdorf's *Das rote Käppchen*, appeared, and these were followed by those for four hands on the Waldstein theme. In fact, Beethoven evidently was in no haste to publish his compositions. It will be remembered from the postscript to the 1794 letter to Eleonore von Breuning that he sent the 'Se vuol ballare' variations to press partly at the request of others and partly to entrap the rival pianists of Vienna. A few years later we shall find him dashing off and immediately publishing variations on popular theatrical melodies; but works of greater scope, and especially his pianoforte concertos, were for the most part long retained in his exclusive possession.

With his old colleague in the Court Orchestra in Bonn, Nikolaus Simrock, though he was a much older man, Beethoven remained in touch after his removal to Vienna. Simrock, who was highly esteemed as man and musician, had embarked in business as a music publisher in Bonn. The *Das rote Käppchen* Variations were published by him in 1793, and the Waldstein Variations the following year. Beethoven's correspondence with Simrock in the summer of 1794 marks the beginning of a long struggle with publishers over revisions and corrections of his works that was to continue until the final year of his life. On 18 June he wrote that he was surprised to hear that Simrock was about to print, or had begun to print, the Waldstein Variations without consulting him. He continues:

'The one thing which I must insist upon is that you now stop the printing and simply write to me whether you had really begun them already. This is so that I may send you the manuscript of them by way of my friend, Count Waldstein, from which you can make the printing, because various things in them have been revised; and I wish to see my works appear in print at least in as perfect shape as possible. Aside from this I have not been willing to have my variations published now since I wanted first to wait until some important works of mine, which will soon be brought out, come into the world.'

The letter ends with a correction for the *Das rote Käppchen* Variations and a complaint that only one copy had been sent him, whereas the publisher Artaria had given him a fee and twelve copies of the variations he had published. The next letter is of 2 August:

'Dear Simrock:
'I deserve a little scolding from you for holding back your variations so long, but, indeed, I do not lie when I say that I was hindered from

correcting them sooner by an overwhelming amount of business. You will note the shortcomings yourself, but I must congratulate you on the appearance of your engraving, which is beautiful, clear and legible. Verily, if you keep on thus you will become chief among cutters, that is, note-cutters —

'In my previous letter I promised to send you something of mine, and you interpreted the remark as being in the language of the cavaliers. How have I deserved such a title? — Faugh, who would indulge in such language in these democratic times of ours? Well, in order to free myself from this declaration that you have made against me, as soon as I have finished the grand revision of my compositions, which will be soon, you shall have something which you will surely engrave —

'I have also been looking about me for an agent and have found a right capable young fellow for the place. His name is *Traeg*. You have only to write to him or to me about what terms you wish to make. He asks of you one-third discount. The devil take all such bargaining — It is very hot here, the Viennese are afraid that soon they will be unable to get *ice-cream*, for since the winter was so mild, ice is scarce. Many persons of *importance* have come here, it was said that a revolution was imminent — But it is my belief that so long as the Austrian has his dark *beer* and *sausage* he will not revolt. It is said that the suburban gates are to be closed at ten o'clock at night. The soldiers' guns are loaded with bullets. No one dares speak aloud, for fear of arrest by the police.

'If your daughters are already grown up, bring one up to be my wife, for if I am to remain single in Bonn I shall not stay long, of a surety; — You must also be living in fear! —

'How is good *Ries*? I shall write to him soon for he can only have an unfavourable opinion of me, but this cursed writing, I cannot get over my antipathy towards it. — *Have you performed my Parthie yet?* Write to me occasionally.

Your Beethoven'

'Please send also a few copies of the first Variations.'

These 'first Variations' obviously are those on the theme from *Das rote Käppchen*; the Parthie whose performance he enquires about is the Octet, Op. 103. The letter, like that written to Eleonore von Breuning, shows that Beethoven was still thinking of the possibility or probability of a return to Bonn. Its cheerful tone discloses a comfortable, satisfied frame of mind.

The reminiscences of Wegeler for the period of his stay in Vienna, excepting those which may be better introduced chronologically in other connections, may well find place here. They are interesting and characteristic in themselves, and indicate, also, the great change for the better in Beethoven's pecuniary condition; for a man who keeps a servant and a horse cannot, if honest, be a sufferer from poverty. Wegeler was another fugitive from the French occupation of Bonn. Though only twenty-nine years of age, he had become Rector of the University. Then he fled to Vienna, where he remained nearly two years, and where he naturally renewed his friendship with Beethoven. He reached that capital in October and found Beethoven not in the 'room on the ground floor' where 'it was not necessary to pay the housekeeper more than 7 florins', but living as a guest in the family of Prince Karl Lichnowsky; and this explains sufficiently the cessation of those records of monthly payments before noticed.

Wegeler says:

'Carl, Prince of Lichnowsky . . . was a very great patron, yes, a friend of Beethoven's, who took him into his house as a guest, where he remained at least a few years. I found him there towards the end of the year 1794, and left him there in the middle of 1796. Meanwhile, however, Beethoven had almost always a home in the country.

'The Prince was a great lover and connoisseur of music. He played the pianoforte, and by studying Beethoven's pieces and playing them more or less well, sought to convince him that there was no need of changing anything in his style of composition, though the composer's attention was often called to the difficulties of his works. There were performances at his house every Friday morning, participated in by four hired musicians . . . Beethoven always listened with pleasure to the observations of these gentlemen . . . Here [his] new compositions, so far as was feasible, were first performed. Here there were generally present several great musicians and music-lovers. I, too, as long as I lived in Vienna, was present, if not every time, at least most of the time.

'Here a Hungarian count once placed a difficult composition by Bach in manuscript before him which he played *a vista* exactly as Bach would have played it, according to the testimony of the owner. Here the Viennese author Förster once brought him a quartet of which he had made a clean copy only that morning. In the second portion of the first movement the violoncello got out [failed]. Beethoven stood up, and still playing his own part sang the bass accompaniment. When I spoke about it to him as a proof of extraordinary acquirements, he replied with a smile: "The bass part *had* to be so, else the author would have known nothing about composition." To the remark that he had played a *presto* which he had never seen before so rapidly that it must have been impossible to see the individual notes, he answered: "Nor is that necessary; if you read rapidly there may be a multitude of typographical errors, but you neither see nor give heed to them, so long as the language is a familiar one."

'After the concert, the musicians generally stayed to dine. Here there gathered, in addition, artists and savants without regard to social position.'

Wegeler describes the outward conditions of the composer thus:

'Beethoven, brought up under extremely restricted circumstances, and as it were, under guardianship, though that of his friends, did not know the value of money and was anything but economical. Thus, to cite a single instance, the Prince's dinner hour was fixed at 4 o'clock. "Now," said Beethoven, "it is desired that every day I shall be home at half-past 3, put on better clothes, care for my beard, etc. – I can't stand that!" So it happened that he frequently went to the taverns, since, as has been said, in this as in all other matters of economy, he knew nothing about the value of money.

'The prince, who had a loud metallic voice, once directed his serving-man that if ever he and Beethoven should ring at the same time the latter was to be first served. Beethoven heard this, and the same day engaged a servant for himself. In the same manner, once when he took a whim to learn to ride, which speedily left him, the stable of the Prince being offered him, he bought a horse.'

Concerning his friend's affairs of the heart, Wegeler had opportunity to make observations in Vienna. He relates that while he was in the capital Beethoven 'was always in love and occasionally made a conquest which would have been very difficult if not impossible for many an Adonis'. Beethoven's antipathy to teaching before he left Bonn has already been noticed. In Vienna he developed a still stronger repugnance to playing in society when requested to do so. He often complained to Wegeler how grievously this put him out of sorts, whereupon the latter sought to entertain him and quiet him by conversation. 'When this purpose was reached,' he continues,

'I dropped the conversation, seated myself at the writing table, and Beethoven, if he wanted to continue the discourse, had to sit down on the chair before the pianoforte. Soon, still turned away from the instrument, he aimlessly struck a few chords out of which gradually grew the most beautiful melodies. Oh, why did I not understand more of music! Several times I put ruled paper upon the desk as if without intention, in order to get a manuscript of his; he wrote upon it but then folded it up and put it in his pocket! Concerning his playing I was permitted to say but little, and that only in passing. He would then go away entirely changed in mood and always come back again gladly. The antipathy remained, however, and was frequently the cause of differences between Beethoven and his friends and well-wishers.'

The following undated letter also belongs to the years of Beethoven's intimate association with Wegeler in Vienna (1794–6). It is significant of Beethoven's character. Though easily offended and prone to anger, no sooner was the first ebullition of temper past than he was so reconciliatory and so open to explanation that usually his contrition was out of all proportion to his fault. For this reason, and because it presents the friend in a light which provoked a protest from his modesty, Wegeler was unwilling to publish the entire letter, which follows:

'Dearest and best one!
'What a detestable image of me you have presented for myself! Oh I acknowledge it, I do not deserve your friendship. You are so noble, so considerate, and this is the first time that I am not allowed to be on an equal footing with you; I have fallen far below you. Ah, for eight weeks I have displeased my best and noblest friend. You think that I have lost some of my goodness of heart, but thank Heaven, no; it was not intentional or deliberate malice which induced me to act as I did towards you, it was my inexcusable thoughtlessness which did not permit me to see the matter in its true light. – Oh how ashamed I am, not only for your sake but also for my own – I scarcely dare to ask for your friendship any more – Ah Wegeler my only comfort lies in this, that you have known me almost from my childhood, and yet, oh let me say this for myself, I was always good, and always strove to be upright and true in my actions. Otherwise how could you have loved me? Could I have changed so fearfully for the worse in such a short time? – Impossible. Could these feelings of goodness and love of righteousness have died for ever in me in a moment? No, dear, best Wegeler. Oh venture again to throw yourself entirely into the arms of your B. – trust in the good qualities you used to find in him. I will guarantee that the pure temple of sacred friendship which you erect shall remain firm for ever, no accident, no storm shall ever shake its foundations – firm – eternal – our friendship – forgiveness – oblivion – a new revival of the dying, sinking friendship – Oh Wegeler, do not reject this hand of reconciliation, place yours in mine – Ah God. – But no more – I am coming to see you and shall throw myself in your arms and entreat you to restore to me

my lost friend; and you will be reconciled to me, to your penitent, loving, never-forgetting

Beethoven again'

'It was only now that I received your letter, because I have just returned home.'

We return to the chronological record of events. The first of these in the year 1795 was Beethoven's first appearance in public as virtuoso and composer. The annual concerts in the Burgtheater established by Gassmann for the benefit of the widows of the Tonkünstlergesellschaft were announced for the evenings of 29 and 30 March. The vocal work selected for performance was an oratorio in two parts, *Gioas, Re di Giuda*, by Antonio Cartellieri; the instrumental, a Concerto for Pianoforte and Orchestra, composed and played by Ludwig van Beethoven. Cartellieri was a young man of twenty-three years who, a year or two since, had come from Berlin to study operatic composition with the then greatest living composer in that field, Salieri. As the direction of these Widow and Orphan concerts was almost exclusively in the hands of Salieri, one is almost tempted to think that he may on this occasion have indulged a pardonable vanity in bringing forward two of his pupils, if we did not know how strong an attraction the name of Ludwig van Beethoven must have been for the public which, as yet, had had no opportunity to learn his great powers except by report. The day of the performance drew near but the Concerto was not yet written out.

'Not until the afternoon of the second day before the concert did he write the rondo, and then while suffering from a pretty severe colic which frequently afflicted him. I [Wegeler] relieved him with simple remedies so far as I could. In the ante-room sat four copyists to whom he handed sheet after sheet as soon as it was finished . . . At the first rehearsal, which took place the next day in Beethoven's room, the pianoforte was found to be half a tone lower than the wind-instruments. Without a moment's delay Beethoven had the wind-instruments and the others tune to B flat instead of A and played his part in C sharp.'

Beethoven also took part in a second concert on 30 March, the minutes of the Tonkünstlerschaft recording that he 'improvised on the pianoforte'; and though busily engaged he also embraced an opportunity to testify to his devotion to the manes of Mozart. On 31 March 1795, Mozart's widow arranged a performance of *La Clemenza di Tito* in the Burgtheater. 'After the first part,' says the advertisement,

'Hr. Ludwig van Beethoven will play a Concerto of Mozart's composition on the Pianoforte.' We opine that this concerto was Mozart's in D minor, which Beethoven loved especially, and for which he wrote cadenzas.

Some other incidents recorded by Wegeler belong to this year. Haydn reached Vienna upon his return from his second trip to England on 20 August 1795. Beethoven had now ready the three Sonatas, Op. 2, and at one of the Friday morning concerts at Prince Lichnowsky's he played them for Haydn, to whom they were dedicated. These sonatas were, therefore, the second group of compositions which Beethoven considered illustrative of his artistic ideals and worthy of publication.

Still another anecdote recorded by Wegeler refers to a further composition of this period:

'Beethoven was seated in a box at the opera with a lady of whom he thought much at a performance of *La Molinara*. When the familiar "Nel cor più non mi sento" was reached the lady remarked that she had possessed some variations on the theme but had lost them. In the same night Beethoven wrote the six variations on the melody and the next morning sent them to the lady with the inscription: "Variazioni, etc. Perdute par la – ritrovata par Luigi van Beethoven." They are so easy that it is likely that Beethoven wished that she should be able to play them at sight.'

The Gesellschaft der bildenen Künstler had, in the year 1792, established an annual ball in the Redoutensaal in the month of November; and Haydn, just then returned covered with glory from England, composed a set of twelve minuets and twelve German dances for the occasion. In 1793, the Royal Imperial Composer Koželuch followed Haydn's example. In 1794, Dittersdorf wrote the same number of like dances for the large hall, and Eybler for the small. In view of this array of great names, and considering that as yet the Trios, Op. 1, were the only works of a higher order than the variations which Beethoven had sent to press, the advertisements for the annual ball to be given upon 22 November 1795 give a vivid proof of the high reputation which the young man had gained as a composer now at the end of his third year in Vienna. These advertisements conclude thus: 'The music for the Minuets and German dances for this ball is an entirely new arrangement. For the larger room they were written by the Royal Imperial Kapellmeister Süssmayr; for the smaller room by the master hand of Hr. Ludwig van Beethoven out of love for the artistic fraternity.' These

A silhouette of the von Breuning family, *c.*1782. From left: Frau Hélène von Breuning, Eleonore, brothers Christoph and Lorenz, the uncle Lorenz and Stephan. *Below left*, Frau von Breuning, from a miniature of 1790, and, *below right*, Count Ferdinand Ernst von Waldstein, an early friend and patron of Beethoven

A view of Bonn, where from the back of his house Beethoven could see the Rhine and the Siebengebirge. The feeling for nature Beethoven discovered there was to find expression in his later compositions. *Below left*, Christian Gottlob Neefe. Beethoven wrote to his teacher in 1793: 'If I ever become a great man yours shall be a share of the credit.' *Below right*, the composer Joseph Haydn, who taught Beethoven in Vienna. The music for Haydn's 'Drum Roll' Symphony lies open on the stand

dances, arranged for pianoforte by Beethoven himself, came from the press of Artaria a few weeks later, as did also Süssmayr's; Beethoven's name in the advertisement being in large and conspicuous type.

As the year began with the first, so it closed with Beethoven's second appearance in public as composer and virtuoso; and here is the advertisement of the performance from the *Wiener Zeitung* of 16 December:

'Next Friday, the 18th instant, Herr Kapellmeister Haydn will give a grand musical concert in the small Redoutensaal, at which Mad. Tomeni and Hr. Mombelli will sing. Hr. van Beethoven will play a Concerto of his composing on the Pianoforte, and three grand symphonies, not yet heard here, which the kapellmeister composed during his last sojourn in London, will be performed.'

One would gladly know what concerto was played. But there was little public criticism then outside of London and very rarely any in Vienna. The mere fact of the appearance of Beethoven at his old master's concert is, however, another proof that too much stress has been laid upon that hasty word spoken by him to Ries and quoted above: Haydn wanted Beethoven to put 'Pupil of Haydn' on the title page of his first works but Beethoven was unwilling to do so because 'though he had taken some lessons from Haydn he had never learned anything from him'. Nothing could be more natural than for Haydn, knowing nothing of the studies of his pupil with Schenk, to express such a wish in relation to the Sonatas dedicated to him, and equally natural that the author should refuse; but to add to the attractions of the concert was a very different matter – a graceful and delicate compliment which he could with pleasure make.

CHAPTER 6

The Years 1796–1799

The narrative resumes its course with the year 1796, the twenty-sixth of Beethoven's life and his fourth in Vienna. If not yet officially, he was *de facto* discharged from his obligations to the Elector Maximilian and all his relations with Bonn and its people were broken off. Vienna had become his home, and there is no reason to suppose that he ever afterwards cherished any real and settled purpose to exchange it for another – not even in 1809 when, for the moment, he had some thought of accepting Jerome Bonaparte's invitation to Cassel.

He had now finished his course of contrapuntal study with Albrechtsberger; he was first of the pianoforte players of the capital and his name added attraction even to the concert which Haydn, returning again from his London triumphs, had given to introduce some of his new works to the Viennese; his 'masterhand' was already publicly recognised in the field of musical composition; he counted many nobles of the higher ranks in his list of personal friends and had been, perhaps even now was, living as one of Prince Karl Lichnowsky's family. The change in his pecuniary condition might have thrown a more equitable temperament than his off its balance. Three years ago he anxiously noted down the few kreutzers occasionally spent for coffee or chocolate 'für Haidn und mich'; now he was keeping his own servant and a horse.

Moreover, by this time the three Beethoven brothers had become reunited, for Vienna had become the new home of Caspar Anton Carl and Nikolaus Johann. Beethoven's first letter to Simrock of 18 June 1794 began: 'Dear Simrock! My brother told me here that you had already printed my variations for four hands or surely would print them.' By this time therefore Caspar Anton Carl had moved to Vienna, and it is prophetic that the first reference to him in correspondence should be in connection with the publication of one of Ludwig's compositions. Nikolaus Johann, the younger brother, made the move eighteen months later. An entry in the Regensburg record of arrivals and departures shows that there arrived on 13 December 1795 '2 Herren Gebrüder Breuning, Kaufleute von Bonn', and the next day 'Herr Bathofen Mediziner aus Göttingen'. Having met at Regensburg these three departed for Vienna on 15 December. But according to police records they were held up in Linz from 18 December (the date that Ludwig was performing in Haydn's concert) to 23 December because they lacked passes and had to be cleared by the police. Due to this complication with the authorities, papers recording their arrival have been found in the Ministry of Justice in Vienna. The late Minister Kurt Smolle of Vienna discovered two half-burned papers from which he was able to decipher: 'concerning the brothers Joseph and [burnt] Breuning who left Bonn two years ago and Johann van B[burnt] who is coming direct from Bonn'. This makes it clear that it was Johann and not Ludwig, as supposed by Wegeler, who was travelling with the Breuning brothers. They arrived in Vienna on 26 December.

The composer's brothers, if at all a burden, were no longer a heavy one. Carl Caspar,* according to the best information now obtainable, soon gained moderate success in the musical profession and, with probably some occasional aid from Ludwig both pecuniary and in obtaining pupils, earned sufficient for his comfortable support; while Johann had secured a situation in that apothecary shop 'Zum Heiligen Geist' which, in 1860, was still to be seen in the Kärnthnerstrasse near the former site of the gate of that name. His wages were, of course, small and we shall soon see that Ludwig offered him assistance if needed, though not to Carl; but Johann's position gradually improved and he was able in a few years to save enough to enable him, unaided by his brother, to purchase and establish himself in a business of his own.

'Fate had become propitious to Beethoven'; and a final citation from the memorandum book will show in what spirit he was determined to merit the continuance of Fortune's favour. If we make allowance for the old error as to his real age, this citation may belong to a period a year or two later; but may it not be one of those extracts from books and periodical publications which all his life long he was so fond of making? This seems to be the more probable supposition. The words are these: 'Courage! In spite of all bodily weaknesses my spirit shall rule. You have lived 25 years. This year must determine the complete man. Nothing must remain undone.'

And now let the chronological narrative of events be resumed. As the year 1795 had ended with a public appearance of Beethoven as pianoforte player and composer, so also began the year 1796; and, as on a former occasion in a concert by Haydn, so this time he played at a concert given by a singer, Signora Bolla, who afterwards became famous, in the Redoutensaal. Again he played a pianoforte concerto.

Also at this time he was doubtless occupied with the last corrections of the Sonatas, Op. 2, dedicated to Haydn, the six Minuets (second

* Caspar Anton Carl was usually referred to as Carl Caspar or Caspar.

part), the Variations on the theme from *Le nozze disturbate* and those on 'Nel cor più non mi sento', all of which works are advertised in the *Wiener Zeitung* in the course of the next two months.

Meanwhile Beethoven had undertaken what turned out to be a concert tour lasting from February to July. Here follows the first record of this trip:

'To my brother Nikolaus Beethoven
to be delivered at the apothecary shop near the Kärnthner Gate
'Hr. von Z. will please hand this letter to the wig-maker who will care for its delivery.

'Prague, 19 February [1796]

'Dear Brother!

'So that you may now at least know where I am and what I am doing I must needs write to you. In the first place I am getting on well – very well. My art wins for me friends and respect; what more do I want? This time, too, I shall earn considerable money. I shall remain here a few weeks more and then go to *Dresden, Leipzig and Berlin*. It will probably be six weeks more before I shall return – I hope that you will be more and more pleased with your sojourn in Vienna; but beware of the whole guild of wicked women. Have you yet called on *Cousin Elss*? You might write to me at this place if you have inclination and time.

'P. Linowski will probably soon return to Vienna; he has already gone from here. If you need money you may go to him boldly, for he still owes me some. For the rest I hope that your life will grow continually in happiness and to that end I hope to contribute something. Farewell dear brother and think occasionally of

Your true faithful brother L. Beethoven'

'Greetings to Brother Caspar. My address is the Golden Unicorn on the Kleinseite.'

This letter, with other considerations, render it well nigh certain that Beethoven had now come to Prague with Prince Lichnowsky as Mozart had done, seven years before, and that upon leaving Vienna he had had no intention of pursuing his journey further; but encouraged by the success thus reported to his brother, he suddenly determined to seek instruction and experience, pleasure, profit and fame in an extended tour.

The musical public of Prague was the same that had so recently honoured itself by its instant and noble appreciation of Mozart, and had given so glorious a welcome to *Figaro, Don Giovanni* and *Titus*. There being no royal or imperial court there, and the public amusements being less numerous than in Vienna, the nobility were thrown more on their own resources for recreation; and hence, besides the traditional taste of the Bohemians for instrumental music, their capital was, perhaps, a better field for the virtuoso than Vienna. 'The considerable money' to be earned would be the presents of the nobility for his performances in their salons, and, perhaps, for composition.

The conception of the aria 'Ah, perfido! spergiuro' is generally associated with Beethoven's sojourn in Prague. The belief rests upon the fact that upon the cover of a copy which he revised Beethoven wrote the words 'Une grande Scène mise en musique par L. v. Beethoven à Prague, 1796'. On the first page is written: 'Recitativo e Aria composta e dedicata alla Signora Contessa di Clari da L. v. Beethoven.' Now, on 21 November 1796, Madame Duschek, the well-known friend of Mozart, at a concert in Leipzig sang 'An Italian Scena composed for Madame Duschek by Beethoven', and it was easy to conclude that the aria was completed by Beethoven for Madame Duschek, one of the circle of Beethoven's friends in Prague.

That Beethoven carried out his intention of stopping at Dresden is shown by two letters from the music dilettante Chamberlain von Schall to the Elector Max Franz. From the first, dated 24 April 1796: 'The young Beethoven arrived here [Dresden] yesterday. He had letters from Vienna for Count Elz; he will play for the court and then go from here to Leipzig–Berlin. He is said to have improved immensely and to compose well . . .' From the second, dated 6 May: 'Beethoven has delayed here almost eight days, everyone who heard him play was enchanted. Beethoven was granted by the Elector of Saxony, a man who knows music, the favour to play in the evening all alone without accompaniment for an hour and a half. HRH was exceedingly well satisfied and presented him with a golden *tabatière*. Beethoven went from here to Leipzig and Berlin . . .' In his answer Maximilian Franz hopes that 'Beethoven will profit more from his trip than Simonetti who was applauded everywhere but never presented with a gift'.

While there is no record of Beethoven's arrival in Leipzig, it can be assumed from von Schall's letter that he left Dresden approximately eight days after his arrival on 23 April and reached his next stop about 1 or 2 May. In a letter to Breitkopf and Härtel of 5 July 1806, Beethoven refers to his acquaintance with the Leipzig musician, August Eberhard Müller, which presumably was made at this time.

His next appearance was in Berlin. In after years he was fond of talking about his sojourn there, and some particulars have thus been preserved. 'He played', says Ries, 'several times at the court (that of King Frederick William II), where he played the two grand sonatas with obbligato violoncello, Op. 5, written for Duport, first violoncellist of the King, and himself. On his departure he received a gold snuff-box filled with louis d'ors. Beethoven declared with pride that it was not an ordinary snuff-box, but such a one as it might have been customary to give to an ambassador.'

This king shared the love for music of his uncle, Frederick the Great, while his taste was better and more cultivated. His instrument was the violoncello, and he often took part in quartets and sometimes in the rehearsals of Italian operas. He exerted a powerful and enduring influence for good upon the musical taste of Berlin. It was he who caused the operas of Gluck and Mozart to be performed there and introduced oratorios of Handel into the court concerts. His appreciations of Mozart's genius, and his wish to attach that great master to his court, are well known; and these facts render credible a statement with which Carl Czerny closes a description of Beethoven's extemporaneous playing, contributed to Cocks's *London Musical Miscellany* (2 August 1852):

'His improvisation was most brilliant and striking. In whatever company he might chance to be, he knew how to produce such an effect upon every hearer that frequently not an eye remained dry, while many would break out into loud sobs; for there was something wonderful in his expression in addition to the beauty and originality of his ideas and his spirited style of rendering them. After ending an improvisation of this kind he would burst into loud laughter and banter his hearers on the emotion he had caused in them. "You are fools!" he would say. Sometimes he would feel himself insulted by these indications of sympathy. "Who can live among such spoiled children?" he would cry, and only on that account (as he told me) he declined to accept an invitation which the King of Prussia gave him after one of the extemporary performances above described.'

Kapellmeister Reichardt had withdrawn himself from Berlin two years before, having fallen into disfavour because of his sympathy with the French Revolution. Neither Himmel nor Righini, his successors, ever showed a genius for chamber music of a high order, and, indeed, there was no composer of reputation in this sphere then living in that quarter. The young Beethoven by his two sonatas had proved his powers and the King may have seen in him precisely the right man to fill the vacancy – no small proof of superior taste and judgement. What the German expression was which the translator of Czerny's letter has rendered 'accept an invitation which the King gave him' there is no means of knowing; but as it stands it suggests an invitation to enter permanently into his service. The death of the King the next year, of course, prevented its being ever renewed.

Friedrich Heinrich Himmel, five years older than Beethoven, whom the King had withdrawn from the study of theology and caused to be thoroughly educated as a musician, had returned the year before and had assumed his duties as Royal Pianist and Composer. As a virtuoso on his instrument his only rival in Berlin was Prince Louis Ferdinand, son of Prince August and nephew of Frederick II, two years younger than Beethoven and endowed by nature with talents and genius which would have made him conspicuous had fortune not given him royal descent. He and Beethoven became well known to each other and each felt and did full justice to the other's musical genius and attainments. Now let Ries speak again:

'In Berlin he [Beethoven] associated much with Himmel, of whom he said that he had a pretty talent, but no more; his pianoforte playing, he said, was elegant and pleasing, but he was not to be compared with Prince Louis Ferdinand. In his opinion he paid the latter a high compliment when once he said to him that his playing was not that of a king or prince but more like that of a thoroughly good pianoforte player. He fell out with Himmel in the following manner: One day when they were together Himmel begged Beethoven to improvise; which Beethoven did. Afterwards Beethoven insisted that Himmel do the same. The latter was weak enough to agree; but after he had played for quite a time Beethoven remarked: "Well, when are you going fairly to begin?" Himmel had flattered himself that he had already performed wonders; he jumped up and the men behaved ill towards each other. Beethoven said to me: "I thought that Himmel had been only preluding a bit." Afterwards they were reconciled, indeed, but Himmel could never forgive or forget. They also exchanged letters until Himmel played Beethoven a shabby trick. The latter always wanted to know the news from Berlin. This bored Himmel, who at last wrote that the greatest news from Berlin was that a lamp for the blind had been invented. Beethoven ran about with the news and all the world wanted to know how this was possible. Thereupon he wrote to Himmel that he had blundered in not giving more explicit information. The answer which he received, but which does not permit of communication, not only put an end to the correspondence but brought ridicule upon Beethoven, who was so inconsiderate as to show it then and there.'

Early in July 1796, the King left Berlin for the baths of Pyrmont, the nobility dispersed to their estates or to watering places, and the city 'was empty and silent'. Beethoven, therefore, could have had no inducement to prolong his stay; but the precise time of his departure is unknown.

Notwithstanding Wegeler's statement that he left Beethoven living as one of the family of Prince Lichnowsky 'in the middle of 1796', it is as certain as circumstantial evidence can well make it that the brother Nikolaus Johann and Christoph von Breuning had returned to Bonn before Beethoven reached Vienna again. On 23 November, Stephan von Breuning wrote to them both from Mergentheim:

'I do not know whether or not Lenz [the youngest Breuning] has written you anything about Beethoven; but take notice that I saw him in Vienna and that according to my mind, which Lenz has confirmed, he has become somewhat staider, or, perhaps I should say, has acquired more knowledge of humanity through travels (or was it because of the new ebullition of friendship upon his arrival?) and a greater conviction of the scarceness and value of good friends. A hundred times, dear Wegeler, he wishes you here again, and regrets nothing so much as that he did not follow much of your advice.'

Except this notice of his bearing and demeanour, there is a complete hiatus in Beethoven's history from June until the following November. There is a story of a 'dangerous illness', which was caused by his own imprudence this summer. 'In the year 1796, Beethoven, on a hot summer day, came greatly overheated to his home, threw open doors and windows, disrobed down to his trousers and cooled himself in a draught at the open window. The consequence was a dangerous illness, which, on his convalescence, settled in his organs of hearing, and from this time on his deafness steadily increased.'

A sickness of the gravity here described seems somewhat improbable in this year in view of the further travels which Beethoven made in the following autumn. We reconsider this notice in connection with the summer of 1797. The most plausible suggestion for the hiatus is that coming back, flushed with victory with the success of his tour, and delighted with the novelty of travelling at his ease, Beethoven made an excursion to Pressburg and Budapest. That this trip took place about four months after his return from Berlin has come to light from a letter written by Beethoven while in Pressburg to Andreas Streicher, dated 19 November 1796, which refers to a concert to be given there by Beethoven on the 23rd. It is here given in full because of its interest concerning the composer's attitude towards the piano, and his relation with the Streichers:

'Dear Streicher!

'The day before yesterday I received your fortepiano which has turned out to be really excellent. Everyone else is anxious to own one, and I – you can laugh all right, I would be lying were I not to tell you that it is too good for me, and why? – because it takes away my freedom to create the tone for myself. Nevertheless it will not keep you from making all your fortepianos in this way, there will probably be fewer people who have such whims.

My Akademie takes place on Wednesday, the 23rd of this m[onth]. If *Stein** would care to come I will be very glad to see him, he can count on spending the night at my house. – Concerning the sale of the fortepiano, this idea had already occurred to me before it had to you and I shall certainly strive to bring it about. – I thank you heartily dear St. for your readiness to serve me so well. I only wish that I were able in some way to return your kindness, and that you, without my having to say it to you, were convinced how much I want the worth of your instruments to become recognised both here and everywhere, and how much I value your friendship and want you to regard me as your loving and warm friend

Beethoven'
'Pressburg 19 November anno 96 post Christum Natum
Everything lovely to your wife.'

From another letter to Streicher, undated, a further insight is gained of Beethoven's attitude towards the pianoforte. This much can appropriately be included here:

'It is certain that the manner of playing the *pianoforte* is still the most uncultivated of all instruments. Often one believes to hear only a harp, and I am glad, my dear, that you are one of the few who comprehend and feel that one may sing on the pianoforte too, if one is but capable of feeling. I hope that the time will come when the harp and the pianoforte will be two totally different instruments.'

November 1796 also marked the publication of a minor work of the composer. This was the year of that astounding series of victories ending at Arcole, gained by the young French general Napoleon Bonaparte. The Austrian government and people alike saw and feared the danger of invasion, a general uprising took place and volunteer corps were formed in all quarters. For the Vienna corps, Friedelburg wrote his 'Abschiedsgesang an Wiens Bürger beim Auszug der

* The noted pianoforte maker.

Fahnen-Division der Wiener Freiwilliger', and Beethoven set it to music. The original printed edition bears the date '15 November 1796'. It does not appear to have gained any great popularity.

The rapid progress of the French army had caused the Germans in Italy to become distrustful of the future and to hasten homeward. Among them were Beethoven's old companions in the Bonn orchestra, the cousins Andreas and Bernhard Romberg, who in the spring of this year (26 May) had kissed the hand of the Queen of Naples, daughter of the Empress Maria Theresia, and then departed to Rome to join another friend of the Bonn period, Karl Kügelgen. The three coming north arrived at Vienna in the autumn; the Rombergs remained there for a space with Beethoven, while Kügelgen proceeded to Berlin. Baron von Braun had heard the cousins the year before in Munich and invited them 'to give Vienna an opportunity to hear them'. There is no notice of their concert in the Vienna newspapers of the period, and the date is unknown. From Lenz von Breuning is gleaned an additional fact which alone gives interest to the concert for us. He writes to Wegeler in January 1797: 'Beethoven is here again; he played in the Romberg concert. He is the same as of old and I am glad that he and the Rombergs still get along with each other. Once he was near a break with them; I interceded and achieved my end to a fair extent. Moreover, he thinks a great deal of me just now.'

It is clear that the Rombergs, under the circumstances, must have largely owed their limited success to Beethoven's name and influence. In February 1797, they were again in their old positions in Schroeder's orchestra in Hamburg.

Beethoven during this winter must be imagined busily engaged with pupils and private concerts, perhaps also with his operatic studies with Salieri, certainly with composition and with preparation for and the over-sight of various works then passing through the press; for in February and April (1797) Artaria advertised the two Violoncello Sonatas, Op. 5, the Pianoforte Sonata for four hands, Op. 6, and the Twelve Variations on a Danse Russe; these last are the variations which he dedicated to the Countess Browne and which gave occasion for the anecdote related by Ries illustrating Beethoven's forgetfulness; for this dedication he had 'received a handsome riding-horse from Count Browne as a gift. He rode the animal a few times, soon after forgot all about it and, worse than that, its food also. His servant, who soon noticed this, began to hire out the horse for his own benefit and, in order not to attract the attention of Beethoven to the fact, for a long time withheld from him all bills for fodder. At length, however, to Beethoven's great amazement he handed in a very large one, which recalled to him at once his horse and his neglectfulness.'

But the war was renewed and the thoughts of the Viennese were soon occupied with matters more serious than the indulgence of their musical taste. On 16 March 1797, Bonaparte forced the passage of the Tagliamento and Isonzo. During the two weeks following he had conquered the greater part of Carniola, Carinthia and the Tyrol and was now rapidly approaching Vienna. On 11 February, Lorenz Leopold Hauschka's 'Gott erhalte unsern Kaiser' with Haydn's music had been sung for the first time in the theatre and now, when on 7 April the Landsturm (local militia) was called out, Friedelberg produced his war-song 'Ein grosses, deutsches Volk sind wir', to which Beethoven also gave music. The printed copy bears the date 14 April, suggesting the probability that it was sung on the occasion of the grand consecration of the banners, which took place on the 17th. Beethoven's music was, however, far from being so fortunate as Haydn's, and seems to have gained as little popularity as his previous attempt; but as the preliminaries to a treaty of peace were signed at Leoben on the 18th, and the armies, so hastily improvised, were dismissed three weeks afterwards, the taste for war-songs vanished.

The little that is known of Beethoven's position as a teacher at this period is very vague and unsatisfactory; enough, however, to render it sufficiently certain that he had plenty of pupils, many of them young ladies of high rank who paid him generously. In the triple capacity of teacher, composer and pianist his gains were large and he was able to write in May to Wegeler that he was doing well and steadily better.

It is very possible that the illness mentioned earlier may have occurred during this summer. But the date, as well as the inference that in it lay the original cause of the composer's subsequent loss of hearing, must be left mainly to conjecture.

From May to October 1797, Beethoven's history is still a blank and nothing but the utter silence of Lenz von Breuning in his correspondence with his family at Bonn on a topic so likely to engage his sympathies as the dangerous illness of his friend, appears to prevent the filling of this blank in part by throwing him upon a bed of sickness. True, Lenz may have written and the letter have been lost or destroyed; or he may have neglected to write because of his approaching departure from Vienna, which took place in the autumn. His album, still preserved, has among its contributors Ludwig and Johann van Beethoven and Zmeskall. Ludwig wrote as follows:

'Truth exists for the wise,
Beauty for a feeling heart.
They belong to each other.

'Dear, good Breuning,

'Never shall I forget the time which I spent with you *in Bonn* as well as here. Hold fast your friendship for me, you will always find me the same.

Your true friend L. v. Beethoven'

'Vienna 1797
1 October'

They never met again. Lenz died on 10 April of the following year.

Early in the year 1798, a political event occurred which demands notice here from its connection with one of Beethoven's noblest and most original works – the *Sinfonia Eroica*.

The extraordinary demands made by the French Directory upon the Austrian government as preliminary to the renewal of diplomatic intercourse, after the peace of Campo Formio – such as a national palace and French theatre for the minister and the right of jurisdiction over all Frenchmen in the Austrian dominions – all of which were rejected by the imperial government, had aroused to a high pitch the public curiosity both as to the man who might be selected for the appointment and as to the course he might adopt. This curiosity was by no means diminished by the intelligence that the new minister was Jean Baptiste Bernadotte, the young general who had borne so important a part in the recent invasion of Istria. He arrived in Vienna on 5 February 1798. The state of the Empress's health, who was delivered of the Archduchess Maria Clementine on 1 March, delayed the private audience of Bernadotte for the presentation of his credentials to the Emperor until the second of that month, and his public audience until 8 April. During the festivities of the court, which then took place, Bernadotte was always present, and a reporter of that day says both the Emperor and Empress held more conversation with him than with any other of the 'cercle'. This familiar intercourse, however, came speedily to an end; for on the 13th Bernadotte had the rashness to display the hated tricolour from his balcony and to threaten to defend it by force. A riot occurred, and it was thought that in the extreme excitement of popular feeling nothing but the strong detachments of cavalry and infantry detailed for his protection saved his life – saved it to ascend the throne of Sweden on the twentieth anniversary of his arrival in Vienna!

Since etiquette allowed a foreign minister neither to make nor receive visits in his public capacity until after his formal reception at court, the General, during the two months of his stay, except the last five days, 'lived very quietly'. Those who saw him praised him as 'well-behaved, sedate and modest'. In his train was Rudolph Kreutzer, the great violinist.

Bernadotte had now just entered his thirty-fourth year; Kreutzer was in his thirty-second; both of them, therefore, in age, as in tastes and acquirements, fitted to appreciate the splendour of Beethoven's genius and to enjoy his society. Moreover, as the Ambassador was the son of a provincial advocate, there was no difference of rank by birth, which could prevent them from meeting upon equal terms. Under such circumstances, and remembering that just at that epoch the young General Bonaparte was the topic of universal wonder and admiration, one is fully prepared for the statement of Schindler upon the origin of the 'Heroic' Symphony: 'The first idea for the symphony is said to have gone out from General Bernadotte, then French Ambassador in Vienna, who esteemed Beethoven very highly. This I heard from several of Beethoven's friends. I was also told so by Count Moritz Lichnowsky (brother of Prince Lichnowsky), who was often in the society of Bernadotte with Beethoven . . .'

Again Schindler adds that in 1823 'Beethoven had a lively recollection that Bernadotte had really first inspired him with the idea of the "Eroica" Symphony.'

It was now no longer the case that Beethoven was without a rival as pianoforte virtuoso. He had a competitor fully worthy of his powers; one who divided about equally with him the suffrages of the leaders in the Vienna musical circles. In fact the excellencies peculiar to the two were such and so different that it depended upon the taste of the auditor to which he accorded the praise of superiority. Joseph Wölffl of Salzburg, two years younger than Beethoven, a 'wonder-child', who had played a violin concerto in public at the age of seven years, was a pupil of Leopold Mozart and Michael Haydn. Being in Vienna, when but eighteen years old he was engaged, on the recommendation of Mozart, by the Polish Count Oginsky, who took him to Warsaw. His success there, as pianoforte virtuoso, teacher and composer, was almost unexampled. But it is only in his character as pianist that we have to do with him; and a reference may be made to the general principle, that a worthy competition is the best spur to genius. When we read in one of Beethoven's letters the words 'I have also greatly perfected my pianoforte playing,' they will cause no surprise; for only by severe industry and consequent improvement could he retain his high position, in the presence of such rivals as Wölffl and, a year or two later, J. B. Cramer. A lively picture of Wölffl by Tomaschek, who heard him in 1799, in his autobiography sufficiently proves that Wölffl's party in

Vienna was composed of those to whom extraordinary execution was the main thing; while Beethoven's admirers were of those who had hearts to be touched. A parallel between Beethoven and Wölffl in a letter to the *Allgemeine Musikalische Zeitung* dated 22 April 1799, just at the time when the performances of both were topics of general conversation in musical circles, and still fresh in the memory of all who had heard them, is in the highest degree apposite to the subject of this chapter. The writer says:

'Opinion is divided here touching the merits of the two; yet it would seem as if the majority were on the side of the latter [Wölffl]. I shall try to set forth the peculiarities of each without taking part in the controversy. Beethoven's playing is extremely brilliant but has less delicacy and occasionally he is guilty of indistinctness. He shows himself to the greatest advantage in improvisation, and here, indeed, it is most extraordinary with what lightness and yet firmness in the succession of ideas Beethoven not only varies a theme given him on the spur of the moment by figuration (with which many a virtuoso makes his fortune) but really develops it. Since the death of Mozart, who in this respect is for me still the *non plus ultra*, I have never enjoyed this kind of pleasure in the degree in which it is provided by Beethoven. In this Wölffl fails to reach him. But W. has advantages in that he, sound in musical learning and dignified in his compositions, plays passages which seem impossible with an ease, precision and clearness which cause amazement (of course he is helped here by the large structure of his hands) and that his interpretation is always, especially in Adagios, so pleasing and insinuating that one can not only admire it but also enjoy . . . That Wölffl likewise enjoys an advantage because of his amiable bearing, contrasted with the somewhat haughty pose of Beethoven, is very natural.'

No biography of Beethoven can omit the somewhat inflated and bombastic account which Seyfried gives of the emulation between Beethoven and Wölffl. Ignaz von Seyfried at the period in question was one of Schikaneder's conductors, to which position he had been called when not quite twenty-one years of age, and had assumed its duties on 1 March 1797. He was among the most promising of the young composers of the capital, belonged to a highly respectable family, had been educated at the University, and his personal character was unblemished. He would, therefore, naturally have access to the musical salons and his reminiscences of music and musicians in those years may be accepted as the records of observation. The unfavourable light which the researches of Nottebohm have thrown upon him as editor of the so-called *Beethoven Studien* does not extend to such statements of fact as might easily have come under his own cognisance; and the passage now cited from the appendix of the *Studien*, though written thirty years after the events it describes, bears all the marks of being a faithful transcript of the writer's own memories:

'Beethoven had already attracted attention to himself by several compositions and was rated a first-class pianist in Vienna when he was confronted by a rival in the closing years of the last century. Thereupon there was, in a way, a revival of the old Parisian feud of the Gluckists and Piccinists, and the many friends of art in the Imperial City arrayed themselves in two parties. At the head of Beethoven's admirers stood the amiable Prince Lichnowsky; among the most zealous patrons of Wölffl was the broadly cultured Baron Raymond von Wetzlar, whose delightful villa (on the Grünberg near the Emperor's recreation-castle) offered to all artists, native and foreign, an asylum in the summer months, as pleasing as it was desirable, with true British loyalty. There the interesting combats of the two athletes not infrequently offered an indescribable artistic treat to the numerous and thoroughly select gathering. Each brought forward the latest product of his mind. Now one and anon the other gave free rein to his glowing fancy; sometimes they would seat themselves at two pianofortes and improvise alternately on themes which they gave each other, and thus created many a four-hand Capriccio which if it could have been put upon paper at the moment would surely have bidden defiance to time. It would have been difficult, perhaps impossible, to award the palm of victory to either one of the gladiators in respect of technical skill. Nature had been a particularly kind mother to Wölffl in bestowing upon him a gigantic hand which could span a tenth as easily as other hands compass an octave, and permitted him to play passages of double notes in these intervals with the rapidity of lightning. In his improvisations even then Beethoven did not deny his tendency towards the mysterious and gloomy. When once he began to revel in the infinite world of tones, he was transported also above all earthly things; his spirit had burst all restricting bonds, shaken off the yoke of servitude, and soared triumphantly and jubilantly into the luminous spaces of the higher ether. Now his playing tore along like a wildly foaming cataract, and the conjurer constrained his instrument to an utterance so forceful that the stoutest structure was scarcely able to withstand it; and anon he sank down, exhausted, exhaling gentle plaints, dissolving in melancholy. Again the spirit would soar aloft, triumphing over transitory terrestrial sufferings, turn its glance upward in reverent sounds and find rest and comfort on the innocent bosom of holy nature. But who shall sound the depths of the sea? It was the mystical Sanskrit language whose hieroglyphs can be read only by the initiated. Wölffl, on the contrary, trained in the school of Mozart, was always equable; never superficial but always clear and thus more accessible to the multitude. He used art only as a means to an end, never to exhibit his acquirements. He always enlisted the interest of his hearers and inevitably compelled them to follow the progression of his well-ordered ideas. Whoever has heard Hummel will know what is meant by this . . .

'But for this [the attitude of their patrons] the protégés cared very little. They respected each other because they knew best how to appreciate each other, and as straightforward honest Germans followed the principle that the roadway of art is broad enough for many, and that it is not necessary to lose one's self in envy in pushing forward for the goal of fame!'

Another interesting and valuable discussion of Beethoven's powers and characteristics as a pianoforte virtuoso at this period is contained in the autobiography of Tomaschek, who heard him both in public and in private during a visit which Beethoven made again this year to Prague:

'In the year 1798, in which I continued my juridical studies, Beethoven, the giant among pianoforte players, came to Prague. He gave a largely attended concert in the Konviktssaal . . . [His] magnificent playing and particularly the daring flights in his improvisation stirred me strangely to the depths of my soul; indeed I found myself so profoundly bowed down that I did not touch my pianoforte for several days . . . I heard Beethoven at his second concert, which neither in performance nor in composition renewed again the first powerful impression. This time he played the Concerto in B flat which he had just composed in Prague. Then I heard him a third time at the home of Count C., where he played, besides the graceful Rondo from the A major Sonata, an improvisation on the theme: "Ah! vous dirai-je, Maman." This time I listened to Beethoven's artistic work with more composure. I admired his powerful and brilliant playing, but his frequent daring deviations from one motive to another, whereby the organic connection, the gradual development of idea was broken up, did not escape me. Evils of this nature frequently weaken his greatest compositions, those which sprang from a too exuberant conception. It is not seldom that the unbiased listener is rudely awakened from his transport. The singular and original seemed to be his chief aim in composition, as is confirmed by the answer which he made to a lady who asked him if he often attended Mozart's operas. "I do not know them," he replied, "and do not care to hear the music of others lest I forfeit some of my originality." '

The veteran Tomaschek when he wrote thus had heard all the greatest virtuosi of the pianoforte, who, from the days of Mozart to 1840, had made themselves famous; and yet Beethoven remained for him still 'the lord of pianoforte players' and 'the giant among pianoforte players'. Still, great as he was now when Tomaschek heard him, Beethoven could write three years later that he had greatly perfected his playing.

Two new and valuable, though but passing, acquaintances were made by Beethoven this year, however – with Domenico Dragonetti, the greatest contrabassist known to history, and John Baptist Cramer, one of the greatest pianists. Dragonetti was not more remarkable for his astounding execution than for the deep, genuine musical feeling which elevated and ennobled it. He was now – in the spring of 1799, so far as the means are at hand of determining the time – returning to London from a visit to his native city, Venice, and his route took him to Vienna, where he remained several weeks. Beethoven and he soon met and they were mutually pleased with each other. Many years afterwards Dragonetti related the following anecdote:

'Beethoven had been told that his new friend could execute violoncello music upon his huge instrument, and one morning, when Dragonetti called at his room, he expressed his desire to hear a sonata. The contrabass was sent for, and the Sonata, No. 2, of Op. 5, was selected. Beethoven played his part, with his eyes immovably fixed upon his companion, and, in the finale, where the arpeggios occur, was so delighted and excited that at the close he sprang up and threw his arms around both player and instrument.'

Cramer, born at Mannheim, 1771, but from early infancy reared and educated in England, was, like Beethoven, in no small degree self-taught. He was so rarely on the Continent that his extraordinary merits have never been fully understood and appreciated there. Yet for a period of many years in the first part of the nineteenth century he was undoubtedly, upon the whole, the first pianist of Europe.

Cramer surpassed Beethoven in the perfect neatness, correctness and finish of his execution; Beethoven assured him that he preferred his touch to that of any other player; his brilliancy was astonishing; but yet taste, feeling, expression, were the qualities which more eminently distinguished him. Beethoven stood far above Cramer in power and energy, especially when extemporising. Each was supreme in his own sphere; each found much to learn in the perfections of the other; each, in later years, did full justice to the other's powers. Thus Ries says: 'Amongst the pianoforte players he [Beethoven] had praise for but one as being distinguished – John Cramer. All others were but little to him.'

Making a visit one morning to him, Cramer, as he entered the ante-room, heard Beethoven extemporising by himself, and remained there more than half an hour 'completely entranced', never in his life having heard such exquisite effects, such beautiful combinations. Knowing Beethoven's extreme dislike of being listened to on such occasions, Cramer retired and never let him know that he had so heard him.

Cramer's widow communicates a pleasant anecdote. At an Augarten Concert the two pianists were walking together and hearing a performance of Mozart's pianoforte Concerto in C minor (K. 491); Beethoven suddenly stood still and, directing his companion's attention to the exceedingly simple, but equally beautiful motive which is first introduced towards the end of the piece, exclaimed: 'Cramer, Cramer! we shall never be able to do anything like that!' As the theme was repeated and wrought up to the climax, Beethoven, swaying his body to and fro, marked the time and in every possible manner manifested a delight rising to enthusiasm.

Schindler's record of his conversations upon Beethoven with Cramer and Cherubini in 1841 is interesting and valuable. He has, however, left one important consideration unnoticed, namely, that the visits of those masters to Vienna were five years apart – five years of great change in Beethoven – a period during which his deafness, too slight to attract Cramer's attention, had increased to a degree beyond concealment, and which, joined to his increased devotion to composition and compulsory abandonment of all ambition as a virtuoso, with consequent neglect of practice, had affected his execution unfavourably. Hence the difference in the opinions of such competent judges as Cramer, describing him as he was in 1799–1800, Cherubini in 1805–6, and two years later Clementi, afford a doubtless just and fair indication of the decline of Beethoven's powers as a mere pianist – not extending, however, at least for some years yet, to his extemporaneous performances.

And now let Schindler speak:

'Cherubini, disposed to be curt, characterised Beethoven's pianoforte playing in a single word: "rough". The gentleman Cramer, however, desired that less offence be taken at the rudeness of his performance than at the unreliable reading of one and the same composition – one day intellectually brilliant and full of characteristic expression, the next freakish to the verge of unclearness; often confused. Because of this a few friends expressed a wish to hear Cramer play several works publicly from the manuscript. This touched a sensitive spot in Beethoven; his jealousy was aroused and, according to Cramer, their relations became strained.'

This strain, however, left no such sting behind it as to diminish Cramer's good opinion of Beethoven both as man and artist, or hinder his free expression of it.

Cramer's musical gods were Handel and Mozart, notwithstanding his lifelong love for Bach's clavier compositions; hence the abrupt transitions, the strange modulations, and the, until then, unheard passages, which Beethoven introduced ever more freely into his works were to him, as to Tomaschek and so many other of his contemporaries, imperfections and distortions of compositions, which but for them were models of beauty and harmonious proportion. It was said: 'If Beethoven emptied his inkstand upon a piece of music paper you would admire it!'

Upon Beethoven's demeanour in society, Schindler proceeds thus:

'The communications of both [Cramer and Madame Cherubini] agreed in saying that in mixed society his conduct was reserved, stiff and marked by artist's pride; whereas among his intimates he was droll, lively, indeed, voluble at times, and fond of giving play to all the arts of wit and sarcasm, not always wisely especially in respect of political and social prejudices. To this the two were able to add much concerning his awkwardness in taking hold of such objects as glasses, coffee cups, etc., to which Master Cherubini added the comment: "Toujours brusque." '

Cramer reached Vienna early in September 1799, and remained there through the following winter; but he does not appear to have given any public concerts, although, during the first month of his stay, we learn from a newspaper, he 'earned general and deserved applause by his playing'. It is needless to dwell upon the advantages to Beethoven of constant intercourse for several months with a master like Cramer, whose noblest characteristics as pianist were the same as Mozart's, and precisely those in which Beethoven was deficient.

CHAPTER 7

Beethoven's Friends and Fellow Musicians

The chronological progress of the narrative must again be interrupted, since no picture of a man's life can be complete without the
lights or shades arising from his social relations – without some
degree of knowledge respecting those with whom he is on terms of
equality and intimacy and whose company he most affects. The
attempt to draw such a picture in the case of Beethoven, during his
first years in Vienna, leaves much to be desired, for, although the
search for materials has not been unsuccessful, many of the data are
but vague and scattered notices. In a Conversation Book, bearing
Beethoven's own date 'on 20 March 1820', some person unknown
writes:

'Would you like to know where I first had the honour and good fortune to see you?'

'More than 25 years ago I lived with Frank of Prague in the
Drachengässel in the old Meat Market.
Several noblemen used to meet there, for instance S. E. van B., Cristen,
Heimerle, Vogl (now a singer), Kisswetter, basso, now Court Council-
lor, Graynstein, who has long been living in France, etc.
There was often music-making, supping and punch-drinking – and at
the conclusion Your Excellency often gave us joy at my PF. I was then
War Court-Councillor.'

'War Court-Councillor Schaller
I have pursued at least 15 thousand professions'

'Did we then meet in Prague?'

'In what year?'

'1796, 3 days.'

There is nothing in the portions of this Conversation Book to show who this man of 'fifteen thousand professions' was, now sitting with Beethoven in an eating-house, and recalling to his memory the frolics of the first year and a quarter in Vienna; nor is there a Frank of Prague sufficiently known to fame as to be now identified. It has been suggested that 'Cristen' was Baron Christ of Ehrenblut (1774–1841); that 'Heimerle' was Joseph v. Haymerle, clerk at the Appellate Court; and that Court Councillor Eberhard Perin v. Gradenstein of the Foreign Office was a possible 'Graynstein'. Johann Michael Vogl, less than two years older than Beethoven, was afterwards a very celebrated tenor of the opera.

The 'Kisswetter, basso' was Raphael Georg Kiesewetter, who lived to be renowned as a writer upon topics of musical history, and to play a part in the revival of ancient music in Vienna. At the period of the 'music-making, supping and punch drinking' by the 'noblemen' in the apartments of Frank of Prague, Kiesewetter was a young man of twenty, engaged, like Vogl, in the study of the law. In the spring of 1794 – and thus the date of these meetings is determined – he received an appointment in the military chancellery, and went at once to the headquarters at Schwetzingen on the Rhine.

More important and valuable during these years, as subsequently, was the warm, sincere friendship of Nikolaus Zmeskall von Domanovecz (1759–1833), an official in the Royal Hungarian Court Chancellery. 'You belong to my earliest friends in Vienna,' writes Beethoven in 1816. Zmeskall was an expert violoncellist, a sound and tasteful composer. That he was a very constant attendant at the musical parties of Prince Karl Lichnowsky and frequently took part in them, may be seen from Wegeler's record. He was eleven years older than Beethoven, had been long enough in Vienna to know the best society there, into which he was admitted not more because of his musical attainments than because of the respectability of his position and character; and was, therefore, what the young student-pianist needed most, a friend, who at the same time could be to a certain degree an authoritative adviser, and at all times was a judicious one. On the part of Zmeskall there was an instant and hearty appreciation of the extraordinary powers of the young stranger from the Rhine and a clear anticipation of his splendid artistic future. A singular proof of this is the care with which he preserved the most insignificant scraps of paper, if Beethoven had written a few words upon them; for, certainly, no other motive could have induced him to save may notes of this kind and of no importance for ten, fifteen, twenty years, as may be seen in the published letters of the composer. On the part of Beethoven, there was sincere respect for the dignity and gravity of Zmeskall's character, which usually restrained him within proper limits in their personal intercourse; but he delighted, especially in the earlier period, to give, in his notes and letters, full play to his queer fancies and sometimes extravagant humour.

Here are a few examples in point:

'Will His Highly Well-born, His Herrn von Zmeskall's Zmeskality have the kindness to say where one might speak with him tomorrow.
We are your most damnably
devoted Beethoven'
'[Address] To His Highly Well-Well-Best-born, the Herr von Zmeskall, Imperial and Royal and also Royal-Imperial Court Secretary'

Also the following:

'My dearest Baron Muckcart-driver,
    'Je vous suis bien obligé pour votre faiblesse de vos yeux. – Moreover I forbid you henceforth to rob me of the good humour into which I occasionally fall, for yesterday your Zmeskall-Domanoveczian chatter made me melancholy. The devil take you, I want none of your moral principles. *Power* is the morality of men who loom above the others, and it is also mine; and if you begin again today I'll torment you until you agree that everything that I do is good and praiseworthy. (For I am coming to the Swan – the Ox would indeed be preferable, but this rests with your Zmeskallian Domanoveczian decision) (Response) Adieu Baron ba . . . ron ron/nor/orn/rno/onr/ (voilà quelque chose from the old pawnshop)'

    At the end of this letter occurs an early example not only of Beethoven's playfulness with letters, but his love of puns in his use of the word 'Versatzamt' (pawnshop). 'Versetzen' also means to transpose (notes, words or letters). Was not the 'quelque chose' from the pawnshop the duet for viola and violoncello?
    Mechanical skill was never so developed in Beethoven that he could make good pens from goose quills – and the days of other pens were not yet. When, therefore, he had no one with him to aid him in this, he usually sent to Zmeskall for a supply. Of the large number of such applications preserved by his friend and now scattered among civilised lands as autographs, here are two specimens:

'Best of Music Counts! I beg of you to send me one or a few pens of which I am really in great need.

'As soon as I learn where really good and admirable pens are to be found I will buy some of them. I hope to see you at the *Swan* today.

Adieu, most precious Music Count'

'His Highness von Z. is commanded to hasten a bit with the plucking of a few of his quills (among them, no doubt, some not his own). It is hoped that they may not be too tightly grown in. As soon as you have done all that we shall ask we shall be, with excellent esteem your

F——

Beethoven'

Had Zmeskall not carefully treasured these notes, they would never have met any eye but his own; it is evident, therefore, that he entered fully into their humour, and that it was the same to him, whether he found himself addressed as 'Baron', 'Count', 'Cheapest Baron', 'Music Count', or simply 'Dear Z.' – which last is the more usual. He knew his man, and loved him; and these 'quips and quiddities' were received in the spirit which begat them. The whole tenor of the correspondence between the two shows that Zmeskall had more influence for good upon Beethoven than any other of his friends; he could reprove him for faults, and check him when in the wrong, without producing a quarrel more serious than the one indicated in the protest, above given, against interrupting his 'good humour'

Another young man who gained an extraordinary place in Beethoven's esteem and affection, and who departed from Vienna before anything occurred to cause a breach between them, was a certain Karl Amenda, from the shore of the Baltic, who died some forty years later as Provost in Courland. He was a good violinist, belonged to the circle of dilettanti which Beethoven so much affected, and, on parting, received from the composer one of his first attempts at quartet composition. His name most naturally suggests itself to fill the blank in a letter to Ries, dated July 1804, wherein some living person, not named, is mentioned as one with whom he (Beethoven) 'never had a misunderstanding'. Their correspondence shows that their friendship was of the romantic character once so much the fashion; and a letter of Amenda's is filled with incense which in our day would bear the name of almost too gross flattery. But times change and tastes with them.

His name appears once in the Zmeskall correspondence, namely, in a mutilated note now in the National Library in Vienna, beginning: 'My cheapest Baron! Tell the guitarist to come to me today. *Amenda* is to make an *Amende* [part torn away] which he deserves for his bad pauses [torn] provide the guitarist.'

Karl Amenda was born on 4 October 1771, at Lippaiken in Courland. He studied music with his father and Kapellmeister Beichtmer, was so good a violinist that he was able to give a concert at fourteen years of age, and continued his musical studies after he was matriculated as a student of theology at the University of Jena. After a three years' course there, he set out on a tour and reached Vienna in the spring of 1798. There he first became precentor for Prince Lobkowitz and afterwards music-teacher in the family of Mozart's widow. How, thereupon, he became acquainted with Beethoven we are able to report from a document still in the possession of the family, which bears the superscription 'Brief Account of the Friendly Relations between L. v. Beethoven and Karl Friedrich Amenda, afterwards Provost at Talsen in Courland, written down from oral tradition':

'After the completion of his theological studies K. F. Amenda goes to Vienna, where he several times meets Beethoven at the table d'hôte, attempts to enter into conversation with him, but without success, since Beeth. remains very *réservé*. After some time Amenda, who meanwhile had become music-teacher at the home of Mozart's widow, receives an invitation from a friendly family and there plays first violin in a quartet. While he was playing somebody turned the pages for him, and when he turned about at the finish he was frightened to see Beethoven, who had taken the trouble to do this and now withdrew with a bow. The next day the extremely amiable host at the evening party appeared and cried out: "What have you done? You have captured Beethoven's heart! B. requests that you rejoice him with your company." A., much pleased, hurries to B., who at once asks him to play with him. This is done and when, after several hours, A. takes his leave, B. accompanies him to his quarters, where there was music again. As B. finally prepared to go he said to A.: "I suppose you can accompany me." This is done, and B. kept A. till evening and went with him to his home late at night. From that time the mutual visits became more and more numerous and the two took walks together, so that the people in the streets when they saw only one of them in the street at once called out: "Where is the other one?" A. also introduced Mylich, with whom he had come to Vienna, to B., and Mylich often played trios with B. and A. His instrument was the second violin or viola. Once when B. heard that Mylich had a sister in Courland who played the pianoforte prettily, he handed him a sonata in manuscript with the inscription: "To the sister of my good friend Mylich." The manuscript was rolled up and tied with a little silk ribbon. B. complained that he could not get along on the violin. Asked by A. to try it, nevertheless, he played so fearfully that A. had to call out: "Have mercy – quit!" B. quit playing and the two laughed till they had to hold their sides. One evening B. improvised marvellously on the pianoforte and at the close A. said: "It is a great pity that such glorious music is born and lost in a moment." Whereupon B.: "There you are mistaken; I can repeat every extemporisation"; whereupon he sat himself down and played it again without a change. B. was frequently embarrassed for money. Once he complained to A.; he had to pay rent and had no idea how he could do it. "That's easily remedied," said A. and gave him a theme . . . and locked him in his room with the remark that he must make a beginning on the variations within three hours. When A. returns he finds B. on the spot but ill-tempered. To the question whether or not he had begun B. handed over a paper with the remark: "There's your stuff!" [*Da ist der Wisch!*] A. takes the notes joyfully to B.'s landlord and tells him to take it to a publisher, who would pay him handsomely for it. The landlord hesitated at first but finally decided to do the errand and, returning joyfully, asks if other bits of paper like that were to be had. But in order definitely to relieve such financial needs A. advised B. to make a trip to Italy. B. says he is willing but only on condition that A. go with him. A. agrees gladly and the trip is practically planned. Unfortunately news of a death calls A. back to his home. His brother has been killed in an accident and the duty of caring for the family devolves on him. With doubly oppressed heart A. takes leave of B. to return to his home in Courland. There he receives a letter from B. saying: "Since you cannot go along, I shall not go to Italy." Later the friends frequently exchanged thoughts by correspondence.'

Though, as we have learned, it was music which brought Beethoven into contact with Amenda, it was the latter's amiability and nobility of character that endeared him to the composer, who cherished him as one of his dearest friends and confided things to him which he concealed from his other intimates – his deafness, for instance.

Count Moritz Lichnowsky, brother of Prince Karl, was another of the friends of those years. He had been a pupil of Mozart, played the pianoforte with much skill and was an influential member of the party which defended the novelty and felt the grandeur of his friend's compositions. Schindler saw much of him during Beethoven's last years, and eulogises the 'noble Count' in very strong terms.

Another of that circle of young dilettanti, and one of the first players of Beethoven's compositions, was a young Jewish violinist, Heinrich Eppinger. He played at a charity concert in Vienna, making his first appearance there in 1789. 'He became, in after years,' says a correspondent of the time, 'a dilettante of the most excellent reputation, lived modestly on a small fortune and devoted himself entirely to music.' At the period before us Eppinger was one of Beethoven's first violins at the private concerts of the nobility. Häring, who became a distinguished merchant and banker, belonged now to this circle of young amateur musicians, and in 1794 had the reputation of being at the head of the amateur violinists. The youthful friendship between him and the composer was not interrupted as they advanced into life, and twenty years later was of great advantage to Beethoven.

But a more interesting person for us is the instructor under whom Beethoven in Vienna resumed his study of the violin – Wenzel Krumpholz. He came to Vienna in 1795 to join the operatic orchestra, and at once became noted as a performer of Haydn's quartets. He was 'a highly sensitive art-enthusiast, and one of the first who foresaw and recognised Beethoven's greatness'.

Krumpholz was a virtuoso on the mandolin, and for that reason, apparently, Beethoven wrote a few pieces for pianoforte and mandolin in these years. Krumpholz concerns us also as the friend through whom the Czerny family became acquainted with Beethoven. Carl Czerny (1791–1857) was shortly to become one of the composer's real students. The following extracts from Carl Czerny's memoirs (1842) show how this introduction led to his long association with the master.

'At that time an old man named Krumpholz (brother of the inventor of the pedal harp) visited us nearly every evening. He was a violinist and as such had a position in the orchestra of the Court Theatre; yet at the same time he was a musical enthusiast whose passion for music was carried to the most extravagant lengths. Nature had endowed him with a just and delicate feeling for the beautiful in tonal art, and though he possessed no great fund of technical knowledge, he was able to criticise every composition with much acumen, and, so to say, anticipate the judgements of the musical world.

'As soon as young Beethoven appeared for the first time, Krumpholz attached himself to him with a persistence and devotion which soon made him a familiar figure in his home, so that he practically spent nearly the whole day with him, and Beethoven, who ordinarily was most reticent with everyone regarding his musical projects, told Krumpholz about all his ideas, played every new composition for him time and again, and improvised for him every day. Although Beethoven often poked fun at the unfeigned ecstasies into which Krumpholz invariably fell, and never called him anything but his jester; yet he was touched by his attachment, which led him to affront the bitterest enmities in order to defend his cause against his adversaries, so numerous in those days. For at that time Beethoven's compositions were totally misunderstood by the general public, and all the followers of the old Mozart–Haydn school opposed them with the most intense animosity.

'This was the man for whom, day by day, I had to play Beethoven's works, and although he knew nothing of piano playing, he was, quite naturally, able to tell me a great deal about their tempo, interpretation, effects, characteristics, etc., since he often heard them played by Beethoven himself, and in most cases had been present when they came into being. His enthusiasm soon infected me and before long I, in turn, was a Beethoven worshipper like himself, learned all that Beethoven had written by heart, and, considering my years, played it with skill and enthusiasm. Krumpholz also invariably told me about the new things Beethoven had "under pen", and would sing or play on his violin the themes he had heard in Beethoven's home during the forenoon. Owing to this circumstance I was always informed at a much earlier date than others with regard to what Beethoven had under way. Later this made it possible for me to realise how long, often for years at a time, Beethoven polished his compositions before they were published, and how in new works he used motives which had occurred to him many years before . . .

'I was about ten years old when Krumpholz took me to see Beethoven. With what joy and terror I greeted the day on which I was to meet the admired master! Even now this moment is vividly present in my memory. It was a winter's day when my father, Krumpholz, and I took our way from Leopoldstadt (where we were still living) to Vienna proper, to a street called *der tiefe Graben* (the Deep Ditch), and climbed endless flights to the fifth and sixth storey, where a rather untidy-looking servant announced us to Beethoven and then admitted us. The room presented a most disorderly appearance; papers and articles of clothing were scattered about everywhere, some trunks, bare walls, hardly a chair, save the wobbly one at the Walter fortepiano (then the best), and in this room was gathered a company of from six to eight persons, among them . . . one of Beethoven's brothers.

Beethoven himself wore a morning coat of some long-haired, dark grey material, and trousers to match, so that he at once recalled to me the picture in Campe's "Robinson Crusoe", which I was reading at the time. His coal-black hair, cut *à la Titus*, bristled shaggily about his head. His beard – he had not been shaved for several days – made the lower part of his already brown face still darker. I also noticed with that visual quickness peculiar to children that he had cotton which seemed to have been steeped in a yellowish liquid, in his ears.

'At that time, however, he did not give the least evidence of deafness. I was at once told to play something, and since I did not dare begin with one of his own compositions, played Mozart's great C major Concerto, the one beginning with chords. Beethoven soon gave me his attention, drew near my chair, and in those passages where I had only accompanying passages played the orchestral melody with me, using his left hand. His hands were overgrown with hair and his fingers, especially at the ends, were very broad. The satisfaction he expressed gave me the courage to play his *Sonata pathétique*, which had just appeared, and finally his "Adelaide", which my father sang in his very passable tenor. When he had ended Beethoven turned to him and said: "The boy has talent. I will teach him myself and accept him as my pupil. Send him to me several times a week. First of all, however, get him a copy of Emanuel Bach's book on the true art of piano playing, for he must bring it with him the next time he comes." Then all those present congratulated my father on this favourable verdict, Krumpholz in particular being quite delighted, and my father at once hurried off to hunt up Bach's book.'

Johann Nepomuk Hummel, the pupil of Mozart, was another of the youths whom Beethoven drew into his circle. In 1795, the elder Hummel brought back his son to Vienna (from that very successful concert tour which had occupied the last six years and had made the boy known even to the cities of distant Scotland) and put him to the studies of counterpoint and composition with Albrechtsberger and Salieri. He seems to have been quietly at his studies, playing only in private, until 28 April 1799, when he again appeared in public both as pianist and composer. 'He performed a symphony besides a melodrama composed for the occasion and between them played prettily *composed* improvisations on the pianoforte.' That the talented and promising boy of seventeen years should, upon arriving home again, seek the acquaintance and favour of one who during his absence had made so profound an impression upon the Vienna public as Beethoven, and that the latter should have rejoiced to show kindness to Mozart's favourite pupil, hardly needs to be mentioned. A chapter of description would not illustrate the nature of their intercourse so vividly, as two short but exceedingly characteristic notes of Beethoven's which Hummel preserved:

I

'He is not to come to me again. He is a treacherous dog and may the flayer get all such treacherous dogs!'

II

'Herzens Nazerl:

'You are an honest fellow and I now see you were right. Come, then, to me this afternoon. You'll find Schuppanzigh here also and we two will bump, thump and pump you to your heart's delight. A kiss from

Your   Beethoven

also called Mehlschöberl'*

In a letter to Eleonore von Breuning, Beethoven described many of the Vienna pianists as his 'deadly enemies'. Schindler's observations upon the composer's relations with the Viennese musicians seem to be very judicious and correct:

'Nobody is likely to expect that an artist who made his way upwards as our Beethoven, although almost confining his activities exclusively to aristocratic circles that upheld him in extraordinary fashion, would remain free from the attacks of his colleagues; on the contrary, the reader will be prepared to see a host of enemies advance against him because of the shining qualities and evidences of genius of our hero, in contrast with the heavy burden of social idiosyncrasies and uncouthness . . . His too small toleration of many eccentricities and weaknesses of high society, and on the other hand his severe demand on his colleagues for higher culture, even his Bonn dialect, afforded his enemies more than enough material to revenge themselves on him by evil gossip and slander.'

Beethoven's instant achievement of a position as artist only paralleled by Mozart and of a social rank which Gluck, Salieri, Haydn had gained only after making their names famous throughout Europe, together with the general impression that the mantle of Mozart had fallen upon him – all this begat bitter envy in those whom his talents and genius overshadowed; they revenged themselves by deriding him for his personal peculiarities and by condemning and ridiculing the novelties in his compositions; while he met their envy with disdain, their criticisms with contempt; and, when he did not treat their compositions with indifference, he too often only noticed them with sarcasm. This picture, certainly, is not an agreeable one, but all the evidence proves it, unfortunately, faithful.

Beethoven was no exception to the general rule, that men of genius delight in warm and lasting friendships with women of superior minds and culture – not meaning those 'conquests' which, according to

* A type of soup dumpling.

Wegeler, even during his first three years in Vienna, he 'occasionally made . . . which would have been very difficult if not impossible for many an Adonis'. Let such matters, even if detail concerning them were now attainable, be forgotten.

In the present connection it is again an old Bonn friend who comes upon the scene. The beautiful, talented and accomplished Magdalena Willmann was invited to sing at Venice during the carnival of 1794. She left Bonn the preceding summer with her brother Max and his wife (Fräulein Tribolet) to fulfil the engagement. After leaving Venice, they gave a concert in Graz, and journeyed on to Vienna. Here Max and his wife remained, having accepted engagements, while Magdalena went on to Berlin. Not suiting the operatic public there she returned to Vienna, and was soon engaged to sing both German and Italian parts in the Court Opera. Beethoven renewed his intercourse with the Willmanns and soon became so captivated with the charms of the beautiful Magdalena as to offer her his hand. This fact was communicated to the author by a daughter of Max Willmann, still living in 1860, who had often heard her father speak of it. To the question, why Magdalena did not accept the offer of Beethoven, Madame S. hesitated a moment, and then, laughing, replied: 'Because he was so ugly, and half crazy!'

Two letters of Beethoven have been preserved from the period before us, addressed to Christine Gerhardi, a young woman of high distinction in society at the time for the splendour of her talents and her high culture. Dr Sonnleithner wrote of her:

'She was the daughter of an official at the court of the Emperor Leopold II . . . an excellent singer, but remained a dilettante and sang chiefly in concerts for charitable purposes (which she herself arranged), or for the benefit of eminent artists. Old Professor Peter Frank was director of the general hospital of Vienna in the neighbourhood of which she lived. He was a great lover of music, but his son, Dr Joseph Frank, was a greater; he made essays in composition and arranged musical soirées at the home of his father at which Beethoven and Fräulein Gerhardi took part, playing and singing. The son frequently composed cantatas, which Beethoven corrected, for the namedays and birthdays of his father, and in which Fräulein Gerhardi sang the soprano solos . . . She was at the time the most famous amateur singer in Vienna, and inasmuch as Haydn knew her well there is no doubt but that he had her in mind when he composed *The Creation*; indeed, she sang the soprano part with great applause not only at Schwarzenberg but also at the first performance in the Burgtheater. All reports agree that she met Beethoven often at Frank's and that he frequently accompanied her singing on the pianoforte. He did not give her lessons.'

Dr Joseph von Frank and Christine Gerhardi were married on 20 August 1798; they moved away from Vienna in 1804.

A few notes upon certain young women to whom Beethoven dedicated compositions at this period of his life may be appropriate here. It was much the custom then for teachers of music to dedicate their works to pupils, especially to those who belonged to the higher social ranks – such dedications being at the same time compliments to the pupils and advertisements for the instructors. Beethoven also followed the custom; and the young ladies, subjects of the following notices, are all known or supposed to have taken lessons of him.

Anna Louisa Barbara ('La Comtesse Babette') was the daughter of Karl Count Keglevics de Busin, of Hungarian Croatian lineage, and Barbara Countess Zichy. She was soon married to Prince Innocenzo d'Erba-Odescalchi. Beethoven's dedications to her are the Sonata, Op. 7 (published in 1797), the Variations 'La stessa, la stessissima' (1799), the Pianoforte Concerto, Op. 15, 1801, and the Pianoforte Variations in F, Op. 34 – the last two to her as Princess Odescalchi.

'Countess Henriette Lichnowsky', writes Count Amade, 'was the sister of the ruling Prince Karl, and was doubtless married to the Marquis of Carneville after the dedication to her of the Rondo (G major, Op. 51, No. 2, published in September 1802); she lived in Paris after her marriage and died about 1830.' The Rondo was first dedicated to Countess Julia Guicciardi, but Beethoven asked for it back in exchange for the C sharp minor Sonata; to this friendship we shall recur presently. Countess Thun, to whom Beethoven dedicated the Clarinet Trio, Op. 11, in 1798, was the mother-in-law of Prince Karl Lichnowsky. She died on 18 May 1800.

To this list should be added the names of the Countesses Therese and Josephine Brunsvik who, with the rest of their family, became such good friends of the composer. Beethoven's relationship with each of the sisters was different, as we shall see, and his friendship also with the brother, Count Franz, was a deep and enduring one. In 1846, Therese started writing her memoirs, which she entitled 'My Half Century', based on a journal which she had kept over the years. Both of these form important sources for the understanding of Beethoven's relationships to the members of this family. The Brunsviks lived in Martonvásár, Hungary, whence the widowed mother brought Josephine and Therese to Vienna for a brief visit in 1799. Both daughters were well educated and trained sufficiently in music so that the mother wanted them, while in Vienna, to have lessons from none other than Beethoven himself. Therese describes these first meetings:

'During the extraordinary sojourn of 18 days in Vienna my mother desired that her two daughters, Therese and Josephine, receive Beethoven's invaluable instruction in music. Adalbert Rosti, a schoolmate of my brother's, assured us that Beethoven would not be persuaded to accept a mere invitation; but that if Her Excellency were willing to climb the three flights of stairs of the house in St Peter's Place, and make him a visit, he would vouch for a successful outcome of the mission. It was done. Like a schoolgirl, with Beethoven's Sonatas for Violin and Violoncello and Pianoforte under my arm, we entered. The immortal, dear Louis van Beethoven was very friendly and as polite as he could be. After a few phrases de part et d'autre, he sat me down at his pianoforte, which was out of tune, and I began at once to sing the violin and the 'cello parts and played right well. This delighted him so much that he promised to come every day to the Hotel zum Erzherzog Carl – then zum Goldenen Greifen. It was May in the last year of the last century. He came regularly, but instead of an hour frequently stayed from twelve to four or five o'clock, and never grew weary of holding down and bending my fingers, which I had been taught to lift high and hold straight. The noble man must have been satisfied; for he never missed a single day in the 16. We felt no hunger until five o'clock. My good mother bore her hunger – the inn-people, however, were indignant, for it had not yet become the custom to eat dinner at five o'clock in the evening.

'It was then that the most intimate and cordial friendship was established with Beethoven, a friendship which lasted to the end of his life. He came to Ofen, he came to Martonvásár; he was initiated into our social republic of chosen people. A round spot was planted with high, noble lindens; each tree had the name of a member, and even in their sorrowful absence we conversed with their symbols, and were entertained and instructed by them.'

While in Vienna the ladies also made the acquaintance of Count Joseph Deym, also known as Herr Müller, who had changed his name to Müller because of a duel (then unlawful) which he had fought before he attained his majority. He was the proprietor of the famed Müller Art Museum in Vienna. The mother thought that this would be a suitable match for Josephine, and unfortunately did not take the time to investigate carefully Deym's financial and social status. 'You, dear Josephine, can make me and your sisters happy,' Therese quotes her mother as saying when urging the marriage upon her daughter. But Josephine herself was far from happy. The hastily arranged marriage took place, and on 29 June 1799, Josephine moved from Martonvásár into quarters in one wing of the eighty-room museum house in Vienna, married to a man thirty years her senior. She wrote to her sisters: 'Separated from you and your love, I shall never be able to be happy, although my husband is very nice, but his education, his outlook, his age are all so different from mine. I want you to choose more successfully than I have, at least to be freer and able to live more according to your own inclination.'

By 1800 the Count had got badly into debt, partially because he had counted upon, but had never received, a large dowry from the Brunsvik family. Legal wrangles threatened, and the mother, who was in Vienna for the birth of Josephine's first child, pressed for a separation, realising too late that the marriage she had forced upon her daughter offered neither social nor financial advantages. Josephine, on the other hand, was a truly honourable woman; amid stormy scenes with her mother she steadfastly refused to dishonour her marriage vows.

Beethoven proved to be a loyal friend to the young Countess in these unhappy circumstances. Therese writes:

'The aristocracy turned its back upon him [Deym] because he had gone into business. He could not hunt up his former rich acquaintances. Beethoven was the faithful visitor at the house of the young countess — he gave her lessons gratis and to be tolerated one had to be a Beethoven. The numerous relatives, the sisters of her father and their children, frequently visited their amiable niece . . . There were musical soirées. My brother came in vacation-time and made the acquaintance of Beethoven. The two musical geniuses became intimately associated with each other, and my brother never deserted his friend in his frequent financial troubles until his, alas! too early death.'

From this it can be seen that Josephine must have derived real comfort from her friendship with the composer, and also that gradually her circle was widening. The following two excerpts from letters written to Therese in the latter part of 1800 confirm this further. On 28 October she writes: 'Beethoven is charming. He has promised that he will come every third day to give me a lesson if I am diligent. And that I really am . . . Beethoven's sonatas are not yet out; as soon as I get them, I will send them to you. I have just learned the first two of the three with violin.' On 10 December:

'We had music in honour of the archduchess . . . Our rooms were so beautiful that you would have been enchanted. All the doors were opened and everything lit up. I assure you it was a splendid sight! Beethoven played the sonata with violoncello, I played the last of the three sonatas [Op. 12, No. 3] with Schuppanzigh's accompaniment, who played divinely like everybody else. Then Beethoven like a true angel let us hear his new still unpublished quartets [Op. 18] which are the most excellent of their kind. The renowned Kraft undertook the 'cello part, Schuppanzigh the first violin. Imagine what a pleasure it was! The archduchess was enchanted and everything came off wonderfully.'

We will return to the subject of Beethoven's friendship with the Countess Deym in 1804; for on 27 January of that year the Count died, and the widow's friendship with the composer developed into an affair of the heart.

The year 1800 is an important era in Beethoven's history. It is the year in which, cutting loose from the pianoforte, he asserted his claims to a position with Mozart and the still living and productive Haydn in the higher forms of chamber and orchestral composition – the quartet and the symphony. It is the year, too, in which the bitter consciousness of an increasing derangement of his organs of hearing was forced upon him and the terrible anticipation of its incurable nature and of its final result in almost total deafness began to harass and distress him. The course of his life was afterwards so modified, on the one hand, by the prosperous issue of these new appeals to the taste and judgement of the public, and, on the other, by the unhappy progress of his malady, each acting and reacting upon a nature singularly exceptional, that some points in his personal character and habits must be made before resuming the narrative of events.

A true and exhaustive picture of Beethoven as a man would present an almost ludicrous contrast to that which is generally entertained as correct. Sculptor and painter in turn has idealised the work of his predecessor, until the composer stands before us like a Homeric god – until those who knew him personally, could they return to earth, would never suspect that the grand form and noble features of the more pretentious portraits are intended to represent the short muscular figure and pock-pitted face of their old friend. In literature evoked by the composer a similar process has gone on, with a corresponding suppression of whatever is deemed common and trivial, until he is made a being living in his own peculiar realm of gigantic ideas, above and apart from the rest of mankind – a sort of intellectual Thor, dwelling in 'darkness and clouds of awful state', and making in his music mysterious revelations of things unutterable! But it is really some generations too soon for a conscientious investigator of his history to view him as a semi-mythological personage, or to discover that his notes to friends asking for pens, making appointments to dinner at taverns, or complaining of servants, are 'cyclopean blocks of granite', which, like the 'chops and tomato sauce' of Mr Pickwick, contain depths unfathomable of profound meaning. The present age must be content to find in Beethoven, with all his greatness, a very human nature, one which, if it showed extraordinary strength, exhibited also extraordinary weaknesses.

It was the great misfortune of Beethoven's youth that he did not grow up under the influence of a wise and strict parental control, which would have given him those habits of self-restraint that, once fixed, are a second and better nature, and through which the passions, curbed and moderated, remain only as sources of noble energy and power. His very early admission into the orchestra of the theatre as cembalist (harpsichordist), was more to the advantage of his musical than of his moral development. It was another misfortune that, in those years, when the strict regulations of a school would have compensated in some measure for the unwise, unsteady, often harsh discipline of his father, he was thus thrown into close connection with actors and actresses, who, in those days, were not very distinguished for the propriety of their manners and morals. Before he became known to the Breuning family and Count Waldstein, he could hardly have learned the importance of cultivating those high principles of life and conduct on which in later years he laid so much stress.

At all events, the consequences of a deficient early moral education followed Beethoven through life and are visible in the frequent contests between his worse and his better nature and in his constant tendency to extremes. Today, upon some perhaps trivial matter, he bursts into ungovernable wrath; tomorrow, his penitence exceeds the measure of his fault. Today he is proud, unbending, offensively careless of those claims which society grants to people of high rank; tomorrow his humility is more than adequate to the occasion. The poverty in which he grew up was not without its effect upon his character. He never learned to estimate money at its real value; though often profuse and generous to a fault, even wasteful, yet at times he would fall into the other extreme. In spite of all his sense of nobility of independence, he early formed the habit of leaning upon others; and this the more, as his malady increased, which certainly was a partial justification; but he thus became prone to follow unwise counsels, or, when his pride was touched, to assert an equally unwise independence. At other times, in the multitude of counsellors he became the victim of utter irresolution, when decision and firmness were indispensable and essential to his welfare. Thus, both by following the impulse of the moment, and by hesitation when a prompt determination was demanded, he took many a false step, which could no longer be retrieved when reflection brought with it bitter regret.

A romantically sentimental admiration of the heroes of ancient classic literature had become widely the fashion in Beethoven's youth. The democratic theories of the French sentimentalists had received a new impulse from the dignified simplicity of the foreign representatives of the young American Republic, Franklin, Adams, Jay. Through the greater part of Central Europe the idea became current of a pure and sublime humanity, above and beyond the influence of the passions, of which Cincinnatus, Scipio, Cato, Washington, Franklin, were the supposed representatives. The playwright Zschokke wrote: 'Virtue and the heroes of antiquity had inspired me with enthusiasm for virtue and heroism'; and so, also, Beethoven. He exalted his imagination and fancy by the perusal of the German poets and translations of the ancient and English classics, especially Homer, Plutarch and Shakespeare; dwelt fondly upon the great characters as models for the conduct of life; but between the sentiment which one feels and the active principle on which he acts, there is often a wide cleft. That Beethoven proved to be no Stoic, that he never succeeded in governing his passions with absolute sway, was not because the spirit was unwilling; the flesh was weak. Adequate firmness of character had not been acquired in early years.

Truth and candour compel the confession, that in those days of prosperity he bore his honours with less of meekness than we could wish; that he had lost something of that modesty and ingenuousness eulogised by Junker ten years before. Traces of self-sufficiency and even arrogance – faults almost universal among young and successful geniuses – are unquestionably visible. No one can read without regret his remarks upon certain persons, with whom at this very time he was upon terms of apparently intimate friendship. 'I value them', he writes to Amenda in 1801, 'only by what they do for me.' He speaks of using them 'only as instruments on which I can play when I please'. His 'somewhat lofty bearing' was matter for jest to the venerable Haydn, who, according to a trustworthy tradition, when Beethoven's visits to him had become few and far between would enquire of other visitors: 'How goes it with our Great Mogul?'

When Beethoven was little known except as a celebrated pianoforte player he went to the house of Prince Lobkowitz at the latter's invitation. In conversation with a gentleman present, Beethoven said in substance, that he wished to be relieved from all bargain and sale of his works, and would gladly find someone willing to pay him a certain income for life, for which he should possess the exclusive right of publishing all he wrote; adding, 'and I would not be idle in composition. I believe Goethe does this with Cotta, and, if I mistake not, Handel's London publisher held similar terms with him.'

'My dear young man,' returned the other, 'you must not complain; for you are neither a Goethe nor a Handel, and it is not to be expected that you ever will be; for such masters will not be born again.' Beethoven bit his lips, gave a most contemptuous glance at the speaker, and said no more. Lobkowitz endeavoured to appease him, and in a subsequent conversation said: 'My dear Beethoven, the gentleman did not intend to wound you. It is an established maxim, to which most men adhere, that the present generation cannot possibly produce such mighty spirits as the dead, who have already earned their fame.'

'So much the worse, Your Highness,' retorted Beethoven; 'but with men who will not believe and trust in me because I am as yet unknown to universal fame, I cannot hold intercourse!'

Beethoven soon gathered about him a circle of young disciples, enthusiastic admirers. Their homage may well have been grateful to him – as such is to every artist and scholar of genius, who, striking out and steadfastly pursuing a new path, subjects himself to the sharp animadversions of critics who, in all honesty, really can see little or nothing of good in that which is not to be measured and judged by old standards. The voice of praise under such circumstances is doubly pleasing. It is known that, when Beethoven's works began to find a just appreciation from a new generation of critics, who had indeed been schooled by them, he collected and preserved a considerable number of laudatory articles. When, however, the natural and just satisfaction which is afforded by the homage of honest admirers and deservedly eulogistic criticism, degenerates into a love of indiscriminate praise and flattery, it becomes a weakness, a fault. Of this error in Beethoven there are traces easily discernible, and especially in his later years; there are pages of fulsome eulogy addressed to him in the Conversation Books, which would make the reader blush for him, did not the mere fact that such books existed remind him of the bitterness of the composer's lot. The failing was also sometimes his misfortune; for those who were most profuse in their flatteries, and thus gained his ear, were by no means the best of his counsellors. But apart from the attractive force of his genius, Beethoven possessed a personal magnetism, which attached his young worshippers to him and, all things considered, to his solid and lasting benefit in his private affairs.

The friends that Beethoven drew around him were of two kinds: those whom he loved and to whom he was able to pour out his heart, like Amenda and Wegeler, and those who were merely useful to him either as contacts, like Prince Lichnowsky, or as helpers in everyday matters. And it is significant that the first kind of friendship was able to exist only with those from whom he was separated. He could write to them as though they existed apart from what he considered the tawdry world around him. The correspondence with Wegeler and Amenda shows the intensity of this kind of friendship; and these two are almost the only close friends that can be named with whom Beethoven did not have a quarrel. One other friend of this type was Stephan von Breuning, and the very fact that he was in Vienna in the years to come made it inevitable that a point would come when he would either have to submit to Beethoven's will or retain his own integrity; in choosing the latter course he forfeited a friendship with Beethoven, which was to be revived only in the last years of his life. Beethoven's inability to enter into a relationship of the heart with any man who was near him was equally true with his friends of the opposite sex. Earlier biographies have stressed the individual woman's reluctance to enter into a close friendship with him, but as time went on, the reluctance was probably equally his own towards establishing a permanent relationship with a woman from whom he could want only that she give herself in service to him with little if anything in return.

Art has been so often disgraced by the bad morals and shameless lives of its votaries, that it is doubly gratifying to be able to affirm of Beethoven that, like Handel, Bach and Mozart, he did honour to his profession by his personal character and habits. Although irregular, still he was as simple and temperate in eating and drinking as was possible in the state of society in which he lived. No allusion is remembered in any of his letters, notes, memoranda, nor in the Conversation Books, which indicates a liking for any game of chance or skill. He does not appear to have known one playing-card from another. Music, books, conversation with men and women of taste and intelligence, dancing, and, above all, his long walks, were his amusements and recreations.

One rather delicate point demands a word. Spending his whole life in a state of society in which the vow of celibacy was by no means a vow of chastity; in which the parentage of a cardinal's or archbishop's children was neither a secret nor a disgrace; in which the moderate gratification of the sexual was no more discountenanced than the satisfying of any other natural appetite – it is nonsense to suppose, that, under such circumstances, Beethoven could have puritanic scruples on that point. Those who have had occasion and opportunity to ascertain the facts, know that he had not, and are also aware that he did not always escape the common penalties of transgressing the laws of strict purity. But he had too much dignity of character ever to take part in scenes of low debauchery, or even when still young to descend to the familiar jesting once so common between tavern girls and the guests.

The names of two married women might here be given, to whom at a later period Beethoven was warmly attached; names which have hitherto escaped the eyes of literary scavengers, and are therefore here suppressed. Certain of his friends used to joke him about these ladies, and it is certain that he rather enjoyed their jests even when the insinuations, that his affection was beyond the limit of the platonic, were somewhat broad; but careful enquiry has failed to elicit any evidence that even in these cases he proved unfaithful to his principles. A story related by Jahn is also to the point, namely, that Beethoven only by the urgent solicitations of the Czerny family was after much refusal persuaded to extemporise in the presence of a certain Madame Hofdamel. She was the widow of a man who had attempted her life and then committed suicide; and the refusal of Beethoven to play before her arose from his having the general belief at the time, that a too great intimacy had existed between her and Mozart.

Beethoven's love of nature was already a marked trait of his character. This was indulged and strengthened by long rambles upon the lofty hills and in the exquisitely beautiful valleys which render the environs of Vienna to the north and west so charming. Hence, when he left the city to spend the hot summer months in the country, with but an exception or two in a long series of years, his residence was selected with a view to the indulgence of this noble passion.

Rochlitz in his letters from Vienna (1822) reports Beethoven's humorous account of his enthusiasm for Klopstock* in his early life:

'Since that Karlsbad summer I read Goethe every day – that is, when I read at all. He killed Klopstock for me. You are surprised? Now you are laughing? Aha, it is because I used to read Klopstock! For years I put up with him, when I took my walks and elsewhere. Well, then, it is true that I did not always know what he was driving at. He hops about so from pillar to post; and he always begins altogether too much from top to bottom. Always *maestoso*, D flat major! Is it not so? Yet he is lofty

* The poet Frederich Gottlieb Klopstock.

and he uplifts the soul. When I did not understand him, then I made my guess and comprehended more or less. If only he did not want to die all the time! Death comes soon enough to all of us. Well, at any rate, what he writes always sounds well, etc.'

Beethoven's correspondence forms so important a portion of his biography that something must be said here upon his character as a letter-writer. A few of his autograph letters bear marks of previous study and careful elaboration; but, in general, whatever he wrote in the way of private correspondence was dashed off on the spur of the moment, and with no thought that it would ever come under any eye but that for which it was intended. It is therefore easy to imagine how energetically he would have protested could he have known that his most insignificant notes were preserved in such numbers, and that the time would come when they would all be made public.

Another striking fact of Beethoven's correspondence, when viewed as a whole, is the proof it affords that, except in his hours of profound depression, he was far from being the melancholy and gloomy character of popular belief. He shows himself here – as he was by nature – of a gay and lively temperament, fond of a jest, an inveterate though not always a very happy punster, a great lover of wit and humour. It is a cause for profound gratitude that it was so; since he thus preserved an elasticity of spirits that enabled him to escape the consequences of brooding in solitude over his great misfortune; to rise superior to his fate and concentrate his great powers upon his self-imposed tasks; and to meet with hope and courage the cruel fortune which put an end to so many well-founded expectations and ambitious projects, and confined him to a single road to fame and honour – that of composition.

Beethoven was seldom without a folded sheet or two of music paper in his pocket upon which he wrote with pencil in two or three measures of music hints of any musical thought which might occur to him wherever he chanced to be. Towards the end of his life his Conversation Books often answered the same purpose; and there are traditions of bills-of-fare at dining-rooms having been honoured with ideas afterwards made immortal.

The sketchbooks performed a twofold office; being not alone the registers of new conceptions, but containing the preliminary studies of the instrumental works into which they were wrought out. One has been thus described:

'[A] volume in oblong folio of 192 pages and bearing 16 staves on each page, and, save a few empty places, containing throughout notes and sketches in Beethoven's handwriting for compositions of various sorts. The volume is not made up, the way many others were, of pages sewn together, but is bound in craftsman's style, trimmed, and has a stout pasteboard cover. It was bound thus before it was used or received the notes. The sketches are for the greater part only one-part; that is, they occupy but a single staff, only exceptionally are they on two or more staves ... It is to be observed that generally Beethoven began a new page with a new composition; and, moreover, that he worked alternately or simultaneously at different movements. As a result, different groups of sketches are crowded so closely together that in order to find room he was obliged to make use of spaces which had been left open, and thus eventually sketches for the most different compositions had to be mixed together and brought into companionship.'

From the sketchbooks one can get an idea of the vast fertility of Beethoven's genius. They are the record of a never ceasing flow of new thoughts and ideas, until death sealed the fountain for ever. There are themes and hints, never used, for all kinds of instrumental compositions, from the trifles, which he called 'Bagatelles', to symphonies, evidently intended to be as different from those we know as they are from each other; and these hints are in such numbers, that those which can be traced in the published works are perhaps much the smaller proportion of the whole. Whoever has the will and opportunity to devote an hour or two to an examination of a few of these monuments of Beethoven's inventive genius, will easily comprehend the remark which he made near the close of his life: 'It seems to me that I have just begun to compose!'

One topic more demands notice before closing this chapter. In the 'Merry-making of the Countryfolk' of Beethoven's 'Pastoral' Symphony, at the point where the fun grows most fast and furious and the excitement rises to its height, an ominous sound, as of distant thunder, gives the first faint warning of the coming storm. So in the life of the composer at the moment of that highest success and prosperity, just when he could first look forward with well-grounded confidence to the noblest gratification of a musician's honourable ambition, a new and discordant element thrust itself into the harmony of his life. This was the symptoms of approaching deafness. His own account fixes their appearance in the year 1799; then they were still so feeble and intermittent, as to have caused him at first no serious anxiety; but in another year they had assumed so much the appearance of a chronic and increasing evil, as to compel him to abandon plans for travel which he had formed, and for which he was preparing himself, with great industry and perseverance, to appear in the twofold capacity of virtuoso and composer. Instead, therefore, in 1801, of having 'before now travelled over half the world', he, for two years, had been confined to Vienna or its immediate vicinity, vainly seeking relief from surgeons and physicians.

CHAPTER 8

The Years 1800 and 1801

A grand concert for which Beethoven had been preparing during the winter took place on 2 April. It was his first public appearance for his own benefit in Vienna, and, so far as is known, anywhere except in Prague. The programme, a copy of which was in the possession of Frau van Beethoven (widow of the composer's nephew) is as follows:

'Today, Wednesday, 2 April 1800, Herr *Ludwig van Beethoven* will have the honour to give a grand concert for his benefit in the Royal Imperial Court Theatre beside the Burg. The pieces which will be performed are the following:

1. A grand symphony by the late Kapellmeister Mozart.
2. An aria from 'The Creation' by the Princely Kapellmeister Herr Haydn, sung by Mlle Saal.
3. A grand concerto for the pianoforte, played and composed by Herr *Ludwig van Beethoven*.
4. A septet, most humbly and obediently dedicated to Her Majesty the Empress, and composed by Herr *Ludwig van Beethoven* for four stringed- and three wind-instruments, played by Herren Schuppanzigh, Schreiber, Schindlecker, Bär, Nickel, Matauschek and Dietzel.
5. A duet from Haydn's 'Creation', sung by Herr and Mlle Saal.
6. Herr *Ludwig van Beethoven* will improvise on the pianoforte.
7. A new grand symphony with complete orchestra, composed by Herr *Ludwig van Beethoven*.

Tickets for boxes and stalls are to be had of Herr van Beethoven at his lodgings in the Tiefen Graben, No. 241, third storey, and of the box-keeper.

Prices of admission are as usual.

The beginning is at half-past 6 o'clock.'

The correspondent of the *Allgemeine Musikalische Zeitung* described the concert as follows:

'Finally on one occasion Herr Beethoven took over the theatre and this was truly the most interesting concert in a long time. He played a new concerto of his own composition, much of which was written with a great deal of taste and feeling. After this he improvised in a masterly fashion, and at the end one of his symphonies was performed in which there is considerable art, novelty and a wealth of ideas. The only flaw was that the wind-instruments were used too much, so that there was more harmony than orchestral music as a whole. Perhaps we might do well to note the following about this concert. The orchestra of the Italian opera made a very poor showing. First, quarrels about who was to conduct. Beethoven thought quite rightly that he could entrust the conducting not to Herr Conti but to Herr Wranitzky. The gentlemen refused to play under him. The faults of this orchestra, already criticised above, then became all the more evident since B's compositions are difficult to execute. When they were accompanying, the players did not bother to pay any attention to the soloist. As a result there was no delicacy at all in the accompaniments and no response to the musical feeling of the solo player. In the second part of the symphony they became so lax that despite all efforts on the part of the conductor no fire whatsoever could be got from them, particularly from the wind-instruments. With such behaviour what good is all the proficiency – which most of the members of this organisation undeniably possess? How, under such circumstances, is even the most excellent composition to be effective?'

Which of the pianoforte concertos Beethoven played on this occasion is not clear. The Symphony in C (the First Symphony) soon became known throughout Germany; while the Septet achieved a sudden popularity so widely extended and enduring as at length to become an annoyance to the composer.

Before the month was out Beethoven again played in public, in a concert given by Johann Wenzel Stich, known as Punto. This Bohemian virtuoso, after several years of wandering, had lately come to Vienna from Paris, via Munich. As a performer upon the horn he was unrivalled by any predecessor or contemporary; but as a composer he was beneath criticism. Beethoven's delight in anyone whose skill afforded him a new experience of the powers and possible effects of any orchestral instrument is known to the reader. Nothing more natural, therefore, than his readiness to compose a sonata for himself and Punto to be played at the latter's concert on 18 April. Ries informs us that 'though the concert was announced with the Sonata the latter was not yet begun. Beethoven began his work the day before the performance and it was ready for the concert.' His habit of merely sketching his own part and of trusting to his memory and the inspiration of the moment, even when producing his grand concertos in public, probably rendered him good service on this occasion. The *Allgemeine Musikalische Zeitung* of 2 July 1800 preserves also the interesting fact that owing to the enthusiastic applause the Sonata was immediately repeated.

These two artists performed together again in Budapest on 7 May. Beethoven was in that city from the end of April to the beginning of July, during which time he was a frequent visitor to the Brunsviks' country estate. From an issue of the *Ofener und Pester Theatertaschenbuch* we quote, 'on this day (7 May) an Akademie of Herr Bethover and Herr Punto . . . Who is this Bethover? The history of German music is not acquainted with such a name. Punto of course is very well known. Punto is his name as an artist, his real name is Wenzel Stich . . . Three weeks before his concert in Ofen-Pest Punto appeared in a concert in Vienna, indeed in the company of a certain *Beethoven*.' From the *Ungarrischer Kurrier* we learn that their appearance on 7 May was the last event in a four-day festival celebrating the birthday of the Archduchess Maria Pawlowna. The notice for this day reads, 'Carousel, after which a concert was given in the *Theatrum* where a famous *Musikus* named Beethoven drew the attention of all present to himself from his artistic performance.' According to the personal chronicle of the aristocratic family Vegh at Vereb, who as keen music-lovers expected both Punto and Beethoven to come to Vereb to perform, 'Punto alone came because there had been a quarrel between him and Herr von Beethoven in Pest, as a result of which Beethoven remained behind.' Nothing further is known of Beethoven's activities during this stay in Hungary.

At the end of February or early in March, the charlatan and touring pianaforte virtuoso Daniel Steibelt gave a concert in Prague which brought him in 1,800 florins. As a result of the way he handled his business affairs, he was widely regarded as a swindler. Thus Ries relates how:

'When Steibelt came to Vienna with his great name, some of Beethoven's friends grew alarmed lest he do injury to the latter's reputation. Steibelt did not visit him; they met first time one evening at the house of Count Fries, where Beethoven produced his new Trio in B flat major for Pianoforte, Clarinet and Violoncello (Op. 11), for the first time. There is no opportunity for particular display on the part of the pianist in this Trio. Steibelt listened to it with a sort of condescension, uttered a few compliments to Beethoven and felt sure of his victory. He played a Quintet of his own composition, improvised, and made a good deal of effect with his tremolos, which were then something entirely new. Beethoven could not be induced to play again. Eight days later there was again a concert at Count Fries's; Steibelt again played a quintet which had a good deal of success. He also played an improvisation (which had, obviously, been carefully prepared) and chose the same theme on which Beethoven had written variations in his Trio. This incensed the admirers of Beethoven and him; he had to go to the pianoforte and improvise. He went in his usual (I might say, ill-bred) manner to the instrument as if half-pushed, picked up the violoncello part of Steibelt's quintet in passing, placed it (intentionally?) upon the stand upside down and with one finger drummed a theme out of the first few measures. Insulted and angered he improvised in such a manner that Steibelt left the room before he finished, would never again meet him and, indeed, made it a condition that Beethoven should not be invited before accepting an offer.'

It was the custom at Vienna for all those whose vocations and pecuniary circumstances rendered it possible, to spend all or some portion of the summer months in the country. The aristocracies of birth and wealth retired to their country seats, lived in villas for the season or joined the throngs at the great watering-places. Other classes found refuge in the villages and hamlets which abounded in the lovely environs of the city, where many a neat cottage was built for their use and where the peasants generally had a spare room or two, cleanly kept and neatly furnished. Beethoven's habit of escaping from town during the hot months was, therefore, nothing peculiar to him. We have reached the point whence, with little if any interruption, Beethoven can be followed from house to house, in city and country, through the rest of his life – a catalogue characterised by his restlessness.

Karl Holz told Jahn: 'He [Beethoven] lived at first in a little attic-room in the house of the bookbinder Strauss in the Alservorstadt, where he had a miserable time.' This attic-room must have been soon changed for the room 'on the ground floor' mentioned in a previous chapter. Thence Beethoven went as a guest to the house occupied by Prince Lichnowsky at 125 Hauptstrasse. In May 1795, Beethoven, in advertising the Trios, Op. 1, gives 'the residence of the author' as the 'Ogylisches Haus in the Kreuzgasse behind the Minorite church, No. 35 in the first storey'. From the memoirs of Countess Therese Brunsvik we learn that by the spring of 1799 Beethoven lived in rooms at St Petersplatz to which one had to climb up three flights on a winding staircase. As has been seen by the concert bill on a preceding page, he was during the winter of 1799–1800 in the Tiefen Graben 'in a very high and narrow house', as Czerny wrote. For the summer of 1800, he took quarters for himself and servant in a house in Unter-Döbling, an hour's walk, perhaps, from town.

An authentic and characteristic anecdote can belong only to this summer. There lived in a house hard by a peasant of no very good reputation, who had a daughter remarkably beautiful, but also not of the best fame. Beethoven was greatly captivated by her and was in the habit of stopping to gaze at her when he passed by where she was at work in farmyard or field. She, however, made no return of his evident liking and only laughed at his admiration. On one occasion the father was arrested for engaging in a brawl and imprisoned. Beethoven took the man's part and went to the magistrates to obtain his release. Not succeeding, he became angry and abusive, and in the end would have been arrested for his impertinence but for the strong representations made by some, who knew him, of his position in society and of the high rank, influence and power of his friends.

Throughout this period of Beethoven's life, each summer is distinguished by some noble composition, completed, or nearly so, so that on his return to the city it was ready for revision and his copyist. Free from the demands of society, his time was his own; his fancy was quickened, his inspiration strengthened, in field and forest labour was a delight. The most important work of the master bears in his own hand the date, 1800, and may reasonably be supposed to have been the labour of this summer. It is the Concerto in C minor for Pianoforte and Orchestra, Op. 37.*

One of the most prolific and popular composers whom Beethoven found in Vienna was Franz Anton Hoffmeister, 'Kapellmeister and RI [Royal Imperial] licensed Music, Art and Book Seller'. He was an immigrant from the Neckar valley and (born 1754) much older than Beethoven, to whom he had extended a warm sympathy and friendship, doubly valuable from his somewhat similar experience as a young student in Vienna. This is evident from the whole tone of their correspondence. In 1800, Hoffmeister left Vienna and in Leipzig formed a copartnership with Ambrosius Kühnel, organist of the Electoral Saxon Court Chapel, and established a publishing house there, still retaining his business in Vienna. Knowing Beethoven personally and so intimately, it is alike creditable to the talents of the one and the taste and appreciation of the other that Hoffmeister, immediately upon organising his new publishing house, should have asked him for manuscripts. To his letter he received an answer dated 15 December 1800, in which Beethoven says:

* Piano Concerto No. 3.

'Dearest Hr. Brother!

'I have been on the point of replying to your enquiry several times, but I am so fearfully lazy about my correspondence and I am loath to write dry letters [of the alphabet] instead of musical notes. Now at last I have prevailed upon myself to comply with your request –

'Pro primo you must know that I am very sorry that you, my dear brother in music, did not let me know something of this earlier so that I might have marketed my quartets with you, as well as many other pieces which I have sold. But if Hr. Brother is as conscientious as many other honest engravers who stab us poor composers to death, you will know how to derive profit from them when they appear – I will now set forth in brief what Hr. B[rother] can have from me. 1. A Septet per il violino, viola, violoncello, contra basso, clarinet, corno, fagotto – tutti obbligati (I cannot write anything non-obbligato for I came into this world with an obbligato accompaniment). This Septet has pleased me greatly. For its more frequent use the three wind-instruments, namely: fagotto, clarinetto and corno might be transcribed for another violin, viola and violoncello. 2. A grand Symphony for full orchestra. 3. A Concerto for pianoforte which I do not claim to be one of my best, as well as another one which will be published here by Mollo (this for the information of the Leipzig critics) because I am for the present *keeping the better ones for myself until I make a tour*. However, it would not disgrace you to publish it. 4. A grand solo Sonata. That is all I can give you at this moment, a little later you may have a Quintet for stringed instruments as well as, probably, quartets and other things which I have not now with me. In your reply you might set the prices, and as you are neither *a Jew nor an Italian*, nor I either one or the other, we shall no doubt come to an understanding.

'Dearest Brother, take care of yourself and be assured of the regard
of your brother

L. v. Beethoven'

The reference to the Quartets, Op. 18, in this letter, taken in connection with the apologies for long delay in writing, indicates conclusively enough that at least the first set, the first three, had been placed in the hands of Mollo and Co. early in the autumn. The following anecdote was told by Karl Amenda:

'After Beethoven had composed his well-known String Quartet in F major he played for his friend [Amenda] [on the pianoforte?] the glorious Adagio [D minor, 9/8 time] and asked him what thought had been awakened by it. "It pictured for me the parting of two lovers," was the answer. "Good!" remarked Beethoven, "I thought of the scene in the burial vault in *Romeo and Juliet*." '

Amenda left Vienna in the autumn of 1799; Beethoven's dedication on the copy which he gave his friend was dated 25 June 1799; thus at this time the first Quartet was ready in its original form.

The chronology of the Quartets may be summed up as follows: the composition was begun in 1798, that in D, the third, being first undertaken. This was followed by that in F and soon after, or simultaneously, work was begun on that in G, which was originally intended as the second; but, as that in F was completed earlier, this was designated as the second by Beethoven, and that in G became in point of time the third. The Quartet in F was finished in its original shape by 25 June 1799, on which day he gave it to Amenda; he revised it later. Whether or not this was also done with the others cannot be said; there is no evidence. The remark made in 1801, that he had just learned to write quartets, is amply explained by his practice on the six Quartets. He wrote the one in A (now No. 5), intending it to be the fourth; in this he seems to have made use of a motif invented at an earlier period. The Quartets in B flat and C minor followed, the latter being, perhaps, the last. The definitive elaboration of the Quartets lasted certainly until 1800, possibly until 1801. The Quartets then appeared in two sets from the press of Mollo.

Notice of a valuable present to Beethoven from his lenient and generous patron, Prince Karl Lichnowsky, naturally connects itself with the story of the Quartets – a gift thus described by Alois Fuchs, formerly violinist in the Imperial Court Orchestra, under date of 2 December 1846:

'Ludwig van Beethoven owned a complete quartet of excellent Italian instruments given to him by his princely patron and friend Lichnowsky at the suggestion of the famous quartet-player Schuppanzigh. I am in a position to describe each of the instruments in detail.

'1. A violin made by Joseph Guarnerius in Cremona in the year 1718 is now in the possession of Mr Karl Holz, director of the *Concerts spirituels* in Vienna.

'2. The second violin (which was offered for sale) was made by Nicholas Amati in the year 1667, and was in the possession of Dr Ohmeyer, who died recently in Hütteldorf; it has been purchased by Mr Huber.

'3. The viola, made by Vincenzo Ruger in 1690, is also the property of Mr Karl Holz.

'4. The violoncello, an Andreas Guarnerius of the year 1712, is in the possession of Mr P. Wertheimber of Vienna.

'The seal of Beethoven has been impressed under the neck of each instrument and on the back of each Beethoven scratched a big B, probably for the purpose of protecting himself against an exchange. The instruments are all well preserved and in good condition. The most valuable one, without question, is the violin by Joseph Guarnerius, which is distinguished by extraordinary power of tone, for which, indeed, Mr Holz has refused an offer of 1,000 florins.'

The four instruments are now on display at the Beethoven Museum in Bonn.

Another proof of the Prince's regard and generosity, however, belongs to this, namely, an annuity of 600 florins to be continued until the composer should find some suitable permanent position.

As for the compositions of the year, it is safe to assume that Beethoven put the finishing touches to the First Symphony, the Septet, Op. 20, and the Quartets, Op. 18. Furthermore, there can be little doubt but that the Sonata for Horn, Op. 17, the Pianoforte Sonata, Op. 22, and the Concerto in C minor belong to this year.

Though the number of new compositions produced in 1800 was small, attention must be directed to the fact that the revision and completion of works for publication, together with the planning of new works, gave a good deal of occupation to Beethoven. The big work of the year was the Concerto in C minor, the autograph of which distinctly bears the date of 1800. Amongst the compositions made ready for the printer were the Quartets, which were not ready till near the end of the year. It is certain, moreover, that Beethoven began working on *Prometheus* and the Sonata in E flat, Op. 27, No. 1, in this year, and the summer must have been a busy one for him.

The tone of Beethoven's correspondence and the many proofs of his untiring industry during the winter 1800–1 and the early part of the succeeding spring, suggest a mind at ease, rejoicing in the exercise of its powers, and a body glowing with vigorous health. But for his own words to Wegeler: 'I have been really miserable this winter', the passing allusions to ill health in his replies to Hoffmeister's letters would merely impress the reader as being half-groundless apologies for lack of punctuality in writing. The following pages will exhibit the young master both as he appeared to the public and as he showed himself in confidential intercourse to the few in whose presence he put aside the mask and laid open his heart; and will, therefore, it is believed, be found fully to justify what has been said of his heroic energy, courage and endurance under a trouble of no ordinary nature.

In the beginning of the year he wrote to Hoffmeister as follows under date '15 January (or thereabouts) 1801':

'... Your enterprises delight me also and I wish that if works of art ever bring profit that it might go to real artists instead of mere shop-keepers – Your purpose to publish the *works of Sebastian Bach* is something which does good to my heart which beats only for the lofty and magnificent art of this patriarch of harmony, and I hope soon to see them in vigorous sale. I hope as soon as golden peace has been declared to be helpful in many ways, especially if you offer the works for sub-scription. – As regards our real business, since you ask it I can meet your wishes by offering the following items: Septet (concerning which I have already written to you, and which can be profitably arranged for piano for greater circulation) 20 ducats – a symphony 20 ducats – a concerto 10 ducats – a grand solo sonata (Allegro, Adagio, Minuetto, Rondo) 20 ducats. (This sonata is a first-class piece, my dearest Herr Brother!) Now for an explanation: you will wonder, perhaps, that I have made no distinction here between sonata, septet and symphony; this is because I find that a septet or symphony has a smaller sale than a sonata, though a symphony ought unquestionably to be worth more. (NB The septet consists of a short introductory Adagio, then Allegro, Adagio, Minuetto, Andante with variations, Minuetto, again a short Adagio introduction and then Presto.) – I put the price of the concerto at only 10 ducats because, as I have already written, I do not consider it one of my best – I do not think the amount excessive for the whole. I have tried, at least, to make the price as moderate as possible for you. – As regards the money order you may, since you leave the matter to me, issue it to Geimüller or Schuller. – The whole sum would thus be 70 ducats; how many thalers in gold that amounts to does not concern me, because I am a really poor businessman and arithmetician. –

'This disposes of the troublesome business, I call it so because I wish things were different in the world. There ought to be only one *art-market* in the world where an artist would need only to carry his art-works and take away with him as much as he needed. As it is one must be half tradesman, and how we must adapt ourselves – good God – that is what I again call *troublesome*. – As regards the Leipzig critics, let them talk, they will certainly never make anyone immortal by their twaddle, nor will they rob anybody of immortality to whom Apollo has decreed it. –

'Now may heaven preserve you and *your associate*. I have not been well for some time now and at present it is difficult for me to write notes, still more so letters of the alphabet. I hope we will have the occasion often to confirm how much you are my friend and I am

your brother and friend

L. v. Beethoven'

'For a speedy answer – goodbye.'

The next letter requires a word of introduction. That military campaign which included the disastrous field of Hohenlinden (3 December 1800) had filled the hospitals in Vienna, and among the various means of raising funds for the benefit of the wounded was a series of public concerts. The two in which they reached their climax took place in the large Ridotto room (Redoutensaal) of the imperial palace. The one arranged by Baron von Braun as Director of the Court Opera was a performance of Haydn's *Creation* conducted by the composer, on 16 January; the other was arranged by Mme Frank (Christine Gerhardi) for 30 January.

In the first public announcement of this second concert printed in the *Wiener Zeitung* the only artist mentioned was 'the famous amateur singer Frau von Frank, née Gerhardi', as the giver of the concert. This called out from Beethoven the following letter:

'Pour Madame de Frank.

'I think it my duty, dear lady, to remind you that in the second announcement of our concert you do not allow your husband to forget again that those who contribute their talents to the same should also be made known to the public. – This is the custom, and I do not see, if this is not done, how the attendance is to be increased, which after all is the chief aim of this concert – Punto is not a little wrought up about the matter, and he is right, and it was my intention even before I saw him to remind you of what must have been the result of grave haste or great forgetfulness. Look after this, dear lady, since if it is not done you will be faced with *real ill humour*. – Because I have been convinced by others as well as myself that I am not a useless factor in this concert, I know that not only I but Punto, Simoni, and Galvani will ask that the public be informed also of our zeal for the philanthropic purposes of this concert; otherwise we must all conclude that we are useless. –

Wholly yours,

L. v. Bthvn'

Whether this sharp remonstrance produced any effect cannot now be ascertained, but the original advertisement was repeated in the newspaper on the 24th and 28th verbatim.

In the state of affairs then existing it was no time to give public concerts for private emolument; but there is still another adequate reason for Beethoven giving no Akademie (concert) this spring. He had been engaged to compose an important work for the court stage.

The second wife of Emperor Franz, Maria Theresia, was a woman of much and true musical taste and culture, and Salvatore Vigano, a dancer and composer of ballets, both action and music, determined to compliment her in a ballet composed expressly for that purpose. Haydn's gloriously successful *Creation* may, perhaps, have had an influence in the choice of a subject, *The Men of Prometheus*, and the dedication of Beethoven's Septet to the Empress may have had its effect in the choice of a composer. At all events, the work was entrusted to Beethoven.

If the manner in which this work has been neglected by Beethoven's biographers and critics may be taken as a criterion, an opinion prevails that it was not worthy of him in subject, execution or success. It seems to be forgotten that as an orchestral composer he was then known only by two or three pianoforte concertos and his first Symphony, and that for the stage he was not known to have written anything. Vigano was a man of real genius and had wrought a reform which is clearly, vigorously and compendiously described in a memoir of Heinrich von Collin, from which we quote:

'The new ballet-master owed his extraordinary triumph over his older rivals to his restoration of his art back from the exaggerated, inexpressive artificialities of the old Italian ballet to the simple forms of nature. Of course, there was something startling in seeing a form of drama with which thitherto there had been associated only leaps, contortions, constrained positions, and complicated dances which left behind them no feeling of unity, suddenly succeeded by dramatic action, depth of feeling, and plastic beauty of representation as they were so magnificently developed in the earlier ballets of Mr Salvatore Vigano, opening, as they did, a new realm of beauty.'

There was nothing derogatory to Beethoven in his acceptance of the commission to compose the music to a ballet by Vigano; but by whom commissioned, upon what terms, and when – concerning these and similar particulars, we know nothing. We only know, that at the close of the season before Easter, on 28 March, *Die Geschöpfe des Prometheus* was performed for the first time for the benefit of the prima ballerina of the ballet corps, Fräulein Casentini, and that the whole number of its performances this year was fourteen, and in 1802 nine. The pecuniary result to Beethoven must therefore have been satisfactory.

Alois Fuchs has preserved a characteristic anecdote which came to him 'from the worthy hand of a contemporary':

'When Beethoven had composed the music to the ballet *Die Geschöpfe des Prometheus* in 1801, he was one day met by his former teacher, the great Joseph Haydn, who stopped him at once and said: "Well, I heard your ballet yesterday and it pleased me very much!" Beethoven replied: "O, dear Papa, you are very kind; but it is far from being a *Creation*!" Haydn, surprised at the answer and almost offended, said after a short pause: "That is true; it is not yet a *Creation* and I can scarcely believe that it will ever become one." Whereupon the men said their adieus, both somewhat embarrassed.'

From the period immediately following we have another letter from Beethoven to Hoffmeister, dated 22 April 1801, in which he says:

'You have good ground for complaint against me and that not a little. My excuse is that I was ill and moreover had a great deal to do besides, so that it was hardly possible for me to think of what I had to send you. Perhaps too, it is the only sign of genius about me that my things are not always in the best of order, and nobody can mend the matter except myself . . .

'So that the works may appear so far as possible in their proper sequence I point out to you that there should be placed

on the solo sonata . . . . . . opus 22
on the symphony . . . . . . opus 21
on the septet . . . . opus 20
on the concerto . . . . opus 19

'– I shall send you the *titles* soon. – Set me down as a subscriber for the works of *Johann Sebastian Bach*, also *Prince Lichnowsky*. The transcription of the Mozart sonatas as quartets will do you honour and certainly prove profitable. I should like to be of greater service *on such occasions* but I am a disorderly individual and with the best of intentions am continually forgetting everything. However I have spoken about the matter here and there, and everywhere have found enthusiasm about it – It would be a fine thing if my good brother besides publishing the Septet were also to arrange it for flute, perhaps as a Quintet. This would help the *amateur flautists*, who have already approached me on the subject, and they would swarm around and feed on it like hungry insects. – To say something of myself, I have just written a ballet in which the ballet-master did not do as well as he might have done. – *Baron von Lichtenstein* has presented us with a product not measuring up to the ideas which the newspapers have spread touching his genius; again another bit of evidence against the newspapers. The Baron seems to have taken for his ideal *Hr. Müller at the Kasperle*, without reaching even *him*. – These are the beautiful conditions under which we poor fellows in Vienna are expected to flourish. – My dear brother make haste to give the world a sight of these works and write to me soon so that I may know whether or not I have forfeited your further confidence by my dilatoriness. To your associate Kühnel all kind wishes. In the future all things will go to you promptly and in order. – The quartets may be published in a few weeks – and with this keep well and continue to love your friend

and brother

Beethoven'

On 22 April 1801 Beethoven wrote to Breitkopf and Härtel:

'Pardon the tardy answer to your letter to me. I was for a time continually indisposed and also overwhelmed with work, and besides since I am not the most industrious of letter writers, this may serve to excuse me also. – As regards your request for compositions by me I regret that at this time I am unable to oblige you. But please be so kind as to tell me what kinds of compositions you would like to have of mine, namely, symphonies, quartets, sonatas, etc., so that I may act accordingly, and should I have what you need or want, be able to place it at your service. – With my permission, 7 or 8 works of mine are about to appear *at Mollo's* in this place; four pieces *at Hoffmeister's* in Leipzig. – In this connection I wish to add that one *of my first concertos* and therefore *not one of the best of my compositions*, is to be published by *Hoffmeister*, and that Mollo is to publish *a concerto which*, indeed *was written later*, but which also does *not* rank among *the best of my works in this form* . . . You should recommend to your Hrn. critics great care and wisdom especially in the products of younger composers. Many a one may have been frightened off who otherwise might have composed more. As far as I am concerned, I am far from thinking that I am so perfect as to be beyond criticism, yet the howls of your critics against me were at first so humiliating that when I compared myself with others I could not get aroused, but remained perfectly quiet, and reasoned that they do not understand their business. It was easier to remain quiet since I saw praise lavished on people who were held of little account here by the better sort, and who have disappeared from sight no matter how worthy they may otherwise have been. – But *pax vobiscum* – peace with you and me – I would not have mentioned a syllable about the matter if you had not yourself done so. –'

Beethoven had just cause for indignation in the treatment which he had received at the hands of the writers for the *Allgemeine Musikalische Zeitung* mentioned in his letter of 15 January 1801. Hoffmeister had evidently written to him on the subject, and his reticence in confining himself in reply to a single contemptuous sentence, though writing in the confidence of private correspondence, is something unexpected; not less so is the manly, dignified and ingenuous style of his answer to Breitkopf and Härtel upon the same topic in the letter of 22 April. The first number of that famous musical journal appeared on 3 October 1798. In the fifteenth (19 January 1799), the name of Beethoven first appears, viz.: in the title of three sonatas dedicated to him by Wölffl. At length, in No. 23, that of 6 March 1799, he is introduced to the readers of the journal as a composer – not of one or more of the eight Trios, ten Sonatas, the Quintet and Serenade, which make up the *opera* 1 to 11 then published – but as the writer of the Twelve Variations on 'Ein Mädchen oder Weibchen', and eight on 'Une fièvre brûlante'.

The criticisms are a perfect reflex of the conventional musical thought of the period and can be read now with amused interest, at least. There is no room here for their production in full. The writer 'M.' recognises the clever pianoforte player in the Variations but cannot see evidences in them of equal capacity as a composer.

No. 33 (15 May) of the *Allgemeine Musikalische Zeitung* contains nearly two pages from the pen of Spazier on Lichtenstein's opera, *Die steinerne Braut*, and a parallel between Beethoven and Wölffl as pianists. Then in the next number the beautiful Trio, Op. 11, finds a reviewer. Here is the whole of his article:

'This Trio, which in part is not easier but more flowing than many other pieces by the same author, makes an excellent ensemble on the pianoforte with accompaniment. The composer with his unusual harmonic knowledge and love for serious composition would provide us many things which would leave many hand-organ things far in the rear, even those composed by famous men, if he would but try to write more naturally.'

Could one say less?

The critics are now ruminating upon the noble Sonatas for Pianoforte and Violin, Op. 12, and No. 36 (June 1799) contains the result:

'The critic, who heretofore has been unfamiliar with the pianoforte pieces of the author, must admit, after having looked through these strange sonatas, overladen with difficulties, that after diligent and strenuous labour he felt like a man who had hoped to make a promenade with a genial friend through a tempting forest and found himself barred every minute by inimical barriers, returning at last exhausted and without having had any pleasure. It is undeniable that Hr. Beethoven goes his own gait; but what a bizarre and singular gait it is! Learned, learned and always learned – and nothing natural, no song. Yes, to be accurate, there is *only a mass of learning here, without good method*; obstinacy, but for which we feel but little interest; a striving for strange modulations, an objection to customary associations, a heaping up of difficulties on difficulties till one loses all patience and enjoyment.'

In June 1801, Beethoven wrote again to the publisher Hoffmeister to this effect:

'I am a little bit amazed at what you have communicated to me through the local representative of your firm; I am almost vexed to think that you consider me capable of such a trick. It would be a different matter if I had sold my wares only to avaricious tradesmen hoping that they would make a good speculation on the sly, but as *artist towards artist* it is a bit harsh to think such things of me. It looks to me as if the whole matter had been thoroughly planned to test me or that it was a mere surmise. In either case I inform you that before you received *the Septet* from me I sent it to London to Hr. Salomon (for performance at his concerts, out of mere *friendship*), but with the understanding that he should have a care that it should not fall into the hands of strangers, because I intended that it should be published in Germany. If you think it necessary, you may make enquiry of him, but in order to prove my honesty *I give you herewith the assurance that I have not sold the Septet, Concerto, the Symphony and the Sonata to anybody but you, Hoffmeister and Kühnel, and that you may consider them as your exclusive property, and to this I pledge my honour.* You may make as much of this assurance as you please – As for the rest I believe as little that Salomon is capable of being guilty of having the Septet printed as I am of having sold it to him – I am so conscientious that I have denied the applications of *various publishers* to print the pianoforte arrangement of the Septet, and yet I do not know whether or not you intend to make use of it.'

In the spring of this year Beethoven removed from the Tiefer Graben into rooms overlooking one of the bastions – there is little, if any doubt, the Wasserkunstbastei – and in one of those houses the main entrances to which are in the Sailerstätte. At a later period of his life he came thither again, and with good reason; for those houses not only afforded a beautiful view over the Glacis and the Landstrasse suburb, but plenty of sun and fresh air.

This year he chose Hetzendorf for his summer retreat. Those who know well the environs of Vienna are aware that this village offers less attraction to the lover of nature than a hundred others within easy distance of the city. There is nothing to invite one, who is fond of the solitude of the forest, but the thick groves in the garden of Schönbrunn some ten minutes' walk distant. It is certainly possible that Beethoven's state of health may have forbidden him to indulge his taste for long rambles, and that the cool shades of Schönbrunn, so easily and at all times accessible, may have determined his choice.

Let us now turn to the important letters written in the summer of 1801, beginning with two written to his friend Amenda. The first, without date or record of place, is as follows:

'How can Amenda think that I could ever forget him – because I do not write or have not written to him? – as if the remembrance of people could be preserved only in that manner!

'A thousand times there comes to my mind the best of all men that I ever knew – yes, along with the two men who had my entire love, of which one lives, you are the third – the memory of you can never be extinguished. You will soon receive a long letter from me concerning my present condition and everything about me that might interest you.

'Farewell, dear, good, noble friend, keep me always in your love, your friendship, as I shall for ever remain
                                   Your faithful Beethoven'

The longer letter which he promised to send to his friend is dated 1 July 1801.

'My dear, my good Amenda, my true friend!

'I received and read your last letter with mixed pain and pleasure – To what shall I compare your fidelity, your attachment to me? Oh, it is so wonderful that you have always been true to me; and yes, I know you as one who is trustworthy and above all others. You are no *Viennese friend*, no, you are one of those who spring from the ground of my native land. How often do I wish you were with me, for your B is living an unhappy life, quarrelling with nature and its creator, often cursing the latter for surrendering his creatures to the merest accident which often breaks or destroys the most beautiful blossoms. Know that my noblest faculty, *my hearing*, has greatly deteriorated. When you were still with me I felt the symptoms but kept silent; now it is continually growing worse, and whether or not a cure is possible has become a question. It is said to be due to the condition of my belly, and so far as that is concerned I am nearly restored to health. I hope, indeed, that my hearing also will improve, but I am doubtful because such diseases are the most incurable. How sad is my lot, I must avoid all things that are dear to me and what is more must live among such miserable and ego-tistical men as Zmeskall, Schuppanzigh, etc. I must say that amongst them all Lichnowsky is the most satisfactory; in the last year he has settled an income of 600 florins on me. This and the good sale of my works enables me to live without care. I could sell everything that I compose five times over and at a good price – I have composed con-siderably of late. As I hear that you have ordered a pianoforte from S., I will send you various things in the box of the instrument so that it need not cost you much. Now a man has recently returned here to my great comfort, with whom I can share the pleasures of a close relationship and an unselfish friendship. He is one of the friends of my youth; I have often spoken of you to him and told him that since I left my fatherland you have been the one person close to my heart. Z. does not appeal to him either, he is and always will be too weak for friendship; and I use him and S. only as instruments on which I can play when I please. But they can never become real witnesses of my internal and external actions any more than they can be real participants in my life; I value them only by what they do for me. Oh, how happy I should be if my hearing were completely restored, then I would hurry to you. How-ever, as it is I must stay away from everything and the most beautiful years of my life must pass by without my accomplishing all that my tal-ent and powers bid me to do – A sad resignation must be my refuge, although, indeed, I am resolved to rise above every obstacle. But how will it be possible? Yes, Amenda, if my infirmity shows itself to be incurable in half a year, I shall appeal to you, you must abandon every-thing and come to me. Then I shall travel (my affliction causes me the least trouble in playing and composing, the most in association with others) and you must be my companion. I am sure my good fortune will not desert me. What is there that I might not accomplish? Since you left I have composed everything except opera and church music. Surely you will not deny me, you will help your friend bear his troubles and his affliction. I have also greatly improved my pianoforte playing, and I hope that this tour will, perhaps, make your fortune too; afterwards you must remain with me forever. – I have received all of your letters, and despite the fact that I have answered so few, you were always with me, and my heart still beats as tenderly for you as it ever did. – *I beg of you to keep the matter of my deafness a profound secret to be confided to nobody no matter whom.* – Write to me very often; your letters, no matter how short, comfort me, do me good, and I shall expect another from you soon, my dear fellow. – Do not lend your quartet to anybody because I have greatly changed it, having just learned how to write quartets properly, as you will observe when you receive them. – Now, farewell my dear, good fellow; if you ever think of anything I can do for you here, you have only to tell

Your faithful and truly affectionate
L. v. Beethoven'

It is not difficult to imagine calamities greater than that which now threatened Beethoven – as the loss of sight to a Raphael or Rubens at the height of his fame and powers; a partial paralysis or other incurable disease of the brain cutting short the career of a Shakespeare or Goethe, a Bacon or Kant, a Newton or Humboldt. Better the untimely fate of a Buckle, than to live long years of unavailing regret over the blasted hopes and promise of early manhood. In such cases there remains no resource; hope itself is dead. But to Beethoven, even if his worst fears should prove prophetic and his infirmity at length close all prospects of a career as virtuoso and conductor, the field of composition still remained open. This he knew, and it saved him from utter despair. Who can say that the world has not been a gainer by the misfortune which stirred the profoundest depths of his being and compelled the concentration of all his powers into one direction?

As the disease made progress and the prospect of relief became less, notwithstanding a grief and anxiety which caused him such mental agony as even to induce the thought of suicide, he so well succeeded in keeping it concealed from all but a few intimate and faithful friends, that no notice whatever is to be found of it until 1802 except in papers from his own hand. They form a very touching contrast to his letters to other correspondents. Neither the head nor the heart is to be envied of the man who can read them without emotion. The two most important are the letters to Wegeler giving full details of his case; doubly valuable because they are not merely letters to a friend, but an elaborate account of the symptoms and medical treatment of his disease, made to a physician of high standing who thoroughly understood the constitution of the patient. They are therefore equally significant for what they contain and for what they omit.

On 29 June, Beethoven sent the following letter to Wegeler:

'Vienna, 29 June

'My good, dear Wegeler,

'How greatly I thank you for thinking of me; I have so little deserved it or tried to deserve anything from you. Yet you are so very good and refuse to be offended by anything, not even by my unpardonable negligence, and remain always my true, faithful and honourable friend. – Do not ever think that I could forget you and all of you who were always so true and dear to me. There are moments when I long for you myself, yes, and would like to spend some time with you. – My fatherland, the beautiful country in which I first saw the light of day, is still as clear and beautiful before my eyes as when I left you. In short, I shall look upon that time when I see you again and greet Father Rhine as one of the happiest moments in my life. – When this shall be I cannot yet tell you, but I want to say this much, that when you see me again it will be only as a great man, not only a greater artist but a better and more accomplished man. If conditions are improved in our fatherland, my art will be used only in the service of the poor. Oh happy moment, how happy I am that I myself can create you, can invoke you – You want to know something about my situation, it is not so bad. In the last year, unbelievable as it may sound when I tell you, Lichnowski, who has always remained my warmest friend (there were little quarrels between us, but haven't they served to strengthen our friendship?), has set aside a fixed sum of 600 florins for me to draw upon so long as I remain without a post suitable for me. My compositions bring me a fair sum, and I may say that I have more commissions than it is possible for me to fill. Besides, I have 6 or 7 publishers after each piece and might have more if I chose; people no longer bargain with me, I ask and they pay. You see how very convenient it is. For instance, I see a friend in need and my purse does not permit me to help him at once; so I have only to get to work and in a short time, help is at hand – Moreover, I am more economical than formerly; if I stay here for good I shall arrange to reserve one day a year for my Akademie, of which I have given several. That evil demon, my bad health, however, has put a spoke in my wheel, namely: my hearing has grown steadily worse during the last three years, which was said to be caused by the condition of my belly, which as you know has always been wretched and has been getting worse, since I am always troubled with diarrhoea, which causes extraordinary weakness. Frank wanted to *tone up* my body by tonic medicines and restore my hearing with almond oil, but *prosit*, nothing happened, my hearing grew worse and worse, and my bowels remained as they had been. This lasted until the autumn of last year, and I was often in despair. Then came a medical ass who advised me to take cold baths for my health; a more sensible one advised the usual lukewarm Danube bath. That worked wonders, my belly improved, but my deafness remained and even became worse. This last winter I was really miserable, since I had frightful attacks of colic and again fell back into my previous condition. Thus I remained until about four weeks ago, when I went to Vering, thinking that my condition demanded a surgeon, and besides I had great confidence in him. He succeeded almost wholly in stopping the awful diarrhoea. He prescribed the lukewarm Danube bath, into which each time I had to pour a little bottle of strengthening stuff. He gave me no medicine of any kind until about four days ago, when he prescribed pills for my stomach and a kind of herb for my ear. Since then I can say I am feeling stronger and better, except that my ears sing and buzz continually, day and night. I can truly say that I am living a wretched life. For two years I have avoided almost all social gatherings because it is impossible for me to say to people "I am deaf ". If I belonged to any other profession it would be easier, but in my profession it is a frightful state. Then there are my enemies, who are numerous, what would they say about this? – In order to give you an idea of this singular deafness of mine, I must tell you that in the theatre I must get very close to the orchestra in order to understand the actor, and if I am a little distant I do not hear the high tones of the instruments or singers. It is curious that in conversation there are people who do not notice my condition at all; since I have generally been absent-minded, they account for it in that way. Often I can scarcely hear someone speaking softly, the tones, yes, but not the words. However, as soon as anyone shouts it is intolerable. Heaven knows what will happen to me, *Vering says that there will be an improvement but not a complete cure* – Already I have often cursed my Creator and my existence; *Plutarch* has taught me *resignation*. If possible I will bid defiance to my fate, although there will be moments in my life when I shall be the unhappiest of God's creatures. – I beg of you to say nothing of my condition to anybody, not even to *Lorchen* [Eleanore von Breuning]. I entrust the secret only to you, but I would be glad if you were to correspond with *Vering* on the subject. If my condition continues like this I shall come to you next spring. You can hire a house for me in some pretty place in the country, and for a half a year I shall become a peasant. This might bring about a change. Resignation, what a wretched refuge, and yet the only one remaining open to me. –

'You will forgive me for burdening you with a friend's troubles when you yourself have sorrow. – Stephan Breuning is here now and we are together almost daily. It does me so much good to revive the old emotions. He has really become a good, splendid young fellow, who knows a thing or two, and like all of us more or less has his heart in the right place. I have very good lodgings now which look on to the Bastei, and are doubly valuable because of my health. I believe I can arrange it for B[reuning] to come and live with me. – You shall have your Antioch* and also many of my musical compositions if you do not think they will cost you too much. Honestly, your love for art still gives me much happiness. If you will write to me how to manage it, I will send you all my compositions, already a goodly number and increasing daily – In return for the portrait of my grandfather which I beg you to send me by mail-coach as soon as possible, I am sending you that *of his grandson*, your good and affectionate Beethoven. It is to be published here by Artaria who has often asked me for one, as have others, including foreign art-dealers. I shall soon write to Stoffel [Christoph von Breuning] and give him a piece of my mind concerning his stubborn frame of mind. I will make his ears ring with the old friendship, he shall promise me by all that is holy not to annoy you further in your present troubled circumstances – I shall also write to good Lorchen. I have never forgotten one of you good people even though I have not written to you, but writing, as you know, was never my forte, even my best friends have not had letters from me in years. I live only in my notes and one composition is scarcely done before another is begun. As I am writing now, I often work on three or four pieces at once. – Write to me often and hereafter I will try to find time to write to you occasionally. Give warmest greetings to all including the good Madame Councillor [Madame von Breuning], and tell her "that I still occasionally have a *raptus*". As regards Koch, I do not at all wonder over the change. Fortune is round like a ball, and therefore does not always fall on the noblest and best – Concerning Ries, to whom I send hearty greetings, I will write to you in more detail about his son, although I think that he would have better luck in *Paris* than in *Vienna*. Vienna is overcrowded and even the most able find it extremely difficult to maintain themselves – In the autumn or winter I shall see what I can do for him, for at that time the public hurries back to the city – Farewell, good, faithful Wegeler; be assured of the love and friendship of

Your

Beethoven'

* Apparently a painting by Friedrich Füger, Director of the Vienna Academy of Art. Whether Beethoven was referring to the original or a popular print of it is not clear.

This letter is important for its descriptions of Beethoven's symptoms of deafness, which strengthen the conclusion that his was a nerve-type deafness. The buzzing in his ears, known as 'tinnitus', is symptomatic of nerve damage. Beethoven stated that he could not hear the *high* tones of the instruments or singers. Nerve degeneration usually starts and is most severe in the high pitches, progressing later to the lower ones. He could hear the tones, but not the words, of conversations, because consonant sounds, so necessary for word identification, are generally high pitched. His mention of the 'intolerable' distress caused when anyone shouted is a phenomenon of nerve-type deafness: up to a certain noise level the person can hear little or nothing, but beyond that level his hearing is as acute as formerly; hence shouting would indeed be intolerable and might cause true pain.

On 16 November he wrote in greater detail to Wegeler:

'My good Wegeler!

'I thank you for the new evidence of your concern on my behalf, all the more since I deserve so little at your hands – You want to know how it goes with me, what I am using. As little as I like to discuss such matters I prefer to do it with you rather than anyone else. – For several months Vering has had *vesicatories* placed on both my arms, which consist, as you know, of a certain bark.* This is a very unpleasant remedy, inasmuch as I am robbed of the free use of my arms for a few days (until the bark has had its effect) to say nothing of the pain. It is true I cannot deny that the buzzing and singing in my ears is somewhat less than formerly, especially in the left ear, where my deafness began. But so far my hearing has not improved in the least, and I am not sure but what it has grown rather weaker – My belly is in a better condition; especially when I have had the lukewarm baths for a few days I feel quite well for 8 or 10 days. I seldom take a tonic for my stomach; I am beginning to use the *herbs on the belly* as you suggested. – Vering will not hear of shower-baths, and I am thoroughly dissatisfied with him. He shows so little care and consideration for such an illness; if I did not go to him, which causes me a great deal of trouble, I should not see him at all. What do you think of [Dr] Schmidt?† I do not like to change, but it seems to me V is much too much of a practitioner to acquire many new ideas from reading – S seems to me a very different sort of man and, perhaps, would not be so negligent. – People speak wonders of

* The bark of the *Daphne Mezereum*.
† Johann Adam Schmidt, since 1784 a professor of anatomy at the Josefakademie for army doctors. In 1796 he became an army medical officer. Dr Schmidt was also the author of a number of scholarly works.

Beethoven was fortunate to find influential patrons among his musical friends at Vienna, such as, *left*, the Elector Maximilian Franz and, *right*, Count Karl Lichnowsky, with whom Beethoven lodged during his early days in the city. *Below*, a view of St Michael's Platz with the Hofburg Theatre, *c*.1800

The Theater-an-der-Wien in 1820, part of Vienna's thriving theatrical and music scene. Beethoven's *Fidelio* was first performed there. *Below*, Mozart and Salieri. While in Vienna Beethoven became acquainted with the composers

galvanism, what do you say to that? – A doctor told me that *in Berlin* he had seen a deaf and dumb child recover his hearing, and a man who had been deaf for seven years get well – I hear even that *your Schmidt* experiments with it. – I am living more pleasantly now, since I mingle more with people. You will scarcely believe how lonely and sad my life has been for the last two years. My bad hearing haunted me everywhere like a ghost and I fled – from mankind. I seemed like a misanthrope, and yet am far from being one. This change has been wrought by a dear fascinating girl who loves me and whom I love. There have been a few blessed moments within the last two years, and it is the first time that I feel that – marriage might bring me happiness. Unfortunately she is not of my station – and now – it would be impossible for me to marry. – I must still hustle about most actively. If it were not for my deafness, I should before now have travelled over half the world, and that I must do. – There is no greater delight for me than to practise and show my art. – Do not believe that I could be happy with you. What is there that would make me happier? Even your solicitude would pain me. I should see pity on your faces every moment and be even more unhappy. – What did those beautiful native regions give me, nothing except the hope of a better situation. This would have been mine now – but for this misfortune – Oh, if I were rid of this affliction I would embrace the world. Really, I feel that my youth is just beginning, for have I not always been in poor health? My physical strength has for some time past been steadily gaining and also my mental powers. Each day I move towards the goal which I sense but cannot describe, only in this way can your B live. – Do not speak of rest – I know of none but sleep, and woe is me that I must give up more time to it than formerly. Grant me but half freedom from my affliction, and then – as a complete and ripened man I shall return to you and renew the old feelings of friendship. You will see me as happy as it is possible to be here below, not unhappy – No, I cannot endure that – I will take fate by the throat, it shall not wholly overcome me – Oh, it would be so beautiful to live life a thousandfold – A quiet life – No, I feel I am no longer made for that. – Write to me as soon as you can – Help *Steffen* to make up his mind to secure an appointment of some kind in the *Teutonic Order*. There is too much wear and tear in the life here for his health, besides, he lives such an isolated existence that I cannot see how he is to get along. You know what it is like here, I will not say that social life might lessen *his fatigue*, but it is impossible to persuade him to go anywhere. A short time ago I had a musicale at my home with a select group, yet our friend – St. – did not turn up. – Advise him to take more rest and seek more composure, I have done my best in this

direction. Without these he will never again be either happy or well. –
Tell me in your next letter whether or not it matters if I send you a
great deal of my music, you can sell what you do not need and so get
back the post-money – my portrait – also – All possible lovely greetings
to L[orchen] – also Mama – also Christoph – You love me a little, do
you not. Be as well assured of this as of the friendship of

Your Bthvn'

In view of the relation in which Wegeler stood to the Breuning
family, Beethoven might have well said more about 'Steffen' but not
easily less. Even in the first letter something of patronising condescension in the tone makes itself felt, which becomes far too pronounced
when he speaks of him in the second letter. One feels that Breuning
had been made sensible, to a painful degree, how great his friend had
grown.

When Beethoven met Stephan von Breuning again in 1801, it was
impossible that it be on such terms as those on which they had parted in
1796. Breuning had passed this interval of five years in a small provincial town, Mergentheim, in the monotonous routine of a petty office,
in the service of the Teutonic Order – a semi-military, semi-religious
institution which had so sunk in grandeur and power as to be little
more than a venerable name – a relic of the past. In the same service he
had now returned to Vienna. How Beethoven had been employed, and
how he had risen, we have seen. Thus, their relative positions in society
had completely changed. Beethoven now moved familiarly in circles to
which Breuning could have access only by his or some other friend's
protection.

Comment should now be made concerning the 'dear fascinating girl
who loves me and whom I love'. This was most probably the Countess
Giulietta (or Julia) Guicciardi, for reasons which will appear. She was
born on 23 November 1784. Her father was an Austrian Court Councillor who was transferred from Trieste to Vienna in 1800; her mother
was born Susanne Brunsvik, an aunt of the two sisters Therese and
Josephine Brunsvik, whom Beethoven had met in May 1799.

Judging from the two letters to Wegeler just cited, one sees that
after withdrawing from society two years before, because of his
oncoming deafness, Beethoven experienced fleeting moments of happiness with this girl and was brought back to the company of men by
its effect. After the Guicciardi family had taken up residence in
Vienna, the meetings were doubtless much more frequent. Meanwhile
with the passing reference to a marriage which gives way to concern
over his work, we find an example of the composer's decision to plunge

into work when faced with the possibility of a permanent attachment with a woman.

The Countess Guicciardi is traditionally described as having had a good share of personal attractions, and is known to have been a fine-looking woman even in advanced years. She appears to have possessed a mind of fair powers, cultivated and accomplished to the degree then common to persons of her rank; but it is not known that she was in any way eminently distinguished, unless for musical taste and skill as a pianist. To come to the capital from a small, distant provincial town when hardly of an age to enter society and to find herself so soon distinguished by the particular attentions and evident admiration of a man of Beethoven's social position and fame might well dazzle the imagination of a girl of sixteen. It might dispose her, especially if she possessed more than common musical taste and talents, to return in a certain degree the affection proffered to her by the distinguished author of the Symphony, the Quartet, the Septet, the *Prometheus* music, and so many wonderful sonatas, by the unrivalled pianist, the generous, impulsive, enthusiastic artist, although unprepossessing in person and unable to offer either wealth or a title. There was romance in the affair. Besides these considerations there are traditions and reminiscences of old friends of the composer all tending to confirm the opinion of Schindler that the 'fascinating girl' was indeed the young Countess Guicciardi.

It is proper to state, before going further, that the young lady married Count Wenzel Robert Gallenberg, a prolific composer of ballet and occasional music, on 3 November 1803. The young pair soon left Vienna for Italy and were in Naples in the spring of 1806; for Gallenberg was one of the composers of the music for the fêtes, on the occasion of Joseph Bonaparte's assumption of the crown of the Two Sicilies.

In November 1852, Jahn had an interview with the Countess Gallenberg. On so delicate a topic as Beethoven's passion for her fifty years before reticence was natural; but had the affair in truth been of the importance that others have given it, some hint must have confessed it. Yet there is nothing of the kind in his notes of the conversation. Here they are:

'Beethoven was her teacher. — He had his music sent to her and was extremely severe until the correct interpretation was reached down to the smallest detail. — He laid stress upon a light manner of playing. — He easily became angry, threw down his music and tore it. — He would accept no pay, though he was very poor, except linen under the pretext that the Countess had sewed it.'

It is hard to believe that this was Beethoven's ordinary attitude towards remuneration for lessons, since in most cases his reason for submitting to the drudgery of teaching was for the money he earned. Therefore, if the Countess's memory is correct, some consideration of his pupil must have dictated this stand. Perhaps it was her relationship to the Countess Deym, to whom he also gave lessons gratis. The notes conclude: 'Beethoven was very ugly, but noble, refined in feeling and cultured. As a rule, Beethoven was shabbily dressed.'

There is but one well-authenticated fact to be added, namely, that Beethoven kept up his intercourse with the family Guicciardi certainly as late as May or June 1803, that is, to within six months of the young lady's marriage. A careful survey and comparison both of the published data and of the private traditions and hints gleaned during a residence of several years in Vienna, result in the opinion (an opinion, note, not a statement resting on competent evidence) that Beethoven at length decided to offer Countess Julia his hand; that she was not indisposed to accept it; and that one of her parents consented to the match, but the other, probably the father, refused to entrust the happiness of his daughter to a man without rank, fortune or permanent engagement; a man, too, of character and temperament so peculiar, and afflicted with the incipient stages of an infirmity which, if not arrested and cured, must deprive him of all hope of obtaining any high and remunerative official appointment and at length compel him to abandon his career as the great pianoforte virtuoso. As the Guicciardis themselves were not wealthy, prudence forbade such a marriage. Be all this as it may, this much is certain: Beethoven did not marry the Countess Julia Guicciardi; Count Wenzel Robert Gallenberg did.

Once again an affair was ended. The testimony of Wegeler, Breuning, Romberg, Ries, has been cited to the point that Beethoven 'was never without a love, and generally deeply engrossed in it'.

In short, Beethoven's experience was precisely that of many an impulsive man of genius, who for one cause or another never married and therefore never knew the calm and quiet, but unchanging affection of happy conjugal life. One all-absorbing but temporary passion, lasting until its object is married to a more favoured lover, is forgotten in another destined to end in like manner, until, at length, all faith in the possibility of a permanent, constant attachment to one person is lost.

CHAPTER 9

The Years 1802 and 1803

The Heiligenstadt Testament –
The 'Eroica' Symphony

The impatient Beethoven, vexed at the tardy improvement of his health under the treatment of Vering, made that change of physicians contemplated in his letter to Wegeler. This was done some time in the winter of 1801–2, and is all the foundation there is for Schindler's story of 'a serious illness in the first months of this year for which he was treated by the highly esteemed physician Dr Schmidt'. The remarkable list of compositions and publications belonging to this year is proof sufficient that he suffered no physical disability of such a nature as seriously to interrupt his ordinary vocations.

Concerning the failure of his project to follow the example set in 1800 and give a concert towards the close of the winter in the theatre, we learn all we know from a letter written by his brother Carl to Breitkopf and Härtel dated 22 April 1802. Therein we read:

'My brother would have written to you himself, but he is ill-disposed towards everything because the Director of the Theatre, Baron von Braun, who, as is known, is a stupid and rude fellow, refused him the use of the Theatre for his concert and gave it to other really mediocre artists. I believe it must vex him greatly to see himself so shabbily treated, particularly as the Baron has no cause and my brother has dedicated several works to his wife.'

Enclosed in the letter was the following message from Beethoven to the firm: 'I reserve the privilege of writing soon to you high-born gentlemen myself – many business matters – and also many vexations – render me utterly useless for some things for a time – meanwhile you may trust my brother *implicitly*, who in fact manages all my affairs.'

Part of a letter written on 13 July to Breitkopf and Härtel affords another illustration of Beethoven's excellent common sense and discrimination in all that pertained to his art.

'. . . Concerning the arrangements of the pieces, I am heartily glad that you rejected them. The *unnatural rage* now prevalent to transplant even *pianoforte pieces* to stringed instruments, instruments so utterly opposite to each other in all respects, ought to come to an end. I insist stoutly that only *Mozart* could arrange his pianoforte pieces for other instruments, and also *Haydn* – and, without wishing to put myself in the class of these great men, I assert the same touching *my pianoforte sonatas also*, since not only would whole passages have to be omitted and changed, but also – things would have to be added, and here lies the obstacle, to *overcome which one must either be the master himself* or at least have the same *skill and inventive power*. – I have transcribed only one of my sonatas for string quartet, yielding to great persuasion, and I certainly know that it would not be an easy matter for another to do as well.'

The difficulties here mentioned, it will be noticed, are those of transcribing pianoforte music for other instruments; the contrary operation is so comparatively easy that Beethoven rarely performed it himself, but left it for the most part to young musicians, whose work he revised and corrected.

When one looked down from the Kahlenberg towards Vienna in the bright, sweet springtime, the interesting country was almost worthy of Tennyson's description:

> 'It lies
> Deep-meadowed, happy, fair with orchard-lawns
> And bowery hollows, crown'd with summer sea.'

Conspicuous were the villages, Döbling, hard by the Nussdorf bounds of the city, and Heiligenstadt, divided from Döbling by a ridge of higher land in a deep gorge.

Dr Schmidt having enjoined Beethoven to spare his hearing as much as possible, he removed for the summer to the place last named. There is much and good reason to believe that his rooms were in a large peasant house still standing, on the elevated plain beyond the village on the road to Nussdorf, then probably quite solitary. In those years, there was from his windows an unbroken view across fields, the Danube and the Marchfeld, to the Carpathian mountains that line the horizon. A few minutes' walk citywards brought him to the baths of Heiligenstadt; or, in the opposite direction, to the secluded valley in which at another period he composed the 'Pastoral' Symphony. The vast increase of Vienna and its environs in population has caused corresponding changes, but in 1802, that peasant house seems to have offered him everything he could desire; fresh air, sun, green fields, delightful walks, bathing, easy access to his physician, and yet a degree of solitude which is now not easy to conceive as having been attainable so near the capital.

The seclusion of Heiligenstadt was of itself so seductive to Beethoven that the prudence of Dr Schmidt in advising him to withdraw so much from society may be doubted; the more, because the benefit to his hearing proved to be small or none. It gave him too many lonely hours in which to brood over his calamity; it enabled him still to flatter himself that his secret was yet safe; it led him to defer, too long for his peace of mind, the bitter moment of his confession; and consequently to deprive himself needlessly of the tender compassion and ready sympathy of friends, whose lips were sealed so long as he withheld his confidence. But, in truth, the secret so jealously guarded was already known, but who could inform him of it?

It was well for Beethoven, when the time came for him to return to the city, and to resume the duties and obligations of his profession. To what depths of despondency he sometimes sank in those solitary hours at Heiligenstadt is shown by a remarkable and most touching paper, written there just before his return to town, but never seen by other eyes until after his death. Although addressed to and intended for both his brothers, it is, as Schindler has remarked, 'surprising and singular' that the name 'Johann' is left utterly blank throughout – not even being indicated by the usual '. . .'. It is couched in terms of energetic expression, rising occasionally to eloquence – somewhat rude and unpolished indeed, but, perhaps, for that reason the more striking. The manuscript is so carefully written, and disfigured by so few erasures and corrections, as to prove the great pains taken with it before the copy was made.

A paragraph by Ries upon Beethoven's deafness, in which he relates a circumstance alluded to in the document, is its most fitting introduction:

'The beginning of his hard hearing was a matter upon which he was so sensitive that one had to be careful not to make him feel his deficiency by loud speech. When he failed to understand a thing he generally attributed it to his absent-mindedness, to which, indeed, he was subject in a great degree. He lived much in the country, whither I went often to take a lesson from him. At times, at 8 o'clock in the morning after breakfast he would say: "Let us first take a short walk." We went, and frequently did not return till 3 or 4 o'clock, after having made a meal in some village. On one of these wanderings Beethoven gave me the first striking proof of his loss of hearing, concerning which Stephan von Breuning had already spoken to me. I called his attention to a shepherd who was piping very agreeably in the woods on a flute made of a twig of elder. For half an hour Beethoven could hear nothing, and though I assured him that it was the same with me (which was not the case), he became extremely quiet and morose. When occasionally he seemed to be merry, it was generally to the extreme of boisterousness; but this happened seldom.'

Following is the text of the document:

'For my brothers Carl and   Beethoven
'Oh you men who think or say that I am malevolent, stubborn or misanthropic, how greatly do you wrong me. You do not know the secret cause which makes me seem that way to you. From childhood on my heart and soul have been full of the tender feeling of goodwill, and I was ever inclined to accomplish great things. But, think that for 6 years now I have been hopelessly afflicted, made worse by senseless physicians, from year to year deceived with hopes of improvement, finally compelled to face the prospect of *a lasting malady* (whose cure will take years or, perhaps be impossible). Though born with a fiery, active temperament, ever susceptible to the diversions of society, I was soon compelled to withdraw myself, to live life alone. If at times I tried to forget all this, oh how harshly was I flung back by the doubly sad experience of my bad hearing. Yet it was impossible for me to say to people, "Speak louder, shout, for I am deaf." Ah, how could I possibly admit an infirmity in the *one sense* which ought to be more perfect in me than in others, a sense which I once possessed in the highest perfection, a perfection such as few in my profession enjoy or ever have enjoyed. – Oh I cannot do it, therefore forgive me when you see me draw back when I would have gladly mingled with you. My misfortune is doubly painful to me because I am bound to be misunderstood; for me there can be no relaxation with my fellow men, no refined conversations, no mutual exchange of ideas. I must live almost alone like one who has been banished, I can mix with society only as much as true necessity demands. If I approach near to people a hot terror seizes upon me and I fear being exposed to the danger that my condition might be noticed. Thus it has been during the last six months which I have spent in the country. By ordering me to spare my hearing as much as possible, my intelligent doctor almost fell in with my own present frame of mind, though sometimes I ran counter to it by yielding to my desire for

companionship. But what a humiliation for me when someone standing next to me heard a flute in the distance and *I heard nothing*, or someone heard a *shepherd singing* and again I heard nothing. Such incidents drove me almost to despair, a little more of that and I would have ended my life – it was only *my art* that held me back. Ah, it seemed to me impossible to leave the world until I had brought forth all that I felt was within me. So I endured this wretched existence – truly wretched for so susceptible a body which can be thrown by a sudden change from the best condition to the very worst. – *Patience*, they say, is what I must now choose for my guide, and I have done so – I hope my determination will remain firm to endure until it pleases the inexorable Parcae to break the thread. Perhaps I shall get better, perhaps not, I am ready. – Forced to become a philosopher already in my 28th year, oh it is not easy, and for the artist much more difficult than for anyone else. – Divine One, thou seest my inmost soul, thou knowest that therein dwells the love of mankind and the desire to do good. – Oh fellow men, when at some point you read this, consider then that you have done me an injustice; someone who has had misfortune may console himself to find a similar case to his, who despite all the limitations of Nature nevertheless did everything within his powers to become accepted among worthy artists and men. – You my brothers Carl and   as soon as I am dead if Dr Schmid is still alive ask him in my name to describe my malady, and attach this written document to his account of my illness so that so far as is possible at least the world may become reconciled to me after my death. – At the same time I declare you two to be the heirs to my small fortune (if so it can be called); divide it fairly; bear with and help each other. What injury you have done me you know was long ago forgiven. To you, brother Carl, I give special thanks for the attachment you have shown me of late. It is my wish that you may have a better and freer life than I have had. Recommend *virtue* to your children; it alone, not money, can make them happy. I speak from experience; this was what upheld me in time of misery. Thanks to it and to my art I did not end my life by suicide – Farewell and love each other – I thank all my friends, particularly *Prince Lichnowsky* and *Professor Schmidt* – I would like the instruments from Prince L to be preserved by one of you, but not to be the cause of strife between you, and as soon as they can serve you a better purpose, then sell them. How happy I shall be if I can still be helpful to you in my grave – so be it – With joy I hasten to meet death – If it comes before I have had the chance to develop all my artistic capacities, it will still be coming too soon despite my harsh fate and I should probably wish it later – yet even so I should be happy, for would it not free me from a state of endless suffering? – Come *when* thou wilt, I shall meet thee bravely – Farewell and do not wholly forget me when I am dead, I deserve this from you, for during my lifetime I was thinking of you often and of ways to make you happy – please be so –

Ludwig van Beethoven
(seal)'

'Heiglnstadt,
6 October
1802'

'For my brothers Carl and
to be read and executed after my death.'

'Heiglnstadt, 10 October 1802, thus I bid you farewell – and indeed sadly – yes, that fond hope – which I brought here with me, to be cured to a degree at least – this I must now wholly abandon. As the leaves of autumn fall and are withered – so likewise has my hope been blighted – I leave here – almost as I came – even the high courage – which often inspired me in the beautiful days of summer – has disappeared – Oh Providence – grant me at last but one day *of pure joy* – it is so long since real joy echoed in my heart – Oh when – Oh when, Oh Divine One – shall I feel it again in the temple of nature and of mankind – Never? – No – Oh that would be too hard.'

De profundis clamavit! And yet in that retirement whence came a paper of such profound sadness was wrought out the Symphony in D (the Second Symphony); a work whose grand and imposing introduction – brilliant Allegro, a Larghetto so lovely, so pure and amiably conceived, written in the scenes which gave inspiration to the divine Pastorale of which its serene tranquillity seems the precursor; a Scherzo as merry, wayward, skipping and charming as anything possible; and a Finale, the very intoxication of a spirit intoxicated with fire – made it, like the Quartets, an era both in the life of its author and in the history of instrumental music. In life, as in music, the more profoundly the depths of feeling are sounded in the Adagio, the more merry to the verge of boisterousness the Scherzo which follows. But who, reading that in October hope had been abandoned and the high courage which had often inspired him in the beautiful days of summer had disappeared, could anticipate that in November, through the wonderful elasticity of his nature, his mind would have so recovered its tone as to leave no trace visible of the so recent depression and gloom?

Perhaps the mere act of giving his feelings vent in that extraordinary *promemoria* may have brought on the crisis, and from that moment the reaction may have begun.

Two interesting anecdotes from Ries may be introduced here:

'Count Browne made a rather long sojourn about this time in Baden near Vienna, where I was called upon frequently to play Beethoven's music in the evening in the presence of enthusiastic Beethovenians, sometimes from notes, sometimes by heart. Here I had an opportunity to learn how in the majority of cases a *name* alone is sufficient to characterise everything in a composition as beautiful and excellent, or mediocre and bad. One day, weary of playing without notes, I improvised a march without a thought as to its merit or any ulterior purpose. An old countess who actually tormented Beethoven with her devotion, went into ecstasies over it, thinking it was a new composition of his, which I, in order to make sport of her and the other enthusiasts, affirmed only too quickly. Unhappily Beethoven came to Baden the next day. He had scarcely entered Count Browne's room in the evening when the old countess began to speak of his most admirable and glorious march. Imagine my embarrassment! Knowing well that Beethoven could not tolerate the old countess, I hurriedly drew him aside and whispered to him that I had merely meant to make sport of her foolishness. To my good fortune he accepted the explanation in good part, but my embarrassment grew when I was called upon to repeat the march, which turned out worse since Beethoven stood at my side. He was overwhelmed with praise on all sides and his genius lauded, he listening in a perturbed manner and with growing rage until he found relief in a roar of laughter. Later he remarked to me: "You see, my dear Ries, those are the great cognoscenti, who wish to judge every composition so correctly and severely. Only give them the name of their favourite; they will need nothing more."

'This march, however, led to one good result: Count Browne immediately commissioned Beethoven to compose three Marches for Pianoforte, four hands, which were dedicated to Princess Esterhazy (Op. 45).

'Beethoven composed part of the second march while giving me a lesson on a sonata – a thing which still seems incomprehensible to me – which I had to play that evening in a little concert at the house of the count mentioned above. I was also to play the marches with him on the same occasion.

'While the latter was taking place, young Count P . . ., sitting in the doorway leading to the next room, spoke so loud and so continuously to a pretty woman, that Beethoven, after several efforts had been made to secure quiet, suddenly took my hands from the keys in the middle of the music, jumped up and said very loudly, "I will not play for such swine!"

'All efforts to get him to return to the pianoforte were in vain; he would not even allow me to play the sonata. So the music came to an end in the midst of a general ill humour.'

According to Jahn's papers the following came from Czerny: 'In composing, Beethoven tested his pieces at the pianoforte until he found them to his liking, and sang the while. His voice in singing was hideous. It was thus that Czerny heard him at work on one of the four-hand marches while waiting in a side-room.'

The following letter to Zmeskall (to which the recipient appended the date, November 1802) is whimsically written on both sides of a strip of very ordinary coarse writing-paper fourteen and a half inches long by four and three-quarters wide:

'You may, my dear Z., talk bluntly to Walter about my affair, first because he deserves it and then because since the belief has gone forth that I am no longer on good terms with Walter I am pestered by the whole swarm of pianoforte makers wishing to serve me – and gratis. Each one wants to build a pianoforte for me just to my liking. Thus Reicha was urgently begged by the man who made a pianoforte for him to persuade me to let him make me one, and he is one of the better people at whose place I have seen good instruments – Give him to understand therefore that I will pay him 30 florins, whereas I might have had one from all the others for nothing. But I will pay 30 florins only on condition that it be of mahogany and I also want the one string [*una corde*] pedal. If he does not agree to this, make it plain to him that I shall choose one of the others from whom I shall order, and I shall also introduce him to *Haydn* so that he may see his instrument. A Frenchman, who is a stranger, is coming to me at about 12 o'clock today. Herr R[eicha] and I will have the pleasure of having to *display my art on a piano by Jakesch – Ad notam –* if you would like also to come we should have a good time, for afterwards we, Reicha, our miserable Imperial Baron and the Frenchman, will dine together – You do not need to don a *black coat* as we shall be *a party of men only*.'

Another letter to Zmeskall (who noted on it the date 13 November 1802) runs as follows:

'Dear Z. – Cancel definitely your *music-making* at Förster's, *nothing else can be done* –

'We shall rehearse at *your house tomorrow morning* at half-past 8 and the production will be at my house at eleven –

'Addio excellent plenipotentiarius regni Beethovenensis.

'The rascals have been jailed as they deserved *in their own handwriting.*'

This second letter makes reference to two separate matters that deserve attention. 'At my house' was no longer in the Hamberger House on the Bastion, but in the one pointed out by Czerny: 'Beethoven lived a little later (about 1802) on the Petersplatz, the corner house beside the Guard-house, *vis à vis* of my present lodgings, in the fourth [?] storey, where I visited him as often as I did [in the Tiefer Graben]. If you will give me the pleasure of a visit (No. 576 beside Daum, second storey) I will show you the windows. There I visited several times every week.'

What whim could have induced Beethoven to remove to this house with the bells of St Peter's on one side and those of St Stephen's sounding down upon him on the other, and he so suffering with his ears?

In his note to Zmeskall, Beethoven referred to 'the production'. Production of what? The new String Quintet, Op. 29, no doubt. The letter ends· 'The rascals have been jailed as they deserved *in their own handwriting.*' The 'rascals' were Artaria and Co., who had unexpectedly made a printing of the Quintet and who were forced to nullify, temporarily, this edition by affixing their signature to a declaration, dated 12 November 1802. The Quintet was dedicated to Count Moritz von Fries who, it will be seen, was implicated along with the publishers in the unpleasantness that developed.

According to Ries:

'Beethoven's Violin Quintet (Opus 29) in C major had been sold to a publisher in Leipzig, but was stolen in Vienna and published suddenly by A. [Artaria] and Co. Having been copied in a single night, it was full of errors; whole measures even were missing. Beethoven's conduct in the matter is without parallel. He asked A. to send the fifty copies which had been printed to me for correction, but at the same time instructed me to use ink on the wretched paper and as coarsely as possible; also to cross out several lines so that it would be impossible to make use of a single copy or sell it. The scratching out was particularly in the Scherzo. I obeyed his instructions implicitly, and A. was compelled to melt the plates in order to avoid a lawsuit.'

A long letter to Breitkopf and Härtel, dated 13 November 1802, gives a lively picture of the excitement which the incident aroused in Beethoven:

'I write hurriedly to inform you of only the most important things — know then, that while I was in the country for my health, the *arch-scoundrel Artaria* borrowed the *Quintet* from *Count Fries on the pretence that it was already published and in existence here* and that they wanted it for the purpose of *re-engraving because their copy was faulty* — as a matter of fact they intended to rejoice *the public* with it a few days ago — Good Count Fr., deceived and not reflecting that a piece of rascality might be in it, gave it to them. He could not ask me, I was not here — but fortunately I learned of the matter in time; it was on *Tuesday of this week.* In my zeal to save my honour and to *prevent* as quickly as possible *your suffering any loss,* I offered two new works to these contemptible persons if they would suppress the entire edition, but a cooler-headed friend who was with me asked, *Do you want to reward these rascals?* The case was finally closed under certain conditions; they assuring me that *whatever you print they would reprint.* These *generous scoundrels* decided therefore to wait three weeks, during which time your copies would have appeared here, before issuing their own (insisting that Count F. had made them a present of the copy). *At the end of this period the contract was to have ended,* and *in return I was to give them a work* which I value at 40 ducats at least. Before this contract was closed, there comes my good brother as if sent by heaven, he hurries *to* C[ount] *F.*; the whole thing is the *biggest swindle* in the world, the *details,* how neatly they kept me out of C[ount] F's way and all the rest in the next letter. — Now I am going to F. too, and the *enclosed Revers* may prove to you that I did all in my power to protect you from injury — and my statement of the case may serve to show you that *no sacrifice was too great* for me to save my honour and *to save you from loss.*

'From the Revers you will see what measures must be adopted, and I think you should make all possible haste to send copies here and if possible at the same price *as that of the rascals.* — Sonnleithner and I will take all further measures which *seem to us good, so that their entire edition may be destroyed.* — Please take good notice that *Mollo and Artaria* are really combined in *one firm,* that is, a whole *family of scoundrels.* — The dedication *to Fries* I hope was not forgotten inasmuch as my brother wrote it on the first sheet. — *I have written the Revers for you myself* since my *poor brother* is so very busy, and yet he *did all he could* to save you and me. In the confusion he lost a faithful dog, which he called his favourite; he deserves to be thanked by you personally as I have done on my own account. – Just remember that from Tuesday to *late last night* I devoted myself almost wholly to this matter; and the mere thought of this rascally stroke may serve to make you realise how unpleasant it is for me to have anything to do with such wretched people –

L. v. Beethoven'

'"Revers

'"The undersigned pledges himself under no circumstances to send out or to sell here or elsewhere the Quintet received from *Herr Graf Fries* composed by Lud. v. Beethoven until the original edition shall have been in circulation *in Vienna* fourteen days.

Vienna, 12 November 1802   Artaria Comp."

'This Revers is signed by the Comp. in its own hand.

'Use the following: to be had à Vienne chez Artaria Comp., à Münich chez Firma Halm, à Frankfort chez Gayl et Hädler, perhaps also in Leipzig chez Meysel – the price is 2 florins, *two gulden Vienna standard*.

'I got hold of twelve copies, the only ones which they promised me from the beginning, and made corrections from them – *the engraving is abominable*. Make use of all this, you see that on every side we have them in our hands and can proceed against them in the courts –

'NB Any measures, even personal, taken against A. will have my approval –'

The composer sought to strengthen his position by the following in the *Wiener Zeitung*, 22 January 1803:

'TO THE LOVERS OF MUSIC

'In informing the public that the original Quintet in C long ago advertised by me has been published by Breitkopf and Härtel in Leipzig, I declare at the same time that I have no interest in the edition published simultaneously by Herrn. Artaria and Mollo in Vienna. I am the more compelled to make this declaration since this edition is very faulty, incorrect, and utterly useless to players, whereas Herren Breitkopf and Härtel, the legal owners of the Quintet, have done all in their power to produce the work as handsomely as possible.'

Artaria felt compelled to defend the integrity of his house by filing a petition in the High Police Court on 14 February 1803, demanding a retraction by Beethoven of his false charges.

Having examined the facts with, perhaps, a somewhat cooler head than Beethoven's, the court ruled on 26 September against him and in favour of the publishers. They ordered the composer to retract his announcement of 22 January in a written statement to be submitted to the court prior to its publication. The court added in a statement on 12 October that should Beethoven fail to comply with this decision, he must realise that it would give full assistance to the plaintiffs to secure their rights through process of law. A report dated 4 December 1803, shows that Beethoven was summoned to court, was told in the clearest way possible to proceed with the disavowal of the announcement so injurious to Artaria and Mollo, yet he remained unwilling to write out the retraction.

On 31 March 1804, however, the following appeared in the *Wiener Zeitung*:

'ANNOUNCEMENT TO THE PUBLIC

'After having inserted a statement in the *Wiener Zeitung* of 22 January 1803, in which I publicly declared that the edition of my Quintet published by Mollo did not appear under my supervision, was faulty in the extreme and useless to players, the undersigned hereby revokes the statement to the extent of saying that Herren Mollo and Co. have no interest in this edition, feeling that I owe such a declaration to do justice to Herren Mollo and Co. before a public entitled to respect.

Ludwig van Beethoven'

Beethoven never did write the retraction of his charges against Artaria despite a further judgment by the Magistrate of Vienna of 8 March 1805, which reiterated the composer's obligation and established the right of the plaintiff to publish himself such a retraction at the expense of the defendant, a right which Artaria never used. Instead, an agreement was signed by the lawyers of the two parties on 9 September 1805 concerning future editions of the work.

It is now necessary to turn to the task of examining a broad tissue of mingled fact and misrepresentation and severing the truth from the error in the matter of the relations which existed between Beethoven and his brothers in these years.

The general charge brought by Ries against Caspar and Johann van Beethoven is this:

'His brothers sought in particular to keep all his intimate friends away from him, and no matter what wrongs they did him, of which he was convinced, they cost him only a few tears and all was immediately forgotten. On such occasions he was in the habit of saying: "But they are my brothers nevertheless," and the friend received a rebuke

for his good nature and frankness. The brothers attained their purpose in causing the withdrawal from him of many friends, especially
when, because of his hard hearing, it became difficult to converse
with him.'

Now, what is really known of Carl Caspar and Johann is not fitted to
convey any very exalted idea of their characters. The same Frau Karth,
who remembered Ludwig in his youth as always 'gentle and lovable',
related that Caspar was less kindly in his disposition, 'proud and presumptuous', and that Johann 'was a bit stupid, yet very good-natured'.
Caspar, like Ludwig, was very passionate, but more violent in his sudden wrath; Johann, slow to wrath and placable. Notwithstanding the
poverty of his youth and early manhood, it is not known that Caspar
was avaricious; but Johann had felt too bitterly the misery of want and
dependence, and became penurious. Now, the onus of Ries's charges is
this: first, that Caspar thrust himself impertinently into his brother's
business; second, that both brothers intrigued to isolate Beethoven
from his intimate friends and that their machinations were in many
cases successful.

To the first point it is to be remarked: besides Beethoven's often
expressed disinclination to engage personally in negotiations for the
sale of his works – although when he did he showed no lack of a keen
eye to profits – his physical and mental condition at this period of his
life often rendered the assistance of an agent indispensable. Accounts
were to be kept with half a dozen publishers; letters received upon
business were numerous and often demanded prompt replies; proof-
sheets were constantly arriving for revision and correction; copyists
required supervision; an abundance of minor matters continually
coming up and needing attention when Beethoven might to be on his
long rambles over hill and dale, the last man to be found in an emer-
gency. One asks with astonishment, how could so obvious a necessity
for a confidential agent have escaped notice? Who should or could this
agent be but his brother Caspar? He held an honourable place in a
public office, he was a musician by education and fully competent to
render valuable service in that 'fearful period of arrangements' – as it
is well known he did. What would have justly been said of Beethoven
if he had passed by one so eminently qualified for the task and had
transferred the burden from his own shoulders to those of other
friends?

In Ries's paragraph upon the efforts of Beethoven's brothers to keep
all the composer's friends away from him it is easy to read between the
lines that it was Ries himself who oft was 'rebuked for his good nature

and frankness', which of itself to some extent lessens the force of the charge. But it is best met by the first half of the Heiligenstadt Will, or Testament, which, along with the confessions to Wegeler and Amenda, open to our knowledge an inner life of the writer studiously concealed from his protégé. In this solemn document, written as he supposed upon the brink of the grave, Beethoven touches upon this very question. We learn from his own affecting words that the cause of his separation from friends lay, *not* in the machinations of his brothers, but from his own sensitiveness. He records for future use what he cannot now explain without disclosing his jealously guarded secret. That record now serves a double purpose; it relieves Caspar and Johann from a portion of the odium so long cast upon their memories, and proves Ries to be, in part at least, in error, without impugning his veracity. It is very probable Ries never saw the Will.

In 1802 began the publication of a polemical literary journal in Berlin called the *Freymüthige*, and an article in No. 58 (12 April), on the 'Amusements of the Viennese after Carnival', informs us: 'Beethoven has for a short time past been engaged, at a considerable salary, by the Theater-an-der-Wien, and will soon produce at that playhouse an oratorio of his composition entitled *Christus am Ölberg*.'

Whether Beethoven had talents for operatic composition, no one could yet know; but his works had already spread to Paris, London, Edinburgh, and had gained him the fame of being the greatest living instrumental composer – Father Haydn of course excepted – and this much might be accepted as certain: viz., that his name alone would secure the theatre from pecuniary loss in the production of *one* work; and, perhaps – who could foretell? – he might develop powers in this new field which would raise him to the level of even Cherubini! He was personally known to the impresario Schikaneder, having played in the old theatre, and his *Prometheus* music was a success at the Court Theatre. So he, too, was engaged. Thus Schikaneder – that strange compound of wit and absurdity; of poetic instinct and grotesque humour; of shrewd and profitable enterprise and lavish prodigality; who lived like a prince and died like a pauper – has connected his name honourably with Beethoven.

The first mention of this appointment is in a letter from brother Johann to Breitkopf and Härtel, dated 12 February 1803: 'You have heard by now that my brother has been engaged by the Wiedener Theatre, he is to write an opera, is in charge of the orchestra, can conduct, when necessary, because there is a director already available there every day.' This was followed by a notice in the 2 August issue of the Leipzig *Zeitung für die Elegante Welt* written by a correspondent under date of 29 June: 'Abbé Vogler is now writing an opera by H[uber], and Beethoven one by Schikaneder.' But in truth Beethoven was still preoccupied with the task of finishing the 'Eroica' and was not able to put his mind on opera until late autumn.

An immediate result of Beethoven's engagement at the theatre was an opportunity to give a concert, for which he composed his oratorio, *Christus am Ölberg*.

The author of the oratorio text was Franz Huber. Beethoven referred to their collaboration in a letter written on 23 January 1824: '*Christus am Ölberg* was written by me and the poet in a period of 14 days, but the poet was musical and had already written many things for music. I was able to consult with him at any moment.' In a letter written nearer the time of composition (to Breitkopf and Härtel in the next year) he speaks of it as the labour of 'a few weeks'. Therefore it seems clear from Beethoven's own references that the oratorio must have been written in a short time, all at once, and probably just before it was to be rehearsed.

The *Wiener Zeitung* of Saturday 26 March and Wednesday 30 March 1803 contained the following:

'NOTICE

'On the 5th (not the 4th) of April, Herr Ludwig van Beethoven will produce a new oratorio set to music by him, *Christus am Ölberg*, in the RI Privil.* Theater-an-der-Wien. The other pieces to be performed will be announced on the large billboard.'

The final general rehearsal was held in the theatre in the morning of the day of performance, Tuesday 5 April. On that morning, as was often the case when Beethoven needed assistance in his labours, young Ries was called to him early – about 5 o'clock. He gives the following description:

'I found him in bed, writing on *separate* sheets of paper. To my question what it was he answered, "*Trombones*". The trombones also played from *these* sheets at the performance.

'Had someone forgotten to copy these parts? Were they an afterthought? I was too young at the time to note the artistic interest of the incident; but probably the trombones were an afterthought, as Beethoven might as easily have had the *uncopied parts* as the copied ones. The rehearsal began at eight o'clock in the morning . . . It was a terrible

* Royal Imperial Privilegen – i.e. the Court Theatre.

rehearsal, and at half-past two everybody was exhausted and more or less dissatisfied.

'Prince Karl Lichnowsky, who attended the rehearsal from the beginning, had sent for bread and butter, cold meat and wine, in large baskets. He pleasantly asked all to help themselves, and this was done with both hands, the result being that good nature was restored again. Then the Prince requested that the oratorio be rehearsed once more from the beginning, so that it might go well in the evening and Beethoven's first work in this genre be worthily presented. And so the rehearsal began again. The concert began at six o'clock, but was so long that a few pieces were not performed.'

The works actually performed were the first and second Symphonies, the third Pianoforte Concerto in C minor and *Christus am Ölberg*. As no copy of the printed programme has been discovered, there is no means of deciding what else had been originally planned; but pieces like the 'Adelaide', 'Ah, perfido!' or the trio 'Tremate, empi, tremate' suggest themselves as vocal pieces well fitted to break the monotony of such a mass of orchestral music. It seems strange – knowing as we do Beethoven's vast talent for improvisation – that no extempore performance is reported.

Beethoven must have felt no small confidence in the power of his name to awaken the curiosity and interest of the musical public, for according to the *Allgemeine Musikalische Zeitung*, he doubled the prices of the first chairs, tripled those of the reserved and demanded twelve ducats (instead of four florins) for each box. But it was his first public appearance as a dramatic vocal composer, and on his posters he had several days before announced that all the pieces performed would be of his composition. The result, however, answered his expectations, for the concert yielded him 1,800 florins.

Seyfried gives a reminiscence of this concert:

'In the playing of the concerto movements he asked me to turn the pages for him; but – heaven help me! – that was easier said than done. I saw almost nothing but empty leaves; at the most on one page or the other a few Egyptian hieroglyphs wholly unintelligible to me scribbled down to serve as clues for him; for he played nearly all of the solo part from memory, since, as was so often the case, he had not had time to put it all down on paper. He gave me a secret glance whenever he was at the end of one of the invisible passages and my scarcely concealable anxiety not to miss the decisive moment amused him greatly and he laughed heartily at the jovial supper which we ate afterwards.'

The impression made upon reading the few contemporary notices of this concert is that the new works produced were, on the whole, coldly received. The short report in the *Freymüthige* said:

'Even our doughty Beethofen, whose oratorio *Christus am Ölberg* was performed for the first time at suburban Theater-an-der-Wien, was not altogether fortunate, and despite the efforts of his many admirers was unable to achieve really marked approbation. True, the two symphonies and single passages in the oratorio were voted very beautiful, but the work in its entirety was too long, too artificial in structure and lacking expressiveness, especially in the vocal parts. The text, by F. X. Huber, seemed to have been as superficially written as the music. But the concert brought 1,800 florins to Beethofen and he, as well as Abbé Vogler, has been engaged for the theatre. He is to write one opera, Vogler three; for this they are to receive 10 per cent of the receipts at the first ten performances, besides free lodgings.'

The report of the *Zeitung für die Elegante Welt* was of the opinion 'that the first symphony is better than the later one [in D] because it is developed with a lightness and is less forced, while in the second the striving for the new and surprising is already more apparent. Less successful was the following Concerto in C minor which Hr. v. B., who is otherwise known as an excellent pianist, performed also not completely to the public's satisfaction.' He found the music to the *Christus* on the whole good; 'there are a few admirable passages; an air of the Seraph with trombone accompaniment in particular makes an excellent effect.' This may well have been the trombone passage, referred to in Ries's account, which Beethoven composed in bed the morning of the performance.

A few days after this we have a sight of Beethoven again in private life. Dr Joh. Th. Held, the famous physician and professor in Prague, then a young man of just the composer's age (he was born on 11 December 1770), accompanied Count Prichowsky on a visit to Vienna. On the morning of 16 April these two gentlemen met Beethoven in the street. He, knowing the Count, invited them to Schuppanzigh's, 'where some of his pianoforte sonatas which had been transcribed as string quartets were to be rehearsed'. In his manuscript autobiography Held writes:

'We met a number of the best musicians gathered together, such as the violinists Krumbholz, Möser (of Berlin), the mulatto Bridgethauer, who in London had been in the service of the then Prince of Wales, also a Herr Schreiber and the 12-year-old Kraft who played second. Even then Beethoven's muse transported me into higher regions, and the desire of all these artists to have our musical director Wenzel Praupner in Vienna confirmed me in my opinion of the excellence of his conducting. Since then I have often met Beethoven at concerts. His piquant conceits modified the gloominess, I might say the lugubriousness, of his countenance.'

The 'Bridgethauer' mentioned by Held – whose incorrect writing of the name conveys to the German its correct pronunciation – was the 'American ship captain who associated much with Beethoven' mentioned by Schindler.

George Augustus Polgreen Bridgetower – a bright mulatto then twenty-four years old, son of an African father and a German or Polish mother, an applauded public violinist in London at the age of ten years, and long in the service, as musician, of the Prince of Wales, afterwards George IV – was never in America and knew as much probably of a ship and the science of navigation as ordinary shipmasters do of the violin. In 1802 he obtained leave of absence to visit his mother in Dresden and to use the waters of Teplitz and Carlsbad, which leave was prolonged that he might spend a few months in Vienna. His playing in public and private at Dresden had secured him such favourable letters of introduction as gained him a most brilliant reception in the highest musical circles of the Austrian capital, where he arrived a few days before Held met him at Schuppanzigh's. Beethoven, to whom he was introduced by Prince Lichnowsky, readily gave him aid in a public concert. It has an interest on account of Beethoven's connection with it; for the day of the concert was the date of the completion and performance of the 'Kreutzer' Sonata. Ries writes:

'The famous Sonata in A minor, Op. 47, with concertante violin, dedicated to Rudolph Kreutzer in Paris, was originally composed by Beethoven for Bridgetower, an English artist. Here things did not go much better [Ries had referred to the tardiness of the composition of the horn sonata which Beethoven wrote for Punto], although a large part of the first Allegro was ready at an early date. Bridgetower pressed him greatly because the date of his concert had been set and he wanted to study his part. One morning Beethoven summoned me at half after 4 o'clock and said: "Copy the violin part of the first Allegro quickly." The pianoforte part was noted down only here and there in parts. Bridgetower had to play the marvellously beautiful theme and variations in F from Beethoven's manuscript at the concert because there was no time to copy it. The final Allegro, however, was beautifully written, since it originally belonged to the Sonata in A major (Op. 30), which is dedicated to Czar Alexander. In its place Beethoven, thinking it too brilliant for the A major Sonata, put the variations which now form the finale.'

Bridgetower, when advanced in years, talking with Mr Thirwall about Beethoven, told him that at the time the Sonata, Op. 47, was composed, he and the composer were constant companions, and that the first copy bore a dedication to him; but before he departed from Vienna they had a quarrel about a girl, and Beethoven then dedicated the work to Rudolph Kreutzer.

When Beethoven removed from the house 'am Peter' to the theatre building, he took his brother Carl Caspar to live with him, as twenty years later he gave a room to his factotum Schindler. This change of lodgings took place, according to Seyfried, before the concert of 5 April. A business letter written by Carl to Simrock from the new lodging shows his activity at this time as agent for his brother.

'Vienna, 25 May 1803
'Highly esteemed Sir:
'I have not been able until now to provide you with three sonatas and something else because your answer to my letter of September of last year arrived here so late. At the moment you can have a grand violin *sonata* under the following conditions; it is to appear simultaneously in London, Leipzig, Vienna and Bonn. A copy of a work of this kind to print costs 30 fl. Then you can have a big *symphony* alone for 400 fl. If you wish to publish the *Sonatas* which appeared in Zurich, write to us and we will send you a list of some 80 mistakes in them.

'Now most of the keyboard music and also the Instrumental pieces by my brother have been arranged with care by a skilful composer, thus already several instrumental pieces have been arranged very usefully for the piano with and without accompanying instruments and others for string quartet. You can have these for about 14 fl apiece. I believe that the offer is very favourable because you could gain great sums of money with little expense.

'Please write to me soon concerning this.

Yours sincerely,
C. v. Beethoven'

'Address
A – Beethoven
in Vienna to be delivered
in the Theater-an-der-Wien, 2nd storey'

When the 'Kreutzer' Sonata was published Carl acknowledged the receipt of a copy in a letter to Simrock, adding that since all the other publishers sent six copies of the works printed by them, he would like five more. Simrock took him to task rather sharply for what he considered a piece of presumption, in a letter which he enclosed to Ferdinand Ries with the statement that he might read it if he wanted to. 'I bought the Sonata of Louis van Beethoven,' says the indignant publisher, 'and in his letter concerning it there is not a word about giving him six copies in addition to the fees – a matter important enough to have been mentioned; I was under the impression that Louis van Beethoven composed his own works; what I am certain of is that I have fully complied with all the conditions of the contract and am indebted to nobody.' In the note to Ries he calls Carl's conduct 'impertinent and deserving of a harsher treatment, for Herr Carl seems to me incorrigible'.

At the beginning of the warm season Beethoven, as was his annual custom, appears to have spent some weeks in Baden to refresh himself and revive his energies after the irregular, exciting and fatiguing city life of the winter, before retiring to the summer lodgings, whose location he describes in a note to Ries as 'in Oberdöbling No. 4, the street to the left where you go down the mountain to Heiligenstadt'.

Beethoven's quarters consisted of an ante-room (which he used as a kitchen) and three rooms, two of which were on the street side. It was a simple wine-grower's house on level ground which at the time was the property of the vinegar-maker, Franz Nusser. The house – Vienna XIX, Döblinger Hauptstrasse No. 92 – still stands, though somewhat changed. In the place of the present front there was a small path through making a narrow connection between the Hofzeile and the Nussdorferstrasse. The street in front of the house was much higher, so that the windows were close to street level. The house is known as the 'Eroicahaus'. In 1803 it had gardens, vineyards or green fields in both front and rear. True, it was half an hour's walk further than from Heiligenstadt to the scenes in which he had composed the second Symphony the preceding summer; but to compensate for this, it was so much nearer the city – was in the more immediate vicinity of that arm of the Danube called the 'Canal' – and almost under its windows was the gorge of the Krottenbach, which separates Döbling from Heiligenstadt, and which, as it extends inland from the river, spreads into a fine vale, then very solitary and still very beautiful. This was the house, this the summer, and these the scenes, in which the composer wrought out the conceptions that during the past five years had been assuming form and consistency in his mind, to which Bernadotte may have given the original impulse, and which we know as the 'Eroica' Symphony.

A young Rhinelander, to whom Beethoven became much attached, and who returned the kindness with warm affection for him personally and a boundless admiration for his genius, became known to the composer also just at this time. Willibrord Joseph Mähler, born at Ehrenbreitstein – who died in 1860, at the age of eighty-two years, as pensioned Court Secretary – was a man of remarkably varied artistic talents. He wrote respectable poetry and set it to correct and not unpleasing music; sang well enough, and painted sufficiently well to be named 'amateur portrait painter'.

Soon after Beethoven returned from his summer lodgings to his apartment in the theatre building, Mähler, who had then recently arrived in Vienna, was taken by Breuning thither to be introduced. They found him busily at work finishing the 'Eroica' Symphony. After some conversation, at the desire of Mähler to hear him play, Beethoven, instead of beginning an extempore performance, gave his visitors the finale of the new Symphony; but at its close, without a pause, he continued in free fantasia for *two hours*, 'during all which time', said Mr Mähler to the present writer, 'there was not a measure which was faulty, or which did not sound original'. He added that one circumstance attracted his particular notice; viz.: 'that Beethoven played with his hands so very still; wonderful as his execution was, there was no tossing of them to and fro, up and down; they seemed to glide right and left over the keys, the fingers alone doing the work.'

He painted a portrait of the composer about 1804–5, and a second around 1814–15. An undated note of Beethoven to Mähler may be inserted here, as an introduction to Mr Mähler's remarks upon the portrait to which it refers:

'I beg of you to return my portrait to me as soon as you have made sufficient use of it – if you need it longer I beg of you at least to make haste – I have promised the portrait to a stranger, a lady who saw it here, that she may hang it in her room during her stay of several weeks. Who can withstand such *charming importunities*, as a matter of course a portion of the lovely favours *which I shall thus garner* will also fall to *you*.'

To the question what picture is here referred to, Mr Mähler replied to me in substance: 'It was a portrait, which I painted soon after coming to Vienna, in which Beethoven is represented, at nearly full length, sitting; the left hand rests upon a lyre, the right is extended, as if, in a moment of musical enthusiasm, he was beating time; in the background is a temple of Apollo. Oh! If I could but know what became of the picture!'

'What!' was my answer, to the great satisfaction of the old gentleman, 'the picture is hanging at this moment in the home of Madame van Beethoven, widow, in the Josephstadt, and I have a copy of it.'

The extended right hand – though, like the rest of the picture, not very artistically executed – was evidently painted with care. It is rather broad for the length, is muscular and nervous, as the hand of a great pianist necessarily grows through much practice; but, on the whole, is neatly formed and well proportioned. Anatomically, it corresponds so perfectly with all the authentic descriptions of Beethoven's person, that this alone proves it to have been copied from nature and not drawn after the painter's fancy. Whoever saw a long delicate hand with fingers exquisitely tapering, like Mendelssohn's, joined to the short stout muscular figure of a Beethoven or a Schubert?

On 22 October 1803, Beethoven, enraged at efforts to reprint his works, issued the following characteristic fulmination in large type, filling an entire page of the journal:

'WARNING

'Herr Carl Zulehner, a reprinter at Mainz, has announced an edition of all my works for pianoforte and string instruments. I hold it to be my duty hereby publicly to inform all friends of music that I have not the slightest part in this edition. I should not have offered to make a collection of my works, a proceeding which I hold to be premature at the best, without first consulting with the publishers and caring for the correctness which is wanting in some of the individual publications. Moreover, I wish to call attention to the fact that the illicit edition in question can never be complete, inasmuch as some new works will soon appear in Paris, which Herr Zulehner, as a French subject, will not be permitted to reprint. I shall soon make full announcement of a collection of my works to be made under my supervision and after a severe revision.'

The publication of a complete edition of his compositions was frequently on Beethoven's mind. In 1806 Breitkopf and Härtel tried to get all of Beethoven's works for publication by them; it is likely that similar efforts on the part of Viennese publishers date back as far as 1803. Later the plan played a role in the correspondence with Probst and Simrock. As late as 1824 it was urged by Andreas Streicher. It has already been said that Beethoven at an early date desired to make an arrangement with a publisher by which he might be relieved of anxiety about monetary matters. He wanted to give all his compositions to one publisher, who should pay him a fixed salary.

The three great works of the year were the oratorio, the 'Kreutzer' Sonata for Violin and the *Sinfonia Eroica*. The title of the second, 'Sonata scritta in uno stilo molto concertante quasi come d'un Concerto', is found on the inner side of the last sheet of the sketchbook of 1803. Beethoven wrote the word 'brillante' after 'stilo' but scratched it out. It is obvious that he wished to emphasise the difference between this Sonata and its predecessors. Simrock's tardiness in publishing the Sonata annoyed Beethoven. He became impatient and wrote to the publisher as follows, under date of 4 October 1804:

'Dear, best Herr Simrock:

'I have been waiting with longing for the Sonata which I gave you – but in vain – please write what is the state of things concerning it – whether or not you accepted it from me merely as food for moths – or do you wish to obtain a special Imperial privilegium in connection with it? – Well, it seems to me that might have been accomplished long ago. –

'Where in hiding is this slow devil – who is to drive out the sonata? – You are generally the quick devil, are known as Faust once was as being in league with the imp of darkness, and for this reason you are *loved* by your comrades. But again – where in hiding is your devil – or what kind of a devil is it – that sits on my sonata and with whom *you* have not come to an agreement? – Hurry, then, and tell me when I shall see the s[onata] given to the light of day – When you have told me the date I will at once send you a little note to *Kreutzer*, which you will please be kind enough to enclose when you send him a copy (as you in any event will send your copies to Paris or even, perhaps, have them printed there) – This *Kreutzer* is a dear, good fellow who during his stay here gave me much pleasure. I prefer his unassuming manner and unaffectedness to *all the extérieur* without *intérieur* of most virtuosi – As the sonata was written for a thoroughly capable violinist, the dedication to him is all the more appropriate – Although we correspond with each other (i.e., a letter from me once a year) – I hope that he will not have learned anything about it yet – I hear that you are improving your lot more and more; that makes me heartily glad. – Greet everyone in your family and all others whom you think would enjoy a greeting from me. – Please answer soon.

Your Beethoven'

In spite of innumerable such petty annoyances, ignorant adverse criticism, dishonest publishers and some appalling performances of his work, the true stature of Beethoven's future greatness was slowly dawning on some of the more percipient. Alone among the critics of *Christus am Ölberg*, that of the *Allgemeine Musikalische Zeitung*, having spoken of the oratorio being received with 'extraordinary approval', went on: 'It confirms my long-held opinion that Beethoven in time can effect a revolution in music like Mozart's. He is hastening towards this goal with giant strides.'

CHAPTER 10

The Years 1804 and 1805

The 'Eroica' Performed – Countess Deym

During the winter of 1803–4 negotiations were in progress the result of which was to put an end for the present to Beethoven's operatic aspirations. For a background to these negotiations let Georg Friedrich Treitschke, poet and Stage Manager of the Court Opera, and a personal actor in the scenes, explain:

'On 24 February 1801, the first performance of *Die Zauberflöte* took place in the Royal Imperial Court Theatre beside the Kärnthnerthor. Orchestra and chorus as well as the representatives of Sarastro (Weinmüller), the Queen of Night (Mme Rosenbaum), Pamina (Demoiselle Saal) and the Moor (Lippert) were much better than before. It remained throughout the year the only admired German opera. The loss of large receipts and the circumstance that many readings were changed, the dialogue shortened and the name of the author omitted from all mention, angered S. [Schikaneder] greatly. He did not hesitate to give free vent to his gall, and to parody some of the vulnerable passages in the performance ... This would be a trifle had it not been followed by such significant consequences; for from that time dated the hatred and jealousy which existed between the German operas of the two theatres, which alternately persecuted every novelty and ended in Baron von Braun, then manager of the Court Theatre, purchasing the Theater-an-der-Wien in 1804, by which act everything came under the staff of a single shepherd but never became a single flock.'

Baron Braun now dismissed the director of the theatre, and the Secretary of the Court Theatres, Joseph von Sonnleithner, for the present acted in that capacity.

In Paris, at the close of the eighteenth century, Othello's 'being taken by the insolent foe and redemption thence' was by far the most popular subject for the stage. Doubtless so many facts stranger than fiction in recent narratives of escape from dungeon and guillotine, rendered doubly fascinating by beautiful exhibitions of disinterested affection, exalted generosity and heroic self-sacrifice, were not without their effect upon public taste. Certain it is that no other class of subjects is so numerously represented in the French drama of that precise period as this. *Les deux Journées* by J. N. Bouilly stands confessedly at its head. In Beethoven's opinion, expressed in 1823, this and *La Vestale* were the two best texts then ever written. Two years before *Les deux Journées* – that is, on 19 February 1798 – the same poet had produced another of that class of texts, which, if less abounding in pleasing and exciting scenes, still contained one supreme moment that cannot readily find its like. This was *Léonore, ou l'Amour conjugal.*

The Italian composer, Ferdinando Paër, who became hofkapellmeister at Dresden in 1802, took up the Leonore plot, rewritten in Italian, and composed his *Leonora, ossia l'amore conjugale*, which was first performed in Dresden on 3 October 1804. Meanwhile, Sonnleithner undertook the translation of the Bouilly text into German, and Beethoven set to work at once to collaborate with the Court Secretary. The start of Beethoven's work on the 'Leonore' subject can be dated January 1804, from the letter written by the composer to the editor Johann Rochlitz in Leipzig. A short time afterwards he wrote a letter to his new collaborator which is interesting enough to be quoted in full:

'Dear Sonnleithner!

'Since it is so difficult to talk with you, I prefer to write to you about the things which we have to discuss . . . I beg you most sincerely to see to it that *the poetical part* of the libretto is ready by the *middle of next April*, so that I can continue to work and the opera can be performed by June at the latest, so that I myself can help you in performance. – My brother has told you of my changing lodgings; I have occupied this one conditionally until a better one can be found. The chance came already some time ago and I wanted to assert my right then . . . at which point Baron Braun became owner of the theatre. – The rooms occupied by the *painter* above and which are clearly adequate only for a servant, need only to be vacated, then my apartment could be granted to the painter, and the affair would be settled. – Since in my apartment the servant must sleep in the kitchen, the servant I now have is already my third – and this one will not stay long with me either; without considering its other inconveniences. – I know beforehand that if it depends upon the decision of Hr. *Baron* again, the answer will be *no*. In that case I shall look for something elsewhere immediately. Already I am used to the fact that he has nothing good to say about me – let it be – *I shall never grovel* – my world is elsewhere. – Now I expect *an answer from you* on this – meanwhile I do not want to stay an hour longer in this fatal hole. *My brother* told me that according to your complaint I am supposed to have spoken against you, but don't listen to miserable *gossip* at the *theatre*. – The one thing which I find at fault with you is that you listen too much to what *some people* say which they certainly don't deserve. – Forgive my frankness. –

Faithfully your Beethoven'

This letter shows first that Beethoven was ready to set the text, waiting only for it to be sent to him; and second that only the 'poetical part of the libretto' was to be set to music.

However, the sale of the theatre made void the contracts with Vogler and Beethoven. It was no time for Baron Braun, with three theatres on his hands, to make new contracts with composers, until the reins were fairly in his grasp, and the affairs of the new purchase brought into order and in condition to work smoothly; nor was there any necessity of haste. The repertoire was so well supplied that the new list of pieces for the year reached the number of forty-three, of which eighteen were operas or *Singspiele*.

Therefore Beethoven, who had already occupied the free lodgings in the theatre building for the year which his contract granted him, was compelled to move. Stephan von Breuning even then lived in the house in which in 1827 he died. It was the large pile of building belonging to the Esterhazy estates, known as 'das rothe Haus', which stood at a right angle to the Schwarzspanier house and church, and fronted upon the open space where now stands the new Votiv-Kirche. Here also Beethoven now took apartments.

The great accomplishment of the year 1803 had been the writing of the Symphony No. 3, the story of which must now be told. Sketches for all four movements are to be found in the so-called 'Eroica' sketchbook. From this it is possible to date the main composition period of the symphony from about May to November 1803. The final shaping of the work probably extended into the beginning of 1804.

Early in the spring a fair copy of the *Sinfonia Eroica* had been made to be forwarded to Paris through the French embassy, so Moritz Lichnowsky informed Schindler. Ries says:

'In this symphony Beethoven had Buonaparte in his mind, but as he was when he was First Consul. Beethoven esteemed him greatly at the time and likened him to the greatest Roman consuls. I as well as several of his more intimate friends saw a copy of the score lying upon his table, with the word "Buonaparte" at the extreme top of the title page, and at the extreme bottom "Luigi van Beethoven", but not another word. Whether, and with what the space between was to be filled out, I

do not know. I was the first to bring him the intelligence that Buonaparte had proclaimed himself emperor, whereupon he flew into a rage
and cried out: "Is he then, too, nothing more than an ordinary human
being? Now he, too, will trample on all the rights of man and indulge
only his ambition. He will exalt himself above all others, become a
tyrant!" Beethoven went to the table, took hold of the title page by
the top, tore it in two and threw it on the floor. The first page was
rewritten and only then did the symphony receive the title: "Sinfonia
eroica".'

The acts of the French Tribunate and Senate, which elevated the
First Consul to the dignity of Emperor, are dated 3, 4 and 17 May. Napoleon's assumption of the crown occurred on the 18th and the solemn
proclamation was issued on the 20th. Even in those days, news of so
important an event would not have required ten days to reach Vienna.
At the very latest, then, a fair copy of the *Sinfonia Eroica* was complete
early in May 1804. That it was a copy, the two credible witnesses, Ries
and Lichnowsky, attest. Beethoven's own score – purchased at the sale
in 1827, for 3 fl. 10 kr., Vienna Standard (less than 3½ francs), by the
Viennese composer Hr. Joseph Dessauer – could not have been the one
referred to above. It is, from beginning to end, disfigured by erasures
and corrections, and the title page could never have answered to Ries's
description. It is this:

[At the top:]   'NB 1. Cues for the other instruments are
                  to be written into the first violin part.
                        SINFONIA GRANDE
                  [here two words are erased]
                        804 im August
                          de Sigr
                  Louis van Beethoven
                  Sinfonie 3   Op. 55'
[At the bottom:] 'NB 2. The third horn is so written that it
                  can be played by by [*sic*] a primario as well
                  as a secundario.'

A note to the funeral march is evidently a direction to the copyist, as are
the remarks on the title page: 'NB The notes in the bass which have
stems upwards are for the Violoncellos, those downward for the bass-
viol.'

One of the two words erased from the title was 'Bonaparte'; and just
under his own name Beethoven wrote with a lead pencil in large letters,

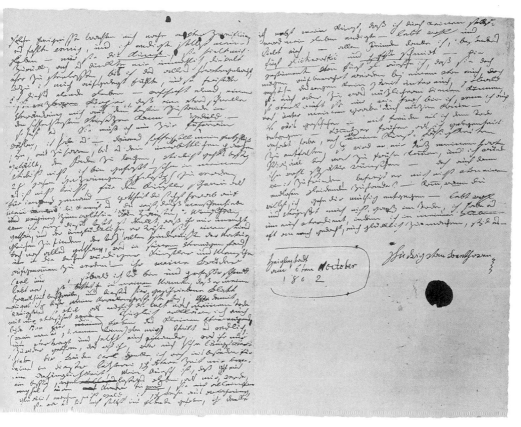

The second and third pages of Beethoven's will, the so-called 'Heiligenstadt Testament', which he wrote on 6 October 1802. *Below left*, Franz Gerhard Wegeler, and, *below right*, Stephan von Breuning, whom Beethoven met again in 1801

Nikolaus Johann van Beethoven, painted in 1841 after his brother's death. *Right*, Count Franz Brunsvik, with whom Beethoven had a long friendship. *Below left*, the countess Giulietta Guicciardi, to whom he dedicated his Rondo in G (Op. 51, No. 2) and with whom he may have had a love affair. *Below right*, a miniature of Beethoven painted by Christian Horneman in 1802, the year of the 'Heiligenstadt Testament'

nearly obliterated but still legible, 'Composed on Bonaparte'. The date '804 im August' is written with a different ink, darker than the rest of the title, and may have been inserted long afterwards, Beethoven's memory playing him false.

'Afterwards', continues Ries, 'Prince Lobkowitz bought this composition for several years' [?] use, and it was performed several times in his palace.' In December the famous Munich oboist Ramm was in Vienna and took part with Beethoven in one of Prince Lobkowitz's concerts.

'Here it happened that Beethoven, who was directing [the "Eroica"] himself, in the second part of the first Allegro where the music is pursued for so many measures in half-notes against the beat, threw the orchestra off in such a way that a new beginning had to be made.

'In the first Allegro occurs a mischievous whim [*böse Laune*] of Beethoven's for the first horn; in the second part, several measures before the theme recurs in its entirety, Beethoven has the horn suggest it at a place where the two violins are still holding a second chord. To one unfamiliar with the score this must always sound as if the horn player had made a miscount and entered at the wrong place. At the first rehearsal of the symphony, which was horrible, but at which the horn player made his entry correctly, I stood beside Beethoven, and, think-ing that a blunder had been made I said: "Can't the damned hornist count? – it sounds infamously false!" I think I came pretty close to receiving a box on the ear. Beethoven did not forgive the slip for a long time.

'On the same evening he played his Quintet for Pianoforte and Wind-Instruments with Ramm as soloist. In the last Allegro there are several holds before the theme is resumed. At one of these Beethoven suddenly began to improvise, took the Rondo for a theme and enter-tained himself and the others for a considerable time, but not the other players. They were displeased and Ramm even very angry. It was really very comical to see them, momentarily expecting the perfor-mance to be resumed, put their instruments to their mouths, only to put them down again. At length Beethoven was satisfied and dropped into the Rondo. The whole company was transported with delight.'

Two works, composed between the autumn of 1803 and 1804, should be mentioned here. The first is the Piano Sonata, Op. 53, which was dedicated to Count Waldstein, and the second is the Concerto for Vio-lin, Violoncello and Piano with orchestra, which was probably written with Beethoven's piano student, the Archduke Rudolph, in mind.

After Beethoven had arrived in Vienna, he saw little of Count Wald-stein, who was travelling between the years 1795 and 1809; but through the connections that the Waldstein family had with other nobility in Vienna, Beethoven had been able quickly to establish contacts with aristocratic patrons.

The middle movement of this sonata was originally to have been an Andante, and sketches for this as well as the first and last move-ments are to be found in the latter part of the so-called 'Eroica' sketch-book.

Ries reports that a friend of Beethoven's said to him that the Sonata was too long, for which he was terribly taken to task by the composer. But after quiet reflection Beethoven was convinced of the correctness of the criticism. The Andante in F major was therefore excluded and its place supplied by the interesting Introduction to the Rondo which it now has. A year after the publication of the Sonata, the Andante also appeared separately. In these particulars Ries is confirmed by Czerny, who adds: 'Because of its popularity (for Beethoven played it fre-quently in society) he gave it the title "Andante favori". I am the more sure of this since Beethoven sent me the proof together with the manu-script for revision.'

Of the Andante Ries continues:

'This Andante has left a painful memory in me. When Beethoven played it for the first time to our friend Krumpholz and me, it delighted us greatly and we teased him until he repeated it. Passing the door of Prince Lichnowsky's house on my way home I went in to tell the Prince of the new and glorious composition of Beethoven's, and was persuaded to play it as well as I could remember it. Recalling more and more of it the Prince urged me to repeat it. In this way it happened that the Prince also learned a portion of the piece. To give Beethoven a surprise the Prince went to him the next day and said that he too had composed something which was not at all bad. In spite of Beethoven's remark that he did not want to hear it the Prince sat down and to the amazement of the composer played a goodly portion of the Andante. Beethoven was greatly angered, and this was the reason why I *never again heard Beethoven play*.'

Sketches for the first movement of the Triple Concerto, Op. 56, appear on the last three pages of the 'Eroica' sketchbook. Further work on all movements is sandwiched in at different places in the so-called *Leonore* sketchbook, dated 1804. The concerto was offered as early as 14 October 1803, to Breitkopf and Härtel by brother Carl, although at this time it is unlikely that Beethoven had more than the form of the work in his mind.

It was bad economy for two young, single men, each to have and pay for a complete suite of apartments in the same house, especially for two who were connected by so many ties of friendship as Breuning and Beethoven. Either lodging contained ample room for both; and Beethoven therefore very soon gave up his and moved into the other. Breuning had his own housekeeper and cook and they also usually dined together at home. This arrangement had hardly been effected when Beethoven was seized with a severe sickness, which when conquered still left him the victim of an obstinate intermittent fever.

Every language has its proverbs to the effect that he who serves not himself is ill served. So Beethoven discovered, when it was too late, that due notice had not been given to the agent of Esterhazy, and that he was bound for the rent of the apartments previously occupied. The question, who was at fault, came up one day at dinner in the beginning of July, and ended in a sudden quarrel in which Beethoven became so angry as to leave the table and the house and retire to Baden with the determination to sacrifice the rent here and pay for another lodging, rather than remain under the same roof with Breuning. 'Breuning,' says Ries, 'a hot-head like Beethoven, grew so enraged at Beethoven's conduct because the incident occurred in the presence of his brother.' It is clear, however, that he soon became cool and instantly did his best to prevent the momentary breach from becoming permanent, by writing – as may be gathered from Beethoven's allusions to it – a manly, sensible and friendly invitation to forgive and forget. But Beethoven, worn with illness, his nerves unstrung, made restless, unhappy, petulant by his increasing deafness, was for a time obstinate. His wrath must run its course. It found vent in the following letters to Ries, and then the paroxysm soon passed. The first of these letters was written in July 1804.

'Dear Riess,
    'Since Breuning did not scruple by his conduct to present my character to you and the landlord as that of a miserable, beggarly, contemptible fellow, I have picked you out first to give my answer to B. by word of mouth. I answer only to one, to the first point of his letter, just in order to vindicate my character in your eyes – Say to him, then, that it never occurred to me to reproach him because of the tardiness of the notice, and that, if B were really to blame for it, each friendly relationship in the world means too much to me for me to give offence to one of my friends because of a few hundred or even more. You know yourself that, in a jocular way, I accused you of being to blame that the

notice did not arrive on time. I am sure that you will remember this. I had forgotten all about the matter. – Then my brother began talking at the table and said that he believed it was B's fault; I denied it at once and said that *you* were to blame. It seems to me that this was clear enough to show that I did not hold B to blame. Thereupon B jumped up like a madman and said he would call up the landlord. This conduct to which I am unaccustomed from any of the persons with whom I associate made me lose my self-control; I also jumped up, upset my chair, went away – and did not return. – This behaviour induced B to put me in such a light before you and the caretaker, and to write me *a letter* also which I have answered only with silence – I have nothing more to say to Breuning. His mode of thought and action in regard to me proves that there never ought to have been a friendly relationship between us, and such will certainly not exist in the future. –

'I have told you all this because your statements have debased my whole way of thinking and acting. I know that if you had known the facts you certainly would not have made them, and this satisfies me. –

'And now, I ask you, dear Ries, immediately on receipt of this letter to go to my brother, the apothecary, and tell him that I shall leave Baden in a few days and that he must engage the lodgings in Döbling the moment you have let him know. – I very nearly came today; I am tired of being here, it revolts me. – Urge him for heaven's sake to rent the lodgings at once because I want to get into them immediately. – Tell B nothing and do not show him any part of what is written on the other page. I want to show him from all points of view that I am not so smallminded as he and have written him only after writing this letter to you, although my resolution to end our friendship is and will remain firm.

Your friend
Beethoven'

Not long thereafter there followed a second letter:

'Baden, 14 July 1804
'If you, dear Riess, are able to find better quarters I shall be glad. Therefore you must tell my brothers that you are not renting these right away – I should very much like to have them on a large quiet square or on the Bastei. – That my brother hasn't yet attended to the wine is unforgivable, since it is so necessary and beneficial for me. I shall take care to be at the rehearsal on Wednesday . . . Farewell, dear Riess. We are having bad weather here and I am not safe from people; I must flee in order to be alone.

Your true friend L. v. Beethoven'

From a third letter, dated 'Baden, 24 July 1804', Ries prints the following excerpt:

'. . . No doubt you were surprised at the Breuning affair, believe me, dear friend, my eruption was only the outburst resulting from many unpleasant encounters with him in the past. I have the talent in many cases of being able to conceal my sensitiveness and to repress it; but if I am irritated at a time when I am more susceptible than usual to anger, I burst out more violently than anyone else. Breuning certainly has excellent qualities, but he thinks he is free from all faults, and his greatest ones are those which he thinks he sees in others. He has a spirit of pettiness which I have despised since childhood. My judgement almost predicted the course which affairs would take with Breuning, since our modes of thinking, acting and feeling are so different. However, I thought these difficulties might also be overcome – experience has refuted me. And now, no more friendship! I have found only two friends in the world with whom I have never had a misunderstanding, but what men! One is dead, the other still lives.* Although we have not known anything of each other for nearly six years I know that I occupy the first place in his heart as he does in mine. The foundation of friendship demands the greatest similarity between the hearts and souls of men. I ask only that you read the letter which I wrote to Breuning and his letter to me. No, he shall never again hold the place in my heart which he once occupied. He who can think a friend capable of such base thoughts and be guilty of such base conduct towards him is not worthy of my friendship . . .'

The reader knows too well the character of Breuning to be prejudiced against him by all these harsh expressions written by Beethoven in a fit of choler of which he heartily repented and 'brought forth fruits meet for repentance'. But, as Ries says, 'these letters together with their consequences are too beautiful a testimony to Beethoven's character to be omitted here.' He writes:

'One evening I came to Baden to continue my lessons. There I found a handsome young woman sitting on the sofa with him. Thinking I might be intruding I wanted to go at once, but Beethoven detained me and said: "Play for the time being." He and the lady remained seated behind me. I had already played for a long time when Beethoven suddenly called out: "Ries, play some love music"; a little later, "Something melancholy!" then, "Something passionate!" etc.

* Lorenz von Breuning and Karl Amenda.

'From what I heard I could come to the conclusion that in some manner he must have offended the lady and was trying to make amends by an exhibition of good humour. At last he jumped up and shouted: "Why, all those things are by me!" I had played nothing but movements from his works, connecting them with short transition phrases, which seemed to please him. The lady soon went away and to my great amazement Beethoven did not know who she was. I learned that she had come in shortly before me in order to make Beethoven's acquaintance. We followed her in order to discover her lodgings and later her station. We saw her from a distance (it was moonlight), but suddenly she disappeared. Chatting on all manner of topics we walked for an hour and a half in the beautiful valley adjoining. On going, however, Beethoven said: "I must find out who she is and you must help me." A long time afterward I met her in Vienna and discovered that she was the mistress of a foreign prince. I reported the intelligence to Beethoven, but never heard anything more about her either from him or anybody else.'

The rehearsal 'on Wednesday' (18th) mentioned in the letter of 14 July, was for the benefit of Ries, who was to play in the first of the second series of the regular Augarten Thursday concerts which took place the next day (19th). Ries says:

'Beethoven had given me his beautiful Concerto in C minor (Op. 37) in manuscript so that I might make my first public appearance *as his pupil* with it; and I am the only one who ever appeared as such while Beethoven was alive ... Beethoven himself conducted, but he only turned the pages and never, perhaps, was a concerto more beautifully accompanied. We had two large rehearsals. I had asked Beethoven to write a cadenza for me, but he refused and told me to write one myself and he would correct it. Beethoven was satisfied with my composition and made few changes; but there was an extremely brilliant and very difficult passage in it, which, though he liked it, seemed to him too venturesome, wherefore he told me to write another in its place. A week before the concert he wanted to hear the cadenza again. I played it and floundered in the passage; he again, this time a little ill-naturedly, told me to change it. I did so, but the new passage did not satisfy me; I therefore studied the other, and zealously, was not quite sure of it. When the cadenza was reached in the public concert Beethoven quietly sat down. I could not persuade myself to choose the easier one. When I boldly began the more difficult one, Beethoven violently jerked his chair; but the cadenza went through all right and Beethoven was so delighted that he shouted "Bravo!" loudly. This electrified the entire audience and at once gave me a standing among the artists. Afterwards while expressing his satisfaction he added: "But all the same you are wilful! If you had made a slip in the passage I would never have given you another lesson." '

A little further on in his book Ries writes: 'The pianoforte part of the C minor Concerto was *never completely written out* in the score; Beethoven wrote it down on separate sheets of paper expressly for me.'

'Not on my life would I have believed that I could be so lazy as I am here. If it is followed by an outburst of industry, something worth while may be accomplished,' Beethoven wrote at the end of his letter of 24 July. He was right. His brother Johann secured for him lodgings at Döbling – presumably the same as those he took the previous summer – where he passed the rest of the summer and worked on the two Sonatas, Op. 54 and 57, certainly 'something worth while'.

In one of the long walks described by Ries,

'in which we went so far astray that we did not get back to Döbling, where Beethoven lived, until nearly 8 o'clock, he had been all the time humming and sometimes howling, always up and down, without singing any definite notes. In answer to my question what it was he said: "A theme for the last movement of the sonata has occurred to me" (in F minor, Op. 57). When we entered the room he ran to the pianoforte without taking off his hat. I took a seat in the corner and he soon forgot all about me. Now he stormed for at least an hour with the beautiful finale of the sonata. Finally he got up, was surprised still to see me and said: "I cannot give you a lesson today, I must do some more work." '

Ries had in the meantime fulfilled Beethoven's wish for a new lodging on the ramparts, by engaging one for him on the Mölkerbastei, three or four houses only from Prince Lichnowsky, in the Pasqualati house – 'from the fourth storey of which there was a beautiful view', namely, over the broad Glacis, the north-western suburb of the city and the mountains in the distance. 'He moved out of this several times,' says Ries, 'but always returned to it, so that, as I afterwards heard, Baron Pasqualati was good-natured enough to say: "The lodging will not be rented; Beethoven will come back." '

Before this time Beethoven and Breuning 'met each other by accident and a complete reconciliation took place and every inimical resolve of Beethoven's, despite their vigorous expression in the two letters, was wholly forgotten' (Ries). And not this alone; he 'laid his peace offering on the altar of reconciliation'. This was the gift of the best picture of himself which exists from those years, a beautiful miniature painted upon ivory by Hornemann, still in the possession of Breuning's heirs. With it he sent the following letter:

'Let all that *passed between us* for a time, my dear St., be hidden behind this picture – I know that I broke *your heart*, but the feelings within me, which you must have noticed, have sufficiently punished me for that. It was not *spitefulness* that I felt towards you, no, if that were so I should never again be worthy of your friendship. It was passion on *your part* and *on mine*. – But mistrust of you arose within me – men came between us who are not worthy of *you* and *me*. – My portrait was long ago intended for you. You know well that I always intended it for somebody; to whom could I give it with so warm a heart as to you, faithful, good, noble Steffen – Forgive me if I have given you pain, I suffered no less myself. Only when I no longer saw you near me for such a long time did I feel to the full how dear to *my* heart you are and always will be. – Surely you will come to my *arms* again as in the past. –'

Nor was the reconciliation on Breuning's part less perfect. On 13 November he wrote to Wegeler and, to excuse his long silence, says:

'He who has been my friend from youth is often largely to blame that I am compelled to neglect the absent ones. You cannot conceive, my dear Wegeler, what an indescribable, I might say, fearful effect the gradual loss of his hearing has had upon him. Think of the feeling of being unhappy in one of such violent temperament; in addition reservedness, mistrust, often towards his best friends, in many things want of decision! For the greater part, with only an occasional exception when he gives free vent to his feelings on the spur of the moment, intercourse with him is a real exertion, at which one can scarcely trust to oneself. From May until the beginning of this month we lived in the same house, and at the outset I took him into my rooms. He had scarcely come before he became severely, almost dangerously ill, and this was followed by an intermittent fever. Worry and the care of him used me rather severely. Now he is completely well again. He lives on the Ramparts, I in one of the newly built houses of Prince Esterhazy in front of the Alstercaserne, and as I am keeping house he eats with me every day.'

Not a word about the quarrel! Not a word to intimate that Beethoven had not occupied his rooms with him until at the usual time for changing lodgings he had crossed the Glacis to Pasqualati's house; not a word of complaint – nothing but the deepest pity and heartiest sympathy.

It is appropriate here to consider the revival of Beethoven's interest in Josephine, Countess Deym. Count Deym had died of pneumonia on 22 January 1804, shortly before the birth of their fourth child. Soon thereafter the widow's health began to fail, and her sister Charlotte came to take care of her. Charlotte wrote to her other sister, Therese von Brunsvik, in June: 'We have visited Beethoven, who appears very well and who has promised to come to see us. He will not travel this summer, but live perhaps at Hütteldorf so that we shall be very near one another.' This visit must have taken place during Beethoven's convalescence from the illness and fever he had had that spring, for at that time he was at nearby Hetzendorf for a short stay. In July, after the quarrel with Breuning, he was at Baden, and later in the summer he chose to go north to Döbling instead of Hütteldorf to the west.

In September, after Josephine had returned to the city, Charlotte wrote to Therese of Josephine's 'dreadful nervous breakdown; sometimes she laughed, sometimes wept, after which came utter fatigue and exhaustion'. By November, however, the sisters' correspondence reveals that she had found a diversion in planning musical evenings. On 10 November Charlotte wrote of Beethoven's taking part in two different occasions. One evening besides participating in his quartet, he was 'so amiable that he played a sonata and variations when asked to'.

On 20 November it is reported that he came almost every other day to give Pepi (Josephine) lessons. A month later Charlotte gives a hint that their friendship was becoming more than that of student and teacher. On 19 December she writes: 'Our small music parties have begun again, finally. Last Wednesday we had the first. Pepi played the clavier excellently, I myself haven't yet found the courage to make myself listen. Beethoven comes quite frequently, he is giving Pepi lessons, it is a bit *dangerous*, I must confess.' Charlotte's worries are also expressed in a letter to her brother Franz written two days later: 'Beethoven is with us almost daily, gives lessons to Pipschen – vous m'entendez, mon cœur!'

There survive thirteen letters from Beethoven to the Countess Josephine Deym, and a fragmentary copy of a letter made by the Countess that is almost certainly from the composer, written between 1804 and 1807. Despite the tone of Charlotte's letters, there is nothing in the first three of Beethoven's letters, which belong to this year, to indicate more than a warm friendship. In the third Beethoven shows that he was encouraging the arrangements at the Countess's house for 'music parties every two weeks', and that the services of Schuppanzigh and Zmeskall had been enlisted to help. But, as we shall see, Charlotte's concern is confirmed by a new tone that enters into the letters that follow, to which we return later in the chapter.

Turn we again to the Theater-an-der-Wien, for a new contract was made with Beethoven, by which his operatic aspirations and hopes were again awakened, and with a better prospect of their gratification. At the end of August Sonnleithner retired from the direction of the theatre and Baron Braun took the extraordinary step of reinstating his former rival and enemy, Schikaneder – a remarkable proof of the Baron's high opinion of his tact and skill in the difficult business of management. It is worth noting that now, when Schikaneder found himself in a strait for novelty and new attractions for his stage, the project of appealing to Beethoven's genius was revived. It will be remembered that Beethoven had started, early in the year 1804, to set Sonnleithner's text of the 'Leonore' subject.

Beethoven, by now, though almost unknown personally beyond the limits of a few Austrian cities – unaided by apostles to preach his gospel, owing nothing to journalist or pamphleteer, disdaining, in fact, all the arts by which dazzling but mediocre talent pushes itself into notoriety – had, in the short space of eight years, by simple force of his genius as manifested in his published works, placed himself at the head of all writers for the pianoforte, and in public estimation had risen to the level of the two greatest of orchestral composers. The unknown student that entered Vienna in 1792, was now in 1804 a recognised member of the great triumvirate, Haydn, Mozart and Beethoven.

He who dwells with wife and children in a fixed abode usually finds himself, as age draws on, one of a small circle of old friends; and hoary heads, surrounded by their descendants, the inheritors of parental friendships, sit at the same tables and make merry where they had gathered in the prime of life. The unmarried man, who can call no spot on earth's surface his own, who spends his life in hired lodgings, here today and there tomorrow, has, as a rule, few friendships of long standing. By divergency in tastes, opinions, habits, increasing with the years, often by the mere interruption of social intercourse, or by a thousand equally insignificant causes, the old ties are sundered. In the memoranda and correspondence of such a man familiar names disappear, even when not removed by death, and strange ones take their places. The mere passing acquaintance of one period becomes the chosen friend of another; while the former friend sinks into the mere acquaintance, or is forgotten. Frequently no cause for the change can be assigned. One can only say – it happened so.

Thus it was with Beethoven, even to a remarkable degree; in part because of his increasing infirmity, in part owing to peculiarities of his character. It was his misfortune, also, that – having no pecuniary resource but the exercise of his talents for musical composition, and being at the same time too proud and too loyal to his ideas of art to write for popular applause – he was all his life long thrown more or less upon the generosity of patrons. But death, misfortune or other causes deprived him of old patrons, as of old friends, and compelled him to seek, or at least accept, the kindness of new ones. A part of this chapter must be devoted to certain new names in both categories, which become prominent in his history in the years immediately before us.

Archduke Rudolph Johann Joseph Rainer, youngest son of Emperor Leopold II, and half-brother of Emperor Franz, was born on 8 January 1788, and therefore was, at the end of 1805, just closing his seventeenth year. Like his unfortunate uncle, Elector Maximilian, he was destined to the Church, and like him, too, he had much musical taste and capacity. In music he, with the children of the imperial family, was instructed by the Royal Imperial Court Composer, Anton Tayber, and made such good progress that he, while still but a boy, played to general satisfaction in the salons of Lobkowitz and others. But an archduke has not much to fear from hostile criticism; a better proof that he really possessed musical talent and taste is afforded by the fact that, so soon as he could emancipate himself from Tayber, he became a pupil of Beethoven.

The precise date of Beethoven's engagement has eluded research, but it is reasonably certain that it occurred at the end of the young Archduke's fifteenth year – that is, in the winter of 1803–4.

In Fräulein Giannatasio's notices from the years 1816–18, she relates:

'At that time Beethoven gave lessons to Archduke Rudolph, a brother of Emperor Franz. I once asked him if the Archduke played well. "When he is feeling just right," was the answer, accompanied by a smile. He also laughingly referred to the fact that he would sometimes hit him on the fingers, and that when the august gentleman once tried to refer him to his place, he pointed for justification to a passage from a poet, Goethe, I think.'

It must have been a mistake of the young lady's to make Beethoven speak here in the present tense; for it is incredible that he should have taken such a liberty in 1816–17, when Rudolph was a man of some thirty years; but, as Ries explains:

'Etiquette and all that is connected with it was never [?] known to Beethoven, nor was he ever willing to learn it. For this reason he often caused great embarrassment in the household of the Archduke Rudolph when he first went to him. An attempt was made by force to teach him to have regard for certain things. But this was intolerable to him; he would promise, indeed, to mend his ways but – that was the end of it. Finally one day when, as he expressed it, he was being tutored [*als man ihn, wie er es nannte, hofmeisterte*] he angrily forced his way to the Archduke and flatly declared that while he had the greatest reverence for his person, he could not trouble himself to observe all the regulations which were daily forced upon him. The Archduke laughed good-naturedly and commanded that Beethoven be permitted to go his own gait undisturbed – it was his nature and could not be altered.'

Meanwhile, however unpopular the composer may have been with his brother musicians in Vienna, he possessed qualities and tastes that endeared him to the best class of rising young men in the learned professions. An example is Dr Johann Zizius, of Bohemia (born 7 January 1772). He appears at the early age of twenty-eight as a professor of political science to the RI Staff of Guards; three years later he has the same professorship in the Theresianum, which he retained to his death in 1824. Dr Sonnleithner made his acquaintance about 1820. In his very valuable and interesting 'Musikalische Skizzen aus alt-Wien' (*Rezensionen*, 1863), he describes Zizius in a way which shows him to have been a man after Beethoven's own heart, and his house a gathering place, until the composer's increasing infirmity excluded him in great measure from mixed society.

Here seems to be the appropriate place to mention a friendship that Beethoven surely made through his close association with Count Browne and his family. Privy Councillor Johannes Büel (1761–1830) was for a long time tutor to the Count's son Moritz. In characterising his friends in Vienna in 1805, Büel wrote: 'Beethoven, full of enthusiasm for his art, original, somewhat of a hypochondriac, who when yesterday Browne read to him a letter from me, freely gave vent to his tears.' In his biography of Büel, Hans Noll has printed a facsimile of an entry that Beethoven made for Büel's album:

> 'Friendship is a shade in
> sunlight and a shelter
> in a downpour of rain.
> Reflect back, my dear Büel,

and you see –
that we saw each other too little –
farewell – and forget not
  your warm friend
  Ludwig van Beethoven'

'Vienna, 29 June 1806'

At the time Beethoven believed his friend was returning to his house in Switzerland, but actually he remained in Vienna until 1817. Büel visited Vienna again in 1821, and at this time wrote, 'If Beethoven only were not completely deaf and so difficult to deal with, I would give G. his address, but now nothing can be done with him.' These are the sad words of a friend who can only treasure a close friendship of the past.

We pass to the notices of Ries, Czerny and others, which record divers characteristic anecdotes and personal traits of the master, not susceptible of exact chronological arrangement but which belong to this period. 'Of all composers,' says Ries, 'Beethoven valued most highly Mozart and Handel, then S. Bach. Whenever I found him with music in his hand or lying on his desk it was surely compositions of these heroes. Haydn seldom escaped without a few sly thrusts.' Compare this with what Jahn heard from Czerny: 'Once Beethoven saw at my house the scores of six quartets by Mozart. He opened the fifth, in A, and said: "That's a work! that's where Mozart said to the world: Behold what I might have done for you if the time were right!" ' And, touching Handel:

'Graun's *Tod Jesu* was unknown to Beethoven. My father brought the score to him, which he played through *a vista* in a masterly manner. When he came to a place where Graun had written a twofold ending to be left to the choice of the performer, he said: "The man must have had the gripes not to be able to say which ending is the better!" At the end he said that the fugues were passable, the rest ordinary. Then he picked up Handel's *Messiah* with the words: "Here is a different fellow!" and played the most interesting numbers and called our attention to several resemblances to Haydn's *Creation*, etc.'

'Once,' says Ries, 'when after a lesson we were talking about fugue themes, I sitting at the pianoforte and he beside me, I played the first fugue theme from Graun's *Tod Jesu*; he began to play it after me with his left hand, then brought in the right and developed it for perhaps half an hour. I am still unable to understand how he could have endured the uncomfortable position so long. His enthusiasm made him insensible to external impressions.'

In another place he relates:

'During a walk I mentioned to Beethoven two pure fifth progressions which sound striking and beautiful in his C minor Quartet (Op. 18). He did not know them and denied that they were fifths. It being his habit always to carry ruled paper with him, I asked him for a sheet and wrote down the passage in all four voices; seeing that I was right he said: "*Well, and who has forbidden them?*" Not knowing how to take the question, I had him repeat it several times until I finally answered in amazement: "But they are first principles!" The question was repeated again, whereupon I answered: "Marpurg, Kirnberger, Fux, etc., etc., all theoreticians!" – "And I allow them *thus*" was his answer.'

And now something more on the subject of Beethoven's improvisations. Says Ries:

'This last was certainly the most extraordinary [performance] anyone was ever privileged to listen to, especially when he was in good humour or excited. Not a single artist of all that I have heard ever reached the plane in this respect which Beethoven occupied. The wealth of ideas which crowded in upon him, the moods to which he surrendered himself, the variety of treatment, the difficulties which offered themselves or were introduced by him, were inexhaustible.'

And Czerny:

'Nobody equalled him in the rapidity of his scales, double trills, skips, etc. – not even Hummel. His bearing while playing was masterfully quiet, noble and beautiful, without the slightest grimace (only bent forward low, as his deafness grew upon him); his fingers were very powerful, not long, and broadened at the tips by much playing, for he told me very often indeed that he generally had to practise until after midnight in his youth.

'In teaching he laid great stress on a correct position of the fingers (after the school of Emanuel Bach, which he used in teaching me); he could scarcely span a tenth. He made frequent use of the pedals, much more frequent than is indicated in his works. His playing of the scores of Handel and Gluck and the fugues of Seb. Bach was unique, in that in the former he introduced a full-voicedness and a spirit which gave these works a new shape.

'He was also the greatest *a vista* player of his time (even in score-reading); he scanned every new and unfamiliar composition like a divination and his judgement was always correct, but (especially in his younger years) very keen, biting, unsparing. Much that the world admired then and still admires he saw from the lofty point of view of his genius in an entirely different light.

'Extraordinary as his playing was when he improvised, it was frequently less successful when he played his printed compositions, for, as he never had patience or time to practise, the result would generally depend on accident or his mood; and as his playing, like his compositions, was far ahead of his time, the pianofortes of the period (until 1810), still extremely weak and imperfect, could not endure his gigantic style of performance. Hence it was that Hummel's purling, brilliant style, well calculated to suit the manner of the time, was much more comprehensible and pleasing to the public. But Beethoven's performance of slow and sustained passages produced an almost magical effect upon every listener and, so far as I know, was never surpassed.'

Pass we to certain minor characteristic traits which Ries has recorded of his master:

'Beethoven had taken lessons on the violin even after he reached Vienna from Krumpholz and frequently when I was there we played his Sonatas for Pianoforte and Violin together. But it was really a horrible music; for in his enthusiastic zeal he never heard when he began a passage with bad fingering.

'In his behaviour Beethoven was awkward and helpless; his uncouth movements were often destitute of all grace. He seldom took anything into his hands without dropping and breaking it. Thus he frequently knocked his ink-well into the pianoforte which stood near by the side of his writing-table. No piece of furniture was safe from him, least of all a costly piece. Everything was overturned, soiled and destroyed. It is hard to comprehend how he accomplished so much as to be able to shave himself, even leaving out of consideration the number of cuts on his cheeks. He could never learn to dance in time . . .

'Beethoven was often extremely violent. One day we were eating our noonday meal at the Swan inn; the waiter brought him the wrong dish. Scarcely had Beethoven spoken a few words about the matter, which the waiter answered in a manner not altogether modest, when Beethoven seized the dish (it was a mess of lungs with plenty of gravy) and threw it at the waiter's head. The poor fellow had an armful of other dishes (an adeptness which Viennese waiters possess in a high degree) and could not help himself; the gravy ran down his face. He and Beethoven screamed and vituperated while all the other guests roared with laughter. Finally, Beethoven himself was overcome with the comicalness of the situation, as the waiter who wanted to scold could not, because he was kept busy licking from his chops the gravy that ran down his face, making the most ridiculous grimaces the while. It was a picture worthy of Hogarth . . .

'Beethoven knew scarcely anything about money, because of which he had frequent quarrels; since he was always mistrustful, and frequently thought himself cheated when it was not the case. Easily excited, he called people cheats, for which in the case of waiters he had to make good with tips. At length his peculiarities and absent-mindedness became known in the inns which he frequented most often and he was permitted to go his way, even when he went without paying his bill.'

Seyfried records:

'Beethoven was much too straightforward, open and tolerant to give offence to another by disapprobation, or contradiction; he was wont to laugh heartily at what did not please him and I confidently believe that I may safely say that in all his life he never, at least not consciously, made an enemy; only those to whom his peculiarities were unknown were unable quite to understand how to get along with him; I am speaking here of an earlier time, before the misfortune of deafness had come upon him; if, on the contrary, Beethoven sometimes carried things to an extreme in his rude honesty in the case of many, mostly those who had imposed themselves upon him as protectors, the fault lay only in this, that the honest German always carried his heart on his tongue and understood everything better than how to flatter . . . When he composed *Fidelio*, the oratorio *Christus am Ölberg*, the Symphonies in E flat, C minor and F, the Pianoforte Concertos in C minor and G major, and the Violin Concerto in D, we were living in the same house and (since we were each carrying on a bachelor's apartment) we dined at the same restaurant and chatted away many an unforgettable hour in the confidential intimacy of colleagues, for Beethoven was then merry, ready for any jest, happy, full of life, witty and not seldom satirical. No physical ill had then afflicted him [?]; no loss of the sense which is peculiarly indispensable to the musician had darkened his life; only weak eyes had remained with him as the results of the smallpox with which he had been afflicted in his childhood, and these compelled him even in his early youth to resort to concave, very strong (highly magnifying) spectacles.'

Other reminiscences form an admirable supplement. Those which belong to the years 1800–5 follow:

'Our master could not be presented as a model in respect of conducting, and the orchestra always had to have a care in order not to be led astray by its mentor; for he had ears only for his composition and was ceaselessly occupied by manifold gesticulations to indicate the desired expression. He often made a down beat for an accent in the wrong place. He used to suggest a *diminuendo* by crouching down more and more, and at a *pianissimo* he would almost creep under the desk. When the volume of sound grew he rose up also as if out of a stage-trap, and with the entrance of the power of the band he would stand upon the tips of his toes almost as big as a giant, and waving his arms, seemed about to soar upwards to the skies. Everything about him was active, not a bit of his organism idle, and the man was comparable to a *perpetuum mobile*. He did not belong to those capricious composers whom no orchestra in the world can satisfy. At times, indeed, he was altogether too considerate and did not even repeat passages which went badly at the rehearsal: "It will go better next time," he would say. He was very particular about expression, the delicate nuances, the equable distribution of light and shade as well as an effective *tempo rubato*, and without betraying vexation, would discuss them with the individual players. When he then observed that the players would enter into his intentions and play together with increasing ardour, inspired by the magical power of his creations, his face would be transfigured with joy, all his features beamed pleasure and satisfaction, a pleased smile would play around his lips and a thundering "Bravi tutti!" reward the successful achievement. It was the first and loftiest triumphal moment for the genius, compared with which, as he confessed, the tempestuous applause of a receptive audience was as nothing. When playing at first sight, there were frequent pauses for the purpose of correcting the parts and then the thread would be broken; but he was patient even then; but when things went to pieces, particularly in the scherzos of his symphonies at a sudden and unexpected change of rhythm, he would shout with laughter and say he had expected nothing else, but was reckoning on it from the beginning; he was almost childishly glad that he had been successful in "unhorsing such excellent riders".

'Before Beethoven was afflicted with his organic ailment, he attended the opera frequently and with enjoyment . . . There he was fascinated more especially by the creations of Cherubini and Méhul, which at that time were just beginning to stir up the enthusiasm of all Vienna. There he would plant himself hard against the orchestra rail and, dumb as a dunce, remain till the last stroke of the bows. This was the only sign, however, that the art work had interested him; if, on the contrary, the piece did not please him he would turn on his heel at the first fall of the curtain and take himself away. It was, in fact, difficult, yes, utterly impossible to tell from his features whether or not he was pleased or displeased; he was always the same, apparently cold, and just as reserved in his judgements concerning his companions in art; his mind was at work ceaselessly, but the physical shell was like soulless marble. Strangely enough, on the other hand, hearing wretched music was a treat to him which he proclaimed by a peal of laughter. Everybody who knew him intimately knew that in this art he was a virtuoso, but it was a pity that those who were near him were seldom able to fathom the cause of such explosions, since he often laughed at his most secret thoughts and conceits without giving an accounting of them.

'... A truly admirable disorder prevailed in his household. Books and music were scattered in every corner; here the remnants of a cold luncheon; here sealed or half-emptied bottles; here upon a stand the hurried sketches of a quartet; here the remains of a *déjeuner*; there on the pianoforte, on scribbled paper the material for a glorious symphony still slumbering in embryo; here a proof-sheet awaiting salvation; friendly and business letters covering the floor; between the windows a respectable loaf of stracchino, *ad latus* a considerable ruin of a genuine Veronese salami – yet despite this varied mess our master had a habit, quite contrary to the reality, of proclaiming his accuracy and love of order on all occasions with Ciceronian eloquence. Only when it became necessary to spend days, hours, sometimes weeks, in finding something necessary and all efforts remained fruitless, did he adopt a different tone, and the innocent were made to bear the blame. "Yes, yes," was the complaint, "that's a misfortune! Nothing is permitted to remain where I put it; everything is moved about; everything is done to vex me; O men, men!" But his servants knew the good-natured grumbler; let him growl to his heart's content, and – in a few minutes all would be forgotten, until another occasion brought with it a renewal of the scene.

'He often made merry over his illegible handwriting and excused himself by saying: "Life is too short to paint letters or notes; and prettier notes would scarcely help me out of needs."

'The whole forenoon, from the first ray of light till the meal hour, was devoted to mechanical labour, i.e., to transcribing; the rest of the day was given to thought and the ordering of ideas. Hardly had he put the last bit in his mouth before he began his customary promenade, unless he had some other excursion *in petto*; that is to say, he hurried in double-quick time several times around the city, as if urged on by a goad; and this, let the weather be what it might.'

It was to the discredit of Vienna, where instrumental performers of rare ability so abounded, that for several years regular public orchestral concerts, save those at the Augarten in the summer, had been abandoned. Sensible of this, the bankers Würth and Fellner during the winter of 1803–4 'had gathered together on all Sunday mornings a select company [nearly all dilettanti] for concerts restricted for the greater part to pieces for full orchestra, such as symphonies [among them Beethoven's First and Second], overtures, concertos, which they played in really admirable style'.

These concerts were renewed the present winter, and the following report appeared in the *Allgemeine Musikalische Zeitung*, 13 February 1805:

'Beethoven's Symphony in C major was performed at Herr von Würth's with precision and ease. A splendid artistic production. All instruments are used excellently, in which an uncommon richness of beautiful ideas are charmingly and splendidly developed, and overall pervades continuity, order and light. An entirely new symphony by Beethoven (to be distinguished from the second which was published some time ago) is written in a completely different style. This long composition extremely difficult of performance, is in reality a tremendously expanded, daring and wild fantasia. It lacks nothing in the way of startling and beautiful passages, in which the energetic and talented composer must be recognised; but often it loses itself in lawlessness. The symphony begins with an Allegro in E flat that is vigorously scored; a Funeral March in C minor follows which is later developed fugally. After this comes an Allegro scherzo and a Finale, both in E flat. The reviewer belongs to Herr van Beethoven's sincerest admirers, but in this composition he must confess that he finds too much that is glaring and bizarre, which hinders greatly one's grasp of the whole, and a sense of unity is almost completely lost.'

Such is the review of the *Sinfonia Eroica* in its first semi-public production! Its first really public performance was in the Theater-an-der-Wien, on Sunday evening, 7 April, where it began the second part of a concert given for his own benefit by Clement. The programme announces it thus: 'A new grand symphony in D sharp by Herr Ludwig van Beethoven, dedicated to his Serene Highness Prince Lobkowitz. The composer has kindly consented to conduct the work.'

Czerny remembered that on this occasion 'somebody in the gallery cried out: "I'll give another kreutzer if the thing will but stop!" ' This is the keynote to the strain in which the Symphony was criticised in communications to the press, that are now among the curiosities of musical literature. The correspondent of the *Freymüthige* divided the audience into three parties:

'Some, Beethoven's particular friends, assert that it is just this symphony which is his masterpiece, that this is the true style for high-class music, and that if it does not please now, it is because the public is not cultured enough, artistically, to grasp all these lofty beauties; after a few thousand years have passed it will not fail of its effect. Another faction denies that the work has any artistic value and professes to see in it an untamed striving for singularity which had failed, however, to achieve in any of its parts beauty or true sublimity and power. By means of strange modulations and violent transitions, by combining the most heterogeneous elements, as for instance when a pastoral in the largest style is ripped up by the basses, by three horns, etc., a certain undesirable originality may be achieved without much trouble; but genius proclaims itself not in the unusual and the fantastic, but in the beautiful and the sublime. Beethoven himself proved the correctness of this axiom in his earlier works. The third party, a very small one, stands midway between the others – it admits that the symphony contains many beauties, but concedes that the connection is often disrupted entirely, and that the inordinate length of this longest, and perhaps most difficult, of all symphonies wearies even the cognoscenti, and is unendurable to the mere music-lover; it wishes that Hr. v. B. would employ his acknowledgedly great talents in giving us works like his symphonies in C and D, his ingratiating Septet in E flat, the intellectual Quintet in D [C major?] and others of his early compositions which have placed B. for ever in the ranks of the foremost instrumental composers. It fears, however, that if Beethoven continues on his present path both he and the public will be the sufferers. His music could soon reach the point where one would derive no pleasure from it . . . but rather would leave the concert hall with an unpleasant feeling of fatigue from having been crushed by a mass of unconnected and overloaded ideas and a continuing tumult by all the instruments. The public and Herr van Beethoven, who conducted, were not satisfied with each other on this evening; the public thought the symphony too heavy, too long, and himself too discourteous, because he did not nod his head in recognition of the applause which

came from a portion of the audience. On the contrary, Beethoven found
that the applause was not strong enough.'

Beethoven refused positively to make any change in the work, but
deferred to public opinion so far, as, upon its publication, to affix to the
title of the Symphony a note to the effect that on account of its great
length it should be played near the beginning of a concert, before the
audience was become weary.

It will be recalled that at the end of 1804, the frequency with which
Beethoven was in the company of Countess Josephine Deym was a
source of concern to her sisters. At the beginning of 1805 Charlotte
Brunsvik in her letters to Therese continued to mention Beethoven's
visits 'almost every day', describing him now as 'exceedingly kind'. 'He
has composed a song for Pepi [Josephine] that she sent you. But she
begged you at the same time to show it to no one nor to say that you have
the notes if you sing it for anyone.' The song was 'An die Hoffnung'
from Tiedge's *Urania*. On 20 January 1805, Therese wrote to Charlotte:

'But tell me, Pepi and Beethoven, what shall become of it? She should
be on her guard! I believe you were referring to her when you under-
lined the specific words: "*Her heart must have the strength to say No*", a
sad duty, if not the saddest of all!! . . . Often one errs and is misunderstood in love. Only one who *experiences* love can form an opinion
concerning it. Love, what an omnipotent feeling, what a new life
within life! – May the grace of God aid Pepi so that she is not tormented with care and her health may improve!'

Of Beethoven's known correspondence with the Countess, four letters and the fragment of a fifth are to be ascribed to the year 1805.

The first one begins with an assurance to Josephine that gossip
about them was not developing. The roots of Josephine's fears were
twofold: first, Prince Lichnowsky had seen in Beethoven's room a copy
of the song 'An die Hoffnung', which evidently bore some message or
inscription to Josephine, for, as Beethoven admits, the Prince concluded that 'I must surely have some affection for you'; second, that
Zmeskall, a good friend of the Brunsvik family, had been asked by the
Prince whether Beethoven and Josephine met very often, a subject
which was subsequently 'magnified' by Zmeskall and Josephine's aunt,
the Countess Susanne Guicciardi. Beethoven made clear that the
Prince had not mentioned the song to Zmeskall, that the latter had
been non-committal in his answer to the Prince, and that no one else
was involved.

Beethoven's letter sheds new light on his friends' concern for him and his creative efforts. He had learned that Zmeskall 'was to have a word with Tante Gui [Countess Guicciardi] – and suggest that she should speak to you so that you might encourage me more earnestly *to finish my opera*, because he believed that this might do a lot of good'. Also he assured Josephine that Prince Lichnowsky wished for a more intimate association between Beethoven and the Countess, for 'such a friendship could not but be advantageous to me.' But the great importance of this letter is the change that it shows in Beethoven's own feelings towards Josephine, whom he now calls 'beloved J' and 'my adored J'. However, it is important to note that in none of these letters is the lady addressed as 'Du', a form of address to a woman used only in the 'Immortal Beloved' letters of 1812.

As with his close friends of the past, Beethoven refers to a period of 'real sorrows and the struggle with myself between death and life, a struggle in which I was engaged for some time', and he longed for the chance, uninterrupted, to unburden to her his private grief – which was of course his deafness.

He wrote that he had been determined not to fall in love but that she had conquered him. The letter ends with the following description of their love:

'Long – long – of long duration – may our love become – For it is so noble – so firmly founded upon mutual regard and friendship – Even the great similarity between us in so many respects, in our thoughts and feelings – Oh you, you make me hope that *your heart* will long – beat for me – *Mine* can only – cease – to beat for you – when – *it no longer beats* – *Beloved J*, I send you all good wishes – *But I also* hope – that *through me* you will gain a little happiness – otherwise I should certainly be – *selfish*.'

Of the remaining four letters for this year, only the fragmentary one continues and indeed exceeds the intensity of the first letter. The others are concerned with such matters as the sending of a gift, the time for next meeting, or the request for the return of some music. Here follows the fragmentary copy made by Josephine Deym of an unsigned letter to her, presumably from Beethoven.

'. . . from her –
the only beloved – why is there no language which can express what is far above all mere regard – far above everything – that we can never describe – Oh, who can name *you* – and not feel that however much he

could speak about *you* – that would never attain – to *you* – only in music – Alas, am I not too proud when I believe that music is more at my command than words – *You, you*, my all, my happiness – alas, no – even in *my music* I cannot do so, although in this respect thou, Nature, hast not stinted me with thy gifts. Yet there is too little for *you*. Beat, though in silence, poor heart – that is all you can do, nothing more – for *you* – always for *you* – only *you* – eternally *you* – only *you* until I sink into the grave – My refreshment – my all. Oh, Creator, watch over her – bless her days – rather let all calamities fall upon me –

'Only *you* – May you be strengthened, blessed and comforted – in the wretched yet frequently happy existence of us mortals –

'Even if you had not fettered me again to life, yet you would have meant everything to me –'

Since none of the letters is dated it is unclear whether Beethoven continued to see a great deal of the Countess as the year progressed, or whether the romance became less intense. However, it is known that they were neighbours at Hetzendorf during the summer. Then in the autumn the Napoleonic invasion forced the Countess to flee the city with her children. She went to the family home at Martonvásár, wintered in Budapest, and did not return to Vienna to live until later in 1806. The nobility of this lady and the conflict that she experienced in her relationship with Beethoven are revealed in her draft of a letter to the composer, dated after the winter of 1804–5:

'The closer relationship with you, dear *Beethoven*, these winter months has left impressions in my heart which neither time – nor circumstances will erase – Are you happy or sad? – can you yourself tell – Also – in regard to your feelings through self-control – or free release – what *you* – could thereby change –

'My soul, already *inspired* about you before I knew you personally – has been nourished by your affection. A feeling that lies deep in my soul and is incapable of expression made me love you; even before I knew you your music aroused *inspiration* within me – your kind *nature* and your affection strengthened it – This favour which you have accorded me, the pleasure of your company would have been the finest ornament of my life if you had been able to love me less sensuously – that I cannot satisfy this sensuous love – does this cause you anger – I would have to break holy vows were I to listen to your desire – Believe me – it is I through the fulfilment of my duty who suffer the most – and my actions have been surely dictated by noble motives.'

The new contract with Baron Braun gave the composer again a right to the apartments in the theatre building, which he improved, at the same time retaining the dwelling at the Pasqualati house. The city directory for 1805 gives his address at the theatre, and there he received visitors; at the Pasqualati house he was accustomed to seclude himself for work, forbidding his servant to admit any person whatever. In the summer he retired to Hetzendorf, and wrought out his opera, sitting in the same crotched oak in the Schönbrunn Garden that he had used, according to Schindler, four years before. Thus again he had three lodgings at the same time, as in the preceding summer; with this difference, that now one was no expense to him.

Before his migration to Hetzendorf – say about the middle of June 1805 – Beethoven had completely sketched the music of his opera. This is made sufficiently certain by one of those whimsical remarks that he was in the habit of making on the blank spaces of whatever manuscript he happened to have before him. In this case he writes: 'June 2nd Finale always simpler. All pianoforte music also. God knows why my pianoforte music always makes the worst impression, especially when it is badly played.' This is in the midst of sketches to the final chorus of the opera, and is written upon the upper outer corner of page 291 of the *Leonore* sketchbook. This sketchbook has been dated for the most part 1804 and has been described thus:

'The sketchbook is filled for the most part with work on the last pieces of the first act and on all pieces of the second act . . . Originally there were four sketchbooks which, because of their similar content, belonged together; the present sketchbook represents the original second and third sections of which the first and fourth are lost. The first must have contained work on the first third of *Leonore*, while the fourth continued work on the second [last] finale and the overture . . . Without counting subsequent changes and the like, Beethoven took up the principal numbers of the opera in the order in which they stand in the 1805 libretto.'

Otto Jahn has summed up the sketch work as follows:

'One is amazed at the everlasting experimentation and cannot conceive how it will be possible to create an organic whole out of such musical scraps. But if one compares the completed art-work with the chaos of sketches one is overwhelmed with wonder at the creative mind which surveyed its task so clearly, grasped the foundation and the outlines of the execution so firmly and surely that with all the sketches and attempts in details the whole grows naturally from its roots and develops. And though the sketches frequently create the impression of uncertainty and groping, admiration comes again for the marvellously keen self-criticism, which, after everything has been tested with sovereign certainty, retains the best. I have had an opportunity to study many of Beethoven's sketchbooks, but I have found no instance in which one was compelled to recognise that the material chosen was not the best, or in which one could deplore that the material which he rejected had not been used.'

He might have added, with truth, that some of the first ideas noted to passages, now among the gems of the opera, are commonplace and trivial to such a degree that one can hardly attribute them to Beethoven. Yet, there they are in his own hand.

In the notices of the *Leonore* sketchbook, made for use in this work, are copied *eighteen* different beginnings to Florestan's air 'In des Lebens Frühlingstagen', and ten to the chorus 'Wer ein holdes Weib'. The studies for that wondrous outburst of joy, 'O namenlose Freude', are numerous; but the first bars of the duet are the same in all of them.

Beethoven's seclusion at Hetzendorf from June to September (probably) and his labour of reducing the chaos of the sketchbook into the order and beauty of the score of *Leonore* – on which, as he told Schindler, he worked in the bright summer days, sitting in the shades of Schönbrunn – are unbroken for us except by his first meeting with Cherubini. Some time in July – for that master arrived in Vienna after the 5th of that month, and Vogler was in Salzburg before the 28th – 'Cherubini, Beethoven and Vogler were gathered together at Sonnleithner's; everybody played, Vogler first, and without ceasing, so that the company meanwhile sat down to table. Beethoven was full of attention and respect towards Cherubini.' Such is Jahn's note of a communication to him by Grillparzer; but Czerny told him: 'B. did not give Cherubini a friendly reception in 1805, as the latter complained to Czerny later.'

At the end of the summer season Beethoven returned to town with his opera ready to be put in rehearsal. Here Ries found him. However, with all of Beethoven's kindness to Ries, Beethoven had neither forgotten nor forgiven the affair of the 'Andante favori'. Ries writes:

'One day when a small company including Beethoven and me breakfasted with Prince [Lichnowsky] after the concert in the Augarten (8 o'clock in the forenoon), it was proposed that we drive to Beethoven's house and hear his opera *Leonore*, which had not yet been performed. Arrived there Beethoven demanded that I go away, and inasmuch as the most urgent appeals of all present were fruitless, I did so with tears in my eyes. The entire company noticed it, and Prince Lichnowsky, following me, asked me to wait in an ante-room, because, having been the cause of the trouble, he wanted to have it settled. But the feeling of hurt to my honour would not permit this. I heard afterwards that Prince Lichnowsky had sharply rebuked Beethoven for his conduct, since only love for his works had been to blame for the incident and consequently for his anger. But the only result of these representations was that Beethoven refused to play any more for the company.'

It so happened that Ries thus lost his only opportunity ever to hear the 'Leonore-Fidelio' music in its original form; but this Beethoven could not anticipate, as he could have no suspicion that they were so soon to be parted. Bonn being now under French rule, Ries was liable to conscription, and notice came that he was among the first drawn. 'He was therefore', says the *Harmonicon* (1824, No. 15), 'obliged to return home immediately, for his disobedience would have exposed his father and family to the risk of ruin.'

Three years will elapse before we meet Ries again in Vienna – the greater part of which period he passed at Paris in such discouraging circumstances that he thought seriously of abandoning his profession.

At the Theater-an-der-Wien none of the new operas produced this season had long kept the stage. It was now autumn and the receipts did not cover the expenses of the theatre. 'From the distance,' says Treitschke, 'the storm of war rolled towards Vienna and robbed the spectators of the calm essential to the enjoyment of an art-work. But just for this reason all possible efforts were made to enliven the sparsely attended spaces of the house. *Fidelio* was relied upon to do its best, and so, under far from happy auspices, the opera was produced on 20 November [1805].'

One can well believe that very considerable difficulties attended the performance, as Treitschke states. His words, as well as certain expressions of Beethoven's a few months later, indicate that the opera was hurriedly put upon the stage, and the inadequacy of the singers thus increased by the lack of sufficient rehearsals. Seyfried says, 'I directed the study of the parts with all the singers according to his suggestions, also all the orchestral rehearsals, and personally conducted the performance.' In 1805 Seyfried was young, talented, ambitious, zealous, and nothing was wanting on his part to ensure success.

Speaking of the rehearsals recalls to mind one of those bursts of puerile wrath, which were passed over with a smile by some of Beethoven's friends, but gave serious offence to others. Mähler remembered that at one of the general rehearsals the third bassoon was absent; at which Beethoven fretted and fumed. Lobkowitz, who was present, made light of the matter: two of the bassoons were present, said he, and the absence of the third could make no great difference. This so enraged the composer that, as he passed the Lobkowitz Palace, on his way home, he could not restrain the impulse to turn aside and shout in at the great door of the palace: 'Lobkowitzian ass!'

Schindler writes:

'It was the overture* in the first place that put our master in a painful situation. It was finished, but the composer himself was not thoroughly satisfied with it, and therefore agreed that it should be tried by a small orchestra, at Prince Lichnowsky's. There it was unanimously pronounced by a knot of connoisseurs to be too light, and not sufficiently expressive of the nature of the work; consequently it was laid aside and never made its appearance again in Beethoven's lifetime.'

The initial performance of the opera was originally scheduled for 15 October. A petition from Sonnleithner to the theatre censor, dated 2 October 1805, sheds much light on the vicissitudes of the production:

'Court Secretary Josef Sonnleithner begs that the ban of this 30 September on the opera Fidelio be lifted since this opera from the French original of Boully (entitled Leonore, ou l'amour conjugal) *has been most especially revised because the Empress had found the original very beautiful and affirmed* that no opera subject had ever given her so much pleasure; secondly: this opera which was revised by Kapellmeister Paër in Italian has been given already in Prague and Dresden; thirdly: *Beethoven* has spent over a year and a half with the composition, also since the ban was completely unanticipated, rehearsals have already been held and other arrangements have been made in order to give this opera on the name-day of the Empress [15 October]; fourthly: the plot takes place in the 16th century, thus there could be no underlying relationship; finally in the fifth place: there exists such a big lack of opera libretti, this one presents the quietest description of womanly virtue and the evil-minded governor is executing only a private revenge like Pedrarias in Balboa.'

On 5 October, the ban was lifted after some changes had been made in the most harsh scenes. But the postponement of the performance

* Now known as the *Leonore* No. 1 Overture.

for another five weeks was due not to censorship problems but to the mechanics of getting the music composed, copied and rehearsed. Let one of the notes from Beethoven to Sebastian Mayer suggest the situation:

'Dear Mayer! The third act quartet is now all right; what has been written out with red pencil must be written over in ink by the copyist right away, otherwise it will fade away! – This afternoon I shall send for the 1st and 2nd acts again because I want to look through them also myself. – I cannot come, because since yesterday I have had *diarrhoea – my usual sickness*. Don't worry about the overture and the rest; if necessary everything could be ready even by tomorrow. In the present *fatal crisis* I have so many other things to do that I must put off everything which is not completely necessary.

Your Friend Beethoven'

This overture could have been none other than the so-called *Leonore* No. 2 since *Leonore* No. 1 had been found to be unsatisfactory at the private hearing at Prince Lichnowsky's. As with *Leonore* No. 3, the autographs for both these overtures have disappeared.

Outside the narrow circle of the playhouse, weightier matters than a new opera now occupied and agitated the minds of the Viennese. On 20 October, Ulm fell. On the 30th Bernadotte entered Salzburg, on his way to and down the Danube; Vienna was defenceless. The nobility, the great bankers and merchants – all those whose wealth enabled and whose vocations permitted it – precisely those classes of society in which Beethoven moved, which knew how to appreciate his music, and of whose suffrages his opera was assured, fled from the capital. On 9 November the Empress departed. On the 10th the French armies had reached and occupied the villages a few miles west of the city. On 13 November, about 11 o'clock in the forenoon, the vanguard of the enemy, Murat and Lannes at the head, 15,000 strong, representing all branches of the service, entered Vienna in order of battle, flags flying and music sounding.

On the 15th, Bonaparte issued his proclamation from Schönbrunn, which he made his headquarters. Murat quartered himself in the palace of Archduke Albert; General Hulin, in that of Prince Lobkowitz. It was just at this most unlucky of all possible periods that Beethoven's opera was produced; on 20, 21 and 22 November. Beethoven desired to retain the original title of the opera, *Leonore*, and the directors of the theatre have been severely censured from that day to this for persisting in giving and retaining the title *Fidelio*.

Concerning the circumstance of the performance, the correspondent for Kotzebue's *Freymüthige* (26 December 1805) describes first the military occupation of Vienna, the officers quartered in the city proper, and the private soldiery in the suburbs. He continues:

'Also in the beginning the theatres were completely empty; gradually the French began to go to them, and they still form the majority of the audience.

'Recently little new of significance has been given. A new Beethoven opera "Fidelio or Die eheliche Liebe" has not pleased. It was performed only a few times and after the first performance [the theatre] remained completely empty. Also the music was really way below the expectations of amateur and professional alike. The melodies as well as the general character, much of which is affected, lack that happy, clear, magical impression of emotion which grips us so irresistibly in the works of Mozart and Cherubini. The music has some beautiful passages, but it is very far from being a perfect, yes, even successful work.'

In the issue of 8 January 1806, the correspondent of the *Allgemeine Musikalische Zeitung* says that he had expected something very different, in view of Beethoven's undisputed talent.

'Up to now Beethoven has sacrificed beauty so many times for the new and strange; thus this characteristic of newness and a certain originality in creative idea was expected from this first theatrical production of his – and it is exactly these qualities that are the least in evidence. Judged dispassionately and with an open mind, the whole is distinguishable neither by invention nor execution. The overture . . . cannot be compared with his overture to the ballet *Prometheus*. As a rule there are no new ideas in the vocal pieces, they are mostly too long, the text repeats itself endlessly, and finally the characterisation fails remarkably . . . The choruses are ineffectual and one, which indicates the joy of prisoners over the sensation of fresh air, miscarries completely . . .'

Joseph August Röckel (1783–1870), a young man educated at the University of Munich, had for some time been private secretary to the Bavarian chargé d'affaires at Salzburg. The approach of the French armies after the fall of Ulm made his position and prospects very uncertain. It was just then that an agent of Baron Braun came thither in search of a young, fresh tenor to succeed Joseph Demmer, who was originally cast as Florestan but whose powers were fast yielding to time. The engagement was offered him and thus it came about that

Röckel, in the autumn of 1805, became first tenor in the Theater-an-der-Wien. After appearing in divers characters with much success, considering his inexperience, he was offered the part of Florestan in the contemplated revival of *Fidelio*. He was present at a stormy six-hour soirée when a group of the composer's friends persuaded him to make major cuts in the opera in order to remove what they perceived as the heaviness of the first act – including the omission of three whole numbers. He later recorded:

'When after their united endeavours from seven till after one o'clock, the sacrifice of the three numbers was accomplished, and when we, exhausted, hungry and thirsty, went to restore ourselves by a splendid supper – then, none was happier and gayer than Beethoven. Had I seen him before in his fury, I saw him now in his frolics. When he saw me, opposite to him, so intently occupied with a French dish, and asked me what I was eating, and I answered: "I don't know!" with his lion-voice he roared out: "He eats like a wolf – without knowing what! Ha, ha, ha!" '

Beethoven felt the loss of Ries very sensibly; but it was in part supplied by young Röckel, to whom he took a great liking. Inviting him to call, he told him he would give special orders to his servant to admit him at all times, even in the morning when busy. It was agreed that, when Röckel was admitted, if he found Beethoven very much occupied he should pass through the room into the bedchamber beyond and there await him a reasonable time; if the composer came not, Röckel should quietly pass out again. It happened one morning upon his first visit that Röckel found at the street door a carriage with a lady in it; and, on reaching the fourth storey, there, at Beethoven's door, was Prince Lichnowsky in a dispute with the servant about being admitted. The man declared he dared not admit anybody, as his master was busy and had given express orders not to admit any person whatever. Röckel, however, having the entrée, informed Beethoven that Lichnowsky was outside. Though in ill humour, he could no longer refuse to see him. The Prince and his wife had come to take Beethoven out for an airing; and he finally consented, but, as he entered the carriage, Röckel noticed that his face was still cloudy.

A remark of Czerny's is as follows:

'When the French were in Vienna for the first time, in 1805, Beethoven was visited by a number of officers and generals who were musical and for whom he played Gluck's *Iphigenia in Tauris* from the score, to which they sang the choruses and songs not at all ill. I begged the score from him and at home wrote out the pianoforte score as I had heard him play it. I still have this arrangement (November 1852). From that time I date my style of arranging orchestral works, and he was always wholly satisfied with my arrangements of his symphonies, etc.'

A lad who, though not yet fifteen years old, was able to write a pianoforte score of such an opera after a single hearing, certainly deserved the testimonial to his talent which, though written by another hand, was signed at the time by Beethoven and sealed.

'We, the undersigned, cannot withhold from the lad Carl Czerny, who has made such extraordinary progress on the pianoforte, far surpassing what might be expected from a boy of fourteen years, that for this reason, and also because of his marvellous memory, he is deserving of all possible support, the more since his parents have expended their fortune in the education of this promising son.

Vienna, 7 December 1805

Ludwig van Beethoven (Seal)'

The master had early and wisely warned him against a too free use of his extraordinary memory. Czerny writes: 'My musical memory enabled me to play the Beethovenian works by heart without exception, and during the years 1804–5 I was obliged to play these works in this manner at Prince Lichnowsky's once or twice a week, he calling out only the desired opus numbers.'

Schindler closes his account of these five years in Beethoven's life with great propriety and elegance by quoting a passage copied by the master from Christian Sturm's *Betrachtungen*. It is made up of scattered sentences:

'To the praise of thy goodness I must confess that Thou hast tried all means to draw me to Thee. Now it hath pleased Thee to let me feel the heavy hand of Thy wrath, and to humiliate my proud heart by manifold chastisements. Sickness and misfortune hast Thou sent to bring me to a contemplation of my digressions. But one thing only do I ask, O God, cease not to labour for my improvement. Only let me, in whatsoever manner pleases Thee, turn to Thee and be fruitful of good works.'

CHAPTER 11

The Years 1806 and 1807

The Fourth and Fifth Symphonies – The Mass in C

Excerpts from a letter written on 2 June 1806, by Stephan von Breuning to his sister and brother-in-law, make a fair opening for the story of the year 1806. In it he reports on *Fidelio*. The letter, though written in the middle of the year, has reference to the period between the original performance late in 1805 and the repetition in the spring of 1806, a period in which it would seem Beethoven was in no mood, or too much occupied otherwise, for correspondence. Von Breuning writes:

'. . . Nothing, perhaps, has caused Beethoven so much vexation as this work, the value of which will be appreciated only in the future . . . Beethoven, who had also observed a few imperfections in the treatment of the text in the opera, withdrew it after three representations. After order had been restored he and I took it up again. I remodelled the whole book for him, quickening and enlivening the action; he curtailed many pieces, and then it was performed three times with great success. Now, however, his enemies in the theatre arose, and as he had offended several persons, especially at the second representation, they succeeded in preventing further performances. Before this, many obstacles had been placed in his way; to let one instance stand as proof for the others, he could not even get permission to secure an announcement of the opera under the changed title *Leonore*, as it is called in the French original, and as it was put into print after the changes were made. Contrary to promise the first title *Fidelio* appeared on the poster. This is all the more unpleasant for Beethoven since the cessation of the performances on which he was depending for his honorarium, which consists in a percentage of the receipts, has embarrassed him in a financial way. He will recover from the setback all the more slowly since the treatment which he has received has robbed him of a great deal of his pleasure in and love for work . . .'

It is noteworthy that Breuning, instead of Sonnleithner, revised the text and made the new disposition of the scenes. Furthermore, in a letter to Sonnleithner near the end of the period of revision Beethoven withheld from him the knowledge of Breuning's share in the rewriting:

'Dear best Sonnleithner!

'I hope you will not refuse me when I beg you very sincerely *to give me a small statement in writing that I may again have the libretto printed with your name* [!] *with its present alterations* – When I made the changes, you were thoroughly occupied . . . and so I made them myself. You would not have had the patience to undertake these changes and it would have made for further delays in the performance of our opera. – Therefore I quietly dared to hope for your consent. *The three acts have been made into only two.* In order to effect this and give the opera a livelier course, I have *shortened everything* as much as possible, the chorus of *prisoners* and music of that sort particularly. – All this made it necessary *to revise only the first act*, and therein lies the *change* in the libretto –

'I will carry the cost of printing, and beg you once again for a *granting of my request* –

respectfully yours   Beethowen'

'PS The time is so short, otherwise I would have sent you the libretto to convince you –'

'PPS Send me, best S , this statement right away by my servant, because I must show it to the *censor*.'

And thus for Beethoven the winter passed. To compete with successful new works which Schikaneder offered the Vienna audiences of 1806 was no light matter; and it is easy to imagine that Beethoven felt this, and determined, at all events in his own field of instrumental composition, to leave no doubt who was master. Hence, that monumental work, the great overture to *Leonore* in its third form. He was, as usual, dilatory in meeting his engagements. January and February passed and March drew to a close, and the overture was not ready. This was too much for Baron Braun's patience. He, therefore, selected the best night of the season – Saturday 29 March, the last before the closing of the theatre for Holy Week and Easter – and gave Beethoven distinctly to understand that if the opera were not performed on that evening, it should not be given at all. This was effectual and the new score was sent in; but so late as to allow but two or three rehearsals with pianoforte and only one with orchestra; and these were directed by Seyfried – the composer appearing at neither.

Beethoven and Breuning supposed that a change of title from *Fidelio* to *Leonore* had been agreed to by the directors, and indeed the new text-book on the occasion was so printed; but it was determined otherwise. By the new arrangement of the scenes, the number of acts was reduced to two. The new playbill therefore substitutes 'Opera in two Acts' for 'three'; excepting this, the change of date, and of Röckel's for Demmer's name as Florestan, it is a facsimile of the previous ones, and announces: 'Fidelio oder die Eheliche Liebe'.

The correspondent of the *Allgemeine Musikalische Zeitung*, under date of 2 April, wrote: 'Beethoven has again produced his opera *Fidelio* on the stage with many alterations and abbreviations. An entire act has been omitted, but the piece has benefited and pleased better.' On Thursday, the 10th, it was given again.

Two notes written to Sebastian Mayer between the two perfor-mances show Beethoven's dissatisfaction with the first performance and with the preparation in general:

'Dear Mayer,
  'Baron Braun tells me that *my opera* is supposed to be performed on *Thursday*; I shall ask you please to see to it that the choruses get more rehearsals, for last time they were full of blunders. Also, we must have another rehearsal on *Thursday in the theatre with the whole orchestra –* The *orchestra* for sure was not at fault, but – *on the stage several were*; but that was too much to ask since the time was too short. But I had to bring it off then for B. Braun had threatened me with the fact that if the opera were not given on Saturday it would not be given any more. I am counting on your loyalty and friendship, which you have shown me in the past, to take care of this opera now; after this the opera will no longer need such rehearsals and you can perform it when you want to. Here are two libretti, I ask you to give one to *Röckel*. Farewell, dear Mayer, and give my affair your attention.
                                        Your friend Beethoven'

In the second note, Beethoven's dissatisfaction had mounted, and the orchestra was sharply criticised:

'Dear Mayer!
  'Please ask Hr. v. Seyfried to conduct my opera today, I want to look at it and hear it from a distance. Thus at least my patience will not be so greatly tried as if I were to hear my music bungled close at hand! I can-not help thinking that it has been done on purpose. I will say nothing about the wind-instruments, but – that all *pp*, crescendos, all *decres.*, and all fortes, *ff*, have been scratched out of my opera! At any rate they

are not all played. All delight in composing departs when one hears one's music played *thus*! Tomorrow or the day after I will fetch you for dinner. Today I am unwell again.

Your friend Beethoven'

'PS – If the opera is to be given the day after tomorrow there must be a rehearsal again *tomorrow* in the room – otherwise it will get worse and worse each day!'

The production of *Fidelio* on Thursday 10 April was the last; for which fact two explanations are given – that in Breuning's letter, and one by Röckel in his letter to the author. Breuning attributes it to the composer's enemies – to a cabal, to 'several persons whom Beethoven had offended, especially at the second representation'; Röckel, to Beethoven's own imprudence and folly.

Breuning, a Secretary in the War Office, could have had little leisure for theatrical matters in those melancholy days during the French occupation and immediately after; it is a cause of surprise that he found time for the revision of the *Fidelio* text; his record, therefore, could hardly have been made except upon the representations of his friend – the last man to admit that he was in fault. But Röckel was behind the scenes in a double sense: he sang the part of Florestan and while Beethoven's 'friends were, most of them, married men, not able to walk and dine out with him like myself, another bachelor, to whom he took a fancy – I could call upon him in the morning and in fine weather stroll and dine with him in the country.'

In the second of the notes to Mayer, Beethoven is guilty of monstrous injustice. A moment's reflection shows this. The orchestra and chorus had duly rehearsed and three times publicly performed *Fidelio* as first written. Since then most of the numbers, perhaps every one, had been more or less changed. Now every musician knows that it is easier to play a piece of new music correctly at sight, than a well-known composition in which material alterations have been made. And yet, because some forty men – playing on a dozen different instruments, and after a single rehearsal at which the composer was not present to explain his intentions – did not effect the impossibility of reading the music correctly and at the same time note all the marks of expression, Beethoven writes: 'I cannot help thinking that it has been done on purpose.'

All things considered, there can be no hesitation in preferring the testimony of the singer of Florestan to that of the Court War Councillor. Röckel writes:

'When the opera was produced in the beginning of the following year, it was exceedingly well received by a select public, which became more numerous and enthusiastic with each new representation; and no doubt the opera would have become a favourite if the evil genius of the composer had not prevented it, and as he, Beethoven, was paid for his work by a percentage, instead of a mere honorarium, an advantage which none enjoyed before him, it would have considerably advanced his pecuniary arrangements. Having had no theatrical experience, he was estimating the receipts of the house much higher than they really were; he believed himself cheated in his percentage, and without consulting his real friends on such a delicate point, he hastened to Baron Braun – that high-minded and honourable nobleman – and submitted his complaint. The Baron, seeing Beethoven excited and conscious of his *one susceptibility* (i.e., suspicious temper), did what he could to cure him of his suspicions against his employees, of whose honesty he was sure. Were there any fraud, the Baron said, his own loss would be beyond comparison more considerable than Beethoven's. He hoped that the receipts would increase with each representation; until now, only the first ranks, stalls and pit were occupied; by and by the upper ranks would likewise contribute their shares.

' "I don't write for the galleries!" exclaimed Beethoven.

' "No?" replied the Baron. "My dear Sir, even Mozart did not disdain to write for the galleries."

'Now it was at an end. "I will not give the opera any more," said Beethoven, "I want my score back." Here Baron Braun rang the bell, gave orders for the delivery of the score to the composer, and the opera was buried for a long time.'

The orchestral parts of the opera, however, evidently remained at the theatre, and a note to Baron Braun, written by Beethoven only a few weeks later, shows the composer in a more conciliatory mood. He asked the Baron's permission to borrow the following:

'. . .*flauto primo*, the three trombones and the four horn parts of my opera. – I need them, but only for a day, in order to have a few *trifles* copied for myself, which *could not be written into the score for want of room*, also because *Prince Lobkowitz is thinking of giving the opera at his house* and has asked me for it. – I am not completely well, otherwise I would have come myself to pay my respects –'

There were other reasons why Beethoven desired to render his score perfect. Whether the opera was performed in the Lobkowitz palace is not recorded; but Breuning ends his letter of 2 June thus: 'I will only write you the news that Prince Lichnowsky has now sent the opera to the Queen of Prussia, and that I hope the performances in Berlin will show the Viennese what they have at home.'

Breuning's hope was vain; the opera was not given in Berlin at this time. In truth, Beethoven had overshot the mark. The overture was too novel in form and grand in substance to be immediately understood; and, in 1806, there was not an audience in Europe able to find, in the fire and expression of the principal vocal numbers, an adequate compensation for the superficial graces and melodic beauties of the favourite operas of the time, which seemed to them to be wanting in *Fidelio*.

In 1836, Schindler conversed with the Fidelio of 1805–6, Madame Milder-Hauptmann, on the subject: 'She said, among other things, that she, too, had had severe struggles with the master chiefly about the unbeautiful, unsingable passages, unsuited to her voice, in the Adagio of the air in E major – but all in vain, until, in 1814, she declared that she would never sing the air again in its then shape. That worked.'

The order of time requires a passing notice of a family event which proved in the end a cause of infinite trouble and vexation to Beethoven and all connected to him by the ties of kindred or friendship. On 25 May 1806 'a marriage contract was closed between Carl Caspar v. Beethoven, RI Officer of the Revenue, and of this city, and Johanna Reiss, daughter of Anton Reiss, civilian, upholsterer'. Their only child, a son, was born on 4 September 1806. Reiss was a man of considerable wealth for one in his sphere of life, and able, it is said, to give his daughter a marriage portion of 2,000 florins. It appears, too, that the valuable house in the Alservorstadt owned by Carl at the time of his death was an inheritance of his wife's from her father's estate; indeed, half the right to the property was legally secured to her. It would seem natural that after his marriage, Caspar should gradually cease to manage his brother's business affairs. The break was not immediate, as is shown by a letter of 5 July to Breitkopf and Härtel in which Beethoven refers to a possible trip of Caspar's to Leipzig 'for his office', at which time the firm was to discuss with him an agreement concerning the possible sale of some compositions. However after this date it seems clear that Carl Caspar no longer took an active part in negotiations with publishers.

The notices of Beethoven's own movements during this year are scanty. *Fidelio* and studies to instrumental works employed him during the winter, but not to the exclusion of social intercourse, as one of his characteristic memoranda indicates. It is written with lead pencil on a page of the new quartet sketches: 'Just as you are now plunging into the whirlpool of society – just so possible is it to compose works in spite of social obstacles. Let your deafness no longer be a secret – even in art.'

Breuning's report (2 June), that Beethoven had lost 'a great deal of his pleasure in and love for work', had even then ceased to be true. On 26 May, the writing out of the first of the Razumovsky Quartets had been begun – and with this came a series of works which distinguished the year 1806 as one of astonishing productiveness.

Two brothers, differing in age by nineteen years, had owed their rise from the condition of singers at the Russian Court into positions of great wealth and political importance to their gratification of the lascivious lusts of two imperial princesses, afterwards known in history as the Empresses Elizabeth Petrovna and Catherine II. Thus the two Razums, born in 1709 and 1728, of half-Cossack parentage, in the obscure Ukraine village of Lemeschi, became the Counts Razumovsky, nobles of the Russian Empire. They were men of rare ability, and, like Shakespeare's Duncan, 'bore their faculties so meek' that none of the monarchs under whom they served, not even those who personally disliked either of them, made him the victim of imperial caprice or ill will. The Empresses provided their paramours with wives from noble families and continued their kindness to the children born of these unions – one of whom came in time to occupy a rather prominent place among the patrons of Beethoven.

Andreas Kyrillovitch (born 22 October 1752), fourth son of the younger Razumovsky, was destined for the navy and received the best education possible in those days for his profession, even to serving in what was then the best of all schools, an English man-of-war. He had been elevated to the rank of captain when, at the age of twenty-five, he was transferred to the diplomatic service. He was Ambassador successively at Venice, Naples, Copenhagen and Stockholm; less famous, perhaps, for his diplomacy than notorious for the profuseness of his expenditures, and for his amours with women of the highest rank, the Queen of Naples not excepted.

Razumovsky was personally widely known at Vienna, where he had married (4 November 1788) Elizabeth, Countess Thun, elder sister of the Princess Karl Lichnowsky, and whither he was transferred as Ambassador early in 1792. He lived in Vienna like a prince, encouraging art and science, surrounded by a luxurious library and other collections and admired and envied by all; what advantages accrued from all this to Russian affairs is another question.

True to the traditions of his family, the Count was a musician and one of the best connoisseurs and players of Haydn's quartets. It would seem a matter of course that this man would be one of the first to appreciate and encourage the genius of the young Beethoven upon his removal from Bonn to Vienna. But the evidence is scanty for the earlier years. The Count may have provided the opportunity at his home for the rehearsal of pieces freshly composed by Beethoven. At any rate, at the end of 1805 Beethoven received a commission for three quartets from the Count. Since he had already returned to the idea of quartet writing, this commission was soon to be fulfilled.

It is quite certain that Beethoven took no summer lodgings in 1806; but he did leave the city at the end of the summer. In a postscript to a letter to Breitkopf and Härtel dated 3 September he writes: 'My present place of sojourn is here in Silesia so long as autumn lasts – with Prince Lichnowsky – who sends greetings to you. My address is L. v. Beethoven in Troppau.' In the main part of the letter Beethoven laid down the conditions under which he would be willing to enter into a contract offered him by the Leipzig publishers which would obligate him 'not to sell any more of my works in Germany to anyone except you'. Breitkopf and Härtel received another letter from Beethoven on 18 November after his return to Vienna, in which he suggested that his word of honour would be preferable to the problem of figuring out the wording of a contract. He writes: 'For the present I offer you three quartets and a pianoforte concerto – I cannot give you the promised symphony yet – because a gentleman of quality has taken it from me, but I have the privilege of publishing it in half a year.' All of these negotiations were without result, and the compositions mentioned were published by the Kunst- und Industrie-Comptoir. These were the Razumovsky Quartets and the Fourth Piano Concerto. The symphony referred to was doubtless the fourth, in B flat, and the 'gentleman of quality' Count von Oppersdorff, to whom it was dedicated.

In October Breuning wrote to Wegeler:

'Beethoven is at present in Silesia with Prince Lichnowsky and will not return till near the end of this month. His circumstances are none of the best at present, since his opera, owing to the cabals of his opponents, was performed but seldom, and therefore yielded him nothing. His spirits are generally low and, to judge by his letters, the sojourn in the country has not cheered him.'

This visit to the Prince came to an abrupt termination in a scene which has been a fruitful theme for the silly race of musical novelette writers. The simple truth was derived by the present writer from a conversation with the daughter of Moritz Lichnowsky:

'When he [Beethoven] did not feel in the mood it required repeated and varied urgings to get him to sit down to the pianoforte. Before he began playing he was in the habit of hitting the keys with the flat of his hand, or running a single finger up and down the keyboard, in short, doing all manner of things to kill time and laughing heartily, as was his wont, at the folly. Once while spending a summer with a Maecenas at his country-seat, he was so pestered by the guests [French officers], who wished to hear him play, that he grew angry and refused to do what he denounced as menial labour. A threat of arrest, made surely in jest, was taken seriously by him and resulted in Beethoven's walking by night to the nearest city, Troppau, whence he hurried as on the wings of the wind by extra post to Vienna.'

To propitiate him for the humiliation which he had suffered, the bust of his patron had to become a sacrifice; he dashed it into pieces from its place on a cabinet to the floor. There is an anecdote which illustrates the feeling which made Beethoven so unwilling to play before the French officers. After the battle at Jena (14 October 1806) Beethoven met his friend Krumpholz, to whom he was warmly attached, and, as usual, asked him, 'What's the news?' Krumpholz answered that the latest news was the report just received that the great hero Napoleon had won another decisive victory over the Prussians. Greatly angered, Beethoven replied to this: 'It's a pity that I do not understand the art of war as well as I do the art of music, I would conquer him!'

A letter by Beethoven, dated Vienna, 1 November, refers to his involvement with a project originally proposed in 1803 by an earnest promoter of good music, George Thomson, a Scottish gentleman – that of making the most extensive collection possible of the music of Scotland. Many compilations, various in extent and merit, had been published, but all of them, as Thomson justly remarks, 'more or less defective and exceptionable'. In one of his prefaces he says:

'To furnish a collection of all the fine airs, both of the plaintive and the lively kind, unmixed with trifling and inferior ones – to obtain the most suitable and finished accompaniments, with the addition of characteristic symphonies to introduce and conclude each air – and to substitute congenial and interesting songs, every way worthy of the music, in the room of insipid or exceptionable verses, were the great objects of the present publication . . .

'For the composition of the symphonies and accompaniments, he [the editor] entered into terms with Mr Pleyel, who fulfilled part of his engagement satisfactorily; but having then stopped short, the editor found it necessary to turn his eyes elsewhere. He was so fortunate, however, as to engage Mr Koželuch, and afterwards, Dr Haydn, to proceed with the work, which they have finished in such a manner as to leave him nothing to regret on Mr Pleyel's breach of engagement . . .'

Doubtless Thomson would have applied sooner to Haydn, had he known that the great master would condescend to such a labour. A very remarkable feature of the enterprise was, that the composers of the accompaniments had no knowledge of the texts, and the writers of the poetry no knowledge of the accompaniments. The poets, in many cases, had a stanza of the original song as a model for the metre and rhythm; in all others, they and the composers alike received the bare melody, with nothing else to guide them in their work but Italian musical terms: allegro, moderato, andante, etc., etc., affettuoso, espressivo, scherzando, and the like. This is also true of the Welsh and Irish melodies. Beethoven began his labours for Thomson with the last named. In the preface to the first volume, dated 'Edinburgh, anno 1814', after describing his work in collecting Irish airs, Thomson says:

'They were sent to Haydn to be harmonised along with the Scottish and Welsh airs; but after that celebrated composer had finished the greater part of those two works, his declining health only enabled him to harmonise a few of the Irish Melodies; and upon his death, it became necessary to find another composer to whom the task of harmonising them should be committed. Of all composers that are now living, it is acknowledged by every intelligent and unprejudiced musician, that the only one who occupies the same distinguished rank with the late Haydn is BEETHOVEN. Possessing the most original genius and inventive fancy, united to profound science, refined taste and an enthusiastic love of his art – his compositions, like those of his illustrious predecessor, will bear endless repetition and afford ever new delight. To this composer, therefore, the Editor eagerly applied for symphonies and accompaniments to the Irish Melodies; and to his inexpressible satisfaction, Beethoven undertook the composition. After years of anxious suspense and teasing disappointment, by the miscarriage of letters and manuscripts, owing to the unprecedented difficulty of communication between England and Vienna, the long expected symphonies and accompaniments at last reached the Editor, three other copies having previously been lost upon the road.'

Following is a translation of the letter to Thomson referred to, which was written in French:

'Vienna, 1 November 1806

'Dear Sir:

'A little excursion to Silesia which I have made is the reason why I have postponed till now answering your letter of 1 July. On my return to Vienna I hasten to communicate to you what I have to say and what I have decided as to the proposals you were so kind as to make me. I will speak with all candour and exactitude, which I like in business affairs, and which alone can forestall any complaint on either side. Here, then, my dear Sir, are my statements:

'1. I am not indisposed, on the whole, to accept your propositions.

'2. I will take care to make the compositions easy and pleasing, as far as I can and as far as is consistent with that elevation and originality of style which, as you yourself say, favourably characterise my works and from which I shall never stoop.

'3. I cannot bring myself to write for the flute, as this instrument is too limited and imperfect.

'4. To give greater variety to the compositions which you will publish, and to give me a freer field in these compositions, in which the task of making them easy would ever thwart me, I can promise you only three trios for violin, viola and violoncello, and three quintets for two violins, two violas and violoncello. Instead of the remaining three trios and three quintets, I shall give you three quartets, and finally two sonatas for pianoforte with accompaniment for two violins and flute, and one quintet. – In a word, I would ask you, in regard to the second series of compositions you ask of me, to rely completely upon my taste and good faith, and I assure you that you will be entirely satisfied – However, if you cannot agree to any of these changes, I do not wish to insist upon them obstinately. –

'5. I should be glad if the second series of compositions were published six months after the first.

'6. I must have a clearer explanation of the statement which I find in your letter that no copy printed under my name shall be introduced into Great Britain; for if you agree that these compositions are to be published in Germany and also in France, I do not see how I can prevent copies from being taken into your country. –

'7. Finally, as regards the honorarium, I understand that you are offering me 100 pounds sterling, or 200 Vienna ducats *in gold* and not in Vienna banknotes, which under the present circumstances entail too great a loss; for if paid in these notes the sum would be too little for the works which I am sending you in proportion to the honorarium which I receive for all my other compositions. – Even the honorarium of two hundred ducats *in gold* is by no means excessive payment for everything that has to be done in order to satisfy your wishes –

'Finally, the best way of making the payment would be for you to send me by post, at the time when I send you the first and again the second series, a bill of exchange for 100 ducats *in gold* drawn upon a banking house in Hamburg; or for you to commission someone in Vienna each time to give me such a bill of exchange at the time he receives from me the first and the second series. –

'At the same time please let me know the date on which you will publish each series, so that I may oblige the publishers who issue these same compositions in Germany and France to abide by the same. –

'I hope that you will find my declarations reasonable and of such a sort that we can reach some definite agreement. – In this case it would be well to draw up a formal contract, which please have the kindness to prepare in duplicate, and of which I shall return you one copy with my signature. –

'I await only your answer before setting to work, and am, with distinguished esteem, my dear Sir,

Your obedient servant,

Louis van Beethoven'

'PS I will also be glad to fulfil your wish to harmonise the little Scottish airs; and in this matter I await a more definite proposal, since it is well known to me that Mr Haydn was paid one pound sterling for each song. –'

Of the various propositions mentioned in this letter, only that of the Scottish songs led to any results.

The Fourth Pianoforte Concerto was offered to Hoffmeister and Kühnel along with *Christus am Ölberg* for 600 florins on 27 March 1806 by brother Carl. The composer himself wrote to Breitkopf and Härtel on 5 July that his brother, who was travelling to Leipzig, would bring with him 'the overture to my opera in pianoforte arrangement, my oratorio and a *new pianoforte concerto*'. It is not known whether this projected trip ever took place. New offers were made in the autumn, still with no results. Thus the work, composed probably by the spring of this year, may not have received its final touches until the end of the year through lack of a publisher.

A song translated by Breuning from Solie's opera *Le Secret* was probably the first fruits of the newly awakened 'desire and love for work', which proved so nobly productive during the summer. But, whether or not this was the first composition after the withdrawal of *Fidelio*, it is certain that just one week before the date of the Breuning letter (to the Wegelers on 2 June, with which this chapter opened),

Beethoven had set resolutely to work upon grander themes. He began to work out the quartets, Op. 59, on 26 May, commissioned by Razumovsky.

These quartets were evidently planned as far back as the autumn of 1804, judging from a letter written by Carl to Breitkopf and Härtel on 24 November of that year: 'I cannot yet say anything definite to you about the quartets, as soon as they are ready, I will write to you immediately.' Sketches for the last three movements of Op. 59, No. 1, especially for the second movement, occur in the latter part of the *Leonore* sketchbook. Thus Beethoven's own words on the autograph of the first quartet – 'Quartetto I^{mo} . . . Begun on 26 May 1806' – probably refer to the final working out of the work. On 5 July 1806, Beethoven wrote to Breitkopf and Härtel: '. . . you may also negotiate with him [Carl] touching some new violin *quartets* of which I have already completed one and now am intending to devote myself almost wholly to this work . . .'

Other sketches for all three quartets exist on thirty-four separate sheets which have been preserved in the Archives of the Gesellschaft der Musikfreunde. On 3 September 1806, Beethoven wrote to Breitkopf and Härtel: '. . . you may have at once 3 *violin quartets* . . .' The opus number, the reports of their performance during the next winter, and, especially, the date of their publication (January 1808), making allowance for Razumovsky's right to them for a year, all point to November or December as the latest possible date for their completion.

Perhaps no work of Beethoven's met a more discouraging reception from musicians than these now famous quartets. One friendly contemporary voice alone is heard – that of the *Allgemeine Musikalische Zeitung* (27 February 1807):

'Three new, very long and difficult Beethoven string quartets, dedicated to the Russian Ambassador, Count Razumovsky, are also attracting the attention of all connoisseurs. The conception is profound and the construction excellent, but they are not easily comprehended – with the possible exception of the 3rd in C major which cannot but appeal to intelligent lovers of music because of its originality, melody and harmonic power.'

Czerny told Jahn that 'when Schuppanzigh first played the Razumovsky Quartet in F, they laughed and were convinced that Beethoven was playing a joke and that it was not the quartet which had been promised'. The Allegretto vivace of the first of these quartets was long a rock of offence. 'When at the beginning of the year 1812', says Lenz, 'the movement was to be played for the first time in the musical circle of Field Marshal Count Soltikoff in Moscow, Bernhard Romberg trampled under foot as a contemptible mystification the bass part which he was to play. The quartet was laid aside. When, a few years later, it was played at the house of Privy Councillor Lwoff, father of the famous violinist, in St Petersburg, the company broke out in laughter when the bass played his solo on *one* note. – The quartet was again laid aside.'

Thomas Appleby, father of Samuel Appleby, collector of valuable papers referring to the violinist Bridgetower, was a leader in the musical world of Manchester, England, and a principal director of concerts there. When these quartets came out in London, Clementi sent a copy of them to him. They were opened and thrown upon the pianoforte. Next day Felix Radicati and his wife, Mme Bertinotti, called and presented letters, they being upon a concert tour. During the conversation the Italian went to the pianoforte, took up the quartets and seeing what they were, exclaimed (in substance): 'Have you got these here! Ha! Beethoven, as the world says, and as I believe, is music-mad; – for these are not music. He submitted them to me in manuscript and, at his request, I fingered them for him. I said to him, that he surely did not consider these works to be music? – to which he replied, "Oh, they are not for you, but for a later age!" '

Young Appleby believed in them, in spite of Radicati, and after he had studied his part thoroughly, his father invited players of the other instruments to his house and the first in F was tried. The first movement was declared by all except Appleby to be 'crazy music'. At the end of the violoncello solo on one note, they all burst out laughing; the next four bars all agreed were beautiful. Sudlow, an organist, who played the bass, found so much to admire and so much to condemn in the half of this second movement, which they succeeded in playing, as to call it 'patchwork by a madman'. They gave up the attempt to play it, and not until 1813, in London, did the young man succeed in hearing the three quartets entire, and finding them, as he had believed, worthy of their author.

The Symphony in B flat, Op. 60, was the great work of this summer season. Sketches prove that its successor, the fifth in C minor, had been commenced, and was laid aside to give place to this. Nothing more is known of the history of its composition except what is imparted by the author's inscription on the manuscript: 'Sinfonia 4ta, 1806. L. v. Bthvn.'

Although the composer did not succeed in bringing his new Symphony and Concerto to public performance this year, an opportunity offered itself for him to give the general public as fine a taste of his

quality as composer for the violin as he had just given to the fre-
quenters of Razumovsky's quartet parties in the Op. 59, namely, the
Violin Concerto, Op. 61. The work was superscribed by its author:
'Concerto par Clemenza pour Clement, primo Violino e Direttore al
Theatro a Vienna, dal L. v. Bthvn., 1806'; – or, as it stands on Franz
Clement's concert programme of 23 December in the Theater-an-
der-Wien: '2. A new Violin Concerto by Hr. Ludwig van Beethoven,
played by Hr. Clement.' It was preceded by an overture by Méhul, and
followed by selections from Mozart, Cherubini and Handel, closing
with a fantasia by the concert-giver. The sketches for the Concerto all
belong to this year and appear alongside sketches for the Violoncello
Sonata, Op. 69, and the Fifth Symphony. When Dr Bertolini told Jahn
that 'Beethoven as a rule never finished commissioned works until the
last minute', he named this Concerto as an instance in point; and
another contemporary notes that Clement played the solo *a vista*, without previous rehearsal.

In singular contrast to these grand works and contemporary with
their completion, as if written for amusement and recreation after the
fatigue of severer studies, are the thirty-two Variations for Pianoforte
in C minor. They belong to this autumn, and are among the compositions which their author would gladly have seen pass into oblivion.
Jahn's notes contain an anecdote in point. 'Beethoven once found
Streicher's daughter practising these Variations. After he had listened
for a while he asked her: "By whom is that?" "By you." "Such nonsense by me? Oh Beethoven, what an ass you were!" '

Among the group of ardent pro-Beethovenists in Vienna, there were a
number of female pianists, some of whom we have already encoun-
tered. At their head stood the Baroness Dorothea von Ertmann, wife of
an Austrian officer who was stationed in those years at or near Vienna.
The Baroness studied Beethoven's compositions with the composer,
and was, as all contemporary authorities agree, if not the greatest
player of these works at least the greatest of her sex.

The composer and kapellmeister to Jerome Bonaparte, Johann
Reichardt, a most competent judge, heard her repeatedly in the winter
of 1808–9 and recorded a highly favourable impression of her from
which we quote:

'A lofty noble manner and a beautiful face full of deep feeling increases
my expectation still further at the first sight of the noble lady; and then
as she performed a great Beethoven sonata I was surprised as almost
never before. I have never seen such power and innermost tenderness

combined even in the greatest virtuosi; from the tip of each finger her soul poured forth, and from her hands, both equally skilful and sure, what power and authority were brought to bear over the whole instrument. Everything that is great and beautiful in art was turned into song with ease and expression! And it was not one of those fine pianos that one finds so frequently here, but the great artist instilled her sensitive spirit into the instrument and forced it to serve her as perhaps no other hands have been able to do.'

Well might the master call her his 'Dorothea-Cäcilia'! In one of his most delightful letters the young Felix Mendelssohn describes his visit at Milan (1831) to the Ertmanns, 'the most agreeable, cultured people conceivable, both in love as if they were a bridal couple, and yet married thirty-four years', where he and the lady delighted each other by turns in the performance of Beethoven's compositions and 'the old General, who now appeared in his stately grey commander's uniform, wearing many orders, was very happy and wept with joy'; and in the intervals he told 'the loveliest anecdotes about Beethoven, how, in the evening when she played for him, he used the candle snuffers as a toothpick, etc.'. In this letter there is one touching and beautiful reminiscence of the Baroness. 'She related', says Mendelssohn, 'that when she lost her last child, Beethoven at first did not want to come into the house; at length he invited her to visit him, and when she came he sat himself down at the pianoforte and said simply: "We will now talk to each other in tones," and for over an hour played without stopping, and as she remarked: "he told me everything, and at last brought me comfort." '

Another member of this group was a young lady, who during her five years' residence in Vienna, became one of the most devoted as well as most highly accomplished players of Beethoven's compositions – Marie Bigot, who was born at Colmar in Alsatia. Her husband took her to Vienna on their marriage in 1804. There she became acquainted with Haydn, and formed a friendship also with Beethoven and Salieri. Such associations naturally fired her ardently musical nature, and at twenty years of age she had already developed great skill and originality. The first time that she played in the presence of Haydn, the old gentleman was so moved that he clasped her in his arms and cried: 'O, my dear child, I did not write this music – it is you who have composed it!' The melancholy genius of Beethoven found an interpreter in Madame Bigot, whose enthusiasm and depth of feeling added new beauties to those which he had conceived. One day she played a sonata which he had just composed, in such a manner as to draw from him the remark: 'That is not exactly the character which I wanted to give this piece; but go right on. If it is not wholly mine it is something better.'

Bigot, according to Reichardt, was 'an honest, cultivated Berliner, Librarian of Count Razumovsky'. As this was precisely in those years when Beethoven was most patronised by that nobleman, the composer and the lady were thus brought often together, and very warm, friendly relations resulted. A very characteristic letter of Beethoven to the Bigots suggests that his attentions to the young wife had at one time the appearance of being a little too pointed.

'Dear Marie, dear Bigot!

'It is only with the deepest regret that I am compelled to recognise that the purest and most harmless feelings can often be misunderstood – Considering, dear M., how you greeted me I never thought of interpreting it otherwise than that you were giving me your friendship. – You must deem me very vain and contemptible if you assume that the kindnesses of such an excellent person as yourself could make me believe – that I had at once won your love – Moreover, it is one of my first principles *never to stand in other than friendly relations with the wife of another man. I do not wish by any other such relations to fill my soul with distrust against her who some day may share her fate with me* – and so ruin for myself the loveliest and purest life. – It is possible that I may have jested a few times with Bigot in a way that was not too refined; I told you myself that I am occasionally ill behaved. I am completely natural with all my friends and hate all restraint. I count Bigot amongst them; if something I do displeases him, the friendship with both of you demands that you tell me so – and I will certainly have a care never to offend him again – but how can good Marie put so bad a construction on my actions? –

'With regard to my invitation to take you and Caroline* driving, it was but natural that I should believe, Bigot having opposed your going with me alone, that both of you deemed it unbecoming or objectionable – and when I wrote to you I had no other purpose than to make you understand that I saw no harm in it. And when I declared that it was a matter of great importance to me that you should not refuse, it was only to persuade you to enjoy the *gloriously beautiful day*. I had your and Caroline's pleasure in mind more than my own, and I thought I could compel you to accede to my wishes when I said that *mistrust on your part or a refusal would really offend me*. – You ought really to ponder how you will make amends to me – for having spoilt for me – a day that was so bright because of my cheerful mood and the cheerful weather. – If I said that you misunderstood me, your present judgement of me shows that I was right, not to mention *what* you yourself thought *in connec-*

* Marie's baby daughter.

tion with it – When I said that *something evil* might come of it if I came to
see you, that was more than anything else a *joke* which had only the one
purpose of showing how everything about you attracts me, that I have
no greater wish than always to live with you, which also is the truth –
Even in case there was a hidden meaning in it, even the most sacred
friendship can yet have secrets, but to *misinterpret* the secret of a friend –
because one cannot at once guess it, that you should *not* do, dear Bigot
and dear Marie. *Never, never* will you find me ignoble; from childhood
on I learned to love virtue – and all that is beautiful and good – You
have hurt me to the quick – It shall only serve to make our friendship
the firmer. – I am really not at all well today and it would be difficult
to see you. Yesterday after the quartets my feelings and imagination
continually called up before me the fact that I had made you suffer. I
went to the Redoute last night to seek distraction, but in vain; everywhere I was haunted by visions of all of you, always saying to me, they
are so good and probably suffering because of you. – Dejected in spirits
I hurried away – Write me a few lines –

Your true and faithful friend Beethoven
embraces you all.'

This friendship continued; within the next year Beethoven wrote
four more notes to Herr Bigot.

The Hungarian Count Peter Erdödy married on 6 June 1796 the
Countess Anna Marie Niczky (born 1779), then just seventeen years of
age. There is nothing to show how or when the very great intimacy
between the Countess and Beethoven began; but for many years she
was prominent among the most useful and valued of his many female
friends. She was described in December 1808 as a

'very beautiful, fine little woman who from her first confinement
(1799) was afflicted with an incurable disease which for ten years has
kept her in bed for all but two to three months but nevertheless gave
birth to three healthy and dear children who cling to her like burrs;
whose sole entertainment was found in music; who plays even Beethoven's pieces right well and limps with still swollen feet from one
pianoforte to another, yet is so merry and friendly and good.'

The manner in which Beethoven received support from the aristocracy is suggested in a report from Vienna, dated 27 February (1807), to
the *Allgemeine Musikalische Zeitung*: 'Beethoven's big symphony in E
flat [the "Eroica"], which has been recently reviewed so scrupulously
and impartially in these pages, will be performed along with the other

two symphonies by this composer (in C and D) and also with a fourth, still unknown symphony by him, in a very select circle that contributed a very considerable sum for the benefit of the composer.' These performances, which took place in March, were described at the beginning of April in the *Journal des Luxus und der Moden*:

'Beethoven gave two concerts at the house of Prince L. at which nothing but his own compositions were performed; namely his first four symphonies, an overture to the tragedy *Coriolan*, a pianoforte concerto and some airs from the opera *Fidelio*. Richness of ideas, bold originality and fullness of power, which are the particular merits of Beethoven's muse, were very much in evidence to everyone at these concerts; yet many found fault with lack of a noble simplicity and the all too fruitful accumulation of ideas which on account of their number were not always adequately worked out and blended, thereby creating the effect more often of rough diamonds.'

The correspondent for the *Allgemeine Musikalische Zeitung* wrote in December 1807, 'A *new* overture by this composer . . . is full of fire and power; according to the inscription, it was intended for Collin's *Coriolan.*' The manuscript of the *Coriolan* Overture bears the composer's own date, 1807. Collin's tragedy was originally performed on 24 November 1802, with 'between-acts music' arranged from Mozart's *Idomeneo*. The next year Lange assumed the leading part with a success of which he justly boasts in his autobiography, and played it so often down to 5 March 1805, as to make the work thoroughly familiar to the theatre-going public. From that date to the end of October 1809, it was played but once – namely on 24 April 1807. The overture was assuredly not written for that one exceptional performance, but it is very likely that the single performance of the tragedy was arranged so soon after the two concerts in order to bring together the composition and the work for which it was written.

Beethoven had at this time written but four overtures – three to *Fidelio*, and that to *Prometheus*, which had long ceased to be a novelty. He needed a new one. Collin's tragedy was thoroughly well known and offered a subject splendidly suited to his genius. An overture to it was a compliment to his influential friend, the author, and, if successful, would be a new proof of his talent for dramatic composition. How nobly the character of Coriolanus is mirrored in Beethoven's music is well enough known; but the admirable adaptation of the overture to the play is duly appreciated by those only who have read Collin's almost forgotten work.

Clementi, called to Rome by the death of his brother, had arrived in Vienna on his way thither, and embraced the opportunity to acquire the exclusive right of publication in England of various works of Beethoven. He reported the results in a letter to his partner, F. W. Collard:

'Messrs. Clementi and Co., No. 26 Cheapside, London
Vienna, 22 April 1807'

'Dear Collard:

'By a little management and without committing myself, I have at last made a compleat conquest of that *haughty beauty*, Beethoven, who first began at public places to grin and coquet with me, which of course I took care not to discourage; then slid into familiar chat, till meeting him by chance one day in the street – "Where do you lodge?" says he; "I have not seen you this *long* while!" – upon which I gave him my address. Two days after I found on my table his card brought by himself, from the maid's description of his lovely form. This will do, thought I. Three days after that he calls again, and finds me at home. Conceive then the mutual ecstasy of such a meeting! I took pretty good care to improve it to our *house's* advantage, therefore, as soon as decency would allow, after praising very handsomely some of his compositions: "Are you engaged with any publisher in London?" – "No" says he. – "Suppose, then, that you prefer *me?*" – "With all my heart." – "Done. What have you ready?" – "I'll bring you a list." In short I agreed with him to take in MSS three quartets, a symphony, an overture and a concerto for the violin, which is beautiful, and which, at my request he will adapt for the pianoforte with and without additional keys; and a concerto for the pianoforte, for *all* of which we are to pay him two hundred pounds sterling. The property, however, is only for the British Dominions. Today sets off a courier for London through Russia, and he will bring over to you two or three of the mentioned articles.

'Remember that the violin concerto he will adapt himself and send it as soon as he can.

'The quartets, etc., you may get Cramer or some other very clever fellow to adapt for the Piano-forte. The symphony and the overture are wonderfully fine so that I think I have made a very good bargain. What do you think? I have likewise engaged him to compose two sonatas and a fantasia for the Piano-forte which he is to deliver to our house for sixty pounds sterling (mind I have treated for Pounds, not Guineas). In short he has promised to treat with no one but me for the British Dominions.'

The quartets, in parts, had been lent to Count Franz Brunsvik and were still in Hungary, which gave occasion to one of Beethoven's peculiarly whimsical and humorous epistles:

'On 11 May 1806 [*sic*]   Vienna on a Mayday
'Dear, dear B.!

'I just want to tell you that I came to a really satisfactory arrangement with *Clementi* – I shall receive 200 Pds. sterling – and besides I am privileged to sell the same works in Germany and France. – He has also offered me other commissions – so that I am enabled to hope through them to achieve the dignity of a true artist while still young. – I need, *dear B.*, the *quartets*. I have already asked your sister to write to you about them. It takes too long to copy them from my score – therefore make haste and send them direct to me by *letter post* – you shall have them back in 4 or 5 days at the latest. – I beg you urgently for them, since otherwise I might lose a great deal. – If you can arrange for the Hungarians to ask me to come for a few concerts, do it – you may have me for 200 florins in gold – then I will bring my opera along – I shall never get along with the princely rabble in the theatres –

'Whenever *we* (several amici) drink your wine, we get drunk on you, that is, we drink your health – Farewell – hurry – hurry – hurry and send me the quartets – otherwise you may embarrass me greatly. – Schuppanzigh has married – it is said to *one very like him*. – What sort of a family???? – Kiss your sister Therese, tell her I fear I shall become great without the help of a monument of hers contributing thereto – Send me tomorrow the quartets – quar – tete – t – e – t – s.

Your friend
Beethoven'

If an English publisher could afford to pay so high a price for the manuscripts of a German composer, why not a French one? So Beethoven reasoned, and, Bonn being then French, he wrote to Simrock and also to Pleyel in Paris proposing a contract like that made with Clementi. The letters expressed a desire to sell six new works to a publishing house in France, one in England and one in Vienna simultaneously, with the understanding that they were to appear only after a certain date. They were a symphony, the overture for Collin's *Coriolan*, a violin concerto, three quartets, one concerto for the pianoforte, the violin concerto arranged for pianoforte 'avec des notes additionelles'. The price, 'very cheap', was to be 1,200 florins.

The only works on this list that were published by Simrock were the Razumovsky Quartets, which appeared in 1808 in Bonn after their first

printing in Vienna by the Kunst- und Industrie-Comptoir, Beethoven's
principal publisher at this time. A series of letters from Beethoven to
Baron Ignaz von Gleichenstein were written during June and July
from Baden, where Beethoven had moved. These letters show the
extent that Gleichenstein had taken over the handling of Beethoven's
affairs at this time and the strain that had developed between him and
his brothers – particularly Johann from whom he had borrowed
money. On 23 June Beethoven wrote to the Kunst- und Industrie-
Comptoir to introduce Gleichenstein as his agent to arrange with the
publishers for an advance payment to him for music which he had
not yet delivered to the firm. Shortly afterwards he wrote the following
letter to his friend:

'Dear good Gleichenstein,
   'Please be so good as to give this to the copyist tomorrow – it concerns
the symphony as you see – in case he is not through with the quartet
tomorrow, take it away and deliver it to the Industrie-Comptoir.
– You may say to my brother that I shall certainly not write to him
again. – I know the cause, it is this. Because he has lent me money and
spent some on my account, he is (*I know my brothers*) already anxious
because I cannot yet pay it back to him: and apparently the other one,
filled with the spirit of revenge against me, stirs him up too. – It would
be best if I were to collect the whole 1,500 florins (from the Industrie-
Comptoir) and pay him with it; then the matter will be at an end –
Heaven preserve me from having to receive benefactions from my
brothers – Farewell – greetings to West* –
                                        Your Beethoven'
'NB I sent the symphony from here to the Industrie-Comptoir. They
have probably received it already – When you next come back, bring
along some good sealing-wax.'

   Before the spring of 1807 Beethoven had received an invitation from
Prince Nikolaus Esterhazy to write a mass in honour of his wife, to be
performed in September for her name-day. On 26 July Beethoven
wrote to Prince Esterhazy from Baden:

'Most Serene and Gracious Prince.
   'Having been told that you my Prince, have enquired concerning
the mass which you commissioned me to write for you, I take the lib-
erty, my Serene Prince, to inform you that you will receive the same at
* Thomas West was the assumed name of Joseph Schreyvogel, a well-known
Viennese writer who is often mentioned in the Conversation Books.

the latest by the 20th of the month of August – This will leave plenty of time to have it performed on the name-day of her Serene Highness, the Princess. – At the time when I was having the misfortune of a benefit date falling through at the theatre, I received an extraordinarily favourable offer *from London* which I felt I must gratefully seize upon due to my impoverished condition; and this retarded the composition of the Mass, much as I wished, Serene Prince, to appear with it before you. Also to this was added an illness of the head, which at first did not permit me to work at all, and now but little. Since people are so eager to misrepresent everything about me, I enclose a letter from my physician. – May I add that I shall deliver the Mass to you with timidity since you, Serene Highness, are accustomed to having the inimitable masterpieces of the great Haydn performed for you. –

'Most serene, most gracious Prince! With high esteem your most devoted and humble

Ludwig van Beethoven'

At the end of July, Beethoven removed from Baden to Heiligenstadt, devoting the time there to the C minor Symphony, the Fifth, and the Mass in C. The name-day of Princess Esterhazy for which he promised to have the Mass ready, was 8 September. In the years when this date did not fall upon a Sunday it was the custom at Eisenstadt to celebrate it on the first Sunday following. In 1807 the 8th fell on a Tuesday and the first performance of Beethoven's Mass, therefore, took place on the 13th. Haydn had written his masses for this day and had gone to Eisenstadt from Vienna to conduct their performance. So Beethoven now, who seems to have had his troubles with the singers here as in Vienna, if one may found such an opinion upon an energetic note of Prince Esterhazy copied and printed by Pohl. In this note, which is dated 12 September 1807, the Prince called upon his vice-kapellmeister, Johann Fuchs, to explain why the singers in his employ were not always on hand at his musical affairs. He had heard on that day with displeasure that at the rehearsal of Beethoven's Mass only one of the five contraltos was present, and he stringently commanded all the singers and instrumentalists in his service to be on hand at the performance of the Mass on the following day.

The Mass was produced on the next day – the 13th. 'It was the custom at this court', says Schindler,

'that after the religious service the local as well as foreign musical notabilities met in the chambers of the Prince for the purpose of conversing with him about the works which had been performed. When Beethoven entered the room, the Prince turned to him with the question: "But, my dear Beethoven, what is this that you have done again?" The impression made by this singular question, which was probably followed by other critical remarks, was the more painful on our artist because he saw the kapellmeister standing near the Prince laugh. Thinking that he was being ridiculed, nothing could keep him at the place where his work had been so misunderstood and besides, as he thought, where a brother in art had rejoiced over his discomfiture. He left Eisenstadt the same day.'

J. N. Hummel was the kapellmeister who had replaced Haydn at the post since 1804, and as Schindler goes on to say, 'the unlucky laugh was not directed at Beethoven, but at the singular manner in which the Prince had criticised the Mass'.

A letter to Countess Josephine Deym in the spring of this year reintroduces the lady to whom Beethoven had expressed his love two years before and starts the last chapter in this affair of the heart. It will be remembered that in his letter of 11 May to her brother Franz, Beethoven mentioned having just written to his sister. Thus, sometime before May Josephine had returned to Vienna from Budapest, where she had been living during the past year. In this first letter, after urging her to write to her brother Franz about the quartets, he complained of poor health which prevented him from coming to see her. For the month of July she moved her family to Baden, where Beethoven was already established. The next letter is written on 20 September from Heiligenstadt, where he had been before and after the performance of the Mass at Eisenstadt. In it he refers to the fact that immediately after his return from Eisenstadt he called on her twice in Vienna '– but I was not so fortunate – as to see you – That hurt me deeply.' He had been trying unsuccessfully to keep a promise with himself to control his feelings for her, but his longing continued, and thoughts of her had followed him to Heiligenstadt and Eisenstadt. He longed to have a long, uninterrupted talk with her so that their hearts and souls could be reunited. At the end of the letter he referred to his improving health and, in the postscript, to the fact that he would be coming to town that day but dared not come to her for fear of being disappointed a third time.

The third letter anticipates the parting of the ways. Beethoven, writing from the country, admitted that at the moment it was better for their peace of mind not to see each other. But another letter is an impassioned plea for frankness and explanation: he had tried to see her again but now did not care to put up with further rebuffs from her servants. He had kept away from her for a while because he thought she desired it; now he would not express himself further until he knew the truth.

A certain amount of time elapsed before the last letter, which we should introduce with a draft of a message from Josephine to Beethoven:

'For a long time I have wanted to hear news of your state of health, and long ago I would have informed myself about it had not modesty held me back – Now tell me how things are going, what are you doing? How is your health, your state of mind, your behaviour? – A deep concern which I have and will continue to have as long as I live about everything to do with you compels me to gain information. Or does my *friend Beethoven*, may I use that term, believe I have changed. – What else would this doubt express to me than that you yourself had not remained the same.'

Beethoven's final letter provides a wistful close to the affair:

'Please deliver the sonata to your brother, my dear Josephine – I thank you for wishing still to appear as if I were not altogether banished from your memory, even though this came about perhaps more at the instigation of others – You want me to tell you how I am. A more difficult question could not be put to me – and I prefer to leave it unanswered, rather than – to answer it *too truthfully* – All good wishes, dear J[osephine].

As always, your Beethoven
who is eternally devoted to you'

A controversy for the possession of the two Court Theatres and that of An-der-Wien involved certain legal questions which, in September 1806, were decided by the proper tribunal against the old directors, who were thus at the end of the year compelled to retire. Peter, Baron von Braun, closed his twelve years' administration with a circular letter addressed to his recent subordinates, dated 28 December, in which, after bidding them an affectionate adieu, he said: 'With imperial consent I have turned over the vice-direction of the Royal Imperial Court Theatre to a company composed of the following cavaliers: the Princes Lobkowitz, Schwarzenberg and Esterhazy, and the Counts Esterhazy, Lodrin, Ferdinand Pálffy, Stephen Zichy and Nikolaus Esterhazy.'

In this change, Beethoven naturally saw a most hopeful prospect of an improvement in his own theatrical fortunes. Acting on a hint from Lobkowitz, he addressed to the new directors a petition:

'To the Worshipful RI Theatre Direction:

'The undersigned flatters himself that during his sojourn in Vienna he has won some favour and approval not only from the high nobility but from the general public as well, and that he has secured an honourable acceptance of his works at home and abroad.

'Nevertheless, he has been obliged to struggle with difficulties of all kinds and has not yet been able to establish himself here in a position which would enable him to fulfil his desire to live wholly for art, to develop his talents to a still higher degree of perfection, which must be the goal of every true artist, and to make certain for the future the fortuitous advantages of the present.

'Inasmuch as the undersigned has always striven less for a livelihood than for the interests of art, the ennoblement of taste and the uplifting of his genius towards higher ideals and perfection, it necessarily happened that he often was compelled to sacrifice profit and advantage to the Muse. Yet works of this kind have won for him a reputation in foreign lands which assures him a favourable reception in a number of important places, and a destiny commensurate with his talents and abilities.

'But in spite of this the undersigned cannot deny that the many years he has spent here, the favour and approval which he has enjoyed from high and low, the wish wholly to fulfil the expectations which he has been fortunate enough to awaken and, let him venture to say, the patriotism of a German have made this very place more estimable and desirable to him than any other.

'Therefore, he cannot forbear, before deciding to leave the city so dear to him, to follow the suggestion kindly made to him by His Serene Highness the ruling Prince Lobkowitz, who intimated to him that the *Worshipful Theatre Direction* would not be disinclined to engage the undersigned under proper conditions for the service of the *theatres* under their management and to ensure his further stay here by offering him the *means of a comfortable livelihood* favourable to the exercise of his talents.

'Inasmuch as this intimation is in perfect accord with the desires of the undersigned, he takes the liberty to submit an expression of his willingness as well as the following conditions for the favourable consideration of the Worshipful Direction:

'1. He promises and contracts to compose every year at least one grand opera, the subject to be selected jointly by the *Worshipful Direction* and the undersigned; in return he asks a fixed remuneration of 2,400 florins per annum and the gross receipts of the third performance of each such opera.

'2. He agrees to deliver gratis each year a small operetta or a *divertissement, choruses* or occasional pieces according to the wishes or needs of the *Worshipful Direction*, but hopes that the Worshipful Direction will not hesitate in return for such works to grant him at least one day per year for a benefit concert in the theatre building.

'If one reflects what an expenditure of time and effort is required for the making of an opera to the absolute exclusion of every other intellectual occupation, and further, that in other cities where the composer and his family have a share in the receipts of every performance, a single successful work may make the fortune of a composer; and still further how small a compensation, owing to the monetary condition and high prices for necessities which prevail here, is at the command of a local artist to whom foreign lands are open, the above conditions can certainly not be thought to be excessive or unreasonable.

'In any case, however, whether the Worshipful Direction confirms and accepts this offer or not, the undersigned adds the request that he be granted a day for a concert in one of the theatre buildings; for should the proposition be accepted, the undersigned would at once require his time and powers for the composition of the opera, and therefore be unable to use them for his profit in another direction. Should this present offer be refused, the undersigned would look upon the fulfilment of last year's promise of a concert, which never took place because of various obstacles which intervened, as the final proof of the great favour heretofore enjoyed by him. He requests that in the first case the day be set on the Feast of the Annunciation, in the second on one of the approaching Christmas holidays.

Ludwig van Beethoven'

'Vienna, 1807'

Neither of these requests was granted directly; one of them only indirectly. Nor is it known whether any formal written reply was conveyed to the petitioner.

Though disappointed in the hope of obtaining the use of the theatre for a concert, Beethoven was not thereby prevented from coming prominently before the public as composer and director. It came about in this way: the want of better opportunities to hear good symphonic music well performed than were afforded by Schuppanzigh's concerts or the occasional hastily arranged Akademies of composers and virtuosi, induced a number of music-lovers early in the winter to form an institute under the modest title 'Concert of Music-Lovers' (Liebhaber Concert). Says the *Wiener Vaterländische Blätter* of 27 May 1808:

'An orchestra was organised, whose members were chosen from the best of the local music-lovers (dilettanti). A few wind-instruments only – French horns, trumpets, etc., were drafted from the Vienna theatres . . . The audiences were composed exclusively of the nobility of the town and foreigners of note, and among these classes the preference was given to the cognoscenti and amateurs . . . In twenty meetings symphonies, overtures, concertos and vocal pieces were performed zealously and affectionately and were received with general approval.'

The works of Beethoven reported as having been performed in these concerts are the Symphony in D (in the first concert), the overture to *Prometheus* in November, the 'Eroica' Symphony and the overture to *Coriolan* in December, and about New Year the Fourth Symphony in B flat, which also had been played on 15 November in the Burgtheater at a concert for the public charities. Most, if not all, of these works were directed by their composer.

CHAPTER 12

The Years 1808 and 1809 –
The Siege of Vienna

The common notion that there was not an understanding or taste for Beethoven's works in Vienna is erroneous. On the contrary, generally in the concerts of these years, Beethoven's works were as often on the programmes as those of Mozart or even Haydn. Few as his published orchestral compositions then were, none were more likely to fill the house. While no other performances of his works at the Liebhaber Concerts are reported, perhaps this was for reasons indicated in a letter from Stephan von Breuning to Wegeler, written in March 1808: 'Beethoven came near losing a finger by a *Panaritium* [felon], but he is again in good health. He escaped a great misfortune, which, added to his deafness, would have completely ruined his good humour, which, as it is, is of rare occurrence.' This is mentioned in Beethoven's own correspondence of the winter. For example, in March he wrote to Heinrich Collin: 'However, yesterday my poor finger had to have a drastic nail operation', and later to Count Oppersdorff: 'I am still under treatment for my *poor innocent finger*, and have not been able to go out for the last two weeks.' He was present, however, at the final concert of the series, on 27 March, at which in honour of Haydn, whose seventy-sixth birthday fell on the 31st, his *Creation* with Carpani's Italian text was given. It is pleasant to know that Beethoven was one of those who, 'with members of the high nobility', stood at the door of the hall of the university to receive the venerable guest on his arrival there in Prince Esterhazy's coach, and who accompanied him as 'sitting in an armchair he was carried, lifted high, and on his entrance into the hall was received with the sound of trumpets and drums by the numerous gathering and greeted with joyous shouts of "Long Live Haydn!"'

Immediately after the close of the Liebhaber Concerts, Mozart's brother-in-law, the singer and actor Sebastian Mayer's annual benefit in the Theater-an-der-Wien opened with the *Sinfonia Eroica*. This was on Monday evening, 11 April. Two days after (13th) the Charity Institute's Concert in the Burgtheater offered a programme of six numbers; No. 1 was Beethoven's Fourth Symphony in B flat; No. 5, his C minor Pianoforte Concerto, played by Friedrich Stein; and No. 6, the *Coriolan* Overture – all directed by the composer; and, at a benefit concert in May, in the Augartensaal, occurred the first known public performance of the Triple Concerto, Op. 56.

The name of Count Franz von Oppersdorff is connected with both the Fourth and the Fifth Symphony, and the little correspondence there is between the Count and the composer sheds light on their history.

Early sketches for the Fifth Symphony are to be found alongside some for the Fourth Piano Concerto and the first act of *Leonore*; the themes for the first and second movements are at a primitive stage and a finale idea is unused.

Further sketches appearing at the end of the 'Eroica' sketchbook show an advancement in the conception of the first movement theme and the establishment of both Scherzo themes. Both sets may be dated 1804. There is also a much later set of sketches for all the movements, which are alongside work for the Violin Concerto and the Cello Sonata in A, Op. 69, and thus may be dated 1806.

In this year plans for the C minor Symphony (the Fifth Symphony) were interrupted in favour of the Symphony in B flat (the Fourth Symphony) which was the work of the late summer and autumn while Beethoven was in Grätz. A receipt from Count Oppersdorff shows that he commissioned this symphony.

> 'Receipt for 500 fl.
> which I received from Count Oppersdorff for a symphony
> which I have written for him –
> > By my own hand and signature
> > > Ludwig van Beethoven'
> '1807, February third'

The Count may well have been influential in arranging its performance at Prince Lobkowitz's a month later, and presumably he was in possession of the score for the customary six-month period judging by Beethoven's letter to Breitkopf and Härtel of 18 November 1806, in which he says: 'I cannot give you the promised symphony yet – because a gentleman of quality has taken it from me, but I have the privilege of publishing it in half a year.'

The next letter from Beethoven to the Count is one which can be dated March 1808 because of the reference to the infection in his finger from which he suffered at this time.

'That you, my *beloved friend*, have fled from me without letting me know anything about your departure has really caused me pain – perhaps you were vexed with me about something, but for *my* part it was certainly not *on purpose* – Today I have little time to write more to you; I only want to inform you that *your symphony* has long been ready, and I will now send it to you by the next post – You may retain 50 florins, for the copying, which I will have done for you, will cost that sum at least – In case you do not want the symphony, however, let me know it before the next post – In case you accept it, rejoice me as soon as possible with the 300 fl. still due me. *The last movement in the symphony* is with 3 trombones and flautini [piccolo] – though not with 3 kettledrums, but will make more noise than 6 kettledrums and better noise at that – I am still under treatment for my *poor, innocent finger*, and because of it have not been able to go out for the last two weeks – Farewell – let me hear something from you soon dearest Count – Things are going badly with me – In haste your most devoted

Beethoven'

The mention of the scoring of the last movement shows that this was the Fifth Symphony which was finally worked out in 1807 and completed in the spring of 1808. Not only did the Count expect this symphony too but the reference to the kettledrums suggests that the Count had discussed the instrumentation of the work with the composer.

The price for the Fifth Symphony was probably again 500 florins of which 200 florins was paid in June 1807, and of the '300 fl. still due me' 150 was paid on 29 March 1808. That neither the balance was paid nor the symphony received by the Count is made fairly certain by the final letter that has survived between the two men:

'Vienna, 1 November 1088[!]

'Best Count!

'You will look at me in a false light, but necessity compelled me to sell to someone else the symphony which was written for you and another as well – but I assure you that I shall soon send you the one intended for you. – I hope that you have been well, and also your gracious wife, to whom I ask you to give my best wishes. – I live right under Prince Lichnowsky at Countess Erdödy's, if you ever wish to give me the honour of a visit. My circumstances are improving – without my *needing the help of people* who would subject *their friends to churlishness* – Also, I have been asked to be kapellmeister to the King of Westphalia, and it is quite possible that I shall accept the call – Farewell and from time to time think of your most devoted friend

Beethoven'

The 'someone else' was Breitkopf and Härtel, to whom Beethoven sold the work in September 1808. During the summer he had reopened negotiations with this firm after somewhat of a lull, and on 8 June he offered them two symphonies (the Fifth and Sixth), the Mass, and the Sonata for Pianoforte and Violoncello, Op. 69, for 900 florins, 'although there have been so many breakings off between us that I am almost convinced that this renewal will again prove fruitless'. The reply of the publishers is not on record, but in early July Beethoven repeated his offer, reduced the fee to 700 florins, and added two pianoforte sonatas 'or instead of these possibly another symphony'. The publishers had evidently demurred at the idea of the Mass, for Beethoven writes:

'You see that I give more and take less – but that is the limit – you must take the Mass, or else I cannot give you my other works – for I am considering honour and not profit merely. "There is no demand for church music," you say, and you are right if you are referring to music from mere thoroughbassists, but if you will only have the Mass performed once you will see whether there will not be music-lovers who will want it . . .'

In midsummer, a third letter offered the above works, only with two trios, 'since such trios are now rather scarce', substituted for the pianoforte sonatas, 'or instead of these trios, a symphony', for 600 florins, and with the Mass given without a fee. The fact that Beethoven was already thinking of writing a seventh symphony is shown both by these letters to the publishers and by the letter to Count Oppersdorff; at the time of the latter letter, he was apparently intending to write it specifically for the Count. Before concluding the negotiations with Breitkopf and Härtel, there must first be considered the history of the Sixth Symphony, also mentioned in each of these letters.

As in the case of the Fifth, ideas later to be used in two different movements of the 'Pastorale' appear in 1803–4 in the 'Eroica' sketchbook. The first is the country-dance theme of the third movement trio. The second is a prophetic indication of the mood, although without the final melody, of the whole second movement.

Further sketches for the symphony appear along with some for the

Mass in C on loose sheets, a few of which were first intended for the score of the B flat Symphony and thus indicate the winter 1806–7. Here the main ideas are established for every movement but the second.

Extended work on all the movements is the work of the autumn of 1807 and spring of 1808. Sketches for the symphony are intermingled with sketches for the cello sonata, Op. 69, and the trios, Op. 70.

From the letters to Breitkopf and Härtel previously quoted we may conclude that by the summer of 1808 the symphony, if not completed, was very nearly so.

The autograph of the Fifth Symphony is in the Berlin State Library, that of the Sixth Symphony in the Beethoven-Haus at Bonn. The first use of the word 'pastoral' is in a violin part that was used at the first performance (still preserved in the Gesellschaft der Musikfreunde) which reads:

> 'Sinfonia Pastorella
> Pastoral-Sinfonie
> oder
> Erinnerung an das Landleben
> Mehr Ausdruck der Empfindung als Mahlerei'

There follow the individual descriptions at the start of each movement.

Those who think programme music for the orchestra is a recent invention, and they who suppose the 'Pastoral' Symphony to be an original attempt to portray nature in music, are alike mistaken. It was never so much the ambition of Beethoven to invent new forms of musical works, as to surpass his contemporaries in the use of those already existing. There were few great battles in those stormy years that were not fought over again by orchestras, military bands, organs and pianofortes; and pages might be filled with a catalogue of programme music, long since dead, buried and forgotten.

A remark that was made by Ries will bear repetition here: 'Beethoven in composing his pieces often thought of a particular thing, although he frequently laughed at musical paintings and scolded particularly about trivialities of this sort. Haydn's "Creation" and "The Seasons" were frequently ridiculed, though Beethoven never failed to recognise Haydn's high deserts', etc. But Beethoven himself did not disdain occasionally to introduce imitations into his works. The difference between him and others in this regard was this: they undertook to give musical imitations of things essentially unmusical – he never.

In the sketches, he has recorded his own views on the subject:

'The hearers should be allowed to discover the situations

  'Sinfonia caracteristica – or recollection of country life

  'A recollection of country life

  'All painting in instrumental music is lost if it is pushed too far

  'Sinfonia pastorella. Anyone who has an idea of country life can make out for himself the intentions of the composer without many titles –

  'Also without titles the whole will be recognised as a matter more of feeling than of painting in sounds.'

On a bright, sunny day in April 1823, Beethoven took Schindler for a long ramble through the scenes in which he had composed his Fifth and Sixth Symphonies. Schindler writes:

'After we had looked at the bath-house and its adjacent garden at Heiligenstadt and he had given expression to many agreeable recollections touching his creations, we continued our walk towards the Kahlenberg in the direction past Grinzing [?]. Passing through the pleasant meadow-valley between Heiligenstadt and the latter village, which is traversed by a gently murmuring brook which hurries down from a nearby mountain and is bordered with high elms, Beethoven repeatedly stopped and let his glances roam, full of happiness, over the glorious landscape. Then seating himself on the turf and leaning against an elm, Beethoven asked me if there were any yellowhammers to be heard in the trees around us. But all was still. He then said: "Here I composed the 'Scene by the Brook' and the yellowhammers up there, the quails, nightingales and cuckoos round about, composed with me." To my question why he had not also put the yellowhammers into the scene, he drew out his sketchbook and wrote:

' "That's the composer up there," he remarked, "hasn't she a more important role to play than the others? *They* are meant only for a joke." And really the entrance of this figure in G major gives the tone-picture a new charm. Speaking now of the whole work and its parts, Beethoven said that the melody of this variation from the species of the yellowhammers was pretty plainly imitated in the scale written down in Andante rhythm and the same pitch. As a reason for not having mentioned this fellow-composer he said that had he printed the name it would only have served to increase the number of ill-natured interpretations of the movement which has made the introduction of the work difficult not only in Vienna but also in other places. Not infrequently the symphony, because of its second movement, had been declared to be child's play. In some places it shared the fate of the "Eroica".'

Equally interesting, valuable and graceful is Schindler's account of the origin of Beethoven's 'Merrymaking of the Countryfolk' in this symphony. Somewhat curtailed it is this:

'There are facts to tell us of how particular was the interest which Beethoven took in Austrian dance-music. Until his arrival in Vienna (1792), according to his own statement, he had not become acquainted with any folk-music except that of the mountains, with its strange and peculiar rhythms. How much attention he afterwards bestowed on dance-music is proved by the catalogue of his works. He even made essays in Austrian dance-music, but the players refused to grant Austrian citizenship to these efforts. The last effort dates from 1819 and, strangely enough, falls in the middle of his work on the "Missa Solemnis". In the tavern "To the Three Ravens" . . . near Mödling there had played a band of seven men. This band was one of the first that gave the young musician from the Rhine an opportunity to hear the national tunes of his new home in an unadulterated form. Beethoven made the acquaintance of the musicians and composed several sets of *Ländler* and other dances for them. In the year mentioned (1819), he had again complied with the wishes of the band. I was present when the new opus was handed to the leader of the company. The master in high good humour remarked that he had so arranged the dances that one musician after the other might put down his instrument at intervals and take a rest, or even a nap. After the leader had gone away full of joy because of the present of the famous composer, Beethoven asked me if I had not observed how village musicians often played in their sleep, occasionally letting their instruments fall and remaining entirely quiet, then awakening with a start, throwing in a few vigorous blows or strokes at a venture, but generally in the right key, and then falling asleep again; he had tried to copy these poor people in his "Pastoral" Symphony.'

The subjects of Beethoven's imitations, even in play, are therefore musical, not incongruous; and in *his* 'Portrait musical de la Nature' are so suggestive as to aid and intensify the 'expression of feelings', which was his professed aim.

The once famous musical wonder-child, Wilhelm Rust, of Dessau, at the time a young man of some twenty-two years, had come to Vienna in 1807. In a letter to his 'best sister, Jette', dated Haking (a village near Vienna), 9 July 1808, he wrote of Beethoven.

'You want much to hear something about Beethoven; unfortunately I must say first of all that it has not been possible for me to get intimately acquainted with him. What else I know I will tell you now: He is as original and singular as a man as are his compositions; usually serious, at times merry but always satirical and bitter. On the other hand he is also very childlike and certainly very sincere. He is a great lover of truth and in this goes too far very often; for he never flatters and therefore makes many enemies. A good fellow played for him and when he was finished Beethoven said to him: "You will have to play a long time before you will realise that you can do nothing." I do not know whether you heard that I also played for him. He praised my playing, particularly in the Bach fugue, and said, "You play that well," which is much for him. Still he could not omit calling my attention to two mistakes . . . It is very possible that Beethoven will leave Vienna; at any rate he has frequently spoken of doing so and said: "They are forcing me to it." He also asked me once how the orchestras were in the North.'

In December Rust, writing to his brother Carl, was obliged to correct what he had said about Beethoven's new opera: 'All new products which have appeared here are more or less mediocre except those of Beethoven. I think I have written to you that he has not yet begun his new opera. I have not yet heard his first opera; it has not been performed since I have been here.' These last sentences of Rust remind us of the once current notion that disgust and disappointment at the (assumed) failure of *Fidelio* prevented Beethoven from ever undertaking the composition of another opera. The error was long since exploded, and, indeed, amply refuted by his proposition to the 'princely theatre rabble' for a permanent engagement. It is now universally known how earnestly Beethoven all his life long sought a satisfactory text for an opera or an oratorio; his friends always knew it; and his essays in vocal composition had, in spite of the critics, so favourably impressed them and the dramatic writers of the day that all were eager to serve him.

The new directors of the theatres began their operatic performances at the Kärnthnerthor on 1 and 2 January, and at the Burg on 4 January 1807, with Gluck's *Iphigenia in Tauris*. It was new to the dramatist Collin and awakened in his mind new ideas of the ancient tragedy, which he determined to embody in a text for a musical drama in oratorio form. He projected one on the Liberation of Jerusalem, to offer to Beethoven for setting; but it was never finished. Another essay in the field was a *Macbeth* after Shakespeare, also left unfinished in the middle of the second act, 'because it threatened to become too gloomy'. There exists a sketch showing that Beethoven had begun its composition. Röckel wrote: 'That Beethoven did not abandon the idea of composing another opera was shown by the impatience with which he could scarcely wait for his friend Collin to make an opera book for him of Shakespeare's "Macbeth".'

However, Collin did complete a grand opera libretto, *Bradamante*, for which he had an unusual predilection. It also was offered to Beethoven, but seemed too venturesome to him in respect of its use of the supernatural; there were probably other reasons why it did not appeal to him.

The consequence of Beethoven's fastidiousness and indecision was that he had no text for a vocal composition when he moved to the country for the summer. This time the move was directly from the Pasqualati house to Heiligenstadt, No. 8 Grinzingerweg. Beethoven's room looked out on the street, while the rooms overlooking the garden were occupied by the Grillparzer family. The poet, Franz, was then seventeen, and the friendship that developed between the two artists probably began at this time.

According to Grillparzer in his own writings, 'The first time I saw Beethoven was in my boyhood – it may have been 1804 or 1805 – and it was at a musical evening in the house of my uncle, Joseph Sonnleithner, partner at that time in an art and music business in Vienna.' Mme Grillparzer, mother of the poet, was a lady of great taste and culture, and was fond of music. She used to stand outside her door in order to enjoy Beethoven's playing, as she did not then know of his aversion to listeners. One day Beethoven, springing from his piano to the door to see if anyone were listening, unfortunately discovered her there. Despite her messages to him through his servant that her door into the common passageway would remain locked, and that her family would use another, Beethoven played no more.

After a long summer at Heiligenstadt, which may have ended with a short trip to Baden, Beethoven returned to Vienna in the late autumn and moved from the Pasqualati house to '1074 Krugerstrasse at Countess Erdödy's'. The circumstance that the composer's new apartments were in the Erdödy lodging strongly suggests the probability that his great intimacy with the Countess dates from the time when he became her near neighbour upon his moving into the Pasqualati house four years before.

The close of the letter to Oppersdorff contains an early allusion to one of the most singular events in Beethoven's life. In the autumn of 1807, Jerome Bonaparte, the Corsican lawyer's youngest son, who had spent his boyhood and youth mostly at sea, and had not yet completed his twenty-third year, found himself at Cassel, bearing the pompous title of 'King of Westphalia'. What could have induced this half-educated, frivolous, prodigal and effeminate young satrap and sybarite to sanction an invitation to his court of the composer most distinguished since Handel for his masculine vigour and manly independence of his art, is one of those small mysteries which seem impenetrable. The precise time when, and by what agency this call was communicated to Beethoven are alike unknown; we only know that before 1 November 1808, Beethoven received the same through 'the High Chamberlain of his Majesty the King of Westphalia, Count Truchess-Waldburg', that it was to the office of first kapellmeister, at a salary of 600 ducats, and that it led to events which will be noticed hereafter.

Razumovsky lived in his new palace on the Donau Canal, into which he had very recently removed from the Wollzeil and in which he had put his domestic establishment on a footing of great splendour. It suited his taste to have the first string quartet of Europe in his service. His own skill rendered him amply competent to play the second violin, which he usually did. Three permanent engagements only were, therefore, necessary, and these now, in late summer or early autumn 1808, were made. To Schuppanzigh – then the first of quartet players, but still without any permanent engagement – was given the appointment for life of *violino primo*, and to him was entrusted the selection of others. He recommended Weiss for the viola, whom Razumovsky accepted and to whom, for himself and family, he granted a suitable lodging in one of the houses connected with the palace.

Schuppanzigh had been so favourably impressed with the talents and skill of Linke as to secure him the place of violoncellist. He was a young man of twenty-five years – slightly deformed in person – an orphan from his childhood. Thus was the Razumovsky Quartet founded.

These were the years (1808–15) when, says Seyfried,

'as is known Beethoven was, as it were, cock of the walk in the princely establishment; everything that he composed was rehearsed hot from the griddle and performed to the nicety of a hair, according to his ideas, just as he wanted it and not otherwise, with affectionate interest, obedience and devotion such as could spring only from such ardent admirers of his lofty genius, and with a penetration into the most secret intentions of the composer and the most perfect comprehension of his intellectual tendencies; so that these quartet players achieved that universal celebrity concerning which there was but one voice in the art-world.'

As in the spring so now in autumn, it was Beethoven's popularity that must ensure success to the Grand Concert for the public charities; it was his name that was known to be more attractive to the Vienna public than any other, save that of the venerable Haydn; and as Haydn's oratorios were the staple productions at the great charity concerts of vocal music in the Burg theatre, so the younger master's symphonies, concertos and overtures formed the most alluring programmes for the instrumental Akademies in the other theatres – at all events, in 1808, this was the opinion of Court Councillor Joseph Hartl, the new theatre director.

A supervisor of the public charities, who at the same time controlled the theatres, he was of course able to secure the highest talent for benevolent concerts on terms advantageous to all parties concerned; and thus it came about, that at the concert for public charities in the Theater-an-der-Wien on the evening of Leopold's day, Tuesday 15 November, Beethoven conducted one of his symphonies, the *Coriolan* Overture, and a pianoforte concerto. In return for Beethoven's noble contribution of his works and personal services to the charity concerts of 15 November 1807 (Fourth Symphony), 13 April and 15 November 1808, Hartl finally gave him the use of the Theater-an-der-Wien for an Akademie on 22 December.

It was advertised in the *Wiener Zeitung* of 17 December as follows:

'MUSICAL AKADEMIE

'On Thursday, 22 December, Ludwig van Beethoven will have the honour to give a musical Akademie in the RI Privil. Theater-an-der-Wien. All the pieces are of his composition, entirely new, and not yet heard in public . . . First Part: 1, A Symphony, entitled: 'A Recollection of Country Life', in F major (No. 6). 2, Aria. 3, Hymn with Latin text, composed in the church style with chorus and solos. 4, Pianoforte Concerto played by himself.

'Second Part: 1, Grand Symphony in C minor (No. 5). 2, Holy, with Latin text composed in the church style with chorus and solos. 3, Fantasia for Pianoforte alone. 4, Fantasia for the Pianoforte which ends with the gradual entrance of the entire orchestra and the introduction of choruses as a finale.

'Boxes and reserved seats are to be had in the Krugerstrasse No. 1074, first storey. Beginning at half-past six o'clock.'

It is unfortunate that the concert of 15 November 1808 was so completely forgotten by all whose contemporary notices or later reminiscences are now the only sources of information; for it is certain that, either in the rehearsals or at the public performance, something happened which caused a very serious misunderstanding and breach between Beethoven and the orchestra; but even this is sufficient to remove some difficulties otherwise insuperable. Ries records that a scene is said once to have happened in which the orchestra compelled the composer to realise his injustice 'and in all seriousness insisted that he should not conduct. In consequence, at the rehearsal, Beethoven had to remain in an ante-room, and it was a long time before the quarrel was settled.' Such a quarrel did arise at the time of the November concert. In Spohr's autobiography is a story of Beethoven's first sweeping off the candles at the piano and then knocking down a choirboy deputed to hold one of them, by his too energetic motions at this concert, the two incidents setting the audience into a 'bacchanalian jubilation' of laughter. It is absolutely certain, however, that nothing of the kind occurred at the concert itself.

But the concert-giver's troubles were not ended even by his yielding to the demands of the orchestra. A solo singer was to be found and vocal pieces to be selected.

Milder was to sing the aria 'Ah, perfido! spergiuro', said Röckel, and accepted the invitation at once. But an unlucky quarrel provoked by Beethoven resulted in her refusal. After other attempts, Röckel engaged Fräulein Josephine Killitschgy, Schuppanzigh's sister-in-law. Being a young and inexperienced singer, her friends wrought her up to such a point that when Beethoven led her upon the stage and left her, stage fright overcame her and she made wretched work of the aria. Reichardt in a letter describes the Akademie:

'I accepted the kind offer of Prince Lobkowitz to let me sit in his box with hearty thanks. There we continued, in the bitterest cold, too, from half-past six to half-past ten, and experienced the truth that one can easily have too much of a good thing – and still more of a loud. Nevertheless, I could no more leave the box before the end than could the exceedingly good-natured and delicate Prince, for the box was in the first balcony near the stage, so that the orchestra with Beethoven in the middle conducting it was below us and near at hand; thus many a failure in the performance vexed our patience in the highest degree.

Poor Beethoven, who from this, his own concert, was having the first and only scant profit that he could find in a whole year, had found in the rehearsals and performance a lot of opposition and almost no support. Singers and orchestra were composed of heterogeneous elements, and it had been found impossible to get a single full rehearsal for all the pieces to be performed, all filled with the greatest difficulties.'

Such a programme, exclusive of the Choral Fantasia, was certainly an ample provision for an evening's entertainment of the most insatiably musical enthusiast; nor could a grander termination of the concert be desired than the Finale of the C minor Symphony; but to defer that work until the close was to incur the risk of endangering its effect by presenting it to an audience too weary for the close attention needful on first hearing to its fair comprehension and appreciation. This Beethoven felt, and so, says Czerny,

'there came to him shortly before the idea of writing a brilliant piece for this concert. He chose a song which he had composed many years before, planned the variations, the chorus, etc., and the poet Kuffner was called upon to write the words in a hurry according to Beethoven's hints. Thus originated the Choral Fantasia, Op. 80. It was finished so late that it could scarcely be sufficiently rehearsed. Beethoven related this in my presence in order to explain why, at the concert, he had had it repeated. "Some of the instruments had counted wrong in the rests," he said; "if I had let them play a few measures more the most horrible dissonances would have resulted. I had to make an interruption." '

Seyfried described the scene thus:

'When the master brought out his orchestral Fantasia with choruses, he arranged with me at the somewhat hurried rehearsal, with wet voice-parts as usual, that the second variation should be played without the repeat. In the evening, however, absorbed in his creation, he forgot all about the instructions which he had given, repeated the first part while the orchestra accompanied the second, which sounded not altogether edifying. A trifle too late, the concert-master, Unrath, noticed the mistake, looked in surprise at his lost companions, stopped playing and called out drily: "Again!" A little displeased, the violinist Anton Wranitsky asked "With repeats?" "Yes," came the answer, and now the thing went straight as a string.'

The *Allgemeine Musikalische Zeitung* reported:

'The wind-instruments varied the theme which Beethoven had previously played on the pianoforte. The turn came to the oboes. The clarinets, if I am not mistaken, make a mistake in the count and enter at once. A curious mixture of tones results. Beethoven jumps up, tries to silence the clarinets, but does not succeed until he has called out quite loudly and rather ill-temperedly: "Stop, stop! That will not do! Again – again!"'

Czerny records: 'In the Pianoforte Fantasia with chorus he called out at the mistake: "Wrong, badly played, wrong, again!" Several musicians wanted to go away.' Beethoven jumped up, ran to the desks and pointed out the place.

Seyfried says further:

'At first he could not understand that he had in a manner humiliated the musicians. He thought it was a duty to correct an error that had been made and that the audience was entitled to hear everything properly played, for its money. But he readily and heartily begged the pardon of the orchestra for the humiliation to which he had subjected it, and was honest enough to spread the story himself and assume all responsibility for his own absence of mind.'

The pecuniary results of this concert to Beethoven are not known.

The Choral Fantasia was obviously finished only a short time before its performance and is plainly one of the few compositions on which Beethoven worked continuously after once beginning it. In the Grasnick sketchbook of 1808 there are sketches for the work consecutively on the first seventy-five pages. The most interesting revelations are that there is no hint of a pianoforte introduction such as Beethoven improvised at the performance; that Beethoven first thought of beginning with the string quartet of the orchestra; that the work was begun before a text was found; and that, as in the case of the Choral Symphony, of which the Fantasia is so interesting a prototype in miniature, Beethoven thought of paving the way for the introduction of the voices by words calling attention to the newcomers among the harmonious company ('*Hört ihr wohl?*'). The introductory pianoforte fantasia which was published to take the place of Beethoven's improvisation at the first performance was composed in 1809.

The offer of an honourable position in Cassel – permanent, so long as

Napoleon's star might remain in the ascendant and his satellite retain his nominal kingship of Westphalia – was one no less gratifying to Beethoven than surprising and perplexing to his friends. Knowing both the strong and the weak points of his character, they saw the extreme improbability that, with his increasing deafness, his removal thither could in the end redound to his profit, honour, or happiness. On the other hand, they saw him forced to consider the question of seeking in a small provincial capital that permanent provision for his future necessities which, in the home of his choice at the end of sixteen years' residence, he saw no hope of obtaining. What an inexcusable, unpardonable disgrace to Vienna would be the departure of Beethoven under such circumstances! It was the first time the question had been presented; but being presented it was promptly met by a request from persons of 'high and the highest rank that he state the conditions under which' he would decline the call to Cassel and remain in Vienna.

Here was one of those happy opportunities for conferences, notes, letters and despatches innumerable, which Beethoven all his life seems to have so eagerly embraced and enjoyed. A letter dated 7 January 1809, by Beethoven to Breitkopf and Härtel, indicates that at the opening of the year 1809, Beethoven was still firmly resolved to go to Cassel. In it occurs this passage:

'... At last I am forced by the intrigues and cabals and contemptible actions of all kinds to leave my only surviving German fatherland. On the invitation of His Royal Majesty of Westphalia, I am going thither as kapellmeister with an annual salary of 600 ducats in gold – Just today I have sent my assurance by post that I will come and am only waiting my decree before making preparations for my journey which will be by way of *Leipzig* – Therefore, in order that my journey may be the more brilliant for me, I beg of you, if not too prejudicial to your interests, not to make anything known of my works *till Easter* ... In all probability abusive letters will again be written from here about my last Akademie to the *Musikalische Zeitung*; I do not ask that all that is against me be suppressed, yet one should realise that nobody has more personal enemies here than I. This is the more easily to be understood, since the state of music here is steadily growing worse – We have kapellmeisters who know so little about conducting that they can scarcely read a score – It is worst of all, of course, at the Theater auf der Wieden – I had to give my Akademie there and all kinds of obstacles were put in my way. – The people in charge of the Widows Concert, out of hatred for me, and Herr Salieri is among the first, played me the nasty trick of threatening to expel every musician who played for me from the company – Notwithstanding the fact that several mistakes were made, which I could not help, the public accepted everything enthusiastically – Nevertheless, scribblers from here will certainly not fail again to send miserable stuff against me to the *Musikalische Zeitung* – The musicians were particularly angry because, when a blunder was made through carelessness in the simplest, plainest place in the world, I stopped them suddenly and loudly called out *"Once again"* – Such a thing had never happened to them before. The public showed its environment at this – but it is daily growing worse. The day before my concert, in the easy little opera "Milton", at the theatre in the city, the orchestra fell into such disorder that kapellmeister and leader and orchestra veritably suffered shipwreck – for the kapellmeister instead of being ahead was behind in his beat and then in came the leader. Give me an answer right away, my friend.

Respectfully your most devoted servant   Beethoven'

It seems likely that the suggestion that formal stipulations for a contract be drawn up under which Beethoven would decline the offer from Cassel and remain in Vienna came from the Countess Erdödy. At any rate Beethoven wrote to Gleichenstein:

'Countess Erdödy is of the opinion that you ought to outline a plan with her according to which she might negotiate in case they approach her as she is convinced they will.

Your friend Lud. Beethoven'
'If you should have time this afternoon, the Countess would be glad to see you.'

The outline of the proposition which was to be submitted to certain noble gentlemen was drawn up by Beethoven for Gleichenstein as follows:

'OUTLINE FOR A MUSICAL CONSTITUTION
'First the offer of the King of Westphalia is to be set forth – B. cannot be held down to any obligation on account of this salary since the chief object of his art, viz., the invention of new works, would suffer thereby – This remuneration must be assured to Beethoven until he voluntarily renounces it – the Imperial title also if possible – to alternate with Salieri and Eybler – the promise of active court service as soon as possible – or adjunction if it be worth while. Contract with the theatres likewise with the title of Member of one of the Committees of Theatrical Direction – A fixed day forever for a concert, even if there

be a change in the directorate in the theatre, in return for which Beethoven binds himself to compose a new work every year for one of the charity concerts as may be thought most useful – or to conduct two – a place at a money-changer's or such kind where Beethoven would receive the stipulated salary – The salary must be paid also by the heirs.'

On some of these points Beethoven changed his mind and wrote again thus:

'. . . Please have everything relate to *the true and for me proper practice of my art*, thus you will write what is in my heart and head – The introduction has what I am to get in Westphalia, 600 ducats in gold, 150 for travelling expenses, for which I have to do nothing except conduct the King's concerts which are short and not numerous – I am not even bound to conduct any opera that I may write – From all this it is clear that I can devote myself wholly to the most important purpose of my art to compose works of magnitude – and also have an orchestra at my disposal.

'NB The title of Member of one of the Theatrical Committees is to be dropped – it would bring nothing but vexation – In regard to the *Imperial duties* I think the point must be handled delicately – nothing about the demand for the title of Imperial Kapellmeister – but only in regard to the fact that once placed in a position through a court salary, I give up the sum which the gentlemen are now paying me. Thus I think that this might best be expressed as a hope and a highest wish sometime to enter the Imperial service, at which time I could at once accept as much less as the sum received from his Imperial Majesty amounts to. –

[on the top of the last page:]
'NB We shall need it tomorrow at 12 o'clock, because we must then go to Kinsky. I hope to see you today.'

Under these instructions the Conditions were drawn up, probably by Gleichenstein. These proving acceptable, the business was concluded and Beethoven retained in Vienna by this

'AGREEMENT

'The daily proofs which Herr Ludwig van Beethoven is giving of his extraordinary talents and genius as musician and composer, awaken the desire that he surpass the great expectations which are justified by his past achievements.

'But as it has been demonstrated that only one who is as free from care as possible can devote himself to a single department of activity and create works of magnitude which are exalted and which ennoble art, the undersigned have decided to place Herr Ludwig van Beethoven in a position where the necessaries of life shall not cause him embarrassment or clog his powerful genius.

'To this end they bind themselves to pay him the fixed sum of 4,000 (four thousand) florins a year, as follows:

His Imperial Highness, Archduke Rudolph . . . . . . fl. 1,500
The Highborn Prince Lobkowitz . . . . " 700
The Highborn Prince Ferdinand Kinsky . . . . " 1,800

Total . . . . fl. 4,000

which Herr van Beethoven is to collect in semi-annual instalments, *pro rata*, against voucher, from each of these contributors.

'The undersigned are pledged to pay this annual salary until Herr van Beethoven receives an appointment which shall yield him the equivalent of the above sum.

'Should such an appointment not be received and Herr Ludwig van Beethoven be prevented from practising his art by an unfortunate accident or old age, the participants herein grant him the salary for life.

'In consideration of this Herr Ludwig van Beethoven pledges himself to make his domicile in Vienna, where the makers of this document live, or in a city in one of the other hereditary countries of His Austrian Imperial Majesty, and to depart from this domicile only for such set times as may be called for by his business or the interests of art, touching which, however, the high contributors must be consulted and to which they must give their consent.

'Given in Vienna, 1 March 1809.

(LS)   Rudolph,
            Archduke
(LS)   Prince von Lobkowitz,
            Duke of Raudnitz
(LS)   Ferdinand Prince Kinsky'

This document bears in Beethoven's hand these words:

'Received
on 26 February 1809
from the hands
of Archduke
Rudolph, RH'

The remarks in a former chapter upon the singular attraction for the young of Beethoven and his works are supported by this contract. Lobkowitz, it is true, was near the master's age, being then thirty-five; but Rudolph and Kinsky were respectively but twenty-one and twenty-seven. Ries, who was then much with Beethoven, asserts that the contract with the King of Westphalia 'was all ready; it lacked only the signature' before his Vienna friends moved in the matter and 'settled a salary on him for life'.

It requires no great sagacity to perceive from the text of the 'Agreement', that none of its signers had any expectation that Beethoven could ever perform the duties of an Imperial Conductor acceptably; and his hope of obtaining the title must have rested upon the influence which he supposed Archduke Rudolph might exert upon Emperor Franz. Be this as it may, the composer was justly elated by the favourable change in his pecuniary condition; and his very natural exultation peeps out in the correspondence of the time.

On 18 March, Gleichenstein received a copy or abstract of the contract enclosed in this:

'You can see from the enclosed, my dear, good Gleichenstein, how honourable my remaining here has turned out for me – the title of Imperial Kapellmeister will also come later, etc. Write to me as soon as possible whether you think that I ought to make the journey in the present warlike state of affairs and whether you are still firmly resolved to travel with me. Several people have advised me against it, but in this matter I shall follow you implicitly. Since you already have a carriage it should be arranged that for a stretch you travel towards me and I towards you – Write quickly – Now you can help me hunt for a wife. If you find a beautiful one in F[reiburg], who yields a sigh to my harmonies, but it must be no *Elise Bürger*, make connections with her in advance – But she must be beautiful, for I cannot love what is not beautiful – else I should love myself. Farewell and write soon. Present my compliments to your parents, your brother – I embrace you with all my heart and remain your true friend

Beethoven'

The jesting on matrimony in this letter and the allusion to the poet Bürger's unlucky marriage with Christine Elizabeth Hahn, attest the writer's lightness of spirit, but are not to be taken seriously. But we shall find in a year's time, when his finances were more secure, that Beethoven was to be definitely considering marriage.

In this connection the following background may be given. At some

point after 1806, when he had returned to Vienna, Gleichenstein introduced Beethoven to a family named Malfatti. The culture, refinement,
musical taste and high character of the parents, and the uncommon
grace and beauty of their two young girls rendered the house very
attractive to the composer. There was less than a year's difference in
the age of the children: Therese was born on 1 January 1792 and Anna
on 7 December of the same year. In 1811 Anna became the wife of
Gleichenstein, and Therese married Court Councillor Wilhelm Baron
von Drosdick in 1817. According to Dr Sonnleithner:

'Frau Therese Baroness von Drosdick, née Malfatti . . . was a beautiful,
lively and intellectual woman, a very good pianoforte player and,
besides, the cousin [actually niece] of the famous physician and friend
of Beethoven's, Dr von Malfatti. Herein lies the explanation of an
unusually kind relationship with Beethoven which resulted in a less
severe regard for conventional forms. Nothing is known of a particular
intimacy between her and Beethoven.'

Through these Malfattis, then, Beethoven became also known personally to the physician of the same name and 'they were great friends
for a long time. Malfatti became Beethoven's doctor after the sudden
death of Dr Schmidt on 19 February 1808. However, towards each
other they were like two hard millstones, and they separated. Malfatti
used to say of Beethoven: "He is a disorderly [konfuser] fellow – but all
the same he may be the greatest genius." '
    The allusions to a tour in the letter to Gleichenstein and the provi-
sion made in the 'Agreement' for the composer's temporary absence
from Austria, acquire a particular significance from one of the notes of
Röckel's conversation, namely: 'Beethoven in those days was full of the
project of travelling, and a plan was marked out of visiting the German
cities, then England and finally *Spain*; upon which last Röckel laid
great stress. He was to have accompanied Beethoven.'
    Relations between Beethoven and his brother Carl Caspar were no
longer on the same footing as they had been before the latter's marriage.
In March 1809, Beethoven, forwarding a letter to brother Johann, in
Linz, enclosed in it an envelope, inside of which he wrote the words:
'Dear Brother – This letter for you has been lying here for a long time.
Would that God would grant the other brother once instead of his
unfeelingness – feeling – I suffer infinitely through him. With my bad
hearing I always need somebody, and whom shall I trust?'
    The breach between Beethoven and his brother Carl was now, in
business matters, complete; and he needed someone to perform for him

the many little offices which he could not with propriety demand to any extent of Zmeskall, Gleichenstein or Röckel, even had they the leisure and the will.

Beethoven's experiment of lodging with Countess Erdödy, as might have been predicted, was not a successful one; he was too irritable, whimsical, obstinate; too ready to take offence, too lax in asking or giving explanations. We have seen in divers cases how, when he discovered himself to be in the wrong, he gladly made every due acknowledgement; but, as in the case of Ries, this was often too late to remedy the mischief already caused. Before the close of the winter, he was evidently becoming discontented; so much so as to take ill even the singular proof of the Countess's goodwill spoken of in the following note:

'I think, my dear Zmeskall, that even after the war is over, if ever it begins, you will be ready to carry on negotiations for peace. What a glorious office!! I leave it wholly in your hands to settle the affair about my servant, but the Countess *Erdödy* must not have the slightest influence over him. She has, as she says, given him 25 fl. and 5 fl. a month *just to make him remain with me*. Now I *must necessarily* believe in this magnanimity – but do not wish it to be continued . . .'

Another note bears Zmeskall's date, '7 March 1809':

'I might easily have thought it –
'About the blows, this is dragged in by the hair of the head – this story is at least three months old – and is by no means – what he now makes of it – The whole miserable affair was brought about by a huckster woman and a few other wretches – but I shall not lose much, because he was really spoiled in the house where I am.'

What cause of dissension, beyond the ill-advised gratifications to the servant, had arisen between Beethoven and the Countess is not known; but something had occurred, the blame of which he soon saw was all his own, and for which he thus humbly expressed his contrition and asked forgiveness:

'My dear Countess:
'I have erred, that is true – forgive me. It was assuredly not intentional malice on my part if I have hurt you – Only since last night have I learned the truth about the matter; and I am very sorry that I acted as I did – Read your note coolly and judge for yourself whether I deserve

this and whether you did not pay me back six-fold since I offended you unintentionally. Send my note back to me today, and write me only one word that you are no longer angry. I shall suffer infinitely if you do not do this. I can do nothing if things are to continue thus — I await your forgiveness.'

There are sufficient grounds for belief that an immediate reconciliation took place; nevertheless, Beethoven decided to go into another lodging, and for a short time he moved into one in the Walfischgasse looking out over the city wall and glacis.

Now the threatening war-clouds became more dense. The French armies not only prevented Ludwig's contemplated journey but affected him disastrously both pecuniarily and professionally. On 4 May, the Empress left Vienna with the Imperial family. Archduke Rudolph accompanied her, and Beethoven mourned his departure in the well-known first movement of the Sonata, Op. 81a. Beethoven's manuscript bears these inscriptions in his own hand: 'The Farewell, Vienna, 4 May 1809, on the departure of his Imperial Highness the revered Archduke Rudolph'; on the Finale: 'The Arrival of His Imperial Highness the revered Archduke Rudolph, 30 January 1810.'

With a garrison of 16,000 troops, 1,000 students and artists, the civil militia and a small number of summoned men, Archduke Maximilian was ordered to defend Vienna. Thus it came about that Beethoven, on 10 May, found himself shut up in a beleaguered city.

The French commanders demanded the capitulation of Vienna, but Archduke Maximilian rejected the demands, and the French erected a battery on the Spittelberg to shell the city. Every shot directed by this battery against the Kärnthnerthor and the Wasserkunst Bastei was liable to plunge into Beethoven's windows.

At 9 o'clock at night (on 11 May) the battery of twenty howitzers opened fire. Rich and poor, high and low, young and old at once found themselves crowded indiscriminately in cellars and fireproof vaults.

Beethoven took refuge in the Rauhensteingasse and 'spent the greater part of the time in a cellar in the house of his brother Caspar, where he covered his head with pillows so as not to hear the cannons', so says Ries. More probably Beethoven took this wise precaution to save his feeble organs of hearing from the effect of the sharp reports of bursting shells, for it does not appear that either the cannons on the bastions or those mounted in the streets were fired. 'At half-past 2 (the afternoon of the 12th) the white flag was sent up as notice of capitulation to the outposts of the enemy.'

The occupation of the capital by the French and the gathering together of opposing armies for the terrible battles of Aspern, Esslingen, Wagram and Znaim produced the inevitable effects of increased consumption and deficient supply of the necessaries of life. Even before the capitulation 'the rate of interest went up fearfully, especially in the sale of food, particularly bread, and because of the disappearance of copper coins'. From the capitulation to the armistice of 12 July, two months, 'the enemy had drawn from the city nearly 10,000,000 florins and demanded enormous requisitions of supplies'. There was one requisition, perhaps more than one, which touched Beethoven directly: 'A forced loan on the houses of the city and the suburbs amounting to one-quarter of the rentals from owners or the parties to a contract for rent on from 101 to 1,000 florins and one-third on from 1,001 to 2,000 florins, etc.' Perhaps at no other time was Beethoven so well able to meet the extraordinary demands upon his purse as now. He had received from Archduke Rudolph 750 florins and from Prince Lobkowitz 350 florins, his first payment of the annuity; and doubtless Breitkopf and Härtel and his other publishers had remitted money or bills. Still he must have felt the pressure of the time severely before Vienna again became free. To whom could he go for aid? The Lichnowskys, Pálffys, Waldstein, etc., were all away; the Erdödys took refuge in Hungary or Croatia. Of personal friends, Breuning seems to have remained – no other is known to have done so. Bigot and his wife went off to Paris, never to return; Zmeskall and the public officials in general had followed the Court and the Ministers to places of safety. The posts were interrupted and for many weeks communication with the country prohibited. For Beethoven, this confinement during this season of the year when he was accustomed to breathe inspiration in vale and forest, was almost intolerable, and increased if possible his old hatred of Napoleon and the French. Young Rust met him one day in a coffee-house and saw him shake his fist at a passing French officer, with the exclamation: 'If I, as general, knew as much about strategy as I the composer know of counterpoint, I'd give you something to do!'

On 31 May Joseph Haydn died. It is not known whether Beethoven was present at any of the funeral services.

During the occupation of Vienna, Beethoven was visited by Baron de Trémont, a French officer and music-lover who in his memoirs left recollections of these meetings:

'. . . I admired his genius and knew his works by heart when, in 1809, as Auditor to the Council of State while Napoleon was making war on Austria, I was the bearer of the Council's despatches to him. Although my departure was hurried, I made up my mind that in case the army should take Vienna I must not neglect the opportunity to see Beethoven. I asked Cherubini to give me a letter to him. "I will give you one to Haydn," he replied, "and that excellent man will make you welcome, but I will not write to Beethoven; I should have to reproach myself that he refused to see someone recommended by me; he is an unlicked bear!" '

The Baron, however, did get himself admitted to Beethoven's lodging, despite his misgivings about Beethoven's reception of anyone who had to do with the French. In fact, Beethoven liked the young Baron enough to arrange several meetings with him during his sojourn in Vienna. Trémont continues:

'I fancy that to these improvisations of Beethoven's I owe my most vivid musical impressions. I maintain that unless one has heard him improvise well and quite at ease, one can but imperfectly appreciate the vast scope of his genius. Swayed wholly by the impulse of the moment, he sometimes said to me, after striking a few chords: "Nothing comes into my head; let's put it off till —" Then we would talk philosophy, religion, politics, and especially of Shakespeare, his idol, and always in a language that would have provoked the laughter of any hearers . . ,

'. . . His mind was much occupied with the greatness of Napoleon, and he often spoke to me about it. Through all his resentment I could see that he admired his rise from such obscure beginnings; his democratic ideas were flattered by it. One day he remarked, "If I go to Paris, shall I be obligated to salute your emperor?" I assured him that he would not, unless commanded for an audience, "And do you think he would command me?" – "I do not doubt that he would, if he appreciated your importance; but you have seen in Cherubini's case that he does not know much about music." – This question made me think that, despite his opinions, he would have felt flattered by any mark of distinction from Napoleon . . .'

On 9 August a letter from Amsterdam was received by the composer, notifying him of his appointment as a Correspondent of the Fourth Class of the Royal Institute of Science, Literature and the Fine Arts. It gave occasion shortly after its receipt (19 September) for a letter to Breitkopf and Härtel in which Beethoven says: '*Do you know that I have become a member of the Society of Fine Arts and Sciences?* – after all a title – ha ha, it makes me laugh.'

Considering the war conditions it is understandable why Beethoven was unable to make his regular move into the country of which he was so fond and which was so important for his health. In his letter to Breitkopf and Härtel of 26 July he writes: 'I still cannot enjoy life in the country, which is so indispensable for me.' Some time before 3 August he had moved once again to new lodgings, for on this date he informs the Leipzig publishers of his new address: 'in the Klepperstall in the Teinfaltstrasse on the third floor, care of the lawyer Gostischa.'

September came and still no payment from Clementi and Co. for the works bought by them in April 1807. Clementi was in Rome and thither, it would seem, Beethoven sent several letters asking for payment. Clementi now came to Vienna and sent a letter to his London partner, Collard, which, though dateless as to year and day, was, no doubt, the result of Beethoven's importunities. In it he complained of having written five or six letters to them for money with which to meet Beethoven's demands, the composer having 'plagued' him with several letters – but in vain. At last a firm of Viennese bankers informed him that a credit for £400 had been sent him, but no letter. He concluded that of this sum £100 were meant for Beethoven and £300 for himself, and that they had received but half of Beethoven's manuscripts. 'A most shabby figure you have made me cut in this affair! – and that with one of the first composers of the day! You certainly might have found means in the course of two years and a half to have satisfied his demands. Don't lose a moment and send me word *what* you have received from him, that I may settle with him.'

It was in the autumn that Beethoven seems to have thought of trying the experiment of living independently of hotels and eating houses, and dining at home. It was therefore of importance to him, if possible, to obtain the joint services of some man and wife, and such a couple, by the name of Herzog, now offered themselves as servant and housekeeper. This is sufficient introduction to the following excerpts from the Zmeskall correspondence:

'. . . Today Herzog, who wishes to become my servant, will come to see you – you may engage him for 30 fl. with his wife *obbligato* – wood, light, small amount of livery. – I must have someone to cook for me, for as long as the present wretched food continues I shall remain ill – Today I am dining at home, because of the better wine. If you will order what you want, I should be glad to have you come to eat with me also – You will get the wine gratis and indeed a better one than that at the beastly Schwan –'

'Here comes Herzog with his wife – Just listen to what these people would agree to do – she must cook when I want her to – also mend, etc., for this is a highly important matter – I shall come to you afterwards in order to hear the result – Perhaps it would be best to ask how much they are willing to do for me? –'

The Herzogs were engaged. All did not go well, however, and Zmeskall, who had previously helped Beethoven with 'peace negotiations' with servants, now had again to officiate in this 'glorious office' with the Herzogs. The following note to Zmeskall undoubtedly refers to troubles with the Herzogs:

'I do not want to see that woman again and although she is *perhaps* better than he I want to hear as little about her as about him – Therefore I am sending you the desired 24 fl. Please add to this the 30 kr., take a 15 kr. piece of stamped paper, have *the servant* write in his own handwriting that *he has received the 24 fl. 30 kr. as money for boots and livery* – You will hear more from me in person concerning how much she has recently lied *to you* – Meanwhile I want you to remember *the respect due yourself as a friend of mine*. Tell them that *it is only from your inducement that more is being given*; otherwise don't have anything to do with them unnecessarily for they are both unworthy of your intercession. – I didn't want to have her husband again but circumstances partly demanded it. I needed a servant; and housekeeper and servant cost too much. Besides I found her several times with her husband down below at the watchmaker's in my house; she even wanted to go out from there with him when I needed her. Therefore, I let him come back, since I had to keep *her* for my lodgings. If I hadn't taken him back I would have been cheated all the more – So the matter ends; *they are both wretched people* – Farewell. I shall see you soon.

Your friend
Beethoven'

The imagination can readily form a lively and correct picture of Beethoven's troubles, partly serious, partly tragi-comic, with people of this kind during that wretched time with all the necessaries of life at famine prices, and they on his hands to be provided for. The situation certainly was not one fitted to sweeten the temper of either party; no doubt both had good cause for complaint. We have, however, only the master's side of the question and not the whole of that.

Meanwhile, Manager Hartl had projected a new charity, a theatrical poor fund, and as usual called upon Beethoven to give attraction to the first public performance for its benefit, by directing one or more of his works. Under these circumstances Hartl might reasonably expect munificent support from the French conquerors for at least one charity concert for the benefit of the actors and their families. Hence, as on 8 September (the Nativity of the Virgin Mary) the Court Theatres would be closed, he selected that day. The programme has eluded search; but one number was the *Sinfonia Eroica*, conducted by its author. Was this selected, in the expectation that Napoleon would be present, to do him homage? If so, it failed of its aim. The day before, Napoleon journeyed from Schönbrunn to Krems and Mölk. Or was it in bitter sarcasm that Beethoven chose it?

An undated letter to Collin should be cited here. In it he asked the Court Secretary to rewrite a note which he had addressed to Beethoven when Hartl gave him the commission for the concert, and which he had lost. Then he continued in part:

'. . . As near as I can recollect the contents were: "that you wrote to me that you had spoken to H. v. Hartl concerning a *day for a concert* and that then he gave you instructions to write to me that if at this year's concert for the theatrical poor, I gave *important works* for the performance, and would myself conduct, I might at once pick out a day for a concert at the Theater-an-der-Wien and that under these conditions I might have a day *every year*. Vive vale . . ." '

'When it was decided', writes Czerny, 'to perform Schiller's "Tell" and Goethe's "Egmont" in the city theatres, the question arose as to who should compose the music. Beethoven and Gyrowitz were chosen. Beethoven wanted very much to have "Tell". But a lot of intrigues were at once set on foot to have "Egmont", supposed to be less adaptable to music, assigned to him. It turned out, however, that he could make masterly music for this drama also, and he applied the full power of his genius to it.'

Perhaps Beethoven's experience with the 'Ode to Joy' earlier and the 'Egmont' just at this time was the origin of a fine remark to Czerny. 'Once, when the talk was about Schiller, he said to me: "Schiller's poems are very difficult to set to music. The composer must be able to lift himself far above *the poet*; who can do that in the case of Schiller? In this respect Goethe is much easier." '

Towards the end of the year Beethoven took ill, as he informed Breitkopf and Härtel in a letter which was dated 4 December (but from which the figure was stricken; the letter may have been delayed or Beethoven become doubtful, as usual, about the day of the month).

In this he writes: 'A fever which shook me up thoroughly, prevented me from sending these tardily found errata [in the two Trios] at once.' On 2 January 1810, he wrote another letter, beginning: 'Scarcely recovered – my illness threw me back again for two weeks – is it a wonder? – we do not even have eatable bread', and concluding with: 'I am too weak today to answer your kind letter more fully, but in a few days I will answer everything else in your letter.'

The great cost of living and the various extraordinary demands upon his purse this year deranged Beethoven's pecuniary affairs seriously; from the same cause the Vienna publishers were not in a position to pay him adequately and in advance for his manuscripts. The dilatoriness of the London publishers has been mentioned. Happily his relations with Breitkopf and Härtel were such that they were ready to remunerate him handsomely for whatever new compositions he might send them; and there seems to have been an arrangement made, under which divers new works of this period were published simultaneously by them in Leipzig and by Artaria in Vienna. Nevertheless, Beethoven was pressed for money, not only from the causes above stated, but from the need of an extra supply, in case a project of marriage, now in his mind, should be effected. Of course he counted with certainty upon the regular payment of his annuity, now that the war was over, and a lasting peace apparently secured by the rumoured union between Napoleon and Archduchess Marie Louise. But a semi-annual payment of this annuity was far from sufficient to meet the expenses of establishing himself as a married man. In a letter dated 'Wednesday the 2nd, Winter month [November] 1809', Beethoven wrote to Breitkopf and Härtel: '. . . I worked for several weeks in succession so that it seemed rather *for death* than *immortality* . . .'

CHAPTER 13

The Years 1810 and 1811

Therese Malfatti – Bettina Brentano and Goethe

Beethoven was to some considerable degree a self-taught man; he had read and studied much, and had acquired a knowledge of the ordinary literary topics of the time, which justified a fine passage in the letter to Breitkopf and Härtel of 2 November 1809; 'There is scarcely a treatise which would be too learned *for me*. Without making the least claim concerning my own learnedness, I have tried since childhood to grasp the *meaning of the better and the wise* of each age. Shame to any artist who does not hold it to be his duty to have at least that amount of proficiency.' Strikingly in point is the interest which he exhibits during these and following years in the Oriental researches of Hammer and his associates. His notes and excerpts prove a very extensive knowledge of their translations, both published and in manuscript; and, moreover, that this strange literature was perhaps even more attractive to him in its religious, than in its lyric and dramatic aspects. In these excerpts – indeed, generally in extracts from books and in his underscoring of favourite passages in them – Beethoven exhibits a keen perception and taste for the lofty and sublime, far beyond the grasp of any common or uncultivated mind.

He was now at an age when men of thoughtful and independent minds have settled opinions on such important subjects as have received their attention, among which, to all men, religion stands pre-eminent. Few change their faith after forty; there is no reason to suppose that Beethoven did; no place, therefore, more fit than this will be found to remark upon a topic to which the preceding observation directly leads – his religious views. Schindler writes:

'Beethoven was brought up in the Catholic religion. That he was truly religious is proved by his whole life, and many evidences were brought forward in the biographical part [of this work]. It was one of his peculiarities that he never spoke on religious topics or concerning the dogmas of the various Christian Churches in order to give his opinion about them. It may be said with considerable certainty, however, that his religious views rested less upon the creed of the Church, than that they had their origin in deism. Without having a manufactured theory before him he plainly recognised the existence of God in the world as well as the world in God. This . . . he found in the whole of Nature.'

As an argument against Schindler and to prove Beethoven's ortho-doxy in respect to the Roman Catholic tenets, the fervid sentiment and sublime devotion expressed in the music of the *Missa Solemnis* have been urged; but the words of the mass were simply a text on which he could lavish all the resources of his art in the expression of his religious feelings. It should not be forgotten that the only mass which could be ranked with Beethoven's in D, was the composition of the sturdy Lutheran, J. S. Bach, and that the great epic poem of trinitarian Chris-tianity was by the Arian, John Milton. Perhaps Schindler would have his readers understand more than is clearly expressed. If he means that Beethoven rejected the trinitarian dogma; that the Deity of his faith is a personal God, a universal Father, to whom his human children may hopefully appeal for mercy in time of temptation, for aid in time of need, for consolation in time of sorrow – if this be Schindler's 'deism', it may be affirmed unhesitatingly that everything known to the present writer, which bears at all on the subject, confirms this view. Beethoven had the habit in moments of temptation and distress of writing down short prayers for divine support and assistance, many of which are pre-served; but neither in them, nor in any of his memoranda or conversa-tions, is there the remotest indication that he believed in the necessity of any mediator between the soul of man and the Divine Father, under whatsoever name known; but an even stronger religious sentiment, a more ardent spirit of devotion, a firmer reliance on the goodness and mercy of God are revealed in them, than Schindler seems to have apprehended.

The topics under last notice have carried us far onward, even to the last years of Beethoven. We now return to the end of 1809 – to the master in the full vigour and maturity of his powers. The princes, whose generosity had just placed him, for the present at least, beyond the reach of pecuniary anxieties, may well have expected the immedi-ate fulfilment of 'the desire that he surpass the great expectations which are justified by his past achievements'. They were bitterly dis-appointed. Kinsky did not live to hear any new orchestral work from that recently so prolific pen; Lobkowitz, whose dissatisfaction is upon record, heard but three; while the Archduke saw the years pass away comparatively fruitless, hardly more being accomplished in ten, than formerly in two – the marvellous year 1814 excepted. The close of 1809 terminated a decade (1800–9) during which Beethoven's works offer a more splendid exhibition of intellectual power than those of any other composer produced within a like term of years; and New Year, 1810, began another (1810–19), which, compared with the preceding, exhibits an astonishing decrease in the composer's productiveness.

Beethoven's studies were now diverted from other works in hand to an order from the directors of the theatres – the *Egmont* music. The persevering diligence of the last months was evidently for the purpose of clearing his desk of a mass of manuscript compositions sold to Breit-kopf and Härtel, before attacking Goethe's tragedy – as decks are cleared for action before a naval battle. The overture bears the composer's own date '1810'; the first performance with Beethoven's music was on the evening of 15 June. Clärchen was played by Antonie Adamberger – a young actress alike distinguished for her beauty, her genius and her virtues. The two songs which Clärchen has to sing necessarily brought Fräulein Adamberger for the moment into personal relations with Beethoven, concerning which she wrote to the present author the following simple and pleasing account in 1867:

'. . . I approached him [Beethoven] without embarrassment when my aunt of blessed memory, my teacher and benefactress, called me to her room and presented me to him. To his question: "Can you sing?" I replied without embarrassment with a decided "No!" Beethoven regarded me with amazement and said laughingly: "No? But I am to compose the songs in 'Egmont' for you." I answered very simply that I had sung only four months and had then ceased because of hoarseness and the fear that continued exertion in the practice of declamation might injure my voice. Then he said jovially with an adoption of the Viennese dialect: "That will be a pretty how do you do!" – but on his part it turned out to be something glorious.

'We went to the pianoforte and rummaging around in my music . . . he found on top of the pile the well-known rondo with recitative from Zingarelli's *Romeo and Juliet*. "Do you sing *that*?" he asked with a laugh which shook him as he sat down hesitatingly to play the accompaniment. Just as innocently and unsuspiciously as I had chatted with him and laughed, I now reeled off the air. Then a kind look came into his eye, he stroked my forehead with his hand and said: "Very well, now I know" – he came back in three days and sang the songs for me a few times. After I had memorised them in a few days he left me with the words: "There, that's right. So, so that's the way, now sing thus, don't let anybody persuade you to do differently and see that you do not put a *mortant* in it." He went; I never saw him again in my room. Only at the rehearsal when conducting he frequently nodded to me pleasantly and benevolently. One of the old gentlemen expressed the opinion that the songs which the master, counting on certain effects, had set for orchestra, ought to be accompanied on a guitar. Then he turned his head most comically and, with his eyes flaming, said, "He knows!" . . .'

Kinsky's active service in the campaign of 1809 and his subsequent duties in Bohemia had prevented him hitherto from discharging his obligations under the annuity contract; but the Archduke, perhaps Lobkowitz also, was promptly meeting his; and these payments, together with the honourable remuneration granted by Breitkopf and Härtel for manuscripts, supplied Beethoven, despite the high cost of living, with ample means for comfort, even for luxury. This led him to contemplate a change of lodgings. It was to his old home in the house of Baron Pasqualati which he had occupied two years before, and which he now took again at an annual rental of 500 florins, on 24 April, the start of the spring renting season.

A number of letters to Gleichenstein and Zmeskall to which attention must now be called seem to show us Beethoven in the character of a man so deeply smitten with the charms of a newly acquired lady friend that he turned his attention seriously to his wardrobe and personal appearance and thought unusually long and frequently of the social pleasures at the home of his charmer. This home was the Malfatti household to which Gleichenstein was a frequent visitor in this year. Beethoven's 'charmer' was Therese Malfatti; the object of Gleichenstein's interest was her younger sister Anna, whom he married in 1811. A letter to Wegeler dated 2 May 1810, to be introduced later, shows that Beethoven was considering marriage.

In one letter to Gleichenstein, Beethoven writes: 'I beg of you to let me know when the M[alfattis] remain home of an evening. You surely had a pleasant sleep – I slept little, to be sure, but I prefer such being awakened to all sleep.'

Another letter reads:

'Dear good Gleichenstein!

'I am sending you 300 fl. – Just let me know if you need more and how much? I'll send it right away – and since I understand so little about these things as it is all so against my nature, please buy for me linen or Bengal for shirts and at least half a dozen neckties. – Use your good judgement but don't delay, you know how I need them – Today I forwarded 300 fl. to Lind and thereby have followed your advice.

'Today *Joseph Henickstein* paid me twenty-seven and a half florins for a pound sterling and *invited you and me along with Clementi to lunch tomorrow. Don't refuse, you know how I like being with you.* However send me word whether I may tell Henickstein that you can surely be counted upon – You won't refuse, will you – Greet everyone who is dear to you and me. How gladly would I like to add and *to whom we are dear*???? This question mark applies at least to me –

'Today and tomorrow I have so much to do that I cannot come to you as I would like to do. Goodbye, be happy – I am not.

Your
Beethoven'

Lind was a tailor, Henickstein the son of a banker. Again he wrote to say that he wished 'Madame M.' would give him permission to pick out a pianoforte for her which she wished to buy 'at Schanz's'. Though it was his rule never to accept commissions on such sales, he wanted to save money for the lady on this purchase.

On another day he writes:

'Here is the sonata I promised Therese. Since I cannot see her today, give it to her – remember me to all of them. I feel so happy with them all and as though they might heal the wounds inflicted upon my soul by wicked people. Thank you, kind G., for having taken me there – Here are 50 fl. for the neckerchiefs. If you need more, let me know. You are wrong if you think that you are the only one that Gigons follows. I too have had the pleasure of having him not leave my side. He has eaten beside me in the evening, and he even accompanied me home. – In short, he provided me with very good entertainment. At least I could never look up, but quite far down – farewell, love me

Your Beethoven'

Gigons was the Malfattis' little dog, and it is evident that Beethoven was pleased by the attention paid him. This is the first of only two allusions which Beethoven makes in all his papers, printed or written relating to him, to a domestic pet animal.

Now we reach the notes to Zmeskall. Beethoven could and did avail himself of Zmeskall's readiness to oblige him to an extent which at length excited misgivings in his own mind that he was really going too far and abusing his friend's kindness. This time Beethoven's want was of a very peculiar nature, namely a looking-glass; that it was not for shaving purposes but for a more general control of his toilet is indicated by the second note:

'Dear Zmeskall,

'Do send me for a few hours your looking-glass which hangs beside your window, mine is broken. If you would be so kind as to buy me one like it today it would be a great favour. I'll recoup you for your expenditure at once – Forgive my importunity dear Z. I hope to see you soon.

Your Bthvn'

'Dear Z., Do not get angry at my little note – don't you recall the situation I am in, like Hercules once at Queen Omphale's??? I asked you to buy me a looking-glass like yours, and beg you as soon as you are not using yours which I am returning to send it back to me for mine is broken – Farewell and don't write again about me as the great man – for I have never felt the strength of human nature as I feel it just now –

Remain fond of me –'

'Do not get vexed, dear Z., because of my continued demands upon you – but let me know how much you paid for the looking-glass?

Farewell, we shall see each other soon at the Schwan as the food is daily growing worse at the [illegible] – I have had another violent attack of colic since the day before yesterday, but it is better today.

Your friend
Beethoven'

In the late spring the Malfatti family moved to their country home, at which time Beethoven wrote the following letter to Therese:

'With this you are receiving, honoured Therese, what I promised, and if there had not been the weightiest difficulties, you would have received more in order to show that I always *do more for my friends than I promise* – I hope and have no doubt that you keep yourself as well occupied as pleasantly entertained – but not so much that you cannot also think of us – It would perhaps be presuming upon your kindness or placing too high a value upon myself if I were to write to you: "Persons are together not only when they are in each other's company, even the distant one, the absent one, is with us." Who would dare to write such a sentiment to the volatile T. who handles everything in this world so lightly? In laying out your plans, do not forget the pianoforte, or music generally; you have so beautiful a talent for it, why not cultivate it exclusively? You who have so much feeling for everything that is beautiful and good, why will you not make use of it in order to learn the more perfect things in so beautiful an art, which always reflects its light upon us? – I live very solitarily and quietly. Although now and then lights try to arouse me, there is still for me a void which cannot be filled since you are all gone and which defies even my art which has always been so faithful to me – Your pianoforte is ordered and you will have it soon – What difference will you have found between the treatment of a theme which I invented one evening and the manner in which I finally wrote it down for you. Figure it out for yourself, but don't get the punch *to help you* –

'How lucky you are to be able to go to the country so soon, I shall not have the pleasure until the 8th, but I rejoice in the prospect like a child. How joyous I am when I walk among bushes and trees, herbs, rocks. Nobody can love the country as I do – since woods, trees, rocks, return the answer which man wants to hear –

'You will soon receive some other of my compositions in which you should not have to complain too much about the difficulties – *Have you read Goethe's Wilhelm Meister, and Shakespeare translated by Schlegel?* One has so much leisure in the country that it might be agreeable were I to send you these works –

'By chance I have an acquaintance in your neighbourhood; perhaps you will see me at your home early some morning for half an hour and then I'll be off. You see I wish to be as little tedious as possible to you. Commend me to the goodwill of your father, your mother, although I have no right as yet to ask it of them, also to your cousin M. Farewell, honoured T, I wish you all that is good and beautiful in life. When you think of me, think of me cheerfully – forget the wild goings-on – Be convinced that no one can wish that your life may be more joyous and more happy than I, even if you have no sympathy for

Your devoted servant and friend

Beethoven'

'NB It would really be very nice of you if you were to write a few lines to say what I can do for you here –'

This does not sound like the letter of a man about to propose marriage, as he does not sound at all sure what his reception may be. Perhaps he felt that as regarded the goodwill of the parents 'I have no right as yet to ask it of them.' However, Beethoven wrote the famous letter of 2 May 1810 to Wegeler in Coblenz, asking him to procure a copy of his baptismal certificate for him. In this letter he says:

'. . . A couple of years ago my quiet, retired mode of life came to an end, and I was forcibly drawn into activities of the world. I have not as yet formed a *favourable* opinion of it but rather one against it – but who is not affected by the storms of the outside world? Yet I should be happy,

perhaps one of the happiest of men, if the demon had not taken possession of my ears. – If I had not read somewhere that a man may not
voluntarily part with his life as long as a good deed remains for him to
perform, I should have long ago been no more – and indeed by my
own hand – Oh, life is so beautiful, but to me it is forever poisoned. –
You will not refuse my friendly request if I beg of you to secure my
baptismal certificate for me – Whatever expense may attach to the matter, since you have an account with Steffen Breuning, you can recoup
yourself at once from that source and I will make it good at once to
Steffen here. – If you should yourself think it worth while to investigate the matter and make the trip from Coblenz to Bonn, charge
everything to me. – But one thing must be borne in mind, namely, that
there was a brother *born before me*, who was also named Ludwig with
the addition Maria, but who died. To fix my age beyond doubt, this
brother must first be found, inasmuch as I already know that in this
respect a mistake has been made by others, and I have been said to
be older than I am. – Unfortunately I myself lived for a time without
knowing my age – I had a family register but it has been lost, heaven
knows how. – Therefore do not be offended if I urge you to attend to
this matter, to find Ludwig Maria and the present Ludwig who was
born after him – The sooner you send me the baptismal certificate the
greater will be my obligation . . .'

Wegeler published a few pages on the occasion of the Beethoven
festival at Bonn in 1845, giving therein a most valuable explanation of
this most important letter:

'It seems that Beethoven, once in his life, entertained the idea of marriage, after having been in love many times . . . Many persons as well as
myself were impressed by the urgency with which in his letter of 10
May [*sic*] he besought me to secure his baptismal certificate for him. He
wanted to pay all the expenditures, even a journey from Coblenz to
Bonn. And then he added explicit instructions which I was to observe
in looking up the certificate in order to get the right one. I found the
solution of the riddle in a letter written to me three months later by my
brother-in-law St. v. Breuning. In this he says: "Beethoven tells me at
least once a week that he intends to write to you; but I believe *his marriage project has fallen through*, and for this reason he no longer feels the
lively desire to thank you for your trouble in getting him the baptismal
certificate." In the thirty-ninth year of his life Beethoven had not given
up thoughts of marriage.'

A short letter to Gleichenstein instructs us slightly touching the conclusion of this psychological drama which, no doubt, tore the heart of
Beethoven. It would seem as if at first Beethoven wanted to visit the
Malfattis at their country home, but at the last preferred to send a formal proposal of marriage by the hands of Gleichenstein. Here is the
letter:

'You are living on a calm and peaceful sea or, possibly, are already in a
safe harbour — You do not feel the distress of the friend who is still in
the storm — or you dare not feel it — What will they think of me in the
star Venus Urania, how will they judge without seeing me — My pride
is so humbled, I would go there with you uninvited — Let me see you at
my lodging tomorrow morning; I shall expect you about 9 o'clock at
breakfast — . . . If you were but franker with me; you are certainly con-
cealing something from me, you want to spare me; and this uncertainty
is more painful than the most fatal certainty — Farewell. If you cannot
come let me know in advance — Think and act for me — I cannot
entrust to paper more of what is going on within me —'

We have no testimony concerning the refusal beyond the cessation of
all correspondence on the subject, and also an utterance of Therese's
niece: 'It is true that Beethoven loved my aunt and wished to marry her,
and also that her parents would never have given their consent.' His
weakness was not in seeking a wife, for this was wise and prudent, but
in the selection of the person; in imagining that the young girl's admiration for the artist — her respect and regard for the friend of her parents
and of Gleichenstein — had with increasing years grown into a warmer
feeling; and in misconceiving the attention, civilities and courtesies
extended to him by all the members of the family as encouragement to a
suit, the possibility of which had, probably, never entered the mind of
any one of them. It placed Gleichenstein in a dilemma of singular difficulty. How he escaped from it, there are no means of knowing; the
affair was, however, so managed, that the rejection of Beethoven's proposal caused no interruption — or at most a temporary one — in the
friendly relations of all the parties immediately concerned.

Beethoven's relations with another fair friend, Bettina Brentano,
now demand attention. In the Vienna suburban road Erdbeergasse
stood the lofty house then numbered 98, its rear windows overlooking
Razumovsky's gardens, the Donau canal and the Prater, whence Elizabeth Brentano (Bettina) wrote to Goethe:

'Here I live in the house of the deceased Birkenstock, surrounded by two thousand copperplate engravings, as many hand-drawings, as many hundred old ash urns and Etruscan lamps, marble vases, antique fragments of hands and feet, paintings, Chinese garments, coins, geological collections, sea insects, telescopes and numberless maps, plans of ancient empires and cities sunk in ruin, artistically carved walking-sticks, precious documents, and finally the sword of Emperor Carolus.'

Joseph Melchior von Birkenstock (born in 1738), the honoured, trusted and valued servant of Maria Theresia and Kaiser Joseph, the friend and brother-in-law of the celebrated Sonnenfels, was pensioned in 1803 and thenceforth lived for science, art and literature until his death, 30 October 1809. His house, filled almost to repletion with the collections of which Bettina spoke, was one of those truly noble seats of learning, high culture and refinement, where Beethoven, to his manifest intellectual gain, was a welcome guest.

Before presenting the account of Bettina's relationship with Beethoven and Goethe it is well to remind the reader of her lively imagination and emotional feeling; her love for her two heroes was matched by her sense of the opportunity for literary expansion that presented itself in the chronicling in letter form all that she could about these two artists. On the one hand, she was sensitive enough to recognise that these two geniuses towered above those around them and she was faithful to this concept until her death. On the other hand, she could not resist weaving herself into all that she described so that in her inexhaustible love for them and their art she made it seem that in their lives she played a much greater role than was actually the case. The impression was furthered to the extent that she edited and revised the correspondence before its publication. Her 'letter' of 28 May which follows, for instance, represents a piecing together of notes that she had written at the time.

One day in May, Beethoven, sitting at the pianoforte with a song just composed before him, was surprised by a pair of hands being placed upon his shoulders. He looked up 'gloomily' but his face brightened as he saw a beautiful young woman who, putting her mouth to his ear, said: 'My name is Brentano.' She needed no further introduction. He smiled, gave her his hand without rising and said: 'I have just made a beautiful song for you; do you want to hear it?' Thereupon he sang – raspingly, incisively, not gently or sweetly (the voice was hard), but transcending training and agreeableness by reason of the cry of passion which reacted on the hearer – 'Kennst du das Land?' He asked: 'Well, how do you like it?' She nodded. 'It is beautiful, isn't it?' he said enthusiastically, 'marvellously beautiful; I'll sing it again.' He sang it again, looked at her with a triumphant expression, and seeing her cheeks and eyes glow, rejoiced over her happy approval. 'Aha!' said he, 'most people are touched by a good thing; but they are not artist-natures. Artists are fiery; they do not weep.' He then sang another song of Goethe's, 'Trocknet nicht Thränen der ewigen Liebe'.

There was a large dinner party that day in the Birkenstock house and Bettina – for it was she – told Beethoven he must change his old coat for a better, and accompany her thither. 'Oh,' said he jokingly, 'I have several good coats', and took her to the wardrobe to see them. Changing his coat he went down with her to the street, but stopped there and said he must return for a moment. He came down again laughing with the old coat on. She remonstrated; he went up again, dressed himself properly and went with her. But, notwithstanding his rather clumsy drollery, she soon discovered a greatness in the man for which she was wholly unprepared. His genius burst upon her with a splendour of which she had formed no previous conception, and the sudden revelation astonished, dazzled, enraptured her. It is just this, which gives the tone to her letter upon Beethoven addressed to Goethe.

'Vienna, 28 May
'When I saw him of whom I shall now speak to you, I forgot the whole world – as the world still vanishes when memory recalls the scene – yes, it vanishes . . . It is Beethoven of whom I now wish to tell you, and who made me forget the world and you; I am still not of age, it is true, but I am not mistaken when I say – what no one, perhaps, now understands and believes – he stalks far ahead of the culture of mankind. Shall we ever overtake him? – I doubt it, but grant that he may live until the mighty and exalted enigma lying in his soul is fully developed, may reach its loftiest goal, then surely he will place the key to his heavenly knowledge in our hands so that we may be advanced another step towards true happiness.

'To you, I am sure, I may confess I believe in a divine magic which is the essence of intellectual life. This magic Beethoven practises in his art. Everything that he can tell you about is pure magic, every posture is the organisation of a higher existence, and therefore Beethoven feels himself to be the founder of a new sensuous basis in the intellectual life; you will understand what I am trying to say and how much of it is true. Who could replace this mind for us? . . .

'He himself said: "When I open my eyes I must sigh, for what I see is contrary to my religion, and I must despise the world which does not know that music is a higher revelation than all wisdom and philo-sophy, the wine which inspires one to new generative processes, and I am the Bacchus who presses out this glorious wine for mankind and makes them spiritually drunken. When they are again become sober they have drawn from the sea all that they brought with them, all that they can bring with them to dry land. I have not a single friend; I must live alone. But well I know that God is nearer to me than to other artists; I associate with him without fear; I have always recognised and understood him and have no fear for my music – it can meet no evil fate. Those who understand it must be freed by it from all the miseries which the others drag about with themselves."

'All this Beethoven said to me the first time I saw him; a feeling of reverential awe came over me when he expressed himself to me with such friendly frankness, seeing that I must have appeared so utterly insignificant to him. I was surprised, too, for I had been told that he was unsociable and would converse with nobody. They were afraid to take me to him; I had to hunt him up alone. He has three lodgings in which he conceals himself alternately – one in the country, one in the city and the third on the bastion. It was in the last that I found him in the third storey, walked in unannounced. He was seated at the pianoforte.

'He accompanied me home and on the way he said the many beautiful things about art, speaking so loud and stopping in the street that it took courage to listen to him. He spoke with great earnestness and much too surprisingly not to make me forget the street . . .'

She continues:

'Since then he comes to me every day, or I go to him. For this I neglect social meetings, galleries, the theatre, and even the tower of St Stephen's. Beethoven says "Ah! What do you want to see there? I will call for you towards evening; we will walk through the alleys of Schönbrunn." Yesterday I went with him to a glorious garden in full bloom, all the hot-beds open – the perfume was bewildering; Beethoven stopped in the oppressive sunshine and said: "Not only because of their contents, but also because of their rhythm, Goethe's poems have great power over me, I am tuned up and stimulated to composition by this language which builds itself into higher orders as if through the work of spirits and already bears in itself the mystery of the harmonies.

' "Then from the focus of enthusiasm I must discharge melody in all directions; I pursue it, capture it again passionately; I see it flying away and disappearing in the mass of varied agitations; now I seize upon it again with renewed passion; I cannot tear myself from it; I am impelled with hurried modulations to multiply it, and, at length I conquer it: – behold, a symphony! Music, verily, is the mediator between the life of the mind and the senses. I should like to talk with Goethe about this – would he understand me? Melody is the sensuous life of poetry. Isn't the intellectual content of a poem transformed into sensuous feeling by the melody? Isn't it through melody that one experiences to the full the sensuous quality of Mignon's Song, and doesn't this emotion in turn stimulate one to fresh creation? The mind wants to expand into the limitless and universal where everything flows into a stream of feelings which spring from simple musical thoughts and which otherwise would die away unheeded. This is harmony, this is what speaks from my symphonies, the sweet blend of manifold forms flows along in a stream to its destination . . . Speak to Goethe about me; tell him to hear my symphonies and he will say that I am right in saying that music is the one incorporeal entrance into the higher world of knowledge which comprehends mankind but which mankind cannot comprehend . . . We do not know what knowledge brings us. The encased seed needs the moist, electrically warm soil to sprout, to think, to express itself. Music is the electrical soil in which the mind thinks, lives, feels. Philosophy is a precipitate of the mind's electrical essence; its needs which seek a basis in a primeval principle are elevated by it, and although the mind is not supreme over what it generates through it, it is yet happy in the process. Thus every real creation of art is independent, more powerful than the artist himself and returns to the divine through its manifestation. It is one with man only in this, that it bears testimony of the mediation of the divine in him . . .

' "I am electrical in my nature. I must interrupt the flow of my undemonstrable wisdom or I might neglect my rehearsal. Write to Goethe if you understand what I have said, but I cannot be answerable for anything and will gladly be instructed by him." I promised to write you everything to the best of my understanding . . . Last night I wrote down all that he had said; this morning I read it over to him. He remarked: *"Did I say that? Well, then I had a raptus!"* '

To this letter Goethe answered:

'Your letter, heartily beloved child, reached me at a happy time. You have been at great pains to picture for me a great and beautiful nature in its achievements and its strivings, its needs and the superabundance of its gifts. It has given me great pleasure to accept this picture of a truly great spirit. Without desiring at all to classify it, it yet requires a psychological feat to extract the sum of agreement; but I feel no desire to contradict what I can grasp of your hurried explosion; on the contrary,

I should prefer for the present to admit an agreement between my nature and that which is recognisable in these manifold utterances. The ordinary human mind might, perhaps, find contradictions in it; but before that which is uttered by one possessed of such a daemon, an ordinary layman must stand in reverence, and it is immaterial whether he speaks from feeling or knowledge, for here the gods are at work strewing seeds for future discernment and we can only wish that they may proceed undisturbedly to development. But before they can become general, the clouds which veil the human mind must be dispersed. Give Beethoven my heartiest greetings and tell him that I would willingly make sacrifices to have his acquaintance, when an exchange of thought and feelings would surely be beautifully profitable; perhaps you may be able to persuade him to make a journey to Karlsbad whither I go nearly every year and would have the greatest leisure to listen to him and learn from him. To think of teaching him would be an insolence even in one with greater insight than mine, since he has the guiding light of his genius which frequently illumines his mind like a stroke of lightning while we sit in darkness and scarcely suspect the direction from which daylight will break upon us . . .

'6 June 1810'

Bettina replied with the following:

'Dearest friend!

'I communicated your beautiful letter to Beethoven so far as it concerned him. He was full of joy and cried: "If there is anyone who can make him understand music, I am that man!" The idea of hunting you up at Karlsbad filled him with enthusiasm. He struck his forehead a blow and said: "Might I not have done that earlier? – but, in truth I did think of it but omitted to do it because of timidity which often torments me as if I were not a real man: but I am no longer afraid of Goethe." You may count, therefore, on seeing him next year . . .'

There are a few letters from this period to which attention may be paid. On 9 July 1810, Beethoven wrote to Zmeskall telling him of his distracted state of mind: he ought to go away from Vienna for the sake of his health, but Archduke Rudolph wanted him to remain near him; so he was one day in Schönbrunn, the next in Vienna. 'Every day there come new enquiries from strangers, new acquaintances, new conditions even as regards art. Sometimes I feel as if I should go mad because of my undeserved fame; fortune is seeking me and on that account I almost apprehend a new misfortune.'

The cessation in Beethoven's productiveness in this period is partly explained by the vast amounts of labour entailed by the preparation of manuscripts for publication, the correction of proofs, etc. Of this there is evidence in a number of letters to Breitkopf and Härtel. On 2 July he wrote demanding an honorarium of 250 ducats for works that he had specified, and sending the first instalment: String Quartet in E flat, Fantasy for pianoforte, two sonatas for pianoforte, five variations for pianoforte and six ariettas (Op. 75) to appear on 1 September. The second instalment, he said, should be a concerto in E flat, the Choral Fantasia and three ariettas (Op. 83) to appear on 1 November. The Sonata 'Farewell, Absence and Return', five Italian ariettas (Op. 82) and the score of *Egmont* would make up the third instalment.

On 21 August 1810, he wrote to the firm at great length. He sent a draft of a plan for a complete edition of his works, in which Breitkopf and Härtel were to figure as the principal publishers. He reiterated the sum of 250 ducats for the works mentioned previously in the letter of 2 July and said it was a small fee. He continues:

'. . . At the time when banknotes were worth only a little less than silver or gold I received a hundred ducats for three sonatas. – NB you yourselves have given me 50 ducats for a quintet – Am I supposed to go backwards instead of forwards, for I certainly hope that I will not receive this reproach in my art – Also no matter what the worth of a ducat in guldens may be for us, there isn't any profit. Now we pay 30 fl. for a pair of boots, 160 or 170 fl. for a coat, etc. The devil with economy in music – Last year before the French came my 4,000 fl. were worth something, this year they're not worth 1,000 fl. in convention coin . . . Yet I love an independent life, and this I cannot have without a small income . . .'

He then gave directions as to the dedications, and of the *Egmont* he says:

'I wrote it purely out of love for the poet, and to show this I accepted nothing from the theatre directors who in turn accepted it, and as a reward, as usual and always, treated my work with *great indifference*. There is nothing *smaller than our great folk*, but I make an exception in favour of Archdukes . . .'

The long, bright summer days, that in other years had awakened his powers to new and joyous activity and added annually one at least to the list of his grandest works, came and departed, leaving no memorial but a few songs and minor instrumental works – the latter apparently to order. True, he wrote to Zmeskall and talked of his art as if great things were in prospect; but he had no heart for such labours. He took no country lodgings this summer – alternating between Baden and Vienna, and indulging in lonely rambles among the hills and forests. We think it must have been in this period that, on such an excursion, he had with him the undated paper containing a selection from the songs in Herder's *Morgenländische Blumenlese* and wrote upon it in pencil: 'My decree [meaning the annuity contract] says only "to remain in the country" – perhaps this would be complied with by any spot. My unhappy ears do not torment me here. It seems as if in the country every tree said to me "Holy! Holy!" – Who can give complete expression to the ecstasy of the woods? If everything else fails the country remains even in winter . . . easy to hire a lodging from a peasant, certainly cheap at this time.'

Let the year 1811 start with a letter from Beethoven to Therese Brunsvik of which we learn from a transcript in a letter written by Therese to her sister Josephine, dated 2 February, as follows:

'Through Franz I have also received a souvenir of our noble Beethoven which gave me much joy; I do not mean his sonatas, which are very beautiful, but a little writing which I will immediately copy literally:
 ' "Even without prompting, people of the better kind think of each other; this is the case with you and me, dear and honoured Therese. I still owe you grateful thanks for your beautiful picture and while naming myself your debtor I must at the same time appear before you in the character of a beggar by asking you if perchance you feel the genius of painting stirring within you to duplicate the little hand drawing which I was unlucky enough to lose. *It was an eagle looking into the sun*; I cannot forget it. But do not think that I am thinking of myself in such a connection, although this idea has been ascribed to me. Many look upon a heroic play without being in the least like it. Farewell, dear Therese, and think occasionally of your truly revering friend
Beethoven" '

Therese tried to comply with Beethoven's request. On 23 February she wrote to her sister: 'My request to you, dear Josephine, is to reproduce that picture which you are able to do; it would not be possible for me to do anything of the kind.' And later she repeated in French: 'You have told me nothing about Beethoven's eagle. May I answer that he shall receive it?'

On 13 February 1810, Josephine had married Baron von Stackleberg, who had been tutor to the two Deym boys. In the following month the Stacklebergs alternatively lived at Witschap in Moravia and at the Müller Gallery in Vienna. Since August 1810, Therese had been in Witschap as governess for the four Deym children and the first Stackleberg child, born on 30 November 1810.

Beethoven's intercourse with the Brentanos kept his interest in Bettina alive. She, meanwhile, had become engaged on 4 December 1810, to the poet Ludwig Joachim von Arnim, and was secretly married to him in 1811.

'Vienna, 10 February 1811

'Beloved, dear Bettine!

'I have already received two letters from you and see from your letters to Toni* that you still think of me, and much too favourably. – I carried your first letter around with me all summer and it has often made me overjoyed. Even if I do not write to you often and you never see me, yet I write you a thousand times a thousand letters in my thoughts – I could have imagined how you feel amidst the cosmopolitan rabble in Berlin even if you had not written about it; a lot of chatter about art without deeds!!!!! The best description of it is in Schiller's poem "Die Flüsse", where the Spree speaks – You are to be married, dear Bettine, or have already been, and I have not been able to see you once more before then. May all the happiness with which marriage blesses the married, flow upon you and your husband . . . If you write to Goethe about me, pick out all the words which express my deepest reverence and admiration for him. I am about to write to him myself concerning *Egmont* for which I have composed music and, indeed, purely out of love for his poems which make me happy. But who can sufficiently thank a great poet, the most precious jewel of a nation? – And now no more, dear good B. It was 4 o'clock before I got home this morning from a bacchanalian feast at which I had to laugh so much that I shall have to weep correspondingly today; boisterous joy often forces me powerfully back in upon myself again . . . Now farewell dear, dear B., I kiss you sadly upon your forehead and thus impress upon you as with a seal all my thoughts of you. – Write soon, soon, often to your friend
                                                    Beethoven'

'Beethoven lives on the Mölker
Bastei in the Pascolati House.'

In the Goethe archives in Weimar there is a letter which Beethoven wrote to the poet.

* Bettina's sister-in-law Antonie.

'Vienna, 12 April 1811

'Your Excellency!

'A friend of mine, who is a great admirer of yours (like myself),
is making a hasty departure from here, and this urgent opportunity
permits me but a moment of time to thank you for the long time that
I have known you (for I have known you since my childhood) – That
is so little for so much – Bettine Brentano has assured me that you
would receive me in a gracious, even a friendly way. But how could
I think of such a reception when I can approach you only with the
greatest reverence and with an unutterably deep feeling for your glorious creations! – You will soon receive the music to Egmont through
Breitkopf and Härtel; this glorious Egmont which through you I have
thought over with the same warmth as when I first read it, and experienced it again by setting it to music. – I would very much like to have
your judgement on it; also your criticism would be beneficial to me
and my art, and would be accepted as gladly as the highest praise. –

Your Excellency's
Great admirer
Ludwig van Beethoven'

Goethe's answer to this letter is worth producing here:

'Karlsbad, 25 June 1811

'Your friendly letter, very esteemed Sir, was received through Herr von
Oliva much to my pleasure. For the kindly feelings which it expresses
towards me I am heartily grateful and I can assure you that I honestly
reciprocate them, for I have never heard any of your works performed
by expert artists or amateurs without wishing that I might sometime
have the opportunity to admire you at the pianoforte and find delight
in your extraordinary talents. Good Bettina Brentano surely deserves
the friendly sympathy which you have extended to her. She speaks rap-
turously and most affectionately of you and counts the hours spent
with you among the happiest of her life.

'I shall probably find the music which you have designed for
Egmont when I return home and am thankful in advance – for I have
heard it praised by several, and plan to perform it in connection with
the play mentioned on our stage this winter, when I hope thereby to
give myself as well as your numerous admirers in our neighbourhood a
great treat. But I hope most of all correctly to have understood Herr
von Oliva, who has made us hope that in the journey which you are
contemplating you will visit Weimar. I hope it will be at a time when
the court as well as the entire musical public will be gathered together.

I am sure that you would find worthy acceptance of your service and aims. But in this nobody can be more interested than I, who with the wish that all may go well with you, commend myself to your kind thought and thank you most sincerely for all the goodness which you have created in us.'

On 28 February 1811, Beethoven sent his friend Mähler an invitation to a concert. Mähler accepted the invitation and received a ticket 'extraordinaire', signed 'Bᵣ. de Neuwirth', admitting him free to three midday concerts on Thursdays, 28 February, 14 and 28 March. Beethoven's elasticity of temperament therefore was doing him good service in enabling him to recover from the disappointment of the preceding year; he was now able not only to find diversion and amusement in society, the theatre and the concert-room, but the spirit of composition was again awakened. In three weeks – 3–26 March – he produced the glorious B flat Trio, Op. 97, which had been sketched in 1810.

There were now, or soon to be, in the hands of Breitkopf and Härtel's engravers the Pianoforte Concerto, Op. 73, the Fantasia, Op. 80, the Sonata 'Les Adieux', Op. 81a, the Ariettas and Songs, Op. 82 and 83, and the *Christus am Ölberg*. The revision of these works for the press, with the correction of the proofs and his duties to the Archduke, are all the professional labours of Beethoven in these months of which we find any trace.

There is a note, which may be dated about the end of March, apologising to the Archduke for his absence, on the ground of having been for two weeks again with his 'tormenting headache'. Soon after he writes:

'Your Imperial Highness! Since despite all my exertions I could find no copyist who would work at my house, I am sending you my manuscript. You would be most kind just to send to *Schlemmer* for a capable copyist who must however copy the trio only in your palace, as otherwise one is never safe from *theft*. I am improving and in a few days I shall again have the honour to wait upon you for the purpose of making up for lost time – I am always anxiously concerned when I cannot be as zealously and as often as I should wish with Your Imperial Highness. It is surely true when I say that it causes me much suffering, but I am not likely to have so bad an attack again soon – Keep me graciously in your memory. Times will come when I shall show you two and threefold that I am worthy of it.'

These professions may well excite a smile; for 'it is surely true' when *we* say that his duties to the Archduke had already become extremely irksome; and that the necessity of sacrificing his previous independence in some small degree to them grew daily more annoying and vexatious; so much so that, in fact, he availed himself of any and every excuse to avoid them.

Here is the place for a letter to Breitkopf and Härtel:

'Vienna, 6 May

'Errors – errors – you yourselves are one large error – I must send my copyist there or else go myself if I do not want my works to appear – as mere errors – It appears as if the musical tribunal at L. is unable to produce a single decent proof-reader, besides which you send out the works before you receive the corrections – At least in the case of larger works with various parts you might count the measures – But the Fantasia shows what can happen – You will see that a whole measure is missing in the piano transcription of the overture to Egmont. – Here is the list of errors.

'My warmest thanks for setting in motion a matter of such interest to me. – Farewell, I hope for improvement – The fantasy has already gone; the sonata also leaves tomorrow. – Make as many errors as you please, permit as many errors as you please – you are still highly esteemed by me. This is of course the custom of men, that we esteem them because they have not made still greater errors –

Your most humble servant

Beethoven'

In 1808 Emperor Franz had sanctioned the building at Budapest of 'an entirely new grand theatre with Ridotto room, casino, restaurant and coffee-house', which it was then thought would be completed in 1810. It was time, therefore to consider the programme for its opening performances, and as no living musician could give the occasion so much splendour as Beethoven, it was of high importance that his consent to compose the music should be secured as early as possible. This, through Brunsvik and other Hungarian friends, was no difficult task. Although not completed in 1810, the enterprise was so far advanced that the authorities began their preliminary arrangements for its formal opening on the Emperor's name-day, 4 October 1811, by applying to Heinrich von Collin to write an appropriate drama on some subject drawn from Hungarian history. Collin declined the commission and the order was then given to the playwright August von Kotzebue, who accepted it, and, with characteristic rapidity, responded with the prologue *Ungarns erster Wohltäter* (Hungary's First Benefactor), the drama

Belas Flucht (Bela's Flight), and the epilogue *Die Ruinen von Athen* (The Ruins of Athens). As Emperor Franz had twice fled from his capital within five years, it is not surprising that '*Bela's Flight* for various reasons cannot be given' and gave place to a local piece, *The Elevation of Pesth [Budapest] into a Royal Free City*. Kotzebue's other two pieces were accepted and sent to Beethoven at the end of July 1811. In a letter to Breitkopf and Härtel on 9 October 1811 Beethoven reported that he started work three weeks later – about 20 August – and that he sent the music off to Budapest on 13 September.

Hartl had now retired from the direction of the Court Theatres, and Lobkowitz and Pálffy* were again at the helms respectively of the theatre next to the Kärnthnerthor and that of An-der-Wien. Beethoven was busy with dramatic compositions and so, very naturally, the project of another operatic work was revived. He had also obtained a subject that pleased him – a French melodrama *Les Ruines de Babylon* – probably from the Prussian Baron Friedr. Joh. Drieberg.

A series of notes from Beethoven, written in June and July 1811, show how the operatic project was shaping itself in his mind. On 6 June, he was anxious to know if Treitschke had read the book, and wished to re-read it himself before Treitschke began work on it. He expressed dismay to Pálffy on 11 June, because he had heard that a performance of the melodrama *Les Ruines de Babilone* was projected for the benefit of an actor, Scholz. 'It is so difficult to find a good libretto for an opera; I have rejected no less than twelve or more in the last several weeks.' Beethoven said that he had told the Archduke about the subject and had even written to foreign newspapers of his intention to set it to music. He hoped the Count would forbid the intended performance. Pálffy evidently co-operated. There the matter seems to have rested, though Beethoven was still thinking about an opera text at Teplitz in September.

'It is said', writes the correspondent of the *Allgemeine Musikalische Zeitung* under the date of 8 January, 'that Beethoven may next Spring undertake a journey to southern skies for the purpose of restoring his health, which has suffered severely during the last few years.' One effect of his maladies was to produce long-continued pains in the head, and it was finally thought best by his physician, Malfatti, to abandon the journey and try the waters of Teplitz. This Beethoven decided to do and to take with him as friend and companion young Oliva.

Beethoven arrived in Teplitz at the beginning of August and stayed

* Count Ferdinand Pálffy von Erdöd, then thirty-six, despite his significant position did nothing to promote or support Beethoven or his music. The composer heartily disliked him.

at the 'Harfe' in the Badgasse. For the first three weeks he was concerned with his cure, plus the correction of proofs, as appears from a letter, dated 23 August, to Breitkopf and Härtel:

'... I have undertaken the revision of the oratorio and the songs and in a few days you will receive both – Here and there the text must remain as in the original. I know that the text is extremely bad, but after one has conceived a complete work even from a bad text, it is difficult to avoid spoiling it by individual changes. And if now there is a single word upon which great stress is laid many times over, it must remain so.'

Varnhagen von Ense, then a young man of twenty-five years and lieutenant in the Austrian service, came from Prague to Teplitz this summer to pass a few weeks with 'the goddess of his heart's most dear delight', Rahel Levin.

In a letter to his regiment commander on 4 September 1811 from Teplitz he wrote:

'I have made Beethoven's acquaintance. The unruly man was very friendly and gentle towards me, said many excellent things and will gladly play for Robert [Rahel Levin] some afternoon, only it is supposed to be kept secret. The strange man lives completely in his art, is very industrious, and is unconcerned about other people. You can be all the more assured by the fact that he greets you with true friendliness and wishes keenly to be excused for his forgetfulness of the moment, but such things probably happen more often with him [than with other people]. He is composing an opera for the Buda theatre for which Kotzebue has written the text. Because of Robert I am twice as well acquainted with him and cherish it three times as much.'

Another visitor at Teplitz was Prince Kinsky; and this gave the composer an opportunity to obtain the arrears of his annuity. On the still existing envelope of the contract of 1809 is written: 'Money drawn from Kinsky last August.'

Also visiting Teplitz was Amalie Sebald, who had come with Countess von der Recke from Berlin. She was said to have a 'fascinatingly lovely singing voice'. Among the friends of Carl Maria von Weber when he was in Berlin in 1812, were Amalie and her sister Auguste, also 'highly musical' and a singer. For the former, Weber conceived a warm and deep affection; and now Beethoven was taken an unresisting captive by her charms. She is mentioned, the reader will note how familiarly – in his letter to the poet Christoph Tiedge, who had been visiting Teplitz. It is dated Teplitz, 6 September 1811:

'Every day the following letter to you, you, you has floated in my mind; I wanted only two words at parting, but not a single word did I receive. The Countess sends a feminine handgrasp; that at least is something to talk about and for it I kiss her hands in my thoughts; but the poet is dumb. Concerning *Amalie*, I know at least that she is alive. Every day I give myself a drubbing for not having made your acquaintance earlier in Teplitz. It is abominable to know the good for a short time and at once to lose it again. Nothing is more insufferable than to be obliged to reproach one's self with one's own mistakes. I tell you that I shall probably be obliged to stay here until the end of this month. Write to me how long you will stay in Dresden. I may feel disposed to take a jump to the Saxon capital. On the day that you went away from here I received a letter from my gracious musically inclined Archduke, that he will not remain long in Moravia and has left it for me to say whether or not I will come. This I interpreted to the best of my wishes and desires and so you see me still within these walls where I sinned so deeply against you and myself. But I comfort myself with the thought that if you call it a sin I am at least a downright sinner and not a poor one . . . Now fare as well as poor humanity may; to the Countess a right tender yet reverential handgrasp, to Amalie an ardent kiss when no one sees us. And we two embrace each other like men who are permitted to love and honour each other. I expect at least one word without reserve, and I am man enough for this.'

A remark made by Beethoven to his friend Cajetan Giannatasio del Rio, on 12 September 1816, refers to this period and should be here considered. Kajetan's daughter Fanny records in her diary: 'My father thought that B. could rescue himself from his unfortunate domestic conditions only by marriage, did he know anybody, etc. Now our long foreboding was confirmed: he was unhappy in love! Five years ago he had made the acquaintance of a person, a union with whom he would have considered the greatest happiness of his life. It was not to be thought of, almost an impossibility, a chimera – "nevertheless it is now as on the first day." ' I believe this reference was to Amalie Sebald.

From the Teplitz guest list, it is clear that Beethoven did not leave Teplitz for Prague until 18 September. From Varnhagen's correspondence with Rahel, we learn that Oliva went on to Vienna on 23 September, without Beethoven, who made a rather wide detour to visit Lichnowsky. Of this visit we learn in one of Jahn's notices, namely:

'In the year 1811, B. was at Prince Lichnowsky's on his estate Grätz near Troppau. The Mass in C was performed at Troppau, for which everything possible was drummed up. The master of athletics was put at the tympani; in the Sanctus Beethoven himself had to show him how to play the solo. The rehearsals lasted three days. After the performance Beethoven improvised on the organ for half an hour to the astonishment of everyone.'

Beethoven returned to Vienna refreshed and invigorated both in body and mind. A letter written from Vienna to Breitkopf and Härtel on 9 October 1811 has so large an interest on many accounts as to merit inclusion:

'From here a thousand excuses and a thousand thanks for your pleasant invitation to Leipzig; I was very sorry not to be able to follow my inclination to go there and to surrounding places. But this time there has been work in every direction. The Hungarian Diet is in session; there is already talk that the Archduke is to become Primate of Hungary and abandon the Bishopric of Olmütz. I have offered to His Imperial Highness, who as Primate of Hungary would have an income of not less than three million, to go through a clean million on my own account (and on account, it is understood, of all the good musical spirits that I would therewith set into action on my behalf). In Teplitz I received no further news, as nothing was known of my purpose to leave the place. I thought concerning the journey which I was contemplating that in view of my attachment for him I must yield (though not willingly), the more since I might be needed at the festivities. Therefore, having chosen the pro*, quick to Vienna, where the first thunderous proclamation that I heard was that my gracious lord had given up all thoughts of priesthood and priestly activities and nothing is to come of the whole business. –

'It is said that soon he is to become a general (an easy thing to understand, you know) and I am to be Quartermaster-General in the battle which I do not intend to lose – what do you say to that? The Hungarians provided me with another incident; in stepping into my carriage to go to Teplitz, I received a parcel from Ofen [Buda] with the request to compose something for the opening of the new theatre at Budapest. Feeling fairly well after spending three weeks in Teplitz, I sat down, in defiance of my doctor's orders, to help the Mustachios, who are heartily well disposed towards me; and sent my packet thither on 13 September, under the impression that the performance was to come off on 1

* Beethoven had written 'pro und contra' and then deleted the last two words.

October, whereas the matter is put off for a whole month. Through a misunderstanding I did not receive the letter in which this was told me until after my arrival here, and yet this theatrical incident also decided me to return to Vienna. – Meanwhile, postponed is not abandoned. I have tasted of travel, it has done me great good, and now already I should like to go away again – I have just received the Lebewohl, etc. I see that after all you have given French titles to other copies. Why? "Lebewohl" is surely something very different from "Les Adieux". The former we say heartily to a single person, the latter to whole gatherings, whole cities – Since you permit me to be criticised so shamefully you must submit to the same treatment. You would also have needed fewer plates, and the turning of pages, which has now been made very difficult, would have been easier. With this, basta – But how in the name of heaven did you come to dedicate my Fantasia with Orchestra to the King of Bavaria? Do answer me that at once. If you are thereby going to procure me an honourable gift, I will thank you, otherwise this is not at all agreeable to me. Did you, possibly, dedicate it yourself? What is the connection? One is not permitted to dedicate things to kings without requesting it. – Besides, there was no dedication of the Lebewohl to the Archduke; and why were not the year, day and date printed as I wrote them? In the future you must agree in writing to retain all superscriptions unchanged as I have written them. Let whomsoever you please review the oratorio and everything else. I am sorry that I ever said a word about those miserable r[eviews]. Who can mind what such r[eviewers] say when he sees how the most wretched scribblers are elevated by them and how they treat most insultingly works of art to which they cannot at once apply their standard as the shoemaker does his last, as indeed they must do because of their unfitness – If there is anything to be considered in connection with the oratorio it is that it was my first work in this form, and an early work, and was composed in fourteen days amidst all possible tumult and other unpleasant, alarming circumstances (my brother was mortally ill).

    'Rochlitz, if I am not mistaken, spoke unfavourably concerning the chorus of disciples "Wir haben ihn gesehen" in C major even before it had been given to you for publication; he called it comic, an impression which here at least was not experienced by the local public, and amongst my friends there are also critics. That I should write a very different oratorio now, than then, is certain – And now criticise as long as you please, I wish you much pleasure; and if it should hurt a little like the sting of a gnat it will soon be over; and when the engraving is over, then it becomes a complete joke. Cri-cri-cri-cri-cri-ti-ti-ci-ci-ci-

ci-cise-cise-cise – *you cannot keep this up for ever*. Therefore, God be
with you . . .'

Something of his old frolicsome humour again enlivened his notes to
Zmeskall: he expected him to dine with him at the Schwan; he begged
for more quills, and promised shortly a whole parcel of them, so that
Zmeskall 'will not have to pull out his own'; he might receive 'the great
decoration of the Order of the 'Cello'; and so on. Beethoven's notes to
Zmeskall are a barometer that indicates very correctly the rising and
sinking of his spirits; they were now high – at composition point – and,
as the Archduke did not return from Pressburg until 7 November, he
had at least one month for continuing without hindrance the studies
that followed the completion of the music for Budapest.

CHAPTER 14

The Years 1812 and 1813

The Austrian Financial Crisis – Letters to the Immortal Beloved

As a result of the war, the Austrian economy was severely strained, and the value of the currency steadily decreased. The depreciation of a national currency to null and its subsequent repudiation by the Government that emitted it is, in effect, a domestic forced loan equal in amount to the sum issued.

Beethoven's annuity contract bore the date 1 March 1809, when one florin in silver was equal to two and forty-eight hundredths in banknotes. Hence his 4,000 shrank to 1,618 in the new paper money. More than this he could not *legally* demand; but the original reasons for the contract, the intentions of the donors and the mutual understanding of the parties gave him a perfect claim *in equity* for the full amount of 4,000 florins in notes of redemption. Nor did the princes hesitate to admit its justice. They were men of honour and this was a debt of honour. Archduke Rudolph immediately gave the necessary order and instructions in writing; and Beethoven's anxiety because the others had not yet given him the same security was justified, although he might have expressed it rather more delicately.

As to Beethoven's third patron, Varnhagen wrote to Oliva from Prague on 9 June 1812:

'Yesterday I had an exhaustive talk with Prince v. Kinsky. Accompanied by expressions of highest praise for Beethoven, he complied at once with his request and from now on he will send him notes of redemption and will pay the arrears and the future sums in this currency. The cashier here will receive the necessary instructions and Beethoven can collect everything here when he passes through, or if he prefers in Vienna as soon as the prince shall have returned.

Prague, 9 June 1812'

But unfortunately this was not carried out. On 2 or 3 November, Kinsky, while riding at Weldus near Prague, was – by the breaking of his saddle-girth – thrown from his horse with such force as to crack his skull, and survived but ten hours. Beethoven's attempts to 'collect everything' after the Prince's death must await discussion until the next chapter.

The opening of the new theatre in Budapest, not having taken place in October as proposed, was deferred to Sunday, 9 February, that it might bear the character of a festivity in honour of the Emperor's birthday (12 February). The performances were repeated on the 10th and 11th to crowded audiences which received Beethoven's music to *König Stephan* and *Die Ruinen von Athen* (reported to be 'very original, excellent and worthy of its master') with clamorous applause. Beethoven had been so favourably impressed with Kotzebue's texts that in January 1812 he applied to him for an opera text:

'Vienna, 28 January 1812

'Highly respected, highly honoured Sir:

'While writing music for the Hungarians to your prologue and epilogue, I could not refrain from the lively wish to possess an opera from your unique talent, romantic, serious, heroico-comic or sentimental, as you please; in short, anything to your liking I would accept with pleasure. True, I should prefer a big subject from history and particularly one from the darker periods, Attila, etc., for instance; but I should accept with thanks anything and any subject coming from you, from your poetical spirit, which I could translate into my musical spirit.

'Prince Lobkowitz, who sends his greetings, and who now has the sole direction of the opera, will certainly grant you an honorarium commensurate with your deserts. Do not refuse my request; you will find that I shall always be deeply grateful for your compliance. Awaiting your favourable and speedy answer, I subscribe myself

Your admirer

Ludwig van Beethoven'

This letter was sent to Breitkopf and Härtel together with one to Goethe (unfortunately lost) with the following request that the two be forwarded to their destinations:

'Vienna, 28 January 1812

'As a punishment for your absolute silence I charge you with the immediate delivery of these two letters. A windbag of a Livonian promised to look after the letter to K. for me, but probably, the Livonians like the Russians being windbags and braggarts, he did nothing of the sort, although he made himself out to be a great friend of his – So I ask this, although I could rightly inflict it as a punishment for all the faulty editions, false titles, negligence and so forth . . . If the three songs by Goethe are not yet printed hurry with them; I should like soon to present them to Princess Kinsky, one of the handsomest and stoutest women in Vienna – And the songs from Egmont, why are they not yet out, really, why is not the whole of E out, out, out? – Do you perhaps want a close tacked on here and there to the entr'actes, this I can do too. Or let it be done by a Leipzig proof-reader of the *Musik-Zeitung*, who cannot make head nor tail out of it – Please charge the postage to me – It seems to me, I hear a whisper, that you are looking out for a new wife. To this I ascribe all the confusion mentioned above. I wish you a Xanthippe like the wife of the holy Greek Socrates, so that I might see a German publisher embarrassed, which is saying a great deal, yes, in real embarrassment.* I hope soon to be honoured with a few lines from you.

Your friend
Beethoven'

Walter Scott somewhere remarks: 'It is seldom that the same circle of personages, who have surrounded an individual at his first outset in life, continue to have an interest in his career till his fate comes to a crisis.' A few years more and this will begin to be very true of Beethoven. The old familiar names will rapidly disappear and new ones take their places; some half a dozen perhaps will remain to the end. But this is not yet. The old friends, Lichnowsky, Razumovsky, Erdödy and that class, Streicher, Zizius, Breuning and their class, are his friends still. We see less of them, because Beethoven is no longer the great pianist performing in the salons of the nobles, or playing his new compositions in the lodgings of his untitled admirers. His astonishing playing in the concert of December 1808 – which completed full thirty years since his appearance in Cologne as a prodigy – proved to be, as it happened, the splendid close of his career as a piano virtuoso.

Beethoven had surely earned the right to retire and leave the virtuoso field to his pupils, of whom Baroness Ertmann and Carl Czerny were pre-eminent as performers of his music. In the more private concerts he had already long given place to the Baroness; and now Czerny began to take it before the public, even to the extent of introducing his last new composition for pianoforte and orchestra, Op. 73, the 'Emperor' Concerto. Theodor Körner, lately arrived in Vienna, writes home under

* One of Beethoven's frequent puns: *Verleger* (publisher) and *Verlegenheit* (embarrassment).

the date 15 February 1812: 'On Wednesday the 11th, for the benefit of the Society of Noble Ladies for Charity, a concert and tableaux, representing three pictures by Raphael, Poussin and Troyes as described by Goethe in his "Elective Affinities", were given. The pictures offered a glorious treat; a new pianoforte concerto by Beethoven failed.'

Castelli's *Thalia* gives the reason why this noble work on this, its first public performance in Vienna, was so coldly received:

'If this composition . . . failed to receive the applause which it deserved, the reason is to be sought partly in the subjective character of the work, partly in the objective nature of the listeners. Beethoven, full of proud confidence in himself, never writes for the multitude; he demands understanding and feeling, and because of the intentional difficulties, he can receive these only at the hands of the knowing, a majority of whom is not to be found on such occasions.'

That was precisely the truth. The work was out of place. The warblings of Fräulein Sessi and Herr Siboni were suited to the occasion and the audience. Instead of Beethoven's majestic work, Kapellmeister Himmel, who had recently been in Vienna, should have been engaged to remain and exhibit his brilliant finger gymnastics.

The new symphony, to which there are allusions in the correspondence of this year, was the Seventh, which he took up and completed this spring (13 May), with the hope of producing it in a concert about the time of Pentecost – but the project fell through. Under the date of London, 14 February 1876, Mr E. Speyer writes: 'My father . . . on a visit to Vienna in 1832, made the acquaintance of the Abbé Stadler, who communicated to him the following curious fact in relation to Beethoven's Seventh Symphony, viz.: that the theme of the Trio was nothing more or less than a Lower-Austrian Pilgrimage Hymn, which the Abbé himself had frequently heard sung.'

Among the sufferers of the financial crisis were the Ursuline nuns at Graz, whose institution, since 1802, had at no time less than fifty wards and always more than 350 pupils. At this juncture they were excessively poor and in debt. In the hope of gaining them some substantial aid, Beethoven's new friend, Varena, now wrote to him offering to pay him properly for the use of some of his compositions in a concert for their benefit to be given on Easter Sunday, 29 March. Beethoven at once presented two of his new compositions to the Art Society of Graz for gratuitous use at charity concerts. At the concert on Easter Sunday there were eight numbers, Beethoven being represented by the overture to *König Stephan*, the march with chorus from *Die Ruinen von Athen*, the overture to *Egmont*, and the Septet. The nuns gained on the occasion the handsome sum of 1,836 fl. 24 kr.

In explanation of the Zmeskall correspondence which follows, it is to be noted that the 'greatest thanks' of one of the notes is merely for keeping his pens in order, and that Zmeskall had been making experiments to determine whether the oscillations of a simple weight and string (without lever) might not answer as a practicable and convenient metrometer.

'[19 January]
'I am coming to the Schwan today, dear Z. Unfortunately I am always so *free* and you *never*.'

'[2 February]
'Not extraordinary but very ordinary, commonplace quill cutter, whose virtuosity assuredly shows a falling off with this specimen. These quills need a few repairs – When will you throw off your chains, when? You think fine things about me; but accursed be for me the life in this Austrian Barbary – I shall now go mostly to the Schwan, as I cannot escape too much attention in the other inns.

'Fare thee well, that is, as well as I wish you to be without me.
                           Your friend
                              Beethoven'
'Most extraordinary one, we beg that your servant find someone to clean out the rooms. As he knows the quarters, he can at once fix the price – But soon – carnival ragamuffin !!!!!!!!!!'

'[8 February]
'Most extraordinary, foremost Oscillator of the world, and that without lever!!!!

'We owe you the greatest thanks for having endowed us with a portion of your oscillatory power. We wish to thank you for the same in person, and therefore invite you to come *to the Schwan* tomorrow, an inn whose name bears evidence that it was made for the occasion when the talk is about such things.
                           Wholly your B.'

'[19 February]
'Dear Z.,
'Only yesterday did I receive a written notice that the Archduke will pay his share in notes of redemption – I beg of you now to note down for me approximately what you said on Sunday so that I may send it to

the other two – It is felt that I should be given a certificate that the Archduke pays in redemption bonds, but I think this unnecessary, the more since these courtiers in spite of their apparent friendship for me say that my demands are not *just*!!!!! Oh heaven help me to bear this; I am no Hercules who can help Atlas bear up the world or do it in his stead. It was only yesterday that I heard in detail how beautifully Herr Baron Kruft had spoken about me at Zizius's, had judged me – Never mind, dear Z., it will not be for much longer that I shall continue the shameful manner in which I am living here. Art, the persecuted one, finds everywhere an asylum. Did not Daedalus, shut up in the labyrinth, invent the wings which carried him *upwards* into the air; and I, too, will find them, these wings –

Always your
Beethoven'

'If you have time, send me the desired form this very morning – For nothing, apparently for nothing have I been kept in suspense with polite words; so the time has already been lost. –'

In a series of notes to the Archduke during the year, he excused his absences from the lessons for varying reasons: for the two previous days because he was 'unexpectedly ill at just the time' when he was about to go to him; he had 'oftener than usual' waited upon him 'in the evening hour, but no one was to be found'; 'certain unexpected circumstances prevent' his attendance today, 'but I shall make use of the gracious privilege of waiting upon you tomorrow evening'. In another letter he writes:

'Your Imperial Highness!
'I was truly upset not to have received the message from YIH to come until very late yesterday evening, in fact not until eleven o'clock. I did not return home in the afternoon contrary to my habit. The beautiful weather had lured me into spending the whole afternoon walking, and in the evening I was seeing *Wanda** at the Wieden, and so it happened that not until I came home again could I know of your wish – Should YIH find it necessary I am at your disposal any moment any hour – I await therefore your gracious command.

Your Imperial Highness's most humble
Ludwig van Beethoven'

The following letter was written perhaps at the end of April:

* A romantic tragedy in five acts with songs by Zacharias Werner.

'Your Imperial Highness!

'Now for the first time, since I have left my bed, am I able to answer your gracious letter of today. Tomorrow it will still not be possible for me to wait upon you, but perhaps the day after tomorrow – I have suffered much during the last few days, twofold I may say because I could not follow my sincerest desire to devote a great deal of time to you. I hope I shall be through with it, though (I mean my illness), this spring and summer.'

This was the year in which Beethoven allowed a mask to be taken, at the desire of Streicher, who wished to add his bust to those which already adorned his pianoforte warerooms. The bust was executed by Professor Klein, a pupil of the famous sculptor Fischer. The gypsum mask passed from the hands of the Streicher family to the sculptor Dietrich who was thus aided in the modelling of his Beethoven busts. After Dietrich's death it was acquired by the Viennese Sculptor Society, and from there the sculptor Zumbusch made use of it in erecting his Beethoven monument. This mask is the most reliable source for Beethoven's likeness in this period.

The cause of an estrangement between Beethoven and Oliva is hinted at in two letters from Oliva to Varnhagen. On 23 March Oliva writes: 'I should like to write you a good deal about the things that sadden me, about Stoll, and Beethoven still more, but I must postpone it – I was ill lately and it moves me greatly to write about things which are so painful.' In a letter of 3 June he says: 'Concerning my unfortunate affairs I can only say that Of.* has treated me very shabbily and I am compelled to seek another engagement; perhaps I shall accept Beethoven's renewed offer and go with him to England. Stoll cheated me in a very miserable manner and even sought to bring about a rupture with Beethoven, in which he was almost successful; I am completely separated from him.'

In May, Bonaparte held court at Dresden and received his father-in-law, Emperor Franz, Frederick William of Prussia, the princes of the Rheinbund, etc. etc. Before the end of June, he had crossed the Niemen with his half million men on his fatal march to Moscow. As if from a presentiment and in the hope of a disastrous failure of the foolhardy invasion of Russia, Teplitz (that neutral ground, but central point of plot and agitation against the parvenu Emperor) became the scene of a virtual congress of imperial personages, or their representatives, accompanied by families, ministers and retinues. Ostensibly they met for health, recreation, social diversion; but views and opinions were

* Offenheimer, the Vienna banker, Oliva's employer.

exchanged and arrangements made for such concerted action as the result in Russia might render politic.

Beethoven left Vienna for Teplitz, going by way of Prague, where he arrived on 2 July in company with Oliva's friend Willisen. As appears from a letter from Beethoven to Princess Kinsky (dated 20 December 1812) Beethoven called upon the Prince, discussed financial matters, and received sixty ducats on account, but unfortunately the definitive settlement of the annuity matter was delayed.

Beethoven's biographers have devoted more thought, research and writing to the next five days in Beethoven's life than to any other period. The reason for this is that Beethoven wrote a three-part letter of such intensity to an unknown lady that ever since its discovery among the composer's possessions after his death, there has been speculation as to when it was written and to whom. While the study of the evidence has now established the year of its writing as 1812, no such success can be claimed for the question of the identity of the intended recipient of this letter.

Early on the morning of 5 July, Beethoven arrived in Teplitz and the next day started the letter.

'6 July, in the morning
'My angel, my all, my very self – Only a few words today and at that with pencil (with yours) – Not till tomorrow will my lodgings be definitely determined upon – what a useless waste of time – Why this deep sorrow when necessity speaks – can our love endure except through sacrifices, through not demanding everything from one another; can you change the fact that you are not wholly mine, I not wholly thine – Oh God, look out into the beauties of nature and comfort yourself with that which must be – Love demands everything and that very justly – *thus it is to me with you, and to you with me*. If only you do not forget that I must live *for me and for you*; if we were wholly united you would feel the pain of it as little as I – My journey was a fearful one; I did not reach here until 4 o'clock yesterday morning. Lacking horses the post-coach chose another route, but what an awful one; at the stage before the last I was warned not to travel at night; I was made fearful of a forest, but that only made me the more eager – and I was wrong. The coach must needs break down on the wretched road, a bottomless mud road. Without such postilions as I had with me I should have remained stuck in the road. Esterhazy, travelling the usual road here, had the same fate with eight horses that I had with four – Yet I got some pleasure out of it, as I always do when I successfully overcome difficulties – Now a quick change to things internal from things external. We shall surely

see each other soon; moreover, today I cannot share with you the thoughts I have had during the last few days touching my own life – If our hearts were always close together, I would have none of these. My heart is full of so many things to say to you – ah – there are moments when I feel that speech amounts to nothing at all – Cheer up – remain my true, my only love, my all as I am yours. The gods must send us the rest, what for us must and shall be –

Your faithful Ludwig'

'Evening, Monday, 6 July

You are suffering, my dearest creature – Just now have I learned that letters must be posted very early in the morning on Mondays – or on Thursdays – the only days on which the mail-coach goes from here to K[arlsbad] – You are suffering – Ah, wherever I am, there you are also – I will arrange it with you and me that I can live with you. What a life!!!! thus!!!! without you – pursued by the goodness of mankind hither and thither – which I as little want to deserve as I deserve it – Humility of man towards man – it pains me – and when I consider myself in relation to the universe, what am I and what is he – whom we call the greatest – and yet – herein lies the divine in man – I weep when I reflect that you will probably not receive the first report from me until Saturday – Much as you love me – I love you more – But do not ever conceal yourself from me – good night – As I am taking the baths I must go to bed – Oh God – so near! so far! Is not our love truly a heavenly structure, and also as firm as the vault of Heaven? –'

'Good morning, on 7 July

'Though still in bed, my thoughts go out to you, my Immortal Beloved, now and then joyfully, then sadly, waiting to learn whether or not fate will hear us – I can live only wholly with you or not at all – Yes, I am resolved to wander so long away from you until I can fly to your arms and say that I am really at home with you, and can send my soul enwrapped in you into the land of spirits – Yes, unhappily it must be so – You will be the more contained since you know my fidelity to you. No one else can ever possess my heart – never – never – Oh God, why must one be parted from one whom one so loves. And yet my life in V[ienna] is now a wretched life – Your love makes me at once the happiest and the unhappiest of men – At my age I need a steady, quiet life – can that be so in our connection? My angel, I have just been told that the mail-coach goes every day – and I must close at once so that you may receive the letter at once – Be calm, only by a calm consideration of our existence can we achieve our purpose to live together – Be

calm – love me – today – yesterday – what tearful longings for you –
you – you – my life – my all – farewell. – Oh continue to love me –
never misjudge the most faithful heart of your beloved.

  ever thine
  ever mine   L.'
  ever ours

This letter is the only known one in which Beethoven used the 'Du'
form of address to a woman. Even his love letters to Josephine Deym
used the more formal 'Sie'. Hence, it is possible that the letter was never
sent, but was preserved by him from the start, as was the Heiligenstadt
Testament. Whoever the lady may have been, the impassioned mood of
the writing forms the last and by far the most vehement expression that
Beethoven gave to his lifelong idealistic concept of union with one of
the other sex. And yet, throughout these three outbursts is revealed
already the hopelessness of this ideal from the composer's point of view.
The tone of the last part of the letter particularly is that of one who is
making up his mind and is attempting to convince one fully in love with
him of the necessity of this decision. It is not surprising to find a sense of
tedium in Beethoven's life as an aftermath to this crisis.

Other letters, to Varnhagen and to Breitkopf and Härtel, reflect
this. To Varnhagen: 'There is not much to be said about Teplitz, few
people and among the few nothing extraordinary, wherefore I live
alone! alone! alone! alone!' To Breitkopf and Härtel: 'How are we? –
on that point much cannot yet be said; on the whole there are not such
interesting people here as were last year and are few – a multitude of
people is less of a bother than are a few.'

A touching letter was drawn from the composer by a child of eight to
ten years, 'Emilie M. at H.' Emilie was a little pianist with such an enthusiasm for Beethoven that she wrote to the composer privately with
the help of her governess enclosing a wallet of her own making which
she shyly offered. Beethoven's answer is dated Teplitz, 17 July 1812:

'My dear good Emilie, my dear friend!

 'My answer to your letter is late in coming; a mass of business and
constant sickness must excuse me. That I am here for the recuperation
of my health proves the truth of my excuse. Do not tear away the laurel
wreaths of Handel, Haydn and Mozart; they possess them, but not I yet.

 'Your wallet will be preserved along with other things of undeserved respect from many people.

 'Keep at it, don't just practise art, but penetrate also to its inner laws;
it deserves it, for only art and science raise men to the Divine. If you

should want something at any time, my dear Emilie, write to me trust-ingly. A true artist has no pride. Unfortunately he sees that art has no limits; he senses darkly how far he is from the goal; and while he is per-haps admired by others, he mourns that he has not yet arrived to the point where his better genius shines as an example like a distant sun. I would rather come to visit you and your people than many rich per-sons who betray themselves with the poverty of their inner selves. If I should come sometime to H., I will come to you and your family. I know no other advantages of a man than those which cause him to be counted among better men. Where I find these, there is my home.

'If you want to write to me, dear Emilie, address it directly here where I will be for 4 weeks more, or Vienna; it is all the same. Consider me as your friend and as a friend of your family.

Ludwig v. Beethoven'

On 19 July, Goethe enters Beethoven's name for the first time among his 'visits' – no doubt those made by him. On the same day he writes to his wife, who had gone on to Karlsbad for a cure: 'Say to his Serene Highness Prince Friedrich, that I can never be with Beethoven without wishing that it were in the *goldenen Strauss*.* A more self-contained, energetic, sincere artist I never saw. I can understand right well how singular must be his attitude towards the world.'

Goethe wrote to a friend concerning Beethoven as follows:

'I made Beethoven's acquaintance in Teplitz. His talent amazed me; unfortunately he is an utterly untamed personality, who is not alto-gether in the wrong in holding the world to be detestable but surely does not make it any the more enjoyable either for himself or others by his attitude. He is easily excused, on the other hand, and much to be pitied, as his hearing is leaving him, which, perhaps, mars the musical part of his nature less than the social. He is of a laconic nature and will become doubly so because of this lack.'

A sifting of fact from legend is necessary to complete the story of the relations between Goethe and Beethoven; such, for instance, as the familiar anecdote according to which, when Goethe expressed his vex-ation at the incessant greetings from passers-by, Beethoven is said to have replied: 'Do not let that trouble your Excellency, perhaps the greetings are intended for me.'

On 26 July, a large portion of the town of Baden, near Vienna, including the palace of Archduke Anton, the cloister of Augustines,

* A well-known inn just outside Vienna.

the theatre and casino, the parochial church and the palace of Count Carl Esterhazy, was destroyed by a conflagration which broke out between noon and 1 o'clock. In all, 117 houses were burned. 'From Karlsbad under the date of 7 August, it is reported,' writes the *Wiener Zeitung* of 29 August, that 'scarcely had the misfortune which recently befell the inhabitants of Baden become known here before the well-known musicians Herr van Beethoven and Herr Polledro* formed the benevolent purpose to give a concert for the benefit of the sufferers'. They seized 'the favourable moment', before those of high station should depart, and 'in the conviction that he who helps quickly helps twofold, this purpose was carried out within twelve hours . . . Universal and rousing applause and receipts amounting to 954 florins, Vienna Standard, rewarded the philanthropic efforts' of the concert-givers.

On 9 August, Beethoven had written a letter to Breitkopf and Härtel. After referring to the concert, and his various moves to follow the doctor's orders, he adds:

'I must refrain from writing more, and instead splash around in the water again. Scarcely have I filled my interior with an ample quantity of it than I must have it dashed around and around over my exterior. I will answer the rest of your letter soon. Goethe is too fond of the atmosphere of the Courts, more so than is becoming to a poet. Why laugh at the absurdities of virtuosi when poets who ought to be the first teachers of a nation, forget all else for the sake of this glitter.'

The letter ended as it began with reference to the dedication to Kinsky of the Mass in C.

In the middle of September Beethoven returned to Teplitz with no amelioration, but rather an increase of his maladies, and was compelled to remain until the end of September. To his great satisfaction, he found there the young lady who had so powerfully attracted him the previous summer. The character of their renewed acquaintance is sufficiently obvious from the series of notes which follow. There are eight in all; six are given here. Only the first one bears a date.

'Teplitz, 16 September 1812

'For Amalie von Sebald:

'Tyrant – I? Your tyrant? Only a misapprehension can lead you to

* Violinist, concert-master in Dresden in 1814, court kapellmeister in Turin in 1824.

say this even if your judgement of me indicated no agreement of thought with me! – But no blame to you on this account, it is rather a piece of good fortune for you – Yesterday I was not wholly well, and since this morning I have grown worse. Something indigestible was the cause, and the irascible part of me appears to seize upon the bad as well as the good. But do not apply this to my moral nature – People say nothing, they are only people, they generally see only themselves in others, and that is *nothing*. Away with this; the good, the beautiful needs no people. It is there without help of any kind and that, after all, appears to be the reason for our agreement. – Farewell, dear A. If the moon shines brighter for me this evening than the sun by day, you will see with you the small, smallest of all men. –

Your friend
Beethoven'

'I only wish to report that the tyrant is chained to his bed *like a slave* – So it is! I shall be glad if I get by with the loss of the present day only. My promenade yesterday at sun-up in the woods, where it was very misty, has increased my indisposition and probably delayed my improvement – Busy yourself meanwhile with Russians, Lapps, Samoyeds, etc., and do not sing too often the song "Es lebe hoch!"

Your friend
Beethoven'

'I cannot yet say anything definite about myself; sometimes I feel better and next things appear to be in the old rut, or to be preparing a long sickness for me. – If I could give expression to my thoughts concerning my sickness as definitely as I can express my thoughts in music, I should soon help myself – Today too I must keep to my bed – Farewell, and rejoice in your good health, dear A,

Your friend
Beethoven'

'[In Amalie Sebald's handwriting.] My tyrant commands an account – here it is:

A fowl	1 fl. VS*
The soup	9 kr.

With all my heart I hope that it may agree with you.'

'[In Beethoven's handwriting.] Tyrants do not pay, but the bill must be receipted, and you can do that best if you come in person, NB, with the bill to your humbled tyrant.'

* Vienna Standard.

'I am already better, dear A. If you think it *proper* to come to me alone, you could give me great pleasure; but if you think it *improper* you know how I honour the liberty of all people. And no matter how you act in this and all other cases, according to your principles or caprice, you will always find me kind and

Your friend
Beethoven'

'Dear, good A!

'After leaving you yesterday my condition grew worse, and from last night till now I have not left my bed. I wanted to send word to you today, but thought it would look as if I wanted to appear important in your eyes, so I refrained – What dream of yours is this that you can be nothing to me? We will talk about that in person, dear A. I have always wished only that my presence might give you rest and peace, and that you would confide in me – I hope to be better tomorrow and then some hours of your stay will still remain for us both to be uplifted and gladdened by Nature – good-night, dear A, many thanks for the proofs of your sentiments towards your friend.

Beethoven'

Beethoven's health must have improved soon after 16 September, for Kapellmeister Glöggl's *Linzer Musik-Zeitung* announces his arrival in Linz on 5 October. 'Now we have had the long wished for pleasure of having within our metropolis for several days the Orpheus and great musical poet of our time, Herr L. van Beethoven; and if Apollo is favourable to us we shall also have an opportunity to admire his art and report upon it to the readers of this journal.' He had come thither, probably direct via Prague and Budweis, to pass a few weeks with his brother Johann, who gave him a large room affording him a delightful view of the Danube with its busy landing place and the lovely country road beyond.

One of Beethoven's memoranda is this: 'In 1812, I was in Linz on account of B.' Supposing this B. to stand for Beethoven's brother it confirms certain very unpleasant information obtained in Linz, from perfectly competent authority, namely, that the principal object of the journey thither was to interfere in Johann's domestic affairs.

Soon after coming to Linz, the apothecary, being unmarried and having a house much too large for his necessities, leased a part of it to a physician from Vienna, whose wife's sister some time later joined them. She, Therese Obermayr, was described as possessing a very graceful and finely proportioned figure, and a pleasing, though not beautiful, face. Johann van Beethoven soon became acquainted with her, liked her, and made her his housekeeper and – something more.

When it is considered that the apothecary was a man of some thirty-five years, that he had gained his present position entirely by his own enterprise, perseverance and good fortune, and that, beyond advice and remonstrance, his brother had no more right to meddle in his private concerns than any stranger, it seems hardly credible that Beethoven, with all his eccentricities of character, could have come to Linz with precisely this purpose in view. But, according to the evidence, this was so. Had the motive of his visit been simply fraternal affection, and had he then and there first discovered his brother's improper connection with Therese, he could justly have employed earnest expostulation and entreaty to the end of breaking it off – but nothing more; if unheeded, he could leave the house. But to come thither for this express object, and employ force to accomplish it, was indefensible. Such, at all events, was Johann's opinion, and he refused to submit to his brother's dictation. Excited by opposition, Ludwig saw the Bishop about it. He applied to the civil authorities. He pushed the affair so earnestly, as at last to obtain an order to the police to remove the girl to Vienna if, on a certain day, she should be still found in Linz. The disgrace to the poor girl; the strong liking which Johann had for her; his natural mortification at not being allowed to be master in his own house; these and other similar causes wrought him up almost to desperation. Beethoven, having carried his point, might certainly have borne his brother's anger with equanimity; might have felt pity for him and sought to soothe him in his trouble. But no; when Johann entered his room with reproaches and upbraidings, he, too, became angry and a scene ensued on which – let the curtain be drawn. It was, unhappily, more disgraceful to Ludwig than Johann. The apothecary, to use the language of the card-table, still had the commanding trump. Should he play it? The answer is in the parochial register at Linz. It is the record of marriage, 8 November 1812, of Johann van Beethoven to Therese Obermayr. There is some slight reason to think that the journey to Linz was suddenly undertaken in consequence of a false report that Johann was about to marry Therese, and with the intention to prevent it. Whether this be true or not he lost the game and immediately hastened away to Vienna, angry and mortified that the measures he had taken had led to the very result which he wished to prevent; had given to the unchaste girl the legal right to call him 'brother', and had put it in Johann's power – should he in the future have cause to rue his wedding-day – to reproach him as the author of his misfortune. Indeed, when that unhappy future came, Johann always declared that

The little town of Heiligenstadt, where Beethoven made
his summer residence.
Left, Franz Grillparzer, who
became acquainted with Beethoven at Heiligenstadt and
who later composed his
funeral oration

A letter from Beethoven to his 'Immortal Beloved', 6 July 1812. The identification of his 'Beloved' remains a mystery. Two women close to Beethoven were, *right*, Josephine Deym (née Brunsvik), and, *below left*, Therese Malfatti. *Below right*, Beethoven's friend, the writer and philosopher Johann Wolfgang von Goethe

Ludwig had driven him into this marriage; how the composer then viewed the matter, we shall see when the time comes. One sister-in-law had already been to Beethoven a bitter source of shame and mortification; and now the other? – Time must show.

Beethoven's professional occupation in Linz was the completion of the Eighth Symphony, which, on Johann van Beethoven's doubtful authority, was wrought out from sketches during walks to and upon the Pöstlingberg. Beethoven had begun to work industriously on the Eighth Symphony before he went to Teplitz; indeed he seems to have reported to Breitkopf and Härtel that he had finished two symphonies. Schindler's account of the origin of the famous Allegretto Scherzando from the Eighth Symphony runs thus:

'In the Spring of the year 1812, Beethoven, the mechanician Mälzel, Count von Brunsvik, Stephan von Breuning and others, sat together at a farewell meal, the first about to undertake the visit to his brother Johann in Linz, there to work out his Eighth Symphony and afterwards to visit the Bohemian baths – Mälzel, however, to journey to England to exploit his famous trumpet-player automaton. The latter project had to be abandoned, however, and indefinitely postponed. The time-machine – metronome – invented by this mechanician was already in such a state of forwardness that Salieri, Beethoven, Weigl and other musical notabilities had given a public testimonial of its utility. Beethoven, generally merry, witty, satirical, 'unbuttoned', as he called it, at this farewell meal improvised the following canon, which was at once sung by the participants.'

Schindler here prints the now well-known canon and adds: 'Out of this canon was developed the Allegretto Scherzando.'

The symphony was composed in 1811 and 1812 with the final working-out in the summer of 1812, thus Schindler's statement that the canon preceded the composing of the second movement is not necessarily correct.

The Conversation Books show, in Schindler's own hand, how he became possessed of the canon. In a Conversation Book (1820) he writes: 'The motif of the canon, 2nd movement of the 8th symphony – I cannot find the original – you will, I hope, have the kindness to write it down for me.' Again in 1824 he writes: 'I am just in the second movement of the 8th symphony – ta, ta, ta – the canon on Mälzel – it was really a very jolly evening when we sang this canon in the "Kamehl" – Mälzel, the bass. At that time I still sang soprano. I think it was the end of 1817.'

Though it may be slightly in advance of strict chronological order, it would seem well to quote here what the violinist, composer and conductor Ludwig Spohr in his Autobiography writes of his personal intercourse with Beethoven. It is interesting and doubly acceptable as the only sketch of the kind belonging to just this period.

'After my arrival in Vienna (about 1 December), I at once hunted up Beethoven, but did not find him and therefore left my card. I now hoped to meet him in one of the musical soirées to which I was frequently invited, but soon learned that since his deafness had so increased that he could no longer hear music distinctly in all its context he had withdrawn from all musical parties and, indeed, become very shy of society. I made another attempt to visit him, but again in vain. At last, most unexpectedly, I met him in the eating-place which I was in the habit of patronising every Wednesday with my wife. I had, by this time, already given a concert (17 December), and twice performed my oratorio (21 and 24 January). The Vienna newspapers had reported favourably upon them. Hence, Beethoven knew of me when I introduced myself to him and greeted me in an extremely friendly manner. We sat down together at a table, and Beethoven became very chatty, which greatly surprised the table company, as he generally looked straight ahead, morose and curt of speech. It was a difficult task to make him understand, as one had to shout so loudly that it could be heard three rooms distant. Afterwards, Beethoven came often to this eating-house and visited me at my lodgings, and thus we soon learned to know each other well. Beethoven was frequently somewhat blunt, not to say rude; but an honest eye gleamed from under his bushy eyebrows.

'After my return from Gotha (end of May 1813), I met him occasionally at the Theater-an-der-Wien, hard behind the orchestra, where Count Pálffy had given him a free seat. After the opera he generally accompanied me home and spent the remainder of the evening with me. There he was pleasant towards Dorette and the children. He very seldom spoke about music. When he did so his judgements were very severe and so decided that it seemed as if there could be no contradiction. He did not take the least interest in the works of others; for this reason I did not have the courage to show him mine. His favourite topic of conversation at the time was severe criticism of the two theatrical managements of Prince Lobkowitz and Count Pálffy. He was sometimes overloud in his abuse of the latter when we were still inside the theatre, so that not only the public but also the Count in his office might have heard him. This embarrassed me greatly and I continually tried to turn the conversation into something else. The rude, repelling conduct of Beethoven at this time was due partly to his deafness, which he had not yet learned to endure with resignation, partly to the un-settled condition of his financial affairs. He was not a good house-keeper and had the ill-luck to be robbed by those about him. So he often lacked necessities. In the early part of our acquaintance I once asked him, after he had been absent from the eating-house: "You were not ill, were you?" – "My boots were, and as I have only one pair I had house-arrest," was the answer.'

Beethoven had other cares, troubles and anxieties in the coming year – to which these reminiscences in strictness belong and serve as a sort of introduction – not then known to Spohr.

Ever since the establishment of the Immortal Beloved love letters as having been written in 1812, the first entries of Beethoven's so-called journal (*Tagebuch*) of the Fischoff manuscript have taken on new meaning. The first entry has only the year 1812 and probably belongs to the end of the year. It begins thus:

'Submission, absolute submission to your fate, only this can give you the sacrifice . . . to the servitude – Oh, hard struggle! – Turn every-thing which remains to be done to planning the long journey – you must yourself find all that your most blessed wish can offer, you must force it to your will – keep always of the same mind . . .
    '*Thou mayest no longer be a man*, not for thyself, only for others, *for thee there is no longer happiness except* in thyself, *in thy art* – O God, give me strength to conquer myself, nothing must chain me to life. Thus everything connected with A [?] will go to destruction.'

The next-following in the manuscript is dated:

'13 May 1813
'To forgo a great act which might have been and remains so – O, what a difference compared with an unstudied life which often rose in my fancy – O fearful conditions which do not suppress my feeling for domesticity, but whose execution O God, God, look down upon the unhappy B., do not permit it to last thus much longer –

    'Learn to keep silent, O friend! Speech is like silver,
    But to hold one's peace at the right moment is pure gold.'

Other causes also joined to render his case now truly pitiable. The result of his interference with his brother Johann, vexatious and mortifying as it was, was of little moment in comparison with the anxiety and distress caused by the condition of his brother Carl Caspar. In 1809, Carl had been advanced to the position of Deputy Liquidator with 1,000 fl. salary and 160 fl. rent money; but all salaries being then paid in banknotes, the minor public officials were reduced to extreme poverty. Carl van Beethoven was already owner of the house in the Alservorstadt near the Herrnalser Linie, which contained lodgings for some ten or twelve small families, enclosed a court-garden with fruit trees, etc.; the whole of this house was rented, and, after deducting interest and taxes, gave him a very desirable addition to his miserable salary. When Beethoven writes that he had wholly to support 'an unfortunate sick brother together with his family', it must be therefore understood *cum grano salis*; but that he had for some time been obliged very largely to aid them in obtaining even the necessaries of life is beyond question. Just now, when his own pecuniary prospects were so clouded, his anxieties were increased by his brother's wretched state of health, which partly disabled him for his official duties, and seems to have forced him to pay for occasional assistance. In March, he appeared rapidly to be sinking from consumption, and he became so hopeless of improvement in April as to induce him – in his wellfounded distrust of the virtue and prudence of his unhappy wife – to execute the following

'DECLARATION

'Inasmuch as I am convinced of the frank and upright disposition of my brother Ludwig van Beethoven, I desire that after my death he undertake the guardianship of my son, Karl Beethoven, a minor. I therefore request the honourable court to appoint my brother mentioned to the guardianship after my death and beg my dear brother to accept the office and to aid my son with word and deed in all cases.

'Vienna, 12 April 1813'

Happily for all parties concerned, spring 'brought healing on its wings'. Carl's health improved; he was advanced to the position of Cashier of the 'Universal-Staats-Schulden Kasse', with 40 fl. increase of rent money; and now, at last, the decree was issued for the payment of all salaries (of public officials) in silver.

The nature of Beethoven's relation to his brother is made vivid by a recollection which Karl van Beethoven, Carl Caspar's son, told his wife in later years. At the time when his father was already very sick, the family were seated at table one day having a meal together. Suddenly the door opened and Beethoven burst in demanding, 'You thief! Where are my notes?' Then followed a violent quarrel, and Karl's mother Johanna had great difficulty separating the brothers. The music in question was produced from a drawer and thrown in front of Beethoven, who then calmed down and begged his brother's pardon. Carl Caspar, however, was still angry and continued to abuse him, whereupon Beethoven rushed from the room without taking the music with him. Carl continued his abuse and the son remembered his saying that he never wished to have that dragon [*Drachen*] in his house again, etc. 'A short time thereafter the uncle [Beethoven] met them on the Ferdinand Bridge and when he noticed the sickly appearance of his brother he fell on his neck and in the public street covered him with kisses so that the people stared in complete bewilderment. Then he put him in a hackney coach and took him home and continued to besiege him almost with kisses in the carriage.'

In a letter to Archduke Rudolph written in January, Beethoven said bitterly: 'neither word, nor honour, nor written agreement, seems binding.' The words relate to non-payments of the Kinsky and Lobkowitz subscriptions to his annuity.

Schindler has enlarged upon Beethoven's inexperience and lack of skill in matters of business, and of his propensity to waste his resources in needless changes of lodgings; Wegeler and others inform us of his ignorance of the value of money; Carl Caspar van Beethoven had been a great expense to him; and five-eighths of his annuity had for some time remained unpaid. Still, it is impossible to account satisfactorily for the very low state of his finances at this time. He must have been strangely imprudent in non-husbanding his resources.

To finish this topic, we pass on to the summer, which the composer spent in Baden, meeting there his friends the Streichers. Frau Streicher afterwards related to Schindler that she found Beethoven in the summer of 1813 in the most desolate state as regards his physical and domestic needs – 'not only did he not have a single good coat, but not a whole shirt', and, adds Schindler, 'I must hesitate to describe his condition exactly as it was.' Frau Streicher, after her return to the city, put his wardrobe and household affairs to rights and, with the help of her husband, saw to the provision of the necessities, and, what was still better, they impressed upon him the necessity of putting money by against the future, and 'Beethoven obeyed in every particular'.

We come now to correspondence with Varena concerning charity concerts at Graz:

'Dear Sir!

'No doubt Rode was right in all that he said about me – my health is not of the best – and, without being my fault, my condition otherwise is probably the unhappiest of my life – But neither this nor anything else shall dissuade me from helping the equally innocent sufferers, the Convent ladies, so far as my modest talents will permit. – To this end, two entirely new symphonies are at your services, an aria for bass voice with chorus, several smaller single choruses – If you need the overture to *Ungarns Wohltäter* which you performed last year, it is at your service. *The overture to Die Ruinen von Athen*, although in a smaller style is also at your service. – Amongst the choruses is a chorus of Dervishes, an attractive thing [literally: "a good signboard"] for a mixed public. – In my opinion you would do best to choose a day on which you could give the oratorio "Christus am Ölberg", which has been performed in a number of places. This would then fill half of the concert, for the second half you could play a new symphony [?], overtures and different choruses, as also the bass aria with chorus mentioned – Thus the evening would not be without variety; but you had better talk this over with the musical councillors in your city and let them decide. – From what you say concerning remuneration for me from a third person, I think I can guess who he is. If I were in my former condition I would flatly say: "Beethoven never takes pay when the benefiting of humanity is concerned"; but now placed in a condition through my great benevolence, the cause of which can bring me no shame, and other circumstances which are to blame, which are caused by men without honesty or honour, I say frankly I would not decline such an offer from a *rich third party* – But there is no thought of a demand, even if *all this about a third party* should prove to be nothing, be convinced that I am just as willing now to be of service to my friends, the reverend ladies, as I was last year without the least reward, and as I shall always be to suffering humanity as long as I breathe – And now farewell, write to me soon and I will care for all that is necessary with the greatest zeal – My best wishes for the convent.

With high esteem your friend
Ludwig van Beethoven'

On 8 April he wrote to Varena again and thanked him for the sum of 100 florins from the nuns. After paying for the copying of parts he planned to send the remainder back to the nuns. And he added:

'I thought that the third person to whom you referred was perhaps the *ex-King of Holland** and – yes, from him who probably took from the Hollanders in a less righteous way I would have had no hesitation in accepting something in my present condition. Now, however, I beg kindly that nothing more be said on the subject. – Write me your opinion as to whether if I came to Graz I could give a concert, for it is not likely that Vienna will long remain my place of residence – perhaps it is already too late, but your opinion on the subject would always be welcome.'

In April, Beethoven sought permission to give two concerts in the hall of the University. The result is shown in a note to Zmeskall dated 19 April:

'The hall of the University, my dear Z., is – refused – I received this information the day before yesterday, but being ill yesterday I could not come to you to talk it over, nor is it possible today. – There remains nothing probably except the Kärnthnerthor theatre or the Theater-an-der-Wien, and at that I fancy for only one A[kademie] – If all that does not work out we must resort to the Augarten. There of course we must give two A[kademies]. Think the matter over a bit, my dear, and give me your opinion – It may be that the symphonies will be rehearsed tomorrow at the Archduke's, if I can go out, of which I shall let you know.

Your friend
Beethoven'

The following letter to Franz Brunsvik, dated by Thayer as 1812, should undoubtedly belong to the summer of 1813. It was this summer in which Napoleon was fighting the Allies in the north and which made Beethoven write: 'If the billows of war roll nearer here, I shall come to Hungary.'

The letter reads as follows:

'Dear friend! Brother!

'I ought to have written to you earlier; I did so 1,000 times in my heart. You ought to have received the T[rio] and S[onata] much earlier; I cannot understand how M. could have detained these so long from you. To the best of my recollection I told you that I would send both sonata and trio. Do as you feel inclined, keep the sonata or send it to Forray as you please. The quartet was designed for you long ago, my disorderliness alone is to blame that you receive it only now, – and

* Then residing in Graz.

speaking of disorder I am unfortunately compelled to tell you that it still persecutes me on every hand. Nothing decisive has been done in my affairs. The unhappy war may delay the final settlement still more or make the matter worse. – At one time I resolve upon one thing, at another time upon a different one. Unfortunately I must remain in the neighbourhood until the matter is settled. – O unhappy decree, seductive as a siren, against which I should have stopped my ears with wax and had myself bound like Ulysses so that I could not sign. If the billows of war roll nearer here, I shall come to Hungary. Perhaps I shall in any event, since I must needs care only for my miserable self; I shall no doubt fight my way through. Away, nobler, loftier plans – Infinite are our strivings, the commonplace puts an end to all! – Farewell, dear brother, be such to me; I have no one to whom I can give the name. Do as much good around you as the evil times will permit. – In the future put the following directions on the coverings of letters to me: "To J. B. v. Pasqualati." The rascal Oliva (no noble r[as]c[al] however) is going to Hungary; do not have too much to do with him. I am glad that this connection which was brought about by sheer necessity, will by this be entirely broken off. – More by word of mouth. – I am now in Baden, now here; – to be found in Baden through the Sauerhof – Farewell, let me hear from you soon –

Your friend Beethoven'

The mechanician and inventor of the metronome, Mälzel, during the past winter, had opened his *Künstkabinett* as a public exhibition. There were marbles, bronzes and paintings and a variety of contributions, scientific or curious, from various artists – among them a large electrical machine with apparatus for popular experiments, but the principal attractions were his own Mechanical Trumpeter and the new Panharmonicon. The Trumpeter executed a French cavalry march with signals and melodies which Mälzel himself accompanied on the pianoforte. The Panharmonicon combined the common instruments then employed in military bands, with a powerful bellows – the whole being enclosed in a case. The motive power was automatic and the keys were touched by pins fixed in a revolving cylinder, as in the common hand-organ or music-box.

The condition of Carl van Beethoven's health forced his brother to defer the contemplated journey to England; and Mälzel, too, found reason to delay leaving for England until the end of the year – the idea of his really very beautiful and striking exhibition, the 'Conflagration of Moscow', had occurred to him and he willingly remained in Vienna to work it out. The change for the better in Carl Caspar's health and pecuniary condition, and the completion of the 'Conflagration', left both Beethoven and Mälzel late in autumn free for their departure.

The mechanician was not only a man of unquestionable inventive genius, but he also understood the public; knew as by instinct how to excite and gratify curiosity without disappointing expectation, and had the tact and skill so to arrange his exhibitions as to dismiss his visitors grateful for an amusement for which they had paid. He was personally both respected and popular. He knew by experience the principal cities of the Continent, and London well enough to foresee that the noble compositions of Handel, Haydn and Cherubini secured the success of his Panharmonicon there; but that if he could add to its repertory some new, striking and popular piece, bearing the now great name of Beethoven, he would increase both its attractiveness and the public interest and curiosity in the composer. Battles and sieges had for many years been favourite subjects for descriptive music, and the grand engagements of the last fifty years were few indeed which had not been fought over again by orchestras, bands and all sorts of instruments.

When, therefore, the news of Wellington's magnificent victory at Vittoria, 21 June 1813, reached Vienna, Mälzel saw instantly that it presented the subject of a composition for his Panharmonicon than which none could be conceived better fitted to strike the popular taste in England. A work which should do homage to the hero, flatter national feeling by the introduction of 'Rule Britannia' and 'God save the King', gratify the national hatred of the French, celebrate British victory and Gallic defeat, bear the great name of Beethoven and be illuminated by his genius – what more could be desired? He wrought out the plan and explained it to the composer, who, for once, consented to work out the ideas of another. In a sketchbook for this composition, having signals for the battle on its first page, we read: 'Wellington's Victory Vittoria, only God save the King, but a great victory overture for Wellington'; and in the so-called *Tagebuch*: 'I must show the English a little what a blessing there is in God save the King'; perhaps, also, another remark just after this was occasioned by his experience on this work: 'It is certain that one writes most prettily when one writes for the public, also that one writes rapidly.' There is nothing in this at all contradictory to Moscheles's positive and unimpeachable testimony on the origin of the work. In a note to his English edition of Schindler's book he writes:

'I witnessed the origin and progress of this work, and remember that not only did Mälzel decidedly induce Beethoven to write it, but even laid before him the whole design of it; himself wrote all the drum-marches and the trumpet-flourishes of the French and English armies; gave the composer some hints, how he should herald the English army by the tune of "Rule Britannia"; how he should introduce "Malbrook" in a dismal strain; how he should depict the horrors of the battle and arrange "God save the King" with effects representing the hurrahs of a multitude. Even the unhappy idea of converting the melody of "God save the King" into a subject of a fugue in quick movement, emanates from Mälzel. All this I saw in sketches and score, brought by Beethoven to Mälzel's workshop, then the only suitable place of reception he was provided with.'

On Beethoven's return to his city lodging in September, his notes to Zmeskall became as usual numerous, the principal topic just now being the engagement of a servant. The preceding winter he had interviewed a man who had formerly worked for Zmeskall – 'I did not remember him, but he told me he had been with you and that you were satisfied with everything except the fact that he could not dress your hair properly . . . For me hair-dressing is, as you know, the least of my worries. First of all it would have to be that my finances were dressed and curled.' Whatever servant he engaged, however, was evidently not a success, for in September he writes:

'Best-born and Bearer of the Grand Cross of Violoncellicity!
  'If your servant is honest and knows of an honest servant for me, it would be a great favour to me, if through your *fine fellow* there could be found a fine fellow for me – In any case I should prefer a married man, for though not necessarily more honesty, at least more orderliness can be expected from such – My present beast of a servant is leaving at the end of the month, the new servant could then come at the beginning of next month . . . As I give no livery except for a cloak, my servant is paid 25 fl. monthly –
  Forgive me, dear Zmeskall
  Your friend   Beethoven'

At length, with the assistance and under the direction of the excellent Streichers, Beethoven got his lodgings and wardrobe into decent order, and with the aid of Zmeskall he obtained that servant spoken of by Schindler,

'who was a tailor and carried on his trade in the ante-room of the composer. With the help of his wife he attended the master with touching care till into the year 1816 – and this regulated mode of life did our friend much good. Would that it might have endured a few years longer.

'At this stage of the case there came also evidences of love and admiration from Prince Lichnowsky, which are well worth more detailed notice. The Prince was in the habit of frequently visiting his favourite in his workshop. In accordance with a mutual understanding no notice was to be taken of his presence, so that the master might not be disturbed. After the morning greeting the Prince was in the habit of looking through any piece of music that chanced to be at hand, watching the master at his work for a while and then leaving the room with a friendly "adieu". Nevertheless, these visits disturbed Beethoven, who occasionally locked the door. Unvexed, the Prince would walk down the three flights of stairs. As the sartorial servant sat in the ante-room, His Serene Highness would join him and wait until the door opened and he could speak a friendly greeting to the Prince of Music. The need was thus satisfied. This is indeed a beautiful counterpart to what we have already learned of the sentiments of Archduke Rudolph. But it was not given long to the honoured Maecenas of Art to rejoice in his favourite and his creations, for already on 15 April of the following year he had departed this life!'

To return to 'Wellington's Victory'. Schindler, supposing the Panharmonicon to have played it, remarked in the first edition of his book: 'The effect of the piece was so unexpected that Mälzel requested our Beethoven to instrumentate it for orchestra.' He is mistaken as to the reason; for Mälzel had only, in Beethoven's words, 'begun to engrave'. In truth, he was musician enough to see from the score how very effective it would be if instrumentated for grand orchestra, and sagacious enough to perceive that the composition in that form might prove of far greater advantage to them in London and probably be more attractive afterwards when performed by the Panharmonicon. But there was another consideration far more important.

Before the age of steam a journey from Vienna to London with the many huge cases required for even a part of Mälzel's collection was a very expensive undertaking. The problem now was, how to provide the necessary funds. Beethoven's were exhausted and his own were very limited. To go alone and give exhibitions at the principal cities on the way, involved little or no risk for Mälzel, as the experience of the next year proved; but to make the journey direct, with Beethoven for his companion, was impossible until in some manner a considerable sum of ready money could be provided.

The only resource of the composer, except borrowing, was, of course, the production of the two new Symphonies, one of which had been copied for trial with small orchestra at the Archduke's, thus diminishing somewhat the expenses of a concert. It was five years since he had had a benefit, and therefore one full house might be counted on with reasonable certainty; but no concert of his had ever been repeated, and a single full house would leave but a small margin of profit. Moreover, his fruitless efforts in the spring to arrange an Akademie were discouraging. Unless the new Symphonies could be produced without cost to himself, and the interest and curiosity of the public so aroused as to ensure the success of two or three subsequent concerts, no adequate fund for the journey could be gained; but if so great a sensation could in some manner be made as to secure this object, the fame of it would precede and nobly herald them in London.

Beethoven was helpless; but Mälzel's sagacity was equal to the occasion. He knew that for the highly cultivated classes of music-lovers, able and ready to appreciate the best, nothing better could be desired than new Symphonies by Beethoven; but such auditors are always limited in number; the programme must also contain something surprising, sensational, to catch the ear of the multitude, and open their pockets. His Trumpeter was not enough. Beethoven alone could, if he would, produce what was indispensable. Time pressed, Mälzel had long since closed his exhibition, and every day of delay was a serious expense. The 'Conflagration of Moscow', the model of his Chronometer and the cylinders for his Panharmonicon were all finished, except the 'Victory', and this would soon be ready. Before the end of the year, therefore, he could be in Munich, as his interest imperatively demanded, provided Beethoven should not be his companion. There was nothing to detain him in Vienna, after the 'Victory' was completed, but his relations to the composer. Him he knew too well to hope from him any work deliberately written with a view to please the multitude, had the time allowed, which it did not.

Mälzel thus formed his plan: if Beethoven would consent to instrumentate the 'Victory' for orchestra – in doing which, being freed from the limitations of the Panharmonicon, he could give free play to his fancy – he (Mälzel) would return to him the score, risk the sacrifice of it for its original purpose, remain in Vienna, and make it the popular attraction of a grand charity concert for the benefit of the Austrians and Bavarians wounded in the battle at Hanau, trusting that it would open the way for two or more concerts to be given for their own benefit. Under all the circumstances, it is difficult to decide whether to admire the more Mälzel's good judgement, or his courageous trust in it and in Beethoven's genius. He disclosed his plan and purposes to the composer, they were approved by him, and the score was returned.

While Beethoven wrought zealously on his task, Mälzel busied himself with the preparations for the concert. His personal popularity, the charitable object in view, curiosity to study Beethoven's new productions, especially the battle-piece, secured the services of nearly all the leading musicians, some of whom were there only in passing or temporarily. Tomaschek, who heard the 'Victory' next year, writes that he was 'very painfully affected to see a Beethoven, whom Providence had probably assigned to the highest throne in the realm of music, among the rudest materialists. I was told, it is true, that he himself had declared the work to be folly, and that he liked it only because with it he had thoroughly thrashed the Viennese.' There is no doubt that this was so; nor that they, who engaged in its performance, viewed it as a stupendous musical joke, and engaged in it *con amore* as in a gigantic professional frolic.

Beethoven wrote to the Archduke to ask that he speak a good word in his behalf through Baron Schweiger to the 'Rector Magnificus' of the University, so that he might secure University Hall for his concerts. This time the use of the Hall was granted and 8 December was fixed for his concert.

Spohr, playing among the violins, for the first time saw Beethoven conduct and was surprised in the highest degree, although he had been told beforehand of what he now saw with his own eyes. He continues:

'Beethoven had accustomed himself to indicate expression to the orchestra by all manner of singular bodily movements. So often as a *sforzando* occurred, he tore his arms, which he had previously crossed upon his breast, with great vehemence asunder. At *piano* he crouched down lower and lower as he desired the degree of softness. If a *crescendo* then entered he gradually rose again and at the entrance of the *forte* jumped into the air. Sometimes, too, he unconsciously shouted to strengthen the *forte* . . . It was obvious that the poor man could no longer hear the *piano* of his music. This was strikingly illustrated in the second portion of the first Allegro of the Symphony. In one place there are two holds, one immediately after the other, of which the second is *pianissimo*. This, Beethoven had probably overlooked, because he began again to beat time before the orchestra had begun to play the second hold. Without knowing it, therefore, he had hurried ten or twelve measures ahead of the orchestra, when it began again and, indeed, *pianissimo*. Beethoven to indicate this had in his wonted manner crouched clean under the desk. At the succeeding *crescendo* he again became visible, straightened himself out more and more and jumped into the air at the point where according to his calculation the *forte* ought to begin. When this did not follow his movement he looked about in a startled way, stared at the orchestra to see it still playing *pianissimo* and found his bearings only when the long-expected *forte* came and was visible to him. Fortunately this comical incident did not take place at the performance.'

Mälzel's first placards announcing the concert spoke of the battle-piece as his property; but Beethoven objecting to this, others were substituted in which it was said to have been composed 'out of friendship, for his visit to London'. No hint was conveyed of Mälzel's share in the composition. The programme was:

1. 'An entirely new Symphony', by Beethoven (the Seventh, in A major).

2. Two marches played by Mälzel's Mechanical Trumpeter, with full orchestral accompaniment – the one by Dussek, the other by Pleyel.

3. 'Wellington's Victory'.

The success of the performances was so unequivocal and splendid as to cause their repetition on Sunday, the 12th, at noon, at the same prices, 10 fl. and 5 fl. The *Wiener Zeitung*, *Allgemeine Musikalische Zeitung* of Leipzig, and the *Beobachter*, contained excessively laudatory notices of the music and vivid descriptions of its effect upon the auditors, whose 'applause rose to the point of ecstasy'. The statements of the contemporary public prints are confirmed by the veteran Spohr, who reports that the Allegretto of the Seventh Symphony 'was demanded *da capo* at both concerts'.

Schindler calls this rightly 'one of the most important moments in the life of the master, at which all the hitherto divergent voices, save those of the professional musicians, united in proclaiming him worthy of the laurel'. 'A work like the battle-symphony had to come,' adds Schindler with good judgement, 'in order that divergent opinions might be united and the mouths of all opponents, of whatever kind, be silenced.'

CHAPTER 15

The Year 1814 – The Congress of Vienna

On the last day of 1813, the *Wiener Zeitung* contained this public notice:

'MUSICAL ACADEMY

'The desire of a large number of music-lovers whom I esteem as worthy of honour, to hear again my grand instrumental composition on "Wellington's Victory at Vittoria", makes it my pleasant duty herewith to inform the valued public that on Sunday, the 2nd of January, I shall have the honour to perform the afore-mentioned composition with added vocal pieces and choruses and aided by the most admirable musicians of Vienna in the RI large Redoutensaal for my benefit.

'Tickets of admission are to be had daily in the Kohlmarkt in the house of Baron v. Haggenmüller, to the right of the court on the ground floor, in the comptoir of Baron v. Pasqualati; parterre 2 fl. gallery 3 fl. Vienna standard.

Ludwig van Beethoven'

Mälzel saw, therefore, that the objects for which he had sacrificed the 'Battle', for which he had spent so much labour and pains, were accomplished in so far as Beethoven's new works were now the subjects of general interest and curiosity, and their repeated performance to large and profitable audiences was secured. To his courage and sagacity this was wholly due. It is thoroughly unjust to deny or ignore the value of his services. What his feelings were now, to find himself deprived of all share in the benefit resulting from them, and therefore left without compensation, may readily be conceived. His Mechanical Trumpeter was discarded with himself, and Beethoven had to find something to take its place on the programme. The result was the selection of Nos. 6, 7 and 8 of the *Ruinen von Athen* music, viz.: the 'Solemn March with Chorus' and the concluding bass aria, sung by Weinmüller, with the choruses. The last was exceedingly appropriate in a concert in the Redoutensaal, it being the number in which the bust of the monarch is made suddenly to appear.

To ensure the effectiveness of this is the object of a humorous note to Zmeskall, on New Year's Day.

'Dear worthy friend!

'All would be well if there were but a curtain, without *it the aria will fall through* ... Let there be a *curtain* even if it be only a bed-curtain, only a sort of *screen* which can be removed for the moment, a *veil*, etc. There must be something; the aria is too *dramatic, too much written for the theatre*, to be effective in a concert; *without a curtain or something of the sort all of its meaning will be lost! – lost! lost! To the devil with everything!* The Court will probably come. Baron Schweiger asked me to go there at once; Archduke Karl admitted me to his presence and promised to *come. – The Empress did not accept nor did she decline.*

'*Hangings*!!! or the aria and I will *hang* tomorrow. Farewell in the new year, I press you as warmly to my heart as in the old – *with or without curtain?*'

The orchestra was for the most part composed of the same professional and amateur artists as had taken part in the two previous concerts, so that the rehearsals were comparatively inexpensive, the only new music being the selections from *Die Ruinen*; but Salieri, as director of the cannonade, gave place to Hummel.

'Only in this room' (the large Redoutensaal), says Schindler, 'was the opportunity offered to put into execution the manifold intentions of the composer in the Battle Symphony. With the help of the long corridors and the rooms opposite to each other the opposing forces were enabled to approach each other and the desired illusion was strikingly achieved.' Schindler was among the listeners on this occasion and gives assurance that the enthusiasm awakened by this performance, 'heightened by the patriotic feeling of those memorable days', was overwhelming.

The composer had every reason to be satisfied with the result, for not only was it pecuniarily profitable but 'the applause was general and reached the highest ecstasy. Many things had to be repeated, and there was a unanimous expression of a desire on the part of all the hearers to hear the compositions again and often.'

So speaks the *Wiener Zeitung* on 9 January.

Among the direct consequences of this sudden and boundless popularity of Beethoven's music was one all the more gratifying, because totally unexpected – the revival of *Fidelio*.

Georg Friedrich Treitschke was born in Leipzig in 1776 and came to the Court Theatre in 1800 as an actor. His talents and fine character raised him in the course of the next two years to the position of poet and stage-manager of the German Court Opera, a post which he continued to hold for many years. He recorded: 'The managing performers of the RI Court Opera, Saal, Vogl and Weinmüller, were granted a performance for their benefit, the choice of a work being left to them, without cost.' The sensation caused by Beethoven's new music suggested *Fidelio*. All three had been in Vienna at its production and therefore knew it sufficiently to judge of its fitness for them as singers, and the probability of its now being successful. At all events the name of Beethoven would surely secure for their night a numerous audience. He goes on:

'Beethoven was approached for the loan of the opera and very unselfishly declared his willingness, but on the unequivocal condition that many changes be made. At the same time he proposed my humble self as the person to make these changes. I had enjoyed his more intimate friendship for some time, and my twofold position as stage-manager and opera-poet made his wish a pious duty. With Sonnleithner's permission I first took up the dialogue, wrote it almost wholly anew, succinct and clear as possible – an essential thing in the case of *Singspiele*.'

Treitschke continues:

'What I am now relating will live for ever in my memory. Beethoven came to me about seven o'clock in the evening. After we had discussed other things, he asked how matters stood with [Florestan's final] aria. It was just finished, I handed it to him. He read, ran up and down the room, muttered, growled, as was his habit instead of singing – and tore open the pianoforte. My wife had often vainly begged him to play; today he placed the text in front of him and began to improvise marvellously – music which no magic could hold fast. Out of it he seemed to conjure the motive of the aria. The hours went by, but Beethoven improvised on. Supper, which he had purposed to eat with us, was served, but – he would not permit himself to be disturbed. It was late when he embraced me, and declining the meal, he hurried home. The next day the admirable composition was finished.'

Concerning this air, Röckel writes:

'The new Florestan (the Italian Radichi) wanted to be applauded after his air, which was not possible nor fitting to the situation nor desirable after the *pianissimo* conclusion of Florestan's air with the *con sordino* accompaniment of the violins. In order to satisfy him in part, without writing a new air, Beethoven first shortened the Adagio and concluded with an Allegro in the high register of the singer. But as the noise of applause would not have been increased by Rocco and Fidelio, who enter at this moment to dig a grave for the supposedly dead man, the composer decided to end the noisy Allegro with a small coda for the orchestra ending with a new *pianissimo*, by which device the silence essential to the succeeding scene was again restored.'

Beethoven's attention was now called away by the concert of which the following two notes speak. The first is to Count Brunsvik:

'13 Febr. 1814

'Dear friend and brother!

'You wrote to me recently; now I write to you – You no doubt are rejoicing over all the victories – also over mine – On the 27th of this month I shall give a second concert in the large Redoutensaal – Come up – now that you know of it – Thus I am gradually rescuing myself from my misery, for from my salaries I have not yet received a penny . . . My opera is going to be performed, but I am writing much of it over. I hope you are living contentedly, no small accomplishment. So far as I am concerned, good heavens, my kingdom is in the air; like the wind, the tones whirl around me, and often in my soul – I embrace you.'

The second note is to Archduke Rudolph.

'Your Imperial Highness!

'I hope for pardon for my non-attendance. Your displeasure would punish me when I am innocent. In a few days I will make it all up – They intend to perform my opera Fidelio again; this gives me a great deal of work, and despite my healthy appearance I am not well.

Ludwig van Beethoven'

The *Wiener Zeitung* of 24 February contains the advertisement of the 'Akademie, next Sunday, the 27th inst. in the large Redoutensaal', announcing 'a new symphony not yet heard and an entirely new as yet unheard terzetto' as novelties. To Hummel, Beethoven writes:

'Best beloved Hummel! I beg of you conduct this time again the drumheads and cannonades with your admirable kapellmeister's and field-marshal's baton – do it, I beg of you, and if ever I am wanted to cannonade you, I shall be at your service body and soul. –

Your friend Beethoven'

The report in the *Allgemeine Musikalische Zeitung* contains the programme in full with a few short and pertinent observations:

'1. The new symphony (the 7th in A major) which was received with so much applause, again. The reception was as animated as at the first time; the Andante (A minor) the crown of modern instrumental music, as at the first performance had to be repeated.

'2. An entirely new Italian terzetto (B flat major) beautifully sung by Mad. Milder-Hauptmann, Hr. Siboni and Hr. Weinmüller, is conceived at the outset wholly in the Italian style, but ends with a fiery Allegro in Beethoven's individual style. It was applauded.

'3. An entirely new, hitherto unheard symphony (the 8th in F major, 3/4 time). The greatest interest of the listeners seemed centred on this, the *newest* product of B's muse, and expectation was tense, but this was not sufficiently gratified after the *single* hearing, and the applause which it received was not accompanied by that enthusiasm which distinguishes a work which gives universal delight; in short – as the Italians say – it did not create a furore. This reviewer is of the opinion that the reason does not lie by any means in weaker or less artistic workmanship (for here as in all of B's works of this class there breathes that peculiar spirit by which his originality always asserts itself); but partly in the faulty judgement which permitted this symphony to follow that in A major, partly in the surfeit of beauty and excellence which must necessarily be followed by a reaction. If this symphony should be performed *alone* hereafter, we have no doubt of its success.

'4. At the close, "Wellington's Victory in the battle of Vittoria" was given again, the first part, the Battle, having to be repeated. The performance left nothing to be desired; and the attendance was again very large.'

Schindler recalls that Beethoven 'often related with much pleasure how, when walking on the Kahlenberg after the performance, he got some cherries from a couple of girls and when he asked the price of one of them, she replied: "I'll take nothing from you. We saw you in the Redoutensaal when we heard your beautiful music." '

The following letter to Treitschke resulted from proposed changes in the scenery of *Fidelio*:

'My esteemed T.! Following your advice I went to the architects and the affair has already been arranged very much to my advantage. It is better to have to deal with *artists* than with *so-called grandees* (wimmeny-pimmenies)! – You will be able to have your song the very moment you give me the word – For everything connected with my opera my thanks hasten on to you. – If the opportunity arises, you might think of giving *Egmont at the Wieden Theatre* for my benefit. The arrival of the Spaniards, which is only suggested in the play, not visibly presented, might be utilised for the multitude to open the *big hole* of the Wieden Theatre [the stage] – and there might be a good deal of *visual spectacle* besides, and the music would not be wholly lost; and I should willingly add something new if it were asked. –

'Esteemed friend! Farewell! Today I spoke with the chief bass-singer of the Austrian Empire, full of enthusiasm for a new opera by – Gyrowetz! In my heart I laughed over the new artistic course which this work will open up.

Wholly your Beethoven'

Towards the end of March, Beethoven received the new text to *Fidelio*. To Treitschke he writes: 'I have read your amendments to the opera with great pleasure; they determine me the more to rebuild the ruins of an old castle.'

Beethoven's attention was now again called away from the opera by a concert in the hall of the Hotel zum Römischen Kaiser, arranged by the landlord and Schuppanzigh for a military charity. Czerny relates that a new grand trio had then for some time been a subject of conversation among Beethoven's friends, though no one had heard it. This work, Op. 97, in B flat major, was to open the second part of the concert and the composer had consented to play in it. Spohr was by chance in Beethoven's rooms at one of the rehearsals and heard him play – the only time. He writes:

'It was not a treat, for, in the first place, the piano was badly out of tune, which Beethoven minded little, since he did not hear it; and secondly, on account of his deafness there was scarcely anything left of the virtuosity of the artist which had formerly been so greatly admired. In *forte* passages the poor deaf man pounded on the keys till the strings jangled, and in *piano* he played so softly that whole groups of tones were omitted, so that the music was unintelligible unless one could look into the [score of the] pianoforte part. I was deeply saddened at so hard a fate. If it is a great misfortune for anyone to be deaf, how shall a musician endure it without giving way to despair? Beethoven's continual melancholy was no longer a riddle to me.'

In those days a well-to-do music-lover, named Pettenkofer, gathered a number of young people into his house every Saturday for the performance of instrumental music. One evening a pupil of Schuppanzigh's requested his neighbour at the music-stand, a youth of eighteen years, to take a note from his teacher next day to Beethoven, proposing a rehearsal of the Trio, and requiring no answer but 'yes' or 'no'. 'I undertook the commission with joy,' he records:

'The desire to be able to stand for even a moment beside the man whose works had for several years inspired me with the greatest reverence for their author, was now to be so unexpectedly and strangely realised. The next morning the bearer of the note, with beating heart, climbed the four flights in the Pasqualati house, and was at once led by the sartorial servant to the writing-table of the master. After he had read the missive, he turned to me and said "Yes"; with a few rapidly added questions the audience came to an end; but at the door I permitted myself to tarry a little while to observe closely the man, who had already resumed his writing.'

This youth was Anton Schindler. He continues his narrative: 'This, almost the most important event in the life-history of the poor student up to that time, was soon followed by the acquaintanceship of Schuppanzigh. He gave me a ticket for the concert of 11 April, given by him , , , On this occasion I approached the great master with more confidence, and greeted him reverently. He answered pleasantly and showed that he remembered the carrier of the note.'

Meantime an event had occurred which doubtless made a strong impression on Beethoven but of which unfortunately there is no indication – Prince Karl Lichnowsky, his old friend and protector, died on 15 April. It is gratifying that the last notice of him in our work is that touching reminiscence by Schindler, which proves that time had neither cooled nor diminished the warm affection that he had conceived twenty years before for the young Bonn pianist.

The following note to Zmeskall was written about this time:

'Dear Z., I am not going on the journey, at least I am not going to hurry – the matter must be pondered more carefully – Meanwhile the work ['Wellington's Victory'] has already been sent to the *Prince Regent* [of England]: *If I am wanted I can be had*, and then *liberty* remains with me to say *yes* or *no*. Liberty !!! What more do I want?

'I should like to consult with you about how to settle myself in my lodging.'

This new lodging, for which Beethoven now left the Pasqualati house, was in the first storey of the Bartenstein house, also on the Mölker Bastei (No. 94); so that he still remained in the immediate vicinity of his friends, Princess Christine Lichnowsky and the Erdödys.

The other matters mentioned in the note call our attention again to Mälzel, who, notwithstanding his bitter disappointment at the turn which his affairs with Beethoven had taken, had still lingered in Vienna several weeks in the hope of making some kind of amicable arrangement with him. As his side of the story was never made public, there is little to add to the information on the subject contained in the papers of Beethoven, preserved by Schindler. From them these facts appear: that Mälzel and he had several interviews at the office of the lawyer, Dr Adlersburg, which had for their subject the 'Battle of Vittoria' and the journey to England; that he made various propositions which Beethoven would not accept 'to get the work, or at least the right of first performance for himself', and the like; that, incensed by the conduct of the composer, he did not appear at the last meeting appointed; and that he obtained by stealth so many of the single parts of the 'Battle' as to be enabled therefrom to have a pretty correct score of the work written out, with which he departed to Munich and there produced it in two concerts on 16 and 17 March.

When this became known in Vienna Beethoven's wrath was excited and, instead of treating the matter with contemptuous silence, or at most making an appeal to the public in the newspapers, he committed the absurdity of instituting a lawsuit against a man already far on his way to the other extremity of Europe. At the same time in all haste he prepared a copy of the 'Battle' and sent it to the Prince Regent of England, so that at least he might prevent Mälzel from producing it there as a novelty. It was a costly and utterly useless precaution; for, on the one hand, Mälzel found in London no inducement to attempt orchestral concerts, and on the other, the score sent by Beethoven lay buried in the library of the Prince, who neither then nor ever took the slightest notice of it or made any acknowledgement to the composer.

Casting aside all extraneous matter contained in Beethoven's documents, the real question at issue is very clear: did the arrangement of the work for orchestra at Mälzel's suggestion and request, transfer the proprietorship? If it did, Beethoven had a basis for his suit; if it did not, he had none. This question was never decided; for after the process had lingered through several years, the two men met, made peace, Beethoven withdrew his complaint, and each paid the half of all expenses incurred!

Thus had been caused a new interruption of the work of *Fidelio*.

'The beneficiaries', says Treitschke, 'urged its completion to take advantage of the favourable season; but Beethoven made slow progress.' To one of the poet's notes urging haste, Beethoven wrote, probably in April:

'Dear worthy T.! The damned Akademie, which I was compelled to give partly because of my bad circumstances, has set me back so far as the opera is concerned . . .

'Now, of course, everything must be done at once; and I could write something new more quickly than add new things to old as now. I am accustomed in my composing . . . to keep the whole in view. But here my whole has – in a certain way – been distributed everywhere and I have got to think myself back into my work ever and anon – It is not likely that it will be possible to give the opera in two weeks' time. I think that it will be in 4 weeks. Meanwhile the first act will be finished in a few days – But there still remains much to do in the second Act, and also a new overture, which will be the easiest because I can compose it entirely new. Before my Akademie a few things only were sketched here and there, in the first as well as the second act. It was not until a few days ago that I could begin to work things out. The score of the opera is as frightfully written as any that I ever saw. I have to look through note after note (it is probably a pilfered one). In short, I assure you, dear T., the opera will secure for me the crown of martyrdom. If you had not given yourself so much pains with it and revised everything so successfully, for which I shall be eternally grateful to you, I would scarcely have been able to bring myself to it – You have thereby saved some good remainders of a ship that was stranded –

'If you think that the delay with the opera will be too long, postpone it till some future time. I am going ahead now until everything is finished, and, just like you, I have been changing and improving everything and making it better, which I see more and more clearly every moment. But it cannot go as fast as if I were composing something new – and in 14 days that is impossible – Do as you think best, but as a friend of mine. There is no want of zeal on my part.

Your Beethoven'

Treitschke wrote again to Beethoven urging him to make haste. Notwithstanding so much was wanting, the rehearsals had begun in the middle of April, and the performance was now fixed for 23 May. Beethoven's memorandum of his revisal of the opera reads: 'The opera Fidelio [?] March to 15 May, newly written and improved.'

'The final rehearsal', says Treitschke, 'was on 22 May, but the promised new overture was still in the pen of the creator.' It was on the 20th or 21st that Beethoven dined with his friend Bertolini. After dinner he took a bill of fare, drew lines on the blank side and began to write. 'Come, let us go,' said Bertolini; 'No, wait a little; I have the idea for my overture,' replied Beethoven, who remained and finished his sketches then and there. Treitschke continues:

'The orchestra was called to rehearsal on the morning of the performance. B. did not come. After waiting a long time we drove to his lodgings to bring him, but – he lay in bed, sleeping soundly, beside him stood a goblet with wine and a biscuit in it, the sheets of the overture were scattered on the bed and floor. A burnt-out candle showed that he had worked far into the night. The impossibility of completing the overture was plain; for this occasion his overture to *Prometheus* [?] was taken and the announcement that because of obstacles which had presented themselves the new overture would have to be dispensed with today, enabled the numerous audience to guess the sufficient reason.'

'The opera was capitally prepared,' says Treitschke, 'Beethoven conducted, his ardour often rushed him out of time, but Kapellmeister Umlauf, behind his back, guided everything to success with eye and hand. The applause was great and increased with every representation.'

'Herr van B.', says the *Sammler*, 'was stormily called out already after the first act, and enthusiastically greeted.' The opera was first repeated on the 26th, when the new overture in E major 'was received with tumultuous applause and the composer again called out twice at this repetition'.

Ignaz Moscheles, then just twenty years of age, was commissioned to make the pianoforte score. Before bidding him farewell for the next half a dozen years, let us look at a few sentences from the preface to the English translation of Schindler's book, partly for the information they impart and partly to prevent a mistake or two from passing into history on his authority. He thus writes:

'In the year 1809 my studies with my master, [Dionysius] Weber*, closed; and being then also fatherless, I chose Vienna for my residence to work out my future musical career. Above all, I longed to see and become acquainted with *that man*, who had exercised so powerful an influence over my whole being; whom though I scarcely understood, I blindly worshipped. I learnt that Beethoven was most difficult of access and would admit no pupil but Ries; and for a long time my anxiety to see him remained ungratified. In the year 1810, however, the

* Director of the Prague Musical Conservatory.

longed-for opportunity presented itself. I happened to be one morning in the music-shop of Domenico Artaria, who had just been publishing some of my early attempts at composition, when a man entered with short and hasty steps, and, gliding through the circle of ladies and professors assembled on business, or talking over musical matters, without looking up, as though he wished to pass unnoticed, made his way direct for Artaria's private office at the bottom of the shop. Presently Artaria called me in and said: "*This is Beethoven!*" and to the composer, "This is the youth of whom I have just spoken to you." Beethoven gave me a friendly nod and said he had just heard a favourable account of me. To some modest and humble expressions, which I stammered forth, he made no reply and seemed to wish to break off the conversation. I stole away with a greater longing for that which I had sought than I had felt before this meeting, thinking to myself – "Am I indeed such a musical nobody that he could not put one musical question to me? – nor express one wish to know who had been my master, or whether I had any acquaintance with his work?" My only satisfactory mode of explaining the matter and comforting myself for this omission was in Beethoven's tendency to deafness, for I had seen Artaria speaking close to his ear . . .

'It was in the year 1814, when Artaria undertook to publish a pianoforte arrangement of Beethoven's *Fidelio*, that he asked the composer whether I might be permitted to make it: Beethoven assented upon condition that he should see my arrangement of each of the pieces, before it was given into the engraver's hands. Nothing could be more welcome to me, since I looked upon this as the long wished-for opportunity to approach nearer to the great man and to profit by his remarks and corrections. During my frequent visits, the number of which I tried to multiply by all possible excuses, he treated me with the kindest indulgence. Although his increasing deafness was a considerable hindrance to our conversation, yet he gave me many instructive hints, and even played to me such parts as he wished to have arranged in a particular manner for the pianoforte. I thought it, however, my duty not to put his kindness to the test by robbing him of his valuable time by any subsequent visits; but I often saw him at Mälzel's, where he used to discuss the different plans and models of a Metronome, which the latter was going to manufacture, and to talk over the "Battle of Vittoria", which he wrote at Mälzel's suggestion.

'Meantime the season had far advanced, the summer heats were approaching, the departure of the nobility and the wealthy for their country-seats was near, and Beethoven thought, perhaps justly, that new attractions must be added to *Fidelio*.'

The earliest hint as to what they might be is found in a note to Treitschke:

'For heaven's sake, dear friend! It seems that you have no instinct for money-making – See to it that Fidelio is not given *before* my benefit. This was the arrangement with *Schreyvogel* – Since Saturday when you last saw me at the theatre, I have been confined to my bed and room, and not until yesterday did I feel a trace of improvement. I might have visited you today did I know that poets like Phaeacians observe Sunday! We must talk about sending out the opera so that you may receive your quarter share and so it is not sent out in stolen copies all over the world. I know nothing of business but think that if we were to sell the score to a publisher here and it were to be printed, the result would be better for you and me. If I understand you correctly I ought to have the song by this time – Please, dear friend, hurry it up! – Are you angry? Have I offended you? If so, it was done inadvertently, and therefore forgive an ignoramus and musician. Farewell, let me know something soon.

Your grateful debtor and friend Beethoven'
'Milder has had her aria for a fortnight, I shall learn today or tomorrow whether she knows it. It will not take her long.'

Beethoven's benefit performance of *Fidelio* took place on Monday evening, 18 July 1814. The song so impatiently awaited could have been no other than Rocco's 'gold aria' which had been sung only in the three performances of 1805.

As to the new piece for Milder, Treitschke says implicitly it was 'a grand aria for Leonore, but as it checked the rapid movement of the rest it was again omitted'. In the advertisement of his benefit Beethoven says only: 'For this performance ... two new pieces have been added.'

The contemporary reports of the performance are numerous and all very eulogistic. Forti, as Pizarro, was 'entirely satisfactory'; the 'gold aria', although well sung by Weinmüller, 'did not make a great effect'; 'beautiful and of artistic value was the aria in E major, [etc.] ... The house was very full; the applause extraordinary; the enthusiasm for the composer, who has now become a favourite of the public, manifested itself in calls before the curtain after every act.'

Another consequence of Beethoven's sudden popularity, was the publication of a new engraving of him by Artaria, the crayon drawing for which was executed by Latronne, a French artist then in Vienna. Blasius Höfel, a young man of twenty-two years, was employed to engrave it. He told the writer how very desirous he was of producing a good likeness – a matter of great importance to the young artist – but that Latronne's drawing was not a good one, probably for want of a sufficient number of sittings. Höfel often saw Beethoven at Artaria's and, when his work was well advanced, asked him for a sitting or two. The request was readily granted. At the time set, the engraver appeared with his plate. Beethoven seated himself in position and for perhaps five minutes remained reasonably quiet; then suddenly springing up went to the pianoforte and began to extemporise, to Höfel's great annoyance. The servant relieved his embarrassment by assuring him that he could now seat himself near the instrument and work at his leisure, for his master had quite forgotten him and no longer knew that anyone was in the room. This Höfel did; wrought so long as he wished, and then departed with not the slightest notice from Beethoven. The result was so satisfactory that only two sittings of less than one hour each were needed. It is well known that Höfel's is the best of all the engravings made of Beethoven. In 1851, Alois Fuchs showed to the writer his great collection, and when he came to this, exclaimed with strong emphasis: 'Thus I learned to know him!'

Höfel in course of the conversation unconsciously corroborated the statements of Madame Streicher, as reported by Schindler, in regard to Beethoven's wretched condition in 1812–13. The effect upon him of his pecuniary embarrassments, his various disappointments, and of a mind ill at ease, was very plainly to be seen in his personal habits and appearance. He was at that time much accustomed to dine at an inn where Höfel often saw him in a distant corner, at a table, which though large was avoided by the other guests owing to the very uninviting habits into which he had fallen; the particulars may be omitted. Not infrequently he departed without paying his bill, or with the remark that his brother would settle it; which Carl Caspar did. He had grown so negligent of his person as to appear there sometimes positively 'schmutzig' (dirty). Now, however, under the kind care of the Streichers, cheered and inspirited by the glory and emolument of the past eight months, he became his better self again; and – though now and to the end, so careless and indifferent to mere externals as occasionally to offend the sensitiveness of very nice and fastidious people – he again, as before quoted from Czerny, 'paid attention to his appearance'.

Beethoven did not get to the country for any lengthy sojourn this summer; he had only a brief stay at Baden. The Congress of Vienna was originally scheduled to meet on 1 August, but was postponed until the early autumn. That Beethoven was bearing this Congress and its visiting dignitaries in mind is shown by the next series of 'occasional

compositions'. Next to Op. 90 in the 'Fidelio' sketchbook are a few
hints for 'Ihr weisen Gründer', which, though called a 'cantata' in the
sketchbook, is but a chorus with orchestra – a piece of flattery intended
for the royal personages at the coming Congress. It was not finished
until 3 September. This was the only work which Beethoven now had
on hand suitable for a grand concert.

The arrival at Vienna of the King of Wurtemburg on 22 September,
of the King of Denmark on the 23rd and the announcement of the
coming of the Russian Emperor with the King of Prussia on Sunday
the 25th, brought Beethoven back to the city. Owing to the failure of
Lobkowitz, the Court Theatres had passed under the management of
Pálffy. If there be any truth whatever in his alleged hostility to Beethoven, it is not a little remarkable that the first grand opera performed
in the presence of the monarchs – Monday the 26th – was *Fidelio*. One
of the audience on that evening, in a published account of his 'Journey
to the Congress', records: 'Today I went to the Court Theatre and was
carried to heaven – the opera *Fidelio* by L. v. Beethoven was given.'
Then follow some fifteen pages of enthusiastic eulogy. That auditor
was Alois Weissenbach, RI Councillor, Professor of Surgery and Head
Surgeon of the St John's Hospital in Salzburg, a man of high reputation. Of him Franz Graeffer writes: 'That Weissenbach was a passionate admirer of Beethoven's is a matter of course; their natures were
akin, even physically, for the Tyrolean was just as hard of hearing . . .
But it was pitiful to hear them shout at each other. It was therefore not
possible thoroughly to enjoy them. Strangely enough in a little room
. . . Weissenbach heard much better, and conversed more freely and
animatedly.'

Weissenbach himself writes:

'Completely filled with the gloriousness of the creative genius of this
music, I went from the theatre home with the firm resolve not to
leave Vienna without having made the personal acquaintance of so
admirable a man; and strangely enough! when I reached my lodgings
I found Beethoven's visiting card upon my table with a cordial invitation to breakfast with him in the morning. And I drank coffee with
him and received his handgrasp and kiss. Yes, mine is the proud privilege of proclaiming publicly, Beethoven honoured me with the
confidence of his heart . . . Beethoven's body has a strength and rudeness which is seldom the blessing of chosen spirits . . . The sturdiness
of his body, however, is in his flesh and bones only; his nervous system
is irritable in the highest degree and even unhealthy. How it has often
pained me to observe that in this organism the harmony of the mind

was so easily put out of tune. He once went through a terrible typhus and from that time dates the decay of his nervous system and probably also his melancholy loss of hearing. Often and long have I spoken with him on this subject; it is a greater misfortune for him than for the world. It is significant that before that illness his hearing was unsurpassably keen and delicate, and that even now he is painfully sensible to discordant sounds; perhaps because he is himself euphony . . . His character is in complete agreement with the glory of his talent. Never in my life have I met a more childlike nature paired with so powerful and defiant a will; if heaven had bestowed nothing upon him but his heart, this alone would have made him one of those in whose presence many would be obliged to stand up and do obeisance. Most intimately does that heart cling to everything good and beautiful by a natural impulse which surpasses all education by far . . . There is nothing in the world, no earthly greatness, nor wealth, nor rank, nor state can bribe it; here I could speak of instances in which I was a witness.'

At this time, before all else Beethoven had to complete his overture for a grand concert before the illustrious attenders of the Congress – the supposed scope and design of which may occupy us a moment.

It is impossible for us to conceive adequately the sensations caused by the downfall of Napoleon at the time of which we are writing. In perusing the history of Bonaparte's campaigns, we become so interested in the 'game' as to forget the attendant ruin, devastation and destruction, the blood, carnage and death, that made all central Europe for twenty long years one vast charnel-house. But only in proportion as the imagination is able to form a vivid picture of the horrors of those years, can it conceive that inexpressible sense of relief, the universal joy and jubilee, which outside of France pervaded all classes of society, from prince to peasant, at the fall of the usurper, conqueror and tyrant. And this not more because of that event, than because of the all-prevailing trust, that men's rights, political and religious – now doubly theirs by nature and by purchase at such infinite cost – would be gladly and gratefully accorded to them. For sovereign and subject had shared danger and suffering and every evil fortune together, and been brought into new and kindlier relations by common calamities; thus the sentiment of loyalty – the affectionate veneration of subject for sovereign – had been developed to a degree wholly unprecedented. The very intoxication of joy and extravagant loyalty then ruled the hour.

It was, as we believe, to give these sentiments musical expression, that Beethoven now took up and wrought out certain themes and motives, noted by him in connection with the memorandum: 'Freude schöner Götterfunken Tochter – Work out the overture!' The poetic idea of the work was not essentially changed – the joy of liberated Europe simply taking the place of the joy of Schiller's poem. But the composer's particular purpose was to produce it as the graceful homage of a loyal subject on the Emperor's name-day. Hence it has become known as the *Namensfeier* Overture (Op. 115).

The theatre had been closed on 29 and 30 September, to prepare for a grand festival production of Spontini's *La Vestale* on Saturday evening, 1 October; but for the evening of the name-day, Tuesday the 4th, *Fidelio* (its fifteenth performance) was selected. It was obviously the intention of Beethoven to do homage to Emperor Franz, by producing his new overture as a prelude on this occasion. What, then, prevented? Seyfried answers this question. He writes: 'For this year's celebration of the name-day of His Majesty, the Emperor, Kotzebue's allegorical festival play, *Die hundertjährigen Eichen* had been ordered. Now, as generally happens, this decision was reached so late that I, as the composer, was allowed only three days, and two more for studying and rehearsing all the choruses, dances, marches, groupings, etc.' This festival play was on the 3rd and rendered the necessary rehearsals of Beethoven's overture impossible. In fact it was not completed until March 1815.

Fidelio was sung for the sixteenth time on the 9th. Tomaschek, one of the auditors on that evening, gave to the public in 1846 notes of the impression made upon him, in a criticism which, by its harshness, forms a curious contrast to Weissenbach's eulogy. Having exhausted that topic, however, Tomaschek then describes his meetings with the composer in an account which has a peculiar interest not only because, though general descriptions of Beethoven's style of conversation are numerous, attempts to report him in detail are very rare. Speaking of von Seyfried:

'B. – My God! There must also be such composers, otherwise what would the vulgar crowd do?

'T. – I am told that there is a young foreign artist here who is said to be an extraordinary pianoforte player.

'B. – Yes, I, too, have heard of him, but have not heard him. My God! let him stay here only a quarter of a year and we shall hear what the Viennese think of his playing. I know how everything new pleases here.

'T. – You have probably never met him?

'B. – I got acquainted with him at the performance of my Battle, on which occasion a number of local composers played some instrument. The big drum fell to the lot of that young man. Ha! ha! ha! – I was not at all satisfied with him; he struck the drum badly and was always behindhand, so that I had to give him a good dressing-down. Ha! Ha! Ha! – That may have angered him. There is nothing in him; he hasn't the courage to hit a blow at the right time.'

Before Tomaschek visited Beethoven again Meyerbeer's opera *Die beiden Kalifen* had been produced at the Kärnthnerthor Theatre. When Tomaschek came to take his farewell, Beethoven was in the midst of preparations for his concert and insisted upon giving him a ticket. Then the conversation goes on:

'T. – Were you at [Meyerbeer's] opera?

'B. – No; it is said to have turned out very badly. I thought of you; you hit it when you said you expected little from his compositions. I talked with the opera singers, and that night after the production of the opera at the wine-house where they generally gather, I said to them frankly: You have distinguished yourselves again! – what piece of folly have you been guilty of again? You ought to be ashamed of yourselves not to know better, nor to be able to judge better, to have made such a noise about this opera! I should like to talk to you about it, but you do not understand me.

'T. – I was at the opera; it began with hallelujah and ended with requiem.

'B. – Ha, ha, ha, ha, ha! It's the same with his playing. I am often asked if I have heard him – I say no; but from the opinions of my acquaintances who are capable of judging such things I could tell that he has agility indeed, but otherwise is a very superficial person.

'T. – I heard that before he went away he played at Herr ——'s and pleased much less.

'B. – Ha, ha, ha, ha! What did I tell you? – I understand that. Let him settle down here for half a year and then let us hear what will be said of his playing. All this signifies nothing. It has always been known that the greatest pianoforte players were also the greatest composers; but how did they play? Not like the pianists of today, who prance up and down the keyboard with passages which they have practised – *putsch, putsch, putsch* – what does that mean? Nothing! When true pianoforte virtuosi played it was always something homogeneous, an entity; if written down it would appear as a well thought-out work. That is pianoforte playing; the other thing is nothing!

'T. – I find it very amusing that ... [Fuss] who himself appears to have a very limited grasp of the instrument, has pronounced him the greatest pianoforte-player.

'B. – He has absolutely no grasp of instrumental music. He is a wretched man; I will tell him to his face. Once he praised an instrumental piece excessively which is fit for the ears of goats and donkeys; I can't help laughing over the uncertainty in his heart. He understands vocal music and should stick to it; outside of that he understands wretchedly little about composition.'

On 30 November, the *Wiener Zeitung* reports: 'At noon yesterday, Hr. Ludwig v. Beethoven gave all music-lovers an ecstatic pleasure. In the RI Redoutensaal he gave performances of his beautiful musical representation of Wellington's Battle at Vittoria, preceded by the symphony which had been composed as a companion-piece. Between the two works an entirely new . . . cantata, *Der glorreiche Augenblick*.' One would like to know what Beethoven said when he read this; for the symphony supposed by the writer to be composed as a companion-piece (*Begleitung*) to the 'Wellington's Victory' was the magnificent Seventh!

'The two Empresses, the King of Prussia' and other royalties were present and 'the great hall was crowded. Seated in the orchestra were to be seen the foremost virtuosi, who were in the habit of showing their respect for him and art by taking part in Beethoven's Akademies.' All the contemporary notices agree as to the enthusiastic reception of the Symphony and the Battle, and that the Cantata, notwithstanding the poverty of the text, was, on the whole, worthy of the composer's reputation and contained some very fine numbers. Vienna at this time was a scene of unparalleled brilliancy. Thus a contemporary observer noted: 'Visited Razumovsky; there innumerable visitors, among others Lord and Lady Castlereagh, Count Münster, Count Westphalen, Mr Coke, the Marquis de Saint-Marsan, Count Castellafu, all the Prussians, etc.' Turn we to Schindler:

'The end of the second period [in Beethoven's life] showed us the composer on a plane of celebrity which may fairly be described as one of the loftiest ever reached by a musician in the course of his artistic strivings. Let us not forget that it was the fruit of twenty years of tireless endeavour. The great moment in the history of the world with which this celebration of his fame was synchronous could not fail to give the incident a brilliancy unparalleled in the history of music . . . Nearly all the rulers of Europe who met at the Vienna Congress placed their seals on our master's certificate of fame . . . He was presented by Prince [Count] Razumovsky to the assembled monarchs, who made known their respect for him in the most flattering terms.

'Wellington's Victory', published in 1816. The conception, design and some of the musical passages of this laudatory piece were the work of Beethoven's friend, the mechanician Johann Nepomuk Mälzel. *Below left*, Beethoven's friend, the musician Carl Czerny. He began teaching Beethoven's nephew Karl, *below right*, in 1816

A view of Teplitz in Böhmen, where Beethoven stayed with his friend Goethe. He wrote to the singer Amalie Sebald, *below left*, from Teplitz. *Below right*, a miniature portrait of an unidentified woman, found in Beethoven's possession after his death. It is thought to be Antonie Brentano, a likely contender for the 'Immortal Beloved'

The Empress of Russia tried in particular to be complimentary to him. The introduction took place in the rooms of Archduke Rudolph, in which he was also greeted by other exalted personages. It would seem as if the Archduke was desirous always to take part in the celebration of his great teacher's triumph by inviting the distinguished foreigners to meet Beethoven.'

CHAPTER 16

The Years 1815 and 1816

Death of Carl van Beethoven – Guardianship of the Nephew

Beethoven might well have adopted Kotzebue's title: 'The Most Remarkable Year of my Life' and written his own history for 1814, in glowing and triumphant language; but now the theme modulates into a soberer key.

In a letter of early December to the Archduke, Beethoven writes: '– then there is the *matter of a new opera* – the *subject* of which I must decide in the next few days –'. The *Sammler* of 13 December explains the allusion to an opera: 'It is with great pleasure that we inform the music-loving public that Herr van Beethoven has contracted to compose an opera. The poem is by Herr Treitschke and bears the title: *Romulus und Remus*.'

Now here was a promising operatic project; but before six weeks had passed came the *Allgemeine Musikalische Zeitung* wherein among the items of Vienna news was a notice that 'Hr. Fuss had composed an opera in three acts entitled *Romulus und Remus* for the Theater-an-der-Wien'! And this was so; but it never came to performance in the theatres of Vienna, perhaps in consequence of measures adopted after the following letter to Treitschke:

'You see this Fuss can attack me in all the newspapers, unless I can produce some written evidence *against him*, or [unless] you – or the director of the theatre undertake to make a settlement with him. On the other hand the business of my contract for the opera is not concluded.

'I beg of you to write me an answer especially as regards Fuss's letter; the matter would be easily decided in a court of *art*, but much as we should like it to be, this is not the case . . .'

The matter was so arranged with Fuss as to leave the text in Beethoven's hands; but how, and on what terms, is not known.

It was about this time (precisely when the painter could not remember when speaking of it in 1860) that Beethoven sat again for his friend

Mähler, who wished to add his portrait to his gallery of musicians.

Notwithstanding that Prince Lobkowitz's financial affairs had been satisfactorily ordered, his return to Vienna was delayed until the spring of 1815, one reason being that (as he states in a letter to Archduke Rudolph, dated Prague, 29 December 1814) an opinion prevailed in the Austrian capital that his presence would be 'unseemly'. In this letter he gives expression to his feelings towards Beethoven as follows:

'Although I have reason to be anything but satisfied with the behaviour of Beethoven towards me, I am nevertheless rejoiced, as a passionate lover of music, that his assuredly great works are beginning to be appreciated. I heard "Fidelio" here and barring the book, I was extraordinarily pleased with the music, except the two finales, which I do not like very much. I think the music extremely effective and worthy of the man who composed it.'

Is this not nobly said?

There is a sketchbook in the Berlin Library, described by Nottebohm, which shows in part what compositions employed Beethoven's thoughts about this time. It contains sketches for marches; an unfinished piano concerto in D; the canon, 'Kurz ist der Schmerz'; the last movement of the Violoncello Sonata, Op. 102 No. 1, the last part of the Overture in C, Op. 115 (evidently at the time of preparing the score); a second version of 'Merkenstein'; the canon, 'Lerne schweigen'; a 'Symphony in B minor'; a 'Sonata pastorale' for pianoforte and violoncello; 'Sonata in C minor'; the second part of 'Meeresstille und glückliche Fahrt'; the last movement of the Violoncello Sonata, Op. 102 No. 2; and various projected fugal movements. The date of these sketches is fixed by a memorandum of Beethoven on the seventh leaf, referring to Smart's production in London of 'Wellington's Victory'. 'In Drury Lane Theatre on 10 February, and repeated by general request on the 13th, *Wiener Zeitung* of 2 March.' This led to enquiry, and Sir George Smart's name, as leader of the Lenten concerts in London, became known to Beethoven, who engaged his friend Häring, who knew Smart intimately, to write the following English letter on his behalf:

'To Sir George Smart,
        Great Portland St., London

'My dear Sir George:
    'I see by the papers that you have brought forth in the theatre Beethoven's battle and that it was received with considerable applause. I

was very happy to find that your partiality to Mr B.'s compositions is not diminished and therefore I take the liberty in his name to thank you for the assistance you afforded in the performance of that uncommon piece of music. He has arranged it for the pianoforte, but having offered the original to his R. H. the Prince Regent, he durst not sell that arrangement to any Editor, until he knew the Prince's pleasure, not only with respect to the dedication, but in general. Having waited so many months without receiving the least acknowledgement, he begged me to apply to you for advice. His idea is to dispose of this arrangement and of several other original compositions to an Editor in London – or perhaps to several united – if they would make a handsome offer – They would besides engage to let him know *the day of the appearance for sale* of the respective pieces, in order that the Editor *here*, may not publish one copy before the day to be mentioned. At the end of this letter follows the list of such compositions, with the price, which the Author expects. I am persuaded, Sir George, you will exert yourself to benefit this great genius. He talks continually of going to England, but I am afraid that his deafness, seemingly increasing, does not allow him the execution of this favourite idea. You are informed without doubt that his opera: Fidelio, has had the most brilliant success here, but the execution is so difficult, that it would not suit any of the English houses.

'I submit here his list with the prices. None of the following pieces has been published, but Nos. 2, 4 and 9 – have been performed with the greatest applause –

1.	Serious Quartetto for 2 violins, tenor and bass	40 guineas
2.	Battle of Vittoria – Score	70 guineas
3.	Battle of Vittoria arranged for the pianoforte	30 guineas
4.	A Grand Symphony – Score	70 guineas
5.	A Grand Symphony arranged for the pianoforte	30 guineas
6.	A Symphony – Key F – Score	40 guineas
7.	A Symphony, arranged for the pianoforte	20 guineas
8.	Grand Trio for the pianoforte, violin and violoncello	40 guineas
9.	Three Overtures for a full Orchestra	each 30 guineas
10.	The Three Arrangements for Pianoforte	each 15 guineas
11.	A Grand Sonata for the pianoforte and violin	25 guineas

The above is the produce of four years labour . . .

'Beethoven happening to call on me just now, he wishes to address a few lines to you which you will find at the bottom of this. My direction is Monsieur Jean de Häring, No. 298 Kohlmarkt, Vienne.

'Poor B. is very anxious to hear something of the English editors, as he hardly can keep those of this city from him, who tease him for his works.'

Häring now writes the following for Beethoven to sign:

'Give me leave to thank you for the trouble you have taken several times, as I understand, in taking my works under your protection, by which I don't doubt all justice has been done. I hope you will not find it indiscreet if I solicit you to answer Mr Häring's letter as soon as possible. I should feel myself highly flattered if you would express your wishes, that I may meet them, in which you will always find me ready, as an acknowledgement for the favours you have heaped upon my children.

Yours gratefully,

Vienna 16 March 1815   Ludwig van Beethoven'

'And now I shall beg, my dear Sir George, not to take this long letter amiss, and to believe that I am always with the greatest regard,

Your most humble and obedient servant,

Vienna 19 March 1815   John Häring'

The works enumerated in this letter, taking them in the same order, are Op. 95, 91, 92, 93, 97, 113, 115, 117 and 96.

In 1810 Tobias Haslinger (of Zell in Upper Austria), who had been one of Kapellmeister Glöggl's singing-boys at Linz and assistant in his music-shop, came to Vienna with the design of establishing himself in business, and there soon became acquainted with the publisher Sigmund Anton Steiner. He detailed to Steiner his purposes and plans and induced him to withdraw his prints and other wares from Grund's bookstore in the Singerstrasse, to open a shop of his own in the narrow passage then existing at the north-east corner of the Graben, and to employ him (Haslinger) as bookkeeper and manager. From this position he soon rose to be partner in the firm, S. A. Steiner and Co.

Beethoven conceived an odd and whimsical liking for the young man. He made his place of business attractive and it became a favourite resort of composers, musicians, singers, writers for the theatre, the public press and the like. In Beethoven's correspondence with the firm the composer was 'Generalissimus', Steiner 'Lieutenant-General', Haslinger 'Adjutant', or rather the diminutive of Adjutant, 'Adjutanter'. Their assistants were 'Subalterns' and the shop, 'Office of the Lieutenant-General'.

In the autumn of 1813 Beethoven had arranged for a loan for his brother Carl through Steiner, and that part of the agreement stated that if the repayment of the loan [1814] reverted to Beethoven, he could have an extension in return for granting Steiner certain privileges with a new unpublished sonata. Thus it would seem that this formed the beginning of their relationship in a business way, since beginning with Op. 90, Steiner published a substantial number of Beethoven's works.

Our first letter to Steiner is dated 1 February 1815, and shows that Carl van Beethoven was somehow involved.

'Most Well-born Lieutenant-General!

'I have received today your letter to my brother and am satisfied with it, but must beg of you to pay *the costs of the pianoforte arrangement in addition*. As I am obliged to pay for *everything* in the world and *more dearly than others*, this would be a hardship for me. Besides I don't believe you can complain about the honorarium of 250 ducats – But neither do I want to complain; therefore arrange for the transcriptions yourself. But all must be looked over by me and if necessary improved. I hope that you are satisfied with this. – In addition to this you might *give my brother the collected pianoforte works of Clementi, Mozart and Haydn*. He needs them for *his little son*. Do this, my dearest Steiner, and be not stone [*Stein*], as stony as your name is – Farewell excellent Lieutenant-General, I am always,

Yours truly, General-in-Chief,

Ludwig van Beethoven'

The correspondence with Steiner and Co. indicates that the task of arranging the orchestral works for the pianoforte was performed by Haslinger and Anton Diabelli, with occasional assistance from Carl Czerny, under Beethoven's superintendence.

Diabelli, born near Salzburg in 1781, had now been for some years one of the more prolific composers of light and pleasing music, and one of the best and most popular teachers in Vienna. He was much employed by Steiner and Co., as copyist and corrector, and in this capacity enjoyed much of Beethoven's confidence, who also heartily liked him as a man. In the composer's comical military staff, he was the 'General Profoss', and in the correspondence his name becomes 'Diabolus' – for Beethoven could never resist the temptation to a play upon words.

About the first of April Beethoven received a package which proved to be an opera text by Rudolph von Berge, sent to him with a letter by his old friend Amenda from Courland. While this letter was under way he received a visit from a friend of Amenda's who, on his departure from Vienna, carried with him a letter for Amenda from Beethoven:

'Vienna, 12 April 1815

'My dear, good Amenda!

'The bearer of this, your friend Count Keyserling, visited me and awoke in me memories of you. You live *happily*, you have *children*, neither of which is true of me. To discuss this would make it too long-winded. More about this another time when you write to me again. – You are one thousand times in my mind with your patriarchal simplicity, and how often I have wanted to have people like you around me. – Unfortunately for my good or that of others, fate denies my wishes in this respect. I can say that I live almost *completely alone* in this greatest city of Germany, since I must live almost in estrangement from all persons whom I love or could love – On what kind of footing is music with you? Have you ever heard any of my great works there? *Great* say I – but compared with the works of the Highest, everything is small – Goodbye, my dear good A, think sometimes of your friend

Ludwig van Beethoven'

'When you write to me, the only address you need is *my name*.'

The opera book sent by Amenda was entitled *Bacchus*, a 'Grand Lyric Opera in Three Acts'. It seems likely that Beethoven gave some thought to the opera and experimented with some themes.

On the approach of warm weather the Erdödys removed for the summer to Jedlersee, never to return to the Schottenbastei; and as Lichnowsky was dead, Beethoven had no inducement to remain in that vicinity and therefore departed from the Mölkerbastei – also never to return. The new lodging was in the third storey of a house then belonging to Count Lamberti, near which he had lived a dozen years before, having the same sunny aspect and the glorious view across the Glacis from the Karlkirche and the Belvedere Gardens, away across the Danube to the blue Carpathian mountains in the distance.

In this house, about the first of June, Häring introduced to Beethoven the very fine English pianist and enthusiastic musician Charles Neate, who after five months' study with Winter in Munich had come to Vienna in the hope of obtaining instruction from the great symphonist. To his application, Beethoven replied in substance: 'I cannot teach, but I will give you an introduction to my master, Förster' (which he did by letter), 'and you may bring your compositions to me for inspection, and I will examine and remark upon them.' In consequence of this permission Neate saw him almost daily. Beethoven spent a part of this summer in Baden, and Neate took a room very near him. There the composer was in the habit of working all the forenoon, dining early

at twelve or one o'clock, and, towards evening, walking with Neate –
sometimes up the Helenenthal, oftener through the fields. Neate,
in the course of his long life – he was nearly eighty in 1861 when he
related these things to the author – had never met a man who so
enjoyed nature; he took intense delight in flowers, in the clouds, in
everything – 'Nature was like food to him, he seemed really to live in
it.' Walking in the fields, he would sit down on any green bank that
offered a good seat, and give his thoughts free course. He was then full
of the idea of going to England, but the death of his brother and the
adoption of his nephew put an end to the project. Neate remembered
the boy as a very beautiful, intelligent lad. Beethoven, at that time, and
as Neate knew him, was charmingly good-tempered to those whom he
liked – but his dislikes were so strong that to avoid speaking to persons
to whom he was not well affected, he would actually increase his pace
in the street to a run. At this time, his dark complexion was very ruddy
and extremely animated. His abundant hair was in an admirable disorder. He was always laughing, when in good humour, which he for
the most part was, as Neate saw him. In their conversations Neate
spoke clearly and found no difficulty in making himself understood if
he spoke into his left ear.

One day Neate spoke to him about the popularity of his Sonatas,
Trios, etc., in England, and added that his Septet was very much
admired: 'That's damned stuff' (or 'a damned thing'), said Beethoven,
'I wish it were burned!' or words to this effect, to Neate's great discomfiture. Another time, walking in the fields near Baden, Neate spoke of
the 'Pastoral' Symphony and of Beethoven's power of painting pictures
in music. Beethoven said: 'I have always a picture in my mind, when I
am composing, and work up to it.'

Neate brought to Beethoven an order from the Philharmonic Society of London – obtained by the exertions of Ries – for three concert
overtures, of which we shall hear more hereafter. It is sufficient to say
here that instead of composing new ones as expected, he gave Neate the
overtures to *König Stephan*, the *Ruinen von Athen* and the so-called
Namensfeier, and received for them seventy-five guineas.

This was the last year of Beethoven's personal intercourse with the
Erdödys, a very interesting memorial of which, namely, a series of
notes and letters, has been preserved and made public by the coolness
and decision of Otto Jahn. Being in Munich in 1852, or about that time,
he learned that this correspondence was in the hands – if our memory
serve – of the widow of Brauchle,* and obtained permission to read it
in the presence of the possessor. Suddenly starting up, he exclaimed (in

* Tutor of the Erdödy children.

effect): 'I will copy this at the hotel', and before the lady, in her amazement and perplexity, could refuse or prevent, he was away, and made
the only copies then known to be in existence. Several of these papers
are only Beethoven's apologies for not coming to Jedlersee 'today' or
'tomorrow' – but all are interesting in the glimpse which they give of
the affectionate intimacy which they show as existing between Beethoven and the family. The following undated letter to Countess
Erdödy is a sample:

'My dear and honoured Countess!
   'You have already given me repeated gifts and that is not right. You
deprive me thereby of the credit of having been able to do the least
thing for you – It is uncertain whether I can come to see you tomorrow,
however much I may want to; but certainly it will be in a few days, but
only in the afternoon. My affairs have become very complicated at present; more of this when I see you – Give my regards to your children,
who are dear to me and press them all to your heart – for the Magister
a slight box on the ears, for the chief bailiff a ceremonious bow. Let the
violoncello apply himself; starting on the left bank of the Danube he is
to play until everyone has crossed from the right bank of the Danube.
In this way the population will soon be increased. What's more I am
confident of the route over the Danube that I have already set; with
courage one may gain any objective if *righteous*. I kiss your hands many
times over. Remember with favour your friend
                                                      Beethoven'
'Do not send a carriage, then; I'd rather *risk* it than a *carriage*! *The
music that I promised is coming from the city.*'

   The Magister was the tutor, Brauchle, and the chief bailiff, or steward, a man named Sperl. The violoncellist was Linke, who passed the
summer at Jedlersee, and whose name probably inspired the drollery
about the left (*linke*) bank of the Danube. The postscript has another
play on words: *Wagen* (carriage) as a verb means 'to risk'.
   A letter to Brauchle is important from a biographical point of view.
It reads:

'I had scarcely returned home before I found my brother making lamentable enquiries about the horses – Please do me the favour to go to
Lang-Enzerdorf about the horses; take horses *at my expense* in Jedlersee, I'll gladly reimburse you – His sickness (my brother's) is
accompanied by a sort of unrest – Let us be of help where we can, I am
obliged to act thus and not otherwise! – I await a speedy fulfilment of my

wishes and a friendly answer on the subject from you – Do not spare expenses; I'll willingly bear them. It is not worth while to let anyone suffer for the sake of a few dirty florins.

Hastily your friend Beethoven'
'Best wishes to the dear Countess.'

Some time around 15 October, Beethoven had returned to Vienna from Mödling where he had been intermittently during the later summer. And now another bitter parting: the Erdödys, accompanied by Brauchle, Sperl and Linke, departed to Croatia.

Turning back to Beethoven's interest in an English market for his compositions, we begin with a letter to an old Bonn acquaintance, Johann Peter Salomon, who since 1781 had been active in London as composer, conductor and violinist:

'Vienna, 1 June 1815

'My respected countryman!

'I have long hoped for the fulfilment of a wish to see *you* in person in London, and to hear you; but the wish has always been frustrated by manifold hindrances – And for this reason, since it is not to be the case, I hope you will not deny my request, which is that you speak with some publisher there, and offer him the following works for me: a Grand Trio for pianoforte, violin and violoncello (80 ducats); Sonata for pianoforte and violin (60 ducats); Grand Symphony in A (one of my most excellent); smaller Symphony in F – a Quartet for 2 violins, viola and violoncello in F minor – a Grand Opera in score, 30 ducats – a Cantata with choruses and solo voices 30 ducats – the score of the Battle of Vittoria on Wellington's victory, 80 ducats and also the pianoforte arrangement (if it has not, as I am assured, already been published) – I have set down the honorarium of a few works which I think fair for England, but leave it to you in the case of these as well as the others, to do what you think best as to my fee.

'I hear, indeed, that *Cramer* is also a publisher but my pupil Ries wrote me recently that he *had publicly expressed himself against my compositions*, I hope for no other reason than *the good of art*, wherefore I have no objection to offer. However if Cramer wants any of these injurious works of art, he is just as agreeable to me as any other publisher. – I only reserve to myself the privilege of also giving the same works to my local publisher so that the works will appear in *London* and *Vienna* only and simultaneously. –

'Perhaps you may be able to point out to me in what manner I may get from the Prince Regent at least the copyist's charges for the *Battle*

Symphony on *Wellington's Victory at the Battle of Vittoria*, which I gave him, for I have long ago abandoned all hope of ever getting anything more, I was not even vouchsafed an answer as to whether I might dedicate the work to the Prince Regent when I publish it. I hear even that the work has already been published in London in pianoforte arrangement, what a fate for a composer!!! While the English and German newspapers are full of reports concerning the success of this work as performed at the Drury Lane Theatre, and the theatre itself has had some takings from it, the composer does not even have a friendly line to show touching it, not even the expense of copying. Besides all this, he has been denied all profit; for if it is true that the pianoforte arrangement is already published, no German publisher will take it. It is probable that the pianoforte arrangement will soon appear in a reprint by a German publisher and I will lose honour and honorarium. Your well-known noble character bids me hope that you will take an interest in the matter and show yourself active in my service. The wretched paper money of our country has already been reduced to one-fifth of its value, so I was treated according to the scale. But after much urging I received the full standard though with a considerable loss. But now we have again reached a point where the currency is worth much less than one-fifth of its value, and I am confronted for the second time with the prospect that my salary will be reduced to *nothing* without recourse of any kind. My only earnings now come from my compositions. If I could count on their sale in England it would be very advantageous to me. Count on my boundless gratitude. I hope for a speedy, a very speedy answer from you.

Your admirer and friend Ludwig van Beethoven'

The letters to Smart, Salomon and Ries were not in vain; through their efforts, especially Salomon's, Mr Robert Birchall, Music Publisher of No. 133 New Bond St, was induced to purchase four of the works enumerated by Häring, viz., the pianoforte arrangements of the 'Wellington's Victory', Op. 91, and Symphony in A, Op. 92; the Trio in B flat, Op. 97, and the Sonata for Pianoforte and Violin, Op. 96, for 'the sum of one hundred and thirty gold Dutch ducats – value in English currency, sixty-five pounds'.

We now reach one of the most important and at the same time most melancholy events in Beethoven's life – an event which exerted the profoundest influence on the rest of his life – the death of his brother Carl Caspar. We introduce it with that brother's last will and testament:

'Certain that all men must die and feeling that I am near this goal, but in the full possession of my understanding, I have freely and voluntarily deemed it good to make these, my last dispositions.

'1. I commend my soul to the mercy of God, but my body to the earth from which it came and desire that it be buried in the simplest manner in accordance with the rites of Christian Catholicism.

'2. Immediately after my death, four holy masses are to be said, to which end set apart 4 florins.

'3. My heirs general are commanded to pay the pious legacies according to law.

'4. As my wife at our marriage brought me and paid over 2,000 fl. in B. bonds, for which I gave no receipt, I acknowledge receipt of these 2,000 fl. in B. bonds and desire that these 2,000 fl. in B. bonds as also the deposit be rectified in accordance with the existing marriage contract.

'5. I appoint my brother Ludwig van Beethoven guardian. Inasmuch as this, my deeply beloved brother has often aided me with true brotherly love in the most magnanimous and noblest manner, I ask, in full confidence and trust in his noble heart, that he shall bestow the love and friendship which he often showed me, upon my son Karl, and do all that is possible to promote the intellectual training and further welfare of my son. I know that he will not deny me this, my request.

'6. Convinced of the uprightness of Hrn. Dr Schönauer, Appellate and Court Advocate, I appoint him Curator for probate, as also for my son Karl with the understanding that he be consulted in all matters concerning the property of my son.

'7. The appointment of heirs being the essential matter in a testament, I appoint my beloved wife Johanna, born Reiss, and my son Karl, heirs general to all my property in equal portions after the deduction of my existing debts and the above bequests.

'8. The wagon, horse, goat, peacocks and the plants growing in vessels in the garden are the property of my wife, since these objects were all purchased with money from the legacy received from her grandfather.

'In witness whereof, I have not only signed this, my last will with my own hand, but to aid in its execution have also called in three witnesses.

'Thus done, Vienna, 14 November 1815.

Carl van Beethoven'

The autograph preserved in the City Archives in Vienna shows that the first sentence in Section 5 read originally: 'Along with my wife I appoint my brother Ludwig van Beethoven co-guardian.' The phrase

'Along with my wife' and the 'co-' were crossed out. The following fragment in Beethoven's writing, preserved at the Beethoven-Haus in Bonn, explains the reason for the change: 'I knew nothing about the fact that a testament had been made; however, I came upon it by chance. If what I had seen was really to be the *original text*, then passages had to be stricken out. This I had my brother bring about since I did not wish to be bound up in this with such a bad woman in a matter of such importance as the education of the child.'

'CODICIL TO MY WILL

'Having learned that my brother, Hr. Ludwig van Beethoven, desires after my death to take wholly to himself my son Karl, and wholly to withdraw him from the supervision and training of his mother, and inasmuch as the best of harmony does not exist between my brother and my wife, I have found it necessary to add to my will that I by no means desire that my son be taken away from his mother, but that he shall always and so long as his future career permits remain with his mother, to which end the guardianship of him is to be exercised by her as well as my brother. Only by unity can the object which I had in view in appointing my brother guardian of my son, be attained, wherefore, for the welfare of my child, I recommend *compliance* to my wife and more *moderation* to my brother.

'God permit them to be harmonious for the sake of my child's welfare. This is the last wish of the dying husband and brother.

'Vienna, 14 November 1815

Carl van Beethoven'

On 20 November 1815, the *Wiener Zeitung* printed the announcement that Hr. Carl van Beethoven, Cashier in the RI Bank and Chief Treasury, aged thirty-eight years, died of consumption on 16 November. And so in his own house died the brother Carl whose last moments came with a suddenness which aroused his brother's suspicions that the end had been hastened by poison! Nor would he be satisfied upon the matter until his friend Bertolini had made a post-mortem examination 'whereby the lack of foundation for the suspicion was proved'.

As above noted, Carl van Beethoven's will was deposited with the proper authorities on the 17th, and 'the RIL Austrian Landrecht [General Court] on 22 November 1815 appointed the widow of the deceased, Johanna van Beethoven, guardian, the brother of the deceased, Ludwig van Beethoven, associate guardian of the minor son Karl'. And so, for the present, we will leave the matter.

There is a striking incongruity between Beethoven's pleas of poverty in his letters to correspondents in England at this period and the facts drawn from official and other authentic sources. Let us tarry a moment on this point.

He was now, at the end of 1815, in the regular receipt of his annuity, 3,400 florins in notes of redemption; in March and April the arrears, 4,987 florins in such notes, had been paid him; the profits of his concerts since 1 January 1814, with presents from crowned heads and others were sufficient in amount to purchase somewhat later the seven bank-shares, which at his death, 'according to the price current on the day of his death', had a value in convention-coin of 7,441 florins; Neate had paid him seventy-five guineas; for the works sold to Steiner and Co. he had 'been wholly compensated'; in March (1816) he received from Mr Birchall sixty-five pounds sterling; and there were payments to him from others, the aggregate of which cannot be determined.

In the following letter to Ries, the reader will observe also a remarkable instance of its writer's occasional great carelessness of statement, where he speaks of his 'entire loss of salary' for several years; for the Archduke's share had throughout been punctually paid; not to mention again the receipt of what had for a time been withheld of the Kinsky and Lobkowitz subscriptions. The omission of these facts in this and other letters, imparted to Ries an utterly false impression; and on their publication in 1838, to the public also. Hence the general belief that Beethoven was now in very straitened circumstances, and that Carl's widow and child had been left in abject poverty. The truth as to them was this: that the property left them produced an annual income, which with the widow's pension amounted at this time to above 1,500 florins. From the day that Beethoven assumed the office of guardian and took possession of the child, he had a valid claim upon the mother for a part of the costs of maintaining him – a claim soon made good by legal process. If he afterwards elected to suffer in his own finances rather than press his sister-in-law, this is no justification of the heedless statements in some of his letters now – a truth to be held in mind. And now the letter to Ferdinand Ries:

'Wednesday, 22 November, Vienna, 1815

'Dear R!

'I hasten to write to you that today I sent the pianoforte arrangement of the Symphony in A by post to the house of Thomas Coutts and Co. As the Court is not here, couriers go not at all or seldom, and this besides is the safest way. The Symphony should appear around March; I will fix the day. It has occupied too much time for me to make the term shorter. More time may be taken with the Trio and the

Sonata for violin, and both will be in London in a few weeks – I urgently beg of you, dear Ries, to make this matter your concern and to see that I get the money. It will cost a great deal before everything gets there and I need it – I had to lose 600 fl. annually of my salary – At the time of the banknotes it was nothing – then came the notes of redemption and because of them I lost the 600 fl. with several years of vexation and entire loss of salary – Now we have reached a point where the notes of redemption are worse than the banknotes were before. I pay 1,000 fl. for house-rent; imagine for yourself the misery caused by paper money – My poor unfortunate brother has just died. He had a bad wife. I may say he had consumption for several years, and to make life easier for him I gave what I may estimate at 10,000 fl. VS. True that is nothing for an Englishman, but very much for a poor German, or rather Austrian. The poor man had changed greatly in the last few years and I can say that I sincerely lament him, and I am now glad that I can say to myself that I neglected nothing in respect of care for him – Tell Hr. B[irchall] to repay Hr. Salomon and you the cost of postage for your letters to me and mine to you. He may deduct it from the sum which he is to pay me. I want those who labour for me to suffer as little as possible –

'Wellington's Victory at the Battle of Vittoria* (this is also the title on the pianoforte arrangement) must have reached Th. Coutts and Co. long ago. Herr Birchall need not pay the honorarium until he has received all the works – Make haste so that I may know the *day* when Hr. B. will publish the pianoforte arrangement – For today, no more except the warmest commendation of my affairs to you; I am always at your service in all respects. – Affectionately Farewell, dear R!

Your friend Beethoven'

On the same day he wrote to Birchall concerning the shipments – promising 'the Trio and the Sonata in a fortnight' and asked that the sum of 130 gold ducats be paid to Thomas Coutts and Co. The Trio and the Sonata, however, were not forwarded until 3 February – a decidedly long 'fortnight'.

In those days £65 was no small sum for the mere right of republication in England of these pianoforte works and arrangements, and Ries richly merited these words of his old master: 'And now my heartiest thanks, dear Ries, for all the kindness you have shown to me, and particularly for the corrections. Heaven bless you and make your progress even greater, in which I take the most heartfelt interest.' Ries, writing on 29 September for Salomon, who had broken his right shoulder in a fall from his horse, informed Beethoven that at that date the three overtures purchased by Neate for the Philharmonic Society had not reached London. Beethoven, in December, repeated this to Neate, who was still in Vienna, adding, in substance, his readiness to make any desired written agreement about these things in England. Salomon's misfortune occurred in August; he lingered only until 25 November. No higher proof of his reputation in England can be given than the fact that the remains of this Bonn violinist rest near those of Handel in Westminster Abbey.

About the first of December, 'a magisterial deputation solemnly delivered' into the hands of Beethoven a certificate conferring upon him the citizenship of Vienna in acknowledgement of his benevolent services on behalf of St Mark's Hospital.

Of noteworthy new friends and acquaintances may be mentioned here Peters, tutor of the young Princes Lobkowitz, and Joseph Karl Bernard, a young littérateur and poet – the reviser of Weissenbach's poem – a great admirer of Beethoven's music, soon to be appointed Editor of the official *Wiener Zeitung*. He is the 'Bernardus non Sanctus' of the Conversation Books; and the two are the friends whom Beethoven set to music in the text:

'Sanct Petrus was ein Fels!
Bernardus war ein Sanct??'*

Another was Anton Halm, 'in whose fresh military nature Master Ludwig took delight', says Schindler.

Young Schindler's acquaintance with Beethoven had now advanced a step: he writes:

'Towards the end of February 1815, I accepted an invitation to become tutor at Brünn. Scarcely arrived there, I was summoned before the police officials. I was questioned as to my relations with some of the tumultuaries of the Vienna University as also certain Italians in whose company I had often been seen in Vienna. As my identification papers, especially the statement concerning the different lectures which I had attended, were not in good order, the latter really faulty – through no fault of mine – I was detained, notwithstanding that a government officer of high standing offered to become my bondsman. After several weeks of correspondence back and forth it was learned that I was not a propagandist and was to be set at liberty. But a whole year of my academic career was lost.

* 'Saint Peter was a rock!
Bernardus was a saint??'

'Again returned to Vienna, I was invited by one of Beethoven's intimate acquaintances to come to an appointed place, as the master
wanted to hear the story of the Brünn happening from my own lips.
During the relation, Beethoven manifested such sympathetic interest in
my disagreeable experiences that I could not refrain from tears. He
invited me to come often to the same place and at the same hour, 4
o'clock in the afternoon, where he was to be found nearly every day –
reading the newspapers. A handgrasp said still more. The place was a
somewhat remote room in the beerhouse "Zum Rosenstock" in the
Ballgässchen. I was there right often and came to know the place as a
quasi-crypt of a number of Josephites* of the first water, to whom our
master presented no discordant note, for his republican creed had
already received a considerable blow through a more intimate acquaintance with the English Constitution. A captain of the Emperor's body-
guard and Herr Pinterics, widely known in musical Vienna, who
played an important role in the life of Franz Schubert, were the closest
companions of the master and, in the exchange of political views, his
seconds actively and passively. From this place I soon began to accompany him on his walks.'

Compared with the years immediately preceding, the year 1816 is
comparatively barren of large incidents in the life of Beethoven; its
recorded history, therefore, is to be found to a still larger extent than
before in the composer's extended correspondence some of which is
likely to make a somewhat melancholy, and to that extent erroneous,
impression. The real record of the writer finds expression in the letters
which he wrote to Zmeskall. These are bubbling over with playfulness
and jocularity, proving that the writer was generally in a cheerful
humour and in this year was anything but the melancholy Beethoven
of the romance writers.

The first letter relates to the oratorio for the Gesellschaft der Musikfreunde:

'Friday, 9 February 1816

'My dear Zmeskall!

'With dismay I observe for the first time today that I have not yet
answered the application of the Gesellschaft der Musikfreunde of the
Austrian capital for an oratorio. The death of my brother two months
ago, the guardianship of my nephew which thereby devolved upon me,
together with many other unpleasant circumstances and occurrences
are the cause of my tardy reply. – Meanwhile the poem by Herr von
Seyfried is already begun and I shall also soon set the same to music.

* Presumably supporters of the Emperor and reactionaries.

That the commission is highly honourable, I scarcely need tell you; that is self-evident, and I shall try to execute it as worthily as my small powers will allow – As regards the *artistic means* to be employed in the performance I shall be considerate, but wish to be allowed to depart *from those already introduced*. I hope that I have made myself understood in this matter. As they insist upon knowing what honorarium I ask, I enquire in turn whether the Society thinks 400 ducats in gold agreeable for such a work. I again beg pardon of the Society for the tardiness of my answer; meanwhile, you, my dear friend have at least reported by word of mouth my readiness to compose the work, before now, which sets my mind measurably at ease – My dear Z. I am with great esteem your friend

Ludwig van Beethoven'

Beethoven's dissatisfaction at the appointment of his sister-in-law as the guardian of her son – now nine years old – was expressed in an appeal to the Upper Austrian Landrecht on 28 November 1815 to transfer the guardianship to himself. That tribunal ordered the petitioner to appear before it in this matter on 13 December. Beethoven then appeared and declared that he could produce 'weighty reasons why the widow should be entirely excluded from the guardianship'. Whereupon, it was ordered that he produce those grounds within three days. Beethoven then signed a petition to the City Magistrates for an official certificate concerning the 'condemnation of his [Karl's] mother, Johanna van Beethoven, on an investigation for infidelity'. The Magistrates answered him that they could not legally grant him a copy of the judgment against her, but would communicate the 'necessary disclosures' to the tribunal. On 20 December, Beethoven wrote a long document to the Landrecht emphasising that the codicil of his brother's will, which divided the guardianship between Johanna and himself, had been forced behind his back upon the dying man for signature by his wife. No further action was taken until 9 January, when a decision was rendered in Beethoven's favour, and he was ordered to appear on the 19th to take the 'vows for the performance of his duties'. He complied, and on the outside of this order is written: 'Today appeared Ludwig van Beethoven as the legally appointed guardian of his nephew Karl and vowed with solemn handgrasp before the assembled council to perform his duties.'

This document also empowered the new guardian to take possession of the boy, who of course was still with his mother. But what to do with him?

A certain Cajetan Giannatasio del Rio was at that time proprietor and manager of a private school in the city for boys, which enjoyed a high and deserved reputation. His family consisted of his wife and two highly accomplished daughters, Fanny and Anna (Nanni), young women of fine talents, of much musical taste and culture, and – especially the elder – enthusiasts for Beethoven's music. The composer, accompanied by his friend Karl Bernard and the boy, visited and inspected the school, and was so much pleased with it and the family that he determined to place him there as pupil and boarder. On 1 February, he wrote to Giannatasio:

'With sincere pleasure I inform you that at last on tomorrow I shall bring to you the precious pledge that has been entrusted to me. – Moreover I beg of you again under no circumstances to permit the mother to exercise any influence. How or when she may see him, all this I will talk over with you tomorrow – You may impress this also on your servants, for *mine* in another matter was *bribed by her*! – More about this will follow by word of mouth, though silence would be preferable to me – But for the sake of your future citizen of the world, this melancholy communication is necessary . . .'

'[In Karl's hand.] I am very glad to come to you, and am your Karl van Beethoven.'

The next day, 2 February, the boy was taken from his mother. The intolerable annoyance caused by her appearing in person daily to take him from the school drew from Giannatasio on the 11th a written application to the guardian for 'a formal authority in a few lines for refusing without further ado to permit her to fetch her son'. In his reply, Beethoven writes: 'as regards the mother I request that on the plea that he is busy you do not admit her to him at all.' The same day, taking Bernard with him, he went to the school, and there meeting Giannatasio, the three prepared a formal petition to the Landrecht, praying that tribunal to grant the guardian plenary authority to exclude the widow and her agents from all or any direct communication with the boy. This was signed by Beethoven and immediately presented. On the 20th, the Landrecht granted this petition; but its decree contained this proviso: that the mother might still visit her son 'in his leisure hours, without disturbing the course of his education or the domestic arrangements, in the company of a person to be appointed by the guardian or the director of the educational institution'. Armed with this authority, Giannatasio on 8 March informed in writing 'Madame Jeannette de Beethoven, Vorstadt, Alsergasse, No. 121', that she has in future 'to apply solely to the uncle as to whether, how and when' she can see her son. And thus this wretched business again for the present rested.

Neate was now gone to London. The document which Beethoven had promised to give him ran as follows:

'Hr. Neate has received from me in the month of July, 1816 [*sic*] three overtures in the name of the Philharmonic Society in London and has paid me an honorarium of 75 guineas for the same in consideration of which I bind myself to permit them *nowhere else* to be published in parts (or in score) although I have the right to perform *the same* wherever I please as well as to publish them in pianoforte arrangement, though not before Hr. Neate shall have written to me that they have been performed in London: – Moreover, Hr. Neate has assured me that he will kindly take it upon himself that the Philharmonic Society after a period of one or two years will permit me to engrave and publish these three overtures *in score and in parts*, inasmuch as I can do this only with their consent – with which I present my compliments to the PS.
Vienna, 5 February 1816   Ludwig van Beethoven'

Works also entrusted to him, as remembered by Mr Neate forty-five years afterwards, were: (1) a copy of the Violin Concerto, Op. 61, with a transcription of the solo for Pianoforte on the same pages, which Beethoven said he himself had arranged and was effective; (2) the two Sonatas for Pianoforte and Violoncello, Op. 102, with a dedication to Neate; (3) the Seventh Symphony in score; (4) *Fidelio* in score; and (5) the String Quartet in F minor, Op. 95 – all in manuscript. On 20 January, Beethoven wrote the following letter to Ries in London:

'Vienna, 20 January 1816
'My dear Riess I see from your letter of 18 January that you have safely received both works – As no couriers are going, the *post* is probably the safest, but it costs a great deal. I will send you the bill for what I have paid here for *copying* and *postage* soon. It is very little for an Englishman but much more for a *poor Austrian musician*! See that Hr. B[irchall] recompenses me for this, since *for England* he has the compositions very cheaply – Neate, who has been about to go every moment, but always remains, will bring the overtures with him. Over and over again I have explained to him the injunctions touching them given by you and our deceased S[alomon] . . .
                    As always, your sincere friend,
                              Ludwig van Beethoven'

It is necessary here to state certain facts, both to explain the failure of Mr Neate to sell any of these works to the London publishers, and to render some of the letters to come intelligible.

The Philharmonic Society was an association of the first musicians of London and its vicinity, and no city on earth could at that time present such an array of great names. Imagine the disappointment of these men, fresh from the performance of the C minor Symphony, when they played through the overtures to *Die Ruinen von Athen* and *König Stephan*, which, however interesting to a Hungarian audience as introductions to a patriotic prologue and epilogue in the theatre, possess none of those great qualities expected from Beethoven and demanded in a concert overture! Nor was the *Namensfeier* thought worthy of its author. And when it became known that none of the three – the *Namensfeier* possibly excepted – was new, and that not one of them had been composed to meet the Society's order, is it surprising that this act of Beethoven's was deemed unworthy of him, disrespectful, nay, an insult to the Society, and resented accordingly?

Another matter was personal with Mr Birchall. That publisher, having at last (early in February) received the last of the works published by him, immediately deposited with Coutts and Co. the sum agreed upon, to the composer's credit, and forwarded the following 'Declaration' to Vienna for signature, leaving the day of the month blank – as it still remains – to be inserted when signed:

'Received . . . March 1816, of Mr Robert Birchall – Music Seller, 133 New Bond Street, London – the sum of One Hundred and Thirty Gold Dutch Ducats, value in English Currency Sixty-five Pounds, for all my Copyright and Interest, present and future, vested or contingent, or otherwise within the United Kingdom of Great Britain and Ireland in the four following Compositions or Pieces of Music composed or arranged by me, viz.:

'1. A Grand Battle Sinfonia, descriptive of the Battle and Victory at Vittoria, adapted for the Pianoforte and dedicated to his Royal Highness, the Prince Regent – 40 Ducats.

'2. A Grand Symphony in the Key of A, adapted to the Pianoforte and dedicated to . . .

'3. A Grand Trio for the Pianoforte, Violin and Violoncello in the Key of B flat.

'4. A Sonata for the Pianoforte with an Accompaniment for the Violin, dedicated to . . .

'And, in consideration of such payment I hereby for myself, my Executors and Administrators promise and engage to execute a proper

Assignment thereof to him, his Executors and Administrators or Assignees at his or their Request and Costs, as he or they shall direct.'

Instead of *this* document, so indispensable for his security, the publisher received a new demand from Beethoven! – one for five pounds additional, as per memorandum:

> 'Copying 1.10.0
> Postage to Amsterdam . . . 1.0.0
> Trio. 2.10.0
> ———————
> £5.0.0'

On 28 February and 3 April he reiterated his demand for the additional ten ducats, equivalent to five pounds. Then he wrote the following letter in May, portions of which were suppressed when printed by Ries:

'Vienna, 8 May 1816

'My dear Ries:

'My answer to your letter comes somewhat tardily; but I was ill, had much to do and it was impossible for me to answer you sooner. Now only the most necessary things – not a heller of the 10 ducats in gold has as yet arrived, and I am already beginning to believe, that the Englishmen, too, are only magnanimous in foreign lands; so also with the *Prince Regent* from whom I have not even received the copyists' fees for *my Battle which was sent* to him, nor even written or oral thanks . . . Tell B this – and see that you yourself get the draft for the 10 ducats, otherwise it will be like the first time – What you *tell me about Neate's undertaking would be desirable for me*. I need it; my salary amounts to 3,400 florins in paper, I pay 1,100 house-rent, and my servant and his wife nearly 900 fl., you can figure out what remains. Moreover, I have got to care wholly for my little nephew. Till now he has been in an Institute; this costs me close to 1,100 fl. and thus is hard for me, so I must establish myself in decent housekeeping and have him live with me – How much one must earn in order to live here! And yet there is never an end for – for – for – you know it already – As to the dedications, I will wait for another time – A few orders as well as an Akademie would also be welcome from the Philharmonic Society – Besides my dear pupil Ries ought to sit down and dedicate *something good* to me to which the *master would also respond and repay in kind* – *How shall I send you my portrait?* I hope to have news from *Neate too; urge him on a bit*. Be assured of my sincere interest in your future. *Urge Neate to get to work and to write – My best regards to your wife*. Unfortunately I have none. I found *only one*, whom I shall doubtless *never possess; but I am not a woman-hater* on that account.

Your true friend, Beethoven'

The £5 had been deposited with Coutts and Co. on 15 March, but month after month passed and still the 'Declaration' with Beethoven's signature did not arrive. Of the justice, propriety, delicacy of this new demand, nothing need be said; its historical importance is due entirely to the very unfavourable effect which it and the correspondence relating to it produced upon the minds of the London publishers. Mr Neate was in some degree prepared for the coldness with which those gentlemen received his proposals on Beethoven's behalf, by a letter written to him after the trial of the overtures. One sentence in it he remembered word for word: 'For God's sake, don't buy anything of Beethoven!' But he was not prepared for the utter refusal in all quarters to listen to him. He besought Mr Birchall to purchase the overtures. The reply was: 'I would not print them, if you would give me them gratis.'

As to the score of the Symphony in A (the Seventh), it was folly to expect that the Philharmonic Society would pay a large sum for the manuscript of a work already (6 March) advertised in Vienna for subscription at the price of twenty-five florins.

It is another instance of Beethoven's unlucky tendency to suspect the conduct and motives of others that seeing in a newspaper a notice of the production of one of his Symphonies by the Philharmonic Society, he at once assumed that it was the Seventh and that Neate had given the use of his manuscript!

Under such circumstances Neate *could* do nothing for Beethoven; nor could he well disclose the true causes of his failure; so the composer characteristically assumed that he *would* do nothing, and, as will be seen, gave vent to his wrath in terms equally bitter and unjust.

On 15 May, a letter of condolence to Countess Erdödy was called out by the sudden death of her son in Padua. The lad burst one morning into his sister's room and, complaining of his head, with a cry of anguish sank dead at her feet. Beethoven laboured sadly in his effort to find words of comfort for the stricken mother. On 13 May, before he heard the news, he had already written to the Countess, so he sent the two letters together. The later letter follows:

'Vienna, 15 May 1816

'Dear honoured friend!

'This letter was already written when today I met Linke and heard of your lamentable fate, the sudden loss of your dear son – How is comfort to be given? Nothing is more painful than the quick unforeseen departure of those who are near us; thus likewise I cannot forget the death of my poor brother. Nothing except – that one can imagine that those who depart quickly suffer less – but I have the deepest sympathy for your irretrievable loss. – Perhaps I have not written to you yet that I have not been well for a long time, to this reason for my long silence is to be added the care for my Karl whom I had often contemplated as a companion to your dear son. – I am seized with grief on your account and on my own since I loved your son. – May heaven watch over you, whose state of health may have failed still further, and not increase your suffering which is already so great. Reflect that your son might have been forced to go into battle and might then, like millions of others, have met his death. Besides you are still *mother* to two dear hopeful children. – I hope soon to have word from you. I weep here with you. Do not, however, listen to all the gossip concerning why I have not written you, nor to Linke, who is certainly devoted to you but *very much of a gossip* – and I feel that no go-between is needed between you dear Countess and myself

in haste and respectfully your friend
Beethoven'

A few days later the following letter to Neate was written in English, probably by Häring, and only signed by Beethoven:

'Vienna, 18 May 1816

'My dear Neate!

'By a letter of Mr Ries, I am acquainted with your happy arrival at London. I am very well pleased with it, and still better I should be pleased if I had learned it by yourself.

'Concerning our business, I know well enough that for the performance of the greater works, as: the Symphony, the Cantata, the Chorus, and the Opera, you want the help of the Philharmonic Society, and I hope your endeavour to my advantage will be successful.

'Mr Ries gave me notice of your intention to give a concert to my benefit. For this triumph of my art at London I would be indebted to you alone; but an influence still wholesomer on my almost indigent life would be to have the profit proceeding from this enterprise. You know that in some regard I am now father to the lovely lad you saw with me; hardly I can live alone three months upon my annual salary of 3,400 florins in paper, and now the additional burden of maintaining a poor orphan – you conceive how welcome lawful means to improve my circumstances must be to me. As for the Quatuor in F minor, you may sell it without delay to a publisher, and signify me the day of its publication as I should wish it to appear here and abroad on the very day. The same you be pleased to do with the two Sonatas, Op. 102, for pianoforte and violoncello; yet with the latter it needs no haste.

'I leave entirely to your judgement to fix terms for both works, to wit, the Quatuor and the Sonatas. The more the better.

'Be so kind to write to me immediately for two reasons; 1st, that I may not be obliged to shrink up my shoulders when they ask me if I got letters from you; and 2ndly, that I may know how you do, and if I am in favour with you. Answer me in English if you have to give me happy news (for example, those of giving a concert to my benefit), in French if they are bad ones.

'Perhaps you find some lover of music to whom the Trio and the Sonata with the violin, Mr Ries had sold to Mr Birchall, or the Symphony arranged for the harpsichord might be dedicated, and from whom there might be expected a present. In expectation of your speedy answer, my dear friend and countryman,

'I am wholly yours,

Ludwig van Beethoven'

Here is the place for some excerpts from the diary of Dr Karl von Bursy, a Courlander, who at this time visited Beethoven with a letter of introduction from his friend Amenda.

'Vienna, 1 June
'. . . Beethoven strongly resembled Amenda, especially when he laughed. He enquired most of all about him and expressed feelings of the warmest friendship for him. "He is a very fine man," he said. "I have the misfortune of having all my friends far away from me and I remain alone in hateful Vienna." He asked me to speak loudly to him because now he was again having particular difficulty in hearing; for that reason he wanted to be in Baden and the country for the summer. He has not been really well for a long time and has composed nothing new. I asked him about Berge's libretto [Bacchus] and he said it was very good and with a few changes would probably be suitable for composition. Until now his illness has not permitted this kind of labour and he wishes to write to Amenda himself about it. I shouted in his ear that for such work one really has to have leisure and work full time. "No," he said. "Nothing I create is done so continuously without interruption. I always work at several things at a time, first I take up this and then that." He misunderstood me very often and, when I spoke, had to pay the greatest attention in order to understand me. Naturally this troubled and embarrassed me very much. He also felt the pressure

and spoke up himself that much more and indeed very loudly. He told
me a great deal about Vienna and his life here. Venom and rancour
raged within him. He defies everything and is dissatisfied with everything and blasphemes against Austria and especially against Vienna.
He speaks fast and with great animation. Often he beat his fist upon
the piano so violently that it made a clear echo in the room. He is not
discreet for he quickly confided in me concerning his personal relations and recounted many things about himself and his friends . . . He
had complaints on several counts of the present times. Art no longer
stands so high above the ordinary, is no longer so respected and above
all is no longer valued in terms of recompense. Beethoven also complained over the bad times in pecuniary matters . . . "Why do you
remain in Vienna when every foreign ruler would have to make a
place for you near his throne?" "Conditions hold me here," he said,
"but here things are shabby and niggardly. It could not be worse, from
top to bottom everyone is a scoundrel. There is nobody one can trust.
What is not down in black and white is not observed by any man, not
even by the one with whom you have made an agreement. Moreover
one has nothing in Austria, since everything is worthless, that is,
paper." At the time of the Congress Beethoven composed an occasion
cantata. The text, he said, was cut and trimmed like a French garden.
And yet it never got a definite performance. After many cabals he
gave a concert in the Redouten-Saal and received an entrance fee of 10
ducats from the King of Prussia. Very shabby! Only the Emperor of
Russia paid respectably for his ticket with the sum of 200 ducats. The
fact that the general manager of the Imperial Theatre, Count Pálfi,
received a little rebuke for this pleased him very much. He particularly dislikes this man . . . He is delighted that his *Fidelio* is given in
Berlin so often and with such success. He is saddened by the loss of
Milder-Hauptmann. "Her place is irrecoverable for us," he said, "the
way she sings cannot be matched by any of the local singers. We could
not pay her, therefore she decided to go to Berlin. Music here is very
much on the decline. The emperor does nothing for art and the
general public puts up with anything . . ." '

Beethoven had now made up his mind to take his nephew from
Giannatasio's care and make a home for him with himself. The
removal was to be made at the end of the approaching quarter, and
meanwhile Karl was to remain where he was so that he might have
proper care during his recovery from the effects of an operation for
hernia. Beethoven notified his purpose to Giannatasio on 28 July 1816,
and admonished his friend that in the interim the old strictness was to

be observed touching the mother's visits. The following passage is from the letter:

'As regards the Queen of Night, matters will remain as they have been, and even if the operation should be performed at your place, as he will be ill for a few days and consequently more susceptible and irritable, she is all the less to be admitted to him since all impressions might easily be renewed in K. which we cannot permit. How little we can hope for improvement in her case is shown by the enclosed insipid scrawl which I send you only that you may see how right I am in pursuing the plan against her that was adopted; but this time I did not answer her like a Sarastro but like a sultan.'

The surgical operation on the boy was performed by Dr Smetana; and under the affectionate care which he received at the hands of the Giannatasios he quickly recovered and in September visited his uncle at Baden, going thither with the Giannatasios. Fräulein Fanny tells the story of the visit simply and gracefully:

'While his nephew was still with us, Beethoven once invited us to visit him at Baden where he was spending the summer months, my father and we two daughters with Karl. Although our host had been informed of our coming we soon noticed that no arrangement had been made for our lodging. B. went with us in the evening to a tavern where we were surprised to note that he argued with the waiter about every roll, but this was because owing to his bad hearing he had frequently been cheated by serving-people. For even then one had to be very close to his ear to make him understand and I recall that I was often greatly embarrassed when I had to pierce through the greyish hairs which concealed his ear. He himself often said: "I must have my hair cut!" Looking at him cursorily one thought that his hair was coarse and bristly, but it was very fine and when he put his hand through it, it remained standing in all directions which often looked comical . . .

'When we came to his lodgings in the afternoon a walk was proposed; but our host would not go along, excusing himself saying he had a great deal to do; but he promised to follow and join us, and did so. But when we came back in the evening there was not a sign of accommodations for our lodging to be seen. B. muttered excuses and accusations against the persons who had been charged with the arrangements and helped us to settle ourselves; O how interesting it was! to move a light sofa with his help. A rather large room in which his pianoforte stood, was cleaned for us girls to use as a bedroom. But sleep remained long absent from us in this musical sanctuary. Yes, and I must confess to my shame that our curiosity and desire to know things led us to examine a large round table which stood in the room. A notebook in particular received our attention. But there was such a confusion of domestic matters, and much of it which to us was illegible that we were amazed; but, behold, one passage I still remember – there it stood: "My heart runs over at the sight of lovely nature – although she is not here!" – that gave us a great deal to think about. In the morning a very prosaic noise roused us out of our poetical mood! B. also appeared soon with a scratched face, and complained that he had a quarrel with his servant who was leaving, "Look," he said, "how he has maltreated me!" He complained also that these persons, although they knew that he could not hear, did nothing to make themselves understood. We then took a walk through the beautiful Helenenthal, we girls ahead, then B. and our father. What follows we were able to overhear with strained ears:

'My father thought that B. could rescue himself from his unfortunate domestic conditions only by marriage, did he know anybody, etc. Now our long foreboding was confirmed: he was unhappy in love! Five years ago he had made the acquaintance of a person, a union with whom he would have considered the greatest happiness of his life. It was not to be thought of, almost an impossibility, a chimera – "nevertheless it is now as on the first day." This harmony, he added, he had not yet discovered! It had never reached a confession, but he could not get it out of his mind! . . . All this happened in September of the year 1816.'

Beethoven's project now was, upon returning to the city, to abandon his tavern life and so arrange his domestic affairs as to have his nephew with him and attend school or study with private tutors – perhaps both. As usual Zmeskall was charged with looking after servants, discovering their qualifications, etc. After Karl should come there would be need of a housekeeper, but meanwhile Beethoven suggested to Zmeskall that he find for him a servant who should be 'good, of decent deportment, well recommended, married and not murderous so that my life may be safe'. He returned to Vienna near the end of September.

Peter Joseph Simrock of Bonn, then twenty-four years of age, was now in Vienna. He was often with Beethoven, in Baden, in his lodging in the Sailerstätte and in the inn 'Zur goldenen Birn', where Beethoven often dined after the removal of Giannatasio to that quarter. Mr Simrock told the writer that he had no difficulty in making Beethoven understand him if he spoke into his left ear; but anything private or confidential must be communicated in writing. On one occasion the composer handed him paper and pencil, remarking that his servant was an eavesdropper, etc. A few days afterwards when Simrock called again, 'Now,' said Beethoven, 'we can talk, for I have given my servant five florins, a kick in the rear and sent him to the devil.' He ate extravagantly at the tavern because he ordered haphazard and sent away what was not to his taste.

Another of Beethoven's visitors just now was Alexander Kyd. This gentleman, since 25 July 1810 a Major-General in the East India Company's Engineer Corps, paid the usual tribute to the climate, and, broken down in health, came to Vienna to put himself under the treatment of Malfatti. He thus made the acquaintance of Dr Bertolini, who gave to Jahn and the present writer the following details:

Kyd was a great lover of music, and, after his long residence in India, enjoyed to the utmost his present opportunities of hearing it. Bertolini took him to Czerny, who during several visits played to him all the pianoforte works of Beethoven then in print. The General was ravished with these compositions and besought Bertolini to introduce him to their author. This took place on 28 September 'in the house next to the Colorado Palace', said Bertolini. They found him shaving and looking shockingly, his ruddy face browned by the Baden sun variegated by razor cuts, bits of paper, and soap. As Kyd seated himself crash! went the chair. In the course of the interview, the General, showing the common belief of Beethoven's poverty, proposed to him through the Doctor, to compose a symphony for which he would pay him 200 ducats (£100), and secure its performance by the London Philharmonic Society, not doubting that the profits of the work to the composer would thus amount to £1,000. He offered also to take him himself to London. To Beethoven's leaving Vienna just now there really seems to have been no serious impediment, other than his nephew; and the boy was certainly in the best of hands so long as he remained with Giannatasio. However, he did not accept the proposition, nor even the order for the Symphony, because Kyd desired to have it rather like the earlier, than the later ones – that is, somewhat shorter, simpler, and more easy of comprehension than these last. The conclusion of the story as told in the Fischoff manuscript corresponds entirely with the Doctor's relation:

'When Bertolini related all this to his friend with sympathetic joy the latter received it in an entirely different spirit. He declared that he would receive dictation from no one; he needed no money, despised it and would not submit himself to the whim of another man for half the world, still less compose anything which was not according to his liking, to his individuality. From that time he was also cool towards Bertolini and remained so.'

When he afterwards quarrelled with and insulted Malfatti he broke entirely with Bertolini. Simrock writes in an autograph notice for this work:

'. . . As an artist he felt himself deeply offended at such an offer and indignantly refused it . . . In his excitement he expressed himself very angrily and with deep displeasure towards a nation which by such an offer had manifested so low an opinion of an artist and art, which he looked upon as a great insult. When we were passing Haslinger's publishing house in the Graben in the afternoon he stopped suddenly and pointing to a large, powerfully built man who had just entered, cried out: "There's the man whom I threw downstairs yesterday!"'

'Whom I threw downstairs' was, of course, meant metaphorically. It is pretty evident that Beethoven in some degree misunderstood General Kyd's proposition and that this ebullition of spleen was rather directed against Neate and the Philharmonic Society than the General. It is greatly to be regretted that this artistic pride had so little restraining effect upon his correspondence when pecuniary matters form the topic – which remark brings us again to Mr Birchall. Beethoven had at last discovered the £5 to his credit in the bank of Fries and Co., and signed a receipt for it on 3 August – too late to prevent the following letter being sent to him:

'14 August 1815

'Sir:
    'Mr Birchall received yours of the 22nd of last month and was surprised to hear you have not yet received the additional £5.0.0 to defray your expenses of copying, etc. . . . .
    'If Mr Beethoven will call on Messrs Fries and Co., no doubt it will be immediately paid, as there is a balance in their favour at Messrs Coutts and Co., of £5.0.0, which was not included in their last Bill on London.
    'Mr Birchall is sorry you have not received it so soon as you ought, but he hopes you will be convinced the fault does not lay [sic] with him, as the money was paid the day after Mr Ries spoke about it.
    'Mr Birchall wished particularly to have the Declaration returned to him as soon as possible.'

Beethoven's reply in English bears all the marks of Häring's pen, being only signed by himself:

'Vienna, 1 October 1816

'My dear Sir:

'I have duly received the £5, and thought previously you would not increase the number of Englishmen neglecting their word and honour as I had the misfortune of meeting with two of this sort . . .

'Concerning the expenses of copying and posting, it is not possible to fix them beforehand, they are at any rate not considerable and you'll please to consider that you have to deal with a man of honour, who will not charge one 6*d*. [sixpence] more than he is charged for himself. Messrs Fries and Co. will account with Messrs Coutts and Co. . . .

'My address or direction is:

Monsieur Louis van Beethoven,
No. 1055 and 1056 Sailerstätte, 3te Stock,
Vienna.'

Beethoven not only complained of Neate to Ries, but now wrote to Smart of him in such bitter terms that that gentleman suppressed the letter entirely except to show it to Neate himself, whose grief and astonishment at the injustice done him are but partly expressed in this next letter:

'London, 29 October 1816

'My dear Beethoven:

'Nothing has ever given me more pain than your letter to Sir George Smart. I confess that I deserve your censure, that I am greatly in fault; but must say also that I think you have judged too hastily and too harshly of my conduct. The letter I sent you some time since, was written at a moment when I was in *such* a state of mind and spirits that I am sure, had you seen me or known my sufferings, you would have excused every unsatisfactory passage in it. Thank God! it is now all over, and I was just on the point of writing to you, when Sir George called with your letter. I do not know how to begin to answer it; I have never been called upon to justify myself, because it is the first time that I ever stood accused of dishonour; and what makes it the more painful is "that I stand accused by the man who, of all the world, I most admire and esteem, and one also whom I have never ceased to think of, and wish for his welfare, since I made his acquaintance". But as the appearance of my conduct has been so unfavourable in your eyes, I must tell you again of the situation I was in previous to my marriage.

'Until the question upon which my whole happiness depended was decided, whether I should be permitted by the family to marry my wife, which I did on 2 October, I was not able to appear as an artist. Now I remain a musician. Also I did not want someone else to negotiate for you from the fear that it would not happen as it should. I am notified that I have not kept my word with you, which is untrue; but I have neglected everyone, everything including myself.

'I remain in my profession, and with no abatement of my love of Beethoven! During this period I could not myself do anything publicly, consequently all your music remained in my drawer unseen and unheard. I, however, did make a very considerable attempt with the Philharmonic to acquire for you what I thought you fully entitled to. I offered all your music to them upon condition that they made you a very handsome present; this they said they could not afford, but proposed to see and hear your music, and then offer a price for it; I objected and replied "that I should be ashamed that your music should be put up by auction and bid for! – that your name and reputation were too dear to me"; and I quitted the meeting with a determination to give a concert and take all the trouble myself, rather than that your feelings should be wounded by the chance of their disapproval of your works. I was the more apprehensive of this, from the unfortunate circumstances of your Overtures not being well received; they said they had no more to hope for, from your other works. I was not a Director last season, but I am for the next, and then I shall have a voice which I shall take care to exert. I have offered your Sonatas to several publishers, but they thought them too difficult, and said they would not be saleable, and consequently made offers such as I could not accept, but when I shall have played them to a few professors, their reputation will naturally be increased by their merits, and I hope to have better offers. The Symphony you read of in the "Morning Chronicle" I believe to be the one in C minor; it certainly was not the one in A, for it has not been played at a concert. I shall insist upon its being played next season, and most probably the first night. I am exceedingly glad that you have chosen Sir George Smart to make your complaints of me to, as he is a man of honour, and very much your friend; had it been anyone else, your complaint might have been listened to, and I injured all the rest of my life. But I trust I am too respectable to be thought unfavourably of by those who know me. I am, however, quite willing to give up every sheet I have of yours, if you again desire it. Sir George will write by the next post, and will confirm this. I am sorry you say that I did not even *acknowledge* my obligation to you, because I talked of nothing else at Vienna, as everyone there who knows me can testify. I even offered my purse, which you generously always declined. Pray, my dear Friend, believe me to remain,

Ever yours, most sincerely,

C. Neate'

Zmeskall, whose patience and forbearance were inexhaustible, had again provided his friend with servants – a man and his wife – and something was done towards making the lodging in the Sailerstätte ready to receive the nephew at the end of the quarter. But this was not yet to be. The circumstances explain the following little letter to Zmeskall of date 3 November 1816:

'Dear Z. Your non-recommendation of the servants engaged by me I can also not recommend – I beg of you at once to hand over to me through Hr. Schlemmer the papers, testimonials, etc., which you have from them. – I have reason to suspect them of a theft. – I have been continually ill since the 14th of last month and must keep to my bed and room. – All projects concerning my nephew have foundered because of these miserable persons. –

As ever yours,

L. v. Beethoven'

Further information is provided by the following letter to Giannatasio:

'Valued friend!

'My household greatly resembles a shipwreck, or threatens to. In brief I have been swindled in reference to these people by one who affects to be a connoisseur. Moreover, my recovery seems to be in no hurry. Under such circumstances, to engage a tutor whose inner and outer life is unknown to me and to leave the education of my Karl to chance I can never do, great as are the sacrifices which in many respects I shall again be called upon to make. I therefore beg you, respected G, to keep my Karl again for this quarter. I shall accept your suggestion regarding his cultivation of music to this extent, that two or even three times a week Karl shall leave you at six o'clock and stay with me until the next morning when he shall return to you again by about 8 o'clock. Every day would be too taxing for K. and, since it would always have to be at the same hour, too wearisome and restricting for me – We shall discuss more in detail during this quarter what would be most practicable for K. and considerate also of me, for, in view of the fact that unfortunately my circumstances are continually getting worse, I must refer to this. If your residence in the garden had been better adapted to my health, everything could have been arranged easily – As regards my indebtedness to you for the last quarter I must beg of you to bring the matter directly to me, as the bearer of this has been blessed by God with a certain amount of stupidity which one might not begrudge him if others were not affected by it – Regarding the other expenses for Karl during his illness or matters connected with it, I beg of you to have patience for a few days as I have large expenditures just now on all sides –

'I should like also to know how matters stand between me and Smetana in view of his successfully accomplished operation. So far as his compensation is concerned if I were rich or not in the condition of all (except the Austrian usurers) whom fate has bound to this country, I would not ask at all. I mean only an approximate estimate – Farewell, I embrace you with all my heart, and will always look upon you as the friend of myself and of my Karl.

Respectfully, Your L. v. Beethoven'

In marked contrast to the sombre tone of his letters to England is the playful character of almost all of the numerous notes to Steiner during the year. Here is a sample:

'Here is a small piece of field equipment which I am sending over – (as a present) – so that it may march right into your arsenal. As for Herr Diabolus, hold on to him for what abilities he has left; whatever has to be changed can be done as it was in the past with the Symphony in F – Concerning a new sonata for pianoforte, present me with 60 well-armed men and the same could be published at once. I also have some variations in mind which would suit a special holiday, and they also could be made to appear with the help of only 40 well-armed men – Now as regards the state debt of 1,300 fl., payment of this cannot yet be considered, moreover the 1,300 fl. would look best if they were transformed into the following figure 0,000 –

'I am astonishingly respectful of the Lt. Gl.

L. v. Beethoven'

First, it is worth noting the size of Beethoven's debt to Steiner during this period, which was not to be paid off for some years. Second, the humorous reference to a number of 'well-armed men' is Beethoven's military paraphrase for the price in ducats.

The 'small piece of field equipment' was the song 'Der Mann von

Wort' on a poem by Kleinschmid. Steiner obliged and the piece did 'march into his arsenal' and appeared in print in November. The new sonata was Op. 101, the first of the great set of late pianoforte sonatas for which, as we shall see, Beethoven was to ponder as to the best word for hammer-action when printing the title.

The following four letters tell of incidents which make up the history of the latter part of the year 1816. The first is to Zmeskall, dated 16 December:

'Here dear Z. you will receive my friendly dedication* which I hope will be a precious souvenir of our long-continued friendship and be accepted as a proof of my respect and not as the end of a long-spun thread (for you are among my earliest friends in Vienna).

'Farewell – Abstain from the decaying fortresses, the attack is more costly than from those well preserved.

As ever, Your friend, Beethoven'

'NB If you have a moment's time please tell me how much a livery will cost now (without cloak) with hat and boot money. The most extraordinary changes have taken place; the man, thank God, has gone to the devil, but on the other hand the wife seems disposed to attach herself here all the more closely.'

The next is to Sir George Smart in London, dictated to Häring:

'Vienna, 18 December 1816 – 1055 Sailerstätte, 3rd Floor
'My dear Sir:

'You honour me with so many encomiums and compliments that I ought to blush, tho' I confess they are highly flattering to me and I thank you most heartily for the part you take in my affairs. They have rather gone a little back through the strange situation in which our lost – but happily recovered – friend, Mr Neate, found himself entangled. Your kind letter of 31 Oct. explained a great deal and to some satisfaction and I take the liberty to enclose an answer to Mr Neate, of whom I also received a letter, with my entreaties to assist him in all his undertakings in my behalf . . .

'I hope he will have it in his power with your assistance to do something for me, which from my illness and from the state of the Austrian finances would be very welcome. – Give me leave to subscribe myself with the greatest esteem and cordiality –

Ludwig van Beethoven'

* To the Quartet in F minor, Op. 95.

The following, to Mr Neate in London, was written in English by Mr Häring, at Beethoven's dictation:

'Vienna, 18 December 1816

'My dear Sir:

'Both letters to Mr Beethoven and to me arrived. I shall first answer his, as he has made out some memorandums, and would have written himself, if he was not prevented by a rheumatic feverish cold. He says: "What can I answer to your warmfelt excuses? Past ills must be forgotten, and I wish you heartily joy that you have safely reached the long wished-for port of love. Not having heard of you, I could not delay any longer the publication of the Symphony in A, which appeared here some few weeks ago. – It certainly may last some weeks longer before a copy of this publication appears in London, but unless it is soon performed at the Phil[harmonic], and something is done for me afterwards by way of benefit, I don't see in what manner I am to reap some good. The loss of your interest last season with the Phil[harmonic], when all my works in your hands were unpublished, has done me great harm – but it could not be helped – and at this moment I know not what to say. Your intentions are good, and it is to be hoped that my little fame may yet help . . . I was very sorry to hear that the three Overtures were not liked in London. I by no means reckon them amongst my best works, (which, however, I can boldly say of the Symphony in A), but still they were not disliked here and in Pest, where people are not easily satisfied. Was there no fault in the execution? Was there no party spirit?

'And now I shall close, with the best wishes for your welfare, and that you enjoy all possible felicity in your new situation of life –

Your true friend,
Louis van Beethoven" '

To the few names which this year have appeared in our narrative, there is still to be added one worthy of a paragraph: that of a wealthy young man from Graz, an amateur musician and composer of that class whose idol was Beethoven – Anselm Hüttenbrenner, who came to Vienna in 1815 to study with Salieri, and formed an intimate friendship with Franz Schubert. His enthusiasm for Beethoven was not abated when the present writer, in 1860, had the good fortune to enjoy a period of familiar intercourse with him and to hear his reminiscences from his own lips. He relates:

'I learned to know Beethoven through the kindness of Hr. Dr Joseph Eppinger, Israelite. The first time Beethoven was not at home; his housekeeper opened to us his living-room and study. There every-thing lay in confusion – scores, shirts, socks, books. The second time he was at home, locked in with two copyists. At the name "Eppinger" he opened the door and excused himself, having a great deal to do, and asked us to come at another time. But, seeing in my hand a roll of music – overture to Schiller's "Robbers" and a vocal quartet with pianoforte accompaniment, text by Schiller – he took it, sat himself down to the pianoforte and turned all the leaves carefully. Thereupon he jumped up, pounded me on the right shoulder with all his might, and spoke to me the following words which humiliated me because I cannot yet explain them: "I am not worthy that you should visit me!" Was it humility? If so it was divine; if it was irony it was pardonable.'

And again: 'A few times a week Beethoven came to the publishing house of Steiner and Co. in the forenoon between 11 and 12 o'clock. Nearly every time there was held there a composers' meeting to exchange musical opinions. Schubert frequently took me there. We regaled ourselves with the pithy, often sarcastic remarks of Beethoven particularly when the talk was about Italian music.'

CHAPTER 17

The Years 1817 and 1818

Almost Sterile Years – A Mother's Struggle for Her Son

Beethoven's splenetic remarks to strangers in his last years upon the music, musicians and public of Vienna have given rise to widely diffused but utterly false conceptions as to the facts. Thus William Henry Fry, a leading American writer on music in the middle of the nineteenth century, did but express a common opinion in the following: 'That composer [Beethoven] worked hard for thirty years. At his death, after the cup of glory had overflowed, his name resounding through Christendom, he left in all a beggarly sum of two or three thousand dollars, having lived as anyone acquainted with his career knows, a penurious life, fitted to his poverty and servile position in Vienna.'

The popular want of appreciation of his merits 'doomed Beethoven to a garret which no Irish emigrant would live in'. It is altogether unnecessary to argue against such statements, as the whole tenor of this biography refutes them; but the public press of Vienna deserves a vindication.

Taking 1821–2 as a medium date, the leading political and literary journals in Vienna in those years were the *Wiener Zeitung*, Joseph Karl Bernard, editor; the *Wanderer*, Ignaz von Seyfried, editor; the *Beobachter*, Joseph Pilat, editor; the *Sammler*, Portenschlag and Ledermeyer, editors; the *Wiener Zeitschrift (Modenzeitung)*, Johann Schickh, editor; and the *Theater Zeitung*, Adolph Bäuerle, editor. Most of these editors were personal friends of Beethoven; and whoever performs the weary task of looking through their myriads of pages sees that all were his admirers and let no opportunity pass unimproved of adding a leaf to his laurels. Still, disappointment at the comparative paucity of matter relating to him follows such an examination. The cause, however, lay in himself; in the small number of his new compositions of high importance, and in the rarity of his appearance before the public.

The correspondence of this and the next two or three years is very voluminous. Schindler says most pertinently of it: 'During these years our composer, instead of writing many notes, as had been his wont, wrote many letters, referring in part to his domestic affairs, in part to the litigation and in part to the education of his nephew. These letters are, in general, among the least encouraging and most deplorable testimonials to the excitement which attended his passionate prosecution of these objects.'

There are few men of whom a most false and exaggerated picture may not be presented by grouping together their utterances, spoken or written at long intervals and in the most diverse moods and states of mind. But there are series of letters covering comparatively short periods of time, which may be grouped and placed apart with no ill consequence. Such is the series to Steiner and Co.; and such to the Streichers and to Zmeskall, for they show, better than any description would, the helplessness of their writer in all affairs of common life; also, by implication, the wretched prospect of any good result to his undertaking the supervision and education of a boy more than usually endowed with personal attractions and mental capacity, but whose character had already received a false bias from the equally indiscreet alternate indulgence and severity of his invalid and passionate father and of his froward and impure mother. Moreover, this undertaking rendered necessary a sudden and very great change in the domestic habits of a man nearly fifty years of age, who, even twenty years before, had not been able, when residing in the family of his Maecenas, Lichnowsky, to bear the restraints imposed by common courtesy and propriety.

Let us again take up the thread of our narrative. We are still to imagine Beethoven living in the lofty, narrow house, Nos. 1055–6 Sailerstätte, entered from the street, but its better rooms on the other side looking over the old city wall and moat and out across the Glacis and little river Wien to the suburb Landstrasse, where, fronting on the Glacis, stood the institute of Giannatasio in which his nephew was a pupil, having been placed there in February 1816.

Carl Friedrich Hirsch was born in 1801, the grandson of J. G. Albrechtsberger, Beethoven's old teacher in counterpoint. At this time the Hirsch family lived in the Renngasse close by the hotel 'zum Römischen Kaiser' where the young Hirsch became acquainted with Beethoven. Due to the family relation to Beethoven's former teacher, Hirsch's father mustered up the courage to approach Beethoven and arrange that his son take lessons from him two or three times a week in what would now be called harmony.

According to Hirsch, Beethoven's deafness had advanced to the point where one had to speak to him very loudly. Beethoven watched his student's hands closely and when a mistake was made he would get very angry, become red in the face, and the vein in his temples and forehead would become swollen; he would also give his pupil a severe pinch through indignation or impatience, and once even bit him in the shoulder. He was very strict during the lesson, and burst forth in anger particularly over 'false fifths and octaves', at which he would spurt out in a great rage 'Well, what are you doing?' After the lesson he was again very 'charmant'.

Hirsch also described Beethoven's appearance in detail. Of powerful build, his face was a healthy red, his eyebrows very thick and his brow low. His nose was very big and broad, especially the nostrils which were finely 'shaped'. His bushy thick hair was already partly grey and stood up from his face. His hands were 'coarse and stout', his fingers short, the veins on the back of his hands thick, and the nails cut short.

Hirsch gave the following account of Beethoven at his lodgings: 'At home Beethoven worked in a flowery dressing-gown, outside the house he wore a dark green or brown coat with grey or dark trousers to match.' For his head he had a kind of low top-hat or in warmer weather a brown or dull gold straw hat. In his whole dress Beethoven was very slovenly. 'In his rooms there was the greatest disorder, notes, sheets, books lying partly on the desk, partly on the floor. Now and then the master used spectacles for reading but he did not wear them continuously.' The pianos upon which Hirsch was taught at Beethoven's were 'first an old five-octave, two-stringed instrument made of cherry wood then a six-octave mahogany one that was completely out of tune'.

There is no record, nor do the sketchbooks show, that in the first half of this year the composer's mind was occupied with any important composition; on the contrary, his time and thoughts were given to the affairs of his nephew, to his purposed housekeeping and to quarrels with his servants, as the frequent letters to the Streichers and Zmeskall show *ad nauseam*.

A curiously interesting picture of the man and his moods is disclosed by the records of Fanny Giannatasio. Of all the members of this family it was the daughter Fanny who recorded the most tender feelings for Beethoven and the most reverence, judging by numerous entries in her diary, of which the following should be quoted here. On 1 March [1817] she writes:

'The fact that Beethoven is angry with us is something which has troubled me a lot ever since, although the way he showed it transformed a sad feeling into one more bitter. It is true that Father has not treated him politely, but to people like us who have shown their respect and love for him every time he should not want to retort with biting sarcasm. He probably wrote that letter in one of his man-hating moods and I excuse it willingly.'

It is not known exactly what was in the letter here referred to. On 6 March, Fanny wrote further:

'. . . Moreover, I feel really hurt on account of Beethoven's behaviour towards us, my bitterness towards him has gone completely and I have only the anxious wish that the stupid affair be cleared up, and that even were I not to see him often, yet I would know that he was thinking of us with a friendly loving heart. I don't know that now and it disturbs Nanni and me in our dreams! The wicked man! If he knew how many troubled moments he has already given us and could understand that in no way have *either of us* deserved this from him and that we have always loved him – he would be compelled in accordance with his affectionate heart – to come here and make everything good between us!'

On 15 March:

'I read over these last lines with an extremely pleasant feeling; for he came – and all is well again. How sorry I am to have to note that Karl is very much to blame for this misunderstanding and sorrier still to see some new signs of his thoughtlessness towards his fine uncle carried out, which were new to him and hurt him all the more. –

'When Nanni asked Beethoven if he was still angry, he replied: I think much too little of myself to get angry. Nevertheless he relaxed after an exchange of explanations, whereupon it was found that the cause of this petty coolness was only a misunderstanding. The lack of delicacy in the way Father had fetched Karl, the reminder of the payment which Karl had delivered to him in front of the piano teacher, along with the lie of the latter [Karl] that he had been forbidden to practise the piano; all these things together so affected his already harassed disposition that, forgetting the confidence he had placed in us, he trusted in appearances rather than lovingly turning to his friends. But he came – he even looked embarrassed; he was probably sorry now about his letter and I am living again in the soothing conviction that he cares about us as much as he used to. Altogether my expectations have never been so fully realised as now. If my fulfilled wish – that Beethoven could understand that we cared for him and then love us in return – if this wish could be extended, it would be to live near him and to be able to brighten whenever possible the many gloomy hours of his life.'

This wish was partially realised on the 24th of the next month when Beethoven moved to the Landstrasser Glacis No. 268, on the second floor, which was not far from either the Streichers or the Giannatasio family.

Letters to Steiner at this time refer to the Pianoforte Sonata in A, Op. 101, which was then in the hands of the printers and appeared in February with a dedication to Baroness Ertmann. The suggestion had gone out that German composers substitute German terms in music in place of Italian. With characteristic impetuosity, Beethoven decided to begin the reform at once, although it seems to have involved the re-engraving of the title page of the new Sonata. He wrote to Steiner in the military style with which we are already familiar:

'To the Well-born Lieut[enant] Gen[eral] von Steiner for his own hands.

'PUBLICANDUM

'After individual examination and taking the advice of our council we have determined and hereby determine that hereafter on all our works with German titles, in place of pianoforte, *Hammerclavier* be printed; our best Lt. Gen. as well as the Adjutant and all others concerned will govern themselves accordingly at once and put this order into effect.

'Instead of Pianoforte, Hammerclavier, which settles the matter once and for all.

Given, etc., etc.   by the
on 23 January 1817   G[eneralissimu]s'

Baroness Ertmann now lived at St Pölten, where the command of her husband lay quartered, and thither Beethoven sent a copy of the 'Hammerclavier' sonata accompanied by the following letter:

'Vienna, 23 February 1816 [*sic*]
'My dear, valued Dorothea-Cäcilia!

'You must often have misunderstood me while I was obliged to appear displeasing to you. This was caused to a great extent by my circumstances, particularly in the days when my muse was less appreciated than it is now. You know the interpretations of the uncalled for apostles who helped themselves along with quite other means than the holy Gospel; I did not want to be counted among them. Receive now what was often intended for you and what may be to you a proof of my affection for your artistic aspirations as well as your person – That I did not hear you play at Cz[erny]'s recently was due to my ill health which at last seems to be giving way before my strength – I hope soon to hear from you, how it goes at Pölten with the Muses, and whether you care anything for your

admirer and friend

L. van Beethoven'

'All things lovely to your worthy *husband and consort*'

Schindler has written of the role that the Baroness played – now so soon to be ended – in the performance of Beethoven's music:

'Through the years – until Colonel von Ertmann became a general in 1818 and was transferred to Mailand – she gathered together around her either at her own place or at other places such as Carl Czerny's a circle of true music-lovers and made the greatest contribution generally among the elite of society to the preservation and cultivation of the purest taste. She was a conservatory all by herself. Without Frau von Ertmann Beethoven's piano music would have disappeared much earlier from the repertory in Vienna; this lady, who was beautiful besides with a tall, fine figure, possessed with the loftiest purpose a feeling for the better things, and resisted the pressure of the new direction in the composition and playing of Hummel and his followers. Thus Beethoven had a double reason to honour her as a priestess of music and call her his "Dorothea Cäcilia".'

Beethoven's correspondence of the winter is full of references to his continued ill health. In several letters he described the 'feverish cold' with which he had been afflicted in October 1816, the effects of which hung on during the winter and spring, limited his activities in the summer, and made his domestic difficulties seem the more intolerable.

He was engrossed with plans of travel throughout the year; he considered a tour of some kind essential to the restoration of his health and the recovery of his creative powers. His chronic dissatisfaction with the conditions which surrounded him in Vienna, as well as the moody mind in which his illness had left him, breathes through the following letter (written in German) to Charles Neate in London:

'Vienna, 19 April 1817

'My dear Neate!

'Since 15 October I have had a severe sickness and I am still suffering from the consequences and not quite recovered. You know that I must live from my compositions alone. Since the time of this sickness I have been able to compose but very little, and therefore to earn almost nothing. It would have been all the more welcome had you done something for me – meanwhile I suspect that the result of everything has been – *nothing*.

'You have even written *complainingly of me to Häring*, which my straightforwardness with you does not deserve in the least – Meanwhile I must justify myself in this, namely: the opera Fidelio had been written for several years, but the book and text were very faulty. The book had to be thoroughly remodelled, wherefore several pieces of the music had to be extended, others shortened, others newly composed. Thus, for instance, the overture is entirely new, as well as various other numbers, but it is possible that the opera may be found in London as it was *at first*, in which case it must have been stolen as is scarcely to be avoided at the theatre. – As regards the Symphony in A, as you did not write me a satisfactory reply, I was obliged to publish it. I should as willingly have waited 3 years if you had written to me that the Philharmonic Society would accept it – but on all sides nothing – nothing. Now, regarding the *Pianoforte Sonatas* with *Violoncello*, for them I give you *a month's time*; if after that I have no answer from you, I shall publish them in *Germany*, but having heard as little from you about them as about the other works, I have given them to a German publisher who importuned me for them. *But I have bound him in writing (Häring has read the document) not to publish the sonatas until you have sold them in London*. It seems to me that you ought to be able to dispose of these 2 sonatas for 70 or 80 ducats in gold at least. The English publisher may fix the day of *publication* in London and they will appear *on the same day in Germany*. It was in this manner Birchall bought and got the Grand Trio and the Violin Sonata from me. I beg you as a last favour *to give me an answer touching the sonatas as soon as possible*. Frau v. Jenny swears that *you have done everything for me*, I too, that is to say I swear that *you have done nothing* for me, are doing *nothing* and will do *nothing* – summa summarum, *Nothing! Nothing! Nothing!!!*

'I assure you of my most perfect respect and hope *as a last favour a speedy reply*.

> Your sincere servant and friend
> L. v. Beethoven'

After the composer's removal to the suburb Landstrasse, his mind was much occupied with a new matter between himself and the widow van Beethoven, namely, her bearing a share of the expenses of her son's education. This was concluded by a contract signed by both parties on 10 May 1817, binding her to pay at once into court 2,000 florins for the lad's education and support, and in the future to pay to the same tribunal every quarter at least one-half of the pension which the widow was to receive, as well as other contributions. Reference is made to this agreement in the following entries in the Fischoff *Tagebuch* in January or February of the next year:

'Karl's mother asked for the contract, the basis of which was that the house should be sold. From the proceeds of the sale it might be counted upon that all debts could be paid out of the one-half and also the half of the widow's income besides the money for Karl's needs and desires, so that she might live not just decently but very well, but inasmuch as the house is not to be sold! which was the chief consideration for the signing of the contract since it was alleged that execution had already been levied against it, my scruples must now cease, and I can well imagine that the widow has cared pretty well for herself, which I most cordially wish her. My duty, O Lord, I have done. –

'It would have been possible without offending the widow, but that was not so, and Thou, Almighty one, seest into my heart, knowest that I have sacrificed the best of my own for the sake of my precious Karl, bless my work, bless the widow, why cannot I wholly follow my heart's inclinations and hereafter for her the widow –

'God, God, my refuge, my rock, my all, Thou seest my inmost heart and knowest how it pains me to be obliged to compel another to suffer by my good labours for my precious Karl!!! O hear me always, Thou Ineffable One, hear me – thy unhappy, most unhappy of all mortals.'

This was the barren result of negotiations which had cost Beethoven, as to any important work, the first half of the year.

In May, the composer took rooms in Heiligenstadt to try the baths for his illness, of which he speaks in the following letter to Countess Erdödy:

'My dear suffering friend,
My most revered Countess!

'Too much of the time I have been upset and overloaded with too many cares. Since October 1816, I have been constantly ill, and since 15 October a severe and feverish catarrh has developed because of which I have had to stay a good deal in bed, and it was several months before I could go out even for a bit. *Up until now* I was *still bothered by the effects.* I changed doctors, since mine, a crafty Italian, had strong designs on me and lacked honesty as well as intelligence; this happened in April 1817. Then every day from 15 April to 4 May I had to take 6 powders, 6 cups of tea; this lasted until 4 May. From this time on I had a kind of powder that had also to be taken 6 times a day, and I had to rub myself three times with a volatile salve, thereupon I travelled here where I am taking the baths. Since yesterday I have been taking a new medicine, namely a tincture of which I must take 12 spoonfuls per day – Each day I hope for the end of this troublesome condition. Although it has improved somewhat, still it seems as though it is going to be a long time before I am completely recovered. How much all of this affects my life you can imagine. My hearing has become worse; and where before I was unable to look after myself and my requirements, now it is even more so. And my cares are still greater because of my brother's child – I have not yet found proper lodgings here; since it is difficult for me to take care of myself, I turn first to this person and then to that, and always I am left as before, and the victim of wretched people. A thousand times I have thought of you dear beloved friend as I do now, but my own misery has depressed me . . . Since my nephew has *vacation time from the last of August* until the end *of October*, it would be *after* that that I *could* visit you if it turns out that I am *cured*. We would of course have rooms for study and would have a comfortable existence, and I would be once again after such a long time among old friends who, unaffected by one or another diabolical human trait, have always sustained *me*. Thus perhaps joy and good health would return to me – Linke must write to me in what way I can make the trip with the least cost. For unfortunately my expenses are so great and my income small because of my illness, during which time I have been able to compose but little . . . Farewell, best and most beloved Countess, let me hear from you soon –

Your true friend
Beethoven'

'Heiligenstadt 19 June 1817'

Beethoven soon moved to Nussdorf, where he remained till the beginning of October. The move was made probably in late June, for on 7 July Beethoven writes to Nanette Streicher from Nussdorf:

'. . . the bad weather kept me from visiting you the day before yesterday when I was in the city; yesterday morning I hurried back here again, but found my servant not at home; he had taken the key to the house along with him. It was very cool, I had nothing to wear from the city but a thin pair of trousers; and so I had to wander about for three hours. This was bad for me and I felt poorly the whole day. – There you see what housekeeping with servants is like! . . .'

Here, too, he received the following highly important letter from Ferdinand Ries, written in London on 9 June 1817:

'My dearest Beethoven:

'For a very long time I have been forgotten by you, although I can think of no other cause than your too great occupation, and, as I was compelled to hear from others, your serious illness. Truly, dear Beethoven, the gratitude which I owe you and always must owe you – and I believe I may honestly say I have never forgotten it – although enemies have often represented me to you as ungrateful and envious – is unalterable, as I have always ardently desired to prove to you in more than words. This ardent desire has now (I hope) been fulfilled, and I hope to find again in my old teacher, my old and affectionate friend. The Philharmonic Society, of which our friend Neate is now also a director, and at whose concerts your compositions are preferred to all others, wishes to give you an evidence of its great respect for you and its appreciation of the many beautiful moments which your great works have so often provided for us; and I feel it a most flattering compliment to have been empowered with Neate to write to you on the subject. In short, my dear Beethoven, we should like to have you with us in London next winter. Friends will receive you with open arms; and to give you at least one proof of this I have been commissioned on behalf of the Philharmonic Society to offer you 300 guineas on the following conditions:

'1. You are to be here in London next winter.

'2. You are to write two grand symphonies for the Philharmonic Society, which are to be its property.

'3. You must bind yourself not to deliver any composition for grand orchestra for any concert in London, nor direct any concert before or during our eight concerts, which begin towards the end of February and end in the first half of the month of June (without the consent of the Philharmonic Society), which certainly will not be difficult . . .

'4. You are not to appear in the orchestra at any concert until our first two concerts are over, unless you want to give a concert yourself, and you can give as many of your own concerts as you please.

'5. You are to be here before 8 January 1818, free from all obligations to the Society except to give us the preference in the future in case we meet the same conditions offered you by others.

'6. In case you accept the engagement and need money for the journey you may have 100 guineas in advance. This is the offer which I am authorised to make to you by the Society.

'All negotiations with publishers are left to you as well as those with

Sir G. Smart, who has offered you 100 guineas for an oratorio in one act, and who has specially commissioned me to remind you of an answer, inasmuch as he would like to have the work for next winter. The intendant of the grand opera, G. Ayrton, is a particular friend of ours. He does not want to commit himself, but he promised us to commission an opera from you.

'Your own concert, or as many concerts as you choose to give, may bring in a handsome sum to you as well as other engagements in the country. Neate and I rejoice like children at the prospect of seeing you here and I need not say that I will do all in my power to make your sojourn profitable and pleasant. I know England, too, and do not doubt your success for a moment.

'Moreover, we need somebody here who will put life into things and keep the gentlemen of the orchestra in order.

'Yesterday evening our last concert took place and your beautiful Symphony in A sharp [B flat] was given with extraordinary applause. It frightens one to think of symphony writers when one sees and hears such a work. Write me very soon an explicit answer and bid me hope to see you yourself here before long.

I remain always

Your thankful sincere friend

Ferd. Ries'

'My hearty greetings to Herr v. Zmeskall, Zizius, Krumpholz and other friends.'

Beethoven was prompt with his answer.

'Vienna, 9 July 1817

'Dear Friend!

'The propositions made in your letter of 9 June are very flattering. You will see by this how much I appreciate them; were it not for my unlucky affliction which entails more attendance and cost than ordinary, particularly while travelling and in a strange land, I would accept the Philharmonic Society's offer *unconditionally*. But put yourself in my place; reflect how many more hindrances I have to contend with than any other artist, and judge then if my demands be unfair. Here they are and I beg of you to communicate them to the directors of the said Society.

'1. I shall be in London in the first half of the month of January 1818, at the latest.

'2. The two grand symphonies, newly composed, shall then be ready and become and remain the exclusive property of the Society.

'3. For them the Society is to give me 300 guineas and 100 guineas for travelling expenses, which will be much more, since I must necessarily take a companion with me.

'4. Inasmuch as I shall go to work on the symphonies at once, the Society is to advance me (on the acceptance of this offer) 150 guineas here so that I may provide myself with a carriage and other necessaries for my journey without delay.

'5. The conditions respecting my not appearing with another orchestra in public, my not conducting and my preferring the Society under equal conditions are accepted by me and in view of my sense of honour would have been understood as a matter of course.

'6. I shall rely upon the support of the Society in the projection and promotion of one, or, if circumstances justify, more benefit concerts. The particular friendship of some of the directors of your esteemed group as well as the kind interest of all artists in my works are a guarantee for this and will increase my zeal to fulfil all their expectations.

'7. In conclusion I ask that the consent or agreement to the above be written out in English and sent to me with the signatures of three directors of the Society.

'You can imagine that I heartily rejoice at the prospect of becoming acquainted with the estimable Sir George Smart and of meeting you and Mr Neate again. Would that I might fly to you instead of this letter!

Your sincere admirer and friend,
L. v. Beethoven'

To this Beethoven appended a postscript as follows:

'I embrace you with all my heart . . . I am convinced of your kind feelings towards me and hope that the Philharmonic Society will approve of my proposition, and you may rest assured that I shall exert all my powers worthily to fulfil the honourable commission of so select a body of artists. How numerous is your orchestra? How many violins, etc., etc., *single or double wind-instruments*? Is the hall large, acoustically good?

Your sincere admirer and friend,
L. v. Beethoven'

Efforts of the widow van Beethoven to keep in touch with her son, and questions of discipline in his bringing-up and education, were matters which weighed heavily on Beethoven's mind during the

summer of 1817. In an undated letter Beethoven explained to Giannatasio that the mother had expressly asked to see Karl at his, the
composer's, house and that certain evidences of indecision on his part
which his correspondent had observed (and apparently held up to him)
had not been due to any want of confidence, but to his antipathy to
'inhuman conduct of any kind', and the circumstance that it had been
put out of the power of the woman to do the lad harm in any respect.
On the subject of discipline he writes:

'As regards Karl, I beg of you to hold him to strict obedience and if he
does not obey you (or any of those whom he ought to obey) to *punish*
him at once, treat him as you would your own child rather than as a
pupil, for as I have already told you, during the lifetime of his father he
could only be forced to obey by blows; this was very bad but it was
unfortunately so and must not be forgotten.'

Beethoven's 'antipathy to inhuman conduct of any kind' seems to
have led him to make concessions to the widow of which he soon
repented. In a letter to Zmeskall dated 30 July, he says: 'After all, it
might pain Karl's mother to be obliged to visit her son at the house of
a stranger and, besides, there is more harshness in this affair than I
like; therefore I shall permit her to come to me tomorrow'; and he
urgently begged his friend to be a witness of the meeting. In a note to
Giannatasio he informed him of his intentions to take Karl to see his
mother at her home, because she was desirous to put herself in a better
light before her neighbours, and this might help. But a fortnight after
the letter to Zmeskall he changed his mind, as witness a letter to Giannatasio dated 14 August, in which he writes:

'I wanted this time to try an experiment to see if she might not be
bettered by greater forbearance and gentleness and I informed Hr. v.
S[chmerling] of this idea of mine. But it has foundered, for on *Sunday* I
had already determined to *adhere to the old necessary strictness*, because
in a moment's time she had communicated some of *her venom* to Karl —
In short we must stick to the zodiac and permit her to see Karl only
twelve times a year ... Once I had believed that by yielding wholly to
her wishes she might be encouraged to better her conduct and appreciate my utter unselfishness.'

Beethoven very naturally took measures that his nephew should
have systematic instruction in music; to this end he employed Carl
Czerny as teacher. Czerny writes:

'In the year 1815 [1816] at his request I began teaching his nephew Karl, whom he had already adopted, and from that time I saw him almost daily, since for the greater part of the time he brought the little fellow to me. From this period I still have many letters written by him, one of which I reproduce here with absolute fidelity because it is musically noteworthy:

' "My dear Czerny!

' "I beg of you to have as much patience as possible with Karl even if matters do not go now as well as you and I might wish; otherwise he will accomplish even less; for (but this he must not know) he is already subjected to too great a strain because of the improper division of his studies. Unhappily this cannot be changed at once. Therefore treat him with as much loving consideration as possible, but with seriousness; *then you will have* better success with Karl in spite of the unfavourable conditions. – In regard to his playing for you, I beg that once he has acquired the correct fingering and can play in time and reads the notes with reasonable correctness, you then direct his attention to the matter of interpretation; and when you have got *that far* don't stop him *because of trifling mistakes* but point them out after he has finished the piece. Although I have given but few lessons I have always followed this method, it soon makes *musicians* which, at the last, is one of the first purposes of art, and gives the minimum of weariness to master and pupil . . . I hope that you may receive all this in the loving spirit in which it is expressed and intended – At any rate I am and will always remain your debtor – May my sincerity be a pledge for future payment so far as possible. –

Your true friend Beethoven" '

Czerny comments:

'Noteworthy in this interesting letter is the very correct view that one ought not to weary the talent of a pupil by too much petty concern (wherein much depends on the qualities of the pupil, it is true) as well as the singular fingering and its influence on interpretation.

'Much more valuable were Beethoven's oral remarks about all kinds of musical topics, other composers, etc., touching whom he always spoke with the greatest positiveness, with striking, often caustic wit and always from the lofty point of view which his genius opened to him and from which he looked out upon his art. His judgement even concerning classic masters was severe, as a rule, and uttered as if he felt his equality. At one lesson which I gave his nephew he said to me: "You must not think

that you will do me a favour by giving him pieces of mine to play. I am
not so childish as to desire that. Give him what you think good for him."

'I mentioned Clementi. "Yes, yes," said he; "Clementi is very good,"
adding, laughingly, "For the present give Karl the regular things so
that after a while he may reach the irregular."

'After such conceits, which he was in the habit of weaving into
nearly every speech, he used to burst into a peal of laughter.'

In August and September the after-effects of the attack of catarrh
and the state of Beethoven's health generally were so distressing and so
depressing upon his spirits that he seemed to be on the verge of despair.
A letter which Zmeskall noted as received by him on 21 August says:

'I am sorry to hear of your illness – As for me, I am in despair so often
and would like to end my life, for there is never an end to all these
afflictions. God have pity on me, I consider myself as good as lost – I
must talk with you also about other things. This servant *steals*, I have
no doubt about this. So he must go. Because of my health I must *eat at
home* and with greater ease. I would like to know your opinion about
this – If my condition does not improve I shall not be in London next
year but perhaps in my grave – Thank God, the part is nearly played –
                              In haste
                              Your L. van Beethoven'

On 11 September, Beethoven was able to report to Zmeskall that
the reply to his letter had been received from the London Philharmonic Society the day before. There was no tone of elation in his note;
it merely mentioned the arrival of the letter and a request for the name
of someone who could translate it for him, it being in English. The
Society rejected the new terms demanded by him, but, as the Society's
records show, repeated the old. These were now at once accepted by
Beethoven.

And did he now sit himself down zealously and perseveringly to
work on a ninth and tenth symphony? Not at all. His thoughts had
become engaged upon a new pianoforte sonata – the great one in B flat,
Op. 106. Sketches were made for the first movement and the scherzo of
the Ninth Symphony during the composing of the sonata between the
autumn and spring of 1817–18; and these will be discussed when the
history of the symphony is told.

That 'indecision in many things', noted by Breuning a dozen years
before, was only aggravated by the lapse of time; and this now was his
bane. There was really nothing to prevent his departing at once except

that the new symphonies were still to be written. If his nephew must remain in or near Vienna, he could nowhere be so well placed as in the school and family of the excellent Giannatasios, who had all the necessary legal power to save the boy from the bad influence of his mother. The effects of such a journey; of a stay of some months in England; of the intercourse of cultivated people; of the enthusiastic admiration which awaited him there, and of the great pecuniary rewards for his labours which were certain, could only have been propitious in the highest degree to both his physical and mental health. But he did not go.

Beethoven's intercourse with a new acquaintance was, doubtless, far more delightful than any other event in his life at this time. This was Frau Marie Pachler-Koschak, who visited him in August or September 1817. Beethoven had already heard from Prof. Schneller, whose pupil she had been, of her extraordinary beauty, talents, intellectual culture and refinement, and of her genius for music.

She was born in 1794, in Graz, the daughter of a respected lawyer, and she attracted attention early in life by her pianoforte playing and talent for composition. In a concert in 1811, she played Beethoven's *Choral Fantasy* and for a long time intended to devote herself completely to the art; but she gave this up in the interests of her family. In 1816 she married the lawyer, Dr Carl Pachler, in Graz. Her house became the centre of a cultivated circle, and she continued to keep up her music as much as her domestic duties would allow. Anselm Hüttenbrenner wrote of her: 'The daughter of the lawyer Koschak was the most beautiful maiden and later for several years the most beautiful woman in Graz and was called "heaven's daughter". She glowed with admiration for Jean Paul, Goethe and Schiller, for Beethoven, Mozart and Schubert.'

In 1817 her wish to meet Beethoven personally was fulfilled; her brother-in-law Anton brought her to him in August or September. She had never been in Vienna, Beethoven never in Graz, so they, of course, had never met previously. But when they did, it could not be as strangers; for his music had been to her like a new divine revelation, and such noble mental and personal qualities as distinguished her always awakened in him feelings akin to worship. Unfortunately absolutely nothing is known of their personal association except that she wrote ten years later that 'they were often in each other's company', and that Beethoven wrote her two notes 'in pencil' – one utterly illegible, and the other in terms placing her as a player of his pianoforte music even higher than Frau von Ertmann.

There are few unmarried men of highly sensitive nature who have not had the bitter experience of a hopeless passion, who have not felt how doubly grateful at such times is intercourse with a glorious creature like Madame Pachler, and how beneficial in preventing the thoughts from continually dwelling on the impossible, and thus aiding reason and conscience to gain the victory over the heart and fancy. Now it happens that one of Beethoven's transient but intense passions for a married woman, known to have occurred in this period of his life, has its precise date fixed by these passages in the so-called 'Tagebuch' from the years 1816 and 1817. 'In the case of T. there is nothing to do but to leave it to God, never to go where one might do a wrong through weakness – to Him, to the all-knowing God, be all this committed.' And again: 'But as kind as possible to T. her attachment deserves never to be forgotten even if the results could never prove advantageous to you.' Let the reader recall the passages in his letters showing a strong desire to leave Vienna and read again: 'Work during the summer for the journey, only thus can you carry out the great task for your poor nephew, afterwards wander through Italy, Sicily, with a few artists – make plans and be of good cheer for the sake of C. . . .' The last initial is uncertain. Other copies have 'L.'; what the original was in Beethoven's handwriting is not now to be determined. As the family name of this lady, whose husband was a man of high position and distinction though not noble by birth, is known to me, it is certain that the 'T' in the above citations is not Therese Malfatti, now Baroness Drosdick; but as her baptismal names have eluded search one can only hint the possibility that the 'T' and 'M' may indicate the same person, and that this last cry of anguish was written a year or two afterwards when the sight of 'M' again, for a moment, tore open a half-healed wound.

On 2 October, Beethoven wrote a letter to Nanette Streicher from Nussdorf which ends: 'Tomorrow I hope to see you for sure, for I am coming in from the country to the Landstrasse just for that reason.' One of the matters to be discussed was a move to the Gärtnergasse which Beethoven had mentioned frequently in his letters to Frau Streicher during the summer. He left Nussdorf for good on 14 October. At some point after this date he left the dwelling on the Landstrasse for one in the house 'zum grünen Baum', first étage, second storey, in the Gärtnergasse, also in the suburb Landstrasse. He was again near both his nephew and the Streichers (in the Ungargasse), and, with the aid of Frau Streicher, he at last brought his domestic arrangements into such a condition that he might take his nephew to himself.

On one side of a large sheet of paper he wrote a list of questions which were painstakingly answered on the opposite page by the friend to whom they were addressed (presumably again Frau Streicher). The questions were as follows:

'What ought one to give 2 servants to eat at dinner and supper both as to quantity and quality?

'How often ought one to give them roast meat?

'Ought they to have it at dinner and supper too?

'That which is intended for the servants, do they have it in common with the victuals of the master, or do they prepare their own separately, i.e., do they have different food from the master?

'How many pounds of meat are to be reckoned for 3 persons?

'What allowance per day do the housekeeper and maid receive?

'How about the washing?

'Do the housekeeper and maid get more?

'How much wine and beer?

'Does one give it to them and when?

'Breakfast?'

Beethoven announced his intention to take his nephew to himself at the end of the current quarter in a letter to Giannatasio dated 1 November 1817. The step involved not only an increase in his expenses, but also an abandonment of his engagement with the London Philharmonic Society and of all the profits which might thence arise. Giannatasio, moved by his complaints of poverty, and probably also by a desire to aid him in the proposed visit to London, kindly offered to keep the boy at a much reduced rate of remuneration for board and instruction. Beethoven's reply shows him to be still undecided as to his movements in the coming spring, and it is possible, could he have made ready the required symphonies, that he might have gone to England; but now the new Sonata had got possession of his imagination, and the symphonies must wait. It was one of the very few compositions begun in this almost sterile year.

Brief mention should be made at this point of Beethoven's increasing deafness. Czerny, who saw Beethoven frequently during these particular years, told Jahn that between 1812 and 1816 it gradually became more and more difficult to make oneself understood without shouting. 'But it was not until 1817 that the deafness became so extreme that he could no longer hear music either, and this condition persisted for about 8 or 10 years until his death.' And further: 'Up to 1816, he was still able (with the aid of machines) to hear himself play, but later even this became more and more difficult, and he had to rely on his inner hearing, his imagination, and experience.'

An entry in an old 'Porter's Book' of John Broadwood and Sons, manufacturers of pianofortes in London, offers an agreeable starting-point for the story of Beethoven's life in 1818. In this book the porter of the firm signs his name, Millet, to the record that on 27 December 1817, he took from the warehouse 'A 6 octave Grand Pianoforte, No. 7362 tin and deal case, Thomas Broadwood, Esq., marked V. B. care of F. E. J. Bareaux and Co., Trieste (a present to Mr van Beethoven, Viene), deliv'd to Mr Farlowes to be shipped.' On 3 January 1818, Mr Broadwood seems to have informed Beethoven that the instrument had been shipped, and exactly one month later Beethoven sent a letter expressing heartfelt gratitude to the generous donor.

The shipper, Joseph Bridi, wrote to Broadwood on 5 February, asking for instructions how to carry out what he understands to be the donor's desire that the instrument be delivered to Beethoven without his being put to any expense whatever, not even for the import duty. The latter charge must have been in the mind of Beethoven when he wrote a letter, without date, to Count Lichnowsky expressing the hope that he be permitted to receive the instrument and proposing to apply by word of mouth to Count Stadion, the Austrian Minister of Finance. The upshot was neither Broadwood nor Beethoven was called on to pay the duty, the Austrian Exchequer remitting the entire charge.

Beethoven's delight in the pianoforte must have been great. Bridi reports to Broadwood that the composer already rejoiced in it in anticipation and expressed a desire to dedicate the first piece of music composed after its reception to the donor, 'convinced that it would inspire something good'. His jealousy of it seems to have been so great that he would not permit anybody to tune it except Stumpff, of London, who came with a letter of introduction from Broadwood.

The case of the instrument, simple, plain but tasteful in design, is of mahogany and the structure generally of a solidity and strength paired with grace which caused no little surprise at the time. The compass is six octaves from C, five leger-lines below the bass staff. Above the keys is the inscription: *Hoc Instrumentum est Thomae Broadwood* (*Londini*) *donum, propter Ingenium illustrissimi Beethoven*. Beethoven kept the instrument as long as he lived. At the sale of his effects it was bought by Spina, the music publisher, for 181 florins; Spina gave it to Liszt, in whose house at Weimar it was up to his death. It is now in the Liszt Memorial Museum in Budapest.

Beethoven's London trip had been abandoned without notice or explanation to the Philharmonic Society, apparently; but Ries must have written to him, renewing the offer previously accepted, for on 5 March Beethoven writes to his old pupil as follows:

'In spite of my desire, it was impossible for me to come to London this year; I beg of you to say to the Philharmonic Society that my poor state of health hindered me; but I hope that I may be entirely well this spring and then take advantage of the renewed offers of the Society towards the end of the year and fulfil all its conditions . . .

'I beg of you to write to me soon. If it is at all possible I shall get away from here sooner in order to escape total ruin and will then arrive in London in the winter at the latest.

'I know that you will stand by an unfortunate friend; had it only been in my power, and had I not been fettered, as always here, by circumstances, I would surely have done much more for you – A hearty farewell, give my greetings to Neate, Smart, Cramer – although I hear that he is a counter-subject to you and me, yet I already know something of the art of treating such and we shall produce an agreeable harmony in London after all.

I greet and embrace you from my heart.

Your friend Ludwig van Beethoven'

'All that is lovely to your dear and (as I hear) beautiful wife.'

The time had come for Beethoven to take his nephew from the home and institute of the Giannatasios. On 6 January he wrote to inform the director that Karl would leave his 'admirable institute' at the expiration of the month and that Giannatasio might rest assured of his and the lad's lifelong gratitude: 'I have observed in Karl that he already feels grateful, and this is a proof that though he is frivolous he is not malicious, and least of all is he bad at heart. I have hopes of all manner of good from him, all the more because he had been under your excellent care for nearly two years.'

Ill-advised and full of evil consequences as was Beethoven's step in taking personal charge of his nephew, it was yet creditable to his heart and bears strong witness to his high sense of duty. His purpose was pure and lofty, and his action prompted by both love and an ideal sense of moral obligation. It was a woeful mistake, however. In the conduct of his own affairs he had always permitted himself to be swayed by momentary impulses, emotions and sometimes violent passions, and he could not suddenly develop the habits of calm reflection, unimpassioned judgement and consistent behaviour essential to the training of a careless and wayward boy. In his treatment of him he flew from one extreme to the other – from almost cruel severity to almost limitless indulgence, and, for this reason, failed to inspire either respect for his authority or deep affection for his person, to develop the lad's self-control or a desire for virtuous living. Very questionable, too, if not utterly unpardonable, were the measures which Beethoven took to separate the boy from his mother in spite of the dying wishes of the father, though there can be no doubt that the woman whom Beethoven called 'The Queen of Night' was wicked and vicious, and that his detestation of her was well founded.

A memorandum in the 'Tagebuch' after 20 February reads: 'Karl's mother has not seen him since 10 August' – a period of more than six months. How often she was allowed to see him during the following months is not on record; we only know from Beethoven himself, in his letters to Frau Streicher, that the mother's instinct drove her to employ the only means by which she could know the condition of her son during the summer in Mödling – i.e., bribing or feeing the servants. That at least is Beethoven's accusation, and exceedingly wroth he was. The following letter deserves to be given in full.

'Best Frau Streicher!

'It was not possible to reply to your last letter sooner. I would have written to you a few days ago when the servants were sent away, but hesitated in my determination until I learned that it was Frau D. in particular who hindered Karl from making full confession. "*He ought to spare his mother,*" she told him; and Peppi co-operated with her.* Naturally they did not want to be discovered; they worked together shamefully and permitted themselves to be used by Frau v. Beethoven; both received coffee and sugar from her, Peppi *money* and the *old one* probably also; for there can be no doubt that she was *herself at the house of Karl's mother*; she said to Karl that *if I drove her away* from my service *she would go straight to his mother*. This happened at a time when I had reproved her for her conduct with which I had frequent occasion to be dissatisfied; Peppi who often played the eavesdropper when I spoke with Karl appears to have tried to tell the truth; but the old one *accused her of stupidity and scolded her stoutly* – and so she remained silent and tried to throw me off the trail – The story of this abominable deception may have lasted about six weeks – they would not have got off *so easy* with a less magnanimous man. Peppi borrowed 9 or 10 florins for stuff for shirts and I afterwards made her a present of the money and instead of 60 she got 70 florins; she might have denied herself these wretched bribes. In the case of the old woman, who was always the worse, hate may have played a part as she always thought herself slighted (although she got more than she deserved) for the *scornful*

* Frau D. and Peppi were the new housekeeper and cook, engaged some time early in the year. The former is also called 'the old woman' by Beethoven in his letters.

smile on her face one day when Karl embraced me, made me suspect *treachery* and how shameless and deceitful such an old woman could be. Just imagine, 2 days before I came here K. went to his mother one afternoon without my knowledge and both the old woman and P. knew it. But now listen to the triumph of a hoary-headed traitress: on the way hither with K. and her, I spoke with K. about the matter in the carriage, although I did not know all; and when I expressed the fear that we should not be safe in Mödling, she exclaimed "*I should only rely upon her.*" O the infamy of it! This was only the 2nd time in the case of a person of such venerable age that *such a thing* happened to me – A few days before when I sent both away I had told them in writing that under no circumstances were they to accept anything for Karl from his mother. Instead of repenting, Peppi tried secretly to take revenge on K., after he had confessed all. This they knew from the fact that in the note mentioned above, I had written that *all had been discovered* – I expected that they would both beg my pardon after this, instead of which they played me one wicked trick after the other. As no betterment was to be expected in such obstinate sinners and I had every moment to fear another piece of treachery, I decided to sacrifice my body, my comfort in order to better my poor misguided Karl; so out of the house they went as a *warning example* to all those servants who may come after – I might have made their certificates of character a little less favourable; but rather I set down the time of service of each at full six months although it was not true. I never practise *vengeance*; in cases where I act *against* the interest of other people, I never do more *against them* than is necessary to protect myself against them or to prevent them from doing further harm. – On account of Peppi's honesty in general I am sorry to have lost her, for which reason I made her certificate more favourable than that of the old woman; also she appears to have been led astray by the old woman. That P.'s conscience was not at ease, however, she showed by saying to Karl that "*she did not dare go back to her parents*", and, in fact, I believe she is still here – I had suspected treachery for a long time until one evening before my departure I received an anonymous letter the contents of which filled me with dread; but they were only suspicions. Karl, whom I took to task in the evening, confessed at once but not everything. As I often treat him harshly though not without cause, he was much too afraid to admit everything completely. In the midst of the struggle we reached here. As I often questioned him, the servants noticed it, and the old woman in particular tried to persuade him *not to admit the truth*. But when I gave Karl my sacred assurance that all would be forgiven if he would but confess the truth, while lying would plunge him into a deeper abyss

than that in which he already was, everything came to the light of day –
Add to this the other data which I gave you before concerning the servants and you will have the shameful story of the two traitresses clearly
before you – K. did wrong, but – mother – mother – even a bad one
remains a mother – To this extent he is to be excused, particularly by
me who knows his intriguing, passionate mother *much too well.* – The
priest here knows already that I know about him, for K. had already
told me. It is likely that he was not fully informed and that he will be
careful; thus we'll guard against K.'s being mistreated by him, since he
appears to be rather a rough man. Enough of that for now. But as K.'s
virtue was put to the test, for there is no virtue without temptation, I
will purposely let the matter go by until it happens again (which I do
not expect), in which case I will so bethwhack his reverence with such
spiritual cudgels, amulets with my sole guardianship and consequent
privileges, that the whole parish will shake – My heart has been terribly shaken up by this affair and I can scarcely recover myself – Now to
the housekeeping; it needs your help – How necessary this is to us you
already know. Do not be frightened away, such a thing might happen
anywhere; but if it has once happened and one is in a position to hold it
up to one's new servants, it is not likely that it will occur again – You
know what we need, perhaps a French woman, and whatever can be
found in the way of a chambermaid; good cooking remains the principal thing – also the matter of economy. For the present we have a
person who cooks for us, but badly. I cannot write you more today. You
will see that *in this matter* I could not act differently; things had gone
too far – I cannot yet invite you to visit me here for everything is still in
confusion; *nevertheless it will not be necessary to send me to a lunatic asylum* – I can say that I already suffered fearfully from this thing while I
was in Vienna, though I kept silence – Farewell; do not let any of this
be known as someone might think prejudicially of K. *Only I* who
know all the driving wheels here can testify *for him* that he was terribly
misled – I beg of you soon to write us something comforting touching
the art of cooking, washing and sewing. I am feeling very ill and in
need of a stomach restorative.

In haste, your friend

Mödling, 18 June 1818 Beethoven'

'K. did wrong, but – mother – mother – even a bad one remains a
mother.' Why did he not follow this thought to its ultimate conclusion?
Why did he permit, if indeed, he did not encourage the lad to speak
disrespectfully of his mother?

Beethoven removed to Mödling on 19 May, taking with him his

nephew and the two servants referred to in the letter above. He found lodgings in the so-called Hafner House in the Hauptstrasse. Beethoven had quarters on the first floor, which consisted of a large room with a view on to the court, two small rooms with a view on to both court and garden, and a small dark kitchen where both servants presumably slept. He began taking the baths two days after his arrival and, the desire and capacity for work soon returning, he took up energetically the Pianoforte Sonata in B flat. Karl was placed in a class of boys taught by the village priest, named Fröhlich, who dismissed him a month later for reasons which became a matter of judicial record before the end of the year. In a document filed as an appendix to Frau van Beethoven's application for the guardianship, Fröhlich set forth that Beethoven had encouraged his nephew to revile his mother, applauding him when he applied vile epithets to her either in writing or by shrieking them into his ear, 'thus violating the fourth divine commandment'; that the boy had confessed to him that while he knew that he was doing wrong he yet defamed his mother to curry favour with his uncle. Once, too, Beethoven came to him (the priest) and in a tone of malicious joy told him that his nephew had that day called his mother a 'Ravenmother' (*Rabenmutter* – meaning a wicked and unnatural mother). Since Karl's training was thus contrary to all moral principles, since he had also displayed indifference to religious instruction, been guilty of unruly conduct in church and in the streets, and since admonitions to the boy and appeals to the uncle had borne no fruit, the priest had been constrained to dismiss him for the sake of his other twelve pupils, who had said 'they did not want to study with the unruly Karl van Beethoven'.

The same summer saw the beginning of the most widely distributed portrait of Beethoven. A young painter named August von Klöber, who was continuing his artistic studies in Vienna, undertook to paint a portrait of the composer. He visited Beethoven at Mödling, after receiving permission to make a drawing of him and found him giving a lesson to his nephew on the Broadwood pianoforte. Though the artist found it impossible to make himself understood unless he wrote his words or spoke them into an ear-trumpet, Beethoven corrected the errors in the lad's playing, compelled him to repeat passages apparently without difficulty. Klöber's account continues:

'After approximately three-quarters of an hour, he grew uneasy ... I knew that it was time to stop and asked him only for permission to come again tomorrow since I lived in Mödling myself. Beethoven was very understanding and said, "Then we can meet often because I do not like to sit long. You must take a good look at Mödling for it is very beautiful here, and, as an artist you must be a lover of nature." On my walks in Mödling I met Beethoven repeatedly, and it was most interesting to see how frequently he stopped, with a sheet of music-paper and a pencil-stump in his hands, as if listening, looked up and down and then scribbled notes on the paper ... Once, just when I was sketching a piece of woodland, I saw him climb up a hill from the hollow which separated us, with his broad-brimmed felt hat pressed under his arm; when he got there, he threw himself down at full length under a pine-tree and for a long time stared heavenwards. – Every morning he sat for me awhile. When Beethoven saw my picture he remarked that the treatment of the hair pleased him very much, the other painters hitherto had always made him look so *well-groomed* ...

'Beethoven's residence in Mödling was extremely simple as, indeed, was his whole nature; his garments consisted of a light-blue frockcoat with yellow buttons, white waistcoat and necktie, as was the fashion at the time, but everything *négligée*. His complexion was healthy and tough, the skin somewhat pock-marked, his hair was of the colour of slightly bluish-grey and very animated – when his hair was tossed by the wind there was something Ossianic-demoniac about him. In friendly converse, however, his expression became good-natured and gentle, particularly when the conversation pleased him. Every mood of his soul found powerful expression instantly in his features.'

Klöber's original painting has disappeared. It was a full-length portrait with a bit of Mödling landscape as a background. The nephew Karl was included, reposing under a tree. The composer was depicted with notebook and pencil.

We now reach an incident in the story of Beethoven's life concerning which much has been written from a biased and frequently erroneous point of view and which it becomes a duty to rectify not only so that the picture of Beethoven as he was may be kept true, but that the better motives and impulses which prompted the woman whom he so cordially detested be placed in their proper light also. The mother of Karl, though she had been convicted and punished for adultery at an earlier period, and though she might not have proved a safe mentor for her son, was yet a mother, his mother. That fact Beethoven was willing to recognise as palliating the conduct of the boy, but he could not bring himself to recognise that it might also palliate if it did not justify the steps which his harshness compelled a mother to take to gratify the need implanted by nature.

After his dismissal from the class of the parish priest at Mödling, Karl van Beethoven was placed in the hands of a private tutor to be prepared for admission to one of the public schools of Vienna – no doubt that known as the academic *Gymnasium*. To enter this school the boy had to pass an examination, and for this purpose Beethoven brought him to Vienna about the middle of August. Frau van Beethoven was now determined to wrest from her brother-in-law the authority, which was his as sole guardian, to keep the boy in his care and to direct his training. She took to her aid Jacob Hotschevar, a Hofconcipist (clerk or scrivener in the government service), and petitioned the Landrecht of Lower Austria to take from Beethoven the authority to direct the future training of his ward. The Landrecht was a tribunal with jurisdiction in litigations and other matters *affecting the nobility*. Acting on the assumption that the Dutch 'van', like the German 'von', was a badge of noble birth, it had listened to Beethoven's plea and appointed him sole guardian of his nephew, removing the widow from the joint guardianship directed in the will of the boy's father on the score of her immorality, as we already know.

The proceedings were begun in September and were dismissed on the 18th of that month. Three days later, that is, on 21 September, she applied to the court again, this time for permission to place her son in the Royal Imperial Seminary, where he would have board, lodging and instruction. She and Beethoven as 'co-guardian' were commanded to appear in court and the latter was directed to bring the report of the lad's examination with him. There was a postponement of the hearing till 30 September, and on 3 October the widow's application was rejected. Thus far victory had gone to Beethoven.

The postponement of the hearing was made in great likelihood to enable Beethoven to change his residence from Mödling to the city (the house on the Gärtnerstrasse). At any rate, Karl was a public school scholar on 6 November, as Fanny Giannatasio records in her diary on that day, together with the fact that her father had met Beethoven, who had shortly before returned from the country. The lad made good progress in his studies, all seemed well and something of the old cordial relations seemed again to be established between Beethoven and the Giannatasios. Fanny writes: 'Yesterday Beethoven was with us once again. We have secured a housekeeper for him. He was here three hours and since his hearing was especially bad this day, we wrote everything down. One cannot be in his company without being impressed with his admirable character, his deep sense of what is good and noble.'

Within a fortnight the diary chronicles the severest trial that the boy had yet caused his uncle: he ran away from home and sought a haven with his mother. The sympathetic Fanny wrote: 'One day B. came in great excitement and sought counsel and help from my father, saying that Karl had run away! I recall that on this occasion amid our expressions of sympathy he cried out tearfully: "He is ashamed of me!" ' The diary entry continued:

'Never in my life shall I forget the moment when he came and told us that Karl was gone, had run away to his mother, and showed us his letter as an evidence of his vileness. To see this man suffering so, to see him *weeping* – it was touching! Father took up the matter with great zeal, and with all my sorrow I feel a pleasurable sensation in the consciousness that now we are *much* to Beethoven, yes, at this moment his only refuge.'

Beethoven went to the mother immediately in the morning to bring back the boy; she promised to release him in the evening; and since Beethoven feared that she would send him away (to Linz or Hungary), he employed the police to get the boy back and turned him over temporarily to Giannatasio again. He was to remain there apparently for the winter.

At the same time the mother was working for her own interests; and on 7 December made a third application to the court:

'Johanna van Beethoven (living at Tiefer Graben No. 238 on the second floor) declares to the RI Landrecht of Lower Austria that her son Karl van Beethoven *ran away from his uncle and guardian, Hr. Ludwig van Beethoven, without her knowledge and participation, but the same was again returned to him by her through the RI chief of police*. At the same time she requested that, since Ludwig van Beethoven according to report intends to send her son to a school and indeed far away from here, perhaps even abroad, he be denied the permission of chief guardianship and that she *once again* will request the sanction to be permitted to send her son to the RI University Seminary for education and board.'

Hotschevar supported these petitions in a document like a modern law brief, explaining his interest in the matter on the grounds that his wife was a stepsister of Frau van Beethoven's deceased mother. He admitted that Frau van Beethoven had years before been guilty of a moral delinquency for which she had been punished, but asserted her right to a standing in court; he then contended: (1) that the mother had illegally been denied all influence over her son and (2) that her son could not remain under the sole influence of his uncle and guardian without danger of suffering physical and moral ruin. In support of these contentions he recited that the brothers van Beethoven were eccentric men, so often at odds with each other that they might better be called enemies than friends, Carl van Beethoven being pleasantly disposed towards his brother only when he was in need of money from him, and that the suspicion lay near that the boy had been an object of traffic between them, inasmuch as an agreement touching the payment of 1,500 florins had been made only on condition that Ludwig van Beethoven surrender a document which appointed him guardian. Carl van Beethoven, moreover, knowing the animosity which his brother felt towards his wife, had in a codicil to his will expressly said that he did not want Ludwig van Beethoven to be sole guardian of his son but joint guardian with the mother. The statement of the village priest Fröhlich was appended to the widow's application as evidence of the physical and moral degeneration of the boy, and for himself Hotschevar says that he had observed after the boy had run away from his uncle that his hands and feet were frostbitten, that he had no seasonable clothing and that his linen and baths had been neglected. The priest's statement was also appealed to to show that the boy had been led into unfilial conduct, indifference towards religion, hypocrisy, untruthfulness and even theft against his guardian – in short, was in danger of becoming a menace to society. He urged that in view of the danger in which the lad was, Beethoven ought to forgo the guardianship or associate with himself either the mother or some other capable person, it appearing from the facts in the case that he was 'physically and morally unfit' for the post.

Already on 9 December the court had summoned the petitioner and also Beethoven and his nephew to appear in court on the afternoon of 11 December at 4 o'clock. Beethoven brought Karl Bernard with him, no doubt to protect him in his deafness. On the same day the widow appealed to the court that in case the guardian of her son should make application touching the plans for his future training, it be not granted without giving her a hearing. All three were examined.

All the old ground was gone over by the court; but towards the end of its examination of Johanna the following exchange took place:

'Was her husband of noble birth?

'So the brothers had said; the documentary proof of nobility was said to be in the possession of the oldest brother, the composer. At the legal hearing on the death of her husband, proofs of nobility had been demanded; she herself had no document bearing on the subject.'

It remains a mystery, if Johanna spoke the truth in answering the final question, how the case ever got into the aristocratic Landrecht in the first place. Beethoven himself, in reply to a question by the court, stated that 'van' was a Dutch predicate not confined to the nobility and that he had no proof of noble birth. His answer, no doubt, raised doubt in the mind of the court touching its jurisdiction. While both parties were awaiting the results of their efforts, the Landrecht made a decision which cut Beethoven to the quick: on 18 December it sent the proceedings down to the lower court of the Vienna Magistracy.

Schindler's comments on the effect of the reference of the case to the Civic Magistrates demand a moment's attention. He says:

'The transfer of the case to the Magistracy was felt as an overwhelming blow by Beethoven. It would be difficult to maintain that Beethoven attached importance to appearing . . . as of noble birth, his origin as well as family conditions being well known . . . But it is certain that he laid great weight upon having his lawsuit adjudicated by the exceptional upper court, partly because as a matter of fact there was in that tribunal a better appreciation of his importance . . . partly because the lower court had an unfavourable reputation which could not inspire in him a hope for the desired outcome. But nevertheless it may be said as sure that neither his genius nor his works of art would have given him the privileged position which he occupied in the circles of the nobility had there not been a presumption that he was an equal. This was variously demonstrated as soon as the occurrence in the aristocratic court became known to the public. Not in the middle classes, but in the upper, the little word "van" had exercised a palpable charm. It is a fact that after the incident in the Lower Austrian Landrecht the great city of Vienna became too small for our aggrieved master, and had he not been restrained by his sense of duty which was placed upon him by his brother's will, the projected journey to England would have been undertaken and his sojourn there perhaps become permanent.'

In one of the Conversation Books used by Beethoven in 1820, there occurs this remark in Beethoven's handwriting: '. . . when [the court] learned that my brother was not of the nobility. It is singular, so far as I know, that there is a hiatus here which ought to be filled, for my nature shows that I do not belong among this plebeian mass.'

Let the rest of the year's history be devoted to Beethoven's creative work. Considering the revival of interest and desire on the part of the composer, the net result, as measured by finished products, was not as large as might have been expected. Two explanations for these circumstances may be offered: the first lies in his domestic miseries and the frame of mind in which they kept him for long stretches at a time — that is obvious; the second may be read in his compositions. He was growing more and more prone to reflection, to moody speculation; his mental processes, if not slower than before, were more protracted, and also more profound, and they were occupied with works of tremendous magnitude. The year produced the Sonata in B flat, Op. 106, and sketches and partial developments of the Symphony in D minor [the 9th].

And not alone the Ninth Symphony, a Tenth also was before his fancy, but with neither of them had Schiller's 'Ode to Joy' been brought into association, though the employment of the human voice in one of them was already under consideration. Notes in the 'Tagebuch' and sketchbooks which, to judge by their context, were written during the summer sojourn in Mödling show the trend of Beethoven's thoughts on religious subjects which were crystallising or about to crystallise in the idea of writing a great mass.

CHAPTER 18

The Years 1819–1821

Karl's Education – The Missa Solemnis – End of the Litigation

The keynote for much that must occupy us in a survey of the year 1819 is sounded by two letters to Archduke Rudolph. The first is a New Year's greeting:

'Everything that can be gathered up into one wish and be called salutary; wealth, happiness and a blessing, is included in my wish which is offered to YIH on this day... A terrible event took place recently in my family affairs, which for a time robbed me of all my reasoning powers; and to this must be charged the circumstance that I have not called upon YIH in person nor made mention of the masterly Variations of my highly honoured and exalted pupil, the favourite of the Muses... May the heavens hear and fulfil my wishes especially for the health of YIH. In a few days I hope to hear the masterpiece that was sent to me performed by YIH himself; and nothing can give me greater joy than to have contributed towards YIH's speedy assumption of the position already prepared for Your Highness atop Parnassus.'

Beethoven had composed a four-measure theme 'O Hoffnung' in the preceding year for the benefit of his patron's creative efforts. The 'masterly Variations' were the Archduke's response to this assignment from his teacher by writing forty variations on this theme and dedicating the work to Beethoven.

The events of the final months of 1818 had indeed been devastating ones for Beethoven, and the 'terrible' one was of course Karl's running away to his mother in early December, which to the uncle was not the natural result of a boy of twelve having been forcibly separated from his mother, but a terrible misfortune and personal affront. Unfortunately the struggle between the mother and the uncle over the boy must occupy many pages in the account of the years ahead.

The second letter to the Archduke, however, takes us to a topic of the highest creative endeavour. It was written in early June, and we quote the pertinent passages:

'Your Imperial Highness!

'On the day when YIH most graciously sent for me, I was not at home, and immediately thereafter I contracted a violent cold, so that I must write to YIH reclining near my bed – Despite the mass of congratulations which may have been pouring in to you, my most gracious Sir, I know full well that it will not be without *sacrifice to YIH* that this new honour is bestowed. But I think of what a widening sphere of action will be opened thereby for you and for your great noble-mindedness. So I can only extend my congratulations about this honour to YIH along with the others. There is almost nothing that is good – without sacrifice, and this appears to apply directly to the nobler, superior man more than others, thereby his virtue becomes tested.

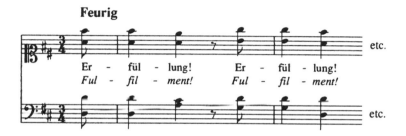

This I might sing out now from the bottom of my heart, were YIH completely recovered; but the new sphere of action, the transformation, the subsequent travels will certainly bring back soon the priceless health of Your Imperial Highness to a perfect state; and then I shall elaborate on the above theme with a hearty A–men or Allelujah – . . .'

Beethoven returns to this subject later in the letter: 'The day when a High Mass of mine shall be performed at the ceremonies for YIH will be for me the most beautiful day of my life, and God will inspire me so that my weak powers may contribute to the glorification of this solemn day – . . . '

The new honour 'bestowed' upon the Archduke was first his elevation to Cardinal and then to Archbishop of Olmütz. The date of his installation was set for 20 March 1820. The following testimony of Schindler determines just when Beethoven started composing his great work which was to be known as the *Missa Solemnis*. Schindler writes:

'Without invitation of any kind Beethoven resolved to compose a mass for the solemnity, thus turning again after the lapse of many years to that branch of his art towards which, after the symphonies – as he himself often said – he felt himself most drawn . . . I saw the score begun late in the autumn of 1818, after the gigantic Sonata in B flat major, Op. 106, had just been finished.'

Now to return to the first topic, the family struggle. The long court procedures had been wearing, and the final blow had been the transfer of the case to the City Magistracy because Beethoven was not of the nobility. Doubtless he was also filled with fear as to what the decision of the new tribunal would be.

At this point a few official data are wanting, but the suspension of Beethoven from the guardianship of his nephew can only be stated as having been determined by the magistrates immediately after the beginning of the new year. In consequence of this, the boy was for a few weeks with his mother. On 10 January, Fanny Giannatasio writes in her diary:

'What Müller tells me about Beethoven pains me deeply. The wicked woman has finally succeeded in triumphing over him. He has been removed from the guardianship, and the wicked son returns to the source of his wickedness. I can imagine Beethoven's grief. It is said that since yesterday he has been entirely alone and eats apart from the others. He ought to know that Karl is glad to be with his mother; it would ease the pain of the separation.'

On 7 January the magistrates summoned Beethoven, the boy, the mother, Hotschevar and the curator, Dr Schönauer, to appear before them on 11 January. Of what action was taken that day there is no record, but Hotschevar's attack brought out a vigorous defence in the shape of a letter sent by Beethoven to the Magistracy, in which he maintained the superiority of the educational plan which he was pursuing over that which had been proposed by the mother, proclaimed the magnanimity and virtuousness of all his acts and discharged a broadside of accusation and insinuation against Frau van Beethoven and the priest who had come to her help.

From the records of the Magistracy and his own words it appears that Beethoven did not send his nephew to a public school, but engaged a private tutor under whose care he continued his studies in an institute conducted by one Johann Kudlich. Beethoven held this man in great esteem judging by his letter to the Magistracy (of 1 February 1819) in which he says 'That Herr v. Kudlich teaches and practises himself the basic methods of the university which all connoisseurs consider the best as I do myself.' Besides the ordinary subjects, Karl received instruction from Kudlich in French, drawing and music; his religious training was entrusted to a priest. This state of affairs lasted till the end of March, when Beethoven announced a desire to resign the guardianship – persuaded to take this step, it is fair to presume, by the magistrates, who, in the end, would have been obliged to remove him. Karl was living with his mother at the time. According to the court records, Beethoven left the matter of education 'entirely to Kudlich', but it was given to him to propose the name of a guardian, either in place of himself or as an associate. He consulted earnestly with his friends as to what was to be done with the boy and who would be his guardian, and they were sorely tried by his constitutional indecision.

The friend who was the most helpful and influential in these affairs was the writer and editor, Joseph Karl Bernard. His acquaintance with Beethoven started at the time of the Vienna Congress, and by 1819 his name was appearing regularly in the Conversation Books. While other members of the circle, such as Oliva, were given the perfunctory jobs of taking dictation and running errands, Bernard was entrusted with a real responsibility: the reworking of the contents of Beethoven's documents until they were legally acceptable. His friendship and advice were invaluable.

In the Conversation Books for March and April 1819, Bernard writes:

'What must be done is to select as guardian a man who has your entire confidence both as respects morality and pedagogical skill, and with whom you may always remain on friendly terms concerning the affair. Since Kudlich has more influence on Karl than . . . Giànatassio [Giannatasio], it is my opinion that you seek no further for someone who would meet every requirement. – It would merely be very troublesome for you.'

Beethoven seemed to be in doubt, for he had a preference for his friend the magisterial Councillor Tuscher. But he seems to have expressed a doubt as to Tuscher's willingness to serve as guardian. Bernard continues: 'Perhaps he might be more easily persuaded if a co-guardian like Kudlich were appointed. It is not necessary to settle everything by tomorrow.'

Tuscher permitted himself to be persuaded, though a bit under protest; he foresaw difficulties. The Magistracy at the suggestion of

Beethoven thereupon appointed the Magisterial Councillor Matthias von Tuscher guardian of the boy on 26 March. He was commanded to place his ward, then 'living with his mother, Johanna van Beethoven', in another place for bringing up and education under proper care, and submit his opinion touching the proposition of the mother and Hotschevar that he be entered in a public institute of learning, that Beethoven contribute to the cost and that the share of the mother's pension and the interest on the money deposited for the boy be applied to this end.

What further could be done? His mind being filled with artistic projects of the greatest magnitude, Beethoven was desirous to pass the summer months again in Mödling, where he moved on 12 May. Now he came to a realisation of the advantages which Giannatasio's institute had offered and in a letter to Giannatasio asked him again to take the lad till other arrangements had been made. The Giannatasio family were fearful lest such a proceeding might work harm to their institution, and on 17 June visited Beethoven at Mödling to tell him that his wishes could not be complied with. 'Grievously as it pained us', Fanny writes in her diary, 'to refuse Beethoven anything, I am yet so convinced of the necessity of the step and that it could do us no good, but on the contrary harm, that I prefer to have it so.'

Thereupon the lad was sent to yet another institute – that of Joseph Blöchlinger in the Landstrasse suburb of Vienna. He appears to have prospered during the early part of his stay at the school. In December 1819 Karl Peters, who was later to assist Beethoven in the litigation, writes in a Conversation Book:

'A great deal has been gained in that the boy has again become orderly in his public studies – Plöchlinger moreover, though not exactly brilliant, seems to be good.
The public school system acts as a restraint on him . . .
Your nephew looks well, handsome eyes – charm, a speaking physiognomy, and excellent bearing. I would continue his education for only two years more . . .'

Tuscher, a member of the Magistracy, was compelled to recognise that his colleagues were wholly under the influence of Frau van Beethoven and Hotschevar; on 5 July, he applied to be relieved of the guardianship which, he said, had become 'in every respect burdensome and vexatious', on the ground that 'the multiplicity of official duties as well as various other considerations would not permit him longer to administer the office'. Beethoven took this action in very bad part, and Tuscher shared the fate of many others of being for a space an object of the composer's critical ill will. Beethoven now served notice on the Magistracy that he would resume the guardianship under the testamentary appointment and that he had placed his ward in Blöchlinger's institution.

He continued, during the summer and autumn, to bombard his friends and those who were helping him with many long letters, containing directives and invectives. Evidently Blöchlinger allowed the boy's mother to visit him at the school, a fact which infuriated Beethoven. Blöchlinger received several violently worded epistles from him on the subject, in which Beethoven refers to himself as 'sole guardian' though he had not been legally appointed as such after Tuscher's resignation. On 14 September he wrote to Blöchlinger: '*Only the following individuals have free access to my nephew, Herr von Bernard, Herr von Oliva, Herr von Piuk, the Referent.*' This last was Franz Xaver Piuk, who was Referent, or Recording Secretary, for the court in this affair. Beethoven had written to him fully and at the time seemed to have enlisted his support. Further in the letter to Blöchlinger he continues: '*My nephew is not to go out of the house without my written permission* – from which it is plain what course is to be followed towards the mother – I insist that in this respect *strict obedience* be given to what the authorities and I have ordained.'

It is not known whether the Magistracy was immediately informed of all of the new steps which Beethoven had taken, though in his draft of the memorandum to the Court of Appeal Beethoven states that he 'wrote' to them that he had resumed the guardianship. Be that as it may, as chief guardian the court determined if possible to put an end to the continual friction and undertook an investigation of all the educational experiments which had been made, arriving at the conclusion that the boy had been 'subject to the whims of Beethoven and had been tossed back and forth like a ball from one educational institution to another'. For this reason it decreed, on 17 September, that Tuscher's request for relief be granted, but that the guardianship should not again be entrusted to Beethoven but to the mother, the natural guardian under the law, with a capable and honest man as co-guardian. To this office Leopold Nussböck, municipal sequestrator, was appointed.

Beethoven protested against the action in a letter which the Magistracy received on 31 October. Having been absent from the city at the time, 'on a matter of business', he had made no objection to the appointment of Herr Nussböck as guardian of his nephew, but, returning with the intention of remaining in Vienna, he wished to resume the guardianship, as this was essential to the welfare of the boy, the

mother having neither the will nor the strength to look after his training. He was the more insistent on a resumption of this duty since he
had learned that owing to lack of money the boy was to be removed
from the institution which he had selected for him. He charged that
the mother wished to take her son to her home so that she might be
able to expend his income, including the half of her pension which she
was obliged to devote to his education, upon herself. He asked that the
intermediary guardianship be taken from Nussböck and be restored to
him without delay.

Acting as a legal adviser to Beethoven at this time was Johann
Baptist Bach, who had helped him since 1816 in his dealings with the
authorities concerning his nephew. A distinguished Vienna lawyer,
Schindler describes him as 'a man of many accomplishments including
a practising lover of music, who was active on more than a dilettante
basis, particularly as violoncellist in a quartet'. Concerning his petition
to the Magistracy, Beethoven wrote to Dr Bach at length on 27 October:

'You will have already received the communication from Frau van
Beethoven. That person is too lacking in moral worth for me to refute
her attacks against me. His Imperial Highness, Eminence and Cardinal, who treats me as a friend and not as a servant, would unhesitatingly bear witness to my morality, and to all the silly twaddle about
Olmütz,* not a word of which is true. So far as one knows, His Highness himself will spend at most six weeks of the year there . . .

'The chief points are that I be recognised at once as sole guardian; I
will accept no co-guardian; that the mother be excluded from intercourse with her son *in the Institute* because in view of her *immorality*
there cannot be enough watchmen there and she confuses the master
by the false statements and lies which she tells him. Also she has led her
son to tell shameful lies and make charges *against me*, and she herself
accuses me of having given him too much or too little; I will substanti-
ate all these statements with evidence – But that the claims of humanity may not be overlooked, she may see her son occasionally at my
home in the presence of the master and other eminent people . . . It is
my opinion that you should insist stoutly and irrevocably that I be *sole*
guardian and that this unnatural mother shall see her son only *at my
house*. My well-known humanity and culture as well as my accustomed
humaneness towards others are a guarantee that my treatment of her
will be no less generous than that given her son. Moreover I think that
all this should be done quickly and that if possible we ought to get the

* Johanna had charged that Beethoven as the Archduke's teacher would now be
obliged to spend most of his time at Olmütz.

Appellate Court to assume the superior guardianship. Since I have brought my nephew into a higher category, neither he nor I belong to the M[agistracy] under whose guardianship are only innmakers, shoe-makers and tailors . . .'

The Magistracy disposed of Beethoven's protest and application on 4 November, by curtly referring him to the disposition made of his petition in September, when he was removed from the guardianship. Beethoven asked for a reconsideration, but without avail, and the only recourse remaining to him was the appeal to the higher court which had already been suggested to Dr Bach. The story of that appeal belongs to the following year.

Citations from the so-called Conversation Books made in the course of the narrative call for some remarks upon this source of information. Schindler wrote: 'Beethoven's hearing had already become too weak for oral conversation, even now with the help of an ear-trumpet, in 1818, and recourse had now to be had to writing. Only in the case of intercourse with Archduke Rudolph, and here because of his gentle voice, the smallest of the ear-trumpets remained of service for several years more.' The Conversation Books, counting in as such those which were really nothing but a sheet or two of paper loosely folded, were only about 400 in number, or less than fifty per annum for the last nine years of Beethoven's life – that being the period which they cover. There is no source of information for the biographer of Beethoven which at first sight appears so rich and productive and yet, to the con-scientious writer, proves so provokingly defective and requires such extreme caution in its use as these Conversation Books.

The larger of them – ordinary blank notebooks – are only of a size and thickness fitted to be carried in the coat pocket. It is obvious, there-fore, on a moment's reflection, that at a single sitting with a few friends in an inn or coffee-house, the pages must have filled rapidly as the book passed from hand to hand and one or another wrote question or reply, remark or statement, a bit of news or a piece of advice. A few such conversations, one sees, would fill a book, all the sooner as there is no thought of economising space and each new sentence is usually also a new paragraph. It strikes one, therefore, that the whole 400 could have contained but a small portion of the conversations of the period they covered. This was so. At home a slate or any loose scraps of paper were commonly used, thus saving a heavy item of expense; moreover, many who conversed with Beethoven would only write upon the slate in order to obliterate it immediately, that nothing should remain exposed to the eyes of others. The books, therefore, were for the most part for use when the composer was away from home, although there were occasions when, it being desirable to preserve what was written, they were also used there. Hence, they can be viewed as little more than scattered specimens of the conversations of the master's friends and companions, most unequally distributed as to time. For months together there is nothing or hardly anything; and then again a few days will fill many scores of leaves. In a few instances Beethoven has himself written – that is, when in some public place he did not trust his voice; and memoranda of divers kinds, even of musical ideas from his pen, are not infrequent.

Though Karl was no longer a member of the Giannatasio household or pupil of the institute, and though there were, in consequence, fewer meetings between Beethoven and his self-sacrificing friends, their relations remained pleasant, and early in 1819 Beethoven found occasion to supplement his verbal protestations of gratitude with a deed. Nanni, the younger daughter of Giannatasio, was married on 6 February 1819, to Leopold Schmerling. When the young couple returned to the house after the ceremony they were greeted by a wedding hymn for tenor solo, men's voices and pianoforte accompaniment. The performers were hidden in a corner of the room. When they had finished they stepped forth from their place of concealment. Beethoven was among them and he handed to the bride the manuscript of the music which he had written for the occasion.

Mödling was chosen again for the annual country sojourn and Beethoven arrived there on 12 May, taking lodgings as before in the Hafner house on the Hauptstrasse. He had, evidently, brought a housekeeper with him and now engaged a housemaid. On the blank leaves of an Almanac for 1819, such as used to be bound in those useful household publications for the reception of memoranda, Beethoven notes: 'Came to Mödling, 12 May!!! *Miser sum pauper...*'

In 1810 Adolf Martin Schlesinger had opened his own bookshop in Berlin. Starting with a music lending library, he soon developed what was to be Berlin's first music publishing house. A few years later his son, Moritz, followed in his father's footsteps and opened a music publishing house in Paris. Father and son worked closely together and often published simultaneously. The Schlesingers were intelligent enough to cultivate Beethoven's friendship and eventually they were to be rewarded with the publication of, among other things, his last three pianoforte sonatas and the string quartets, Op. 132 and Op. 135. In 1819 the father sent Moritz to Vienna to become acquainted with Beethoven. According to young Schlesinger's reminiscences:

'After getting out of the wagon I went to the inn and found Beethoven there, who came out of the door in a fury and slammed it hard behind him. After I had dusted off a bit I went to the house which was designated as his dwelling. His housekeeper told me that it would be better not to speak to him as he had returned home in a rage. I gave her my visiting card which she brought to him, and after a few minutes to my great astonishment she came out again and bade me enter. Inside I found the great man at his writing desk. Immediately I *wrote* that I was glad to make his acquaintance. This (the fact that I *wrote*) made a favourable impression. He let himself go immediately and told me that he was the most miserable man in the world; a minute ago he came out of the inn where he had asked for a piece of *veal* which he especially desired; but *there was none there* – all this with a very serious and dark expression. I comforted him; we spoke (I always writing) of other things and so he detained me for two hours; then feeling that I would tire or upset him I wanted often to get up but he always held me back. After leaving him I hurried back to Vienna in my wagon and asked my inn boy if there was any roast veal available. Upon finding there was I left it on the platter, well covered up, and, without writing a word, I gave it to the man waiting with the carriage to take to [Mödling] and present to Beethoven in my name. One morning soon afterwards I was still lying in bed when in came Beethoven, who kissed and embraced me and said I was the best fellow he had ever met; never had anything made him so happy as this veal for which at that moment he had had such a longing.'

Beethoven, as letters to the Archduke dated 15 July and 31 August show, was not in the best of health, but was hard at work on the Mass, with an excursion now and then into the Symphony (Ninth). Schindler presents us with a pathetic, impressive, almost terrifying picture of the state to which his labours lifted him:

'Towards the end of August, accompanied by the musician Johann Horzalka still living in Vienna, I arrived at the master's home in Mödling. It was 4 o'clock in the afternoon. As soon as we entered we learned that in the morning both servants had gone away, and that there had been a quarrel after midnight which had disturbed all the neighbours, because as a consequence of a long vigil both had gone to sleep and the food which had been prepared had become unpalatable. In the living-room, behind a locked door, we heard the master singing parts of the fugue in the *Credo* – singing, howling, stamping. After we had been listening a long time to this almost awful scene, and were about to go away, the door opened and Beethoven stood before us with distorted features, calculated to excite fear. He looked as if he had been in mortal combat with the whole host of contrapuntists, his everlasting enemies. His first utterances were confused, as if he had been disagreeably surprised at our having overheard him. Then he reached the day's happenings and with obvious restraint he remarked: "Pretty doings, these [*Saubere Wirtschaft*], everybody has run away and I haven't had anything to eat since yesternoon!" I tried to calm him and helped him to make his toilet. My companion hurried on in advance to the restaurant of the bathing establishment to have something made ready for the famished master. Then he complained about the wretched state of his domestic affairs, but here, for reasons already stated, there was nothing to be done. Never, it may be said, did so great an artwork as is the *Missa Solemnis* see its creation under more adverse circumstances!'

In a conversation of late March or early April, someone, probably Oliva, writes:

'– Is the oratorio finished?
I cannot understand how he is so occupied; his professional work amounts to nothing and other than that he does nothing, and yet he talks all the time about so much work and business.'

The author in question was Bernard, who had been designated to write the text for the oratorio which Beethoven had been commissioned to write for the Gesellschaft der Musikfreunde. As we shall see, the writing of the libretto remained an obstacle for this project. Meanwhile, on 15 June Beethoven had received an advance payment for the work, for on this date he wrote the following note to the society:

'Dear esteemed Sir!
    'I am lying in bed and from here cannot immediately elaborate on the subject of the oratorio – Meanwhile I shall write to you about it in a few days or speak to you in person. I confirm for you herewith by virtue of my own signature that I have received 400 fl. VS.
                    Respectfully and most sincerely
                                    Beethoven'

Pathetic and diverting are the incidents which Karl Friedrich Zelter relates in letters to Goethe of his attempts to form a closer acquaintance with Beethoven. On 29 July he writes concerning his journey to Austria:

'Beethoven, whom I would like to see once during my lifetime, lives in the country and no one can tell me where.' On 16 August he writes:

'. . . It is said that he is intolerably *maussade*. Some say he is a lunatic. It is easy to talk. God forgive us all our sins! The poor man is reported as being totally deaf. . . Lately Beethoven went to an eating-house; he sat himself down to a table and lost himself in thought. After an hour he calls the waiter: "What do I owe?" – "The gentleman has not eaten anything yet, what shall I bring?" – "Bring anything you please, but let me alone!"'

Then on 14 September he writes:

'The day before yesterday I wanted to pay a visit to Beethoven in Mödling. He wanted to go to Vienna, so we met en route, climbed out and embraced one another affectionately. The poor fellow is practically stone deaf and I could hardly restrain my tears. Then I went on to Mödling and he to Vienna. – I must tell you about an episode that amused me considerably. – With me on this trip was Steiner, the music publisher, and since it is rather hard to converse with a deaf man on a country road, we arranged a proper meeting with Beethoven at four o'clock in the afternoon in Steiner's music store. After eating we drove back to Vienna at once. Full as a badger and tired as a dog I lay down and slept away the time, slept so soundly that not a thing entered my mind. Then I went to the theatre and when I saw Beethoven there I felt as if I had been struck by lightning. The same thing happened to him at sight of me, and this was not the place for explanations with a deaf man. Now comes the point: in spite of the things of which Beethoven is accused justly or unjustly, he enjoys a popular respect such as is be-stowed only upon the most excellent. Steiner had given it out that Beet-hoven would appear in his little office, which will hold only six or eight persons, for the first time in person at 4 o'clock, and invited guests so generously that in a room crowded to the street, half a hundred brilliant people waited in vain. I did not get an explanation till next day, when I received a letter from Beethoven in which he begged my pardon, for he, like me, had passed the time set for the meeting in blissful sleep.'

In August, Johann van Beethoven bought the Wasserhof estate near Gneixendorf. This would bring the brothers closer together in the period to follow. That Beethoven was also interested in acquiring some property at this time is shown by a letter which he wrote to Steiner:

'Mödling, 10 October 1819

'Dear Steiner!

'The day before yesterday I left you a note asking you to come here before the sale of the house; you would really be doing me a great kindness. The sale is on the 13th, thus next Wednesday. It is not possible for me to undertake anything to do with this without your help. The capital cannot be in any way reduced through this since naturally my nephew, who will devote himself to learning, needs support after my death for the continuation of his studies. – If you have had the record of baptism made through a notary, I will gratefully repay you the expense of it. –

To the WORTHY

LITTLE TOBIAS*

I have spoken about the Archduke var., I have proposed *you* for them since I do not believe that you will incur a loss from them and it is always honourable to print something from such a Principe Professore. – As to the corporal I beg you to tell him that he is not to sell anything of which I have notified him until I come to the city; also he must not forget to notify those who are moving and the landlady at the Landstrasse that the bell and window shades are mine. – I hope to see you tomorrow or the day after; mornings are the best since we must talk with H. v. Carbon, at which time we could also get a look at the house; and you could examine everything, if necessary also at the registry, and you could act as a judex since my decision will be based completely upon your judgement. –'

The house in question must have been an old ecclesiastical house called 'Christof' which was in secular possession by 1819 and advertised for sale in August. Beethoven was evidently outbid by Johann Speer, who bought the house and rented the apartment on the first floor to Beethoven the following summer.

The variations composed by the Archduke were, it will be remembered, on a theme composed by Beethoven and given to his imperial pupil as a lesson, and had called forth the obsequious remarks previously quoted in his New Year's letter to the Archduke. His remark to Steiner is explained by the fact that on 31 August he had written to the Archduke as follows:

'. . . As regards the masterly variations of YIH I think they might be published under the following title, namely:

* Presumably Tobias Haslinger, Steiner's partner.

'Theme, or Task
set by L. v. Beeth.
forty times varied
and dedicated to his teacher
by the *Most Serene Author*

'There are so many requests for them, and eventually this honourable work will reach the public in garbled copies. YIH will yourself not be able to avoid presenting copies here and there; therefore, in the name of God, among the many consecrations which YIH is receiving and of which the world is being informed, let the consecration of Apollo (or in Christian terms Cäcilia) also be made known. True, YIH may accuse me of *vanity*; but I can assure you that although this dedication is precious to me and I am really proud of it, this is not at all my ultimate aim. Three publishers have appealed for it; Artaria, Steiner and a third whose name does not come to me. Considering but the first two, to which shall the Variations be given? On this point I await the commands of YIH. Both of them have offered to print the variations at *their own cost*. The question now is whether YIH is *satisfied with the title?* To the question whether or not the variations ought to be published, YIH ought to close your eyes; if it is done, YIH *may call it* a misfortune; but *the world will think the contrary . . .*'

Steiner printed the archducal work in the seventh number of his *Musée musical des Clavicinistes* under a slightly changed title, viz.: 'Theme [*Aufgabe*] composed by Ludwig van Beethoven, varied forty times and dedicated to the author by his pupil R[udolph], A[rch-] D[uke].' Other evidences of Beethoven's interest in Archduke Rudolph's studies in composition are shown by a letter to his patron dated 29 July 1819. It deserves to be given in full because of passages which, although vaguely worded, give some indication of Beethoven's attitude towards his art.

'Your Imperial Highness!
'I was indeed sorry to receive the news of a new indisposition of Your Highness; and since I have had no further definite news, I am very much upset – I was in Vienna in order to look in the library of YIH for some things most useful for me. The central plan is a *quick recognition* of the essential coupled with a *greater artistic unity* in respect of which practical considerations sometimes compel an exception as we may learn in a twofold way from the old composers, where we find stress laid chiefly upon the artistically valuable (among these only the *German*

Händel and *Sebastian Bach* had genius). But *freedom, progress,* these are the aims in the world of art as in the whole great universe. Even if we moderns are not so far advanced in *sound technique* [*Festigheit*] as our *forefathers,* yet refinement in manners has opened many new things to us. My exalted pupil in music, already a fellow-contestant for the laurel of fame, must not subject himself to the accusation of one-sidedness – et iterum venturus judicare *vivos* – et *mortuos.* – Here are three poems of which YIH could perhaps set one to music. The Austrians now know already that the *spirit of Apollo* has newly awakened in the Imperial family. From all quarters I receive requests for something [by you]. The *proprietor of the Modenzeitung* will appeal to YIH *in writing,* I hope I *shall not be accused of bribery – at court and no courtier, what possibilities??!!!* In my search for music in Vienna I found some resistance from *His Excellency the Chief Steward.* It is not worth the trouble to burden YIH in writing about it; I only must say this much, that because of this, many talented, good and noble men would be frightened away from YIH, who did not have the good fortune to become acquainted with your excellent qualities of spirit and heart – I wish YIH a speedy, speedy recovery and some news of it for the sake of *my peace of mind.* –

Your Imper. Highness's most obedient and faithful servant

L. v. Beethoven'

That his mind was full of his Mass is indicated by the quotation from the text of the *Credo* and that he was consulting authorities on ecclesiastical music for this purpose is suggested by his reference to Bach and Handel.

In the autumn of this year was painted probably the best known portrait of Beethoven: the oil painting by Ferdinand Schimon. Concerning the origin of this picture Schindler has this explanation. Schimon had permission through Schindler to set up his easel in the chamber adjoining Beethoven's workroom, the composer resolutely having refused a sitting because he was busy on the Mass. From this point of vantage he made his studies and had finished all but the eyes – the most striking feature in the portrait. Out of this dilemma Beethoven unconsciously helped him. He had evidently been impressed with the discretion, or independence, of the young artist who came without a 'good morning' and went without a 'good evening', and invited him to coffee. Thus Schimon had ample opportunity to supply the one deficiency in his sketches. Schindler adds: 'From an artistic point of view Schimon's work is not a distinguished work of art, yet full of characteristic truth. In the rendering of that particular look, the majestic forehead, this dwelling-place of mighty, sublime ideas, of hues, in the drawing of the firmly shut mouth and the chin shaped like a shell, it is truer to nature than any other picture.'

According to Schindler it was at the end of October that Beethoven returned to Vienna from Mödling. His new lodging is described by him in a Conversation Book of March 1820, as 'opposite the Auersperg palace in the same house where the coffee-house is in the Josephstadt Glacis'. This move was made so that he could be near the Blöchlinger institute; and Fanny Giannatasio del Rio writes in her diary on 1 December 1819: 'Beethoven, whom we do not hear of now at all lives ... in the Josefstadt naturally because of the boy.' But Beethoven may have had a second lodging at the same time since his home is recorded in two court records dated 30 October 1819 and 7 January 1820 as 'im Blumenstöckel' near the newspaper office.

It is remarkable that Beethoven, under the circumstances which have been set forth, could continue his labours on the Mass which were his principal occupation during the year; it was but another proof of the absorbing possession which the composition of a great work took of him when once fairly begun. So diligently did he apply himself that he had hopes not only of finishing it in time for the installation of the Archduke as Archbishop of Olmütz, but he wrote to Ries on 10 November that he had already nearly completed it and would like to know what could be done with it in London. To Schindler, however, in expressing a doubt that he would have it done in time for the ceremonial, he said that every movement had taken on larger dimensions than had originally been contemplated. Schindler says also that when the day came, not one of the movements was finished in the eyes of the composer.

That he worked occasionally on the Ninth Symphony, especially in the early part of the year, has already been said. Another work which was not to be completed until a later time was probably conceived in this year. In a letter to Simrock dated 10 February 1820, Beethoven offered his wares which included, characteristically, works that were far from completion. On this list besides the Mass, which he was offering for an honorarium of 125 louis d'or, Beethoven mentions some 'big variations on a well-known "Deutsche", which, however, I cannot promise you as yet and if you wish them will notify you later of the honorarium'. This refers to the variations on a waltz by Diabelli, who conceived the idea of inviting several composers to contribute variations to his theme for a collection to be published as a monument to Austrian talent. Beethoven was not to complete his variations until 1823, but as already mentioned there are sketches for the work alongside those for the *Kyrie* of the Mass, which may be dated 1819.

*

Beethoven had become a lonely man – an enforced seeker of solitude. No doubt many who would have been glad to give him their friendship were deterred by the widespread reports of his suspicious, unapproachable, almost repellent nature. But a miracle happened. Driven in upon himself by the forces which seem to have been arrayed against him, introspection opened wider and wider to him the doors of that imagination which in its creative function, as Ruskin tells us, is 'an eminent beholder of things when and where they are not; a seer, that is, in the prophetic sense'.

But to take up the story of the incubus which oppressed the composer's mind, the clog which impeded his creative activities much of the year – the legal proceedings concerning the guardianship of nephew Karl. Fortunately the end is not distant.

Two applications made by Beethoven to the Court of Magistrates had been denied and he now asked for a review of these decisions by the Court of Appeals. The action of the Magistracy had grievously pained him, so he informed the superior tribunal, and not only had his rights been set aside, but no regard had been shown for the welfare of his nephew. Against this he now sought relief, and he set forth his grievances: (1) he was testamentary appointee and the Landrecht had confirmed him and excluded the mother; (2) the higher education which his nephew's talents demanded neither the mother nor Nussböck could direct; (3) having no child of his own, his hopes were set on the boy, who was unusually talented. Being 'somewhat hard of hearing' communication with him was difficult and therefore he had asked that a co-guardian be appointed in the person of Herr Peters, councillor to Prince Lobkowitz, whose knowledge and moral character would assure such a training and education as were justified by the boy's capacity. 'I know of no more sacred duty than the care and education of a child,' he observes. He would offer no objection to the mother's having a 'sort of joint-guardianship', but its duties and privileges should be limited to her visiting him and learning what plans were being made for his education; to permit more would be to compass the ruin of the boy.

This petition was filed on 7 January 1820; three days later the Appellate Court commanded the Magistracy to file a report of the proceedings held before it, together with all minutes and documents. The Magistracy complied, reiterating its decision of 17 September 1819.

In a Conversation Book at the beginning of the year, Bernard writes: 'The case will soon reach a firm decision since the Appellate Court has intervened.' To strengthen his case for this court, Beethoven spent several weeks on a 'memorial' which describes the history of the case from his point of view. In turning to Bernard for help in the editing of this document, Beethoven was also confident of its success in the near future. He writes:

'Dear Bernard! As I find myself alone again today in these to me confusing circumstances, a true understanding of my memorial has come to me for the first time. Without wishing to be resplendent in another person's feathers, still I believe I should leave it to your discretion to handle everything according to your superior judgement, since you in a few words can say as much or more as I can in sheets. The case would become more forceful and intelligible for the judges as a result. But this must be completed soon. Consider that you are labouring for Karl's happiness and for the only possible state of contentment for me and contributing to it for *the last time* – Once again do as you like with my raw material according to your judgement. In any case you write more clearly than I and the copy would soon be ready.

Your friend and admirer Beethoven'

The Court of Appeals demanded a more explicit report. The Magistracy complied on 28 February, taking advantage of the opportunity to review the proceedings held before the Landrecht from the beginning, and to make severe strictures on the conduct of Beethoven in filing an exhibit (F) with his petition in support of which no evidence was offered.

'Exhibit F' has not been found and its contents can only be guessed at from the allusions to it in the documents. Obviously it contained aspersions on the moral character of Frau van Beethoven, and it probably was true that they were unsupported by evidence and therefore undeserving of consideration in a court either of law or equity. On the other hand, it is singular that the Magistrates in their final effort to justify their course had nothing to say about the present moral standing of the woman whose legal and natural right they claimed to be upholding. Were they in ignorance of what we now know, that her conduct had not only been reprehensible in 1811 (though condoned by her husband) but continued so after her husband's death? Schindler says that she gave birth to a child while the case was pending, and that is confirmed by a statement of nephew Karl's widow that in her old age Frau van Beethoven lived in Baden with this illegitimate daughter, who was also a dissolute woman.

On 6 March Beethoven writes to Karl Winter, a Councillor of Appeal:

'I have the honour of informing you that I have written a memorial

consisting of information about Fr. van Beethoven, about the Magistracy, about my nephew, about myself, etc. which I will send you within
a few days. I *believed* that I owed this to myself to expose the falsity of
the many slanders which have been uttered *against me* and to lay bare
the intrigues of Frau van Beethoven *against me* to the injury of her own
child, as also to place in its proper light the conduct of the Magistrates'
Court.'

He asked that the charges against him be re-examined.

The case to the Appellate Court was prepared shrewdly, carefully
and most discreetly by Dr Bach, who seems to have advised Beethoven
to visit two of the judges and himself had an interview with the boy,
who told his uncle what the advocate had questioned him about.

For the nonce Karl was on his good behaviour. Blöchlinger reported
favourably on his studies to Bernard, and in a Conversation Book the
boy apologised to his uncle for some statements derogatory to him
which he had made to the Magistrates. 'She promised me so many
things', he said, 'that I could not resist her; I am sorry that I was so
weak at the time and beg your forgiveness.'

The magisterial commission which followed on 29 March had
plainly been held at the instance of the Appellate Court. Beethoven was
solemnly admonished, and in answer to questions declared: (1) that he
still demanded the guardianship of his nephew under the will and
would not relinquish his claim; (2) that he requested the appointment
of Councillor Peters as associate guardian; (3) that he demanded that
Frau van Beethoven be excluded from the guardianship as she had
been by the Landrecht; and (4) he reiterated his readiness to provide
financially for the care of his ward.

On 8 April the reviewing court issued its decree in Beethoven's
favour, he and Peters being appointed joint guardians, the mother and
Nussböck being deposed. The widow now played her last card: she
appealed to the Emperor, who upheld the Court of Appeals. There was
nothing for the Magistracy to do except to notify the result of the
appeals to Beethoven, Frau van Beethoven, Peters and Nussböck. This
was done on 24 July.

Beethoven had won at last. But at what a cost to himself, his art, the
world! What time, what labour, what energy had he not taken away
from his artistic creations! What had he not expended in the way of
peace of mind, of friendship, of physical comfort, of wear of brain and
nerve-force, for the privilege of keeping the boy to himself, of watching unmolested over his physical welfare and directing his intellectual
and moral training unhindered! At the present moment, however, his

joy was unbounded, and he gave it expression in the following letter to his friend Karl Pinterics:

'Dear Herr v. Pinterics!

'I am reporting to you that the civil senate was authorised by the high Appellate Court to inform me of their decision which gives me complete satisfaction. – Dr Bach was my representative in this affair, and this *brook* [in German: *Bach*] was joined by the sea, with lightning, thunder and storm, and the magisterial brigantine suffered complete shipwreck.

Yours faithfully,
Beethoven'

Schindler says that 'his happiness over the triumph which he had won over wickedness and trickery, but also because of the supposed salvation from physical danger of his talented nephew, was so great that he worked but little or hardly at all all summer – though this was perhaps more apparent than real, the sketchbooks disclosing from now on only empty pages'. A wise qualification, for though the sketchbooks may have been empty, there is evidence enough elsewhere of hard work. Yet the Mass was not finished, and for this unfortunate circumstance the guardianship trial was no doubt to blame.

Peters, who was appointed joint guardian with Beethoven of the nephew, was a tutor in the house of Prince Lobkowitz and had been on terms of friendship with Beethoven since 1816. His appointment by the court is a confirmation of Beethoven's tribute to him as a man of intellectual parts and of good moral character.

Nephew Karl remained at Blöchlinger's institute and continued to cause worry and anxiety to his uncle. Reports to Beethoven concerning his conduct and studies were variable from different persons and at different times. According to Blöchlinger he was unsteady and inclined to be lazy, and it was with great difficulty that he had again been made to work. He writes in March: 'Since he has been with us, he has always been treated strictly, otherwise we would not have progressed as far as we now have.' There must have been further bad experiences for again in April someone writes: 'Karl has little spirit and NB despite the knowledge for which he is praised, little intelligence – that is probably the key to this otherwise unpardonable behaviour.'

Meanwhile work on the Mass was continuing, as the sketchbooks show. Exactly what condition it was in at that time we have no means of knowing; it was, however, in a sufficient state of forwardness to enable Beethoven to begin negotiations for its publication. In a letter

to the firm of Simrock on 10 February Beethoven offered the Mass
for 125 louis d'or. He repeated the offer in a letter of 9 March and
suggested on 14 March that perhaps he could ask for a lower figure.
What was offered by Simrock as a counter-offer is made clear from
Beethoven's answer which follows:

'Vienna, 18 March 1820

'Dear Herr Simrock!

'I don't know whether I discussed everything completely in my last
letter – I am writing to you briefly therefore that I can extend the date
for the edition of the variations, if you find it necessary. – As regards
the Mass, I have pondered the matter carefully and might give it to you
for the honorarium of 100 louis d'or which you offered me, provided
you agree to a few conditions which I shall propose and which, I think,
you will *not* find burdensome. We have gone through the plan for publication here and believe that with a *few modifications* it can be put into
effect very soon. This is very necessary, wherefore I shall make haste to
inform you of the necessary changes soon – Since I know that dealers
like to save post money, I enclose 2 Austrian folk-tunes here as change
with which you can do what you like. The accompaniments are mine –
I think a folk-song hunt is better than a man-hunt of such exalted
heroes – My copyist is not here now; I hope you will be able to read it –
in fact you could have many things from me, for which you could show
me another favour –

In haste   Yours
Beethoven'

The enthronement of Beethoven's imperial pupil as Archbishop of
Olmütz took place on 20 March. The Mass which was to have been the
composer's tribute was still unfinished.

At this time some new portraits were made of the master, including
a half-length drawing in chalk by the artist Hippius which, according
to his family, was based on a sitting with the composer. It is almost life-
size and is similar to the Schimon in the interpretation of Beethoven's
features.

Another of the portraits of Beethoven which have been made familiar by reproductions was begun in 1819. Joseph Stieler, who enjoyed
wide reputation as a portrait painter, had made the acquaintance of
Beethoven through a letter of introduction probably given to him by
Brentano. Beethoven took a liking to him and gave him three sittings,
but because Beethoven refused to sit longer, Stieler had to exercise his
imagination or memory in painting the hands. In fact, the painting

never received the finishing touches but remained, as those who have seen it testify, 'sketchy'. In April 1820, Stieler asks the question: 'In what key is your mass? I want to write on the sheet Mass in –.' Beethoven writes the answer 'D, Missa solemnis in D', and Stieler: 'A quarter-hour after it has been exhibited I shall send it to Brentano* – I thank you thousands and thousands of times for so much patience.' Beethoven's friends refer frequently to the picture in their written conversations with Beethoven. Schindler writes that he prefers the portrait by Schimon: 'There is more character in it – all agree on that – You were very well two years ago; now you are always ailing.' J. Czerny writes: 'We were just talking about your portrait. – Oliva thinks it is a very good resemblance.' The artist visited Beethoven again at Mödling in July and writes: 'Before the exhibition I shall paint your portrait again, but full life-size. Your head makes an excellent effect full face, and it was so appropriate because Haydn was on one side and Mozart on the other.' Schindler says it reproduces Beethoven's characteristic expression faithfully and that it met with approval, though fault was found with the pose. Beethoven's contemporaries were not used to seeing him with his head bowed down as Stieler represents him; on the contrary, he carried his head high even when suffering physical pain.

By February Beethoven had returned to live in the house on the Josephstädter Glacis where he stayed until May. In this period the Giannatasio family followed up their intention to visit Beethoven. On 19 April 1820, Fanny writes in her journal:

'Tonight we visited Beethoven after not seeing him for almost a year. It seemed to me that he was glad to see us again; on the whole things seem to be going well for him now, at least it is a period in which he is free from the vexations of Karl's mother. I lament exceedingly that every connection with this excellent man has been given up; I was stirred more and more by his genuineness in every regard. His hearing has become a little worse. I wrote everything. He gave me a new beautiful song: "Abendlied unter dem gestirnten Himmel", which gave me very much pleasure.'

In the summer of 1820 Beethoven went to Mödling again, but he did not take lodgings in the Hafner house for the very sufficient reason that the proprietor had served notice on him in 1819, that he could not have it longer on account of the noisy disturbances which had taken place there. He took a house instead in the Babenbergerstrasse and

* Franz Brentano, half-brother of Bettina, inherited a large import business and used it to render financial assistance to Beethoven on several occasions.

paid twelve florins extra for the use of a balcony which commanded a view which was essential to his happiness. Here again he took the baths. He worked chiefly on the Mass, which was far from finished. His friends thought that he was further along than he was, and he was frequently asked if it was finished and when it would be performed. Some hurried sketches belonging to the *Credo* are found amongst the remarks of his friends, and also sketches for the *Agnus Dei*. Schindler asks him in August: 'Is the *Benedictus* written out in score? – Are those sketches for the *Agnus*?'

There was at this time considerable talk in the Conversation Book of publishing a complete edition of Beethoven's works. Bernard told him that Steiner was already counting on it, and Schindler, who was enthusiastic over the project, gave it as his opinion that arrangements must be made with a Vienna publisher so as to avoid voluminous correspondence. Bernard remarks: 'Eckstein will so arrange it that you will always get all the profits and will also publish your future works as your property. He thinks that every fourth or fifth piece should be a new one.' Since the beginning of the year, there had also been negotiations with Simrock concerning this idea. A letter written to this firm on 5 August from Vienna shows that Beethoven had just made one of his short visits to the city. He writes: '. . . Regarding the edition of my complete works we believe here that it would be good to add a *new work* to each type of composition; e.g., to the variations a new work of this kind, to the sonatas, each etc. etc. . . .' The plan appealed strongly to Beethoven, but nothing came of it at the time.

Karl came to visit his uncle in Mödling, presumably during his school vacation. When the Giannatasio family made a visit to Mödling on 5 October, they saw 'our good Beethoven' returning Karl to the city.

Towards the end of October, Beethoven returned to Vienna and took lodgings at No. 244 Hauptstrasse in the Landstrasse, 'the large house of the Augustinians' beside the church. There he was visited by Dr W. Chr. Müller of Bremen, a philologist and musical amateur who had long admired Beethoven and, with the help of his 'Family Concerts', established in 1732, had created such a cult for Beethoven's music as existed in no city in Germany in the second decade of the nineteenth century. Müller's daughter Elise played the sonatas exceptionally well and was largely instrumental with her father in creating this cult. On his journey to Italy, Müller came to Vienna where he was in October and early November 1820. He not only visited Beethoven but also saw and observed him from a distance as is shown by an article which he published entitled 'Some Things about Beethoven', from which we quote:

'This sense of cosmopolitan independence and consideration for others might have been the reason why over and over again he continued a conversation, already started, in restaurants, where he often had his frugal lunch, and expressed opinions freely and candidly about everything, the government, the police, the manners of the aristocracy in a critical and mocking manner. The police knew it but left him in peace either because he was a fantastic or because he was a brilliant artistic genius. Hence his opinion and assertion that nowhere was speech freer than in Vienna. His ideal of a [political] constitution was the English one.'

It was through Dr Müller that we know somewhat of Beethoven's views on the subject of analytical concert programmes. Among the zealous promoters of the Beethoven cult in Bremen was a young poet named Dr Karl Iken, editor of the *Bremer Zeitung*, who conceived the idea of helping the public to an understanding of Beethoven's music by writing programmatic expositions of the symphonies for perusal before the concerts. Some of his lucubrations were sent to Beethoven by Dr Müller, and aroused the composer's ire. In the Seventh Symphony, Dr Iken professed to see a political revolution.

'The sign of revolt is given; there is a rushing and running about of the multitude; an innocent man, or party, is surrounded, overpowered after a struggle and haled before a legal tribunal. Innocency weeps; the judge pronounces a harsh sentence; sympathetic voices mingle in laments and denunciations – they are those of widows and orphans; in the second part of the first movement the parties have become equal in numbers and the magistrates are now scarcely able to quiet the wild tumult. The uprising is suppressed, but the people are not quieted; hope smiles cheeringly and suddenly the voice of the people pronounces the decision in harmonious agreement . . .'

It is scarcely to be wondered at that such balderdash disgusted and even enraged Beethoven. In the autumn of 1819, he dictated a letter to Müller – it has, unfortunately, been lost – in which he protested energetically against such interpretations of his music.

Beethoven's complaints concerning his financial condition were chronic and did not cease even in periods where extraordinary receipts make them difficult to understand. That the lamentations in his letters during the two years which we have in review were well founded, however, is no doubt true. With so engrossing a work as the *Missa Solemnis* on hand there could not have been much time for such potboilers as he mentions and the other sources of revenue were not many.

A letter from Steiner to the composer shows that he had sent Beethoven a statement of account, and Beethoven had evidently been unreasonable in his reply. His letter ran:

'Vienna, 29 Dec. 1820

'Most highly esteemed sir and friend Beethoven!

'Enclosed are the three overtures in score with the request that you go through them at your convenience as you yourself suggested and correct any errors that may have crept in. – As soon as we have received these corrections we will proceed to engrave and print them in order to bring out the first edition as quickly as possible.

'I cannot rest content with your remarks concerning the account sent you; for the cash money loaned you I have charged you only 6% interest, while for the money which you deposited with me I paid you 8% promptly in advance and also repaid the capital promptly. What is sauce for the goose is sauce for the gander [*Was also dem Einen recht ist, muss dem Andern billig sein*]. I am not in a position to lend money without interest. As a friend I came to your help in need, I trusted your word of honour and believe that I have not been importunate, nor have I plagued you in any way; wherefore I must solemnly protest against your upbraidings. If you recall that my loan to you was made in part 5 years ago, you will yourself confess that I am not an urgent creditor. I would spare you even now and wait patiently if I were not on my honour in need of cash for my business. If I were less convinced that you are really in a position to give me relief and able to keep your *word of honour* I would, difficult as it would be for me, right gladly remain patient a while longer; but when I remember that I myself returned to you 4,000 florins, conventional coin, or 10,000 florins, Vienna Standard, as capital 17 months ago and at your request did not deduct the amount due me, it is doubly painful to me now to be embarrassed because of my goodwill and my trust in your word of honour. Every man knows best where the shoe pinches and I am in this case; wherefore I conjure you again not to leave me in the lurch and to find means to liquidate my account as soon as possible . . .'

In a letter to Haslinger written on 5 September, presumably in 1822, Beethoven writes: 'I beg Steiner to go to Dr Bach tomorrow afternoon where the 600 fl. CM may be received, the other 600 will be available also from Dr Bach as soon as possible.' But the conflict between Steiner and Beethoven was again to come to a head in the year 1823. The three overtures mentioned in Steiner's letter were undoubtedly those to the

Ruinen von Athen and *König Stephan*, and the *Namensfeier* Overture. The increasingly strained relations between Steiner and Beethoven are demonstrated by the fact that after the Symphonies No. 7 and No. 8 and the Pianoforte Sonata in A, Op. 101, no big works were given to Steiner.

The negotiations for the publication of the Mass had already begun; as we know from the letter of 18 March to Simrock, the Bonn publisher was supposed to receive it for 100 louis d'or along with certain conditions. But entries in the Conversation Books show that in Beethoven's circle there was decreasing enthusiasm for the offer, yet increasing need for the money.

On 23 April Beethoven asked again that the 100 louis d'or be sent to Brentano and stated that Simrock would receive the Mass 'by the end of May or beginning of June'.

But it was not to be: Simrock always was to be but never was blest with the score.

The information in 1821 concerning Beethoven's life is comparatively meagre. Not only have no Conversation Books of this year survived but also the number of letters existent is very small.

A final word should be said concerning his old love, Josephine née Brunsvik, since 1810 Baroness von Stackelberg. After the financial misfortunes which followed his marriage, Stackelberg's situation improved at the end of 1815 when he inherited his brother's property in Russia. Josephine refused to leave Vienna, and he departed with their three daughters who were left with their governess in Bohemia. Stackelberg returned with the children to Vienna in 1817 and then left Austria for good. Josephine died on 31 March 1821. Her sister Therese wrote in her journal on 12 July 1817: 'If Josephine doesn't suffer punishment on account of Luigi's woe – his wife! What wouldn't she have made out of this hero!' During all of these years did the two meet again? There is no known evidence of any communication after Ludwig's poignant close to their correspondence in 1807; it is known only that Josephine's last years were years of suffering from ill health.

The beginning of the year 1821 found Beethoven still at his home in the suburb Landstrasse, and, it would seem, working as hard as his health permitted. In the *Novellistik* section of the *Allgemeine Musikalische Zeitung*, 10 January 1821, appears: 'Herr von Beethofen was sick with a rheumatic fever. All friends of true music and all admirers of his muse feared for him. But now he is on the road to recovery and is working actively.' A letter of 7 March to Adolf M. Schlesinger in Berlin starts:

'Noble Sir!

'Perhaps you are thinking disparagingly of me, but you may soon change when I tell you that for six weeks I have been laid up with a severe rheumatic attack; but now it is much better. You can imagine how many things have come to a standstill. Soon I shall catch up with everything . . .'

For the summer he went first to Unterdöbling. He had suffered from rheumatism during the preceding winter and now became a victim of jaundice. This attack may have been an *avant-courier* of the disease of the liver which brought him to the grave six years later. He wrote the following letter to the Archduke on 18 July:

'Your Imperial Highness!

'I heard yesterday of the arrival here of Your Highness, which would have given me so much pleasure, but now has become a sad event for me since it may be a rather long time before I can be lucky enough to wait upon YIH. After feeling poorly for a very long time, a *full case of jaundice* finally developed, a disease that is extremely loathsome to me. I hope at least that I will be cured enough to see YIH before your departure – Also last winter I had a very bad rheumatic fever – Much of this is linked up with the sad situation as regards my economic circumstances. Up until now I had hoped by struggling to the utmost to emerge finally victorious over it. God, who knows my heart and knows how sacredly I as a man fulfil all the duties imposed upon me by humanity, God and nature, will some day free me from this affliction – The Mass will be delivered to YIH while you are here. Please let me spare YIH the causes of its delay. The details might prove anything but pleasant to YIH . . .'

The rest of the letter consists of further expressions of concern about his relationship with his patron.

In order to take a cure prescribed by his physician, Dr Staudenheim, Beethoven moved to Baden on 7 September.

In 1820 Professor Blasius Höfel, who had engraved the Latronne portrait of Beethoven for Artaria, was appointed to a professorship of drawing in Wiener Neustadt. A year or two afterwards he was one evening with several colleagues in the garden of the tavern 'Zum Schleifen', a little way out of town. The Commissioner of Police was a member of the party. It was autumn and already dark when a constable came and said to the Commissioner: 'Mr Commissioner, we have arrested somebody who will give us no peace. He keeps on yelling that he is Beethoven; but he's a ragamuffin, has no hat, an old coat, etc. – nothing by which he can be identified.' The Commissioner ordered that the man be kept under arrest until morning, 'then we will examine him and learn who he is.' Next day the company was very anxious to know how the affair turned out, and the Commissioner said that about 11 o'clock at night he was awakened by a policeman with the information that the prisoner would give them no peace and had demanded that Herzog, Musical Director in Wiener Neustadt, be called to identify him. So the Commissioner got up, dressed, went out and woke up Herzog, and in the middle of the night went with him to the watchhouse. Herzog, as soon as he cast eyes on the man, exclaimed, 'That *is* Beethoven!' He took him home with him, gave him his best room, etc. Next day came the burgomaster, making all manner of apologies. As it proved, Beethoven had got up early in the morning, and, slipping on a miserable old coat and, without a hat, had gone out to walk a little. He got upon the towpath of the canal and kept on and on; seemed to have lost his direction, for, with nothing to eat, he had continued on until he ended up at the canal-basin at the Ungerthor. Here, not knowing where he was, he was seen looking in at the windows of the houses, and as he looked so like a beggar the people had called a constable who arrested him. Upon his arrest the composer said, 'I am Beethoven.' 'Of course, why not?' said the policeman; 'You're a tramp: Beethoven doesn't look like that.' Herzog gave him some decent clothes and the burgomaster sent him back to Baden in the magisterial state-coach.

A letter written from Baden on 10 September 1821 to Tobias Haslinger accompanying a canon on the words 'O Tobias dominus Haslinger, O, O!' deserves to be given here to show that Beethoven's high spirits could at times dominate him in spite of his general misery.

'Very best fellow!

'Yesterday, in the carriage on the way to Vienna, I was overcome by sleep, naturally enough, since (because of my early rising here) I had never slept well. While thus slumbering I dreamed that I had made a long journey – to no less distant a country than Syria, then to India, back again, even to Arabia; finally I reached Jerusalem. The Holy City aroused in me thoughts of Holy Writ and small wonder that the man Tobias now occurred to me, and how natural that our little Tobias should enter my mind and the pertobiasser, and now during my dream journey the following canon came to me:

'But scarcely awakened, away went the canon and nothing of it would come back to my memory. But when, next day, I was on my way hither in the same conveyance (that of a poor Austrian musician) and continued the dream journey of the day before, now awake, behold, according to the laws of association of ideas, the same canon occurred to me again. Now fully awake I held it fast, as once Menelaus held Proteus, only allowing it to change itself into 3 voices.

'Farewell. Presently I shall send you something on Steiner to show you that he has no stony [*Steinernes*] heart. Farewell, very best of fellows, we ever wish that you will always belie your name of publisher [*Verleger*] and never become embarrassed [*verlegen*] but remain a publisher [*Verleger*] never at a loss [*verlegen*] either in receiving or paying –

Sing the epistles of St Paul every day, go to pater Werner,* who will
show you the little book by which you may go to heaven in a jiffy. You
see my anxiety for your soul's salvation; and I remain with the greatest
pleasure from everlasting to everlasting,

Your most faithful debtor   Beethoven'

The reference to the Mass in the letter of 18 July to the Archduke
could suggest that it was almost ready; but unfortunately that was not
the case, for he was working on it constantly during this and the following year. The slow progress is explained partly through his illnesses
and partly that he had taken up other composition projects simultaneously. Back in Vienna Beethoven wrote the following letter to Franz
Brentano which sheds light on these matters:

'Vienna, 12 November 1821
'Honoured friend!
'Don't consider me a shabby or thoughtless genius – For the past year
up to the present I have been continually ill; likewise during the summer. I had an attack of jaundice, which lasted until the end of August.
Following Staudenheim's order I had to go to Baden in September.
Since it soon became cold there I was overtaken by a case of diarrhoea
that was so violent that I could not keep up the course of treatment and
had to flee here. Now thank God things are better and it appears that I
am to be cheered up by the return of health and may live again for my
art, which for the last two years has certainly not been the case not only
from lack of health but also on account of many other human miseries –
The Mass might have been sent before this, but had to be *carefully looked
through*, for the publishers in other countries do not get along well with
my manuscript, as I know from experience. A copy for the engraver
must be examined note by note. Moreover, I could not do this because
of illness, the more since despite everything I have been compelled to
make a considerable number of *potboilers* (as unfortunately I must call
them) – I think I am justified in making an attempt to get Simrock to
reckon the louis d'or at a higher rate, inasmuch as several applications
have been made from other quarters, concerning which I shall write to
you soon. As for the rest, do not question my honesty; frequently I think
of nothing except that your kind advance may soon be repaid –
with sincere gratitude and respect your friend
and servant Beethoven'

* The dramatic poet Zacharias Werner, who had become a convert to Roman
Catholicism and, now an ordained priest, was preaching to great crowds of
Viennese.

It seems a fair inference from his concluding remark, together with the advice of his friend or friends in the Conversation Book of the previous summer concerning a collection through Brentano as soon as the Mass had been handed over to the stage-coach, that Beethoven had got an advance from Brentano on the money which was awaiting the arrival of the work in Frankfurt. The following letter to Brentano strengthens the inference:

'Vienna, 20 December 1821

'Noble man!

'I am awaiting another letter respecting the Mass, which I shall send you to give you an insight into the whole affair. In any event the honorarium will be paid to you whereupon you will please deduct the amount of my indebtedness to you. My gratitude to you will always be unbounded – I was so presumptuous as not to ask before dedicating a composition of mine to your daughter Maxe. Please accept the deed as a mark of my continual devotion to you and your entire family – do not misinterpret the dedication as prompted by my own interest or as a recompense – this would pain me greatly. There are nobler motives to which such things may be ascribed if reasons must be found –

'The new year is about to begin; may it fulfil all your wishes and daily increase your happiness as pater familias in your children. I embrace you cordially and beg you to present my compliments to your excellent, one and only glorious Toni –

Your most respectful faithful Beethoven'

'I have received from here and elsewhere offers of 200 ducats in gold for the Mass. I think I can get 100 florins VS more. On this point I am waiting for a letter which I will send you at once. The matter might then be presented to Simrock, who certainly will not expect me to lose so much. Till then please be patient and do not think that you have acted towards an unworthy man.'

CHAPTER 19

The Years 1822 and 1823

The Missa Solemnis Finished – Progress of the Ninth Symphony

Bernard Romberg, Beethoven's old colleague and friend in Bonn, was in Vienna at the beginning of the year, giving concerts with his daughter Bernhardine and his eleven-year-old son, Carl, who was also a violoncello virtuoso. Concerning one of the last of these concerts Beethoven wrote to him on 12 February:

'This last night I have again been *suffering from one of my earaches* which habitually occur in *this season, even your tones* would *today* be merely *painful to me*; this alone is to blame if you do not see me in person – Perhaps I shall be better in a few days in which case I shall still be able to say goodbye to you – Moreover, if you have not received a visit from me, remember the remoteness of my house, my almost ceaseless affairs, all the more since I have been ill for the whole past year, because of which I have been held up on so many works already begun – And, after all, between us there is no need for superficial compliment – I wish for a full tribute of applause to you for your high art and also a *metallic recognition* which nowadays is seldom the case – If I can for a little while, I will see you together with your wife and children whom I greet affectionately herewith.

'Farewell   great artist
as always your Beethoven'

The 'metallic recognition' was made, and according to Hanslick, Romberg's earnings during the Vienna season amounted to 10,000 florins.

And now to resume the story of the Mass. At the beginning of 1822 the work was completed in sketch form, by the end of the year the autograph score was made, and on 19 March 1823, a beautiful copy was sent to the Archduke. Meanwhile negotiations for the publication of the Mass continued not only with Simrock but with a number of other firms as well.

On 13 May 1822, Simrock became impatient and wrote the following letter from Bonn:

'To Herr Louis van Beethoven!
          in Vienna!

'It is now a year since you promised me for sure that I would receive the Mass completely finished at the end of April. Since 25 October 1820 I have had 100 louis d'or on deposit in Frankfurt from which you should have received your payment immediately. On 19 March you wrote me expressly that you had been bedridden for 6 weeks and had not yet fully recovered. I was supposed to be completely assured; you wrote this only so that I should think nothing differently. Next I asked Brentano [about it] at the autumn fair and again at this Easter fair, but nothing has arrived as usual. So I beg you now to write some words about it once and for all: I write about this so that you will not believe that I have died, which nearly happened this past winter!

'Every so often I have taken up the idea of publishing your six symphonies in score, which by now should have been done several times – even publicly advertised; but had not been done because there was no profit in it. I know this very well; but I have wanted to make a worthy monument to my worthy old friend and I hope that you will be satisfied with the edition since I have done all I can with it! I have had the first two appear at the same time and will send you a copy along with the first shipment to Vienna!

'We thought that we would see you here during the past summer as you had promised in your letter of 19 March, but this has not happened either.

'We all greet you sincerely.

                                        N. Simrock'

What Beethoven said in reply to this letter is not known; it can be surmised, however, from the recital given to Brentano in a letter from Beethoven dated 19 May. He had been troubled by 'gout in the chest' for four months, he said, and able to do but little work; nevertheless the Mass would be in Frankfurt by the end of the next month, that is, by the end of June 1822. There was another reason for the delay. Cardinal Rudolph did not want the Mass published so early and had returned to the composer the score and parts only three days before. Here we have a very significant statement. What may be called the official copy of the Mass in D was formally presented to Archduke Rudolph on 19 March 1823; here, ten months earlier, he speaks of a score and parts which the Archduke had returned to him three days before. The Mass, therefore, must have had what, for the time being (Beethoven never considered it finished so long as it was in his hands), was looked upon as a definitive shape at the time when Beethoven promised to send it to Brentano for Simrock. The Archduke returned it, as Beethoven says, so that the publication might not be hindered. How long it had been in the hands of the Archduke no one can tell. Now, said Beethoven to Brentano, the score will be copied again, carefully examined, which would take some time owing to his ill health, but it would be in Frankfurt at the end of June 'at the latest'. He had received better offers from Vienna and elsewhere, but had rejected all of them because he had given his word to Simrock and would abide by the agreement even if he lost money. Brentano communicated with Simrock at once and received a letter from the publisher on 29 May expressing regret that sickness had been partly responsible for the delay. He had been expecting the Mass every day for more than a year.

Thus on 19 May, Beethoven told Brentano that he would keep the faith with Simrock even at a sacrifice. On 1 May, however, he had written to Schlesinger in Berlin:

'... as to the Mass I beg of you to get everything in readiness as other publishers have asked for it and many approaches have been made to me ... For the present I ask of you only that you signify to me whether you accept my last offer of the Mass together with the two songs ... I must insist upon an early answer, chiefly because two other publishers who want to have it in their catalogues have been waiting for a definite answer from me for a considerable time ...

Respectfully yours   Beethoven'

Schlesinger answered:

'... Everything is in order about the Mass, and I beg you to send it and the two songs as soon as possible and draw on me at fourteen days' sight for 650 rthlr., I will honour the draft at once and pay it, for I have no opportunity to make payment to you there [Vienna] ...'

Schlesinger's son, who had established himself in business in Paris, wrote to Beethoven on 3 July and in the course of the letter asked him if a third movement of the Pianoforte Sonata in C minor (Op. 111), which he was publishing, had not been forgotten at the copyist's. He, like his father a little later (letter of 13 July), evidently suspected that they had not received as much music as they had paid for! The incident may have angered Beethoven; but there must have been a

further incursion of Beethoven's displeasure to account for the fact
that Beethoven resolved about this time to have nothing more to do
with Schlesinger *père*. On 26 June he wrote to Peters of Leipzig, with
whom he had now entered into negotiations and to whom he had just
also offered the Mass, 'In no event will Schlesinger ever get *anything
more from me*; he has played me a Jewish trick, but aside from that he
is not among those who might have received the Mass.' Beethoven's
threats were frequently mere *brutum fulmen*; the Schlesingers, *père et
fils*, remained his friends to the end and got two of the last Quartets.

On 22 August 1822, Simrock wrote to Beethoven again. Beethoven's
answer followed on 13 September and it contains more than a mere
implication why he refused to abide by his contract:

> 'Baden, 13 September 1822
> 'My dear and valued Simrock:
> 'You will receive this letter from Baden, where I am taking the
> baths, as my illness which has lasted two and a half years has not yet
> ended . . . As regards the Mass you know that at an earlier date I wrote
> to you that a larger honorarium had been offered me. I would not be so
> sordid as to haggle with you for a few florins, but my poor health and
> many other unpleasant circumstances compel me to insist upon it. The
> minimum that at least four publishers have offered me for the Mass is
> 1,000 florins CM [Convention Money] at the rate of twenty, or count-
> ing the florin at 3 Austrian CM at twenty. Much as I shall regret it if we
> must part just because of this work, I know that your loyalty will not
> allow me to lose money on this work, which is perhaps the greatest that
> I have composed . . . I very much wish to have the matter about the
> Mass settled as soon as possible, for I have had to endure plots of all
> sorts on account of it . . . I hope, my dear Simrock, whom I consider the
> richest of all these publishers, will not permit his old friend to go else-
> where for the sake of a few hundred florins . . .
> Cordially your old friend, Beethoven'

This was evidently answered by Simrock, who, despairing of ever
getting the Mass, may have suggested that he would accept other works
in lieu of it, for on 10 March 1823, Beethoven wrote again saying that
he should surely receive *a* mass, for he had written two and was only
undecided which one to send. He asked Simrock to be patient until
Easter, when he would send one of them to Brentano. He intended also
to write a mass for the Emperor. He adds: 'You will surely receive one
of these two grand masses which are already composed; only be patient
until after Easter, by which time I shall have decided which to send.'

This is the last letter between Beethoven and Simrock which has been found. It leaves the composer promising *a* mass instead of delivering *the* Mass, and that promise unfulfilled; of a necessity, for the work, though described as 'already composed', was never written.

In 1814 C. F. Peters had purchased the Bureau de Musique, publishers of a number of Beethoven's compositions. On 18 May 1822, Peters addressed a letter to Beethoven in which he said that he had long wished to publish some of his work but had refrained from applying to him because he did not wish to offend the Viennese publishers; seeing now, however, that he was going outside with his compositions and giving them 'even to the Jew Schlesinger', he would no longer give heed to such considerations. He had spoken to Steiner on the subject at the last fair, who had offered no objections, had, indeed, said that he would be glad if he (Peters) got the works instead of Schlesinger, and had offered his services as intermediary between him and Beethoven, and asked for a list of compositions which he wanted. Thereupon he had given Steiner such a list: symphonies, pianoforte quartets and trios, pianoforte solos 'among which there might be small pieces', songs, etc. – anything, in short, which Beethoven should send him would be welcome, for he wanted honour, not profit, from the association. Beethoven replied that he had met Steiner only a few days before and that he had said not a syllable about Peters's approach. He continued with a detailed list of work he was willing to sell to Peters.

Peters's reply is dated 15 June. He regretted to hear of Steiner's duplicity and expressed hope that his conduct might have been harmless in intention and caused by his weakness. The works which he wanted and of which he had given a list to Steiner were a quartet for strings, a trio of the same kind, a concert overture for full orchestra, songs, and some small solos for pianoforte 'such as capriccios, divertissements', etc. Then he took up Beethoven's detailed offer of compositions:

'The most admirable among them is your Grand Mass, which you offer me together with the pianoforte arrangement for one thousand florins CM which I admit I am ready to accept at this price... Between honest men like us there is no need of a contract, but if you want one send it to me and I will return it *signed*. If not, please state to me in writing that I am to receive the *Mass in question* together with the *pianoforte score* for *1,000 florins* at the 20 florin rate and indicate when I am to receive it and that it is to be my *sole* property *for ever*.'

For the present, Peters added, he did not want to publish larger vocal works by Beethoven nor the Mass singly but along with other works, to show the Viennese publishers that there was a contract between him and Beethoven which obliged the latter to send him compositions.

Beethoven answered, agreeing to give him the Mass, which he would receive by the end of July, for the stipulated fee, and enclosed an agreement form which had been prepared by Steiner.

Peters answered this letter on 3 July. He was distressed about Beethoven's financial affairs and wanted to help him. 'It is wrong that a man like you is obliged to think about money matters. The great ones of the earth should long ago have placed you in a position free from care, so that you would no longer have to live on art but only for art.'

Peters was prompt in his remittance of the money. On 25 July, Piringer, associate conductor of the *Concerts spirituels*, who was on terms of intimacy with Beethoven, wrote him as follows:

'*Domine Generalissime!*

'*Victoria* in Döbling – fresh troops are advancing! The wholesalers, Meisl Bros. here in the Rauhensteingasse, their own house, 2nd storey, have received advices from Hr. Peters in Leipzig to pay several hundred florins to Herr Ludwig van Beethoven – I hasten . . . to convey this glad report to *Illustrissimo* at once. – Today is the first sad day in the Viennese calendar, because yesterday was the last day of the Italian opera.'

Now there enters a new element into the story of the Mass which is introduced by Beethoven near the end of a letter to Peters dated 'Vienna, 22 November 1822':

'. . . This is the state of affairs with regard to the Mass: already I have finished *one* completely but another is *not yet* finished. There will always be *gossip* about such as us and you have been misled by it. *I do not yet* know which of the two you will receive – Pressed on all sides I must declare the opposite of 'the spirit weighs nothing' – I greet you most heartily and hope that a relationship which is profitable and not dishonourable to *me* may exist in the future between us both.

Yours faithfully   Beethoven'

The gossip against which Beethoven warned Peters, it is safe to assume, related to the compositions which the latter had purchased but not received; in great likelihood rumours about the Mass had reached

Leipzig. Peters was in communication with Steiner and others; and that he knew that the Mass had been planned for the installation of Archduke Rudolph as Archbishop of Olmütz he had indicated when he expressed the belief that it was something 'really excellent' because it had been composed for an occasion. The mass which Beethoven had promised to deliver by the end of July 1822 could therefore have been none other than the Mass in D.

Peters was getting importunate, and on 20 December Beethoven wrote to him that nothing intended for him was entirely ready; there had been delays in copying and sending, but he had no time to explain. The songs and marches would be sent 'next week'.

During February and March 1823, Beethoven finally sent on to Peters three songs, six bagatelles, three tattoos (Turkish music) and a march. Peters wrote that he was distressed by the manuscripts that he had received and that he was sending back the three songs since they were not what he had asked for. His objections were that he had wanted extended songs with pianoforte accompaniment and 'that I want to have good choice things from you'. Just when Beethoven received the songs back is not clear, since he was offering songs to Simrock in his letter of 10 March 1823, which must have been these three, the only ones yet unpublished.

On 20 March 1823 Beethoven wrote again to Peters, referring to the marches, bagatelles and Peters's request for a string and a piano quartet:

'As regards the Mass I will also send you a document which I beg you to sign, for in any event the time is approaching when you will receive one or the other. Besides yourself there are two other men who also desire each a mass. At present I am resolved to write at least three; the first is entirely finished, the second *not yet*, the third not even begun. – But in view of this I must have an understanding so that I may be secured in any case, you may have the Mass whenever you pay 1,000 CM . . .'

Peters published none of the works sent to him and did not receive the Mass. One of the 'two other men' was, in all likelihood, Artaria, Beethoven's old publisher. On 22 August 1822, Artaria received a letter which seems to stand alone so far as the Mass is concerned:

'Being just now overwhelmed with work, I can only say briefly that I have always returned your favours whenever possible. As regards the Mass, I have been offered 1,000 florins CM for it. The state of my affairs do not permit me to take a smaller honorarium from you. All

that I can do is to *give* you the *preference*. Rest assured that I do not *take a heller more* from you than has been *offered me by others*. I could prove this to you in writing. You may think this over but I beg of you to send me an answer by *tomorrow noon* as tomorrow is post-day and my decision is expected in other places – I will make a proposition to you concerning the 150 florins CM which I owe you, but the sum must not be deducted *now*, as I am in urgent need of the 1,000 florins – In addition I beg of you to keep everything secret about the Mass. As always
your grateful friend Beethoven'

Here *the* Mass (*Missa Solemnis*) is implied and not *a* mass. When Beethoven wrote this letter he had offered the Mass to Peters, earlier to Simrock, and had indicated the same purpose to Schlesinger. Thus there were not less than four publishers who hoped to receive the Mass. Also he raised their hopes for works which were not ready or even hardly begun.

Because of these striking facts it is appropriate to consider Beethoven's personality and the circumstances under which he lived. The painstaking work that Beethoven put into the works of these late years came from his innermost heart and he never felt that he had done enough. While he was absorbed with this kind of work he was free of his cares and guided only by the demands of his art. To Peters he was to write: 'It is another thing during the work itself, since I never think of gain, thank God, but only *how to compose*.' These were his principles.

Then too there was his health and the duress already described which cramped the elasticity of his nature and diminished his delight in creating. 'To begin a great work makes me shudder,' he is once supposed to have said. His income had diminished due to the reduced payments on the pension supplied by his princely admirers and due to his limited productivity of the last few years; consequently, he was in need of straight cash. Hence came the necessity to get the highest possible fees for his works, for dealings unfortunately with many parties at once, and for acceptance of advance payments. He owed money, among others, to Steiner and Artaria. To the former he owed nearly 3,000 florins, and this explains not only the painful relations with Steiner but also Beethoven's wish to have his new works published by foreigners.

These circumstances invite one's deepest sympathy; the noble impulses of his heart on all other levels and the reasons which necessitated his doing everything to better his affairs are well known; yet the conscientious reporter cannot ignore the actual, public facts and, hard as it is, cannot acquit Beethoven of the reproach that his conduct did not agree with the principles of strict honour and justice.

Beethoven finally borrowed money from his brother and asked his help in the sale of his works. This circumstance brings Johann van Beethoven back significantly into this history. The brother had grown rich enough in the interim to buy some farm property near Gneixendorf and to make his winter residence in Vienna. Because of his relationship to his famous brother, and also because of his idiosyncrasies, habits and public behaviour, he became a conspicuous and rather comical figure in Vienna. Gerhard von Breuning describes him thus:

'His hair was blackish-brown; hat well brushed; clothing clean but suggesting that of a man who wishes to be elegantly clad on Sundays; somewhat old-fashioned and uncouth, an effect which was caused by his bone-structure, which was angular and unlovely . . . His nose was large and rather long, the position of his eyes, crooked, the effect being as if he squinted a little with one eye. The mouth was crooked, one corner drawn upwards giving him the expression of a mocking smile. In his garb he affected to be a well-to-do elegant, but the role did not suit his angular, bony figure. He did not in the least resemble his brother Ludwig.'

Beethoven's friends used to ridicule him to his face. In a Conversation Book of early 1823 Count Moritz Lichnowsky writes: 'Everybody thinks him a fool; we call him only the Chevalier . . . all the world says of him that his only merit is that he bears your name.' It is very likely that he was not at all musical and that his affectation of appreciation of his brother's works made him a fair subject for ridicule. In a conversation in 1824 the nephew relates that his uncle had been present at a chamber concert. Beethoven wanted to know what he was doing there, and the nephew replies: 'He wants to acquire taste; he is continually crying *bravo*.'

Exactly when Beethoven went to Oberdöbling in the summer of 1822 is not known, but he was there in July. In the spring or early summer he wrote the following letter to Johann:

'I was counting on seeing you – but in vain – on Staudenheim's orders I am still having to take medicine, and am not allowed to move about much – I beg you instead of going to the Prater today to come to me with your wife and daughter – I only wish that the benefits which are certain to result from our being together may be achieved without hindrance. I have enquired about lodgings; there are tolerably good ones to be had and you won't have to pay much more than before. From a purely financial point of view, how much can be saved on both sides without our having to sacrifice our pleasure – I have nothing against your wife, I only wish that she would see how much you too might benefit from being with me and that we need not be troubled by all the petty miseries of life . . .

Your true brother Ludwig'

'I have been ailing for three and one half months and am very, yes extremely sensitive and irritable. But away with everything which *cannot promote* the object, which is that I and my good Karl maintain a moderate way of life . . .'

Here there is no mention of business matters and hence it may be assumed that the letter dates from an early period in the reunion of the brothers. But business considerations prompted two long letters at the end of July:

'Dear brother!

'Because I have been extremely busy and thoroughly uncomfortable with respect to my dwelling and my servants, both of whom are extremely awkward, I have not yet been able to write you. As for my health, it is better. I have been having to drink Johannes spring-water, take powder 4 times a day, and now I am supposed to go to Baden to take 30 baths; I will go there by 6 or 7 August if it is *possible* to do so. If you could only come for a few days to help me, yet the dust and the heat would be too much for you. If it weren't for that you could stay with me in Baden for some 8 days, ad tuum libitum . . . [Negotiations with Peters are summarised.] Also Breitkopf and Härtel have sent the Saxon Chargé d'Affaires to me concerning my works. Also I have received requests from Paris for my works and again from Diabelli in Vienna; in short, people are scrambling for my works; what an *unfortunate fortunate* man I am!!! – That *Berliner* has also turned up – If my health would return I might yet feather my nest. –

'The Archduke Cardinal is here, I go to him twice a week. Though there is nothing to be expected from him in the way of magnanimity or money, I am on such a good and confidential footing with him that it would be extremely painful not to show him some agreeable attention . . . Before I go to Baden, I need some clothes because I am really lacking in them, especially in shirts as you have already seen. Ask your wife what she thinks of this linen, it costs 48 kr. VS per ell . . . Write to me as soon as you receive this; give my greetings to your family. If I did not have to go to Baden, I would certainly have visited you during the coming month, but now things cannot be otherwise. Do come if

you can, it would be a great relief for me. – Write at once – Farewell –
I embrace you with all my heart
                    and am as ever your true brother Ludwig'

On 31 July, Beethoven writes:

'Best little brother! Most high and mighty property holder!
     '. . . I should be glad if you would write to me whether you can spare
me something so that I will not be prevented when the time comes
from going to Baden, where I must stay for at least a month . . . The
Steiner people are pushing me into a corner. They wish to have in writing that I shall give all my works to them. They are willing to pay for
each printed sheet; but I have explained to them that I will not enter
into such an arrangement with them until they cancel the debt. For
that I have offered them 2 works which I wrote for Hungary and
which can be considered as two small operas, from which they have
already accepted 4 pieces. The debt amounts to about 3,000 fl., but they
have outrageously charged me interest, to which I do not agree. I have
taken over from Karl's mother a part of her debt since I want to do
everything I can for her insofar as it isn't against Karl's interest. If you
were here, these things would soon be disposed of . . . It would be wonderful if you could come and visit Baden with me for 8 days, only you
must write immediately what you think about it. Meanwhile get the
kitchen and cellar well stocked; for presumably my little son and I will
make our headquarters at your house and we have the noble resolve to
eat you out of house and home . . .
                    Your faithful brother Ludwig'
'I, secretarius embrace you with all my heart and hope to see you soon
again. Karl'

There must now be recorded some of the facts connected with the
visit to Beethoven of Friedrich Rochlitz, distinguished musical *littérateur* and first editor of the Leipzig *Allgemeine Musikalische Zeitung*. He
wrote two letters to Gottfried Härtel about his experiences in the Austrian capital, one from Vienna and the other from Baden. He had never
seen Beethoven in the flesh and was eager for a meeting. A friend to
whom he went told him that Beethoven was in the country and had
grown so shy of human society that a visit to him might prove unavailing; but it was Beethoven's custom to come to Vienna every week and
he was then as a rule affable and approachable. He advised Rochlitz to
wait, and he did so until the following Saturday. The meeting was a
pleasant one and enabled Rochlitz to study Beethoven's appearance and

manner; but the interview was suddenly terminated by Beethoven in the midst of the visitor's confession of his own admiration and the enthusiasm which Beethoven's symphonies created in Leipzig. From the beginning Beethoven had listened, smiled and nodded; but after he had curtly excused himself on the score of an engagement and departed abruptly, Rochlitz learned that his auditor had not heard or understood a word of all that he had said. Rochlitz continues:

'Some two weeks later I was about to go to dinner when I met the young composer Franz Schubert, an enthusiastic admirer of Beethoven. The latter had spoken to Schubert concerning me. "If you wish to see him in a more natural and jovial mood," said Schubert, "then go and eat your dinner this very minute at the inn where he has just gone for the same purpose." He took me with him. Most of the places were taken. Beethoven sat among several acquaintances who were strangers to me. He really seemed to be in good spirits and acknowledged my greeting, but I purposely did not cross over to him. Yet I found a seat from which I could see him and, since he spoke loud enough, also could hear nearly all that he said. It could not actually be called a conversation, for he spoke in monologue, usually at some length, and more as though by hapchance and at random.

'Those about him contributed little, merely laughing or nodding their approval. He philosophised, or one might even say politicised, after his own fashion. He spoke of England and the English, and of how both were associated in his thoughts with a splendour incomparable – which, in part, sounded tolerably fantastic. Then he told all sorts of stories of the French, from the days of the second occupation of Vienna. For them he had no kind words. His remarks all were made with the greatest unconcern and without the least reserve, and whatever he said was spiced with highly original, naïve judgements or comical fancies. He impressed me as being a man with a rich, aggressive intellect, an unlimited, never resting imagination.'

After finishing his meal Beethoven approached Rochlitz and beckoned him into a little ante-room, where conversation was carried on with the help of a tablet which Beethoven produced.

'He began by praising Leipzig and its music; that is to say the music chosen for performance in the churches, at concerts and in the theatre. Otherwise he knew nothing of Leipzig and had only passed through the city when a youth on his way to Vienna. "And even though nothing is printed about the performances but the dry records, still I read them with pleasure," he said. "One cannot help but notice that they are intelligent and well inclined toward all. *Here*, on the contrary ..." Then he started in, rudely enough, nor would he let himself be stopped. He came to speak of himself: "You will hear nothing of me here." "It is summer now," I wrote. "No, nor in winter either!" he cried. "What should you hear? *Fidelio*? They cannot give it, nor do they want to listen to it. The symphonies? They have no time for them. My concertos? Everyone grinds out only the stuff he himself has made. The solo pieces? They went out of fashion here long ago, and here fashion is everything. At the most Schuppanzigh occasionally digs up a quartet, etc." And despite all the exaggeration in what he said a modicum of reason and truth remains. At last he had relieved himself and harked back to Leipzig. "But", said he, "you really live in Weimar, do you not?" He probably thought so because of my address. I shook my head. "Then it is not likely that you know the great Goethe?" I nodded my head vigorously. "I know him, too," said Beethoven, throwing out his chest, while an expression of the most radiant pleasure overspread his face.

' "It was in Karlsbad that I made his acquaintance – God only knows how long ago! At that time I was not yet altogether deaf, as I now am, though I heard with great difficulty. And what patience the great man had with me!" He told numerous little anecdotes and gave the most enjoyable details. "How happy it all made me at the time! I would have died for him ten times over. Then, while I still was head over heels in trouble, I thought out my music for his *Egmont* and I did make a success of it, did I not? ... Since that Karlsbad summer I read Goethe every day – that is, when I read at all. He killed Klopstock for me. You are surprised? Now you are laughing? Aha, it is because I used to read Klopstock! For years I put up with him, when I took my walks and elsewhere. Well, then, it is true that I did not always know what he was driving at. He hops about so from pillar to post; and he always begins altogether too much from top to bottom. Always *maestoso* and in D flat major! Is it not so? Yet he is lofty and he uplifts the soul. When I did not understand him, then I made my guess and comprehended more or less. If only he did not want to die all the time! Death comes soon enough to all of us. Well, at any rate, what he writes always sounds well. But Goethe – he is alive, and he wants us all to live with him. That is why he can be set to music. There is no one who lends himself to musical setting as well as he ..." '

At this point Rochlitz believed that the opportunity had arrived to present Härtel's proposal and wrote it out. This was to write music for

Goethe's *Faust* similar to that for *Egmont*.

'He read it. "Ha!" he cried and flung up his hand. "That would be a piece of work! That might yield something!" He went on in this fashion for a time, picturing the thought to himself in a manner anything but inept, while, with his head thrown back, he stared at the ceiling. "But", he next began, "for some time past I have been carrying about with me the idea of three other great works. Already I have hatched out much in connection with them, that is to say, in my head. These I must first get rid of: two great symphonies each different from the other, and each also different from all my other ones, and an oratorio. And that will be a long-winded affair; for you see, for some time past I find I no longer settle down to write so easily. I sit and think and think and what I have to say is all there, but it will not get down to paper. I dread beginning works of such magnitude. Once I have begun, then, all goes well ..." '

Rochlitz continues his description:

'Our third meeting was the merriest of all. He came here, to Baden, this time looking quite neat and clean and even elegant. Yet this did not prevent him – it was a warm day – from taking a walk in the Helenenthal. This means on the road that all travel, even the Emperor and the imperial family, and where everyone crowds past everyone else on the usually narrow path; and there he took off his fine black frockcoat, slung it across his shoulder from a stick, and wandered along in his shirtsleeves. He stayed from about ten in the forenoon to six o'clock in the evening ... During the entire visit he was uncommonly gay and at times most amusing, and all that entered his mind had to come out. ("Well, it happens that I am unbuttoned today," he said and the remark was decidedly in order.) His talk and his actions all formed a chain of eccentricities, in part most peculiar. Yet they all radiated a truly childlike amiability, carelessness, and confidence in everyone who approached him. Even his barking tirades – like that against his Viennese contemporaries, which I already have mentioned – are only explosions of his fanciful imagination and his momentary excitement. They are uttered without haughtiness, without any feeling of bitterness and hatefulness – and are simply blustered out lightly, good-humouredly, the offsprings of a mad, humorous mood. In his life he often shows – and for the sake of his own subsistence only too often and too decidedly – that to the very person who has grievously injured him, whom he has most violently denounced one moment, he will give his last thaler the next, should that person need it.

'To this we must add the most cheerful recognition of merit in others, if only it be distinctive and individual. (How he speaks of Handel, Bach, Mozart!) He does not, however, where his greater works are concerned, allow others to find fault (and who would have the right to do so?) yet he never actually overvalues them; and with regard to his lesser things is more inclined, perhaps, to abandon them with a laugh than any other person. He does this the more since once he is in the vein, rough, striking witticisms, droll conceits, surprising and exciting paradoxes suggest themselves to him in a continuous flow. Hence in all seriousness I claim he even appears to be amiable. Or if you shrink from this word, I might say that the dark, unlicked bear seems so ingenuous and confiding, growls and shakes his shaggy pelt so harmlessly and grotesquely that it is a pleasure, and one has to be kind to him, even though he were nothing but a bear in fact and had done no more than a bear's best.'

Rochlitz concludes by describing his parting with Beethoven, when he had 'thrust our good Beethoven into the carriage':

'This time my reflections did not turn only, as on the first time I met him, on the grievous complaint with which fate had afflicted Beethoven. After all, I realised that he also had his hours of great gladness and perfect happiness. In other hours, also good ones, he lived in his art or in his plans and dreams regarding it; the evil hours, however, are thrown into the bargain and he takes them, pours out his soul with regard to them and then forgets them. After all, who may claim to be any better off?'

Although little is known of the subsequent relation between Beethoven and Rochlitz, yet an appreciation of this spirited writer remained until the days of Beethoven's last illness when, in answer to a question, he explained that he would choose Rochlitz for his biographer.

Beethoven had a meeting with another man this year which is of even more interest. This man was Rossini. His operas had been on the current list in Vienna for several years, and with the coming of the composer in person, in the spring of 1822, the enthusiasm for him and his music had grown into a fanatical adoration. Rossini was on his wedding trip and his elegant manners and brilliant conversation had made him the lion of aristocratic drawing-rooms in the Austrian capital.

Several of Beethoven's utterances concerning the musician, who no doubt did much to divert the taste of the masses away from the German master's compositions, have been preserved. Seyfried recorded that in answer to the question, 'What is Rossini?' Beethoven replied, 'A good scene painter.' To Freudenberg at Baden in 1824 he remarked: 'Rossini is a talented and a melodious composer; his music suits the frivolous and sensuous spirit of the times, and his productivity is so great that he needs only as many weeks as the Germans need years to write an opera.'

The Rossini craze was no doubt largely responsible for some of Beethoven's outbreaks concerning the taste of the Viennese, but on the whole he does not seem seriously to have been disturbed by it. Schindler cites him as remarking on the change in the popular attitude: 'Well, they cannot rob me of my place in musical history.'

In 1867 Dr Eduard Hanslick visited Rossini with two friends in Paris. Concerning the interview, Hanslick wrote:

'Suddenly, as if he intentionally wanted to call attention to something loftier, he asked if the Mozart monument at Vienna was finished? And Beethoven's? We three Austrians looked rather embarrassed. "I remember Beethoven well," continued Rossini after a pause, "although it is nearly half a century ago. On my visit to Vienna I hastened to look him up."

' "And he did not receive you, as Schindler and other biographers assure us."

' "On the contrary," said Rossini, correcting me . . . "He received me at once and very politely. True, the visit did not last very long, for conversation with Beethoven was nothing less than painful. His hearing was particularly bad on that day and in spite of my loudest shoutings he could not understand me; his little practice in Italian may have made conversation more difficult." '

On 31 August, Beethoven wrote to his brother that he was leaving for Baden the next day or at the most the day after next. In Baden he lived for a while at the inn 'zum goldenen Schwann'.

Here he began the work which was to call him back into public notice. This was the music for the opening of the Josephstadt Theatre in Vienna, which the director of the theatre, Carl Friedrich Hensler, asked of him immediately after his arrival at the watering-place. Carl Meisl had written two festival pieces for the opening, which had been set down for 3 October 1822, the name-day of the Emperor. The first piece was a paraphrase of Kotzebue's *Ruinen von Athen*, written for the opening of the theatre in Budapest in 1812, for which Beethoven had composed the music. Meisl took Kotzebue's text and made such alterations in it as were necessary to change *Die Ruinen von Athen* into *Die Weihe des Hauses*. The new words did not always fit the music and caused Beethoven considerable concern. A choral dance was introduced and to this Beethoven had to write new music, which he did in September. He also revised, altered and extended the march with chorus. Beethoven wrote a new overture also, that known as *Die Weihe des Hauses*, putting aside the overture to the *Ruinen von Athen* because that play had served as a second piece, or epilogue, at Budapest. Schindler has an anecdote about the origin of the overture:

'Meanwhile September was come. It was therefore time to go to work on the new overture, for the master had long ago seen that the one to the *Ruinen von Athen* was for obvious reasons unsuitable. One day, while I was walking with him and his nephew in the lovely Helenenthal near Baden, Beethoven told us to go on in advance and join him at an appointed place. It was not long before he overtook us, remarking that he had written down two motives for an overture . . . one in the free style and one in the strict, and, indeed, in Handel's. As well as his voice permitted he sang the two motives and then asked us which we liked the better. This shows the roseate mood into which for the moment he was thrown by the discovery of two gems for which, perhaps, he had been hunting a long time. The nephew decided in favour of both, while I expressed a desire to see the fugal theme worked out for the purpose mentioned. It is not to be understood that Beethoven wrote the overture to the *Weihe des Hauses* as he did because I wanted it so, but because he had long cherished the plan to write an overture in the strict, expressly in the Handelian, style . . . The newly organised orchestra of the Josephstadt Theatre did not receive it till the afternoon before the opening, and with innumerable mistakes in every part. The rehearsal, which took place in the presence of an almost filled parterre, scarcely sufficed for the correction of the worst of the copyist's errors.'

Beethoven's stay in Baden was interrupted by the performance of the *Weihe des Hauses*, which took place in Vienna, as projected, on 3 October, the eve of the Emperor's name-day. Beethoven had reserved the direction for himself and sat at the pianoforte, the greater part of the orchestra within view, his left ear turned towards the stage. He was still able to hear a little with that ear. Kapellmeister Franz Gläser stood at his right, and Schindler, who had recently abandoned the law, led the first violins. The rehearsal and the performance demonstrated plainly, Schindler says, that under no circumstances was Beethoven able longer to conduct large bodies of performers. The representation, despite the enthusiasm of the performers, stimulated by Beethoven's encouraging speeches, was not a success. Beethoven would take none of the fault to himself, however, though his anxiety led him to hold back the music despite the exertions of his two leaders, whom he admonished against too much precipitancy, of which Schindler protests they were not guilty. There were demonstrations of enthusiasm at the close and Beethoven was led before the curtain by Director Hensler.

The revival of *Fidelio* which took place on 3 November, after an absence from the stage of three years, was a benefit performance for Wilhelmine Schröder, then seventeen years old. Later as the famous dramatic singer, Madame Schröder-Devrient, she was reputed to be the greatest of all the Fidelios; but she did not reach her full artistic stature until after Beethoven's death. Schindler tells a pathetic tale concerning the dress rehearsal. Together with his friends, mindful of the happenings in the Hall of the University in 1819 and in the Josephstadt Theatre only a short time before, Schindler advised Beethoven not to attempt to conduct the performance. He hesitated for a few days, then announced his intention to direct with the help of Kapellmeister Umlauf. Schindler escorted him to the rehearsal. The overture went well, the orchestra being well trained in it, but at the first duet it became painfully manifest that Beethoven heard nothing of what was being sung on the stage. He slackened his beat and the orchestra obeyed; the singers urged the movement onward. Umlauf stopped the performance at the rappings on the gaoler's lodge-gate but gave no reason to Beethoven. Let Schindler continue the narrative:

'The impossibility of going ahead with the author of the work was evident. But how, in what manner inform him of the fact? Neither Duport, the director, nor Umlauf was willing to speak the saddening words: "It will not do; go away, you unhappy man!" Beethoven, already uneasy in his seat, turned now to the right now to the left, scrutinising the faces to learn the cause of the interruption. Everywhere a heavy silence. Then he summoned me. I had approached near him in the orchestra. He handed me his notebook with an indication that I write what the trouble was. Hastily I wrote in effect: "Please do not go on; more at home." With a bound he was in the parterre and said merely: "Out, quick!" Without stopping he ran towards his lodgings . . . Inside he threw himself on the sofa, covered his face with his hands and remained in this attitude till we sat down to eat. During the meal not a word came from his lips; he was a picture of profound melancholy and depression. When I tried to go away after the meal he begged me not to leave him until it was time to go to the theatre. At parting he asked me to go with him next day to his physician, Dr Smetana, who had gained some repute as an aurist.'

Wilhelmine Schröder-Devrient wrote an account of her debut as Leonore from which we quote in part:

'Under the guidance of my talented mother many of the traits in Leonore's character became clear to me; however I was still too young, too little developed within to have a full understanding of what took place in Leonore's soul, emotions for which Beethoven had conceived his immortal harmonies. At the rehearsals which were led by Umlauf who was then kapellmeister, the limits of my underdeveloped young voice soon became known and many things in my part were changed for me so that the effect did not suffer too much. The last rehearsals were set, when I learned before the dress rehearsal that Beethoven had asked for the honour of conducting the work himself in celebration of the day. On hearing this news a great fear came over me, and I also remember my frightful awkwardness which nearly drove my poor mother, as well those who were working with me, to despair. But Beethoven sat in the orchestra and waved his baton over everyone's heads, and I had never seen the man before! At that time the master's physical ear was already closed to all sounds. With a bewildered face and unearthly inspired eyes, waving his baton back and forth with violent motions, he stood in the midst of the performing musicians and didn't hear a note! If he thought it should be *piano* he crouched down almost under the conductor's desk and if he wanted *forte* he jumped up with the strangest gestures, uttering the weirdest sounds. With each piece our courage dwindled further and I felt as though I were watching one of Hoffmann's fantastic figures appear before me. The inevitable happened: the deaf master threw the singers and orchestra completely off the beat and into the greatest confusion, and no one knew any longer where they were ... I found him at the performance on the following night sitting in the orchestra behind Umlauf lost in profound thought ... Beethoven followed the whole performance with eager attention, and he looked as if he were trying to see from each of our gestures whether we had even half understood him ...

'The next day he came himself, the great master, to bring me his thanks and his congratulations. With hot tears I moistened the hand that he offered me, and in my joy, I would not have exchanged anything in the world for this praise from Beethoven's lips! He promised at that time to write an opera for me, but unfortunately it remained nothing but a promise.'

Following Schindler's narrative we learn that Beethoven's woeful experience at the rehearsal led to a resolution on his part to make another effort to be healed of his deafness. He went to Dr Smetana, who prescribed medicaments to be taken inwardly, thereby indicating, as Schindler asserts, that he had no expectation of effecting a cure, but wanted only to occupy Beethoven's mind, knowing what to expect from so impatient, wilful and absent-minded a patient; for Beethoven was as unready to follow a physician's advice as a musician's, and was more likely to injure himself with overdoses of drugs than to invite the benefit which the practitioner hoped for by obedience to the prescription. The usual thing happened; not only with Dr Smetana's treatment, but also with that of the priest, Pater Weiss, whom he had consulted some eighteen years before and to whom he now returned. For a while he thought that the oil which the priest dropped into his ears was beneficial, and Pater Weiss himself expressed the belief that the left ear, at least, might permanently be helped; but Beethoven grew sceptical, as he always did unless he experienced immediate relief, his work monopolised his attention, and despite the priest's solicitations he abandoned the treatment and yielded himself to his fate. Thenceforward no one heard him lament because of his deafness.

The compositions which were in Beethoven's hands at the close of the year were those which had occupied him in the earlier months. The Mass, several times completed but never complete so long as it was within reach, received what must now be looked upon as its finishing touches.

On 2 September, Beethoven had received a letter from Charles Neate concerning the publication in London of three quartets. Letters from Ries refer to the same quartets, which as yet existed only in Beethoven's intentions. Neate says that he had found it difficult to obtain subscriptions for the works. He thought, however, that he might still be able to raise £100, but could not get any money before the arrival of the works in London. Beethoven had referred to a quartet and possibly some successors in his correspondence with Peters, so that it is more than likely that a determination to return to the quartet field had been formed by Beethoven before the practical and material incentive came to him in the last month of the year from Prince Galitzin – the incentive to which we owe three of the last five quartets, which many regard as the master's greatest achievement.

Prince Nicolas Galitzin, born in 1794 in Moscow, was an influential force in the musical life of St Petersburg. He played the violoncello, and his wife was an admirable pianist. Prince Galitzin was an ardent admirer of Beethoven's music and had arranged some of his pianoforte works for strings. On 9 November 1822, he wrote the following letter to Beethoven:

'Monsieur!

'I take the liberty of writing to you, as one who is as much a passionate amateur in music as a great admirer of your talent, to ask if you will not consent to compose one, two or three new quartets for which labour I will be glad to pay you what you think proper. I will accept the dedication with gratitude. Would you let me know to what banker I should direct the sum that you wish to get. The instrument that I am cultivating is the violoncello. I await your answer with the liveliest impatience. Could you please address your letter to me as follows

'To Prince Nicolas de Galitzin at S. Petersburg care of Messrs Stieglitz and Co. Bankers.

'I beg you to accept the assurance of my great admiration and high regard.

Prince Nicolas Galitzin'

Beethoven's reply was written in French in Karl's hand and the composer supplied the date and his signature:

'Vienna 25 January 1823

'Your Highness!

'I would not have failed to answer Your letter of 9 Nov. sooner if the multitude of my affairs had not prevented me from writing to you. It was with great pleasure that I found that Your Highness is interested in works of my creation. You wish to have some quartets; since I see that you are cultivating the violoncello, I will take care to give you satisfaction in this regard. Inasmuch as I am constrained to live by the products of my mind, I must take the liberty of setting the honorarium for one quartet at 50 ducats. If this is agreeable with Your Highness, I beg you to inform me soon and to direct this sum to the banker Hénikstein in Vienna; I bind myself to finish the 1st quartet by the end of the month of February or at the latest by the middle of March.

'In expressing to you my real interest in your musical talent, I thank Your Highness for the regards that you have been willing to indicate, in choosing me to increase, if it is possible, your love for music. I have the honour of being

Your Highness's very humble servant
Louis van Beethoven'

*

This period in Beethoven's life was great in inspiration and creation. The great Mass was ready, needing only corrections and a few alterations. Work continued on the new symphony, and the stimulation to write some new string quartets, the big labour of the last years, was already upon him.

The progress of the Mass and the negotiations, still inconclusive, towards its publication have been sketched for the preceding years. Now at last it was possible for the work to reach its destination. It was intended, as we have long known, for Archduke Rudolph; since the plan was first formulated, four years had elapsed. On 27 February 1823, he wrote of his intention to pay him a visit and apologised that he had not written for such a long time:

'. . . but I have been wanting to wait until I had sent the Mass; but then there were really terrible mistakes in it and to such an extent that *every part* had to be read over; it was delayed further by many other affairs that could not be put off, which led to still other circumstances to hinder me, for so much confronts a man when he least expects it. However, that I have had YIH continually in mind is shown by the copies of some new publications that are being sent which have been ready for YIH for several months; but I did not want to send them on ahead of the Mass. This *last* is being bound and after that will be respectfully handed over by me to YIH . . .'

This took place on 19 March 1823, the evening before the anniversary day of the enthronement of the Archduke as Archbishop of Olmütz, for which solemnisation the Mass was supposed to have been ready four years before. That he had been sincere in his original purpose to provide a mass for the installation ceremonies themselves is to be found in a letter to the Archduke in which he says:

'The day on which a high mass of my composition is performed at the ceremony for YIH will be to me the most beautiful in my life and God will enlighten me so that my poor powers may contribute to the glory of this solemn day.'

Something was said earlier in this biography concerning the views

Beethoven entertained on the subject of religion. His attitude towards the Roman Catholic Church becomes an almost necessary subject of contemplation in a study of the *Missa Solemnis*. The obedient church-man of a Roman Catholic country will attach both less and more importance, than one brought up in a Protestant land, to the fact that he admonished his nephew when a lad to say his prayers and said them with him (as the boy testified in the guardianship proceedings), that he himself at least once led him to the door of the confessional, that he consented to the summoning of a priest when *in extremis* and that he seemed to derive comfort and edification from the sacred function. It is not necessary, however, to go very deeply into a critical study of the Mass in order to say that while the composition shows respect for traditions in some portions and while it is possible to become eloquent without going beyond the demonstration contained in the music itself, in describing the overwhelming puissance of his proclamation of the fatherhood of God and belief in Him as the Creator of all things visible and invisible, the most obvious fact which confronts the analytical student is that Beethoven approached the missal text chiefly with the imagination and the emotions of an artist, and that its poetical, not to say dramatic elements were those which he was most eager to delineate.

One example of this may be found in the *Agnus Dei*. Among the sketches for the movement is found the remark: 'dona nobis pacem darstellend den *innern* und äussern Frieden' ('delineating internal and external peace'), and in agreement with this he superscribes the first Allegro vivace in the autograph with the same words. In the later copy this phrase is changed to 'Prayer for internal and external peace', thus showing an appreciation of the fact that the words alone contain the allusion to peace which in its external aspect is disturbed by the sounds of war suggested by the instruments. The petition for peace is emphasised by the threatening tones of military instruments accompanying the agonising appeal for mercy sent up by the voices. The device is purely dramatic.

By the end of 1822, Beethoven had made the plan of postponing the publication of the Mass in order to sell manuscript copies of it by subscription to the sovereigns of Europe. In the first week of the new year Beethoven sent his brother Johann with a letter to Griesinger of the Saxon Legation asking him to give advice on the subject of subscription to the bearer of the letter, apologising for not coming in person on the grounds of indisposition. Whether or not Griesinger came to his assistance we do not know, but within a fortnight work on the project had been energetically begun. Schindler was now called upon to write, fetch and carry as steadily and industriously as if he were, in fact, what he described himself to be – a private secretary. Among his papers in Berlin are found many billets and loose memoranda bearing on the subject, without date, but grouped as to periods by Schindler himself and provided with occasional glosses touching their contents. Beethoven took so much of his time that he offered to pay him fifty florins after the collection of one of the subscription fees, but Schindler never received them nor would he have accepted them. He was, as he informed the world for many years afterwards on his visiting card, 'L'Ami de Beethoven', and his very considerable and entirely unselfish labours were 'works of friendship' for which he wanted no remuneration; but he was very naturally rejoiced when Beethoven presented him with several autograph scores.

The invitations to the courts were issued in part before the end of January. A letter to Schindler, evidently written in that month, asked him to draw out a memorandum of courts from an almanac in which the foreign embassies stationed at Vienna were listed. The invitations were posted on the following dates: to the courts at Baden, Wurtemburg, Bavaria and Saxony on 23 January; 'to the other ambassadors' (as Beethoven notes) on 26 January; to Weimar on 4 February; to Mecklenburg and Hesse-Darmstadt on 5 February; to Berlin, Copenhagen, Hesse-Cassel and Nassau on 6 February; to Tuscany on 17 February, and to Paris on 1 March. The invitation to the court at Hesse-Cassel had been written on 23 January, but it was not sent because, as Schindler says, 'it had been found that nothing was to be got from the little courts'. The letter came back to Beethoven and its preservation puts in our hands the formula which, no doubt was followed in all the formal addresses. We therefore give it here:

'The undersigned cherishes the wish to send his latest work, which he regards as the most successful of his intellectual products, to the Most Exalted Court of Cassel.

'It is a grand solemn mass for 4 solo voices with choruses and complete grand orchestra in score, which can also be used as a grand oratorio.

'He therefore begs the High Embassy of His Royal Highness, the Elector of Hesse-Cassel, to be pleased to procure for him the necessary permission of your Exalted Court.

'Inasmuch, however, as the copying of the score will entail a considerable expense the author does not think it excessive if he fixes an honorarium at 50 ducats in gold. The work in question, moreover, will not be published for the present.

Vienna, 23 January 1823   Ludwig van Beethoven'

There were ten acceptances. The first came from the King of Prussia. Prince Hatzfield acted in the matter for Berlin. Court Councillor Wernhard, Director of the Chancellery of the Embassy at Vienna, brought the report to Beethoven and asked him if he would not prefer a royal order to the fifty ducats. Without hesitation, Beethoven replied 'fifty ducats', and after Wernhard had gone he indulged in sarcastic comments on the pursuit of decorations by various contemporaries – 'which in his opinion were gained at the cost of the sanctity of art'. Beethoven received the money, but the score was not delivered, owing, no doubt, to delay in the copying, and in July Prince Hatzfield felt compelled to remind the composer of his remissness. Prince Radziwill in Berlin also subscribed, but he did not receive his copy till more than a year later. On 28 June 1824, a representative of the Prince politely informed Beethoven that he had sent a cheque for fifty ducats to him with a request for a receipt and a copy of the score, but had received neither. Schindler says the fault lay with the copyists; in every copy many pages had to be rewritten.

King Friedrich August of Saxony subscribed for the Mass, and on 31 July Archduke Rudolph wrote to his music-master: 'My brother-in-law Prince Anton has already written to me that the King of Saxony is expecting your beautiful Mass.'

The Grand Duke of Hesse-Darmstadt was appealed to directly under date of 5 February; the letter, signed by Beethoven, was forwarded through the Hessian ambassador, Baron von Türckheim. The composer, Louis Schlösser, was in Vienna at the time, and Baron von Türckheim, knowing that he wanted to make Beethoven's acquaintance, gave him the opportunity by asking him to carry the information that the invitation had been accepted to Beethoven, handing him the despatch with the Grand Ducal seal affixed for that purpose. Schlösser went to Beethoven, 'No. 60 Kothgasse, first storey, door to the left'. Beethoven read the document with great joy and said to Schlösser: 'Such words as I have read do me good. Your Grand Duke speaks not only like a princely Maecenas but like a thorough musical connoisseur of comprehensive knowledge; it is not alone the acceptance of my work which rejoices me but the estimation which in general he places upon my works.'

No success was met with at the cultivated Court of Weimar, though here Beethoven invoked the assistance of no less a dignitary than Goethe, in a letter in which this passage occurs:

'Now I am no longer alone but have for six years been father to the son of my deceased brother, a promising youth in his sixteenth year, wholly devoted to learning and already at home in the rich literature of ancient Greece. But in these regions such things cost a great deal and, in the case of young students, not only the present but also the future must be borne in mind; and as much as I formerly kept my thoughts directed aloft I must now also turn my gaze *earthwards* – My income is *worthless* – My poor health has for several years made it impossible for me to make professional journeys or to seize upon the many opportunities which yield *profit*! Could I completely recover my health, I might expect other and better things . . .'

No answer to this letter was ever received; nor did the Grand Duke subscribe.

Bavaria's story is a short one. In a Conversation Book towards the close of May, Schindler writes: 'A negative answer has come from Bavaria.' To the King of Naples, Beethoven sent a French copy of the letter of invitation practically identical with the formula, and also to the King of France. King Louis XVIII not only subscribed for the Mass but within less than a year sent Beethoven a gold medal weighing twenty-one louis d'or, showing on the obverse side the bust of the King and on the reverse, within a wreath, the inscription: 'Donnée par le Roi à Monsieur Beethoven.'

No subscription was received from the King of Naples. The negotiations with the Grand Duke of Tuscany were more successful, though they dragged on into the next year. They were a subject of discussion in the Conversation Book in which Count Lichnowsky, brother Johann and nephew Karl took part. From remarks there recorded it appears that an appeal was also made to Empress Maria Louisa, Duchess of Parma. It looks also as if the case of the Grand Duke of Tuscany had been exceptional, in that the Mass had been forwarded before the subscription had been received.

Schindler says that Beethoven sent a carefully written letter to the King of Sweden to accompany the invitation; but nothing came of it. The King of Denmark subscribed, but as we hear nothing of the particulars, it is most likely that everything went smoothly in his case.

Prince Galitzin had been asked to make a plea to the Russian Court and reported in a letter to Beethoven, dated 2 June, that the invitation had been accepted and the official notification would follow in due course through the Russian Embassy. The money came soon afterwards. On 9 July, Schindler writes in a jocular vein, using a metaphor which had already done service in Beethoven's correspondence:

'I take pleasure in reporting to you herewith, that by command of the Emperor of all the Russias, 50 horsemen in armour are arrived here as a Russian contingent to do battle under you for the Fatherland. The leader of these choice troops is a Russian Court Councillor. Herr Stein, pianoforte maker, has been commissioned by him to quarter them on you. Rien de nouveau chez nos voisins jusqu'ici.

Fidelissimus Papageno'

Impatience at the non-delivery of the Mass at the expected time must have been expressed by the Russian Embassy, for in a note which Schindler dates 'in the winter of 1824', Beethoven says:

'Mr v. Schindler:
  'Here is the Paquett for the Russian Embassy. Please look after it at once – moreover say that I shall soon visit him in person, inasmuch as it hurts me that lack of confidence has been felt in me. I thank God I am in a position to prove that I do not deserve it in any way nor will my honour permit it! –'

Prince Galitzin, meanwhile, also became a subscriber, and in a letter of 3 August proposed that the Mass be published by popular subscription at four or five ducats, as there were not many amateurs who could afford to pay fifty ducats for a written copy. 'All that I can do', the Prince writes in conclusion, 'is to beg you to put me down among your subscribers and to send me a copy as soon as possible so that I may produce it at a concert for the benefit of the widows of musicians which takes place annually near Christmas.' Plainly, the Prince's subscription was in the existing category; there was no other, and Beethoven, in view of the invitation to the courts, could not at once entertain the subject of a popular subscription for a printed edition. The score was in the hands of Prince Galitzin on 29 November, but the performance which he projected did not take place until 6 April 1824. It was the first complete performance of the Mass anywhere.

A special invitation to subscribe to the Mass was not extended to the Austrian court for reasons which, no doubt, were understood between Beethoven and Archduke Rudolph and which may have been connected with efforts which were being made at the time to secure a court appointment for the composer. At the request of Artaria, however, an invitation was sent to Prince Paul Esterhazy. Beethoven had little confidence in the successful outcome of the appeal, probably with a recollection in his mind of the Prince's attitude towards him on the occasion of the production of the Mass in C in 1807. His lack of faith in the enterprise was justified; Esterhazy did not subscribe.

No invitation was sent to the English court, probably because

Beethoven cherished his grudge in that quarter over the 'Wellington's Victory' affair.

There were, therefore, ten subscribers, namely: the Tsar of Russia, the Kings of Prussia, Saxony, France and Denmark, the Grand Dukes of Tuscany and Hesse-Darmstadt, Princes Galitzin and Radziwell with the addition of the Cäcilia Society of Frankfurt to whom Schindler had also written. Beethoven's receipts, 500 ducats, were very materially reduced, how much we cannot say, by the costs of copying. In this work his principal helper was a professional copyist named Schlemmer, who could best decipher his manuscript. But Schlemmer was sickly and died before the year was over; his successor was named Rampel, and seems to have caused Beethoven a great deal of annoyance; he probably was made to bear a great deal of the blame for the tardiness of the work, for which, also, the composer's frequent alterations were in part responsible.

The story of Beethoven's plan to get private subscriptions to the Mass has taken the reader well into the year 1823. It is now time to turn back and take up the other events of the year, presenting them as much as possible in chronological order.

The Symphony in D minor, the Ninth, on which he was working industriously, had been the subject of correspondence between himself and Ries (in London) for some time before the year opened. On 6 July 1822, Beethoven had enquired of his old pupil: 'What would the Philharmonic Society be likely to offer me for a symphony?' Ries, evidently, laid the matter before the directors of the society who, at a meeting on 10 November, 'resolved to offer Beethoven fifty pounds for a MS symphony'. Ries conveyed the information to Beethoven in a letter dated 15 November. In a reply dated 20 December 1822, Beethoven writes:

'My dear Ries!

'Overwhelmed with work I could not answer your letter of 15 November until now – I accept with pleasure the offer to write a new symphony for the Philharmonic Society even though the honorarium from Englishmen cannot match that of other nations; for I myself would write gratis for the first artists of Europe, if I were not still poor Beethoven. If I were in London, what would I not write for the Philharmonic Society! For Beethoven can compose, God be thanked – though he can do nothing else in this world. If God gives me back my health, which at least has improved somewhat, I shall yet be able to comply with all the requests which have come from all parts of Europe, even from North America; and I might yet make my way in the world.'

A glimpse into the occupations, cares and perplexities which beset Beethoven at this period is given by a letter to Ries written in the new year – on 5 February 1823:

'My dear good Ries!

'I have no further news to give you about the Symphony; but meanwhile you may confidently count on receiving it, since I have made the acquaintance here of a very amiable and cultivated man, who holds an appointment in our Imperial Embassy at London [Herr Bauer]. He will undertake later to forward the Symphony to you in London, so that *it will soon be in London*. Were I not so poor that I am obliged to live by pen I would accept nothing at all from the P. Soc; as it is I must wait until the fee for the Symphony is deposited here ... And now another request: my brother here, who keeps a horse and carriage, wanted to derive advantage from me and so, without asking me, he offered the Overture in question to a publisher in London named Boosey. Let him be told that at present it is impossible to say whether he can have the Overture or not, I will write to him myself. – It all depends on the Philharmonic Society. Say to him please that my brother made a mistake in the matter of the *Overture* – As to the other works which he wrote to him about, he may have them. He *bought* them of me in order to *profit from them*, as I now see – O frater! ...'

How Johann became involved with transactions concerning his brother's compositions becomes clear from a letter to Schott in the next year in which Beethoven says 'I have given to my brother, to whom I am indebted for many kindnesses, instead of a sum of money which I owe him, the following works'; and he listed an overture (Op. 124), three songs and some bagatelles.

On 22 March Ries was informed that the symphony would be finished in two weeks, and on 25 April that it would be received soon along with thirty-three variations (Op. 120) dedicated to his wife.

Not long afterwards Beethoven wrote another letter to Ries which has been preserved only in part:

'– in addition to these hardships I have many debts to pay, for which reason I would be glad to have the honorarium paid to me if you have disposed of the Mass. By then the London copy will have been made. There need be no scruples because of the few souverains who are to get copies of it. If a local publisher made no objections, there ought to be still fewer in London, since I bind myself in writing that not a note of it shall appear in print or otherwise ... Attend to everything soon for your poor friend; I await also your plan of travel. Things have become too awful. I am tormented by the Cardinal worse than before; if I don't go there, it is a crimen legis majestatis. As for payment, I must draw my wretched salary with the aid of a *stamp* – Since you apparently wish a dedication from me, how happy I am to gratify a wish from you, much happier than one from the *finest of fine gentlemen*, entre nous; the devil only knows how one can keep from falling into their hands. The dedication of the new symphony will be *to you* – I hope eventually to receive *yours* to me . . .'

Neither husband nor wife received a dedication; the Ninth Symphony was dedicated to the King of Prussia and the Diabelli Variations (Op. 120) to Antonie Brentano.

Of the earlier inaction of King George IV upon receiving the score of *The Battle of Vittoria* there has already been mention. Before leaving for England, the 'amiable and cultivated' Bauer visited Beethoven and an entry of his in a Conversation Book of middle February refers again to this matter: 'I am of the opinion that the King had it performed, but perhaps nobody reminded him that on that account he ought to answer.'

His next entry reads: 'I will carry a letter to the King and direct it in a channel which will ensure its delivery, since I cannot hand it over in person.'

The character of the address to the King can be guessed at from the following draft for an earlier letter which was found amongst Schindler's papers:

'In thus presuming, herewith, to submit my most obedient prayer to Your Majesty, I venture at the same time to supplement it with a second.*

'Already in the year 1813, the undersigned took the liberty, at the frequent requests of several Englishmen then living here, to send to Your Majesty his composition entitled "Wellington's Battle and Victory at Vittoria" which no one possessed at that time. The then Imperial Russian Ambassador, Prince Rasoumowsky, undertook to send the work to Your Majesty by a courier.

'For many years the undersigned cherished the sweet wish that Your Majesty would graciously make known the receipt of his work to him; but he has not yet been able to boast of this happiness, and had to content himself with a brief notice from Herr Ries, his former worthy

---

* The first request, presumably, was to have been an invitation to subscribe to the Mass in D; but Beethoven had decided subsequently to strike the King of England from his list.

pupil, who reported that Your Majesty had been pleased graciously to deliver the work to the then Musical Director Herr Salomon and Herr Smart for public performance in Drury Lane Theatre. This appears also from the English journals, which added, as did Herr Ries, that the work had been received with extraordinary favour not only in London but elsewhere. Inasmuch as it was extremely humiliating to the undersigned to learn all this from indirect sources, Your Majesty will surely pardon his sensitiveness and graciously permit him to observe that he spared neither time nor cost to lay this before Your Exalted Person in the most proper manner in order to provide a pleasure for Your Majesty.

'From this the undersigned concludes, that it may have been improperly submitted to Your Majesty and inasmuch as the most obedient petition which is now submitted enables him again to approach Your Majesty, he takes the privilege of handing to Your Majesty an accompanying printed copy of the Battle of Vittoria in score, which has been set aside for this highest purpose ever since 1815 and which has been retained so long because of the uncertainty felt by the undersigned concerning the matter.

'Convinced of the lofty wisdom and graciousness which Your Majesty has hitherto shown towards art and artists to their appreciation and good fortune, the undersigned flatters himself that Your Majesty will graciously condescend to take all this in consideration and grant his most humble petition . . .'

Among the friends who were offering Beethoven advice in the handling of his affairs was Count Moritz Lichnowsky. According to Schindler, there was a difference of opinion between the count and the composer concerning the signing of an agreement with Steiner, whereupon Beethoven improvised the following canon in the much frequented tavern 'zur goldenen Birne':

'Written on Febr. 20 1823 in the coffee house zur Birn on the Landstrasse [note by Schindler]'

Beethoven, however, was not always in such a gay mood; financial difficulties were now crowding in on him. First of all, the debt remained to his friend Franz Brentano in Frankfurt. Meanwhile, Steiner, now that Beethoven was offering his works to other publishers, pressed him for the money which he had lent him and threatened to sue him for the balance of the debt. Beethoven presented a counter-claim and demanded that Steiner publish a number of compositions which he had purchased but had not issued. Steiner, now the owner of the works, refused. Beethoven appealed to his brother Johann to go security for him, but he refused. Then he consulted Dr Bach, who advised him to dispose of one of his shares of bank stock. Beethoven resisted this advice as long as he could, since he considered these shares not his own but his nephew's, so he attempted instead to use them as security for a loan. Schindler was called upon to act as agent in this matter, as is shown by the following notes.

'Very best optimus optime!
'. . . Try to find some philanthropist who will make me a loan on a bank share, so that, first, I need not put too severe a strain on the generosity of my special friends the B[rentanos] and may not myself be subjected to need because of the withholding of this money, due to the beautiful arrangements and precautions made by my *dear* brother! – It would be lovely if you appeared at Mariahilf this afternoon around 3.30 or even in the forenoon –
'It must not be apparent to people that the *money* is needed –'

In another note he writes:

'Dear S,
'Do not forget the BS [bank-share], it is highly necessary. I should not like to be sued for no reason whatsoever. The conduct of my brother is worthy of him – The tailor is coming today and I hope to hold him off with kind words.
Very hastily yours'

The Conversation Books of this period show that Schindler, despite his devotion to the master, was stubborn, and unlike the other close friends, dared express criticism or a contrary opinion as the following entries show: the first, in January:

'Don't be so undecided, my dear Master! –
'now what do you wish me to do in regards to a bank-share and how much is one worth?

'I would arrange for it right away today in order to have done every-thing to achieve this purpose.'

In April he writes: 'Don't think night and day about your debts, when you are well you'll pay them without any pain.'

It was while in this distressful state concerning his debts that Beet-hoven took the first step towards making his nephew his legal heir. On 6 March 1823, he wrote to Bach:

'Dear honoured friend!

'Death might come unannounced and give no time to make a legal will, therefore I hereby attest with my own hand that I declare my beloved nephew Karl van Beethoven to be my universal heir and that after my death everything without exception *which can be called my property shall belong to him* – I appoint you to be his curator, and if there should be no testament after this you are also authorised and requested to find a guardian for my beloved nephew K. v. Beethoven – to the exclusion of my brother Johann van Beethoven – and secure his appointment according to law. I declare this writing to be valid for all time as being my last will before my death – I embrace you with all my heart –

Your true admirer and friend
Ludwig van Beethoven'

In this period the alluring vision of a new opera presented itself, haunted the minds of Beethoven and his friends for a space and then disappeared in the limbo of unexecuted projects. *Fidelio* had been revived on 3 November 1822, at the Kärnthnerthor Theatre. Its success was so great that the management of the theatre offered a commis-sion to Beethoven for a new opera. Beethoven viewed the proposition favourably and his friends hailed it with enthusiasm. Beethoven's love for classic literature led him to express a desire for a libretto based on some story of the antique world. He was told that such were all worn threadbare. In the Conversation Books we see what suggestions were offered by others: a text by Schlegel; Voltaire's tragedies; Schiller's *Fiesco*. Local poets and would-be poets were willing to throw them-selves into the breach.

In the forefront of those urging Beethoven was Count Moritz Lich-nowsky. In February he writes in a Conversation Book: 'Recently I was with a certain Madam Neumann. 2 to 3 years ago she wrote a libretto, *Alfred the Great*, it is said to be very beautiful, I will bring it in 3 or 4 days'; and the count goes on to describe the work which contains, he has heard, a 'fabulous spectacle'. At the same time he reports that he has been in touch with Grillparzer and writes a few pages later: 'I am eager for an answer from Grillparzer. He has a beautiful command of language, a lot of fire and imagination and [is] qualified to write a big poetic work . . . This would be something for a second opera. If he writes something for you, his composition would be the winner.'

Franz Grillparzer (born in 1791) by this time was well known to the Viennese as a dramatic poet through his plays *Sappho, The Ancestress* and *The Golden Fleece*; he was now completing his tragedy *Ottokar*. Already he and Beethoven had met several times, and, being musically educated, he admired the composer very highly.

Grillparzer has left us an account of his attempt to collaborate with Beethoven on an opera in his *Reminiscences of Beethoven* (written in 1840). According to this account it was Count Moritz Dietrichstein, director of both court theatres, who informed him that Beethoven was turning to him for a new libretto.

'This request, I must confess, gave me no little embarrassment. Once I had the idea of writing a libretto, still remote enough in itself, I began to doubt if Beethoven who meanwhile had become completely deaf and whose latest compositions without detracting from their high worth possessed a quality of harshness, who to me seemed to be in conflict with the treatment of the singing voice; I doubted, I say, if Beethoven was still capable of composing an opera. The thought, however, of giving to a great man the opportunity for a work which would be at any rate of the first interest overcame all considerations and I agreed.

'From the dramatic material which I had set aside for future adaptation, there were two which, if necessary, would permit of operatic treatment. One was set in the realm of most intense emotion. But aside from the fact that I knew no lady singer who would be able to rise to the main role, I also did not want to give Beethoven the opportunity to step still closer to the extreme limits of music which lay nearby, threatening like precipices, in partnership with material that was semi-diabolical.'

This was, as the Conversation Books show, *Drahomira*, a story drawn from Bohemian legendary history. The second subject was the fable of Melusine.

Grillparzer describes the visit to Beethoven at his lodgings in the Kothgasse which he made in company with Schindler:

'I found him lying in soiled nightwear on a disordered bed, a book in his hand. At the head of the bed was a small door which, as I observed later, opened into the dining-room and which Beethoven seemed in a manner to be guarding, for when subsequently a maid came through it with butter and eggs he could not restrain himself, in the middle of an earnest conversation, from throwing a searching glance at the quantity of the provisions served – which gave me a painful picture of the disorder prevailing in his domestic economy.

'As we entered Beethoven arose from the bed, gave me his hand, poured out his feelings of goodwill and respect and at once broached the subject of the opera. "Your work lives here," said he, pointing to his heart; "I am going to the country in a few days and shall at once begin to compose it. Only, I don't know what to do with the hunters' chorus which forms the introduction. Weber used four horns; you see, therefore, that I must have eight; where will this lead to?" Although I was far from seeing the need of such a conclusion I explained to him that without injury to the rest of the book the hunters' chorus could be omitted, with which concession he seemed to be satisfied, and neither then nor later did he offer any objection to the text or ask that a change be made. He even insisted on closing a contract with me at once. The profits of the opera should be divided evenly between us, etc. I declared to him, and truthfully, that I had not thought of a fee or anything of the kind while at work . . . Least of all was it to be the subject of conversation between us. He was to do with the book what he pleased   I would never make a contract with him. After a good deal of talk back and forth or rather of writing, for he could no longer hear speech, I took my leave . . .

'I had hoped that he had given up all thoughts of business in regard to the matter; but a few days later my publisher, Wallishauser, came to me and said that Beethoven insisted upon the execution of a contract. If I could not make up my mind, Wallishauser suggested that I assign the property-right in the book to him and he would arrange with Beethoven, who was already advised of such a step. I was glad to get rid of the business, let Wallishauser pay me a moderate sum, ceded to him all the author's rights, and banished the matter from my thoughts.'

On 13 April 1823, the boy Franz Liszt, who was studying with Carl Czerny and had made his first public appearance on the first day of the year, gave a concert in the small Redoutensaal. A few days earlier he along with his father was presented to Beethoven by Schindler. There is an entry in a Conversation Book which, because of the handwriting and courtly language, was probably written by the father: 'I have often expressed the wish to Herr von Schindler to make your high acquaintance and am rejoiced to be able now to do so. As I shall give a concert on Sunday the 13th I most humbly beg you to give me your high presence.'

The day before the concert, Schindler writes in a Conversation Book:

'Little Liszt has urgently requested me humbly to beg you for a theme on which he wishes to improvise at his concert tomorrow.'

'He will not break the seal till the time comes.'

'The little fellow's free improvisations cannot yet, strictly speaking, be interpreted as such. The lad is a true pianist; but as far as *improvisation* is concerned, the day is still far off when one can say that he improvises.'

'Czerny Carl is his teacher.
Just eleven years.'

Beethoven did attend the concert, went afterwards upon the stage, lifted up the prodigy and kissed him. At the concert, however, the theme upon which he improvised was not one by Beethoven but a rondo theme of some twenty measures. According to the reviews the improvisation did not please.

Amid the account of the negotiations concerning subscriptions to the Mass there was mentioned the name of Louis Schlösser who at this time was friendly with Beethoven and whose reception by him provides a fine example of the cordiality that Beethoven could offer to young artists. For months he was unsuccessful in his attempts to meet the master. Finally on 4 November 1822, at the second performance of *Fidelio* he got his chance to see him at least from a distance. He was leaving the theatre with his friend Franz Schubert.

'Together with us, three gentlemen, to whom I paid no further attention because their backs were turned to me, stepped out of a lower corridor; yet I was not a little surprised to see all those who were streaming by towards the lobby crowding to one side, in order to give the three plenty of room. Then Schubert very softly plucked my sleeve, pointing with his finger to the gentleman in the middle, who turned his head at that moment so that the bright light of the lamps fell on it and – I saw, familiar to me from engravings and paintings, the features of the creator of the opera I had just heard, Beethoven himself. My heart beat twice as loudly at that moment; all the things I may have said to Schubert I now no longer recall; but I well remember that I

followed the Desired One and his companions (Schindler and Breuning, as I later discovered) like a shadow through crooked alleys and
past high, gable-roofed houses, followed him until the darkness hid
him from sight.'

The opportunity to visit Beethoven was finally made by the Hessian
Ambassador, Baron von Türckheim, who gave Schlösser the commission of reporting to Beethoven the acceptance of the subscription to the
Mass from that court. Climbing up the dark stairs to the first storey of
the Kothgasse No. 60, Schlösser turned as instructed to the door on the
left. Finding no servant or maid, he opened the door which led into the
kitchen

'through which one had to pass to gain the living-rooms ... After
repeatedly knocking in vain at the real living-room door, I entered and
found myself in a rather commodious but entirely undecorated apartment; a large, four-square oak table with various chairs, which presented a somewhat chaotic aspect, stood in the middle of the room.
On it lay writing-books and lead-pencils, music-paper and pens, a
chronometer, a metronome, an ear-trumpet made of yellow metal and
various other things. On the wall at the left of the door was the bed,
completely covered with music, scores and manuscripts. I can recall
only a framed oil-painting (it was a portrait of Beethoven's grandfather,
for whom, as is known, he had a childlike reverence) which was the sole
ornament I noticed. Two deep window-niches, covered with smooth
panelling I mention only because in the first a violin and bow hung
from a nail, and in the other Beethoven himself, his back to me, stood
busily writing down figures and the like on the wood, already covered
with scribblings.'

Schlösser continues:

'The deaf Master had not heard me enter, and it was only by stamping
vigorously with my feet that I managed to attract his notice and he at
once turned around, surprised to see a young stranger standing before
him. Yet before I could address a single word to him, he commenced
to excuse himself in the politest manner imaginable because he had
sent out his housekeeper, and no one had been in attendance to
announce me, the while quickly drawing on his coat; and then first
asking me what I wished. Standing so near this artist, crowned with
glory, I could realise the impression which his distinguished personality, his characteristic head, with its surrounding mane of heavy hair

and the furrowed brow of a thinker, could not help but make on everyone. I could look into those profoundly serious eyes, note the amiably smiling expression of his mouth when he spoke, my words always being received with great interest.

'My visit probably occurred shortly after he had eaten breakfast, for he repeatedly passed the napkin lying beside him across his snow-white teeth, a habit, incidentally, in which I noticed he often indulged. Steeped in my contemplation of him I entirely forgot the unfortunate man's total deafness, and was just about to explain my reason for being there to him when, fortunately, I recalled the uselessness of speaking at the last moment, and instead reverentially handed him the letter with its great seal.'

Having expressed pleasure over the letter and the visit from him, Beethoven, continues Schlösser,

'seized his ear-trumpet, so I explained the unbounded veneration accorded his genial works, with what enthusiasm they were heard, and what an influence the perfection of his intellectual creations had exercised on the cultural level of the day. Though Beethoven was so impervious to flattery of any kind, my words which came stammering from the depths of my soul, nevertheless seemed to touch him, and this induced me to tell him of my nocturnal pursuit of him after the performance of "Fidelio". "But what prevented you from coming to see me in person?" he asked. "I am sure you have been told any amount of contradictory nonsense; that I have been described as being an uncomfortable, capricious and arrogant person, whose music one might indeed enjoy, but who personally was to be avoided. I know these evil, lying tongues, but if the world considers me heartless, because I seldom meet people who understand my thoughts and feelings, and therefore content myself with a few friends, it wrongs me."

'He had put down his ear-trumpet, for speaking into it agitated his nerves too greatly; his complaint, so he insisted, did not lie in the weakness of the auditory canals, but was seated in the intestines; his physicians in treating him had made a false diagnosis their point of departure, etc.'

From then on, Schlösser wrote his questions on sheets of paper lying at hand. Beethoven spoke of particular passages in his works – would that Schlösser had preserved these remarks! —of the superficial art currents in Vienna, under Italian influence, the 'speechlessness' of princely gentlemen. Then he asked Schlösser to show him his compo-

sitions, and after inviting him to a meal two days from then (3 March)
he dismissed him with the greatest amiability. 'Do not hesitate to avail
yourself of me whenever I can be useful to you or be of service to you in
any way,' were his parting words.

On the morning of 3 March, Beethoven surprised his admirer by
mounting the four flights of steps to pay a return visit. Schlösser writes:

'What I did and said in my first confusion I do not know; he, on the
other hand, well aware of my embarrassment, at once began to speak:
he had called, in order since it was such a pleasant day, to take me along
for a little walk before dinner, and to improve the occasion by making
the acquaintance of my lodgings, instruments, music and pictures of
my parents, which I had mentioned to him. And he actually began to
turn the pages of my copy-books of contrapuntal exercises, to look over
my little hand-library, in which he found his favourites, Homer and
Goethe, and I even had to submit to him a drawing of mine, and all of
these things he examined attentively and praised.'

Beethoven's meal ended with coffee which he himself had prepared
with a newly discovered machine, the construction of which he explained. Afterwards there was talk of his abandoned trip to England,
his difficulties with the pension payments, *Fidelio* and the attempt to
find a good new opera libretto, his new compositions; and as his guest
left, he called out 'To our next meeting!'

According to Schlösser, Beethoven was living

'alternately in the delightful Helenenthal near Baden, where in
Nature's open, his creative powers drew their richest nourishment
among the hills and the heavily-laded woods, and where ideas, as he
expressed himself, flowed to him in quantity. I visited him there, for he
felt himself much indisposed: the germ of his future illness was even
then present in his body, and yet I could not help but admire the
strength of soul with which he fought against it. Nothing about him
betrayed his suffering during our excursions in common through the
surrounding country; the pictures of the landscapes captured completely his eyes and his feelings . . .'

He continues:

'Only a few weeks later we met in the Kärnthnerstrasse. His keen eye
discovered me first; and coming up to me he at once seized me by the
arm with the words: "If you can spare the time then accompany me to

the Paternostergässchen, to Steiner's (the music shop of Steiner and Haslinger) whom I want to give a good set-down. These publishers always have all sorts of excuses handy. When it comes to bringing out my compositions they would like to put it off until I am dead, because they think they would do a better business with them; but I shall know how to meet them" (literally). At this encounter I had been so surprised at the very onset to find Beethoven, usually so careless about his attire, dressed with unwonted elegance, wearing a blue frock-coat with yellow buttons, impeccable white knee-breeches, a vest to match, and a new beaver hat, as usual on the back of his head. I left him at the entrance to the shop, which was crowded with people while, thanking me for escorting him, he entered Mr Steiner's office with the latter. I could not resist telling my teacher Mayseder, who lived in the neighbourhood, about the striking metamorphosis of Beethoven's elegant appearance, an event which, however, caused Mayseder far less surprise than it had caused me, for he said with a smile: "This is not the first time that his friends have taken his old clothes during the night and laid down new ones in their place; he has not the least suspicion of what has happened and puts on whatever lies before him with entire unconcern" . . . I shall only add, to what has gone before, the last conversation I had with this profoundly serious thinker. One day I brought him a new, somewhat complicated composition I had written, and after he had read it he remarked: "You have given too much, less would have been better; but that lies in the nature of heaven-scaling youth, which never thinks it possible to do enough. It is a fault maturer years will correct, however, and I still prefer a superfluity to a paucity of ideas." "What shall I do to find the right way and – how did you yourself attain that lofty goal?" I added, timidly. "I carry my thoughts about with me for a long time, sometimes a very long time, before I set them down," he replied. "At the same time my memory is so faithful to me that I am sure not to forget a theme which I have once conceived, even after years have passed. I make many changes, reject and reattempt until I am satisfied. Then the working-out in breadth, length, height and depth begins in my head, and since I am conscious of what I want, the basic idea never leaves me. It rises, grows upward, and I hear and see the picture as a whole take shape and stand forth before me as though cast in a single piece, so that all that is left is the work of writing it down. This goes quickly, according as I have the time, for sometimes I have several compositions in labour at once, though I am sure never to confuse one with the other. You will ask me whence I take my ideas? That I cannot say with any degree of certainty: they come to me uninvited, directly or indirectly. I could almost grasp them in my hands, out in Nature's open, in the woods, during my promenades, in the silence of the night, at the earliest dawn. They are roused by moods which in the poet's case are transmuted into words, and in mine into tones, that sound, roar and storm until at last they take shape for me as notes." '

After the labours and vexations of town life in the winter, the call of the country in the summer was even more than usually imperative, because the work which had long occupied Beethoven's mind – the Ninth Symphony – was demanding completion. His brother Johann had invited him to visit him on his estate near Gneixendorf, but he had declined. His choice for the summer sojourn fell upon Hetzendorf, a village not far from Vienna, where he removed on 17 May. After much hesitation, he finally decided upon a villa, surrounded by a beautiful park, which belonged to Baron Müller-Pronay. There was some haggling about the rent and some questioning about the post service – an important matter in view of the many negotiations with publishers, in all of which Schindler was depended on – but eventually all was arranged. Ill health marred the Hetzendorf sojourn. Beethoven's other ailments were augmented by a painful affliction of the eyes which called for medical treatment, retarded his work and caused him no small amount of anxiety. Complaints on this score began in April and were continued through July, on the 15th of which month he writes to the Archduke, 'My eyes are better, but improvement is slow ... It would be more rapid if I were not obliged to wear glasses. It is an unfortunate circumstance and has delayed me in everything'; and later, when on a short visit to Vienna: 'I have just heard that YIH is coming here tomorrow. If I cannot obey the wishes of my heart, please ascribe it to my eyes. I am much better, but I must not breathe the town air for many more days, for it would have an ill effect on my eyes.' In August, very shortly before his departure for Baden: 'I am feeling really badly and not only because of my eyes. I propose to drag myself to Baden tomorrow to take lodgings and in a few days will have to go there to stay. The town air has an injurious effect on my entire system and I hurt myself by going twice to my physicians in the city.'

In his *Reminiscences of Beethoven*, Grillparzer writes of his promise, after visiting Beethoven, to visit him in Hetzendorf. The poet kept his promise, going thither with Schindler. Part of his account may best be given in his own words:

'We took a promenade and entertained each other as well as was possible half in conversation, half in writing, while walking. I still remember with emotion that when we sat down to table Beethoven went into an adjoining room and himself brought forth five bottles. He set down one at Schindler's plate, one at his own and three in front of me, probably to make me understand in his wild and simple way that I was master and should drink as much as I liked. When I drove back to town without Schindler, who remained in Hetzendorf, Beethoven insisted on accompanying me. He sat himself beside me in the open carriage but instead of going only to the edge of the village, he drove with me to the city, getting out at the gates and, after a cordial handshake, starting back alone on the journey of an hour and a half homeward. As he left the carriage I noticed a bit of paper lying on the seat which he had just vacated. I thought that he had forgotten it and beckoned him to come back; but he shook his head and with a loud laugh, as at the success of a ruse, he ran the faster in the opposite direction. I unrolled the paper and it contained exactly the amount of the carriage-hire which I had agreed upon with the driver. His manner of life had so estranged him from all the habits and customs of the world that it probably never occurred to him that under other circumstances he would have been guilty of a gross offence. I took the matter as it was intended and laughingly paid my coachman with the money which had been given to me.'

Following are excerpts from a Conversation Book used during the visit to Hetzendorf. The first permits us to observe the poet's ideas on the music for his own libretto:

'Are you still of the opinion that something else ought to be substituted for the first chorus of the opera?'

'Perhaps a few tones of the hunting-horns might be continued by an invisible chorus of nymphs.'

'I have been thinking if it might not be possible to mark every appearance of Melusine or of her influence in the action by a recurrent and easily grasped melody. Might not the overture begin with this and after the rushing Allegro the introduction be made out of the same melody.'

'I have thought of this melody as that to which Melusine sings her first song.'

'Drahomira'

'I will send you the plot of this Drahomira in writing.'

Grillparzer made many observations concerning music and musicians which must have interested Beethoven even when he did not agree with him. Earlier he had asserted that on the whole the North Germans knew little of music – they would never produce anything higher than *Der Freischütz*.

Among the cheering incidents of the summer were the reports which reached him of the production of *Fidelio* under the direction of Weber in Dresden. Most unfortunately all the letters between them have disappeared, and the only hints we have as to their contents are from the draft for Weber's first communication:

'*Fidelio*. To Beethoven. The performance in Prague under my direction of this mighty work, which bears testimony to German grandeur and feeling, gave me an intimacy, as inspiring as it was instructive, with the essence through which I hope to present it to the public in its complete effectiveness here, where I have all possible means at my command. Every representation will be a festival day on which I shall be privileged to offer to your exalted mind the homage which lives in my heart, where reverence and love for you struggle with each other.'

Weber had received the score of the opera on 10 April from Beethoven, who had to borrow it from the Kärnthnerthor Theatre, whose musical archives were in the care of Count Gallenberg. Through Schindler, Gallenberg sent word to Beethoven that he would send the score, provided two copies were on hand; if not, he would have a copy made. Schindler, reporting the message to Beethoven, adds that Gallenberg had said he thought Beethoven himself had the score: 'But when I assured him that you did not have it he said that its loss was a consequence of your irregularity and many changes of lodgings.' Nevertheless, Weber got the score and after fourteen rehearsals the representation took place with great success. Von Könneritz, Director-General of the Royal Chapel, reported the triumph to Beethoven and sent him a fee of forty ducats. Beethoven, in acknowledging receipt on 17 July, was emboldened 'by the account which my dear friend Maria Weber gives me of the admirable and noble motives of Your Excellency' to ask his intercession with the Saxon court on behalf of the Mass in D; through the good offices of von Könneritz and the Archduke, the King of Saxony duly subscribed, as already recorded in this chapter.

Another pleasant experience for Beethoven may be recorded here. In 1822 the Royal Academy of Music of Sweden had elected Beethoven to a foreign membership. The consent of the Austrian government was necessary to his acceptance of the honour and this seems to have been deferred an unconscionably long time. When permission eventually came he wrote notes to the editors of the newspapers *Beobachter* and *Wiener Zeitung*, asking them to announce the fact of his election; these letters were to be delivered by Schindler, to whom Beethoven wrote instructions in the following note:

'Very best L[umpen]k[er]l from Epirus no less than from Brundusium etc!

   'Give this letter to the Beobachter. His name must be written on it by you – At the same time ask him whether his daughter has progressed well on the pianof[orte] and whether I might perhaps be of service to her with a copy of my compositions? – I have written down *honorary member*, but I do not know whether this is right or whether just to put *as a foreign member, not knowing* about such things and *never* noticing.

   'You have also something to deliver to Bernardum non Sanctum concerning this story. But also ask Bernard about this rascal Rupprecht. Explain the chit-chat to him and ask how one can apply the leather to such scandalous people.

   'Ask both philosophical newspaper writers if this is an *appointment to Honorary or Dishonorary Membership?* –

   'I am eating at home, if you want to come, do so –

   'Beg pardon of Herr Beobachter that the letter looks so confused – There is really too much to be done.

   'Find out also whether a copy of the Beobachter can be bought.'

About this time Franz Schoberlechner, a young pianist, appealed to him for letters of recommendation to be used on a concert tour. The letter reached Beethoven through Schindler, to whom he returned it with the curt endorsement: 'A capable fellow has no need of recommendation other than from one good house to another.' Schindler importuned him again and Beethoven answered: 'It must be plain to you that I do not want to have anything to do with this matter – as for "being noble" I think I have shown you sufficiently that I am that on principle; I even think that you must have observed that I have never been otherwise.' That ended the matter.

Beethoven's domestic affairs continued to plague him. While at Hetzendorf he had the services of a housekeeper whom he described as 'the swift-sailing frigate Frau Schnaps'. He had no end of trouble about his town lodging in the Kothgasse where Schindler was living, and was compelled to write long letters to his factotum on the subject. Here is one sent from Hetzendorf on 2 July:

'The continuous brutality of the landlord from the beginning and for as long as I have been in the house calls for the help of the RI police. Go to them direct. As regards the storm windows, the housekeeper was ordered to look after them and particularly after the recent severe rain-storm to see if they were necessary to prevent rain from entering the room. But she found that it had neither rained in nor could rain in. Believing this, I put on the lock so that the brutal fellow could not open my rooms in my absence as he threatened to do – Tell them further how he behaved towards you and that he posted [up] the bill without notice, which he has no right to do before St James's day. –

'He has also refused to give me a receipt from St George's to St James* as this paper shows, because of the demand that I pay a charge for lighting of which I knew nothing. This abominable lodging with-out a *stove-flue* and with the most wretched sort of *main chimney* has cost me at least 250 florins VS for extra expenses above the rent, in order to make it habitable while I was there in the winter.

'It was an intentional cheat, inasmuch as I never saw the lodgings in the first storey but only in the second, for which reason many objec-tionable things remained unknown to me. I cannot comprehend how it is possible that *so shameful a chimney, ruinous to human health, can be tol-erated by the government*. You remember how the walls of your room looked because of smoke, how much it cost to get rid of some, but not all, of the nuisance – The chief thing now is that he be commanded to take down the notice and to give me the receipt for the rent paid at any rate, since under no circumstances will I pay for that wretched light-ing. Furthermore, I had other large expenses in order to make life endurable in that lodging – My sore eyes cannot yet stand the town air, otherwise I would go myself to the imperial police.

Yours faithfully

L. v. Beethoven'

Schindler obeyed instructions. In a letter to Beethoven dated 3 July, he reported that the police director, Ungermann, sent his compliments to Beethoven, granted all his wishes in advance, but advised him to pay the six florins for lighting to prevent a scoundrelly landlord from having any kind of hold upon him. The poster came down, but Beet-hoven had had enough and moved to new lodgings in the autumn.

Beethoven's nephew Karl pursued his studies at Blöchlinger's Insti-tute till August and then spent his vacation with his uncle at Baden. He made himself useful as amanuensis and otherwise, and his words are occasionally found among the notes of conversation. His mother

* i.e., for the second quarter-year rental period, 24 April–25 July.

remained in the background for the time being, which is providential, for Beethoven had trouble enough with his other sister-in-law, the wife of Johann, whose conduct reached the extreme of reprehensibleness in the summer of 1823, during a spell of sickness which threw her husband on his back. The woman chose this time to receive her lover in her house and to make a shameless public parade of her moral laxness. The stepdaughter was not less neglectful of her filial duties.

Schindler, who in Beethoven's lodgings was living next door to Johann, wrote a letter on 3 July from which we quote:

'As I have been visiting him [Johann] three to four times a day since he took to his bed, and have entertained him by the hour, I have had an opportunity carefully to observe these two persons; hence I can assure you on my honour that, despite your venerable name, they deserve to be shut up, the old one in prison, the young one in the house of correction . . . This illness came opportunely for both of them, to enable them to go their ways without trammel. These beasts would have let him rot if others had not taken pity on him. He might have died a hundred times . . . He often wept over the conduct of his family and once he gave way completely to his grief and begged me to let you know how he is being treated so that you might come and give the two the beating they deserve . . . It is most unnatural and more than barbarous if that woman, while her husband is lying ill, introduces her lover into his room, prinks herself like a sleigh horse in his presence and then goes driving with him, leaving the sick husband languishing at home. She did this very often. Your brother himself called my attention to it, and is a fool for tolerating it so long.'

Further accounts of his sister-in-law's misconduct reached Beethoven's ears, and he was frank in his denunciation of her to his brother. Schindler was asked by Beethoven to lay the matter before the police, but he managed to postpone that step for the time being.

Burdened with these difficult relationships, with physical suffering of different kinds, and with other vexations as well, Beethoven laboured at Hetzendorf on the great work which, already begun, was supposed to be nearing its end: the *Symphony for England* or, as we are used to naming it, the Ninth Symphony. In a letter to Archduke Rudolph on 1 July, Beethoven writes: 'I am now writing a new symphony for England, for the Philharmonic Society, and hope to have it completely done in a fortnight.' The work claimed his attention to such a degree that he strove for solitude and wished if possible to see no one, not even Schindler.

This deep concentration on his big work resulted in much disturbance in his domestic affairs. 'Completely preoccupied, he roamed through fields and pastures, sketchbook in hand, without giving a thought to the arranged hour for meals. When he returned he was repeatedly without his hat, which never happened formerly even in the moments of highest inspiration. Up to the middle of August were to be seen big notebooks with notations for his new work.' So Schindler writes. The ideas for the symphony had been growing in his mind for a long time before the writing out in this summer; otherwise he would not have been able to write to Ries on 25 April 1823: 'Right now I am not well because of many vexations that I have had to endure, yes even pain in my eyes! But do not worry; you will have the symphony soon; it is really this miserable situation alone that has been the fault.' During the labour on this work there was room for nothing else in his mind; it was so ever-present with him that there was neither paradox nor hyperbole in his words, 'I am never alone when I am alone.'

To the distractions already mentioned there came another which is related by Schindler: 'Then the "raptus" seized him to want to leave the beautiful villa of Baron Pronay and move to beloved Baden; the reason "because the Baron made deep bows to him every time they met".' Here Schindler cites the phrase 'Humility of man towards man – it pains me' from the second letter to the 'Immortal Beloved'.

Beethoven may have formed the plan earlier in the year – probably had – but the Baron's excessive politeness helped to turn his departure into something like a bolt. Schindler continues:

'There appeared one morning his swift-sailing frigate, the good old housekeeper, in my room (it must be remembered that since September 1822 Beethoven had shared his room with me in the Pfarrgasse [Kothgasse], Vorstadt Leimgrube) and brought the message: the master feels that he is unable to work any longer in Hetzendorf and must depart from there; he expected me the next day to be with him at 5 o'clock in the morning so that I could help him in the search for a house in Baden. As evidence there were the following lines in his hand: "Samothracian L – K – Come, the weather is just right. But it is better earlier than later, presto prestissimo, we are leaving from here."

'This trip from Hetzendorf to Baden and the business there are among my most singular experiences with the great eccentric. Forthwith he began to reminisce over the long list of dwellings which he had already occupied there and their inconveniences and unpleasantnesses. There was only one of all that he had occupied which he now wanted; "but the people have declared in years past that they do not want to take me [Beethoven] in again." But such declarations had come from other houses there several times already. When we had arrived he requested me to proceed as a go-between to the desired house and in his name to give a promise of better order and respect for other occupants (a chief cause of the complaint). This promise, however, received no attention. I was refused. My persevering friend was deeply troubled by this. Once again the bearer of the flag of truce was sent to the stronghold of the coppersmith with new assurances of good conduct. This time he found a willing ear. One specific stipulation, however, was made, that in order to have the room overlooking the street as in past years, Beethoven must provide it with window shutters. We tried in vain to learn the reason for this strange demand. Meanwhile, since the procurement of this requisite proved necessary for the prevention of bright sunlight for the composer's ailing eyes, this demand was willingly agreed to. A few days later the move took place.'

Schindler then gives the reason for the request. Beethoven was in the habit of scrawling all kinds of memoranda on his shutters in lead pencil – accounts, musical themes, etc. A family from North Germany had noticed this in the previous year and had bought one of the shutters as a curiosity. The thrifty smith had an eye for business and disposed of the remaining shutters to other summer visitors. When Beethoven was informed by an apothecary at Baden of this strange transaction, he broke into Homeric laughter.

The day of Beethoven's move to Baden was 13 August. Excerpts from a letter to his brother Johann show his mood at this time:

'Baden, 19 August

'Dear Brother:

'I am rejoiced at your better health. As regards myself, my eyes are not entirely recovered and I came here with a disordered stomach and a frightful catarrh, the first due to the arch-pig of a housekeeper, and the second to a beast of a kitchen-maid whom I had once sent away but whom I took back . . .

'I received your letter of the 10th through the hands of the miserable scoundrel *Schindler*. You need only to give your letters directly to the post, from which I am certain to receive them, for I avoid this mean and contemptible fellow as much as possible – Karl cannot come to me before the 29th of this month when he will write to you. You cannot be wholly unadvised as to what the two *canailles*, Lout and Bastard,* are doing to you, and you will have had letters on the subject from me and

* Meaning Johann's wife and stepdaughter.

Karl, for, little as you deserve it I shall never forget that you are my brother, and a good angel will yet come to rid you of these two *canailles*, this former and present strumpet who slept with her fellow no less than three times while you were ill, and who, in addition to everything else, has your money wholly in her hands. O infamous disgrace, isn't there a spark of manhood in you?!!! – Now concerning another matter. You have my own manuscript of some pieces for the "Ruinen von Athen", which I want urgently because the copies of the score made for the Josephstadt lack several things which are to be found in these manuscript scores of mine. Since I am writing something similar, I want this most urgently, so write where I can get these manuscripts, I particularly ask this of you. About coming to you I will write another time. Ought I so to degrade myself as to associate with such bad company? Mayhap this can be avoided and we might yet pass a few days with you?! About the rest of your letter another time. Farewell. Unseen I hover over you and work through others so that these *canailles* shall not strangle you. –

As always your faithful

Brother'

At Baden Beethoven's health improved. In a letter to the Archduke, dated 22 August, he complained of a catarrhal trouble, the misery in his bowels and the trouble with his eyes, but adds: 'Thank God, the eyes are so much improved that I can again use them considerably in the daytime.' He was characteristically optimistic about the completion of his symphony as is shown in a letter to Ries dated 5 September in which he reports: 'The score of the symphony has been completed by the copyists during the last few days and consequently Kirchhoffer and I are merely waiting for a good opportunity to send it off.' At this time the symphony was not ready, let alone copied; but in his head it was far advanced and in July he was already working out the third movement. Franz Christian Kirchhoffer was a bookkeeper in the Ofenheimer wholesale firm in Vienna. Beethoven wrote several letters to him at this time and both now and later he acted as intermediary between Beethoven and Ries. On 5 September the composer wrote to Kirchhoffer that he would receive the score of the symphony in fourteen days at the most, but that what was really important now was the speedy delivery of the Mass to Ries.

There were several visitors to Beethoven at Baden in the summer of 1823 who have left accounts of their experiences. One was an Englishman, Edward Schulz, who published his story in the *Harmonicon* in January 1824. Schulz visited Beethoven on 28 September in the company of Haslinger. He describes it as a *dies faustus* for him and, as Schindler shrewdly observes, it must have also been one for Beethoven, since he managed to hear the conversations of his visitors without the aid of an ear-trumpet. He talked with great animation, as was his wont when in good humour, but says the English visitor, 'One unlucky question, one ill-judged piece of advice – for instance, concerning the cure of his deafness – is quite sufficient to estrange him from you for ever.' He asked Haslinger about the highest possible note on the trombone, but was dissatisfied with the answer which he received; introduced his nephew and showed his pride in the youth's attainments by telling his guest that he might put him to 'a riddle in Greek' if he liked. At dinner during a visit to the Helenenthal he commented on the profusion of provisions at dinner, saying: 'Why such a variety of dishes? Man is but little above other animals if his chief pleasure is confined to the dinner-table.' An excerpt from the letter will serve to advance the present narrative:

'In the whole course of our table-talk there was nothing so interesting as what he said about Handel. I sat close by him and heard him assert very distinctly in German, "Handel is the greatest composer that ever lived." I cannot describe to you with what pathos, and I am inclined to say, with what sublimity of language, he spoke of the *Messiah* of this immortal genius. Every one of us was moved when he said, "I would uncover my head, and kneel down at his tomb!" H. and I tried repeatedly to turn the conversation to Mozart, but without effect. I only heard him say, "In a monarchy we know who is the first"; which might or might not apply to the subject. Mr C. Czerny – who, by the by, knows every note of Beethoven by heart, though he does not play one single composition of his own without the music before him – told me, however, that B. was sometimes inexhaustible in his praise of Mozart. It is worthy of remark that this great musician cannot bear to hear his own earlier works praised; and I was apprised that a sure way to make him very angry is to say something complimentary of his Septetto, Trios, etc. His latest productions, which are so little relished in London, but much admired by the young artists of Vienna, are his favourites. His second Mass he looks upon as his best work, I understood . . . He appears uniformly to entertain the most favourable opinion of the British nation. "I like", said he, "the noble simplicity of the English manners," and added other praises.'

A few days after the one just recorded Beethoven received a visit from a man of much greater moment than the English traveller. The new visitor was Carl Maria von Weber. He wrote an account of the visit, which took place on 5 October, to his wife as follows:

'I was right tired but had to get up yesterday at 6 o'clock because the excursion to Baden had been appointed for half-past 7 o'clock. This took place with Hasslinger, Piringer and Benedict; but unfortunately the weather was atrocious. The main purpose was to see Beethoven. He received me with an affection which was touching; he embraced me most heartily at least six or seven times and finally exclaimed enthusiastically: "Indeed, you're a devil of a fellow! – a good fellow!" We spent the afternoon very merrily and contentedly. This rough, repellent man actually paid court to me, served me at table as if I had been his lady. In short, this day will always remain remarkable in my memory as well as of those present. It was uplifting for me to be overwhelmed with such loving attention by this great genius. How saddening is his deafness! Everything must be written down for him. We inspected the baths, drank the waters, and at 5 o'clock drove back to Vienna.'

Max Maria von Weber in his account of the incident says that Beethoven, in the conversation which followed his greeting of the 'devil of a fellow', railed at the management of the theatre, the concert impresarios, the public, the Italians, the taste of the people, and particularly at the ingratitude of his nephew. Weber, who was deeply moved, advised him to tear himself away from his discouraging environment and make an artistic tour through Germany, which would show him what the world thought of him. 'Too late!' exclaimed Beethoven, shaking his head and going through the motions of playing the pianoforte. 'Then go to England, where you are admired,' wrote Weber. 'Too late!' cried Beethoven, drew Weber's arm into his and dragged him along to the Sauerhof, where they dined. At parting, Beethoven embraced and kissed him several times and cried: 'Good luck to the new opera; if I can I'll come to the first performance.'

A generation later Sir Julius Benedict, who had also put his memory of those Vienna days at the service of Weber's son, wrote down his recollections for this work in these words:

'I endeavour, as I promised you, to recall the impressions I received of Beethoven when I first met him in Vienna in October 1823. He then lived at Baden; but regularly, once a week, he came to the city and he never failed to call on his old friends Steiner and Haslinger, whose music shop was then in the Paternostergässchen, a little street, no longer in existence, between the Graben and the Kohlmarkt.

'If I am not mistaken, on the morning that I saw Beethoven for the first time, Blahetka, the father of the pianist, directed my attention to a stout, short man with a very red face, small, piercing eyes, and bushy eyebrows, dressed in a very long overcoat which reached nearly to his ankles, who entered the shop about 12 o'clock. Blahetka asked me: "Who do you think that is?" and I at once exclaimed: "It must be Beethoven!" because, notwithstanding the high colour of his cheeks and his general untidiness, there was in those small piercing eyes an expression which no painter could render. It was a feeling of sublimity and melancholy combined. I watched, as you can well imagine, every word that he spoke when he took out his little book and began a conversation which to me, of course, was almost incomprehensible, inasmuch as he only answered questions pencilled to him by Messrs Steiner and Haslinger.'

Towards the close of October Beethoven returned to Vienna. He removed to new lodgings in the Landstrasse on the corner of the Bockgasse (now Beatrixgasse) and the Ungargasse, where his nephew remained with him as long as he continued a student at the University. Here he worked at the Ninth Symphony, more particularly on the last movement.

After the conversations with Grillparzer at Hetzendorf on the subject of *Melusine*, there were many others with whom Beethoven discussed the opera and who came to him to tell him of their desire to see it written. Duport, who had directed *Fidelio* the previous year, was greatly interested, wanted to read the book with care, and asked Beethoven's terms; Lichnowsky was willing to risk the financial outcome; 'I will go security', he says in October, 'for the money which you want for the opera. After selling the opera to the director you can still reserve the right of disposing of it at home and abroad.' And again: 'If you do not compose the opera, German opera is finished – everybody says that.'

Grillparzer mentions that Beethoven told him in Hetzendorf that his opera was ready (whether he meant in his head or in its essential elements in the numerous sketchbooks, the poet could not say), but after the composer's death not a single note was found which could indubitably be assigned to their common work. Why didn't Beethoven compose *Melusine*? Many reasons must be obvious to those who have followed this narrative closely: illness; vexation of spirit; loss of initiative; a waning of the old capacity to assimilate conceptions and ideas which did not originate in his own consciousness and were not in harmony with his own predilections. Moreover, it was the period of his greatest introspection; he was communing more and more with his own soul, and separating himself more and more from all agencies of utterance except the one which spoke most truthfully and directly within him, and to which he entrusted his last revelations – the string quartet.

CHAPTER 20

The Year 1824

The First Performance of the Ninth Symphony – The First Full Performance of the Missa Solemnis

The year 1823 ended with Beethoven in his new lodging on the corner of the Ungargasse, occupied with work upon the Ninth Symphony, which was approaching completion, oppressed with anxiety concerning his health and worried about his brother's domestic affairs. His eyes continued to trouble him till late in March; Schindler cautioned him not to rub them, as that might increase the inflammation; Karl suggested buying a shade to protect them from the glare of the light; and when Count Brunsvik wanted to take him along with him to Hungary, Schindler advised him to take the trip, as it might be beneficial for his eyes.

About this time Beethoven took an unusually charitable attitude towards Karl's mother. She had been ill for some time as is shown by a remark by Bernard in a Conversation Book of February–March 1823: 'Have you heard nothing concerning your sister-in-law? My house-keeper has told me that she is sick and things are going very badly with her. The doctor has told it to her himself. He said that she could not pay for the medicine. You should have enquired before how the matter stands.' That Beethoven seems to have followed up this suggestion is shown by an undated letter to Bernard:

'Dear Friend!

'I beg of you before the day is over to make enquiries about Frau van Beethoven and if it is possible, to have her assured through her physician that from this month on *so long as I live* she shall have the enjoyment of the whole of her pension, and I will see to it that if I die first, Karl shall not need the half of her pension – It was, moreover, always my intention to permit her to keep the whole of her pension as soon as Karl left the Institute, but as her illness and need are so great she must be helped at once. God has *never* deserted me in this heavy task and I shall continue to trust in Him. If possible I beg you to send me information today and I will see to it that my tenacious brother also makes a contribution to her –

Yours sincerely
Beethoven'

Beethoven wrote to her on 8 January 1824, possibly in answer to an entreating letter from her:

'Many affairs have prevented Karl and myself from sending you our good wishes for the New Year, but I know that, nevertheless, you expect nothing but the best wishes for your welfare from me as well as Karl –

'Concerning your need, generally I would have been glad to help you out with a sum, but unfortunately I have too many expenses and debts and am still waiting for a certain amount of money and so am unable right now to prove to you my willingness to give you immediate help – Meanwhile I assure you herewith in writing that you can keep Karl's half of your pension from now on. We will hand over to you each month the receipt whereupon you can collect it yourself since there is indeed no shame (and I know that several of my acquaintances receive their pensions every month) in receiving it monthly. Should I be in a position later on to give you a sum from my bank for the improvement of your circumstances, it will certainly be done – the 280 fl. 25 kr. which you owe Steiner I have likewise taken over already as you have probably been told – Moreover, for some time you have not had to pay any interest on the loan –

'You have received two months of pension from me through Schindler – On the 26th of this month or some time after that you will receive the pension payment for this month . . .

'We wish you all possible good, Karl as well as myself –

Your most willing to help L. v. Beethoven'

Beethoven seems to have regretted his magnanimity soon afterwards. In another letter to Bernard he writes:

'Dear Bernard!

'With so little time it is too much trouble for me to write to the doctor myself, to whom, however, I send best greetings herewith. Now briefly, what she has for sure, pension 406 fl. 30 kr. VS and the interest on 6,700 fl. VS yearly [which comes to] 335 VS; she is also to receive 480 fl. VS yearly from *Hofbauer*. Since, as I hear, the latter considers her child as his, *he is probably right*. And since she has become such a prostitute I believe that I and Karl even more should be sensitive to the guilt of *her bad behaviour*. Hence if this 480 fl. of Hofbauer's is true, I believe she should not be given the whole other half of the pension. Perhaps such an eminent man as the doctor could clarify the thing; at any rate I do *not* want *to come into contact with her*. I am sending her herewith 11 fl. CM and ask you to deliver it to her via the *doctor* and further that she does not know from whence it comes . . .'

The nephew was now attending the philological lectures at the university and living in the winter and spring months with his uncle. He had left Blöchlinger's Institute in August 1823, and matriculated at the university. He was active in the service of Beethoven, doing work as his amanuensis, carrying messages, making purchases, and so on; in fact Beethoven seems to have taken up more of his time than was good for his studies. Karl's involvement is shown by the following excerpts in his hand from the Conversation Books: 'Every time that you have trouble with the servants, I have to carry the blame for it . . . If you had made decisions, everything would have been different long since.' Beethoven loved his nephew tenderly and was unceasingly thoughtful of his welfare; but the jealousy of his affection led him to exercise a strictness of discipline over him which could not fail to become irksome to a growing stripling. He never seems to have realised that Karl had outgrown the period when he could be treated as a child, and it was a child's submission which he asked of him.

Grillparzer's libretto was a frequent subject of conversation between Beethoven and his friends in the early months of 1824 as already mentioned, but petitions and advice were alike unfruitful. He did not go to work upon it nor yet upon a composition which presented a more urgent obligation. This was the oratorio which he had agreed to write for the Gesellschaft der Musikfreunde and on which he had received an advance of money in 1819. Here the fatal procrastination was not altogether his fault. Bernard began the book, but seems to have put it aside after a few weeks.

Reference has already been made to the fact that in 1819 Oliva could not understand Bernard's inaction in the matter. In April 1820, Bernard himself writes: 'I must finish the oratorio completely this month so that you can begin on it at Mödling.' His intentions were not carried out, however.

Finally towards the close of October 1823, Bernard gave a copy of the complete text of the oratorio, which was entitled *Der Sieg des Kreuzes* ('The Victory of the Cross'), to Beethoven and also one to Sonnleithner for the society. After waiting nearly three months, the directorate of the society took action, the nature of which was notified to both Beethoven and Bernard.

The society wrote to Bernard that as it had left the choice of the text which he was to compose to Beethoven, it could not say whether or not it would make use of the poem which he had sent until Beethoven had set it to music, and the censor had given his sanction. He was also asked to co-operate with the society in stimulating Beethoven to finish the work 'so long expected by the musical world'.

The letter from the society to Beethoven follows:

'Dear Sir!

'When the Society of the Friends of Music of the Austrian Empire invited you to write an oratorio four years ago, which proposal you accepted along with its terms; it left to you the choice of a poem and a poet. Soon thereafter it was learned that Hr. Bernard had undertaken the writing of the poem. As often as we turned to you in this long interim and asked if you were already occupied with this work, we heard that the poem was not yet in your hands. We could not expect that a composer of your stamp should sketch the plan of his musical composition before he had been entrusted with the whole of the poem and had found it worked out and finished according to his wish; therefore we could only turn to Hr. Bernard and urge him on. Finally he handed in the complete poem to the society near the end of October 1823, and explained that he had also given a copy over to you. Since on the one hand we could only make use of the text if you, the composer, not only have actually chosen it for composition but also have actually completed the composition; but on the other hand the resolve has been expressed repeatedly by you to deliver such a work to the society, which has been confirmed by the part-payment made on request; we request consequently Your Well-born to inform the society categorically whether you will set to music the poem delivered by H. Bernard and at what time we may hope to receive this work to which every friend of music and admirer of your great talent has been looking forward for such a long time with keen expectation.

'Receive assurances of the most distinguished respect.'

Beethoven wrote the following answer to the society on 23 January:

'Dear Sirs!

'Since I have been overloaded with business and still plagued continually by an eye trouble, please be good enough to excuse my late answer – Concerning the oratorio . . . *I did not* choose Hr. v. B[ernard] to write the text; I was assured that the Society had commissioned him . . . It has been difficult to confer with him much. It has become a long story, however, very irksome in fact for me, since Hr. v. B. had written nothing other than "Libussa" for music, which at that time had not yet been performed. I have known it, however, since 1809 and since that time it has become very much altered; thus I couldn't with full confidence view the undertaking with him as anything but difficult. On account of this I was forced all the more to hold out until I had the whole text; at one point I finally received the first part. But according to B's disposition it had to be changed again, and I had to give it back again, that much I remember. Finally I received the whole at the same time that the Society did, with other obligations having occurred which I could not fulfil because of earlier illness. I have now really had to hurry to keep my word, all the more since you know that I *unfortunately can live only from works that I write. But now a variety of passages have to be altered* in B's oratorio. I have already indicated some and soon will finish and then acquaint B with them. For, though I find the material good and the poem has some value, it cannot remain *as it is*. "Christus am Ölberg" was written by me in collaboration with the *poet* in 14 days, but that poet was musical and had written several things for music and I could consult him at any moment . . . As soon as I am through with making changes in the oratorio with B, I shall have the honour to inform you of the fact and at the same time let the society know when it may with certainty count upon it. That is all I can say about it at present . . .'

Beethoven was frequently urged to set to work on the music of *Der Sieg des Kreuzes*; but he was also advised not to compose it. Archduke Rudolph accepted the dedication of the poem and wrote to Beethoven telling him of the fact and expressing a wish that he would set it to music. But the editor Schickh said to him: 'If I were Beethoven I would *never* compose the extremely tiresome text of his oratorio.' Beethoven never set seriously to work upon it, though at the end of a letter of 23 September 1824 he reiterated his promise so that he might, with mock solemnity, attest it by affixing his hand and seal.

The book of the *Sieg des Kreuzes* was based upon the ancient story of the apparition of the cross and the legend '*In hoc signo vinces*' to Constantine the Great, who had crossed the Alps into Italy and lay encamped confronting his enemy Maxentius before Rome. His daughter Julia, who was represented as wife to Maxentius, attempted to avert the battle, but the vision strengthened Constantine's resolve. Julia heard the angelic canticles which accompanied the apparition and was converted to the true faith, persisting in it to martyrdom, to which she was condemned by her husband. Schindler says that Beethoven's failure to set the book caused a rupture of the friendship which existed between him and Bernard. The directors of the Gesellschaft der Musikfreunde dropped the matter, neither importuning Beethoven more nor taking any steps to recover the money paid on account. The society afterwards elected him to honorary membership.

During the account of the oratorio project, we learned that the new symphony was ready or almost ready and that an Akademie had already been planned for a performance of the new work. Schindler, who was an eyewitness of events at this time, gives the termination date for the Ninth Symphony as February 1824, and adds that the conclusion of the work had a cheering effect upon Beethoven's spirits. He no longer grudged himself occasional recreation and was again seen strolling through the streets of Vienna, gazing into the shop-windows through eyeglasses which dangled at the end of a black ribbon, and, after a long interregnum, greeting friends and acquaintances as they passed. The history of the work is far more interesting than that of any other of his compositions, with the possible exception of the Mass in D.

Thoughts of a symphony to succeed the Symphonies in A and F major (Nos. 7 and 8) were in the composer's mind while he was making sketches for those two works in 1812; but the memoranda there found tell us only in what key the new symphony was to be; they are mere verbal notes: '2nd Sinfonie, D minor' and 'Sinfonie in D minor – 3rd Sinfonie'. A fugue-theme, identical, so far as the first three measures go, with that of the Scherzo of the Ninth Symphony, presented itself to him and was imprisoned in his notebook in 1815.

The fugue-theme appeared again in 1817 in an altered form but with the same rhythmic outline. Both versions of the D minor theme reappeared in later sketches for the symphony, the composition of which really began when the beginning of the first movement was sketched. Of this fragments are found on loose leaves belonging to the year 1817. By the end of that year and the beginning of 1818 extended sketches of the movement were made. The principal subject was definitely fixed, but the subsidiary material was still missing. The fugue-theme was assigned to the third movement. There was no suggestion of the use of Schiller's 'Ode to Joy', but a plain intimation of an instrumental finale.

In 1818 a plan was outlined for the introduction of voices into the slow movement of a further symphony which was to *follow* the Sinfonie in D. It is as follows:

'ADAGIO CANTIQUE

'Pious song in a symphony in the ancient modes – Lord God we praise Thee – alleluia – either alone or as introduction to a fugue. The whole 2nd sinfonie might be characterised in this manner in which case the vocal parts would enter in the last movement or already in the Adagio. The violins, etc., of the orchestra to be increased tenfold in the last movement, in which case the vocal parts would enter gradually – in the text of the Adagio Greek myth, *Cantique Ecclesiastique* – in the Allegro, feast of Bachus.'

Schiller's hymn was still absent from his mind. These sketches were all likewise excursions undertaken while Beethoven was chiefly occupied with the composition of another work. What progress, if any, was made with the Symphony during the next four years cannot well be determined. The work was interrupted by the composition of the Mass in D, the last three Pianoforte Sonatas and the Overture, Op. 124.* It was not until the Mass and the Josephstadt music were finished in the sketches that he gave his whole attention to the Symphony.

In the sketches of 1822, there are evidences of considerable progress on the first movement, little if any on the Scherzo, the fugue-themes of 1815 and 1817 appearing in them almost unchanged. There is no hint as yet of the slow movement, but among the sketches appears the beginning of the melody of the 'Ode to Joy' with the underlying words, assigned as a finale. The thought of using the Ode for a concluding movement had presented itself, but only tentatively, not as a fixed determination.

The conclusions to be drawn from the sketches thus far are that, as was the case in 1812 when the Seventh and Eighth Symphonies were brought forth as a pair, Beethoven was again contemplating the almost simultaneous production of two symphonies. With the exception of a portion of the first movement, the Ninth Symphony was still in a chaotic state. Taken in connection with negotiations which had been concluded with the Philharmonic Society of London, it may be assumed, however, that the present Symphony in D minor was associated in Beethoven's mind with the English commission, and that the second was to have been a 'Sinfonie allemand'. For a time, at least, Beethoven is not likely to have contemplated a choral movement with German words in connection with the symphony for the London Philharmonic Society: this was to have an instrumental finale. The linguistic objection would be invalid in the case of the German symphony, however, and to this was now assigned the contemplated setting of Schiller's poem.

* *The Consecration of the House.*

Work now proceeded with little interruption, and most of the first half of 1823 was devoted to the first movement, which was nearly complete in sketch-form before anything of the other movements appeared beyond the themes which have already been cited. When the foundation of the work is firmly laid we have the familiar phenomenon of work upon two or three movements simultaneously. In a general way it may be asserted that the year 1823 saw the birth of the Symphony, though work was carried over into 1824.

Sketches for the Finale show that Beethoven had made considerable progress with the setting of Schiller's Ode before he decided to incorporate it with this, and not the contemplated Tenth, Symphony.

When he began work on the Finale, Beethoven took up the choral part with the instrumental variations first and then attacked the instrumental introduction with the recitatives. Once the present 'Joy' melody, as noted in the autumn of 1822, was adopted, the tune underwent many transformations in the second part before its definitive form was established.

The entire Symphony was finished in sketch-form at the end of 1823 and written out in score in February 1824. The time which had elapsed between the beginning of the first movement (1817–18) and the time of completion was about six and a half years. Within this period, however, there were extended interruptions caused by other works.

For the chief facts in the story of the first performance of the D minor Symphony in Vienna we are largely dependent on Schindler, who was not only a witness of it but also an active agent. Beethoven was thoroughly out of sympathy with the musical taste of Vienna, which had been diverted from German ideals by the superficial charm of Rossini's melodies. He wanted much to produce his symphony, but despaired of receiving adequate support or recognition from his home public. His friends offered him encouragement, but his fear and suspicion that his music was no longer understood by the Viennese and he no longer admired, had grown into a deep-rooted conviction. The project of a concert at which the Mass in D should be performed had been mooted months before.

Since 1822, Beethoven had been acquainted with the young singers, Karoline Unger and Henriette Sontag. On 8 September of that year he wrote to his brother Johann, 'Two singers visited us today and since they wanted by all means to kiss my hands and were really pretty, I proposed that they kiss my mouth.' Judging from the Conversation Books he saw them a good deal in 1823, and they vied with one another in their expressions of devoted veneration for the master. Unger did come alone in December and again in January, and on 25 January 1824 she wrote in a Conversation Book:

'When are you going to give your concert? When one is *once* possessed by the devil, one can be content.'

'If you give the concert, I will guarantee that the house will be full.'

Still a moody suspicion, which the lady thinks it her right to rebuke: 'You have too little confidence in yourself. Has not the homage of the whole world given you a little more pride? Who speaks of opposition? Will you not learn to believe that everybody is longing to worship you again in new works? O obstinacy!'

In this mood, Beethoven had turned to Count Brühl in Berlin and enquired whether or not a performance of the new Mass and Symphony might be given in that city, and Brühl had favoured the plan. When news of this fact became known in Vienna, twenty-seven of Beethoven's friends addressed him in a written memorial, declaring him to be one of an immortal trio, with Mozart and Haydn, and pleading most eloquently that a performance of the great new work should be delayed no longer.

Among the signatories were Court Secretary von Felsburg and J. N. Bihler, a tutor in the imperial household. These gentlemen waited upon Beethoven one afternoon to present the address, and talk over its suggestions. Beethoven said he wanted to read it when alone. Later Schindler went to him and found him with the letter in his hand. He was manifestly moved by its expressions and handed it to Schindler to read while he went to the window and gazed out for quite a while. Then he returned to Schindler, said briefly: 'It is very beautiful! – it rejoices me greatly!' and when Schindler also had expressed his delight added: 'Let us go out for a walk.' During the walk he remained sunk in thought.

The object had in view by the designers of the memorial was accomplished; Beethoven was lifted out of his despondent mood and inspired with new determination. By March Schindler had been informed that the concert would be given in Vienna. He lauded Beethoven's decision and begged him not to distress himself with vain imaginings about the outcome – everything would go gloriously and everybody would esteem it an honour to participate. Expressions of satisfaction poured in on the composer from all quarters, and also offers of help. Beethoven's friends discussed the details in the liveliest fashion – the time, the place, the programme, the choir and orchestra, who should sing the solos, the copying of the music in which Beethoven laid great stress on the supervision of the parts, the price of seats, the number of rehearsals. The concert season was drawing to a close and delay was hazardous; but delay there was, for Beethoven was vacillating, full of doubtings and suspicions, and there was a too great multiplicity of counsellors. Schindler was kept extremely busy; Lichnowsky and Schuppanzigh bestirred themselves mightily; brother Johann came to the fore with advice and suggestions, especially about the business administration; nephew Karl, much to Schindler's dissatisfaction, not only ran errands but volunteered his opinion on many topics.

At first it was agreed that the place should be the Theater-an-der-Wien. The director, Count Pálffy, who had signed the memorial, was willing to provide the theatre and all the forces, vocal as well as instrumental, for 1,200 florins, let Beethoven have as many rehearsals as he desired and fix the prices of admission. But a difficulty presented itself at once. At the Theater-an-der-Wien Seyfried was kapellmeister and Clement leader of the orchestra. Beethoven wanted Umlauf to be general conductor of the concert and Schuppanzigh leader of the orchestra. Count Pálffy was willing to sacrifice Seyfried, but not Clement — at least, he asked that if Clement was to be displaced it be done with as little injury to his feelings as possible. He therefore suggested that Beethoven write a letter of explanation to Clement, which he felt sure would solve the difficulty. Meanwhile Schindler had begun negotiations with Duport, director of the Kärnthnerthor Theatre. Duport was favourably inclined towards the enterprise and also towards Schuppanzigh; but troublesome questions of another kind were now precipitated — questions about prices of admission, the solo singers and the number of rehearsals. On all these points Beethoven was so irresolute that the project seemed likely to fall by the wayside; in which crisis the leading spirits thought themselves entitled to resort to a stratagem to give stability to the wavering mind of Beethoven.

It was now planned that Lichnowsky, Schindler and Schuppanzigh should simultaneously call upon Beethoven as if by accident, turn the conversation on the points on which it was necessary for Beethoven to reach a decision and that his utterances should then be put into writing and he be asked, half in jest, half in earnest, to affix his signature to the document. The ruse succeeded but after the conspirators had gone away, Beethoven saw through the trick which had been played on him, and scenting treachery as was his wont, decided off-hand to abandon the concert. He issued his *pronunziamento* to the three friends in this characteristic fashion:

'[To Count Moritz Lichnowsky.]
  'I despise treachery –
Do not visit me any more. There will be no concert –'

'[To Herr Schuppanzigh.]
  'Let him not visit me more. I shall give no concert.'

'[To Schindler.]
  'I request you not to come again until I send for you. There will be
no concert.'

The three friends refused to take umbrage at Beethoven's rudeness;
they gave him time to get over his wrath and suspicion and then went
on with the preparations for the concert. In the Conversation Book
there appears a record of consultation which was opened formally by
Schindler as follows:

'Present:
  Mr L. van Beethoven, a *musikus*.
  Mr Count v. Lichnowsky, an amateur.
  Mr Schindler, a fiddler.
Not yet present today:
  Mr Schuppanzigh, a fiddler representing My lord Fallstaff.'

At this consultation Schindler reported an offer from Pálffy to furnish the Theater-an-der-Wien, orchestra, lights, etc., *appertinenta* for
1,000 florins, provided a second or third concert be given. The receipts
would be 4,000 florins, which would yield a profit of 2,000 florins at the
first concert and about 3,000 at the second, when there would be no
copying charges. The prices would not be so high as at the Redoutensaal. If Duport were to charge only 300 florins, there would still be a
further charge of 300 florins for building the platform. Pálffy wanted
only his expenses. Would Beethoven authorise him [Schindler] and
Lichnowsky to complete arrangements with Pálffy? Haste was necessary, for a supervisor must be appointed – Umlauf or somebody else –
so that rehearsals might begin.

But matters were not so easily arranged with Clement as Pálffy
had anticipated and Schindler had imagined. He did not want to be
deprived of the honour of playing at the concert, the orchestra of the
Theater-an-der-Wien sided with him and declared that it would not
play under Schuppanzigh. Schindler appealed to Count Pálffy, who
said that he could command the men to play under Schuppanzigh, but

he did not want to be answerable for the mischief which would result. Schindler advised Beethoven that if Pálffy stood by Clement the contract for the Kärnthnerthor Theatre be closed with Duport. Up to late in April it was as good as settled that the concert would be given at the Theater-an-der-Wien, though Beethoven's fatal indecision left the point uncertain. With negotiations pending with both theatres, the Redoutensaal came up for consideration, and finally (it would seem as a consequence of advice by the Steiner firm), also a fourth locale. This was the Landständischersaal, a small room in which the *Concerts Spirituels* took place.

Lichnowsky, when he heard that Beethoven was considering such a step, hurried to him with representations that if the hall were taken there would be trouble with Pálffy and he himself humiliated and embarrassed, since he had come to an agreement with the manager in his name. He as well as Schindler was sorely tried by the new turn of affairs and represented to Beethoven that the room was too small, holding only 500 persons, and that the court would not go there. But nephew Karl favoured the hall because its choice would avoid the difficulties incident to the selection of either of the theatres. Lichnowsky and Schindler did not seek to hide their displeasure from Beethoven because of his willingness to take the advice of brother Johann, nephew Karl and Steiner in preference to theirs, but at length circumstances compelled him to abandon all other plans and agree to take the Kärnthnerthor Theatre.

There were to be twenty-four violins, ten violas, twelve contrabasses and violoncellos, and the number of wind-instruments was to be doubled, for which reason room would have to be provided for the orchestra on the stage. Duport was requested to fix the date not later than 3 or 4 May and was informed that the reason why the agreement with Count Pálffy had been cancelled was that the Theater-an-der-Wien was lacking in capable solo singers and that Pálffy wanted Clement to lead the orchestra, whereas Beethoven had long before selected Schuppanzigh for the post. With a change of date to 7 May this arrangement was formally confirmed.

It was originally intended that the programme should consist of the new Overture (Op. 124), the Mass in D and the new Symphony; but realising that this would make the concert unduly long Beethoven first decided to omit the *Gloria* of the Mass, and after the rehearsals had already begun he curtailed the list still more by eliding the *Sanctus*. The church authorities were opposed to the performance of missal music in a theatre and the censor therefore withheld his approval of the programme. So, in April, at the suggestion of Schindler, Beethoven wrote a letter to the censor, Sartorius, in which he pleaded for his consent to the performance on the ground that he had involved himself in costs by reason of the copying, there was no time in which to produce other novelties, and if consent were refused he would be compelled to abandon the concert and all his expenditures would have been in vain. The three ecclesiastical pieces which were to be performed were to be listed on the programme as hymns.

The letter failed of its mission; not until an appeal was made to Count Sedlnitzky, the Police President, through the agency of Count Lichnowsky, was the performance sanctioned.

The rehearsals were now in progress. Dirzka* was making good headway with the choruses and was satisfied; Schuppanzigh was holding rehearsals for the strings in the rehearsal-room of the Ridotto; the solo singers were studying under the supervision of Beethoven, sometimes in his lodgings, Umlauf assisting. Accustomed to Rossini's music, the principal singers found it difficult to assimilate the Beethovenian manner, especially as it is exemplified in the concluding movement of the symphony. They pleaded with the composer for changes which would lighten their labours, but he was adamant. Unger called him a 'tyrant over all the vocal organs' to his face, but when he still refused to grant her petitions she turned to Sontag and said: 'Well, then we must go on torturing ourselves in the name of God!' At the final meeting on 6 May, Beethoven was 'dissolved in devotion and emotion' at the performance of the *Kyrie*, and after the Symphony stationed himself at the door and embraced all the amateurs who had taken part. The official announcement of the concert read as follows:

'GRAND

MUSICAL CONCERT

by

HERR L. V. BEETHOVEN

which will take place

Tomorrow, 7 May 1824

in the RI Court Theatre beside the Kärnthnerthor

The musical pieces to be performed are the latest works of Herr Ludwig van Beethoven.

First: A Grand Overture.

Second: Three Grand Hymns with Solo and Chorus Voices.

Third: A Grand Symphony with Solo and Chorus Voices entering in the finale on Schiller's Ode to Joy.

The solos will be performed by the Demoiselles Sontag and Unger and

* Choral Director of the Kärnthnerthor Theatre.

the Herren Haizinger and Seipelt. Herr Schuppanzigh has undertaken the direction of the orchestra, Herr Kapellmeister Umlauf the
direction of the whole and the Music Society the augmentation of
the chorus and orchestra as a favour.

Herr Ludwig van Beethoven will himself participate in the general
direction.

Prices of admission as usual
Beginning at 7 o'clock in the evening'

The overture was that to the *Weihe des Hauses*; the hymns were the
Kyrie, Credo, and *Agnus Dei* from the Mass in D.

The theatre was crowded in every part except the imperial box; that
was empty. Beethoven had gone in person, accompanied by Schindler,
to invite the Imperial Family, and some of its members promised to
attend; but the Emperor and Empress had left Vienna a few days
before and Archduke Rudolph, who had naturally displayed interest
in the affair, was in Olmütz. But we hear of several of Beethoven's present and former friends seated in various parts of the house; poor,
bedridden Zmeskall was carried to his seat in a sedan chair. Some
of the foremost musicians of Vienna were in the band. The performance was far from perfect. There was lack of a homogeneous power,
a paucity of nuance, a poor distribution of lights and shades. Nevertheless, strange as the music must have sounded to the audience, the
impression which it made was profound and the applause which it
elicited enthusiastic to a degree. At one point in the Scherzo, presumably at the startling entry of the tympani at the *ritmo di tre battute*, the
listeners could scarcely restrain themselves, and it seemed as if a repetition then and there would be insisted upon. To this Beethoven, no
doubt engrossed by the music which he was following in his mind, was
oblivious. Either after the Scherzo or at the end of the Symphony,
while Beethoven was still gazing at his score, Fräulein Unger, whose
happiness can be imagined, plucked him by the sleeve and directed his
attention to the clapping hands and waving hats and handkerchiefs.
Then he turned to the audience and bowed.

The incident is variously related. I personally talked to the pianist
Thalberg in Paris in 1860. He told me he was present at Beethoven's
concert in the Kärnthnerthor Theatre, 1824. Beethoven was dressed
in black dress-coat, white neckerchief, and waistcoat, black satin
small-clothes, black silk stockings, shoes with buckles. He saw after the
Scherzo of the Ninth Symphony how Beethoven stood turning over
the leaves of his score utterly deaf to the immense applause, and Unger
pulled him by the sleeve, and then pointed to the audience when he

turned and bowed. Umlauf told the choir and orchestra to pay no attention whatever to Beethoven's beating of the time but all to watch him.

After the concert Beethoven's friends, as was natural, came together to exchange comments and felicitate him. From Schindler Beethoven received a report which is preserved in the Conversation Book. It gives us a glimpse of his own joy and the composer's happy pride in having been more enthusiastically greeted than the court:

'Never in my life did I hear such frenetic and yet cordial applause.'

'Once the second movement of the Symphony was completely interrupted by applause.'

'and there was a demand for a repetition.'

'The reception was more than imperial'

'for the people burst out in a storm four times. At the last there were cries of Vivat!'

'When the parterre broke out in applauding cries the fifth time the Police Commissioner yelled Silence!'

'My triumph is now attained; for now I can speak from my heart. Yesterday I still feared secretly that the Mass would be prohibited because I heard that the Archbishop had protested against it. After all I was right in at first not saying anything to the Police Commissioner. By God, it would have happened!'

'The whole audience was impressed, crushed by the greatness of your work.'

'In Paris and London the concert would certainly have yielded from 12 to 15 thousand florins; here it may be as many hundreds.'

'When Karl comes home at noon, be so good as to instruct him [to come] after his lectures, this at five o'clock, to the box-office where I will be waiting for him. The box-office will be opened in his presence and he will receive the money.'

'Then I will fetch him at the university at 5 o'clock.'

The financial results of the concert fell far short of Beethoven's expectations. The gross receipts were 2,200 florins in the depreciated Vienna money, of which only 420 florins remained after paying the cost of administration and copying; and against this pitiful sum some petty expenses were still chargeable. Beethoven was not only disappointed; he was chagrined and thrown into a fuming ill humour. He invited Schindler, Umlauf and Schuppanzigh to dine with him at the restaurant 'Zum wilden Mann' in the Prater. The composer came with his nephew; 'his brow was clouded, his words were cold, peevish, captious,' says Schindler. He had ordered an 'opulent' meal, but no sooner had the party sat down to the table than the 'explosion which was imminent' came. In plainest terms he burst out with the charge that the management and Schindler had cheated him. Umlauf and Schuppanzigh tried to convince him that that was impossible, as every penny had passed through the hands of the two theatre cashiers, whose accounts tallied, and that though it was contrary to custom, his nephew had acted on behalf of his brother as comptroller. Beethoven persisted in his accusation, saying that he had his information from an entirely credible source. Thereupon Schindler and Umlauf abruptly left the room. Schuppanzigh remained behind just long enough to get a few stripes on his broad back and then joined his companions in misery. Together they finished their meal at a restaurant in the Leopoldstadt.

It is more than likely that Beethoven's 'credible' informant was his brother Johann. He was jealous of Schindler's participation in the composer's business affairs and probably took advantage of a favourable opportunity to strengthen Beethoven's chronic suspicion and growing distrust of what the composer himself looked upon as Schindler's officiousness.

A second concert had been contemplated from the outset, or at least since the opening of negotiations with Pálffy. Schindler says that Duport offered to pay all expenses and guarantee 500 florins with the understanding that the profits should be divided equally between Beethoven and the exchequer of the theatre. But he wanted a change made in the programme. To this change, obviously designed as a concession to the popular taste, Beethoven seems to have given his consent. The concert took place on Sunday, 23 May, at midday with the following programme:

'First: A Grand Overture [Op. 124].
Second: A new Terzetto, composed by Herr Ludwig van Beethoven, sung by Mad. Dardanelli, Herren Donzelli and Botticelli ["Tremate, empi, tremate"].

Third: A Grand Hymn, sung by Dlles. Sontag, Unger, Herren Haizinger, Seipelt and assembled chorus [Kyrie from the Mass in D].

Fourth: Aria, "Di tanti palpiti", sung by Herr David [from Rossini's *Tancredi*].

Fifth: A Grand Symphony with Solo and Chorus Voices entering in the Finale on Schiller's Ode to Joy.'

The delightful weather lured the people into the open air, the house was not half full and there was, in consequence, a deficit of 800 florins. Nor was the popular demonstration of enthusiasm over the music as great as at the first concert, and Beethoven, who had not favoured the repetition, was so disheartened that he was with difficulty persuaded to accept the 500 florins which Duport had guaranteed to him. He was also vexed to find his old trio, 'Tremate, empi, tremate', announced as a novelty.

Meanwhile a copy of the Symphony was sent to the London Philharmonic Society, through Kirchhoffer; the date may be determined by Beethoven's receipt of £50 from Kirchhoffer 'for my symphony delivered to him for the Philharmonic Society in London', dated 27 April 1824.

During the preparations for the concerts, thought was also given to the usual summer sojourn, and various places were canvassed in consultation with Beethoven by his friends. In all of the excursions which were made in the vicinity of Schönbrunn in search of a summer home, Schindler accompanied the composer to see, to advise, to negotiate. The choice fell upon Penzing, where an apartment was found in the first storey of the house numbered 43 belonging to a tailor in Vienna named Johann Hörr, who was rejoiced to have so distinguished a tenant. Beethoven took it for the summer, beginning on 1 May. The lodgings were in all things adapted to his needs and Beethoven, entirely satisfied, moved into them soon after the second concert. But the house lay close to a footbridge over the little stream called the Wien Fluss and people crossing it frequently stopped to gaze into his rooms. He could have saved himself the annoyance by drawing the curtains, but instead he flew into a rage, quarrelled with his landlord, against whom he recorded his anger by scrawling the epithet 'Schurke' (rogue, wretch, scoundrel, etc.) under his name on the receipt, and removing to Baden (Gutenbrunn).

The move had taken place by 27 May. He stayed there on and off until November; thus he was again paying rent for three lodgings at the same time.

During the summer Karl was continuing his philological studies at the university. On one of his visits to his uncle not long after the concerts the conversation proceeded from the progress of Karl's studies to the question of his choice of a career. Karl writes:

'I will not do anything without your consent and will, if you wish, continue to study, or even more begin something new.'

'You will find my choice rather strange, but I will speak freely, nevertheless, as I prefer to do. The profession which I would like to choose is not a *common* one. On the contrary, it *also* demands study; only of a different kind; and one that is to my liking, I believe.'

'Soldier'

'The regulation is certainly very strict. And mathematics and the science of fortification are certainly not among the lowest.'

Later on there is further conversation about Karl's studies which shows, even though only Karl's side of the conversation is recorded, that there was conflict between them: Beethoven worried over Karl's effort and use of time; Karl answered that he was exerting himself to the utmost and not seeing anyone but his fellow student Erik with whom he read Greek and Latin.

On 1 August Beethoven wrote to his lawyer friend, Dr Bach, concerning his nephew and his will:

'Most worthy friend!
'My heartfelt thanks for your kind recommendation here; I am really well taken care of – I must remind you of the part of my will concerning Karl. I think that I might have a stroke some day, like my worthy grandfather whom I take after. Karl is and remains the sole heir of all that I have and that may be found after my death. However, since one must leave something to one's relatives, even when they are quite uncongenial, my *brother* is to receive my French piano from *Paris* – Karl could bring the will on Saturday if it doesn't inconvenience you in any way – As far as Stein [Steiner] is concerned, he will be satisfied to have his debt completely paid off at the end of this month and at the end of September – For if something comes of the Mainz affair, it will take no longer than that, and the first 600 fl. should at any rate be paid back to two of the most generous human beings* who, when I was

* Undoubtedly the Brentanos.

nearly desperate, kindly advanced me this sum without any interest whatsoever.

With fondest wishes I embrace you.

Respectfully your friend Beethoven'

Towards the end of September, Johann Andreas Stumpff, a native of Thuringia but a resident of London, was among the visitors at Baden who were admitted to intimate association with Beethoven. (This was another Stumpff, not the one who came to Vienna in 1818 with a letter from Thomas Broadwood, and who tuned the new English pianoforte.) He was a manufacturer of harps and an enthusiastic admirer of Beethoven's music. Anticipating a meeting with the composer, he had provided himself with a letter of introduction to Haslinger, whose help to that end he asked. He had also received a letter from Streicher, whose acquaintance he had made in London. He accomplished his end and wrote a long and enthusiastic account of his intercourse with Beethoven at Baden, whither Haslinger had accompanied him on his first visit. He was received by Beethoven with extraordinary cordiality. The composer accepted an invitation to dinner, entertained his host at dinner in return, played for him on his Broadwood pianoforte, and at parting gave him a print of one of his portraits and promised to alight at his house if ever he came to London. Much of his conversation, which Stumpff records, is devoted to a condemnation of the frivolity and bad musical taste of the Viennese, and excessive laudation of everything English. 'Beethoven', Stumpff remarks, 'had an exaggerated opinion of London and its highly cultured inhabitants', and he quotes Beethoven as saying: 'England stands high in culture. In London everybody knows something and knows it well; but the man of Vienna can only talk of eating and drinking, and sings and pounds away at music of little significance or of his own making.' He spoke a great deal about sending his nephew to London to make a man of him, asked questions about the cost of living there and, in short, gave proof that an English visit was filling a large part of his thoughts. The incidents of the conclusion of the dinner which he gave to Stumpff may be told in the latter's words:

'Beethoven now produced the small bottle. It contained the precious wine of Tokay with which he filled the two glasses to the brim. "Now my good German-Englishman, to your good health." We drained the glasses, then, extending his hand, "A good journey to you and to a meeting again in London." – I beckoned to him to fill the glasses again and hurriedly wrote in his notebook: "Now for a pledge to the welfare of the greatest living composer, Beethoven." — I arose from my chair, he followed my example, emptied his glass and seizing my hand said: "Today I am just what I am and what I ought to be, all unbuttoned." . . . Thereupon I took up the pencil and wrote in very distinct letters:

' "Whom do you consider the greatest composer that ever lived?"

' "Handel," was his instantaneous reply; "to him I bow the knee," and he bent one knee to the floor.

' "Mozart," I wrote.

' "Mozart", he continued, "is good and admirable."

' "Yes," wrote I, "who was able to glorify even Handel with his additional accompaniments to *The Messiah*."

' "It would have lived without them," was his answer.

'I continued writing. "Seb. Bach."

' "Why is he dead?"

'I answered immediately: "He will return to life again."

' "Yes, if he is studied, and for that there is now no time."

'I took the liberty of writing: "As you yourself, a peerless artist in the art of music, exalt the merits of Handel so highly above all, you must certainly own the scores of his principal works."

' "I? How should I, a poor devil, have got them? Yes, the scores of *The Messiah* and *Alexander's Feast* went through my hands."

'If it is possible for a blind man to help a cripple, and the two attain an end which would be impossible to either one unaided, why might not in the present case a similar result be effected by a similar co-operation? At that moment I made a secret vow: Beethoven, you shall have the works of Handel for which your heart is longing if they are anywhere to be found.'

Stumpff relates that Beethoven's brother, who came into the room during his visit, seemed glad to greet him and begged him most amiably to call on him, as he desired to talk with him about a number of things. At parting, Beethoven accompanied Stumpff to the door and said: 'That is my brother — have nothing to do with him — he is not an honest man. You will hear me accused of many wrong actions of which he has been guilty. Farewell!' Stumpff returned to London on 6 December. He fulfilled his vow touching the gift of Handel's works two years later.

Two notes to Haslinger in October show that a new element had entered into Beethoven's worries concerning his nephew. The first is dated 'Baden, evening of 6 October':

'Dear Tobias!

'I beg of you most fervently to enquire right away at the house in the Johannesgasse, into which we are going to move, whether Karl slept there yesterday and today, and, if he is at home, to give him this note immediately; if not, to leave it with the caretaker there to give to him – He has been away since yesterday and this evening neither he nor the housekeeper are here. I am alone with a person who can neither speak, read nor write, and I can find scarcely a thing to eat dining out – Once already I have had to go in from here to fetch Karl in Vienna; once he has gone somewhere it is hard to bring him away. I beg of you to notify me right away what you can. I would like to have had a few more peaceful days here; unfortunately I will have to return to the city on account of him. At any rate I beg of you to let no one know of this. God is my witness as to what I have had to endure already because of him. If there is no information from the caretaker in the Johannisgasse, then send someone to the Landstrasse, where I lived before, to ask the care-taker where Frau von Niemetz* lives, in order to find out there if he has been to her place or is coming there, so that she will direct him here at once.

'Naturally I shall remunerate your servant as well as pay the cost of postage for the letters – Also I beg of you to take care of the letter to my Cain-brother – I beg of you to answer immediately whether or not he has been found.

Most hastily your friend Beethoven'
'For God's sake an answer immediately.'

The second letter dated 'Baden, the day after 6 October 1824' deter-mines the year date of the first. Touching is the expression of relief expressed in this letter, the first part of which is given here:

'Best one!

'Our Benjamin arrived here early today, on which account I am firing off 17 and a half cannons – Earlier events through no fault of his et sine mea culpa made me anxious, thank heaven everything goes well and opportunely at times despite my agitatos! With these wretched arrangements it is no wonder one gets anxious about a growing young man, and with it the poisoned breath dragons! –'

Four years earlier at the Blöchlinger Institute, Karl had made the friendship of a fellow student named Niemetz. By now they were close friends and Karl invited him to join in one of his visits to Baden. The

* The mother of Karl's friend Niemetz, who will be mentioned shortly.

following discussion about Niemetz, in a Conversation Book, marked by Schindler 'Autumn of 1824 in Baden', has a particular interest in that it includes Beethoven's part in the conversation:

'*Beethoven:* I am very ill-pleased with your choice of this friend. Poverty certainly deserves sympathy, but not invariably. I would not want to be unfair to him but to me he is a burdensome guest, lacking completely in decency and manners, which belong in some degree to all well brought up youths and men. – Besides I suspect that his interests are more with the housekeeper than with me – Besides I love quiet; also the space here is too limited for several people since I am constantly busy, and he cannot engage my interest at all. – You still have a very weak character.

'*Karl:* Concerning my choice, I believe that a close acquaintance of four years' duration is really sufficient to get to know a man from *all angles*, especially a boy who cannot possibly remain disguised for such a long time – Thus there cannot be a question of lack of conviction, but merely of the reasons which led me to it, and they are in a word: the very great similarity of character and tastes. If he has been unable to please you, you are free to send him away, but he has not deserved what you have said about him.

'*Beethoven:* I find him rough and common. These are no friends for you.

'*Karl:* If you find him rough, you are mistaken. In any event, I wouldn't have thought that he had given you the opportunity to think it. Also I do not intend to exchange him for another which would be a clear sign of weakness of character, for which you reproach me certainly with injustice; for of all the students at Blöchlinger's I have found *no one* but him who would have cheered up my own, often dreary home, and consequently I feel that I am gratefully indebted to him.

'*Beethoven:* You are not yet in a position to discriminate.

'*Karl:* It is really useless to quarrel over a subject, especially over a [person's] character concerning which I will never abandon my conviction, *so long as I can consider that I myself am not a bad man*, for if there is something good in *me*, he possesses it in at least as high a degree as I, and it would be unfair to be angry with him if you do not judge *me* likewise. For my part I will not stop loving him as I would my brother, if I had one.'

Here Beethoven's part in the conversation stops; but this talk shows the boy, just turned eighteen, was in mature command of himself in these inevitable scenes with his uncle.

At some point in the first part of November, Beethoven returned
again with Karl to Vienna, where he took up his new residence – at 969
Johannesgasse, in a house owned by a family named Kletschka. There,
he had quarrels with both the housekeeper and his nephew, which led
to noisy scenes; further 'at times the deaf master pounded the piano
(presumably out of tune) quite unmercifully.' As a result of these disturbances, Frau Kletschka finally had to send her young daughter,
Nanette, to her boarders to serve notice. But here the story of Beethoven's dwellings is unclear. On the one hand it would appear that he
remained at this address throughout the winter, since this address is
given as late as 18 April 1825, in a letter from Beethoven to Dr Braunhofer. Yet from two other sources we learn that Beethoven moved to
the Krugerstrasse. Because of the expense it seems unlikely that Beethoven was once again occupying two dwellings at the same time. But it
may well be that, having been ousted temporarily from the Johannesgasse and forced to live elsewhere, he was later allowed to return.

The state of Beethoven's health is suggested by the following letter
to Archduke Rudolph, dated 18 November 1824:

'Your Imperial Highness
'Since I was ill when I returned here from Baden I was prevented
from betaking myself, as I wished to do, to YIH because I was forbidden to go outside. Yesterday was the first day that I could walk in the
free air again – Your gracious letter caught me just when I was confined to my bed. As I was in a state of perspiration at that moment,
since my poor health resulted from a chill, it was impossible for me to
get up, nevertheless I know that YIH is convinced that I never could
neglect the regard due you – Tomorrow at noon I shall have the pleasure of paying my respects; moreover, means will not be lacking to
arouse YIH's musical spirit which can be nothing but beneficial for art
– my refuge – God be praised –
Your Imperial Highness's truly most obedient servant Beethoven'

The main composition of the year 1824 was the Quartet in E flat, Op.
127, the history of which is inevitably wound up with the history of
Prince Galitzin's request to Beethoven for three string quartets. Ideas
for the work were probably in the composer's head when he offered a
quartet to Peters in June 1822. The invitation from Galitzin in November 1822 undoubtedly spurred the work forward. Then the composition and performance of the Ninth Symphony delayed work until the
summer of 1824. The main work was done in the second half of 1824
and the beginning of 1825, and the work was first performed on 6

March 1825. By this time there were also preliminary sketches for the first and last movements of the second of the final quartets (Op. 132).

On 3 August 1823, Prince Galitzin had first expressed his desire for the score of the Mass so that he could perform the work at St Petersburg. When the score arrived, however, there was missing a page of the *Gloria*, a precaution that Beethoven had taken against his manuscript being stolen while copied. Beethoven wrote a letter of apology and explanation to the Prince on 13 December 1823, with assurances that the missing page would soon arrive, and with further notices concerning the *Gloria* section.

In his answer of 30 December, Galitzin indicated that his performance of the Mass would take place in February or Easter. The Prince added: 'Let me know whether you need 50 for the 1st quartet, [if so] I will make it immediately available to you.' In his next letter, dated 11 March 1824, Galitzin was more impatient and worried as to whether Beethoven was ill and consequently unable to fulfil his promises; he reiterated his wish that if Beethoven should need money, he should feel free to draw it on account with M. M. Stieglitz and Co.; and he announced that the performance of the Mass, which was a benefit for musicians' widows, would take place on 7 April. Galitzin's next letter described what was in fact the first full performance in the world of the Mass in D. It deserves to be given in full:

'Petersburg, 8 April 1824
'Monsieur, I am eager to give you an account of the performance of your sublime masterpiece which we presented here to the public the night before last. For several months I have been extremely impatient to hear this music performed, the beauties of which I foresaw from the score. The effect of this music on the public cannot be described and I doubt if I exaggerate when I say that for my part I have never heard anything so sublime; I don't even except the masterpieces of Mozart which with their eternal beauties have not created for me the same sensations that you have given me, Monsieur, by the Kyrie and Gloria of your Mass. The masterly harmony and the moving melody of the Benedictus transport the heart to a plane that is really blissful. This whole work in fact is a treasure of beauties; it can be said that your genius has anticipated the centuries and that there are not listeners perhaps enlightened enough to experience all the beauty of this music; but it is posterity that will pay homage and will bless your memory much better than your contemporaries can. Prince Radziwill, whom you know is a great amateur of music, arrived just a few days ago from Berlin and was present at the performance of your mass which he had

not known before; he was enraptured with it just like myself and all those present. – I hope that your health is restored and that you are going to give us many more products of your sublime genius. – Excuse the nuisance that I often cause by my letters, but it is a sincere tribute from one of your greatest admirers.

P. Nicolas Galitzin'

Beethoven's next (and last surviving) letter to the Prince is dated 'Vienna, 26 May 1824'.

'My dear and honoured Prince!

'So many of your charming letters unanswered! – [Please] attribute it only to the overwhelming load of business, and certainly not to neglect on my part – Having been entreated to give a few concerts in which I lost time and money; and to the shame of our present organisation in Vienna, I had to be sacrificed to a former dancer Duport, who is leaseholder at the Kärnthnerthor. Let me off from repeating a description of the vulgar details, which anyway would revolt and disgust you as it does me. But allow me to tell you that it was a waste for me of much time and money – Here I have learned that the Mass is going to be given in St Petersburg as a great oratorio. My circumstances force me, since here they do nothing at all *for me*, but rather *against me*, to try a second subscription on this work, and in fact, as Your Excellency once suggested to me, to offer a printed copy of the score for 5 ducats in gold, which could be printed and delivered in a half-year. I cannot send you this invitation until the next post – You will soon receive your quartet, promised so long ago to you, perhaps also the others. If only the enquiries and encouragements from all sides for big works were not so strong . . . I will send Your Excellency a new overture and a trio which was sung by three local Italians and performed excellently. Should you wish a new big symphony with a finale in which occurs chorus and solo parts, I would have a score of it copied. The cost would be nothing more than a reimbursement for the cost of copying – Perhaps it would be possible through your efforts to be able to have the Mass dedicated to His Majesty the Emperor of Russia; perhaps such a generous monarch as the Russian Emperor would even settle on me a yearly pension for which I would first deliver all my big works to His Majesty and would also fulfil speedily His Majesty's commissions and thereby would be able to have helped suffering mankind –

'Enclosed is an impression of the medal from His Majesty from France as a sign of his satisfaction with my Mass. The medal weighs a half a pound in gold; and [has] Italian verses about me – which . . . the side of genius which outside is radiantly white, only the . . . [missing]

With all the esteem and devotion

from Your Highness's faithful Beetho[ve]n'

Replying on 16 June, Galitzin accepted Beethoven's offer of the symphony, the overture and the trio. He added that to secure permission to dedicate a work to the Emperor one must write to Count Nesselrode, and that he would be glad to distribute as many printed copies of the Mass as possible, but that the difficulty of its performance precluded a large sale. Considering the later history between Beethoven and Galitzin, the postscript is interesting: 'If you ever find yourself in the least kind of difficulty, apply quickly to me. I will be only too glad to be able to be of help to you.'

In his next letter, dated 28 July, he wrote:

'Right now I am convinced that if you wanted to travel in Europe without any treasures other than your compositions, and without any recommendations other than your immortal masterpieces, you would take the world by storm. Your presence alone at Paris, London would eclipse everything else, and the concerts which you would give would not resemble those in Vienna.'

As regards the quartet, he was becoming impatient: he announced that fifty ducats were being remitted to Count von Lebzeltern, minister of Austria, for remittance to Beethoven and that Beethoven could expect it soon. This then was the second payment of fifty ducats and was specifically for the first quartet. Beethoven must have written to him in the autumn concerning his poor health, for Galitzin answers: 'I am really very much vexed that you have suffered so from poor health, but suffering is an indispensable part of human life, and it seems that geniuses like yourself ought to impose on nature and force her to respect those like you who are distinguished from the rest of mankind.'

By the end of the year the quartet was sent and was acknowledged by Galitzin on 29 April 1825, after having 'performed it several times'.

CHAPTER 21

The Year 1825

Increasing Trouble with His Nephew –
The Three Galitzin Quartets

In the early part of 1824, thoughts of a visit to England had been
revived by a letter from Charles Neate; it had been determined that the
visit should be undertaken in the autumn and that Schindler should
accompany him. When nothing developed, Neate wrote another letter
on 20 December 1824, bringing with it an invitation from the Philharmonic Society of London which kept the thought of an English visit
alive in Beethoven's irresolute mind for a considerable space longer.
Neate wrote in an extremely cordial vein. He had long wished to see
Beethoven in England, he said, where he believed that his genius was
appreciated more than in any other country; and now he had received
the pleasant charge from the Philharmonic Society to invite him to
come. It was disposed to give him 300 guineas for conducting at least
one of his works at each of the Society's concerts in the coming season,
and composing a new symphony and a concerto which were to be produced during his visit but to remain the composer's property. As an
additional pecuniary inducement he held out that Beethoven could
give a concert of his own at which he would make at least £500, besides
which there were many other avenues of profit open to him. If he were
to bring along the quartets about which he had written, they would
yield him £100 more, and he might therefore be sure of carrying back a
large sum of money, enough, indeed, to make all the remainder of his
life much pleasanter than the past had been. He told Beethoven that
the new Symphony had arrived and the first rehearsal of it was set for
17 January. He hoped that Beethoven would be on hand to direct it at
the first concert of the Society and trusted that a report that a copy of it
was in Paris was not true.

Beethoven replied on 15 January and again on the 27th. The first
letter follows:

'Monsieur!
'With the greatest pleasure I received your letter of – [December 20]
through which you had the kindness to inform me that the Philhar-

monic Society, with its distinguished artists is inviting me to come to London. I am well satisfied with the conditions made to you by the society, but I wish to propose that besides the 300 guineas that it has promised me I be sent 100 more guineas for travelling expenses; for I need to buy a carriage; also I need to be accompanied by someone. You can see clearly that that is necessary; besides I beg you to let me know the inn at which I may stay in London. I will take a new quartet along with me.

'As for the rumour that you wrote about, that there is a copy of the 9th Symphony in Paris, there is no foundation in it at all. It is true that this symphony will be published in Germany, but not before the year has come to an end during which time the Society will be playing it. On this point I must inform you again to have only small rehearsals of this composition, with the four string parts for example; for it is the only way to study well such a work; above all the choruses should be rehearsed. There are still some errors, a list of which I will send you by the next post. –

'It seems to me that in the second movement of the Symphony it has been forgotten that at the repetition of the minore after the Presto one must begin again at the sign and continue without repetition right to the ferma, then one goes directly to the Coda.

'I beg you to reply as quickly as possible for I am being asked to write a big new composition which I will not begin, however, without hearing from you.* – I have to write all the time, not to accumulate wealth – only to provide for my needs.

'Now I need to have assurance on this point. – I will be charmed to see you and to know that noble nation, England. I am your sincere friend,

Monsieur,
with the highest regards
Louis van Beethoven'

To this letter Neate replied on 1 February. He had conveyed the contents of Beethoven's letter to the directors of the Philharmonic Society and had now regretfully to report that they had declined to make any change in their offer. He was personally willing to give the advance asked, but the individual directors were not masters of their conduct in all things; they had to abide by the laws of the Society. He hoped that under the circumstances Beethoven would come; he was sure the trip would pay him, and the directors would impatiently await his presence at the second concert, it being already too late for the first. There was to be another rehearsal of the Symphony that evening.

* This was the oratorio on Bernard's text *Der Sieg des Kreuzes*.

Again Beethoven had to struggle with the question as to whether or not he should make the journey to London. He was strongly urged by his desire to earn a large sum of money. His friends pressed him with arguments in favour of the trip. Karl admonished him to make up his own mind without giving heed to the insatiable avarice of his brother, but reminded him that Neate had assured him he would make enough money to be free of care the rest of his life. Johann did not talk of the financial advantage alone but said that he would benefit physically, travel being good for the health. Apparently answering an objection of Beethoven's on the score of his age, Karl reminded him that Haydn also went to London when he was fifty years old – and he was 'not so famous'. Schuppanzigh burst out with his brusque third person singular: 'I wish he would pick up enough courage to make the trip; he would not regret it.' Who should accompany him? Schindler had been recommended by Neate, but his name does not occur in these conversations; instead there was talk of Schuppanzigh and young Streicher. But as it turned out, no one was to accompany him, nobody alight with him at either the house of Stumpff or the Hotel de la Sablonière in Leicester Square which Neate had recommended as a French house much visited by foreigners. His doubts, suspicions, fears for his health, anxiety about his nephew, his fatal indecision, prevailed. On 19 March he wrote to Neate that he would make the visit some other time – perhaps in the autumn; two days later the Symphony was performed for the first time in London. From that time on there was no further mention of the trip.

In this same letter, however, Beethoven kept alive the idea of selling the quartets in England and wrote that he was satisfied with Neate's offer for them provided that he would be allowed to publish the quartets in a year and a half or two years. On 25 May he reaffirmed his satisfaction with the price already offered of £100 for three quartets but warned that the first quartet was much in demand by different artists and had already been promised them for their benefit; he urged Neate to let him know whether he was satisfied with his conditions, so that he could send the first quartet right away.

The absence of Ries's name in the negotiations with England is explained by the fact that he was no longer in London. He had purchased an estate in Godesberg, near Bonn, and removed thither in 1824. From there he wrote to Beethoven inviting him to visit him for a while; he also made various enquiries concerning Beethoven's compositions, for which a word of explanation is needed. In 1817 there had come into being the Lower Rhenish Musical Festival. For the seventh annual meeting in 1824, which was to be held at Aix-la-Chapelle, Ries had been invited to be the conductor. During that year reports of the Vienna performance of the Ninth Symphony had spread and it was desired to make the symphony a feature of the festival scheme. Ries was asked to write to Beethoven for a manuscript copy. He also asked for the metronome markings of *Christus am Ölberg*. Beethoven's answer came in February:

'Dear Ries!

'... It will be a great pleasure to indicate the tempi of *Christus am Ölberge* for you by metronome, even though this indication of time is so unstable. As for the Symphony I will make you now a more general offer. My situation forces me to seek resolution of my *needs* [*Nöthen*] through my *notes* [*Noten*]. Would it be possible for you to arrange the affair *in this way?* I would send *you* my score of the Symphony or a good copy, also a score of the Mass, and the overture which I wrote for the Phil. Society. Also I could give you several small things for orchestra, and for chorus. In this way such a society would be in a position to give two or three concerts instead of one. Perhaps 40 carolins would not be too much for it – I leave the whole matter to you. This concept does not come from *me* but from those who want to rescue me from my *needs* through my *notes* – I take the deepest interest in your property in Godesberg; no one could have a more envious joy over it than I whose deepest desires would be realised by such a property. However, it appears that my destiny is not to be quite the way I want it. Greet your old father heartily for me. I am overjoyed on account of his happiness. I embrace you heartily and hope to be able to write you more soon.

As always your true friend

Beethoven'

'You write soon too.'

Beethoven consented to Ries's request and about 11 March sent the score of the first three movements but only the individual parts of the finale.

Ries waited in vain for the full score of the finale and finally had to have one made from the parts. In a letter dated 9 April, Beethoven explained more specifically that it was an approaching concert that prevented him from sending his score of the finale; at the same time he enumerated what was being sent: a revised copy of *Opferlied*, the chorus-master's score of the symphony finale, and an overture in C, 6/8 time; by the next post the *Kyrie* and the *Gloria*, and an Italian duet. He was still to send a grand march and chorus and might have added an overture which was yet unknown outside of Vienna, but thought he had sent enough. The overture in C was, of course, Op. 115; the march and chorus were from the *Ruinen von Athen*.

The performance took place on 23 May 1825, the second day of the festival, with the following programme: (1) The Ninth Symphony; (2) Mozart's *Davidde penitente*; (3) Overture to *Die Zauberflöte*; (4) *Christus am Ölberg*. The time was too short for the difficult music to be learned thoroughly and at the performance portions of the slow movement and the Scherzo of the Symphony were 'regretfully' omitted, a fact that, it is to be hoped, was never known to Beethoven. There were 422 performers in chorus and orchestra, and the popular reception of the music was enthusiastic enough to enable Ries to report to Beethoven that the performance had been a success; and he sent him forty louis d'or as a fee. Ries recognised the Symphony as a work without an equal and told Beethoven that had he written nothing else it would have made him immortal. 'Whither will you yet lead us?' he asked.

In a letter to the publishers Schott, dated 26 January 1825, which was concerned primarily with corrections of the Mass in D, Beethoven wrote a postscript indicating passages in the *Agnus Dei* where the appoggiaturas had been written incorrectly as eighth notes rather than sixteenth notes. It ends thus: 'From this you can observe what copyists I am left with now; the fellow is a stupid Bohemian, a pandour, doesn't understand a thing; at first he writes quarters in the appoggiaturas, then finally eighths. Since I was no longer supervising [the work] I noticed this as it was being hastily wrapped.'

This was probably the copyist Wolanek against whom the composer had railed repeatedly. In delivering some uncompleted manuscripts by messenger some time before Easter, Wolanek ventured a defence of his dignity in a letter which, though couched in polite phrases, was nevertheless decidedly ironical and cutting:

'To Herr Ludwig v. Beethoven!

'Since I cannot add the finale to the score until Easter and you will no longer need it at this time, I am sending over the complete parts along with what has already been begun for your favourable disposition.

'I remain gratefully obliged for the honour rendered by your employment of me; as for more concerning the discordant behaviour towards me, I can only regard it smilingly as a good-natured outburst to be accepted. In the ideal world of tones there are so many dissonances, shouldn't they exist also in the real world?

'My one comfort is the firm conviction that with Mozart and Haydn, those celebrated artists, I would have shared a similar fate as with you in the position of copyist.

'I request only not to mix with those common copyists who consider themselves happy to be able to maintain their existence by being treated as slaves.

'At any rate be assured that I will never have the least bit of cause to blush in front of you on account of my behaviour.

Respectfully yours Ferd. Wolanek'

Beethoven read the letter, and, in a rage, drew lines across its face from corner to corner. Then in letters two inches long he scrawled over the writing the words: 'Dummer, Eingebildeter, Eselhafter Kerl' ('Stupid, Conceited, Asinine Fellow'). That was not enough. There was a wide margin at the bottom of the sheet, just large enough to hold Beethoven's next ebullition: 'Compliments for such a good-for-nothing, who pilfers one's money? – better to pull his asinine ears.' Then he turned the sheet over. A whole page invited him – and he filled it up the middle with 'Dirty Scribbler! Stupid Fellow! Correct the blunders which you have made in your ignorance, insolence, conceit and stupidity, this would be more to the purpose than to try to teach me, which is as if a *Sow* were to try to give lessons to Minerva.' The margins were still available: on the right – '*Do you do honour* to Mozart and Haydn by never mentioning *their names*.' On the left: 'It was decided yesterday and even before then *not to have you* write *any more* for me.'

The story of the events leading up to the first performance of the E flat Quartet (Op. 127) may be summarised here. In January 1825, Schuppanzigh was starting another subscription series of quartet concerts and was anxious to have his quartet give the first performance of the work at the opening concert. Beethoven consented, to the delight of Schuppanzigh, who must have assumed that the quartet was ready, for the following notice appeared on 20 January in Bäuerle's *Theater Zeitung*:

'The famous musical artist Herr Schuppanzigh will continue his popular quartet performances but in the small *Vereinssaal beim roten Igel*. The first concert is on Sunday, 23 January; the most distinguished of the new musical works are: the new renowned double quartet by L. Spohr as introduction, a new quintet [*sic!*] by Ludw. van Beethoven (still in manuscript) and in conclusion by common request the most famous and popular Septet by the same artist.'

Schuppanzigh rushed this into print no doubt because he knew how easily Beethoven's decisions could be altered. His fear was justified. At

the urging of Johann and Karl, Beethoven had promised the quartet to
Linke for a benefit concert. The conflict was discussed and Beethoven
was persuaded to let Linke have it first and then let Schuppanzigh perform it as often as he liked. Thereupon Schuppanzigh was invited to
lunch to learn the decision. He wrote in the Conversation Book:

'This affair with the quartet is accursed.'

'That doesn't matter; he can also give it to Linke. His music can be
heard more often than once.'

'I wouldn't say anything if it were not already in the newspaper.'

'I cannot call it off.'

'Linke has said nothing about it to me. If he had spoken to me I would
not have asked him for it.'

'But he certainly hasn't promised him because that isn't his habit; he has
perhaps given him a half-consent, still that is not yet a solemn promise.'

'It is no disadvantage for Linke if he gives it to him now too.'

   Schuppanzigh succeeded in swinging the decision back in his
favour, and Linke was given the hope of getting the A Minor Quartet
(Op. 132), which was realised in the autumn. In the meantime he was
annoyed and held Schuppanzigh responsible for the change. However,
by the middle of January the quartet still was not ready so that for his
first concert Schuppanzigh had to substitute the Quartet in F Minor,
Op. 95.
   During January and February there was also much conversation
concerning another set of spring concerts of Beethoven's works, in
which Schuppanzigh played a prominent part. He became worried not
only about the delay in starting rehearsals for these concerts – which
were never to materialise – but also the delay in receiving the new
quartet for the second concert on 6 March. In the middle of February
he asks: 'How is the quartet getting on?'
   In fact, the quartet was sent less than two weeks before performance. In view of what happened at the performance, and afterwards,
it is clear that Schuppanzigh did not have enough time for proper
rehearsing of such a difficult new work.
   The performance took place on 6 March, and the result was disap-

pointing. The music was not understood either by the players or the public and was all but ineffective. Schuppanzigh was held responsible and his patience must have been severely taxed by Beethoven's upbraidings and his determination to have an immediate repetition by other players. Schuppanzigh defended himself as vigorously as possible and was particularly vexed because Beethoven cited his brother's opinion of the performance – that of a musical ignoramus. He wanted to play the Quartet a second time; he could easily master the technical difficulties, but it was hard to arrive at the spirit of the work: the ensemble was faulty, because of this fact and too few rehearsals. Beethoven decided that the next hearing should be had from Böhm, and though Schuppanzigh had acquiesced, he harboured a grievance against the composer for some time.

Joseph Böhm had been leader of the quartet concerts in Vienna during Schuppanzigh's long absence from the city. He has left an account of his connection with the work as follows:

'. . . The affair did not come off well. Schuppanzigh, who played first violin, was weary from much rehearsing, there was no finish in the performance, the quartet did not appeal to him . . . Few were moved, it was a weak *succès d'estime*.

'When Beethoven learned of this – for he was not present at the performance – he became furious and let both performers and the public in for some harsh words. Beethoven could have no peace until the disgrace was wiped off. He sent for me first thing in the morning – In his usual curt way, he said to me: "You must play my quartet" – and the thing was settled. – Neither objections nor doubts could prevail; what Beethoven wanted had to take place, so I undertook the difficult task. – It was studied industriously and rehearsed frequently under Beethoven's own eyes: I said Beethoven's *eyes* intentionally, for the unhappy man was so deaf that he could no longer hear the heavenly sound of his compositions. And yet rehearsing in his presence was not easy. With close attention his eyes followed the bows and therefore he was able to judge the smallest fluctuations in tempo or rhythm and correct them immediately. At the close of the last movement of this quartet there occurred a *meno vivace*, which seemed to me to weaken the general effect. At the rehearsal, therefore, I advised that the original tempo be maintained, which was done, to the betterment of the effect.

'Beethoven, crouched in a corner, heard nothing, but watched with strained attention. After the last stroke of the bows he said, laconically, "Let it remain so," went to the desks and crossed out the *meno vivace* in the four parts.'

The quartet was performed finally and received with a real storm of applause. It was played three times by Böhm with the other three members of the Schuppanzigh quartet: once for a small audience, twice a few days later for a larger audience in an evening concert on 23 March. Then Böhm asked Beethoven's permission to use the quartet in a benefit concert for himself, which he clearly deserved. On 28 April the *Theater Zeitung* made a report on Schuppanzigh's concert and on Böhm's, which follows:

'. . . Herr Prof. Böhm . . . now performed the wonderful quartet, twice over on the same evening, for the same very numerous company of artists and connoisseurs in a way that left nothing to be desired, the misty veil disappeared and the splendid work of art radiated its dazzling glory. Although Prof. Böhm had a lighter touch, yet this composition was heard from a master.'

Beethoven was completely satisfied and, no doubt, went to work on its successor with a contented mind.

It now becomes necessary to pay attention to the new friend of Beethoven – the successor of Schindler, as he had been of Oliva, in the office of factotum in ordinary. This was Karl Holz, a young man (he was born in 1798) who occupied a post in the States' Chancellery of Lower Austria. He had studied music with Glöggl in Linz; yet Schuppanzigh also called him his pupil. He was a capable violinist and had already been for some time a member of Böhm's quartet group; then upon Schuppanzigh's return from Russia in 1823, he became a second in the latter's quartet. He seems to have come into closer contact with Beethoven early in the spring of 1825, probably when, having to conduct a performance of the B flat Symphony (the Fourth Symphony) at a concert in the Redoutensaal, he asked an audience of the composer in order that he might get the tempi for that work. Emboldened by the kindness with which he was first received he gradually drew nearer to the composer and in August 1825 an intimate friendship seemed imminent. He was good at figures, a quality which made him particularly serviceable to Beethoven (who was woefully deficient in arithmetic) at a time when he was dealing with foreign publishers and there was great confusion in money values and rates of exchange. He was also a well-read man, a clever talker, musically cultured, a cheery companion, and altogether an engaging person. All these qualities, no less than the fact that he was strong and independent in his convictions and fearless in his proclamation of them, recommended him to Beethoven, at a time when the composer had begun to feel a growing antipathy to Schindler.

In a short time Holz made himself indispensable and acquired great influence over the composer. He aided him in the copying of his works, looked into the affairs of nephew Karl and reported upon them, advised him in his correspondence, and directed his finances at a time when he was more than ordinarily desirous to acquire money so that he might leave a competency on his death to his foster-son. In time Beethoven came to entrust weighty matters to his decision, even the choice of publishers and his dealings with them. His prepossessing address, heightened by his independence of speech, made it less easy to contradict him than Schindler. Moreover, the recorded conversations show that he was witty, that he had a wider outlook on affairs than Beethoven's other musical advisers, that his judgements were quickly reached and unhesitatingly pronounced. His speeches were not free from frivolity nor always from flattery, but he lived at a time and among people accustomed to extravagant compliments, and there can be no doubt of his reverence for Beethoven.

We owe much of our knowledge of the relations between Beethoven and Holz to Schindler's statements. But many of his utterances show ill feeling, which it is not unfair to trace back to a jealousy dating from the time when Holz crowded Beethoven's 'Secretary sans Salary' out of Beethoven's service and good graces. There was no open rupture between Beethoven and Schindler, but a feeling of coolness and indifference which grew with the advancement of the younger man in the favour of the composer. The results of Beethoven's fellowship with a cheery companion were certainly not so great as Schindler says, nor so evil and grievous as he intimates. Beethoven was accustomed to drink wine from youth up, and also to the companionship which he found in the inns and coffee-houses of Vienna. It was, moreover, undoubtedly a charitable act to drag him out of his isolation into cheerful company. Beethoven's table habits were thus described by Holz to Jahn: 'He was a stout eater of substantial food; he drank a great deal of wine at table, but could stand a great deal, and in merry company he sometimes became tipsy. In the evening he drank beer or wine, generally the wine of Vöslau or red Hungarian. When he had drunk he never composed. After the meal he took a walk.'

Beethoven's letters to Holz bear witness to his fond regard for the man. His name, which in German signifies 'wood' and in the literature of the Church also 'cross', provided Beethoven with a welcome chance to indulge his extravagant fondness for punning. Thus, in the composer's jovial address book, not distinguished by reverence in anything sacred or profane, Holz becomes 'Best Mahogany', 'Best Splinter from the Cross of Christ', 'Best lignum crucis'. Holz had his entire confidence, and when the great catastrophe of 1826 came, Holz was the strongest prop upon which he leaned.

The E flat Quartet had been successfully performed, a summer home for Beethoven was in prospect, and considerable progress had been made in the draft for the second quartet designed for Prince Galitzin, when an illness befell Beethoven from about the middle of April to the middle of May 1825. In the middle of April Schindler writes: 'I believe that this is the result of your exertions in recent days and the disorder in your way of living. – Dear master, think of the future. What will be the result of your working at night?'

The distinguished Viennese doctor, Anton Braunhofer, had been giving medical attention to Beethoven periodically since 1820. On 18 April he received the following letter from the composer:

'My honoured friend,
   'I am feeling poorly and hope you will not deny me your help since I am suffering great pain. Is it possible for you to visit me as early as today, this I beg of you from the bottom of my heart –
   With everlasting gratitude and respect, your
                                                        Beethoven'

Dr Braunhofer was so blunt and forceful in his demands for obedience that Beethoven was somewhat awed, and beneficial results followed.

'No wine, no coffee; no spices of any kind. I'll arrange matters with the cook.'

'Then I will guarantee you full recovery which means a lot to me, understandably, as your admirer and friend.'

'A sickness does not disappear in a day. I shall not trouble you much longer with medicine, but you must adhere to the diet, you'll not starve on it.'

The doctor inspired him with courage and hope, and admonished him to keep quiet and patient. In dry weather he was to take walks, but even after going to Baden he must take no baths as long as the weather remained damp and symptoms of his illness remained.

'When you have been in Baden for a while, it will be better, and should there be a recurrence, let me know. When are you going?'

'Do not forget the bit of music, just something unimportant, what matters is that it is your handwriting.'

'You should be striving to get to the country soon.'

'It will give you fresh air, the walks here are too fatiguing.'

In the beginning of May Beethoven's condition had improved sufficiently for him to make the long-planned move to Baden, which he did on 7 May.

It is clear that Beethoven took his condition seriously and longed to get working again. This happened soon thereafter; on 17 May he wrote to his nephew, 'I am beginning to write a bit again.' The work taken up was the A Minor Quartet, the progress of which had been interrupted by the illness. In a Conversation Book used in May or June 1825, Beethoven writes: 'Hymn of Thanksgiving to God of an Invalid on his Convalescence. Feeling of new strength and reawakened feeling.' As will appear, these words, slightly modified, formed the title of a newly planned second movement to the quartet, the 'Song of Thanksgiving in the Lydian mode'.

It was while Beethoven was ill in Vienna that Ludwig Rellstab made several visits to him, of which he has left enthusiastic reports. He was twenty-six years old at the time and had made a mark as essayist and poet.

The most interesting incident of the meetings occurred when Rellstab told that he had been deeply moved by the Quartet in E flat, which he had heard performed twice in succession. He continues:

'Beethoven read and remained silent; we looked at each other mutely, but a world of emotions surged in my breast. Beethoven, too, was unmistakably moved. He arose and went to the window, where he remained standing beside the pianoforte. To see him so near the instrument gave me an idea which I had never before dared to harbour. If he – Oh! he needed only to turn half-way around and he would be facing the keyboard – if he would but sit down and give expression to his feelings in tones! Filled with a timid, blissful hope, I approached him and laid my hand upon the instrument. It was an English pianoforte by Broadwood. I struck a chord lightly with my right hand in order to induce Beethoven to turn around; but he seemed not to have heard it. A few moments later, however, he turned to me, and, seeing my eyes fixed upon the instrument he said: "That is a beautiful pianoforte! I got it as a present from London. Look at these names." He pointed to the crossbeam over the keyboard. There I saw several names which I had not before noticed – Moscheles, Kalkbrenner, Cramer, Clementi, Broadwood himself . . . "That is a beautiful gift," said Beethoven looking at me, "and it has such a beautiful tone," he continued and moved his hands towards the keys without taking his eyes off me. He gently struck a chord. Never again will one enter my soul so poignant, so heart-breaking as that one was! He struck C major with the right hand and B as a bass in the left, and continued his gaze uninterruptedly on me, repeated the false chord several times in order to let the sweet tone of the instrument reverberate; and the greatest musician on earth did not hear the dissonance! Whether or not Beethoven noticed his mistake I do not know; but when he turned his head from me to the instrument he played a few chords correctly and then stopped. That was all that I heard from him directly.'

During the summer at Baden, there was increasing tension between Beethoven and his nephew. In the winter of 1824–5 Karl had still been pursuing his studies in philology at the University of Vienna. In the spring of 1825 Karl again tried to make a shift in his studies. He wanted to enrol in a training school for a mercantile career, and this time he was successful in persuading his uncle.

He entered the Polytechnic Institute of Vienna about Easter, 1825, and Beethoven arranged to have the vice-director, Dr Reisser, appointed as co-guardian in place of Peters. Karl was placed under the supervision of a government official named Schlemmer, with whom the lad took lodgings. According to reports from Dr Reisser and Karl himself, he made a good beginning in his studies, although he was hampered by the fact that he had entered late in the term and therefore had a good deal of back work to cover.

After Beethoven's move to the country, Karl was expected to visit his uncle in Baden on Sundays and holidays, but conflict on this point soon developed. Furthermore, now that the two were separated, Beethoven worried about Karl's whole way of life and sought to keep tight control over him, despite the fact that the young man was nearly nineteen. In an undated letter to Schlemmer, Beethoven voiced the suspicion that Karl mingled with bad company in the evenings. He continues: 'I request you hereafter to watch out and under no pretext to let him outside of the house at night unless you have received something through Karl in writing from me.'

Of Karl's feelings we learn mainly from the Conversation Books; of Beethoven's from a remarkable series of letters that he wrote to his nephew from Baden. In a Conversation Book entry Karl showed the strain he was feeling from the demands on his time made both by his uncle and by his studies. Beethoven had evidently come to Vienna on business. Karl writes:

'It is impossible to get everything done today if I also have some things to attend to with you. But I will take some things along because we are very much overloaded and on Sundays have to write out everything that has been presented during the whole of the week.'

'I really would like to go out with you today but it is almost impossible to do much out there because it is so much trouble to take along all the books and papers that I need; besides since I must go along with you to see about the lodging, there remains but little time for me.'

The first series of notes from Beethoven to Karl, written in May, were concerned with the poor weather, his feelings of weakness, household matters about which he asked Karl's help, and mentions of his projected weekend visits. On 22 May, however, only fifteen days after his move, there was an abrupt change in the tone of Beethoven's letters upon his hearing that Karl had been seeing his mother. He writes:

'Until now [it was] only conjecture although someone assured me that there were secret dealings again between you and your mother – Am I to experience once again the most abominable ingratitude? No, if this bond is to be broken, so be it, but you will be despised by all impartial men who hear of this ingratitude . . . Shall I get involved again in these vulgarities? No, never again . . . I turn you over to Divine Providence. I have done my job and upon this I can appear before the mightiest of all judges. Do not be afraid to come to me tomorrow, I can still presume, God grant, that *nothing of this* is true, for if it were truly your unhappiness would be unending, light-heartedly as my rascally brother and your – mother would take this matter –

I am expecting you for sure – along with the old woman.'*

At the end of the next letter, written nine days later, he was still bitter:

'. . . God is my witness, I dream only of being completely removed from you and from this wretched brother and this abominable family to which I am attached – God grant me my wish, for I *cannot* trust *you* any more –

Unfortunately your Father or better not your Father'

* Presumably the housekeeper.

One more letter from the earlier part of the summer deserves to be cited in full, containing as it does one of Beethoven's references to death:

'Baden, 9 June 1825

'I wish at least that you would come here Saturday, I ask for an answer to no avail – God be with you and with me

as always your faithful Father'

'I have written to Hr. v. Reissig [Dr von Reisser] to ask you to come here on Saturday. The carriage leaves Vienna around six o'clock and in fact *from the Kugel auf der Wieden*. Consequently you have only to get some work or study done before so that you will not lose anything by this. I am sorry to cause you this trouble – In the afternoon around five o'clock you will return again by the same carriage to Vienna. It is paid for already beforehand. In the morning you can shave here and also get a shirt and necktie in order to arrive there conveniently – Farewell, although I am sulky with you it is not without reason, and I would have liked not to have spent so much in order to have given to the world an *ordinary man* – I hope to see you without fail – Moreover *if the intrigues have already developed*, explain yourself openly and naturally and you will find one who is concerned consistently with what is good . . .

'You know how I live here, with the cold weather to boot. The continual solitude weakens me even more, for often through my weakness I am really on the verge of feebleness. Oh do not pain me more; the man with the scythe will not be giving me much more time.'

In September, there are some entries by Karl Holz in the Conversation Books which suggest the role he was playing as Beethoven's helper:

'On Sunday I was with Karl in order to give him your note; it was evening and I learned from the maid that he had gone out in the early morning and had not come back home to eat –'

'I have a plan to attach him closer to myself, I would like to win him over to my side; perhaps in this way I will learn to know him and his way of life more easily.'

'I have lured him into going to a beerhouse with me because I [wanted] to see if he drinks much; but that does not appear to be the case. Now I will invite [him] at some point to play billiards; then I will see immediately if he has already been practising a long time –'

Beethoven, by Willibrord Joseph Mähler, 1815

'I felt as if I were watching one of Hoffmann's fantastic figures,' wrote the soprano Wilhelmine Schröder-Devrient of Beethoven's conducting during the dress rehearsal of *Fidelio* in 1814, in which she played the title role of Leonore. *Right*, a music sketch on one of the 'Conversation Books' for the *Missa Solemnis*, *c*.1819. *Below*, a contemporary lithograph of the apocryphal episode in which Beethoven embraced the young Liszt after the boy's recital in 1823

The letters continued through the summer alternating between tenderness and reproach. With the young man's sense of money he had no patience whatever, and insisted upon a strict accounting for every florin which he allowed him. In September he was enraged when he heard that Karl had resorted to borrowing from the servants:

'. . . You also borrowed again last Sunday 1 fl. 15 kr. from the house-keeper, that vulgar old kitchen-wench – It was long ago forbidden – Everywhere it is the same. I should have got along two years with the frock-coat. True, I have the bad habit of wearing an old coat at home, but Herr Karl, oh fie the shame of it, and why? The money-bag Herr L. v. B—n is here only for this purpose –'

On the other hand, Beethoven apparently trusted Karl enough to delegate to him not only minor household errands, but important cor-respondence and negotiations. Throughout this summer's correspon-dence, along with the scoldings and the reproaches, there are instances of Beethoven's instructing Karl what to do about letters to Galitzin, Peters and Schlesinger, and of his using Karl to represent him in finan-cial transactions.

In early October the letters became even more emotional. On the 5th of the month Beethoven writes from Baden:

'Precious, dear son!

'I have just received your letter. Filled with anxiety I had today determined to hasten to Vienna – God be thanked, it is not necessary. Do but obey me, and love and happiness of the soul paired with human happiness will be at our side; and you will unite an intensive inner exis-tence with the external, but it were better that the *former* dominate the *latter* – il fait trop froid – I shall see you on Saturday then. Write whether you are coming in the morning or the evening so that I may hasten to meet you –

'I embrace you and kiss you a thousand times not as my *prodigal but as my newly born son* – I wrote to Schlemmer. Do not think harshly on that account – I am still so filled with anxiety – My anxiety and my worry over finding you again will show you that your father is full of love.'

Beethoven moved from Baden into the Schwarzspanierhaus, his final residence, on 15 October, a Saturday. His letters to Karl during those final ten days in Baden alternate between instructions for mov-ing possessions into the new rooms from the brother's apartments and violent reproaches for his conduct.

Just before he had made the move, he reminded Karl: 'It pained me especially that you came out so late on Sunday and hurried off again so early.' Then came the move and with it an additional emotional outburst written from Vienna:

'My precious son!
 'Go no further – Come but to my arms, not a harsh word shall you hear. O God, do not rush away in your misery. You will be received as lovingly as ever. What to consider, what to do in the future, these things we will talk over affectionately. On my word of honour no reproaches, since they would in no case do good now. Henceforth you may expect from me only the most loving care and help – Do but come – come to the faithful heart of
your father Beethoven'

'Volti sub[ito]'

Karl had clearly absented himself and it can be presumed that he had gone to his mother. At this point the correspondence stops, and the only other letter of the autumn is a matter-of-fact note concerning payment of money to Frau Schlemmer, and a request for some of his nephew's time for some letter-writing.

During the summer Beethoven received a number of visitors whose meetings with the composer have been recorded either by themselves or in the Conversation Books. One of them was Karl Gottfried Freudenberg, a young musician who visited Beethoven in July. The master spoke of Bach: 'His name ought not to be Bach [brook] but Ocean, because of his infinite and inexhaustible wealth of combinations and harmonies. He was the ideal of an organist.' This led Beethoven into the subject of music for the church. 'I, too, played the organ a great deal in my youth,' he said, 'but my nerves could not stand the power of the gigantic instrument. I place an organist who is master of his instrument, first among virtuosi.' Pure church music, he remarked, ought to be performed only by voices, unless the text be a *Gloria* or something of the kind. For this reason he preferred Palestrina to all other composers of church music, but it was folly to imitate him unless one had his genius and his religious beliefs; moreover, it was practically impossible for singers today to sing the long-sustained notes of this music in a cantabile manner.

Beethoven's greatest desire now must have been the completion of the order from Prince Galitzin for three quartets. As we already know, the first one, in E flat, was finished and already performed. The sketches for the second one, in A minor (Op. 132), date back to 1824.

The work was originally to have the customary four movements; labour on it was interrupted by the illness of April and then the plan for the middle movements was changed to include the 'Song of Thanksgiving in the Lydian mode', the short march before the last movement, and the minuet. The work was finished by August at the latest. Immediately Beethoven set to work on the third quartet for Prince Galitzin. The story of this work comes later, while events must now be told which lead to the first performance of the second Galitzin Quartet.

The quartet was to have its first public performance in a benefit concert for the cellist Linke after it had first been given a private hearing. Holz took the responsibility of having the work copied speedily and sent to Beethoven for corrections. The following letter from Beethoven to Karl shows that this arrangement did not result in his always being free of worry:

'Baden on 11 August

'Dear Son!

'I am worried to death about the quartet, namely the 3, 4, 5 and 6th movement,* Holz has taken them along. The first measures of the 3rd movement have been left here, that is to say 13 in number – *I hear nothing from Holz* – I wrote to him yesterday. Usually he writes. What a terrible misfortune if he should have lost it. *Just between us, he is a hard drinker* . . . for God's sake give me some peace of mind concerning the quartet; what a terrible loss. The main ideas have been written on nothing but small scraps of paper, and I shall never be able to write out the whole thing again in the same way.

Your true father'

'I also point out to you that the coming *Sunday and Monday* are both holidays, thus you can arrange accordingly. With this opportunity you could perhaps [drive] here with me *Saturday* in the evening if I come in. Thus you gain the whole morning.'

On 4 September Beethoven received a visit from the Paris publisher, Moritz Schlesinger; he wanted to publish the two new quartets. In mid-July Beethoven had written to Adolf Schlesinger in Berlin, mentioning 'two new grand violin quartets' and offering them for eighty ducats each. He could only have meant the A minor, Op. 132, and the B flat major, Op. 130, not yet composed. Schlesinger was eager to know of the quartets; he asked if he could attend a rehearsal of the A minor quartet. His pertinacity on this matter evidently aroused Beethoven's

* In its final form the Quartet had only five movements.

suspicions, and his pride revolted at the thought that a publisher should ask to hear a work of his which he proposed to buy.

Schlesinger had his way, however, for it was rehearsed at his rooms at the tavern 'zum Wilden Mann' on Wednesday 7 September, preparatory to its performance to a small group (which may have been a sort of dress rehearsal) on the 9th. Beethoven had originally wanted the players to come to his lodging at Baden, but had agreed that this was impractical and suggested they all meet at Schlesinger's. Meanwhile, arrangements for the rehearsals had been made independently of Beethoven, and on the 8th Holz arrived in Baden to report to him the progress of the rehearsal the day before. He mentioned the fact that Karl was present, and also Johann Nepomuk Wolfmayer and Tobias Haslinger, for Wolfmayer 'at the Adagio wept like a child' and 'Tobias scratched his head when he heard the quartet; he certainly regrets that the Jew Steiner did not take it.' He continued about the arrangements for the performance the next day, which was to take place at noon, and stated that the innkeeper had arranged for them to have a larger room. This took place as scheduled, and on 11 September the quartet was performed for a larger group, also at 'zum Wilden Mann'.

We have an account of both the 9 September and 11 September occasions from the English visitor whom Beethoven received at this time. This was Sir George Smart, who, in the summer of 1825, made a tour of Germany in company with Charles Kemble. Sir George recorded the performances of his meetings with Beethoven in his journal, from which the following excerpts are taken:

'Friday, September 9th . . . We then went to Mecchetti's music shop, they, too, are publishers, and bought three pieces for Birchall . . . Mr Holz, an amateur in some public office and a good violin player, came in and said Beethoven had come from Baden this morning and would be at his nephew's – Karl Beethoven, a young man aged twenty – No. 72 Alleegasse . . . At twelve I took Ries to the hotel Wildemann the lodgings of Mr Schlesinger, the music seller of Paris, as I understood from Mr Holz that Beethoven would be there, and there I found him. He received me in the most flattering manner. There was a numerous assembly of professors to hear Beethoven's second new manuscript quartette, bought by Mr Schlesinger. This quartette is three-quarters of an hour long. They played it twice. The four performers were Schuppanzigh, Holz, Weiss, and Lincke. It is most chromatic and there is a slow movement entitled "Praise for the recovery of an invalid". Beethoven intended to allude to himself I suppose for he was very ill during the early part of this year. He directed the performers, and took off his coat, the room being warm and crowded. A staccato passage not being expressed to the satisfaction of his eye, for alas, he could not hear, he seized Holz's violin and played the passage a quarter of a tone too flat ... About fourteen were present ... I fixed to go to Baden on Sunday and left at twenty-five minutes past two ...

'Sunday, September 11th ... From hence I went alone to Schlesinger's, at the "Wildemann", where was a larger party than the previous one ... When I entered Messrs C. Czerny, Schuppanzigh and Lincke had just begun the Trio, Op. 70, of Beethoven, after which the same performers played Beethoven's Trio, Op. 97 ... Then followed Beethoven's quartette, the same that I had heard on September the 9th and it was played by the same performers. Beethoven was seated near the pianoforte beating time during the performance of these pieces. This ended, most of the company departed, but Schlesinger invited me to stop and dine with the following party of ten: Beethoven, his nephew, Holz, Weiss, C. Czerny, who sat at the bottom of the table, Lincke, Jean Sedlatzek – a flute player who is coming to England next year, and has letters to the Duke of Devonshire, Count St Antonio, etc. – he has been to Italy – Schlesinger, Schuppanzigh, who sat at the top, and myself. Beethoven calls Schuppanzigh Sir John Falstaff, not a bad name considering the figure of this excellent violin player.

'We had a most pleasant dinner, healths were given in the English style. Beethoven was delightfully gay ... He was much pleased and rather surprised at seeing in the oratorio bill I gave him that the "Mount of Olives" and his "Battle Symphony" were both performed the same evening. He believes – I do not – that the high notes Handel wrote for trumpets were played formerly by one particular man ... After dinner he was coaxed to play extempore, observing in French to me, "Upon what subject shall I play?" Meanwhile he was touching the instrument thus

to which I answered, "Upon that." On which theme he played for about twenty minutes in a most extraordinary manner, sometimes very fortissimo, but full of genius. When he arose at the conclusion of his playing he appeared greatly agitated. No one could be more agreeable than he was – plenty of jokes. He was in the highest of spirits. We all wrote to him by turns, but he can hear a little if you halloo quite close to his left ear.'

Smart accepted Beethoven's invitation to visit him at Baden on 16 September. Though he had been warned not to write in Beethoven's book, Sir George did not, or was not always able to, obey the injunction. A considerable portion of the conversation at the meeting is preserved in a Conversation Book which covers three dates, 16, 19 and 24 September. From this book some excerpts are made here, since they bear on the subject which filled so large a place in the plans of Beethoven for several years, and was in his mind up to the time of his death – the English tour. No doubt Beethoven gave expression, as he frequently had done, to his admiration for the English people and possibly also for their national hymn, for Karl translates the stanza:

> 'Long may he reign!
> May he defend our laws,
> And ever give us cause
> To sing with heart and voice:
> God save the king!'

The one-sided conversation proceeds:

'*Smart:* You understand English writing?'

'*Karl:* He would like to know the tempi of the finale of the last symphony.'

'Haven't you it here?'

'How long have you worked on the symphony?'

'How long does it last? – 1 hour and 3 minutes'

'3/4 hour'

'We are now going to take a walk.'

According to Smart's journal, Beethoven now ordered dinner 'with his funny old cook', told his nephew to look after the wine, and the party of five took a walk. 'Beethoven was generally in advance humming some passage . . .' Holz talked to Beethoven now about Schlesinger, telling him that it was the publisher's purpose to print the quartets in succession, which would postpone the appearance of the thirteenth for two years, and advised Beethoven hereafter to make immediate publication a condition of purchase. The conversations continued:

'*Karl:* He asked why you had not come before now; he said the £300 of the Philhar. Society were not to be looked upon as the principal thing. For that you needed only to appear 2 or 3 times in the orchestra and make money with your own concerts.'

'He said that in a short time you could make at least £1,000 and carry it away with you.'

'You can do better business with the publishers there than here.'

'And you'll find 1,000 friends, Smarth says, who will do everything to help you.'

'. . . We'll wait till the year is over before going to England.'

'. . . You'll not leave London so quickly if we are once there.'

We shall let Smart conclude the story of the meeting.

'On our return [from the walk] we had dinner at two o'clock. It was a most curious one and so plentiful that dishes came in as we came out, for, unfortunately, we were rather in a hurry to get to the stage coach by four, it being the only one going to Vienna that evening. I overheard Beethoven say, "We will try how much the Englishman can drink." *He* had the worst of the trial. I gave him my diamond pin as a remembrance of the high gratification I received by the honour of his invitation and kind reception and he wrote me the following droll canon as fast as his pen could write in about two minutes of time as I stood at the door ready to depart.

Ars   lon - ga   vi - ta   bre - vis

' "Written on 16 September 1825, in Baden, when my dear talented musical artist and friend Smart (from England) visited me here.
                              Ludwig van Beethoven." '

After securing the A minor Quartet for publication and an assurance that he should also have that in B flat, Schlesinger said that he would purchase the first of the three quartets from Schott and Sons so as to have all three for his proposed Complete Edition. Karl, in reporting the fact to Beethoven, expressed his belief that the Schotts would sell for fear that if they did not Schlesinger would reprint the work in Paris without permission. The latter made a strenuous effort to get the autograph score of the A minor, but had perforce to content himself with a copy. Beethoven expressed indifference as to which publisher got the works so long as he was promptly paid.

The house into which Beethoven moved on 15 October – the Schwarzspanierhaus – derived its name from the fact that it had been built by the Benedictines of Spain. In it Beethoven occupied four rooms on the second floor, besides a kitchen and servants' quarters. One of the most important results of Beethoven's removal to these quarters was a re-establishment of the intimate relations which had existed for so many years with the friend of his youth Stephan von Breuning, a Councillor in the War Department of the Austrian Government, who lived hard by. Though there had been no open rupture between him and Beethoven an estrangement had existed from the time when von Breuning had advised against Beethoven's assumption of the guardianship over his nephew. They had met occasionally *ad interim*, but it was not until they became neighbours that the intimate friendship which had existed in earlier years was restored. Concerning the relations which existed between Beethoven and her father's family, Marie, a daughter of Stephan von Breuning, wrote many years after:

'My mother once met Beethoven when on her way to the Kaiserbad on the Danube; he accompanied her for the rather long distance from the Rothes Haus, where she lived. She spent about an hour in the bathhouse (the bath being a warm one) and on coming out was surprised to find Beethoven waiting to accompany her home. She often said that he was always gallant towards women and had paid court to her for a while.

'She related, too, that his animated gestures, his loud voice and his indifference towards others surprised the people in the street, and that she was often ashamed because they stopped and took him for a madman. His laugh was particularly loud and ringing.

'My mother often and repeatedly deplored the fact that she had never heard him play – but my father, in his unbounded tenderness, always replied when she expressed a desire to hear him: "He doesn't like to do it, and I do not want to ask him because it might pain him not to hear himself."

'Beethoven repeatedly invited my mother to coffee, or, as the Viennese say, *zur Jause*; but my mother almost always declined, as his domestic arrangements did not appear altogether appetising.

'My mother often said to my father that Beethoven's habit of expectorating in the room, his neglected clothing and his extravagant behaviour were not particularly attractive. My father always replied: "And yet he has a great deal of success, especially with women."

'Beethoven often told my mother that he longed greatly for domestic happiness and much regretted that he had never married.'

There can be no doubt that the renewed association with von Breuning frequently turned his thoughts to his old home and his boyhood friends in the Rhine country, and his delight must have been keen when at the end of December he received letters from Wegeler, whom he had not seen since he left Vienna twenty-eight years before, and his wife, who had been Eleonore von Breuning. They were tender letters, full of information about their family, each other, friends and relations – real home letters telling of births, marriages, careers and deaths.

On 25 November, Beethoven wrote to Schott and Sons promising to send them the metronome marks for the Mass in D soon, telling them to print the list of subscribers before the dedication, asking delay in the matter of the dedication of the Ninth Symphony, and requesting that the publication of both works be postponed three months. He gives the title of the Mass as follows:

'MISSA
composita, et
Serenissimo ac Eminentissimo Domino Domino
Rudolpho Joanni Caesareo Principi et Archiduci Austriae SRE
tit. S. Petri in monte aureo Cardinali et Archiepiscopo Olomucensi
profundissima cum veneratione dedicata
a
Ludovico van Beethoven'

In a Conversation Book at the very end of the year, in the midst of remarks about New Year's greetings, Beethoven wrote the following:

'It is very interesting that the opening idea for the Quartet in C sharp minor (Op. 131) should thus appear before the close of 1825.'

Underneath Beethoven writes: 'Only the praise of one who has enjoyed praise can give pleasure,' – a relic, no doubt, of some of the composer's classic readings.

CHAPTER 22

The Year 1826 Through to the Autumn

Prince Galitzin – The Nephew's Attempt at Suicide

The year which witnessed the last of Beethoven's completed labours, and saw what by general consent might be set down as the greatest of his string quartets, that in C sharp minor, Op. 131, beheld also the culmination of the grief and pain caused by the conduct of his nephew. The year 1826 was a year of awful happenings and great achievements; a year of startling contradictions, in which the most grievous blows which an inscrutable Providence dealt the composer as if utterly to crush him to earth, were met by a display of creative energy which was amazing not only in its puissance but also in its exposition of transfigured emotion and imagination.

There was a good deal of talk concerning the performance of Beethoven's works at the beginning of the year, at the Schuppanzigh evening concerts and the *Concerts spirituels*, etc. The new Quartet in B flat major, Op. 130, was ready to be rehearsed; and at the home of the rich music-lover Dembscher, there were quartet parties at which the A minor Quartet was played. There was talk of new compositions – oratorios on the old text by Bernard and on a new one by Kuffner, the opera on Grillparzer's *Melusine*, a requiem, and a new symphony. Beethoven's thoughts, however, were not with such things but in the congenial region of the string quartet. Having fulfilled his commission for Prince Galitzin by writing the Quartets in E flat, A minor and B flat (Op. 127, 132, 130) he had started to work on the Quartet in C sharp minor (Op. 131). That he could continue to write amidst all the disturbing circumstances of this year in the higher and purer regions of chamber music was a source of admiration and wonder to his friends.

The figure which stands out in the highest relief throughout the year beside that of the composer is that of Holz, whose concern for his welfare went into the smallest detail of his unfortunate domestic life. Schindler appears at intervals, but with jealous reserve, chary of advice, waiting to be asked for his opinion and pettishly protesting that after it once had been given it would not be acted upon. Stephan von Breuning appears in all the nobility of his nature; and in the attitude and acts of Brother Johann, there is evidence of something as near affectionate sympathy and interest as Beethoven's paradoxical conduct and nature invited of him.

The year was not far advanced before Beethoven's health was bothering him again; he complained of pains in the bowels and found locomotion difficult. He suffered also from his eyes. Dr Braunhofer was called in and advised his patient to abstain from wine for a few days and from coffee, which he was told was injurious because of its stimulating effect on the nerves; also to eat freely of soups. Small doses of quinine were prescribed.

In a note to Braunhofer, Beethoven refers to his trouble as 'rheumatism or gout'. Frequent visits from the doctor and admonitions from his friends to be cautious continued until March, during which month he appeared to improve and to take an interest again in musical events and other things that were going on in the world.

The event that was personally important to Beethoven at this time was the first performance of his Quartet in B flat – the last of the three Galitzin Quartets, Op. 130. Schuppanzigh and his fellows had taken it in hand. They found the concluding fugue extremely troublesome, but the Cavatina entranced them at once. The performance took place on 21 March 1826. The second and fourth movements had to be repeated, but the fugue proved a crux as, no doubt, the players had expected it would. Some of Beethoven's friends argued that it had not been understood and that this objection would vanish with repeated hearings; others, plainly a majority, asked that a new movement be written to take its place. Johann van Beethoven told the composer that the 'whole city' was delighted with the work.

The doubts about the effectiveness of the fugue felt by Beethoven's friends found an echo in the opinions of the critics. Matthias Artaria, the publisher, went to Beethoven with the suggestion that he write a new finale and that the fugue be published as an independent piece, for which he would remunerate him separately. Beethoven listened to the protests unwillingly, but, 'Vowing he would ne'er consent, consented.'

There was talk of other performances of the Quartet. Schuppanzigh was indisposed to venture upon a repetition, but Böhm and Mayseder were eager to produce the work at one of their quartet parties at Dembscher's house. But Dembscher had neglected to subscribe for Schuppanzigh's concert and had said that he would have it played at his house, since it was easy for him to get manuscripts from Beethoven for that purpose. He applied to Beethoven for the Quartet, but the latter refused to let him have it, and Holz told Dembscher that Beet-

hoven would not let him have any more music because he had not
attended Schuppanzigh's concert. Dembscher stammered in confusion
and begged Holz to find some means to restore him to Beethoven's
good graces. Holz said that the first step should be to send Schuppanzigh fifty florins, the price of the subscription. Dembscher laughingly asked, 'Must it be?' ('Muss es sein?') When Holz related the
incident to Beethoven he too laughed and instantly wrote down the
following canon:

Out of this joke in the late autumn of the year grew the finale of
the last of the last five quartets, that in F major, Op. 135, to which Beethoven gave the superscription: 'Der schwer gefasste Entschluss' ('The
difficult resolution'). The story that the phrases: 'Muss es sein? Es muss
sein', and 'Der schwer gefasste Entschluss' had their origin in a scene
frequently repeated when Beethoven's housekeeper came to him of a
Saturday for the weekly house-money, was spread by Schindler. Holz
was an actor in the scene and is the better witness, being confirmed,
moreover, by the Conversation Book. The joke played a part in the
conversations with Beethoven for some time.

With the Quartet in B flat, Beethoven had completed the three
works of its kind which he had been commissioned to compose by
Prince Nicolas Galitzin. He had taken three years to perform the task,
but in the end the patience of his patron had been nobly rewarded.

Meanwhile the Prince had been privileged to shine in the musical circles of St Petersburg as one who stood peculiarly close to the greatest of living composers. During the delay, Prince Galitzin's conduct was in the highest degree honourable. In his letters he was most generous in his offers of assistance, practically giving Beethoven *carte blanche* to draw on his bankers in case of need. After the first performance of the *Missa Solemnis*, for which he had been primarily responsible, he presented his copy of the written score to the Philharmonic Society of St Petersburg. He was so proud of his collection of Beethoven's music that he applied to the composer himself to help him make it complete. Too eager to wait for the publishers, he commissioned Beethoven to have copies made for him of new works, like the Ninth Symphony and the overture to the *Weihe des Hauses*, at his expense. He entertained the idea of repeating in St Petersburg the concert which Beethoven had given in Vienna, at which the Symphony had received its first performance.

After an exchange of letters between Prince and composer in June, there is a break in the correspondence until the beginning of 1826. In the summer of 1825 Beethoven had two overtures, *Zur Namensfeier* and the *Weihe des Hauses*, sent to the Prince with a dedication to his patron on the latter. The A minor Quartet, Op. 132, had received its first public performance on 6 November 1825 in Vienna. That the Prince had heard of this performance is shown by his next letter:

'St Petersburg, 14 January 1826
'Dear, respected Monsieur van Beethoven,
    'I am much at fault for not having yet acknowledged the receipt of the overtures which you had the kindness to send me. I was waiting for the shipment of the quartet to express my thoughts all at once. Since that time I have been very ill and then I was obliged to make a trip into the heart of Russia. All these circumstances and unexpected changes here have prevented me from writing to you up until now. I have just read in the musical Gazette of Leipzig that the new Quartet in A minor was performed in Vienna, and I am so impatient to get acquainted with this new masterpiece that I beg you to send it to me by post, like the preceding one, without further delay.
    'I will remit the amount of 75 ducats to M. Stieglitz to be remitted to you by M. Fries; 50 for the quartet and 25 for the overture which is magnificent and which I thank you very much for dedicating to me. The Leipzig journal referred to your new quartet in such flattering terms that I could not be more impatient to get acquainted with it. Would you forward it as soon as possible, for soon I am leaving for the

coronation in Moscow, and then I will send you my address.

   'I wish you a good and happy new year.

Your devoted friend
Prince Nicolas Galitzin

The A minor Quartet was sent in February, the B flat Quartet shortly thereafter. But Beethoven waited in vain to be paid for them, and this was a matter of concern to him and those close to him during the months to come.

Holz knew a courier named Lipscher who often went to St Petersburg, and he volunteered in January to obtain his services if the money did not arrive soon. In March Johann suggested that his brother write another letter, which he himself would post, for fear that the last quartet had never been received.

In May, Holz writes in the Conversation Books:

'The courier Lipscher, who took the third quartet and was supposed to bring back the money, has written from Petersburg: he went to the home of the Prince, who excused himself, he had no time, he could come another day; Lipscher then went 5 or 6 times but was never received; all kinds of excuses were given. A so-called blue note for 5 florins given to a servant helped him finally to get through to the Prince again; he was embarrassed again, fumbled through his scores and finally said that Lipscher might come to him before his departure for Vienna and receive the money.'

In June, Holz writes:

'The courier Lipscher has written: "7 times I went to see the scamp, the last time it turned out that he had left for the coronation in Moscow – merely a Russian trick." '

'Several couriers have told me that there has been little action from the embassy; it does not want to have a quarrel with this gentleman.'

Lipscher advised Beethoven to turn to the banker Stieglitz in Vienna, who could exert more pressure than the Embassy. On 13 August Stieglitz answered a letter of 2 August from Beethoven reporting that the Prince was not at home but probably near Koslov in the Tambov region and that the matter would be attended to upon his return.

Finally in November a letter arrived:

'10/22* November 1826

'My dear and respected Monsieur van Beethoven!

'You must think I am very inconsistent and fickle to let so much time go by without writing to you especially since I have received from you two new masterpieces of your immortal and inexhaustible genius. But the unhappy circumstances that I find myself in, partly from great losses which have brought me several bankruptcies, partly from other considerations that I cannot explain to you, have drawn me away from my usual occupations.

'Now I am living in the country in the heart of Russia, and in a few days I will be leaving for Persia to participate in the war there. Before this I will definitely dispatch the sum of 125 ducats to be remitted to you, and I can only offer you my thanks for your masterpieces and my excuses for having taken so long to give you any sign of life. Please let me keep on hearing from you, it means a lot to me. Always write to me at the old address, and tell me, I beg of you, what new things you are composing.

'Accept the esteem and regard of one of your greatest admirers.

Pce Nicolas Galitzin'

Since this letter was written before his return to St Petersburg, it shows that he had received both of the last two quartets before his trip and that he recognised his debt to be fifty ducats for each of those quartets and twenty-five ducats for the dedication of the overture *Weihe des Hauses*. On the outside of this letter there is a notation, probably written by Breuning: 'Enquiry sent on 10 January 1827 to Stieglitz and Company, requesting the delivery of the sum of 125 ducats or a report.' Stieglitz answered this enquiry on 18 January reporting that he had sent another reminder to the Prince in Koslov. A final appeal to Stieglitz was written on 21 March 1827, which Beethoven signed on his deathbed.

Holz said that when he once remarked to Beethoven that the one in B flat was the greatest of the three Galitzin Quartets (Op. 127, 130, 132) the composer replied: 'Each in its way. Art demands of us that we shall not stand still. You will find a new manner of voice treatment (part writing) and thank God there *is less lack of fancy than ever before.*' Afterwards he declared the C sharp minor Quartet (Op. 131) to be his greatest. The first form of the fugue-theme in this work, as has been noted, was written down in a Conversation Book in the last days of December 1825. The quartet was the main work of the next month, and indeed for the first half of 1826 with interruptions only from sick-

* The same day by the Russian and Austrian calendars.

ness, preparations for the performance of the B flat Quartet, and a four-hand arrangement for the pianoforte of the Fugue (Op. 133).

In a letter to Schott and Sons, the Mainz publishers, dated 20 May, Beethoven complained of ill health and pressing affairs which prevented him from completing the quartet until now. On 12 July he wrote that the quartet was ready for delivery upon receipt of the draft of the second instalment of the fee. The score was turned over to Schott's agent in Vienna on 12 August. On the copy Beethoven had written: 'Put together from pilferings from one thing and another.' Because this had alarmed the publishers, Beethoven writes on 19 August: 'You wrote to me that the quartet must be an original one. I felt rather hurt, so as a joke I wrote on the copy that it was put together from pilferings. Nevertheless, it is *brand new* —.' It was published by Schott after Beethoven's death.

Now we turn to the projects which the composer's friends tried unsuccessfully to persuade him to undertake. First, there was Bernard's *Der Sieg des Kreuzes* which Beethoven had promised to write for the Gesellschaft der Musikfreunde. At the end of 1825 advice had been sought and an abbreviation of the text recommended. The Society gave its approval to the revision. In April Kuffner told Beethoven that he had read Bernard's oratorio book but could not find in it even a semblance of an oratorio, much less half-good execution. These protests could only strengthen Beethoven's distaste for the text. At any rate the plan was definitely laid aside. According to Holz, he never worked earnestly on the subject and yet, at the same time, showed his intention to write no more 'Opern' and piano pieces, but only oratorios. Holz further relates that Beethoven, in reference to his last sonatas, said: 'In the future I shall write in the manner of my grand-master Handel annually only an oratorio or a concerto for some string or wind instrument, provided I have completed my tenth symphony (C minor) and my Requiem.'

His friends also urged him to compose a requiem mass and such a composition belongs in the category with the oratorio as a work which he had been paid to undertake. Among the ardent admirers of Beethoven and most zealous patrons of the Schuppanzigh Quartets was Johann Nepomuk Wolfmayer, a much respected cloth merchant. One of the methods chosen by Wolfmayer to show his appreciation of the composer was occasionally to have a new coat made for him which he would bring to Beethoven's lodgings, place upon a chair and then see to it that an old one disappeared from his wardrobe. It is said that Wolfmayer sometimes had difficulty in getting the composer's consent to the exchange, but always managed to do it. Early in the second decade of the century Wolfmayer commissioned Beethoven to write a Requiem for him and paid him 1,000 florins as an advance on the honorarium. Beethoven promised, but never set to work: though Holz says he was firmly resolved to do so and, in talking about it, said that he was better satisfied with Cherubini's setting of the Mass for the Dead than with Mozart's. A requiem, he said, should be a memorial of the dead and have nothing in it of the noises of the last trumpet and the Day of Judgement.

There was still talk of an opera, and the matter was constantly being broached by different members of his circle. Duport, director of the Court Opera, sent word that Grillparzer's *Melusine* would be acceptable to him.

Beethoven evidently had expressed the intention or wish to the older Schlesinger to write an opera for Berlin. This information was passed on to the General Intendant of the Berlin Theatre, Count von Brühl, who wrote a letter to Beethoven on 6 April expressing the honour it would bring his stage to have a work written for it by such an artist as Beethoven. The letter was evidently never answered.

An adaptation to operatic uses of Goethe's *Claudine von Villa Bella* was discussed, apparently with favour, but Kanne, who was designated to take the adaptation in hand, was afraid to meddle with the great poet's drama. So nothing came of the Berlin project or of *Melusine*. To Schindler, Beethoven once held out a prospect that 'something would come' of the idea of music for *Faust* which had been implanted in Beethoven's mind four years before; but it shared the fate of opera and oratorio.

The sketchbooks bear witness, though not voluminously, to other works of magnitude which were in Beethoven's thoughts in this year but never saw completion. These were a symphony and overture. In a book used towards the end of 1825, containing sketches for the last movement of the Quartet in B flat, there is a memorandum of a Presto in C minor, 3/4 time, and of a short movement in A flat, Andante, which Schindler marked as belonging to 'the tenth symphony'. He published the sketches of the symphony after Beethoven's death and started the story of an uncompleted tenth symphony. Lenz says that Holz wrote to him that Beethoven had played 'the whole of the Tenth Symphony' for him on the pianoforte, that it was finished in all of its movements in the sketches, but that nobody but Beethoven could decipher them. Holz, however, made no such broad statement to Otto Jahn, a much more conscientious reporter than Lenz. To Jahn he said that there was an introduction in E flat major, a soft piece, and then a powerful Allegro in C minor, which were complete in Beethoven's head and which he had played to him (Holz) on the pianoforte. This is very different from an entire symphony.

Among Beethoven's intimate friends was Abbé Stadler, an old man and an old-fashioned musician, the horizon of whose aesthetic appreciation was marked by the death-date of his friend Mozart. Castelli says that he used to call Beethoven's music 'pure nonsense'; certain it is that he used to leave the concert-room whenever a composition by Beethoven was to be played. Holz, telling Beethoven in February 1825 that as usual he had left the room when an overture by Beethoven was about to be played, added: 'He is too old. He always says when Mozart is reached, "More I cannot understand." ' But once he stayed and not only listened to a Beethoven piece but praised it. It was the Trio for Strings, Op. 9, which had been composed nearly a generation before! But Stadler now had occasion to court Beethoven's favour, or at least to betray the fact that even if he could not appreciate his music he yet had a vast respect for his genius and reputation. In 1825, Gottfried Weber had written an essay attacking the authenticity of Mozart's *Requiem*. The article angered Beethoven. Stadler published a defence of Mozart, 'Vertheidigung der Echtheit des Mozartschen Requiems', and sent a copy to Beethoven, who replied with fiercely expressed approval.

Later, Beethoven and Abbé Stadler met at Steiner's. About to depart, Beethoven knelt before the Abbé and said: 'Reverend Sir, give me your blessing.' Stadler, not at all embarrassed, made the sign of the cross over the kneeling man and, as if mumbling a prayer, said: 'Nutzt's nicht, so schadt's nix' ('If it does no good, 'twill do no harm'). Beethoven thereupon kissed his hand amid the laughter of the bystanders.

Different proposals for Beethoven's move to the country were already being offered early in the year. In February Johann invited him again to his country house. It is not surprising that Beethoven did not consider it at this time. He was waiting for the money from Prince Galitzin and Karl writes: 'If the sums of money should come, you could probably go to the country.' Among many possibilities was a move to Ischl. In June and July there is talk of the baths there which are beneficial to those suffering from gout. Holz offered also to find a house in Baden for him. It had been planned to make a move for the summer, but the place had not yet been decided upon when an event took place which suddenly changed all such thoughts: an attempt by Karl to take his life.

Since he had enrolled late in the term at the Polytechnic Institute, Karl employed a tutor to help him, and apparently still needed his help a year later. At the time of the change to the Institute, Beethoven made the remark that the expense of the tutor, along with the board at

Schlemmer's, would amount to 2,000 florins a year. Entries in the Conversation Book of 1825 show that the matter was under discussion and that Beethoven had registered his disapproval of the tutor to Schlemmer. Later, there appears in Schlemmer's hand:

'I can assure you that as yet he has never stayed away overnight. Also I must tell you that your nephew is at home daily in the evening, and that he goes out early only if it is time for school. But if he were going out to play, then it would have to be instead of school. Otherwise he is at home and he cannot play. In the time that he has been here he has been changing his ways favourably. He said today at lunch that the tutor was not really satisfied, he is negligent in his studies.'

Beethoven's alternation between strong reproaches, moral sermons and excessive emotional expressions of love served only to diminish bit by bit his authority over the boy, and as a result Karl saw less and less of his uncle. Beethoven felt this keenly and asked his brother Johann to find out the reason. At the beginning of March Johann writes in the Conversation Book:

'Today I spoke with him earnestly about why he had been to see you so little.'

'His answer was approximately as follows. He would very much like to be with you but he fears the frequent rows and reproaches for his mistakes of the past, also the frequent rows with the servants. However, please do not reproach him with this; otherwise he would no longer be candid with me. From here, however, I think that only you can draw him to yourself completely.'

He continues: 'In 4 months Karl will be ready with everything, then you must urge him to go immediately into a local or foreign business house, for otherwise he will become a lout [*ein Lump*] and will let himself live off you as long as you are living; then he could idle away his time.'
Johann advised that in the latter case the guardianship should be placed in the hands of Dr Bach, because 'You are as little able as I to be always running after him.' In these conversations we also find Schindler once again, to whom Beethoven had voiced his fears. Schindler replies: 'I am sorry to hear it, what all are we to live through with Karl, if it goes on like this.' And he advised Beethoven not to depend upon Holz in the management of this affair.

Meanwhile Karl explained again how much work he had to do – for example, 'The professors assign so much work over the holidays that one can scarcely get it done. The fair copying is the most disagreeable part because it takes a lot of time' – and its effect on his visits and his participation in outside events. In June he writes: 'There is much to be done because the examinations are soon.' Holz adds: 'Now Karl does not have much longer to study.'

Another form of duress came from the uncle's suspicion of the nephew in money matters. Beethoven asked to see the receipts of last month's payment to Schlemmer and expressed misgivings over Karl's demands for funds. Karl writes:

'If the receipt is not in my room, Schlemmer can give it to me along with the receipt for this month.'

'It will show up all right.'

'When I go walking and have a drink and the like. I don't have any other expenses.'

This last answer from Karl must have been to a demand from his uncle as to how he used money, and must be weighed against a statement by Schlemmer in the Conversation Books, and later again by Breuning, that the principal reason that circumstances had become intolerable for Karl was that he was heavily in debt.

There were violent scenes, evidently in Karl's rooms, which deeply embittered him. Shortly afterwards his uncle visited him again to break down his obstinacy. Here follows Karl's part of the dialogue, which shows what tension had been reached over Beethoven's persistence:

'You consider it insolence if, after you have upbraided me for hours undeservedly, this time at least, I cannot turn from my bitter feeling of pain to jocularity. I am not so frivolous as you think. I can assure you that since the scene on Sunday in the presence of this fellow I have been so depressed that the people in the house noticed it. The receipt for the 80 florins which were paid in May I now positively know, after a search at home, that I gave you, as I already said on Sunday; it must and no doubt will be found.'

'If I continue to work while you are here it is not in a spirit of insolence, but because I believe that you will not be offended if I do not permit your presence to keep me from my labours, which are now really piling up on me, all the more since we see each other *here*, where there is time, enough to talk over all needful things. You are mistaken, too, when you think that I wait for your coming to *become industrious*. You also seem to accept as *my views* what I repeat to you as the opinions of *others* as, for example, the word of *Haslinger* and the twaddle of Frau Passy.'

At one point Karl seems to have raised his hand in physical violence against his uncle. Holz writes:

'I came in just as he took you by the breast.'

'At the door, as he was coming out. '

It is the only allusion to the incident in the book and we know none of the particulars; but it and other scenes of tumult and the utterances which they provoked must have inspired the dreadful conflict of emotions which finds expression in a letter written at this time:

'If for no other reason than that you obeyed me, at least, all is forgiven and forgotten; more today by word of mouth, very quietly – Do not think that I am governed by anything but thoughts for your well-being, and from this point of view judge my acts – Do not take a step which might make *you* unhappy and shorten *my* life – I did not get to sleep until 3 o'clock, for I coughed all night long – I embrace you cordially and am convinced that soon you will no longer *misjudge* me; I thus judge your conduct yesterday – I expect you without fail today at one o'clock – Do not give me cause for further worry and apprehension – Meanwhile farewell!
Your real and true Father'
'We shall be alone, for I shall not permit H[olz] to come – the more so since I do not wish anything about yesterday to be known. Do come – do not permit my poor heart to *bleed any longer*.'

At this time Karl was also seeing his mother, which, of course, was directly contrary to Beethoven's wishes. There he saw his friend, Niemetz, with whom his mother had become acquainted. At this time Beethoven wrote a short note to Holz:

'Please come as soon as possible, thereupon we can arrange everything. It is no small matter, he wanted to go away again early today.
Most hurriedly
Your Beethoven'

The force of circumstances had made Karl sullen and angry. Schindler writes in the Conversation Book that once when he was admonished by his teachers at the Institute and reminded of his duty to his uncle he replied, 'My uncle! I can do with him what I want, some flattery and friendly gestures make things all right again right away.' According to Holz, Karl said that he could wrap his uncle around his finger. A note to Niemetz was subsequently found in which Karl writes: 'I had to write to you in such a great hurry from fear and worry of being discovered by the old fool.'

In the last days of July, Beethoven was notified that Karl had disappeared and was intending to take his life. Evidently Karl had left the house leaving a hint of his purpose. Schlemmer learned of this, and from him Holz, who went to report to Beethoven. They both went to Schlemmer's house where Holz writes out:

'I will fetch the police.'

'Still he must be moved away from here. He certainly will not take the examination.'

'Shall I have Schlemmer fetched?'

Then Schlemmer reports:

'The story in brief, since you have heard it already from Hr. Holz: I learned today that your nephew intended to shoot himself before next Sunday at the latest. As to the cause I learned only this much, that it was on account of his debts, but not completely, only in part was he admitting that they were the consequences of former sins.'

'I looked to see if there were signs of preparations; I found in his chest a loaded pistol all right, together with bullets and powder. I tell you this so that you may act in this case as his father. The pistol is in my keeping.'

'Be lenient with him or he will despair.'

To the question of possible debts to him, Schlemmer answers: 'I have been paid completely – up to the present month, but not yet for August.'

Holz questions further, while looking through papers:

'This is not his handwriting, yet everything is paid for till the end of July.'

'There is still a great deal more to be learned.'

Holz then went to the Institute to find Karl and returned to report:

'He is not staying here.'

'I could not detain him; he said he would come again to Schlemmer's, but he wanted to get his papers from a friend, meanwhile I talked with Reisser.'

'I said that I could not wait more than a quarter of an hour.'

Beethoven apparently rebuked him for letting his ward out of his sight. He answers:

'He would have run away from you just the same.'

'I think that if he has made up his mind to injure himself, no one can prevent him.'

'He has till 3 September to make up his examinations.'

Holz evidently continued his search among Karl's papers: 'Here is 30 kr. more for the rest of Schlemmer's board. He [Karl] said to me, "What good will it do you to detain me? If I do not escape today, I will at another time." '
Subsequently Schlemmer writes:

'I will unload the gun. My wife has the second pistol.'

'Because I was not at home when it was found.'

A new suspicion now seized upon the mind of Beethoven. For some reason, though he may also have uttered it orally, he wrote it down in the book: 'He will drown himself.' Probably he did not want the bystanders to know his thoughts, and the fear was therefore committed to the written page for the instruction of Holz. What else was said at the same time we do not know, for the book here shows a mutilation; some pages are missing. Perhaps Schindler removed them in later years to save the integrity of his account; or they may have been torn out by Beethoven himself when, some weeks later, Holz advised him to look through his books against their possible demand for examination by the police magistrate; they might contain references to affairs which he did not want to bring into public discussion. The missing pages might have helped us in the chronology of the story, but the main facts are before us without them. It was resolved first to go to the house of Niemetz, who it was thought might be privy to Karl's intentions, and then if necessary, to call in the help of the police.

Meanwhile Karl, having given Holz the slip, went straight to a pawnbroker and pledged his watch. From Holz's subsequent account we know that this took place on a Saturday – i.e. 29 July. With the money he bought two new pistols, powder and balls. He did not dare go to his lodgings for the pistols which he had in readiness for the contemplated deed, and the new ones were therefore necessary. He drove out to Baden, and spent the night in writing letters. One was to his uncle, and this he enclosed in one to his friend Niemetz. The next morning, it being a Sunday, he climbed up to the ruins of Rauhenstein, in the lovely Helenenthal which his uncle loved so well, and there discharged both pistols towards his left temple. He was a bungler with firearms. The first bullet flew past harmlessly; the second ripped up the flesh and grazed the bone, but did not penetrate the skull. Holz said afterwards that, had he taken with him the pistols which he was obliged to leave at his lodgings, he would have been a dead man; their barrels were charged with powder and ball to above the middle. A wagoner came upon him lying among the ruins and, no doubt at his request, carried him to his mother's house in the city.

It was there that Beethoven found him. And to his uncle's questions he answers:

'It is done. Now, only a surgeon who can hold his tongue. Smetana, if he is here.'

'Do not plague me with reproaches and lamentations; it is past. Later all matters may be adjusted.'

'She has sent for a doctor, but he is not at home. Holz will soon bring another one.'

Then Beethoven asks: 'When did it happen?' and the mother writes the answer:

'He has just come. The wagoner carried him down from a rock in Baden and has just driven out to you . . . I beg of you to tell the surgeon not to make a report or they will take him away from here at once, and we fear the worst.'

'There is a bullet in his head on the left side.'

Smetana was the physician who had treated Karl when he was a boy at Giannatasio's school. To him Beethoven writes:

'Most honoured Herr von Smetana,
    'A great misfortune has happened, which Karl accidentally inflicted upon himself. I hope that he can still be saved, especially by you if you come quickly. Karl has a *bullet* in his head; how, you shall learn – But quick, for God's sake, quick.
                              Yours respectfully,
                                        Beethoven'
'In order to give help quickly, it was necessary to take him to his mother's, where he now is. The address follows herewith.'

    Holz took this letter for delivery but, before he left, a surgeon named Dögl had been called in. Returning, Holz had a message from Smetana saying that Dögl was a capable practitioner and that in order not to compromise him he would not come unless Dögl desired to see him in consultation. Karl expressed himself as satisfied and the case was left for the time being in Dögl's hands.
    Beethoven went home, but Holz remained some time longer. The matter had to be reported to the police and Holz thought it best to do this himself, as he wanted to be able to inform Beethoven what the consequences of the young man's act were likely to be in case of his recovery. He learned, and so reported, that there would be a severe reprimand and thereafter police surveillance. He also told Beethoven that, after he had left, Karl had said, 'If only he would not show himself again', and 'If he would only quit his reproaches!' He had also threatened to tear the bandage from the wound if another word were spoken to him about his uncle.
    On 7 August, the day being a Monday, the wounded youth, who by his act was in the hands of the law, was removed from his mother's house to the general hospital by the police authorities. If Beethoven was forced to leave the would-be suicide in the hands of his mother for an entire week it was most likely because the police authorities commanded it; he did not yield her a day after her son came out of the hospital.

Meanwhile Holz reported regularly on Karl's condition:

'Four of the most skilful doctors come four times daily.'

'He is getting unfailing care.'

'As yet there is no fever, but if it should come, then there would be a dangerous crisis.'

'The Magistrate as a criminal court is now concerned with this.'

Under the Austrian code an attempt at suicide was an offence against the Church and guilty persons were remanded to the care of priests who imparted religious instruction until a profession of conversion could be recorded.

'The priest will be sent by the Magistrate, you need not concern yourself with this any more.'

'He will not be released until he has passed a complete examination in religious instruction and has been completely converted, so that there is no longer fear of a relapse.'

'In such cases the police treat the misguided one with the greatest possible forbearance in order not to arouse stubbornness.'

'But custody must not be as a punishment but as a means of security for himself.'

Strenuous efforts were made by Beethoven through Holz and others to discover what direct cause had led the misguided young man to attempt to end his life. The enquiries made of him at the hospital during the weeks spent there brought scarcely more information from his lips than the first question asked by his mother. Schindler seems to have been persuaded that it was his failure to pass the examinations at the Institute; but this theory is not tenable. Aside from the fact that he had till 3 September to make up his neglected studies, he never himself advanced this as an excuse nor an explanation, but explicitly denied it. In the hospital he told Holz that it would have been easy for him to make himself fit to pass, but that, having made up his mind to do away with himself long before, he had not thought it worth while to continue his studies. 'He said that he was tired of life', Holz reports to Beethoven, 'because he saw in it something different from what you judiciously and righteously could approve.' He also phrased it thus: 'Weariness of imprisonment.' To the examining police magistrate Karl said that his reason for shooting himself was that Beethoven 'tormented him too much', and also 'I grew worse because my uncle wanted me to be better.' To Beethoven's question if Karl had railed against him, Schlemmer replied: 'He did not rail, but he complained that he always had trouble.' Holz's explanation many years after to Otto Jahn was that 'Beethoven was rigorous to excess in his treatment and would not allow him the slightest extravagance.' Beethoven stinted him in the matter of pocket-money, and the scores of reckonings in the Conversation Books show how close was the watch kept upon every kreutzer placed in his hands. So he had recourse to borrowing and no doubt, though the fact does not appear in the books, he went into debt at the places he frequented for pleasure. When he shot himself he had paid his lodging bill for the month but owed his tutor. In a Conversation Book there was talk of a sale of books, which did not belong to Karl but to his uncle. Since this constituted a penal offence, a bad conscience along with fear of punishment could have been providing further pressure before the catastrophe. Beethoven, in his efforts to find an explanation that was excusable on moral grounds, wanted to advance a cause of mental disturbance. In his hand appears a note in a Conversation Book: 'Mental aberration and insanity; the heat too – afflicted with headaches since childhood.'

Stephan von Breuning's son, Gerhard, has described the shattering effect of this attempted suicide upon Beethoven.

'The pain which he received from this event was indescribable; he was cast down as a father who has lost his much-loved son. My mother met him on the Glacis completely undone. "Do you know what has happened? My Karl has shot himself!" – "And – is he dead?" – "No, it was a glancing shot, he is still living, there's hope that he can be saved; but the disgrace that he has brought upon me; and I loved him so." '

Evidently Gerhard was sent to the master soon after, for he writes in a Conversation Book: 'You must come to us for all your meals so that you will not be alone.'

Schindler wrote that the blow bowed the proud figure of the composer, and that he soon looked like a man of seventy. To add to his suffering he was compelled to learn that many persons placed part of the blame for the rash act upon him.

The surgical section in which Karl was placed in the hospital was under the care of a Dr Gassner, whose assistant, Dr Seng, had supervision over Karl. He related the following subsequently to Gerhard von Breuning:

'In the late summer of 1826 there came to me one day during my inspection a man in a grey coat whom at first glance I took to be a simple peasant. He asked me in a dull voice, "Are you Assistant Doctor Seng? I was referred to you in the reception office. Is my nephew with you, the dissolute fellow, the scoundrel?" etc. After learning the name of the patient, I answered in the affirmative and told him that he was lying in a room in the three-florin ward, was bandaged for gunshot wound, and asked if I could direct him to him. Whereupon he said, "I am Beethoven." And, while I led him to him, he spoke further, "I did not really want to visit him for he does not deserve it, he has given me too much vexation, but . . ." and then he continued to talk about his nephew's conduct and how he was altogether too spoiled, etc. But I was astonished to have these things expressed to me by the great Beethoven, and I promised him that I intended to give his nephew the best possible care.'

There was no delay in discussing plans for the future of the boy. In fact, prompt decision was necessary, for it was the penal aspects of the case which held the greatest terrors for Beethoven. Shortly after Karl had been put into the hospital, Holz writes:

'Here you see ingratitude as clear as the sun; why do you want further to restrain him? Once with the military, he will be under the strictest discipline, and if you want to do anything more for him you need only make him a small allowance monthly. A soldier at once.'

'Do you still doubt? This is a marvellous document.'

It seems likely that this last remark may have been called out by the letter written by the nephew on the eve of his attempt – a letter which has never been found.

Holz also urged him to give up the guardianship. He pointed out that it would be the Magistrate's responsibility to find a replacement and that Beethoven, relieved of his duties, would be free to decide what more, if anything, he would want to do for the boy.

As court councillor in the war department, Stephan von Breuning's opinion had especial weight. 'A military life will be the best discipline for one who cannot endure freedom; and it will teach him how to live on little,' is one of Breuning's first utterances. As we shall see, this opinion, shared by Schindler and Holz, prevailed. As for the guardianship, Dr Bach joined these three in advising Beethoven to relinquish it, but there was no immediate change as Karl's cure took its course.

The composer's friends, Holz in particular, made many efforts to divert Beethoven's mind from his disappointment and grief. They accompanied him on brief excursions into the country which he loved so passionately and which had been closed to him, for the customary happy seasons, by his nephew's act. Again did his brother offer him a haven at Gneixendorf in August, only to receive the curt answer: 'I will not come. Your brother??????!!!! Ludwig.'

Meanwhile Beethoven was far from idle. He had begun a new quartet, in F major, and Schlesinger, *père*, who had come from Berlin, negotiated with him for its publication. He had the new finale for the B flat Quartet on his mind and several other works occupied him. With Schlesinger he talked about the Complete Edition and some military marches which the King of Prussia was to pay for, as they were to be written for the Royal Band.

Meanwhile a recurring subject of conversation during the summer was the question of Karl's future. As has been mentioned, Breuning, Holz and Schindler favoured placing him in the army, while Dr Bach urged that he be sent off at once to some business house in Trieste, Milan or Hamburg.

There was also the immediate question of where Karl would go when he first left the hospital. During the investigation by the court, Holz kept Beethoven informed about all the proceedings and discussions with the counsel in charge. He reported that the question of where young Beethoven should stay in the future could present difficulties. There was the possibility that he would wish to be with his mother, which the court viewed as a natural response to instinct. At one point Beethoven, after considering the possible measures that might be taken by the court and the police, writes: 'My only intent was that he improve; if he is abandoned now, something terrible could still happen.'

Beethoven was unalterably opposed to the nephew's being with the mother for even a day. In an interview with Karl he brought the subject up and began to berate her as usual, but the young man interrupted him: 'I do not want to hear anything that is derogatory to her; it is not for me to be her judge. If I were to spend the little time I shall be here with her, it would be only a small return for all that she has suffered on my account.' He repeated his desire for the new career and his wish to leave Vienna as soon as possible. He made clear that his mother would offer no objection to the military career: 'All the less, therefore, can I deny her wish to be with me during these days, as I shall in all likelihood not be here again soon. It is self-evident that this will not prevent you and me from seeing each other as often as you wish.'

Very reluctantly Beethoven gave his consent that his nephew should become a soldier. But he spilled out his feelings to Holz, reiterating his dislike of the army as a career. Meanwhile Breuning, in pursuance of his own plan, consulted Baron von Stutterheim and persuaded him to give the young man a cadetship in his regiment. Having carried the day with his plan, Breuning agreed to accept the guardianship, which had been relinquished by Reisser. Beethoven now set down his terms for the cadetship in a pencilled note for Breuning:

'I believe that there are three points to be observed with Karl. First, he is not to be treated as a culprit, which would have exactly the opposite result from what we want; second, in order to become promoted to a higher rank, one cannot live too modestly and meanly; third, too great a limitation on his eating and drinking might have a harsh effect upon him. I am not trying to obstruct you.'

Now the plans for this disposition were made. He was to be presented to von Stutterheim as soon as he was discharged from the hospital, take the oath of service the next day, and leave Vienna for Iglau, where von Stutterheim's regiment was stationed, within five or six days. Breuning, as guardian, now found himself confronted by a serious embarrassment. Where should the young man be sent while the preparations for his entry into the military service were being made? Karl did not want to go to his uncle's, nor did von Breuning want to send him there, and he frankly tells Beethoven the reason: 'If he were here you would talk to him too much and that would cause new irritation; for he testified in the police court that the reason why he had taken the step was because you harassed him too much.'

Beethoven, on the other hand, was still fearful that the magistrate might allow him to go to his mother's, and to guard against this he wrote two letters to that official, a man kindly disposed to him, appealing against such an eventuality.

Late in September Beethoven's brother was again in Vienna. He repeated his offer to give the composer a temporary home and his nephew a harbour of refuge at Gneixendorf. This time Beethoven accepted. Karl was discharged from the hospital on 25 September, and on the 28th Beethoven and his nephew set off for Gneixendorf with Johann for what was supposed to be a visit of a week. A night was passed at a village en route, and Johann's estate was reached in the afternoon of the next day but not too late for the composer to walk through the fields with his brother to take a look at the property. The next day the walk was extended to the vineyards on the hill in the forenoon and to Imbach in the afternoon.

Gneixendorf was a little village on a high plateau of the Danube valley about an hour's walk from Krems. It was a mean hamlet, with only one street and that narrow, rough and dirty. The houses were low huts. Wasserhof, the Beethoven estate, lay opposite the village, and was reached by a wagon road which ran a large part of the way along the edge of a ravine, which had been made by torrents cutting into the clay soil. The plateau was almost treeless but covered with fields and vines. There were two houses on the estate, both large and handsome, each with its garden and surrounding wall, and separated from each other by a road. Beethoven's rooms had a magnificent view of the Danube valley stretching to the distant Styrian mountains. A lover of hills and forests like Beethoven must have found the flat expanses dreary and monotonous in the extreme, yet the distant view of the Danube seems to have compensated him in a measure, for in a letter to Schott he writes: 'The scenes among which I am sojourning remind me somewhat of the Rhine country which I so greatly long to see again, having left them in my youth.'

Johann had made repeated efforts to persuade his brother to come to Gneixendorf ever since he had acquired the estate in 1819. In 1823 Beethoven wrote: 'He always wants me to come to his people – *non possibile per me*.' The obstacle was Johann's wife, about whose behaviour, it will be remembered, Beethoven had become very concerned in 1823. Urged on by Ludwig, Johann had made himself master of his household, for he wrote in a Conversation Book of 1824: 'My wife has surrendered her marriage contract and entered into an obligation permitting me to drive her away without notice at the first new acquaintance which she makes.' Beethoven perhaps suggested that he do this very thing, for Johann continued: 'I cannot do that. I cannot know but that some misfortune might befall me.'

Beethoven was sick when he went to Gneixendorf. He had not recovered from his illness of the early months of the year when Karl attempted to kill himself, and this was not calculated to improve the physical or mental condition of so nervous and irritable a being as he. He had never been a comfortable or considerate guest or tenant at the best.

Johann's wife had assigned Michael Krenn, son of one of her husband's vinedressers, to look after Beethoven's wants. At first the cook had to make up Beethoven's bed. One day, while the woman was thus

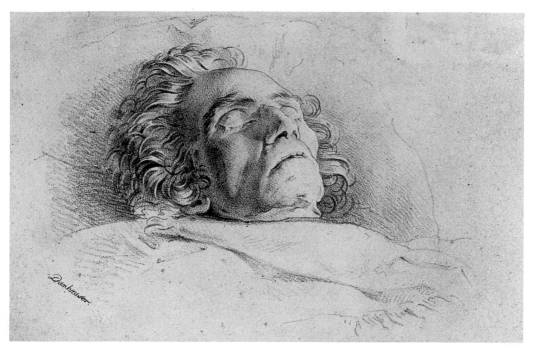

Beethoven on his deathbed in the Schwarzspanierhaus, a study made by
Joseph Danhauser two days after the composer's death in March 1827. The
following day the artist Johann Nepomuk Höchle made a sketch, *below*, of
Beethoven's room

A 'life-mask' of Beethoven made in 1812. *Right*, Beethoven's friend and publisher, Tobias Haslinger, for whom he wrote his humorous canon 'O Tobias!', 1821. *Below*, Beethoven's funeral procession leaving the Schwarzspanierhaus (to the right of the church), the composer's last residence. A contemporary watercolour by Franz Stöber

occupied, Beethoven sat at a table gesticulating with his hands, beating time with his feet, muttering and singing. The woman burst into a laugh, which Beethoven observed. He drove her out of the room instanter. Krenn tried to follow her, but Beethoven drew him back, gave him three twenty-kreutzer pieces, told him not to be afraid, and said that hereafter he should make the bed and clean the floor every day. Krenn said that he was told to come to the room early, but generally had to knock a long time before Beethoven opened the door. It was Beethoven's custom to get up at half-past 5 o'clock, seat himself at a table and write while he beat time with hands and feet and sang. This frequently stirred Krenn's risibles, and when he could no longer restrain his laughter he used to leave the room. Gradually he grew accustomed to it. The family breakfast was eaten at half-past 7 o'clock, after which Beethoven hurried out into the open air, rambled across the fields shouting and waving his arms, sometimes walking very rapidly, sometimes very slowly and stopping at times to write in a sort of pocketbook. At half-past 12 Beethoven would come home for dinner, after which he went to his room until about 3 o'clock; then he roamed over the fields until shortly before sunset, after which he never went out of doors. Supper was at half-past 7, and after eating he went to his room, wrote till 10 o'clock and then went to bed.

One day the wife of the landowner sent Michael with five florins to buy wine and a fish; but Michael was careless and lost the money. He came back to Gneixendorf in consternation. As soon as Frau van Beethoven saw him she asked for the fish, and when he told her of the loss she discharged him from her service. When Beethoven came into dinner he asked at once for his servant and the lady told him what had happened. Beethoven grew fearfully excited, gave her five florins, and angrily demanded that Michael be called back at once. After that he never went to table any more but had his dinner and supper brought to his rooms, where Michael had to prepare breakfast for him. Even before this occurrence Beethoven scarcely ever spoke to his sister-in-law and seldom to his brother. Beethoven would have liked to have taken Michael with him to Vienna.

Two old peasants told the owner of Wasserhof in 1862 stories which confirm Krenn's account of Beethoven's unusual behaviour in the fields. Because of his unaccountable actions they at first took him for a madman and kept out of his way. When they had become accustomed to his singularities and learned that he was a brother of the landlord they used to greet him politely; but he, always lost in thought, seldom if ever returned their greetings. One of these peasants, a young man at the time, had an adventure with Beethoven of a most comical nature.

He was driving a pair of young oxen, scarcely broken to the yoke, from the tile-kiln towards the manor-house when he met Beethoven shouting and waving his arms about in wild gesticulations. The peasant called to him: '*A bissel stada!*' ('A little quieter') but he paid no attention to the request. The oxen took fright, ran down a steep hill and the peasant had great difficulty in bringing them to a stand, turning them and getting them back on the road. Again Beethoven came towards them, still shouting and gesticulating. The yokel called to him a second time, but in vain; and now the oxen rushed towards the house, where they were stopped by one of the men employed there. When the driver came up and asked who the fool was who had scared his oxen the man told him it was the proprietor's brother. 'A pretty brother, that he is!' was the answering comment.

The Quartet in F (Op. 135) was also completed at Gneixendorf; as was the new finale for the Quartet in B flat – though it, too, had been worked out almost to a conclusion in Vienna. Schuppanzigh gave it a private performance in December and told Beethoven that the company thought it exquisite (*köstlich*) and that Artaria was overjoyed when he heard it.

It is probable that the first sketches for the Quartet and the canon 'Muss es sein?' were written about the same time. But it cannot be determined whether or not the motif of the canon was destined from the first for the finale of the Quartet. It may have been in Beethoven's mind for that purpose and the sudden inspiration on hearing the story of Dembscher's query 'Muss es sein?' may have gone only to the words and the use of them with the music for the canon. That the Quartet was to be shorter than the others was known before Beethoven left Vienna. Holz once said to Beethoven before the departure that Schlesinger had asked about the Quartet and that he had replied that Beethoven was at work upon it and added 'You will not punish him if it is short. Even if it should have only three movements it would still be a quartet by Beethoven, and it would not cost so much to print.'

CHAPTER 23

December 1826–1827 – Finale

The Conversation Books add nothing to the account of Beethoven's sojourn in Gneixendorf as it has been drawn from other sources. They indicate that there were some days of peace and tranquillity, and that not only Johann, but his wife and nephew also, were concerned with making the composer comfortable. Several times there was mention of trips in the carriage, such as to nearby Krems where there was some sort of city life; yet travel was not always possible because the carriage was in need of repair. Johann had business which took him occasionally to Vienna. Beethoven was supplied with writing materials from Krems by his nephew, who also found there the opportunity to play billiards. Johann met Holz and Linke in Vienna; the latter was anxious to have the new finale for the B flat Quartet for an Akademie. The money for this movement was in the hands of the baker, Leopold Obermayr, brother of Johann's wife, Therese. Beethoven accepted Therese's offer to go to Vienna and bring the money back to him.

But there were also strong scenes between uncle and nephew as could be expected. For example:

'You ask me why I do not talk.'

'Because I have had enough.'

'Yours is the right to command, and I must endure it all.'

'I can only regret that I can give no answer to anything you have said today, since I know of nothing better to do than to listen and to remain silent as is my duty. You must not consider this insolent.'

It can be imagined how sensitive Beethoven became to the increasingly cold weather in Gneixendorf, and how he must have longed for his customary way of living. But the Conversation Books do not make clear Beethoven's attitude on this score beyond occasional complaints about the food. Meanwhile Johann was becoming increasingly concerned about the effect of this life upon his nephew. To avoid an argument with his brother, he wrote him a letter on the subject near the end of November:

'My dear Brother:

'I cannot possibly remain silent concerning the future fate of Karl. He is abandoning all activity and, grown accustomed to this life, the *longer* he lives as at present, the more difficult it will be to bring him back to work. At his departure *Breuning* gave him a fortnight in which to recuperate, and now it is two months. – You see from Breuning's letter that it is his decided wish that Karl *shall hasten* to his calling; the longer he is here the more unfortunate will it be *for him*, for the harder it will be for him to get to work, and it may be that we shall suffer harm . . .'

Ludwig took his brother's suggestions with bad grace; and before his departure from Gneixendorf there was an exceedingly acrimonious quarrel between the brothers, growing out of Ludwig's demand that Johann make a will in favour of Karl, thus cutting off his wife.

The question of returning to Vienna was now discussed with Karl, whose attitude is shown by the following entry:

'I cannot argue against it since we have been here longer than was planned; but *Breuning* himself has said that I cannot go to the Field-Marshal until I am able to appear without any visible sign left of what happened to me, because he wants to overlook the whole affair. This is almost accomplished now except for a little bit which really won't take much more time . . .'

During this period of decision there was great strain between uncle and nephew. Beethoven asks:

'What is the matter? Why are you hanging your head now? . . .'

'The idea of going from here continues to pain you and I have also taken this into consideration.'

Apparently this was followed by further strong reproaches, for Karl writes:

'Did you see me speak a word? Hardly – for I was not disposed at all to speak, everything that you say about me needs no refutation. So I beg of you once and for all to leave me alone. If you want to go, good.'

'If not, good again.'

'But I beg of you once more not to torment me as you are doing; you might regret it, for I can endure much, but too much I cannot endure. You treated your brother in the same way today without cause. You must remember that other people are also human beings.'

'These everlastingly unjust reproaches!'

That the means of conveyance back to Vienna were discussed is proved by a remark of Johann's and also by a report made by Karl to the composer: 'There is no postchaise to Vienna, but only to St Pöl-ten . . . From here there is no opportunity except by a stagecoach.'

Exactly how the travellers set out is not clear. Schindler writes: 'This return journey, which that late in the year could not be made in one day, took place in an open carriage since, as Beethoven himself assured me, his brother denied him the use of his closed carriage.'

Dr Wawruch, Beethoven's attending physician during the illness which ended in his death, writes: 'Oppressed by the sad prospect of a gloomy future, being helpless in the case of sickness in the country, he longed to return to Vienna and used for his trip home the most wretched vehicle of the devil, a milk-wagon, as he humorously put it.'

Beethoven arrived in Vienna on Saturday, 2 December, and as there is a reference to only one night spent in transit, it is likely that he left Gneixendorf early in the morning of Friday, 1 December. Dr Wawruch continues:

'That December was raw, damp, cold and frosty; Beethoven's clothing anything but adapted to the unfriendly season of the year, and yet he was urged on by an eternal unrest and a gloomy foreboding of misfor-tune. He was compelled to spend a night in a village tavern where, besides wretched shelter, he found an unwarmed room without winter shutters. Towards midnight he experienced his first fever-chill, a dry hacking cough accompanied by violent thirst and cutting pains in the sides. When seized with the fever he drank a few measures of ice-cold water and longed, helplessly, for the first rays of the morning light. Weak and ill, he permitted himself to be lifted into the *Leiterwagen* and arrived, at last, weak, exhausted and without strength, in Vienna.'

He immediately went to his lodgings in the Schwarzspanierhaus. The first thing to be done was to get a doctor. According to Johann, Beethoven himself wrote to his old doctor, Braunhofer, who gave as his reason for not coming that the distance was too great. Then Dr Stau-denheim was sent for; he promised to come but failed to do so. Then

Dr Wawruch of the General Hospital was called, and came directly. 'I was not called until the third day,' he writes in his report.

The Conversation Book records the following in the handwriting of Holz:

'I have had Professor Wawruch called for you . . . I do not know Wawruch personally, but he is known here as one of the most skilful physicians.'

'He is professor in the hospital.'

'He will come after dinner.'

Wawruch came and introduced himself with the following words in a Conversation Book: 'One who greatly reveres your name will do everything possible to give you speedy relief. Prof. Wawruch.' Then in his presence the necessary questions to the patient were written out by Karl, including probably the question of the abdominal complaint. Wawruch's report continues:

'I found Beethoven afflicted with serious symptoms of inflammation of the lungs. His face glowed, he spat blood, his respiration threatened suffocation and a painful stitch in the side made lying on the back a torment. A severe counter-treatment for inflammation soon brought the desired relief; his constitution triumphed and by a lucky crisis he was freed from apparent mortal danger, so that on the fifth day he was able, in a sitting posture, to tell me, amid profound emotion, of the discomforts which he had suffered. On the seventh day he felt considerably better, so that he was able to get out of bed, walk about, read and write.'

Wawruch's report shows that Beethoven had weathered an attack of pneumonia. Before its continuation, account may be made of one or two letters.

Beethoven's old friends, Franz and Eleonore Wegeler, had written to him almost a year ago, and now he finally answered. They begin the closing chapter to a friendship which, along with that of Stephan von Breuning, was one of the earliest and one of the most tender.

'Coblenz, 20 December 1825
'My dear old Louis!
    'I cannot have one of the 10 Ries children travel to Vienna without recalling memories of you. If you have not received a long letter every

2 months within the 28 years since I left Vienna, you may consider your silence on top of mine as the cause. This is not right at all, and all the less now when we older people want to live so much in the past and delight ourselves to the utmost with scenes of our youth. To me at least my acquaintance and childhood friendship with you, which was limited but blessed because of a good mother, is a very bright point in my life which I contemplate with pleasure and with which I become completely preoccupied when travelling. Now I look up to you as a hero and am proud to be able to say: I was not without influence on his development; he confided in me his wishes and dreams; and when later he was so frequently misunderstood, I knew well what he wanted. Thank God that I have been able to talk with my wife and now more recently with my children about you; yet the house of my mother-in-law was more your house than mine, especially after you lost your own noble mother. Just speak to us once again: yes, I think of you in your gay and in your dark moods! Is it that man is happy, even if he has such a great stature as yours, still but one time in his life, namely in his youth; the rocks of Bonn, Kreuzberg, Godesberg, the Baumschul etc. have been a sounding board for you from which you have been able joyfully to shape many ideas.

'Now I will tell you something about myself, about us in order to give you an example of how you must write to me in reply.

'After my return from Vienna in 1796, things went rather badly for me; for several years I had to live from my practice alone, and this lasted for some years in the poorest environment until I could support myself. Then I became a salaried professor and married in 1802. A year later I received a daughter, who is still living and who has married well. With much genuine intelligence she has the cheerfulness of her father and likes best to play Beethoven sonatas. This gift perhaps is not to her credit but simply hereditary. In the year 1807 a boy was born to me, who is now studying medicine in Berlin. Four years from now I will send him to Vienna, will you receive him? Concerning the family of your friend, my father died on 1 Jan. 1800 in his 70th year. Concerning that of my wife, the schoolteacher died four years ago at the age of 72 . . . I myself celebrated my 60th birthday in August in the company of some 60 friends and acquaintances, among whom were some of the foremost people of the town. – Since 1807 I have been living here, have a fine house now and a beautiful place. My superiors are satisfied with me and the King gave me decorations and medals. Lore and I are pretty well.

'Now I have brought you up to date all at once with our situation; if you want to continue it, please write. – Of our acquaintances Court

Councillor Stupp died three weeks ago, Fischenich is Councillor of State in Berlin; Ries and Simrock are two fine old men, but the latter is in much weaker health than the former . . .

'Why haven't you avenged the honour of your mother when, in the Encyclopedia and in France, you were set down as a love-child? The Englishman who wished to vindicate you gave this slander a box in the ears, as we say in Bonn, and [showed that] your mother [would have had to] carry you for 30 years since the King of Prussia, your alleged father, had been dead since 1740. – Won't you ever come to see the Stephens steeple? Has travelling no attraction for you? Don't you ever want to see the Rhine again? – All the warmest regards from Frau Lore as well as myself.

Your ancient friend Wglr.'

Enclosed was a note from Eleonore Wegeler:

'For so long a time dear Beethoven!
'It was my wish that Wegeler should write to you once again – now that this wish is fulfilled, I must still add a few words – not only to bring myself more vividly to your memory but to repeat the important question: do you have no desire to see the Rhine and your birthplace once again? – You will be most welcome as our guest at any time and at any hour – and this would give Weg. and me the greatest joy – Our Lenchen is grateful to you for so many happy hours – listens so gladly to our stories about you – knows all the small details of our happy youth in Bonn – of the quarrels and reconciliations – How happy she would be were she able to see you! Unfortunately the girl has no musical talent but through great industry and perseverance she has progressed to the point where she can play your sonatas, variations and the like; and since music continues to be the greatest relaxation for Weg., she has given him many happy hours through this. Julius does have musical talent, but until now has neglected it – and just in the last half year he has been learning the violoncello with pleasure and delight – Since he has a good teacher in Berlin, I am confident that he will continue to learn – Both children are big and like their father – also with the gay, cheerful frame of mind which thank heaven Weg. still hasn't completely lost – He gets great pleasure in playing the themes of your variations, the old ones are his favourites but he has been practising a lot and with unbelievable patience on a new one – your Opferlied stands at the top – He never enters the living room without going to the piano – still, dear Beethoven! if you could see the way the lasting memory of you lives on with us – Just tell us once that it means some-

thing to you and that you haven't completely forgotten us – If it were not so difficult to satisfy our greatest desire, we would already have made a visit to our brother in Vienna which would certainly have included the pleasure of seeing you – But such a trip is not possible now since our son is in Berlin – Weg. has told you how things are with us – We would be wrong to complain – Even the most difficult period was easier for us than for 100 others – the greatest luck is that we are healthy and the children are good and well – Neither of them have ever given us any trouble and we are of good cheer – Lenchen has experienced just one great grief – that was when our poor little boy died – a loss which none of us will ever forget. Goodbye, dear Beethoven, and think of us with kind, friendly thoughts –

Eln. Wegeler'

Beethoven's reply, a long time in coming, was dictated to Karl:

'Vienna, 7 October 1826

'My old beloved friend!

'I cannot convey the pleasure which the letters from you and your Lorchen gave me. Truly an answer should have followed with the speed of an arrow; but I am after all somewhat negligent as a writer because I think that the better people know me without it. I often form an answer in my head, yet when I want to write it down in most cases I throw the pen away because I am incapable of writing the way I feel. I remember all the love that you have constantly given me; for example how you had my room whitewashed and gave me such a pleasant surprise; – thus it was with the Breuning family. If we were separated one from another that was the force of circumstances; each had to follow the object of his goal and try to reach it; but the eternally firm and unshakeable principles of the good bind us together ever fast. Unfortunately I cannot write you today as much as I should like since I am bedridden and must limit myself to answering some points of your letter . . . You write of your son. It goes without saying that if he should come here, he will find in me a friend and father; and whenever I am in a position to serve him or help him in anything, I shall do it with joy.

'I still have the silhouette of your Lorchen, so you see how precious even now are all the dear, good memories of my youth . . .

'My beloved friend! rest content now, for the memory of the past has taken hold of me; and not without many tears first will you be receiving this letter. The beginning has now been made and soon you will get another letter; and the more often you write to me, the more pleasure you will give me. On account of our friendship no kinds of demands are needed, and so goodbye. I beg of you to embrace and kiss for me your dear Lorchen and your children and thereby think of me. God be with you all!

As ever your faithful friend who reveres you

Beethoven'

Dr Wawruch's report continues:

'On the eighth day I was alarmed not a little. At the morning visit I found him greatly disturbed and jaundiced all over his body. A frightful choleric attack had threatened his life in the preceding night. A violent rage, a great grief because of sustained ingratitude and undeserved humiliation, was the cause of this mighty explosion. Trembling and shivering he bent double because of the pains which raged in his liver and intestines, and his feet, thitherto moderately inflated, were tremendously swollen. From this time on dropsy developed . . . Gentle entreaties from his friends quieted the threatening mental tempest, and the forgiving man forgot all the humiliation which had been put upon him. But the disease moved onward with gigantic strides. Already in the third week there came incidents of nocturnal suffocation; the enormous volume of collected water demanded speedy relief and I found myself compelled to advise tapping in order to guard against the danger of bursting.'

At this point we may consider who was in attendance to the sick man. His brother had arrived in Vienna about 10 December and thereafter was in regular attendance. As an apothecary he felt he could contribute to the decisions concerning the choice of food for his brother. The Conversation Books show that Karl was closely involved with Dr Wawruch's care of the patient. In mid-December there are scattered entries in Karl's hand:

'The doctor has allowed rice-soup . . .'

'You may eat fruit.'

'The maid says that you have been drinking water at night, that will not do you any good.'

'During the enema you must hold your breath, otherwise it will run out . . .'

'Take a breath.'

'Do not hold your breath, draw it in.'

'Hold it in hard, but longer.'

'Now hold on, then the enema will work.'

Since Holz was now married, his visits were not as numerous, but he still found time to look after the correction and publication of the last compositions and to collect the composer's annuity. Schindler found his way back to the composer's side within a fortnight and seems, at least at first, to have been given more menial labours to carry out. Stephan von Breuning's visits were interrupted by illness and official labours, but his son, the thirteen-year-old Gerhard, frequently lent a gracious touch to the scene by his familiar mode of address and his gossip about his father's domestic affairs.

After Dr Wawruch had reached his decision, Dr Staudenheim was called in consultation and he confirmed the attending physician's opinion as to the necessity of an operation. Beethoven was told; 'after a few moments of serious thought he gave his consent.' Wawruch had retained Dr Seibert, principal surgeon at the hospital, to perform the operation, which took place on 20 December. Those present were Johann, Karl and Schindler. Beethoven's sense of humour did not desert him. When, the incision having been made, Dr Seibert introduced the tube and the water spurted out, Beethoven said: 'Professor, you remind me of Moses striking the rock with his staff.'

The operation made necessary renewed care and a close watch on the patient's diet. He was allowed to drink almond milk, but not in too great quantities, and also only a little coffee. During this period he had to remain in a near-lying position while it was being determined whether a second operation would be necessary.

One joyful event brightened the solitary gloom of the sick-chamber in the middle of December. From Johann Andreas Stumpff, of London, Beethoven received the forty volumes of Dr Arnold's edition of the works of Handel which the donor had resolved to send Beethoven on his visit in 1824. Gerhard von Breuning pictures the joy of Beethoven at the reception of the gift, which he described as royal. One day the boy was asked to hand the big books from the pianoforte where they rested to the bed. 'I have long wanted them,' said the composer to his faithful little friend, 'for Handel is the greatest, the ablest composer that ever lived. I can still learn from him.' He leaned the books against the wall, turned over the pages, and ever and anon paused to break out into new expressions of praise.

After saying his goodbyes and New Year greetings, Karl left for Iglau to join his new regiment. Beethoven's thoughts went swiftly towards his self-assumed duty of providing for the young man's future. The very next day he wrote the following letter to Dr Bach:

'Vienna, Wednesday 3 January 1827
'Before my death I declare Karl van Beethoven, my beloved nephew, my sole and universal heir of all the property which I possess in which is included chiefly seven bank shares and whatever money may be on hand. – If the laws prescribe a modification in this I beg of you as far as possible to turn it to his *advantage*. – I appoint you his *curator* and ask you along with his guardian, Hofrat von Breuning, to take the place of a father to him – God preserve you – A thousand thanks for the love and friendship which you have shown me. –
Ludwig van Beethoven'

After the close of the letter there is noted the following: 'This had to be opened by Dr Bach *today* in whose presence copies were made for the preservation of the declared will of Herr Ludwig van Beethoven – By the Viennese Magistrate, 27 March [1]827. Schütz'

Thus the will was read immediately after Beethoven's death, and the testamentary disposition, to which we return later. Beethoven had his letter to Bach sent to Breuning to read, who answered as follows:

'Dearest friend!

'I am still too weak to write much to you, but I think that the following few words from a candid heart should be said to you. Since through Gerhard you have told me that I should read the letter to Hr. Dr Bach, I have done so and return it to you for the time being with the following observations. That you name Karl as heir in the event, hopefully far distant, that we all leave this life, is appropriate considering your way of thinking and what you have already done for him. But Karl has shown himself up until now to be very reckless, and one doesn't know how his character will shape itself at present; thus I would be of the opinion that for his own good and for the security of his future you limit his power to dispose of capital either during his whole life or at least for a few years more until he has become 24 years old, the age of his majority. In any case he would have enough yearly income at hand and the limitation would protect him from the consequences of reckless actions before he reaches maturity. Speak about this with Hr. Dr

Bach, whom I should think it would be best for you to have visit you. He will arrange everything in the simplest way . . .
I embrace you warmly.'

Beethoven received a letter from his nephew in Iglau on 13 January, which begins:

'My dear Father,
'I have received your letter written by Schindler, I ask only that in the future you include the date so that I can estimate the speed of the post. Concerning your state of health I am glad to know that you are in good hands; I, too, had felt some distrust of the treatment of your former (or perhaps present?) physician; I hope improvement will follow.'

He reported about his situation in the regiment, asked for money and for the flute part of the Pianoforte Concerto in B flat (Op. 19), which one of the officers of the regiment wished to play.

Communications from the young man were not many, and Schindler's rebukes and complaints in the Conversation Books about his undutifulness were probably only a reflex of Beethoven's moods and utterances. One cause of dissatisfaction was the fact that a letter to Smart had been sent to him for translation and was not promptly returned. On 4 March he wrote another letter:

'My dear Father,
'I have just received the books that you sent me and thank you very much for them.
'You will have received the translation of the letter to Smart; I don't doubt that it will have favourable results.
'Just today a cadet, who had been in Vienna on leave, returned to his battalion; and he reports having heard that you had been saved by a frozen punch and are feeling well. I hope that this last is true no matter what the means may have been.
'There is little new about myself to tell; the service goes its usual way with the difference only that the weather is much milder, thus the watches also are easier.
'Write to me very soon about the state of your health; also please give my hearty greetings to Hr. Hofrat [von Breuning]. I kiss you.
Your loving son Charl'
'PS Please stamp your letters because I have to pay a lot of postage here for which I hardly have enough from my account.'

Karl van Beethoven never saw his uncle in life again, nor even in death, for he was not present at the funeral – as indeed in those days of tardy communication and slow conveyance he could not be.

As the year 1826 ended, Beethoven's friends were discussing with Dr Wawruch the necessity of a second tapping. The surgeon Seibert evidently advised a postponement of the operation. There were now signs of Beethoven's dissatisfaction with his doctor. According to Gerhard von Breuning, Wawruch's visits were ungraciously received; when his name was announced, Beethoven would turn his face to the wall and exclaim, 'Oh, the ass!'

The second operation took place on 8 January, according to Schindler, who was present. There were no complications; the tapping was accomplished without difficulty, and Dr Seibert reported that the water was clearer and the outflow greater than the first time. Ten measures were drawn off.

Before the year's end Schindler was putting in his voice for more medical advice. He writes:

'Yesterday I urged your brother earnestly to hold a medical council of men who have known your constitution longer.'

'Staudenheim, Braunhofer and Malfatti, three capable men whose judgement is not to be rejected.'

On 11 January the desired council of physicians took place and included Dr Malfatti, who 'prescribed for B. nothing hereafter but frozen fruit punch and rubbing of the abdomen with ice-cold water, a remedy with which Malfatti is said to have completely cured a similar patient'. It had become an ardent wish of Beethoven's that Malfatti undertake his case, but Malfatti had refused, pleading professional ethics, but no doubt actuated by reasons of a more personal character. Many years before, probably as early as 1813, he had been not only Beethoven's physician but also his friend; indeed he was an uncle of the Therese Malfatti to whom the composer once made an offer of marriage. Beethoven was ever a disobedient and irritable patient. He became dissatisfied with Dr Malfatti's treatment and commented upon it and him in such a manner as to cause a serious and lasting estrangement.

Dr Wawruch, after describing Beethoven's lack of appetite and loss of fluids, writes:

'Then Dr Malfatti, who thenceforth supported me with his advice, and who, as a friend of Beethoven's of long years' standing understood his predominant inclination for spirituous liquors, hit upon the notion of administering frozen punch. I must confess that the treatment produced excellent results for a few days at least. Beethoven felt himself so refreshed by the ice with its alcoholic contents that already in the first night he slept quietly throughout the night and began to perspire profusely. He grew cheerful and was full of witty conceits and even dreamed of being able to complete the oratorio "Saul and David" which he had begun.

'But this joy, as was to have been foreseen, did not last long. He began to abuse the prescription and applied himself right bravely to the frozen punch. The spirits soon caused a violent pressure of the blood upon the brain; he grew soporous, breathed stertorously like an intoxicated person, began to wander in his speech, and a few times inflammatory pains in the throat were paired with hoarseness and even speechlessness. He became more unruly, and when, because of the cooling of the bowels, colic and diarrhoea resulted, it was high time to deprive him of this precious refreshment.'

Schindler now tried to effect a reconciliation between Dr Malfatti and Beethoven. His account is clearly prejudiced against Dr Wawruch's treatment:

'Never shall I forget the harsh words of that man which he [Dr Malfatti] commissioned me to bear to the friend and teacher who lay mortally ill, when after the second operation (8 January) I repeatedly carried to him the urgent requests of Beethoven that he come to his help or he should die. Dr Wawruch did not know his constitution, was ruining him with too much medicine. He had already been compelled to empty 75 bottles, without counting various powders, he had no confidence in this physician, etc. To all of these representations Malfatti answered me coldly and drily: "Say to Beethoven that he, as a master of harmony, must know that I must also live in harmony with my colleagues." Beethoven wept bitter tears when I brought him this reply, which, hard as it was, I had to do, so that he might no longer look for help to that quarter . . .'

We learn more from Schindler's letter to the composer of 19 January:

'My great master!
'Since I have a rehearsal today at half-past eight from which I cannot be absent, I must report the result in writing of my second visit to Malfatti.
'He is coming to you today at half-past nine. Knowing perfectly well

that the professor has a lecture until ten, I told him [Malfatti] that we are inviting him [Wawruch] to come at half-past nine. In order that we don't get into a pickle, you just have to offer the excuse to Malf. that today for the first time you have learned from the Professor that because of his lecture he couldn't come before ten o'clock. Malf. has a meeting in the city at ten o'clock; therefore you have the opportunity that you want to speak with him alone –

'What I am asking you, however, is to make a complete reconciliation with him concerning the past for it still rankles with him to a certain extent; only today he again gave me to understand that he could not forget this planned offence, as he called it. – Some words of explanation from you will get everything to rights and bring it back on the old, friendly track . . .'

A reconciliation took place. Beethoven no doubt, in the warm glow of a recovered friendship, gave the physician a full measure of confidence and hailed in him much more than the ordinary professional leech. It is also safe to assume that Malfatti knew from the beginning that a cure was impossible and strove at once for temporary relief, which in Beethoven's case was the surest of means for cheering him up and reanimating hope within him. By administering frozen punch he stimulated the jaded organs more successfully than Wawruch had succeeded in doing; at the same time he warned against excess in its use and forbade the patient taking it in a liquid form. But this was only at the beginning; when he saw the inevitable end approaching he waived all injunctions as to quantity. Schindler says:

'The quantity of frozen punch permitted in the first weeks was not more than one glass a day. Not until after the fourth operation (27 February), when it was seen that the case was hopeless, were all restrictions removed. The noble patient, feeling the marked effects of a doubled and even trebled allowance meanwhile, thought himself already half saved and wanted to work on his tenth symphony, which he was allowed to do to a small extent.'

Gerhard von Breuning, prejudiced as he was against Dr Wawruch, was yet far from unqualified in his praise of Malfatti. He says:

'But the usually brilliant physician seems to have been little inspired in the presence of Beethoven. The frozen punch which he prescribed on his first visit to restore the tone of the digestive organs, excessively weakened by Wawruch's overload of medicaments, had, indeed, the desired restorative effect; but it was too transient. On the other hand a sort of sweat-bath prescribed a few days after the [third] operation was so obviously injurious to the patient, filled with longing and hope, that it had to be abandoned after the first application. Jugs filled with hot water were arranged in a bathtub and covered thickly with birch leaves on which the patient was seated, all of his body but the head being covered with a sheet. Malfatti hoped for a beneficial action upon the skin and to put the organs into a productive perspiration. But the very opposite effect resulted. The body of the patient, which had been emptied of water by the scarcely completed tapping, attracted the moisture developed by the bath like a block of salt; it swelled visibly in the apparatus and in a few days compelled the introduction anew of the tube into the still unhealed puncture.'

The third tapping took place on 2 February. Malfatti received the report of the operation from the surgeon. Schindler writes:

'I am just wondering whether Malfatti won't want to check up today on the condition of your liver and belly. It would therefore be very good as a matter of caution if Hr. Seybert were sent for at 5 o'clock. He said naturally that he wants to see you again today.'

'Perhaps to check up. The water is going through the liver.'

'Then the well-being of the liver is the key to the whole sickness.'

Thus there was talk now of the liver among Beethoven's friends. But it is not possible to determine how long before it had occurred to them that this organ was the seat of the trouble.

Among other friends who visited Beethoven during this period, the Conversation Books show Tobias Haslinger, Piringer, later Schickh, Streicher, Bernard, and the singer, Nanette Schechner. This last arranged through Schindler at the end of February a short visit to tell the composer of her great admiration for his music. She described her successes in *Fidelio* in Munich, and stated that it was through singing in *Adelaide* that she had won her way to the operatic stage.

On 1 February there came to the composer a cheery letter from his old playmate Wegeler, calling to his mind some of his early flames – Jeannette d'Honrath and Fräulein Westerholt – and playfully outlining a plan by which the old friends might enjoy a reunion: he would send, he said, one of his patients to Carlsbad and go there with him as soon as Beethoven should arrange also to go there for his convalescence.

Then, after a three weeks' trip through South Germany, there should be a final visit to the home of their childhood. And, as before, Eleonore sent a postscript emphasising the pleasure of the reunion.

Zmeskall, faithful to the old friendship, a bound prisoner to his room through gout, sent greetings and enquiries through Schindler. From his sickbed Beethoven wrote a short answer, dated by Zmeskall 18 February:

'A thousand thanks for your sympathy. I do not despair. The most painful feature is the cessation of all activity. No evil without its good side – May heaven but grant you relief in your painful existence. Perhaps health is coming to both of us and we shall meet again in friendly intimacy.

Warm regards from your old sympathising friend.

Beethoven'

Though Beethoven had received the Handel scores in December, he does not seem to have had an opportunity to enjoy Stumpff's gift thoroughly until he turned to them for intellectual refreshment on his bed of pain. He wrote to Stumpff under the date of 8 February.

'Most worthy friend!

'What great joy was given to me by your sending the works of Handel as a present – for me a royal present! – This my pen cannot describe . . . Unfortunately I have been laid up with the dropsy since 3 December. You can imagine in what a situation this places me! Generally I live from the proceeds of my brain only, and thus provide all things for myself and my Karl. Unhappily for a month and a half I have not been able to write a note.

'My salary suffices only to pay my semi-annual rent, after which there remains only a few hundred florins. Remember also that it cannot yet be determined when my illness will be over and I again will be able to sail through the air on Pegasus under full sail. Doctor, surgeon, everything must be paid –

'I recall right well that several years ago the Philharmonic Society wanted to give a concert for my benefit. It would be fortunate for me if they would come to this decision now. I might still be saved from the poverty which now confronts me. On this account I am writing to Mr S[mart]. And if you, dear friend, can do anything towards this end I beg of you to co-operate with Mr S. A letter will also be written about this to Moscheles and if all my friends unite I believe that something can be done for me in this matter . . .

'I thank you again for your glorious gift, at the same time I beg of you to tell me if I can be of any service to you here; this I would do with all my heart . . . I wish you everything that is good and beautiful.

Very respectfully yours,

Beethoven'

It is evident that Stumpff went at once to Smart and Moscheles, and knowledge of Beethoven's condition and request was communicated to the directors of the Philharmonic Society forthwith. The quick and sympathetic action of the Society was no doubt due to his initiative. The directors held a meeting on 28 February. Mr Dance presided, and those present, as recorded in the Society's minutes, were F. Cramer, Horsley, Moralt, Dragonetti, Neate, Dizi, Beale, T. Cooke, Sir G. Smart, Welsh, Latour, Spagnoletti, Calkin, J. B. Cramer, Cipriani Potter and Watts. The minutes continue:

'It was moved by Mr Neate, and seconded by Mr Latour:

' "That this Society do lend the sum of One Hundred Pounds to its own members to be sent through the hands of Mr Moscheles to some confidential friend of Beethoven, to be applied to his comforts and necessities during his illness."

'Carried unanimously.'

Schindler says that the appeal to London, which had been suggested by Beethoven, had been discussed with the composer by himself and Breuning, who agreed in questioning the advisability of the step which, they said, would make a bad impression if it became known. They reminded Beethoven of his bank-shares, but he protested vigorously against their being touched; he had set them apart as a legacy for his nephew which must not be encroached upon.

There are evidences outside of the importunate letter to Stumpff that Beethoven had frequent spells of melancholy during the period between the crises of his disease, which culminated in the third operation on 2 February, and the fourth. Some of them were, no doubt, due to forebodings touching the outcome of his illness; some to the anxiety which his financial condition gave him (more imaginary than real in view of the easily convertible bank-shares), and some presumably to disappointment and chagrin at the conduct of his nephew. Breuning warned Beethoven that to give way to melancholy was to stand in the way of recovery. We learn this from the Conversation Books which also give glimpses of friendly visits calculated to divert the sick man's mind and keep him in touch with the affairs of the city, theatre and the world at large. Schuppanzigh, and apparently Linke also, came; Beethoven showed them the Handel scores and the conversation ran out into a discussion of international politics. Moritz Lichnowsky made a call and entertained him with the gossip of the theatres. Gleichenstein made several visits, and once brought with him his wife and son. The Countess was a sister of Therese Malfatti, and was disappointed when Beethoven did not recognise her. About the middle of February Beethoven was given a print-picture of Haydn's birthplace; Beethoven showed it to his little friend Gerhard von Breuning and said: 'Look, I got this today. See this little house, and in it so great a man was born!'

Pathetic is the picture of the sufferer in his sick-room at the time of the fourth operation on 27 February. So wretched were his surroundings that it is scarcely possible to avoid the conviction that not poverty alone but ignorance and carelessness were contributory to the woeful lack of ordinary sick-room conveniences. Gerhard von Breuning wrote that after the operation the fluid which was drained from the patient's body flowed half-way across the floor to the middle of the room; and in the Conversation Books there is mention of saturated bedclothing and a suggestion by the physician that oilcloth be procured and spread over the couch. Beethoven now gave up hope. Dr Wawruch says: 'No words of comfort could brace him up, and when I promised him alleviation of his sufferings with the coming of the vitalising weather of spring he answered with a smile: "My day's work is finished." '

Among Beethoven's visitors in February was Wolfmayer, whose coming must have called up a sense of a long-standing obligation and purpose in the composer's mind. It will be remembered that Wolfmayer had commissioned him years before to write a requiem, and had paid him for it. On 22 February he dictated a letter to the Schotts asking that the Quartet in C sharp minor be dedicated to 'my friend Johann Nepomuk Wolfmayer'. The letter then proceeds:

'Now, however, I come with a very important request. – My doctor has ordered me to drink very good old Rhine wine. To get a thing of that kind unadulterated is not possible at any price. If, therefore, I were to receive a small number of bottles I would show my gratitude to you in the [musical journal] *Cäcilia*. I think something might be done for me at the customs so that the transport would not cost too much . . . I am now just in the period when the fourth operation is about to be performed. – The sooner, therefore, that I receive the Rhine wine, or Moselle, the more beneficial it will be to me in my present condition; and I beg of you most heartily to do me this favour for which I shall be under grateful obligation to you.

With the greatest respect I remain your every devoted

Beethoven'

On 8 March the Schotts answered that they had forwarded a case of twelve bottles of Rüdesheimer Berg of the vintage of 1806, via Frankfurt, but in order that he might receive a slight refreshment, they had sent that day four bottles of the same wine, two pure and two mixed with herbs, to be used as a medicine which had been prescribed for his disease.

A few days later Beethoven finally received the great and urgent gift of £100 from London and dictated the following acknowledgement to Schindler:

'Vienna, 18 March 1827

'My dear good Moscheles:

'I cannot describe to you in words with what feelings I read your letter of 1 March. The generosity with which the Philharmonic Society almost anticipated my petition has touched me in the innermost depth of my soul. – I beg you, therefore, my dear Moscheles, to be the agent through which I transmit my sincerest thanks to the Philharmonic Society for the particular sympathy and help.

'I found myself constrained to collect at once the entire sum of 1,000 florins CM, as I was in the unpleasant position of being about to borrow money, which would have brought new embarrassments.

'Concerning the concert which the Philharmonic Society has resolved to give for my benefit, I beg the Society not to abandon this noble purpose, and to deduct the 1,000 florins already sent to me from the proceeds of the concert. And if the Society is disposed graciously to send me the balance, I will pledge myself to return my heartiest thanks to the Society by binding myself to compose for it either a new symphony, which lies already sketched in my desk, or a new overture or something else which the Society would like.

'May heaven very soon restore me to health, and I shall prove to the generous Englishmen how greatly I appreciate their interest in my sad fate.

'Your noble act will never be forgotten and I shall follow this with special thanks to Sir Smart and Mr Stumpff.

'Farewell! With kindest remembrances

From your friend who highly esteems you

Ludwig van Beethoven'

Schindler relates that Beethoven a few days later whispered to him,

'Write to Smart and Stumpff,' and that he would have done so on the morrow had Beethoven been able to sign his name.

The money, as is to be seen from Beethoven's acknowledgement, was collected by the composer at once. Herr Rau, of the banking house of Eskeles to whom it had been entrusted, called upon Beethoven immediately on receiving advices from London. It was on 15 March, and two days later he enclosed Beethoven's receipt in a letter to Moscheles which the latter transmitted to Mr W. Watts, Secretary of the Philharmonic Society. Rau writes:

'I have with the greatest surprise heard from you, who reside in London, that the universally admired Beethoven is so dangerously ill and in want of pecuniary assistance, while we, here at Vienna, are totally ignorant of it. I went to him immediately after having read your letter to ascertain his state, and to announce to him the approaching relief. This made a deep impression upon him, and called forth true expressions of gratitude. What a satisfactory sight would it have been for those who so generously relieved him to witness such a touching scene! I found poor Beethoven in a sad way, more like a skeleton than a living being. He is suffering from dropsy, and has already been tapped four times; he is under the care of our clever physician Malfatti, who unfortunately gives little hope of his recovery.

'How long he may remain in his present state, or if he can at all be saved, cannot yet be ascertained. The joyous sensation at the sudden relief from London has, however, had a wonderful effect upon him; it made one of the wounds (which since the last operation had healed) suddenly burst open during the night, and all the water which had gathered since a fortnight ran out freely. When I came to see him on the following day he was in remarkably good spirits and felt himself much relieved. I hastened to Malfatti to inform him of this alteration and he considers the event as very consolatory. He will contrive to keep the wound open for some time and thus leave a channel for the water which gathers continually. Beethoven is fully satisfied with his attendants, who consist of a cook and housemaid. His friend and ours, Mr Schindler, dines with him every day and thus proves his sincere attachment to him. S. also manages his correspondence and superintends his expenses . . .'

In a letter, dated 24 March, Schindler wrote to Moscheles:

'. . . In short, care and anxiety vanished at once when the money arrived, and he said quite happily, "Now we can again look forward to

a comfortable day once in a while"; for there were only 340 fl. VS left
in the cash-box, and we had economised for some time in the amount
of beef and vegetables, which, more than anything else, made him suffer. The other day, it was Friday, his favourite dish of fish was cooked
so that he could nibble from it. In short, his delight on receiving this
noble gift from the Phil. Society resembled that of a child. Also a large
so-called easy-chair had to be procured, which cost 30 fl. VS in which
he could stay at least a half-hour per day so that his bed could be properly made up . . . whatever remains of the 1,000 fl. we want to apply
towards a respectable burial, without commotion, in the . . . [church-
yard] at Döbling where he ever delighted to roam . . .'

Schindler at one time had expressed the opinion that Schubert was a
greater song-composer than Beethoven and excited criticism thereby.
He wrote, in defence of his opinion:

'As the illness to which Beethoven finally succumbed after four
months of suffering from the beginning made his ordinary mental
activity impossible, a diversion had to be thought of which would fit
his mind and inclinations. And so it came about that I placed before
him a collection of Schubert's songs, about 60 in number, among them
many which were then still in manuscript. This was done not only to
provide him with a pleasant entertainment, but also to give him an
opportunity to get acquainted with Schubert in his essence in order to
get from him a favourable opinion of Schubert's talent, which had
been impugned, as had that of others by some of the exalted ones. The
great master, who before then had not known five songs of Schubert's,
was amazed at their number and refused to believe that up to that
time (February 1827) he had already composed over 500 of them. But
if he was astonished at the number he was filled with the highest
admiration as soon as he discovered their contents. For several days he
could not separate himself from them . . . With joyous enthusiasm he
cried out repeatedly: "Truly, a divine spark dwells in Schubert; if I
had had this poem I would have set it to music"; this in the case of the
majority of poems whose material contents and original treatment by
Schubert he could not praise sufficiently. Nor could he understand
how Schubert had time to "take in hand such long poems, many of
which contained ten others", as he expressed it . . . In short, the respect
which Beethoven acquired for Schubert's talent was so great that he
now wanted to see his operas and pianoforte pieces; but his illness had
now become so severe that he could no longer gratify this wish. But he
often spoke of Schubert and predicted of him that he "would make a

great sensation in the world", and often regretted that he had not learned to know him earlier.'

Another incident recorded about Beethoven by Gerhard von Breuning deserves to be told here:

'One time, as so often happened when I came, I found him sleeping. I sat down on the bed, keeping quiet in order not to awaken him from a sleep that was hopefully giving him strength. I turned the pages of a Conversation Book that was lying on the bed still in use in order to find out who had been here during that time and what had been said. And I found there among other things the entry: "Your Quartet which Schuppanzigh played yesterday did not please" – When he awoke a short time later, I held this passage before his eyes and asked him what he had to say about it. "It will please them some day" was the laconic reply.'

Johann Hummel had heard in Weimar that Beethoven was hopelessly ill. He came in haste to see him, reaching Vienna on 6 March; two days later he visited his dying friend. His young pupil Ferdinand Hiller, who accompanied him, later wrote:

'Through a spacious ante-room in which high cabinets were piled with thick, tied-up parcels of music we reached – how my heart beat! – Beethoven's living room, and were not a little astonished to find the master sitting in apparent comfort at the window. He wore a long, grey sleeping-robe, open at the time, and high boots reaching to his knees.* Emaciated by long and severe illness he seemed to me, when he arose, of tall stature; he was unshaven, his thick, half-grey hair fell in disorder over his temples. The expression of his features heightened when he caught sight of Hummel, and he seemed to be extraordinarily glad to meet him. The two men embraced each other most cordially. Hummel introduced me. Beethoven showed himself extremely kind and I was permitted to sit opposite him at the window. It is known that conversation with Beethoven was carried on in part in writing; he spoke, but those with whom he conversed had to write their questions and answers. For this purpose thick sheets of ordinary writing-paper in quarto form and lead-pencils always lay near him. How painful it must have been for the animated, easily impatient man to be obliged to wait

* In 1860 Hüttenbrenner told me that when Hummel came, Beethoven said, 'I cannot receive him in bed,' immediately got up, put on a sleeping robe, and received him with due respect.

for every answer, to make a pause in every moment of conversation, during which, as it were, thought was condemned to come to a standstill! He always followed the hand of the writer with hungry eyes and comprehended what was written at a glance instead of reading it. The liveliness of the conversation naturally interfered with the continual writing of the visitor – I can scarcely blame myself, much as I regret it, for not taking down more extended notes than I did; indeed, I rejoice that a lad of fifteen years who found himself in a great city for the first time, was self-possessed enough to regard any details. I can vouch with the best conscience for the perfect accuracy of all that I am able to repeat.

'The conversation at first turned, as is usual, on domestic affairs, the journey and sojourn, my relations with Hummel and matters of that kind. Beethoven asked about Goethe's health with extraordinary solicitude and we were able to make the best of reports, since only a few days before the great poet had written in my album. Concerning his own state, poor Beethoven complained much. "Here I have been lying for four months," he cried out, "one must at last lose patience!" Other things in Vienna did not seem to be to his liking and he spoke with the utmost severity of "the present taste in art", and "the dilettantism which is ruining everything". Nor did he spare the government, up to the most exalted regions. "Write a volume of penitential hymns and dedicate it to the Empress," he remarked with a gloomy smile to Hummel, who, however, made no use of the well-meant advice... He asked about my studies and, encouraging me, said: "Art must be propagated ceaselessly," and when I spoke of the exclusive interest in Italian opera which then prevailed in Vienna, he gave utterance to the memorable words: "It is said *vox populi, vox dei*. I never believed it."

'On 13 March Hummel took me with him a second time to Beethoven. We found his condition to be materially worse. He lay in bed, seemed to suffer great pains, and at intervals groaned deeply despite the fact that he spoke much and animatedly. Now he seemed to take it much to heart that he had not married. Already at our first visit he had joked about it with Hummel, whose wife he had known as a young and beautiful maiden. "You are a lucky man," he said to him now smilingly, "you have a wife who takes care of you, who is in love with you – but poor me!" and he sighed heavily. He also begged of Hummel to bring his wife to see him, she not having been able to persuade herself to see in his present state the man whom she had known at the zenith of his powers...

'Shortly after our second visit the report spread throughout Vienna that the Philharmonic Society of London had sent Beethoven £100 in order to ease his sickbed. It was added that this surprise had made so great an impression on the great poor man that it had also brought physical relief. When we stood again at his bedside, on the 20th, we could deduce from his utterances how greatly he had been rejoiced by this altruism; but he was very weak and spoke only in faint and disconnected phrases. "I shall, no doubt, soon be going above," he whispered after our first greeting . . . He spoke of projects and hopes which were destined not to be realised. Speaking of the noble conduct of the Philharmonic Society and in praise of the English people, he expressed the intention, as soon as matters were better with him, to undertake the journey to London. "I will compose a grand overture for them and a grand symphony." Then, too, he would visit Madame Hummel (she had come along with her husband) and go to I do not know how many places. It did not occur to us to write anything for him. His eyes, which were still lively when we saw him last, dropped and closed today and it was difficult from time to time for him to raise himself. It was no longer possible to deceive one's self – the worst was to be feared.

'Hopeless was the picture presented by the extraordinary man when we sought him again on 23 March. It was to be the last time. He lay, weak and miserable, sighing deeply at intervals. Not a word fell from his lips; sweat stood upon his forehead. His handkerchief not being conveniently at hand, Hummel's wife took her fine cambric handkerchief and dried his face several times. Never shall I forget the grateful glance with which his broken eye looked upon her.'

The consultations between Beethoven and his legal advisers, Bach, Breuning and others, concerning the proper disposition of his estate by will, had not been brought to a conclusion when it became apparent to all that it was high time that the document be formally executed. Haste was necessary, and on 23 March von Breuning made a draft of a will which, free from unnecessary verbiage, set forth the wishes of the testator in three lines of writing. Beethoven had protested against the proposition of his friends that provision be made that Karl should not be able to dissipate the capital or surrender any portion of it to his mother. To this end a trust was to be created and he was to have the income during life, the reversion being to his legitimate heirs. With this Beethoven declared himself at length satisfied; but when Breuning placed the draft before the dying man, who had yielded unwillingly, he copied it laboriously but substituted the word 'natural' for 'legitimate'. Schindler says the copying was a labour, and when Beethoven finished it and appended the signature he said: 'There; now I'll write no more.'

Signatures were necessary to several documents – the will, the transfer of the guardianship of the nephew to von Breuning and the letter of 3 January, which also made a testamentary disposition of Beethoven's property. These signatures were all obtained with great difficulty. After von Breuning, Schindler and the dying man's brother had indicated to Beethoven, who lay in a half-stupor, that his signature was required, they raised him as much as possible and pushed pillows under him for support. Then the documents, one after the other, were laid before him and von Breuning put the inked pen in his hand. 'The dying man, who ordinarily wrote boldly in a lapidary style, repeatedly signed his immortal name, laboriously, with trembling hand, for the last time; still legibly, indeed, but each time forgetting one of the middle letters – once an *h*, another time an *e*.'

On the day which saw the signing of the will, Beethoven made an utterance, eminently characteristic of him. The date is fixed as 23 March by Schindler's letter to Moscheles of 24 March in which he says: 'He feels the end coming for yesterday he said to me and Hr. v. Breuning, "Plaudite, amici, comoedia finita est." '* Gerhard von Breuning writes of this scene: 'Schindler told me that Beethoven had called out these words as the doctors were taking their leave after a long consultation. He spoke them in his favourite sarcastic-humorous manner as though to imply: nothing can be done . . .'

When Beethoven's friends saw the end approaching, they were naturally desirous that he receive the spiritual comfort which the offices of the Roman Catholic Church offer to the dying, and it was equally natural that Beethoven, brought up as a child of the Church though careless of his duties towards it, should, at the last, be ready to accept them. Johann van Beethoven relates that a few days after 16 March, when the physicians gave him up for lost, he had begged his brother to make his peace with God, to which request he had acceded 'with the greatest readiness'. Confirmation of this is found in Dr Wawruch's report. Wawruch had, at the beginning of his studies, intended to enter the priesthood. At the crisis described by Johann he says he called Beethoven's attention to his impending dissolution 'so that he might do his duty as a citizen and to religion'. He continues: 'With the greatest delicacy I wrote the words of admonition on a sheet of paper (for only so were we able to communicate one to another). Beethoven read the writing with unexampled composure, slowly and thoughtfully, his countenance like that of one transfigured; cordially and solemnly he held out his hand to me and said: "Have the priest called." Then he lay quietly lost in thought and amiably indicated by a nod his "I shall soon

---

* 'Applaud, my friends, the comedy is finished': a common closing line in Roman comedy.

see you again." ' Shortly afterwards, Beethoven received the viaticum in the presence of Schindler, von Breuning, Dr Johann Baptist Jenger and Therese, the wife of his brother Johann.

About one o'clock on 24 March the special shipment of wine and wine mixed with herbs came from Mainz, and Schindler placed the bottles upon the table near the bed. Beethoven looked at them and murmured, 'Pity, pity – too late!' He spoke no more. A little of the wine was administered to him in spoonfuls at intervals, as long as he could swallow it. Towards evening he lost consciousness and the death-struggle began. It lasted two days. 'From towards the evening of the 24th to his last breath he was almost continually *in delirio*,' wrote Schindler. We have a description from Gerhard von Breuning:

'During the next day and the day following the strong man lay completely unconscious, in the process of dissolution, breathing so stertorously that the rattle could be heard at a distance. His powerful frame, his unweakened lungs, fought like giants with approaching death. The spectacle was a fearful one. Although it was known that the poor man suffered no more it was yet appalling to observe that the noble being, now irredeemably a prey to the powers of dissolution, was beyond all mental communication. It was expected as early as the 25th that he would pass away in the following night; yet we found him still alive on the 26th – breathing, if that was possible, more stertorously than on the day before.'

Anselm Hüttenbrenner, who was a witness of Beethoven's death, writes: 'When I entered Beethoven's bedroom on 26 March 1827 at about 3 o'clock in the afternoon, I found there Court Councillor Breuning, his son, Frau van Beethoven, wife of Johann van Beethoven, landowner and apothecary of Lenz, and my friend Joseph Teltscher, portrait painter. I think that Prof. Schindler was also present.'

Gerhard von Breuning says that Beethoven's brother was in the room, and also the housekeeper Sali; Schindler adds a nurse from Dr Wawruch's clinic. No doubt all were present at one moment or another; they came and went as occasion or duty called. Hüttenbrenner says that Teltscher began drawing the face of the dying man, which grated on Breuning's feelings and he made a remonstrance, whereupon the painter left the room. Then Breuning and Schindler went away to choose a spot for the grave. Hüttenbrenner continues:

'Frau van Beethoven and I only were in the death-chamber during the last moments of Beethoven's life. After Beethoven had lain unconscious, the death-rattle in his throat from 3 o'clock in the afternoon till after 5, there came a flash of lightning accompanied by a violent clap of thunder, which garishly illuminated the death-chamber. (Snow lay before Beethoven's dwelling.) After this unexpected phenomenon of nature, which startled me greatly, Beethoven opened his eyes, lifted his right hand and looked up for several seconds with his fist clenched and a very serious, threatening expression as if he wanted to say: "Inimical powers, I defy you! Away with you! God is with me!" It also seemed as if, like a brave commander, he wished to call out to his wavering troops: "Courage, soldiers! Forward! Trust in me! Victory is assured!" When he let the raised hand sink to the bed, his eyes closed half-way. My right hand was under his head, my left rested on his breast. Not another breath, not a heartbeat more! The genius of the great master of tones fled from this world of delusion into the realm of truth! – I pressed down the half-open eyelids of the dead man, kissed them, then his forehead, mouth and hands. – At my request Frau van Beethoven cut a lock of hair from his head and handed it to me as a sacred souvenir of Beethoven's last hour. Thereupon I hurried, deeply moved, into the city, carried the intelligence of Beethoven's death to Herr Tobias Haslinger, and after a few hours returned to my home.'

When Breuning and Schindler left the dying man, they went to the cemetery of the little village of Währing, and selected a place for Beethoven's grave in the vicinity of the burial plot of the Vering family, to which Breuning's first wife had belonged. Their return was retarded by the storm. When they re-entered the sick-room they were greeted with the words: 'It is finished!'

Breuning, Schindler, Johann van Beethoven and Holz later met in the lodgings to gather up the dead man's papers, particularly to look for the seven bank-shares which the will had given to the nephew. In spite of strenuous search they were not found, and Johann let fall an insinuation that the search was a sham. This angered von Breuning and he left the house in a state of vexation and excitement. He returned to the lodgings in the afternoon and the search was resumed. Then Holz pulled out a protruding nail in a cabinet, whereupon a drawer fell out and in it were the certificates. With them were found the letter to the 'Immortal Beloved' and the portrait of the Countess von Brunsvik.

The funeral took place at 3 o'clock in the afternoon of 29 March. It was one of the most imposing functions of its kind ever witnessed in Vienna. In the Archives of the Vienna Supreme Court there is a document containing a full account:

'Beethoven died on Monday, 26 March 1827 about 5.45 p.m. Two men kept the death-watch. On Tuesday morning Dr Johann Wagner dissected the corpse. Then it was clothed and laid in a polished oak coffin which rested on ball-shaped gilded supports. On the cover was constructed a gilded cross. The head of the deceased, adorned with a wreath of white roses, rested on a white silk pillow. The face, framed with grey curls, was very lifeless because of the dissection. The folded hands grasped a wax cross and a large lily. And near the body a large lily was placed on the right side and on the left. Over the coffin was spread a coverlet half pulled back. The bier stood in the room in which he died, with his head facing the "composition room" [music room]. There were eight candles burning on both sides of the coffin. On a table at the foot stood a crucifix and holy water for aspersion together with ears of corn. The good faithful Sali, the Master's maid, tirelessly received the many who wished to pay their last respects to the deceased.

'Thursday was the time of departure. [Around noon] Andreas Zeller,* the director of ceremonies . . . stepped into the room and distributed to the invited guests rose bouquets with white silk stitches. They were placed on the left sleeve. Near 3 o'clock poems by Castelli and Seidl were given out as keepsakes. In the morning by order of Breuning Mathias Mann with 5 others had cleaned the roomy court. In this area were gathered Barbaja's singers of the Italian Opera. Before 3 o'clock the house-gate was closed, the court filled to overflowing, and outside the crowd stormily demanded entrance. The military assistance from the Alser Barracks, procured by Breuning, was hardly able to ward off the crowd. Even the schools were closed.

'At 3 o'clock the coffin was closed, carried down and placed in the court. The pall, ordered by Anton Schindler from the 2nd Civil Regiment, was spread over the coffin, the cross was adorned with a 'very beautiful' wreath, and the Evangelical book and the 'very beautiful' civic crown set up. The contour of the coffin was hidden by a group of wreaths. Nine priests from the Schottenstifte blessed the dead. Thereupon Barbaja's court singers sang a funeral song: a chorale by B. Anselm Weber . . . These singers also carried the coffin into the church. Now the door was opened; the crowd was so jammed that only with the greatest difficulty was the director of ceremonies with his helpers able to organise the procession. Even those standing near the deceased became pressed from their places of honour behind the coffin. From here hung down broad white silk bands. The ends of the pall (not the points) were taken by eight kapellmeisters – the honour

* The author of this account.

escort of the sleeping master. They carried candles wrapped in crepe. On both sides of the coffin came the torchbearers [who included] Bernard, Böhm, Castelli, Czerny, Grillparzer, Grünbaum, Holz, Linke, Schubert, Schuppanzigh, [and] Wolfmayer, with lily bouquets adorning their shoulders. The torches were decorated with flowers.

'Now the procession, which had been formed with so much trouble, started to move, beginning with the carriers of the crosses decorated with flowers. Members of welfare institutions followed. Behind them strode the trombonists ... Then followed Assmayer's choir ... [who] sang the *Miserere*, the refrain of which was blown by the trombonists. This *Miserere* was the work specified as music for All Souls' Day, which Beethoven had written at Linz in 1812 at Glöggl's request. During the evening of 26 and 27 March Seyfried arranged it for voices. *Amplius lava me** was also sung. The parish crucifer was followed by the nine priests from the Schottenstifte, striding slowly before the coffin. The cross-carriers, priests, corporation, and director of ceremonies wore rose bouquets. Behind the coffin in the middle of the boisterous crowd followed Johann and Therese van Beethoven, Stephan and Gerhard v. Breuning, Hofrat v. Mosel, the students of Drechsler, Kapellmeister of St Anna, the pupils of the Conservatory, and numerous friends and admirers of the deceased. At the end of the procession came the "very lovely ceremonial carriage" pulled by 4 horses which had been ordered from the office of Kirchenmeister of St Stephan Cathedral. Thus the procession reached the Alsergasse. Gerhard von Breuning ... estimated the crowd at 20,000; the *Sammler* at 10,000. When the procession turned into the Alsergasse, a brass band played the "Marcia funebre" from Op. 26. The church was filled to capacity; the soldiers on duty did not want to admit anyone after the coffin had been carried in. The relatives and friends of the master succeeded only with difficulty to get inside the church. Those who had fainted from the pressure of the crowd were taken across to the hospital.

'The inside of the church shone with candlelight ... But Johann Wolfmayer had candles at all altars, wall brackets, and chandeliers lit at his own expense. The nine priests from the Schottenstifte sang the *Libera* by Seyfried. Then the bier was carried by the bearers, led by the trombonists and priests and followed by the funeral guests. It was taken through the nave and to the door. The ceremony was over.

'After the religious service the ceremonial carriage took the coffin. A part of the crowd was dispersed but thousands closed in on the procession going slowly along the hospital street. It crossed the Alserbach by

---

* Also written by Beethoven for Glöggl and arranged for voices by Seyfried. The singers and trombonists alternated in the performance.

the Namentur, passed by the almshouse and the brick-kiln, reached the Währing line, crossed it, reached the right bank of the Währing Brook and went along the brook to the village parish church. The minister, Johann Hayek, and a second priest were waiting there. The procession stopped; the coffin was carried into the church and blessed by both of the priests, candles were burning on three altars. After the ceremony the parish singers sang the *Miserere* [motets] and the *Libera* . . . Now the bearers again took the bier. Many people were still following the procession, the village schoolchildren were there, supervised by the school assistants; then came the local poor people. Before the coffin went the priests, the sacristan, and the acolyte with the censer. The funeral guests followed the coffin accompanied by the prayer leader. The Währing master of ceremonies arranged the procession. With the brook on the right and a slope falling gently on the left, the funeral procession approached the fields of the parish cemetery amid the sound of bells. Before the gates . . . the bearers put their load down. Before the coffin stepped the great tragedian, Heinrich Anschütz, and delivered the gripping obituary by Grillparzer. Thereupon a poem by Schlechta was passed out. And now the great man joined the other dead. The priests consecrated the tomb and blessed the corpse for the last time. By the last light of the spring day the coffin was lowered into the earth . . . Tobias Haslinger had brought three laurel wreaths which Hummel placed on the grave. According to an old custom, those standing near threw earth on the grave and the torches were extinguished.'

On 3 April Mozart's *Requiem* was sung at the Church of the Augustinians, under the direction of Lablache. On 5 April a further observance was made with a performance of the Cherubini *Requiem* at the Karlskirche. The grave in the cemetery at Währing was marked by a simple pyramid bearing the one word

'BEETHOVEN'

It fell into neglect, and on 13 October 1863 the Gesellschaft der Musikfreunde of Vienna caused the body to be exhumed and reburied. On 21 June 1888 the remains of Beethoven and Schubert were removed to the Central Cemetery in Vienna, where they now repose side by side.

FINIS

Index of Beethoven's Works

Beethoven is referred to as B in subentries throughout this index.

General Index

Beethoven is referred to as B in subentries throughout this index.